D0912616

AN ARCHITECTURAL GUIDEBOOK TO

LOS ANGELES

AN ARCHITECTURAL GUIDEBOOK TO
LOS ANGELES

by DAVID GEBHARD AND ROBERT WINTER

Edited and updated by Robert Winter

Gibbs Smith, Publisher
Salt Lake City

In memory of
David Gebhard, historian
Esther McCoy, critic
Tom Owen, librarian
Ira Yellin, developer

On the cover: Walt Disney Concert Hall, 1998–2003, Downtown, Civic Center;
Frank O. Gehry and Associates; photograph © 2003 by Alex Vertikoff.

First Edition
07 06 05 04 03   5 4 3 2 1

Published by
Gibbs Smith, Publisher
P.O. Box 667
Layton, Utah 84041

Orders: (1-800) 748-5439
www.gibbs-smith.com

Edited by Linda Nimori
Designed by Kurt Wahlner
Produced by J. Scott Knudsen, Park City, Utah

Printed and bound in Korea

Library of Congress Cataloging-in-Publication Data

Winter, Robert, 1924–
  An architectural guidebook to Los Angeles / Robert Winter and David Gebhard ;
edited and updated by Robert Winter.— Rev. ed.
     p. cm.
  Includes bibliographical references and index.
  ISBN 1-58685-308-2
  1. Architecture—California—Los Angeles—Guidebooks.
  2. Los Angeles (Calif.)—Buildings, structures, etc.—Guidebooks.
  I. Gebhard, David. II. Title.
  NA735.L55 G44 2003
  720'.9794'93—dc21
                            2003002032

Contents

Preface

David Gebhard, my old friend and coauthor, died in 1996, not long after the last revision of the guide was published. To me his loss was both professional and personal. We met in 1962 in the living room of Carl Sheppard, the chair of the art department at UCLA where I was then teaching. Carl had seen the mimeographed list of important Southern California buildings that I had compiled from an old AIA guide to early modern buildings in L.A., and from the lecture notes of Hugh Morrison, my professor of architectural history at Dartmouth. Hugh had visited Los Angeles, probably intending to see the houses that Frank Lloyd Wright had designed in the 1920s. He also encountered the buildings of Wright's son, Lloyd, and of Charles and Henry Greene as well as the early Modernists R. M. Schindler, Richard Neutra, and Harwell Hamilton Harris. I had seen his slides of their work when I was his student in the mid-1940s.

David liked my list, and together we expanded it. The result was our first Guide (1965) subsidized by the Los Angeles County Museum of Art, which had only recently moved into its new quarters designed by William Pereira. Being naughty boys, we thought his three pavilions were so stupid that we did not include them in the Guide. In our later additions (1977, 1985, and 1994) we relented on the grounds that they were evidence of what to avoid. How David would have enjoyed the museum trustees' recent decision to tear them down and replace them with a new building designed by Rem Koolhaas, a modern-day master!

In our first Guide, we tried to cover the best in Southern California architecture. Since timing of the Guide was intended to be linked to the first national meeting of the Society of Architectural Historians ever to be held in Los Angeles, we consciously excluded most Victorian architecture from the listing, thinking that the registrants would be more interested in the early modern architecture that easterners were just beginning to recognize as California's gift to architectural history. What we produced was intended to be the crème de la crème of local building, mainly from the 1920s to the present.

By the next edition (1977), we knew more and our decision to cover much more architecture caused the book to become quite a bundle—the Los Angeles pundit, Jack Smith, called it "The Blue Brick." Since then we have limited it to Los Angeles County in order to include more buildings in a limited space. The present edition is the result of my condensing and rewriting much of the old material at the front of the book and eliminating entries for buildings that no longer exist. This editing has allowed me to add buildings that have been erected since 1994 and also ones that we missed in our earlier Guide.

Another reason for the bulkiness of the earlier book was the fact that David was a very generous person who wanted the Guide to be representative of the best work of the past and at the same time to credit the best contemporary work. He and I both wanted to include buildings designed by young architects, especially women. We put in some things that don't look as good now as they did ten years ago. I have eliminated only a few buildings that do not seem to pass muster and will probably be pilloried for this action by generations yet unborn. So be it. As we have said before, we expect this Guide, like the others, to be a period piece with enough absolute truth in it to have to be dealt with by future critics and historians.

That being said, this Guide is, like the earlier ones, by no means a complete listing of works by major architects. We have always tried to limit it to buildings that can be seen from the street, though a luxuriant nature is always trying to cover them up. A few that cannot be seen have been included because they are of major importance in the history of architecture or in the aesthetic development of an architect. You may have a chance to see them on the few occasions that they are open to the public.

Very early in our studies, David and I found it very difficult to map everything in a logical manner. The general order of the book is a listing of the beach cities from north to south; then we go inland and move up to the northern tier of cities and then east to Claremont. The maps follow this order. But to map everything in a completely logical fashion is impossible. Unless you plan trips carefully, you will often find that you were only a few blocks away from an important building, but you missed it because it was on another map. We advise the purchase of the *Thomas Guide* that is revised every year, but in such difficult areas as Silver Lake, the curving streets and rolling hills create problems that even the Thomas people cannot solve. Good luck!

Finally, a plea: the inclusion of buildings in this Guide does not mean that the owners have given permission to enter the building or even the grounds of private property. Some people love to show you through their houses, honored to think that you would notice them, but this attitude is becoming increasingly rare, especially among owners of famous buildings by famous architects. Some people don't even want their houses to be photographed from the street even though that is perfectly legal. Diplomacy will, however, open many doors. If the building is of recent vintage, its architect may help you to visit it. A note to the occupant may also have good results. But please respect the privacy of the people who live and work in fine architecture.

Naturally I hope that nothing really important has been omitted from this Guide. I know, though, that because I cannot cover every highway and byway, I have missed some good things. Let me know about them. They will be attended to in the next edition.

–R. W.

Acknowledgments

In a book so full of details as this one, the final copy must be a compilation of the work and intelligence of many people, most of whom will have to be unsung unless they recognize themselves in its pages. We are grateful for the many leads that we have received in telephone calls, after lectures, and in casual conversation. People who have helped us over the years include the following:

Gregory Ain
Robert Alexander
Timothy Andersen
Margaret Bach
Max A. Balgooy
Mary and Reyner Banham
John Beach
Mary Ann Beach
Mary Borgerding
Ken Breisch
Harriette von Breton
Lauren Weiss
    and David Bricker
Jeannine Burk
Douglas Byles
Regula Campbell
David Cameron
Richard Carrott
Carol Chapman
Alson Clark
Norman Cohen
John Crandall
Richard Crissman
Jeff Cronin
Jane Ellison
Charlie Fisher
Patricia Gebhard
Frank O. Gehry
Justin Gershuny
Ray Gervigian

Joseph Giovannini
Paul Gleye
Calvin Gogerty
Barbara Goldstein
Betty Goldwater
Ann Gray
Tim Gregory
Ken and Kathy Grobecker
Marlene Grossman
Stephen Harby
Harwell H. Harris
Kurt Helfrich
Allen Hess
Leslie Heumann
Thomas Hines
T. M. Hotchkiss
Warren Iliff
Shelley Kappe
Chase Langford
Paul Laszlo
Stephen Laughlin
Ruthann Lehrer
Eugene Lesner
Sally Lesner
Ann Scheid Lund
Kevin Mc Mahon
Robert Magiligan
James Marrin
Janeen Marrin
Cliff May

Margaret Meriwether
John Merritt
Kennon Miedema
Denver Miller
Charles W. Moore
Dion Neutra
Dione Neutra
Jay Oren
Nicholas Ouroussoff
Merry Ovnick
Tom Owen
Helen Park
John Pastier
Jean Bruce Poole
James Pulliam
Carolyn Ramsay
Marvin Rand
John August Reed
John Ripley
Elizabeth Sampson
Pauline Schindler
Julius Shulman
Kathryn Smith
David A. Stupplebech
Michael Webb
Msgr. Francis J. Weber
Jay Weiser
John Willeim
Mary Jo Winder
Betty Lou Young

I have had expert help in dealing with mechanical problems. Jennifer Johnson, the slide librarian at Occidental College, and her assistant, Garrett Keith, have scanned the collection of my photographs, which are now the property of the College. In many ways they have improved them.

And how can I possibly express my debt to my neighbor and former student Marcie

Chan who has done all the typing and rearranging of my revisions and kept her patience with an author who is kind of cranky and only recently a convert to the computer.

I am indebted to another neighbor and longtime friend, Ann Scheid Lund, who has chauffeured me all over Los Angeles County so that I might check on old buildings and see new ones. Being an architectural historian who expresses her ideas in no uncertain terms, she has made me think and thus is a leading contributor to this book.

What a pleasure it has been to work with Madge Baird, who directed the production of this book, and her fine staff. In editing the book, Linda Nimori's attention to detail has been exemplary.

Los Angeles

In their *California of the South* (1888), Walter Lindley and J. P. Widney wrote: "The health-seeker who, after suffering in both mind and body, after vainly trying the cold climate of Minnesota and the warm climate of Florida, after visiting Mentone, Cannes, and Nice, after traveling to Cuba and Algiers, and noticing that he is losing ounce upon ounce of flesh, that his cheeks have grown more sunken, his appetite more capricious, his breath more hurried, that his temperature is no longer normal, . . . turns with a gleam of hope toward the Occident"—by which they meant Southern California. Many people followed that gleam and found it something more than hope.

Behind the hyperbole is the promise of health, a practical matter, but this is confused with the dream of California as an earthly paradise—and the authors do not fill out the reality. Casual California living hinges on a harmonious interplay of cool ocean breezes and warm desert air. A protracted period of Santa Ana winds (when air is drawn down and baked on the mountain slopes, then suffused over the foothills) can be disastrous, as can an overly wet rainy season. Rain usually appears in good amounts (often causing landslides) in the winter months, but when it does not (and often it does not), water must be hoarded in almost all of Southern California *except* Los Angeles, which in the early twentieth century bought the Owens River Valley to the north and drew off its water in order to get a constant supply from the High Sierra.

The Big Orange—as Jack Smith, the newspaper columnist and local sage, used to call Los Angeles—uses the water of the Colorado River and more recently the Feather River, which it pipes hundreds of miles to the semidesert and its people. All this costs millions of dollars, but it has worked so far. Nevertheless, because the water might quickly be cut off, Los Angeles is utterly at the mercy of human caprice or error—not to mention divine intervention. The great Nietzsche told us to live dangerously. In Los Angeles there is no alternative.

If the supreme existential predicament exists in this area, its residents are all but oblivious to it. They are intent upon an individualistic hedonism rarely experienced since Sodom and Gomorrah. At first it might seem that people who, like the Athenians, live outdoors and swarm at malls, paseos, and beaches would develop public virtues to a high point. Not so. Southern Californians are among the most privacy-conscious people on earth. Outdoor living means backyard swimming pool areas, not the Grecian agora.

Southern California is the realization of the myth of the self-made, self-reliant, and self-oriented individual. Its denizens are disciplined by the most ingenious and complex commercial, industrial, and transportation systems, yet they accept this marvelous concatenation of forces as a given, assuming that its reason for being is to serve individual needs.

This attitude has some negative ramifications, the most important being a gross shirking of social responsibility, as the riots of 1965 and 1992 demonstrated. Signs of this lack of public concern are everywhere, especially in central Los Angeles. The breaking up of communities, urban renewal, and the destruction of the remains of the past in the name of progress are only the most glaring signs. When faced with this problem, Southern Californians say that in a real emergency they will come together—in the meantime, hands off. Sometimes they are right, but often they are not and they reap the whirlwind.

The freeway is another agency of individualistic hedonism. It services real estate promotion, but it also serves to get people away from cities and into the landscape where they can roam to their hearts' content. Ironically the freeway also tends to obliterate the landscape to which they were fleeing, but it gives Southern California its identity. That is a reason why it is absurd to compare Los Angeles to other cities save perhaps London. Unless you can tolerate and, indeed, appreciate the mobility provided by freeways, you will never understand Los Angeles.

Freeways, though appearing on the scene rather late, are closely related to another much-older embodiment of the ideal of individualism— the single-family dwelling. It is significant that in America the terms "house" and "home" are often used interchangeably and that when viewing American architectural history, domestic architecture is usually given more space than public architecture. A sentiment for the freestanding single-family dwelling continues even as we see more apartment houses and condominiums rising. What has drawn people to Southern California is the ideal of a house standing on a good-sized lot providing space for a garden and a swimming pool. The semblance of an estate surrounds the humblest bungalow, and even with the coming of multiple housing units, it is significant that the developer likes to call them garden apartments, even though the garden may be a few pots filled with artificial flowers.

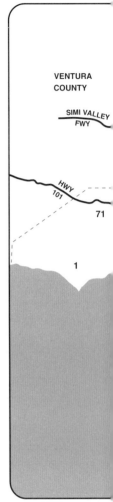

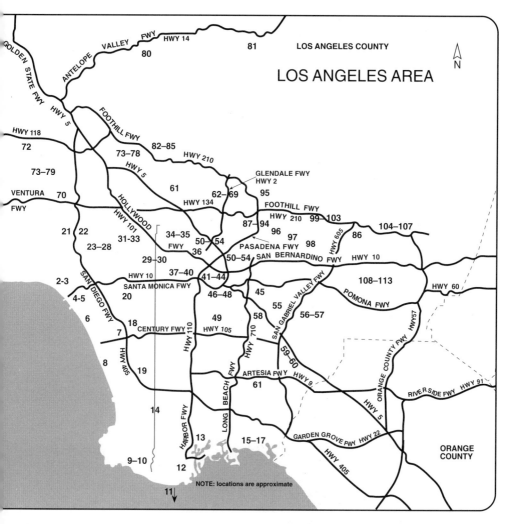

LOS ANGELES AREA

LOS ANGELES COUNTY

NOTE: locations are approximate

1. Malibu
2–3. Pacific Palisades
4–5. Santa Monica;
Ocean Park
6. Venice
7. L.A. Int'l Airport
8. South Beach Area
9–10. Palos Verdes
11. Santa Catalina Island
12. San Pedro
13. Wilmington
14. Torrance
15–17. Long Beach
18. Inglewood; Hawthorne
19. Gardena
20. Baldwin Hills;
Culver City

21. Brentwood
22. Bel Air
23–28. Westwood–
Century City
29–30. Carthay
31–33. Hollywood
34–35. East Hollywood–
Silver Lake
36. Angelino Heights–
Elysian Park
37–40. Wilshire–
MacArthur Park
41–44. Downtown
45. Boyle Heights
46–48. Exposition Park;
USC
49. Vernon–Watts

50–54. Highland Park–
Alhambra
55. Montebello;
Pico Rivera
56–57. Whittier;
Santa Fe Springs
58. Downey
59–60. Norwalk; Artesia
61. San Fernando Valley
62–69. Glendale–Encino
70. Tarzana;
Woodland Hills
71. Calabasas–
Westlake Village
72. Simi Valley
73–79. Canoga Park–
San Fernando

80. Newhall–Valencia
81. Palmdale;
Lancaster
82–85. La Crescenta
Valley–La Cañada
86. San Gabriel Valley
87–94. Pasadena
95. Altadena
96. South Pasadena;
San Marino
97. San Marino
98. San Gabriel
99–103. Sierra Madre–
Bradbury
104–107. Azusa–La Verne
108–113. Temple City–
Claremont

A Brief History of Los Angeles Architecture

In 1781 Felipe de Neve, the Spanish governor of California, founded the pueblo of Los Angeles on what is now called the Los Angeles River. Placing the settlement inland on the river plain was a logical move, for the distance from the Pacific Ocean made the site less open to attack. Furthermore, the presence of a Gabrielino Indian (Yangna) village nearby offered a source of cheap labor.

Adobe structures were built around a plaza in the typical Spanish fashion. Later, a rectangular grid of streets was platted around this central feature. Unfortunately, the river that provided a steady supply of water also flooded the town so that the plaza had to be moved several times; thus, the present plaza is not the original one.

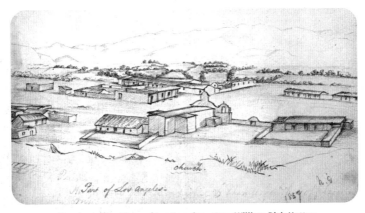

Drawing of the Plaza of Los Angeles, 1847, William Rich Hutton.
Courtesy of the Henry E. Huntington Library.

A church was built on the existing plaza in 1818. It has been rebuilt, enlarged, and imaginatively remodeled so many times since then that it is difficult to establish its original appearance except from old rough drawings that exhibit a simplification of Spanish Neoclassical architecture. Similarly, the churches built at the San Fernando and San Gabriel Missions are watered-down versions of the early-nineteenth-century religious architecture of Spanish Mexico.

By the 1860s the Spanish-Mexican influence in the architecture of Southern California was set aside by the invasion of Yankees and Jews who began settling on the land even before the American annexation of California in 1848. The adobe building method, often employed by Yankees as well as Mexicans in the early years, was replaced by fired-brick and wood-frame construction, and the latest East Coast styles were introduced. A case in point was the Pico House, a hotel built in 1869–70 by Pio Pico, the last Mexican governor of Alta California. He commissioned a Yankee, Ezra F. Kysor, to design it in a sophisticated version of the Italianate style that was popular in the rest of the United States at that time.

Left:
Italianate—
Pico House, 1869–70,
Downtown Los Angeles;
Ezra Kysor

Lower left:
Mansard—
Shaw House (Valley Knudson
Memorial House), circa 1877,
Heritage Square,
Highland Park

Lower right:
Queen Anne—
Wright-Mooers House, 1894,
818 Bonnie Brae,
MacArthur Park

From then on into the twentieth century, Southern California echoed the styles of the East—Mansard, Queen Anne, Eastlake, Anglo-Colonial Revival, Beaux-Arts, etc.— to the point that in 1900, except for some subtropical foliage in Southern California, you would not see much difference between Main Street in Los Angeles and Main Street in Davenport, Iowa. All of these styles were picturesque and superficial in the sense of being engaging façades. They were strong on show but weak on substance or what the nineteenth century called character.

Victorian

Bradbeer & Ferris (Los Angeles)
Ernest Coxhead (Los Angeles)
Ezra Kysor (Los Angeles)
Seymour Locke (Pasadena)

Merithew and Ferris (Los Angeles)
Joseph Cather Newsom (Los Angeles)
W. F. Norton (Los Angeles)
A. N. W. Parkes (Pasadena)
Harry Ridgeway (Pasadena)

A major exception to this generalization was a style that you rarely encounter in Southern California these days—Richardsonian Romanesque, named for H. H. Richardson whose Trinity Church (1874–77) in Boston along with his other public buildings caused a sensation in the architecture of American cities and even small towns, where churches, town halls, libraries, schools, and houses were built in a style indebted to Richardson's assured principles of design.

**RIchardsonian Romanesque—
Stimson Block, 1893**

Most Richardsonian buildings in Los Angeles have disappeared. Until 1900 Los Angeles was a small city. As it grew, many of the Richardsonian buildings downtown were destroyed, leaving the exterior of the Bradbury Building (1893) as one of the few shards of Richardsonian Romanesque in the central city. Just a block away was the Richardsonian Stimson Block (1893), which was also the first steel-frame building in the city. It was destroyed in 1963 to make way for a parking lot. The Richardsonian Courthouse and High School are long gone. A few relics remain—the Stimson House (1893) near the corner of Figueroa and West Adams, and in outlying Pasadena the Holliston Avenue Methodist Church (1901).

The Richardsonian Romanesque was a strong style, assertive, confident, and solid. It was also a national style, to be found in every state in the union. But even in the 1890s it was in competition with the Beaux-Arts architecture imported from France and glorified by Chicago architect Louis Sullivan. It is clear from the buildings, mainly in downtown Los Angeles, that the Beaux-Arts won. The architectural division of the École de Beaux-Arts in Paris stressed rational planning and organization, and is best known for its influence on late-nineteenth- and early-twentieth-century museums that have an entrance rotunda topped by a dome, with balancing wings containing the art. In Los Angeles, the old Los Angeles County Historical and Art Museum (see right), now simply a wing of the Museum of Natural History, is the best example.

**Beaux-Arts—Museum of Natural History, 1910–13, Exposition Park;
Hudson and Munsell**

But it was an interpretation of this idea for the façades of buildings constructed along Spring Street, Broadway and other streets that really affected Los Angeles architecture. Again, H. H. Richardson was the inspiration. His commercial buildings—the Marshall Field Wholesale Store (1885–87) in Chicago was the most important—were organized with the same rationalism as the museums except that the organization was applied to the façade whose model was a classical column with base, shaft, and capital: the first two floors, usually looking strong, formed the base; the floors above, all treated the same, were the shaft; the top floor, housing machinery and often expressed with more lavish decoration than the rest, comprised the capital. The whole surface was covered with ornament from a variety of styles—in the early 1900s the Los Angeles architects preferred Baroque, though in the twenties they veered toward Art Deco.

3rd and Broadway, Downtown Los Angeles

Beaux-Arts

John C. Austin (Los Angeles)
Robert Farquhar (Los Angeles)
Hudson & Munsell (Los Angeles)

Morgan, Walls, and Clements
(Los Angeles)
Walker & Eisen (Los Angeles)

Beaux-Arts designs for medium-rise buildings were popular in the period between 1890 and 1930 when the Great Depression held up building downtown. But in the 1890s another style that competed with the Beaux-Arts and the Richardsonian Romanesque was introduced—the Mission Revival, the use of details from Mission churches on all varieties of new buildings. In a sense it was just as superficial as the Beaux-Arts, but it had literary pretensions giving it a local significance that other styles did not offer. Helen Hunt Jackson's widely read novel *Ramona* (1884) popularized the author's conception of a better California before the arrival of Yankees whose invasion had, according to her view, broken up the happy relationship between the American Indians and the Spanish colonizers, the builders of the missions. Her fantasy was published just as the missions were moldering into dust, but Jackson's romantic suggestion of a quieter, simpler day was very attractive to readers who were becoming critical of industrialization and other aspects of modernization that in the late nineteenth century seemed to them to be in conflict with values of an earlier time. The missions represented an epoch of rest.

Left:
Mission Revival—
Wilson House, 1916,
Chester Place,
Exposition Park;
Dennis and Farwell

Lower right:
Mission Revival—
Abbey San Encino,
1909–25,
Highland Park;
Clyde Browne

     This idea was partly a reflection of an eastern colonial revival inspired by the centennial of the Declaration of Independence in 1876 and celebrated in a great exposition in Philadelphia that introduced Anglo-Colonial architecture. It was almost inevitable that Yankees in California would try to find an indigenous colonialism to complement the eastern phenomenon. Under the leadership of Charles Fletcher Lummis, an eastern emigrant who had become a booster for the West, a California Landmarks Club was founded in 1894 to save and preserve the California mission churches.

     The restoration of the missions was accompanied by a revival of the use of mission arches, tile roofs, gables, domes, and quatrefoil windows not only on new churches but also on new commercial buildings, city halls, and, rather oddly, even new houses. Among the most fervent Los Angeles advocates of the Mission Revival were Lummis' friends and fellow Landmarks Club members Sumner Hunt and A. B. Benton, the latter being the designer of the greatest monument of the Mission Revival—the Mission Inn (1902 and later) in Riverside.

Mission Revival	Sumner Hunt (Los Angeles)
A.B. Benton (Los Angeles)	Lester S. Moore (Pasadena)
Irving J. Gill (Los Angeles)	Frederick Louis Roehrig (Los Angeles)

Exactly contemporaneous with the Mission Revival and closely related to it was the Arts and Crafts movement, also called the Craftsman movement in acknowledgment of the importance of Gustav Stickley's *The Craftsman* magazine (1901–16) in furthering the cause. The Mission Revivalist's nostalgia for a simpler, better day was also part of the Craftsman rhetoric, and it was symbolized in beautifully crafted wood-shingled houses with wood-paneled interiors. The works of Charles and Henry Greene, most of them in Pasadena, are the best known relics of the Craftsman aesthetic, but there were a great many architects working in the same vein—usually with less wealthy clients! In fact, the bungalow in the period before World War I was a modest demonstration of Craftsman principles extended to the working class. It was this woodsy one or one-and-a-half-story cottage that got the name "California bungalow" and was built all over the United States.

Arts and Crafts
Joseph J. Blick (Pasadena)
Irving J. Gill
  (Los Angeles and San Diego)
Charles and Henry Greene
  (Pasadena)
Arthur S. and Alfred Heineman
  (Pasadena)
Sylvanus Marston (Pasadena)
Ross Montgomery (Los Angeles)
Frederick Louis Roehrig
  (Los Angeles)

Duncan-Irwin House, 1900, 1906, Pasadena;
Charles and Henry Greene

After World War I, fanciful interpretations of past styles took over in both public and domestic architecture. In a way these Period Revivals were extensions of the eclecticism that had been a constant movement in American architecture. But a more immediate source of this phenomenon, particularly the reproduction of Spanish architecture, was the popularity of the Panama-California Exposition in San Diego in 1915. There, Bertram Goodhue and the

California Building, Panama-California Exposition, 1915.
Courtesy San Diego Historical Society.

architects under his supervision introduced Spanish Plateresque and Churrigueresque forms that had rarely been seen above the border with Mexico. Their flamboyance was attractive to California architects, who used them mainly in commercial and religious structures with great dramatic effect.

At the same time, a different quieter Hispanicism was introduced into domestic architecture. Here, the source was the Spanish farmhouse. David Gebhard has called this the "Spanish Colonial Revival," suggesting the influence of Mexican forms. A greater contribution came directly from Spain as the result of the work of young architects such as Austin Whittlesey, who traveled in Spain just before and during World War I and made sketches of Spanish rural architecture as well as the more colorful urban baroque. They produced books showing traditional Spanish farmhouses with white stucco walls and picturesque asymmetry. These books became the source and inspiration for many California residences.

But these Hispanicists were not purists. To the abstract forms of the farmhouses they sometimes added Churrigueresque flourishes around doorways. In fact they went beyond

Spanish Revival (Mediterranean)—Baldwin House, 1925, San Marino;
George Washington Smith

Spain to southern France, Italy, and even North Africa for ideas and eventually coined the term "Mediterranean" as a catchall for their designs. They were truly eclectic.

The result was a new wave of an architecture of entertainment in the American tradition. The intensity of this movement was probably due to the widely popular movies where backdrops were often modeled on exotic buildings and streets. In fact, streets such as Lombardy in Pasadena and San Marino resembled a series of stage sets. Even Frank Lloyd Wright, who claimed to hate California "medievalism," caught the spirit and drew upon Mayan sources for his Los Angeles houses of the 1920s.

Period Revivals

Allison & Allison (Los Angeles)

John Byers (Santa Monica)

Roland Coate (Pasadena)

Elmer Grey (Pasadena)

Myron Hunt (Los Angeles)

Reginald Johnson (Pasadena)

Gordon B. Kaufmann
(Pasadena and Beverly Hills)

Marston, Van Pelt & Maybury
(Pasadena)

Ross Montgomery (Los Angeles)

Wallace Neff (Pasadena)

Parkinson & Parkinson
(Los Angeles)

George Washington Smith
(Pasadena and Santa Barbara)

Like H. H. Richardson, there were California architects who took issue with the superficiality of the Period Revivals. Such a person was Irving J. Gill. He had worked for a short time with Louis Sullivan in Chicago and had taken seriously Sullivan's dictum that, in order to get back to the fundamentals of architecture, ornament should be banished—a rule that Sullivan himself found difficult to follow. Gill came to California in the 1890s when the Mission Revival was in full swing. He took that style and eliminated all its detail except arches, thereby developing a mode that was in general appearance very close to the lessons in geometry produced at the European Bauhaus at about the same time—the so-called "International Style." Although the Europeans used the machine image to define their design principles, something Gill never did, Gill's simplification of the

Mission Revival—Dodge House; Irving Gill

Mission Revival was related to the spirit of reductionism that seemed to be in the air in the teens and twenties.

At the same time, Gill was no radical. He made no fiery pronouncements; instead, he wrote for *The Craftsman* magazine as if he were following the principles of the Arts and Crafts movement. The radicals who would break with history in order to get a modern architecture were in Europe.

Even as the Craftsman movement flourished in the first two decades of the twentieth century there was a spirit of modernism arising. The European Art Nouveau had few takers in the United States, but its successor, the Art Deco, certainly attracted many American architects. Eastern cities, especially New York, were (and are) alive with the Zigzag Moderne, as David Gebhard labeled the Art Deco. Like Art Nouveau, it was an applied decorative motif. In fact, that is why it was so attractive during the 1920s when the architecture of

Art Deco—Selig Retail Store (now Crocker-Citizens National Bank Branch Offices), 1931, MacArthur Park; Arthur E. Harvey

entertainment flourished. It was a sort of people's modern, vertical, and in a vaguely Gothic style so that everyone could understand it, but it also celebrated the future in a Buck Rogers sort of way.

The greatest Art Deco landmarks in Los Angeles are the Wiltern Theater Building (1930–31; Morgan, Walls, and Clements) and the Bullocks-Wilshire Department Store (1928; Parkinson & Parkinson), now recycled as a law library. The great Richfield Building (1929; Morgan, Walls, and Clements) was demolished long ago, but there are many other Art Deco buildings on Wilshire Boulevard and other places in the Los Angeles area.

In the 1930s the Art Deco was followed by the Streamline Moderne (at the time called Modernistic) and a number of other Modernes, the PWA and Regency being the most conspicuous. All evoked an idea of the future. But in the twenties there was also the International Style, a serious modern architecture coming from Europe that, as with the work of Gill, was less easily understood by the general public because of its intended radical break with history and its concern with abstraction and the elimination of ornament, either historic or contemporary.

It is significant that when the International Style came to Los Angeles in the twenties, its propo-

International Style—Lovell House, 1927, Newport Beach; R. M. Schindler

nents, R. M. Schindler and Richard Neutra, both educated in Viennese radicalism, would also be admirers of Frank Lloyd Wright, who claimed that he despised the International Style. Wright would soften the radicalism of his admirers. Schindler came to America first and worked for Wright, in fact arriving in Los Angeles in 1919 to supervise the construction of Wright's Hollyhock House for Aline Barnsdall. He set up his own practice in 1922 and encouraged his friend Richard Neutra to join him, which Neutra did, bringing along his wife and their child. The Neutras lived at the Schindler's house and the two men were associated with each other on a number of projects until their temperaments clashed, and they went their separate ways.

Schindler was the more imaginative of the two. But Neutra got the publicity and the rich clients that Schindler rarely acquired. Being successful, Neutra employed a number of able young architects, such as Raphael Soriano, Gregory Ain, and Harwell Hamilton Harris, who carried the torch of Modernism in Los Angeles well past World War II. In fact, it is not exaggerating to say that Los Angeles in the thirties, forties, and fifties was the center of the Modernist movement in American domestic architecture.

International Style—Lovell House, 1929, Hollywood; Richard Neutra

Just after World War II, John Entenza, the editor of *Arts and Architecture,* fearing the conservatism that always follows wars, inaugurated his famous Case Study House program (1945–60). He projected a series of Modernist houses being built and then opened for tours, after which they would be sold and the proceeds would then go to the commissioning of more International Style houses. He feared public apathy, but was astonished and delighted when 368,554 people visited the first six houses. As Esther McCoy noted (*Perspecta* 15, 1975), the popularity of these buildings spread to the furniture they exhibited, much of it being the same pieces hauled from house to house for photographic purposes. A number of retail outlets for the furniture of Charles and Ray Eames, Harry Bertoia, Eero Saarinen, and Hendrick Van Keppel were opened with great success.

Naturally, a style as clearly arbitrary ("less is more") as the International Style would have its critics. Cliff May's ranch houses, strongly expressing a warm Arts and Crafts modernism, would contradict their machine-image critics. Schindler and Neutra, while avant-garde and notably Modernist, were considerably less arbitrary than their teachers. In fact, they were criticized for their expressionist tendencies by such purist critics as Philip Johnson and Henry-Russell Hitchcock, when they were organizing their "International Style"

International Style—Kubly House, 1965, Pasadena; Craig Ellwood

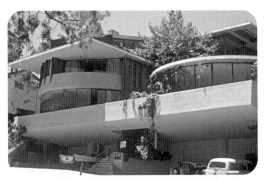

Expressionist—Sheets (L'Horizon) Apartments, 1949,
Westwood; John Lautner

Expressionist—Beckman Auditorium, 1963,
Caltech, Pasadena; Edward D. Stone

exhibition that opened at the Museum of Modern Art in New York in 1932.

After World War II, just at the moment of International Style triumph, some even more blatant attacks on its Spartan doctrine appeared in the designs of architects that were eventually labeled Postmodern, an unfortunate term since it suggests that its practitioners were futuristic. Actually, many of them, such as Charles Moore, dipped into historicism, with ironic overtones to be sure. Historicism certainly returned with a vengeance when architects Langdon and Wilson, with the help of Norman Neuerberg's research, designed the J. Paul Getty Museum (1972–73; now called the Old Getty), strongly based on the ancient Villa dei Papyri near Herculaneum. The museum building may be simply a projection of Getty's conservative taste, but the appreciation of it by the general public is significant. Many admirers find it an excellent background for Getty's Greek and Roman sculptures. Also, the view of the Pacific Ocean from its pergola is more magnificent than that from most Roman villas. Moreover, it is grand.

As indicated earlier, the followers of Frank Lloyd Wright, represented in Los Angeles by John Lautner, had always scoffed at European radicalism in their pursuit of "organic" architecture. And a curious vogue of Edward Durell Stone, just when he was becoming passé on the East Coast, showed unease with Bauhaus principles.

In the seventies and eighties the upholders of the International Style aesthetic were, of course, looking back many years, one school to the geometry and clean lines of the Bauhaus, the larger one literally exploiting the image of the machine in details derived from industrial objects. The latter school, associated with Postmodernism, took its inspiration from Le Corbusier and from the Place Pompidou, which, if we can believe Reyner Banham, was in its turn simply an ordering of the disparate forms of the San Onofre Power Plant in Southern California.

The greatest monument of the Postmodern in the Los Angeles area is, of course, Frank Gehry's Chiat-Day-Mojo Building (1985–91) in Venice. Its central entrance for automobiles is a pair of binoculars designed by Claes Oldenburg and Coosje van Bruggen. On the north side of this Pop Art is a wing that looks back to the layered, white International Style. The south wing, on the other hand, is a building in decadent purple that looks as if it were about to collapse—perhaps Gehry's notion of Deconstructionism that never really took hold in Southern California. The whole congeries seems to be a comment on what was going on in architecture at the time the building took shape.

Postmodern—Chiat-Day-Mojo Building, 1985–91, Venice; Frank O. Gehry and Associates

Postmodern— J. Paul Getty Center for the Arts (New Getty), 1984–97, Brentwood; Richard Meier

The local monument of the return to the revival of the International Style is, of course, Richard Meier's vast new Getty Museum (1992–99) in Brentwood. It is so big, Spartan, white, and assertive that it is almost a parody of Le Corbusier's work. Better examples of the return to the twenties are the condominiums (1982) that Mark Mack and Drew Batey designed on Bellevue Avenue in Pasadena and Mack's own house on the Venice canals. An even more beautiful recent evocation of the International Style is Glen Irani's house nearby—*with color*!

Postmodern— Mack House 419 Howland Canal Venice; Mark Mack

Postmodern—St. Matthew's Episcopal Church, 1982–83,
Pacific Palisades; Charles W. Moore

Hard to place in the history of Los Angeles architecture is the important work of
Charles Moore. His residential architecture shows the influence of the International Style
filtered through the tradition of the California barn and strongly affected by Moore's own
sense of humor, a gesture toward the Postmodern. In the eighties, while he was teaching
at UCLA, he seemed to become more serious in his St. Matthew's Episcopal Church
(1982–83) in Pacific Palisades, with its almost Romanesque feeling on both the exterior
and interior. His First Church of Christ, Scientist (1989), in Glendale was positively
serene—then he went to Texas!

The two most recent additions to the significant landmarks list are Rafael Moneo's
Roman Catholic Cathedral of Our Lady of the Angels (2002) and, of course, Frank Gehry's
Walt Disney Concert Hall (1993–2003). When it began to take form on the south side of

the San Bernardino Freeway, the cathedral looked like a resurrection of New Brutalism, and it remains austere, perhaps as it should be in its urban environment. The interior is magnificently sculptured space and suffused light in the Gothic tradition. But it remains a Spanish interpretation of the American Catholic church and, for all its beauty, seems a little out of place.

The headliner is Gehry's new home for the Los Angeles Philharmonic (see cover). Although its basic design (much modified since the building was first projected) antedates that of Gehry's Guggenheim Museum in Bilbao, Spain, the resemblance between the two is obvious. The similarity suggests that both buildings embody Gehry's anxiety to break with tradition, national or international, and to create architecture that will lift the spirit rather than refer to previous notions of what architecture should be.

Looking to recent work, especially that of the younger architect, it appears that the most imaginative architecture is being created on the west side of Los Angeles—Culver City, Santa Monica, Venice, and West Hollywood. A great many of the avant-garde architects have their offices in Santa Monica. It would seem that the presence of Frank Gehry there provides at least some inspiration for the emergence of a quantity of extremely interesting work. The area is also the home of the Southern California Institute of Architecture, a school that welcomes radical ideas as advanced by its faculty and student body. Maybe it is the sea air that nourishes the mind, although it should be remembered that this same west side was hardly the home of creativity in architecture until at least the 1980s.

Unfortunately some of the best work, especially that of the youngest architects, is only on paper and has not been put into forms. Also, it is significant and sometimes sad that when they do get jobs, they seem, to a notable degree, to be used mainly as interior designers, especially of restaurants that, having a short life span, require trendy remodelings as they come and go. Perhaps as the economy improves, we will see a new wave of building that will employ these good minds, but it is dangerous to predict the future. Suffice to say that the spirit and intelligence are at hand. At the moment, the promise is refreshing, even if it is not yet fulfilled.

Cathedral of Our Lady of the Angels, 2002, Downtown Los Angeles; Rafael Moneo

International Style

Gregory Ain (Los Angeles)
Charles & Ray Eames
Craig Ellwood
Harwell H. Harris (Los Angeles)
A. Quincy Jones (Los Angeles)
Raymond Kappe (Pacific Palisades)
Pierre Koenig (Los Angeles)
Lotery/Boccato (Los Angeles)
Richard Meier (Los Angeles)
Richard Neutra (Los Angeles)
R. M. Schindler (Los Angeles)
Raphael Soriano (Los Angeles)
Smith & Williams (Pasadena)

Neo-Expressionism (Postmodernism)

Belzberg Architects
Rebecca Binder
Cavaedium
Chu + Gooding
Daly, Genik Architects
Steven Ehrlich Architects
Ellerbe Becket
Frederick Fisher and Partners
Frank O. Gehry and Associates
Gensler Architecture
Bruce Goff
David Lawrence Gray
Melinda Gray
Grinstein/Daniels Architects
Hodgetts + Fung
Glen Irani
Franklin D. Israel
John Lautner
Johnson, Favaro
Kanner Architects
Koning Eizenberg Architecture
Ricardo Legoretta
Mark Mack
Michael Maltzan
Marmol Radziner & Associates
Charles Moore
Morphosis
Eric Owen Moss
I. M. Pei
Cesar Pelli
Pugh + Scarpa
Michael Rotondi (RoTo)
Hak Sik Son
Syndesis (David Hertz)
Venturi, Scott-Brown & Associates
Mehrdad Yazdani

Historic Preservation in Los Angeles

Organized preservation efforts have had a long history in Los Angeles. The California Landmarks Club, founded in 1894 under the leadership of Charles F. Lummis and the architects Arthur B. Benton and Sumner Hunt, pioneered conservation of historic architecture, though, to be sure, these efforts were largely limited to a few missions.

Avila Adobe, Olvera Street, watercolor circa 1900, by Edith Scott Fenyes.
Courtesy Pasadena Museum of History.

In the late 1920s Christine Sterling and many local merchants set out to save and restore notable structures in the Old Plaza area including Olvera Street, a project in which the city, county, and state took an interest in the 1950s and administered jointly for a while. Saddened by the destruction of a Victorian Bunker Hill in the same period, a group of citizens founded the Cultural Heritage Foundation (1969) and moved the last two derelicts on the Hill to a newly designated Heritage Square located on an unused piece of land next to the Arroyo Seco and the Pasadena Freeway in Highland Park.

In 1978 the private nonprofit Los Angeles Conservancy appeared as a watchdog and galvanized preservation energy throughout the city. In fact, the 1970s and 1980s saw an active development of urban conservation programs, notably in Pasadena, South Pasadena, Santa Monica, Claremont, and more recently Long Beach.

The Conservancy, now having a 7,000-plus constituency and a good-sized staff, is a real force in the community. Its intervention has stopped the destruction of many notable buildings. Probably its most celebrated victory was in finding an institution that would recycle and reuse the Bullocks-Wilshire Department Store, a monument of the Art Deco

Bullocks-Wilshire Department Store, 1928, MacArthur Park; John and Donald Parkinson; Feil and Paradice; Jock Peters

style of the late 1920s. The store had been bought by Macy's, was badly damaged in the rioting of April 1992, and was then stripped by Macy's of chandeliers and other appointments, which were dispersed. The Conservancy, with help from city authorities, succeeded in retrieving most of these relics and interested the Southwestern School of Law in buying the store in order to hold its library. The building is now functioning well and tours can be arranged through the Conservancy. Long Beach, with its large number of disused hotels and other buildings, has converted them to multiple-family housing.

Not all such efforts have happy endings. Occasionally in their zeal to protect the heritage, members of the Conservancy have wasted their time trying to preserve old things that have very little historical significance and even less beauty. But the general effect of the Conservancy's vigilance has been to advance preservation causes and to alert the general public and politicians to the danger of losing the past.

The Los Angeles Cultural Heritage Foundation, whose Heritage Square was dubbed "an architectural petting zoo" by one critic, has been criticized for its inactivity, limited scope, and tendency to channel its monies into moving houses onto a rather undesirable piece of land. These charges lack in appreciation the fact that the foundation has saved some very distinguished pieces of architecture that otherwise would have been destroyed by the bulldozer or vandals.

Longfellow-Hastings ("Octagon") House, 1893, Heritage Square, Highland Park

The historic Plaza in downtown Los Angeles is another matter. Until recently, the effect of the tripartite administration of the Plaza area has been a disaster for true preservation to the point that, although Olvera Street is a business success, the nearby Pico House, Garnier Block, Masonic Lodge, and Merced Theater are unfinished and, except for the theater, unused. Not all the blame can rest on managerial rivalry. Even ethnic jealousies have entered the fray, and now that the project is under the city's administration, it is obvious that the problems, now mainly political, have not ended.

Pico House (1869–70), Merced Theater (1870), Masonic Lodge (1858), Downtown Plaza (photographer not identified)

All the while, the official city agency responsible for urban conservation has been the Los Angeles Cultural Heritage Board (now Commission). Founded by ordinance in 1962 it is one of the oldest such municipal agencies in the country and, among the large cities of the United States, one of the weakest. Ironically, when the ordinance was written, largely by Carl Dentzel (then-director of the Southwest Museum) and William L. Woolett (of the American Institute of Architects), it was one of the strongest. Under its provision that the board may withhold permits for demolition or extensive remodeling for up to one year if progress is shown in efforts to preserve them, many old and treasured buildings are today standing that otherwise would be demolished. But, until recently, the board has felt limited by the ordinance to designate "cultural-historic monuments" and under the ordinance has been specifically barred from owning property or handling money.

An excellent Historic District Ordinance has been established by the City Council. Historic Preservation Overlay Zones may now be set up under the supervision of the Planning Department. Fifteen zones have their machinery in order and five others have been recommended to the city council. Long Beach also has a very successful program for preserving historic districts, as does Pasadena.

In 1980 an inventory of the historic resources of Los Angeles was begun. For a time the city's Department of Engineering administered it. More recently the J. Paul Getty Institute has initiated a program to foster the completion of the survey and has organized a Blue Ribbon Committee to raise money for that purpose. The effort to survey a huge, sprawling city is almost overwhelming, but it is necessary. Much smaller Pasadena has a better record, especially in the central city.

As we have noted, a number of preservation programs have been developed by the cities of Los Angeles County. Pasadena passed a historical preservation ordinance in 1976 and a new, much stronger one began its passage into law by the Pasadena City

Council in August 2002. Its private preservation organization is Pasadena Heritage, a pressure group that has gone beyond campaigns to prevent demolitions and has actually moved buildings that would otherwise have been razed. The Gartz bungalow court and the house of Charlotte Perkins Gilman have been moved, rehabilitated, and sold to sympathetic owners.

The people of Pasadena, through the good offices of the city as well as private organizations, have developed a conscience about preservation that is unmatched by any other city in the county. This may have something to do with the stability of its economic position. Nevertheless, as elsewhere, zealous developers are always at hand and continue to destroy valuable vestiges of the past, so eternal vigilance is necessary. Strong neighborhood associations, usually in upper-class neighborhoods, guard against intrusions to the point that such large residential tracts as the Arroyo Seco and Oak Knoll districts are treated with a respect usually reserved for sacred objects. Lower-class neighborhoods do not fare so well, although the city Historic Preservation Commission can sometimes hold up demolitions.

Other parts of the county, especially the city of Los Angeles proper, have fewer safeguards against chaotic economic growth. For many years Los Angeles has been one of the few American cities to sustain economic expansion even in periods of recession. It is very difficult to talk preservation when there is a need for new buildings.

Extremely heartening is the participation of state and national governments in furthering preservation. Since 1977 the California Historical Property Contracts Program (Mills Act) has helped to attract owners of historical landmarks to preservation and renovation projects in the City of Los Angeles. It provides approximately a one-half property tax reduction to Historical-Cultural Monuments and Historic Preservation Overlay Zones. On March 5, 2002, California voters approved Proposition 40, which provides $267.5 million for historic and cultural resources. The only sour note heard during the campaign for Proposition 40 was struck by the pollsters who indicated that they found that historic preservation did not score as high as clean air, open space, and clean water in the voters' reasons for voting for the proposition.

When everything is considered, the decision to retain old buildings is made by individuals who may be swayed by public opinion but in the end they make the commitment. That is why developers such as Wayne Ratkovitch, Tom Gilmore, and Ira Yellin as well as preservation architects such as Brenda Levin are so important. They have shown that it is possible to advance the public good and at the same time to make a profit.

Planning

According to folk wisdom, Los Angeles grew without a plan. This is nonsense. In 1781, when the Spanish established a pueblo on the banks of the Porciúncula (now Los Angeles) River, the colonists brought with them the traditional Spanish idea of a central plaza set into a grid of streets. The gridiron (without plaza) was also the Yankee pattern for laying out towns so that as Los Angeles grew, this regular plan was used as it was for the small settlements that came to surround Los Angeles proper in the nineteenth century. As places such as Highland Park, Wilmington, and Santa Monica enlarged and touched the grid of Los Angeles, it was not always a close fit, thus making it necessary to link streets by curves and awkward angles. But, except in hilly areas where streets had to be laid out on the contours of the land, the gridiron was the accepted plan.

With the coming of the World's Columbian Exposition of 1893 in Chicago, the people of Los Angeles were just as impressed by its magnificence and planning as was the rest of the nation. They saw monumental buildings set on lagoons and a more complex plan than the grid system. Daniel Burnham, a Chicago architect, and Frederick Law Olmsted, a New York landscape architect, had devised a plan that included not only verticals and horizontals but also streets that ran diagonally through the grid. They called it "the great white city" or, more often, "the City Beautiful."

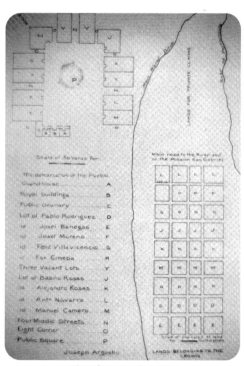

Plan of Los Angeles, 1781

Actually a model existed before the fair—Pierre L'Enfant's plan (1791) for Washington, D.C., was extended beyond L'Enfant's boundaries in the period after the fair. The City Beautiful movement touched almost every city in the United States in the teens and twenties. Burnham's grand plan for Chicago was unveiled in 1909, and, even though actual building on it barely began, it was a great source of enthusiasm.

Although Burnham's Chicago Plan was never applied to a whole city, it was instrumental in developing civic centers, the one in San Francisco (1912–36) being among the

first. But the most successful application of Beaux-Arts ideas in this country happened
in Los Angeles County in the twenties—the civic center of Pasadena. As David Gebhard
used to say, "The Pasadena Civic Center plan is second only to Edwin Lutyen's plan for
New Delhi."

As early as 1900 the City Beautiful movement affected thinking about a civic center
in the city of Los Angeles. From that time onward, numerous plans were drawn up and
then discarded or ignored. Nevertheless, a commission was appointed in 1918 to select a
site. Its members chose the present location, near the old plaza but significantly not on it. A Neoclassical Hall of Justice was erected in 1924 and the present Goodhuesque City Hall was constructed nearby in 1928. It was assumed that the City Hall would be the center of the plan, which would extend from it along north/south and east/west axes.

Pasadena City Hall, 1925–27;
John Bakewell Jr. and Arthur Brown Jr.

In 1939 this idea was warmed over and extended by Sumner Spaulding and a number of other architects, but nothing much was done about it until after World War II when planning became closely involved with urban renewal. Seeing the Victorian housing on Bunker Hill near which the civic center was proposed, the planners decided that these ancient houses must go. By the end of the forties they were being demolished, and
the top of the hill itself was shaved off for the construction of high-rise that some people
thought would give a focus to the central city.

For the civic center, the Spaulding plan was revised. Some extremely boring buildings
were built in the fifties along the north and south sides of the east/west axis to provide a
courthouse, law library, and state building. Then in the sixties, the north side of the axis
was completed with a Hall of Records, Hall of Administration, and Criminal Court
Building. At the west end of the axis, "Mrs. Chandler's Acropolis" arose, with the Music
Center spread out below the Department of Water and Power that, like the Parthenon,
stood sentinel over the whole operation.

The visual impact of this interpretation of Beaux-Arts planning is not happy. The
buildings seem loose and unrelated to each other. The center of the grand allée leading
up the hill, covered over for parking garages on which gardens were planted and sculpture
strewn, is uninviting—a kind of big, eerie no-man's-land.

A few smaller Beaux-Arts projects have been more successful. Lawrence Halprin's grand staircase (see right) leading down Bunker Hill to the north door of Goodhue's Public Library is marvelous. On the other hand, Ricardo Legorreta's refashioning of Pershing Square, although based on good intentions, is a symbolic and aesthetic disaster.

Areas of the county outside the city have had better luck. One of the most interesting plans was more English landscape than Beaux-Arts—the Palos Verdes Estates. Here, the planning developed by Myron Hunt and the Olmsted Brothers set up a community whose winding streets followed the contours of the land. Even more radically the town fathers set up a jury, still in existence, that reviewed landscaping and architectural ideas and imposed restrictions on property owners. Some critics have found these harsh and even silly, but the impression on most viewers is of coherent beauty.

Bunker Hill Steps, 1989–90, Downtown Los Angeles; Lawrence Halprin

In his *Los Angeles: The Architecture of Four Ecologies* (1971), the English architectural historian and critic Reyner Banham suggested that the developing transportation system for Los Angeles County organized the growing city far more significantly than the decisions of professional planners. He pointed out that Los Angeles, cut off from the rest of the world by deserts and mountains, first came together as a community as a result of the short lines of railroads that struck out from the central city between 1868 and 1875 to Wilmington, Anaheim, Pomona, San Fernando, and Santa Monica. None of them went very far, but they did act as links to downtown Los Angeles. As Banham wrote, "Lines were hardly laid before commuting began along them; scattered communities were joined together in a diffuse and unprecedented super-community."

Consolidation proceeded with the development of the Pacific Electric Railroad, an interurban light-rail much more extensive than the early system of railroads. By the twenties Los Angeles County had one of the finest public transportation systems in the country. To quote Banham again: "Local electric services by street railways and interurban lines were to make almost every piece of land in the Los Angeles basin conveniently accessible and thus profitably exploitable . . ." The ageing of the Big Red Cars and the popularity of the motorcar doomed the Pacific Electric. The last run was in 1961. It was replaced by the freeways, the Pasadena Freeway being the first. By the 1970s almost everyone in Los Angeles was less than four miles from a freeway.

In the last few years, nothing really dramatic has developed in the field of planning. The *Los Angeles Times* occasionally carries articles about major projects intended for Skid Row or South Central Los Angeles or Hollywood, but nothing seems to come from them. When prosperity returns, we will undoubtedly see a renewal of interest in proposals for a more orderly city.

Landscape Architecture

Among its many attributes, including some rather embarrassing ones, California has always suggested paradise, even if it is paradise lost. At its best it is Eden, a garden of perfection. Nevertheless, there has always been a human arrogance that believes that nature can be improved. Thus, landscape architecture—gardening.

Northern California has certain attractions, but Southern California, especially the Los Angeles area, has the climate. It is semidesert, but with enough water, the desert blossoms as

the rose. If it doesn't rain enough, we just tap the Owens River Valley for water from the High Sierra. The other requirement for the garden beautiful is a fertile soil. Unfortunately, the soil is not rich except for areas where cattle graze. But fertilizer is plentiful and fairly cheap. Almost everything grows. The result is that we go for the exotic, disdaining native plant materials and adopting things like eucalyptus

Doheny House (landscape), 1898–1900, Chester Place, Exposition Park; Theodore A. Eisen and Sumner P. Hunt

trees that the Lord never intended to grow in Southern California. But they do grow—and quite beautifully—so they become the symbols of our land.

The Victorian settlers were the first to discover the potential versatility of the land and the gifts of nature. They usually built their houses on flat surfaces and then set out plants and trees in clumps without much relation to the gardening theory, which in its rudimentary form they knew from books but which they ignored in their desire to show off. Pictures of lawns such as those around the Banning Mansion (1864) in Wilmington show no attempts to create vistas toward garden architecture nor do they contain winding paths that give the impression of informality. An alternative design, the formal Italo-French garden, was also ignored. In the Victorian era, Los Angelinos simply exulted in what Southern California could produce, whatever its source, and planted it where they wanted.

With the advent of professional landscape architects in the early twentieth century, a number of extensive gardens were developed that showed the influence of high theory. Almost all of these have disappeared or have lost their coherence. Many are beautifully illustrated in Eugene O. Murmann's *California Gardens* (1914), but Murmann does not identify them by owner or place. It is clear from the exotic plant materials, however, that his illustrations are almost all Southern California gardens, and it is possible in many cases to recognize well known gardens such as those of Charles and Henry Greene at the Blacker House (1907) in Pasadena and of Myron Hunt at the Wattles House (1905) in Hollywood. Photographs of the Busch Gardens (1907 and later) are illustrated as they existed in their early years.

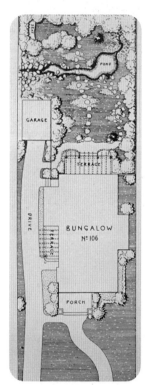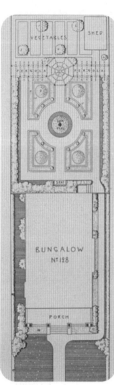

Probably the most interesting section of Murmann's book is devoted to plans of gardens for bungalows that almost always were on small lots that offered the least opportunity for elaborate planning. But Murmann gives his attention to formal gardens, Japanese gardens, and landscape gardens as well as variations on these styles. Unfortunately, almost none of his ideas seem to have been carried out, but they are there in his book, ready to be used by present-day members of the cult of the bungalow.

Landscape plans, *California Gardens*, 1914;
Eugene O. Murmann

In the 1920s Montecito's rich settlers planted many elaborate gardens, some of them magnificent. But in the Los Angeles area the relatively high value of the land limited the size of the plantings, the result being that the expansive English landscape garden with its winding paths and other aspects of "irregular symmetry" was rarely realized. Most Los Angeles gardens were formal essays in geometry. The *Architectural Digest,* founded in 1920, carried photographs of the finest gardens of that period, as did Winifred Starr Dobyns in her *California Gardens* (1931). Remarkable also in the twenties was the number of women who, following in the steps of Gertrude Jekyl in England, found a significant place in the field of landscape architecture when there were still only a few professions open to them.

Japanese Garden, begun in 1911,
Henry E. Huntington Art Gallery,
Library and Gardens,
San Marino

Although nature usually cooperates, the art of gardening is not easy in Southern California. Changes in climate occur sometimes every few miles so that fuchsia, which blooms beautifully in Santa Monica's moist ocean air, has to be coddled if planted a mile or so inland. The soil also plays tricks. Pasadena is noted for its roses, but in one part of the city near the Arroyo Seco the soil is so sandy and so full of oak root fungus that roses can be raised only with constant care. Every landscape architect and gardener must be a student of place and a constant experimenter. But the result is worth the effort.

Landscape Architects

Nineteenth Century—
Charles Gibbs Adams
Francesco Franceschi
Joseph Sexton

Early Twentieth Century—
Robert Gordon Fraser
William Hertrich
Myron Hunt
Olmsted and Olmsted

Twenties and Thirties—
Katherine Bashford
Ralph D. Cornell
Lucille Council
Beatrix Farrand
A. E. Hanson
Edward Huntsman-Trout
Kate Sessions
Paul Thiene
Lloyd Wright
Florence Yoch

Post–World War II—
Campbell and Campbell
Eckbo, Dean and Associates
Nancy Goslee Power
Emmett Wemple

1 • Malibu

Malibu Beach did not begin its development until 1929, when the Pacific Coast Highway was finally pushed through the Rindge Ranch. After that, Malibu became a fashionable place to have a beach house. The hilly coastland of the West remained basically rural until the 1960s. Increasingly in recent years, the area between the highway and the beach is being filled with numerous large-scale houses. In the 1960s and early 1970s, most of these houses were loosely Modern in imagery, but in recent years historicism (usually grossly misunderstood) ranging from the Medieval to the Spanish Revival has prevailed. The land adjacent to the highway is slowly being condominiumized, with disappointing versions of varied architectural styles. In the early 1990s, Malibu was incorporated as an independent city. It will be interesting to see how it develops its own personality in the years to come.

Malibu continues to acquire houses of distinguished design, but the colony is a private, well-guarded world and is not open to the public.

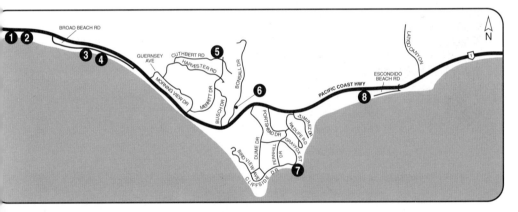

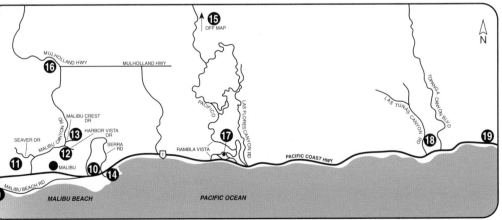

1. Sagheb House, 1990
John Lautner
32402 Pacific Coast Highway

Since the 1960s, John Lautner has designed a number of houses on the Malibu coast. Most of these are of reinforced concrete in a highly organic (and unusual) form. Unfortunately, these houses are not easy to see from the road, but at low tide, an adventuresome person wandering along the beach can catch an occasional glimpse of them. Other Lautner houses in the Malibu area are the Krause House (1983) at 24444 Malibu Road, and the Segel House (1983) at 22426 Pacific Coast Highway.

2. Pierson House, 1961–64
Craig Ellwood
32320 Pacific Coast Highway

The Pierson house is a precise, carefully delineated volume, closed off from the road by thin, paper-like walls and an intervening courtyard. It has an urban design on three sides and an open beach pavilion on the west.

3. Berns House, 1951
Gordon Drake
31654 W. Broad Beach Road
Trancas Beach

A screened patio forms the center of this dwelling. The frame is articulated by vertical wood posts having an infill primarily of glass. Rational, but warm. In recent years the house has been remodeled by Gerald Frost.

4. Downey House, 1991
Melinda Gray
31616 Broad Beach Road
Trancas Beach

The three main sections of this two-story dwelling suggest not a single building but an informal group of buildings. Gray wrote of the house that it was a "playful series of pavilions created by vaults, gables, cylinders, and squares connected by the landscape elements that start out formally and drift into casual directedness." The house is sheathed in natural and pink-colored stucco combined with a thin slate base.

5. Davis House, 1972
Frank O. Gehry and Associates
29715 W. Cuthbert Road
Trancas Beach

A trapezoidal building covered by a low-pitched shed roof creates a neutral interior space that can be arranged at will. The exterior, including roof, is sheathed in corrugated metal. The shape as you see it from a distance creates some unusual problems of perspective.

6. LeBrun House, 1963
Thornton M. Abell
6339 Bonsall Drive
Zuma Beach

An entrance gallery, small courtyard, and office connect the living wing to the studio section of the house. Enclosed terraces and gardens effectively carry the interior space outward. Certainly one of Abell's most successful houses.

7. Lyndon House, 1950
Maynard Lyndon
28820 Cliffside Drive
Paradise Cove

A 1950s Modern ranch house expressing the classic post-and-beam tradition of the Case Study Houses.

8. Holiday House Motel, 1950
Richard J. Neutra;
1954
Dion Neutra
27400 Pacific Coast Highway

Two layouts of living/sleeping rooms, each with its own balcony, look out over the ocean. The upper unit has two stories, the lower has one. Balconies are supported by L-shaped outriggers, and the buildings are sheathed in board and batten. The original buildings plus the twelve units added by Dion Neutra in 1954 are effectively worked into the hillside bluff.

9. Hunt House, 1955–57
Craig Ellwood
24514 Malibu Beach Road

The Case Study House image of the 1950s—Miesian, cardboardy, and fragile. Facing the road are two boxes, each of which houses a garage; a small entrance court is enclosed between them. A wooden bridge leads down to the house. The plan of the house is the Modernist H-scheme. The front leg of the H contains the two bedrooms, both of which look out on a court. A wood decked terrace extends along the beach side of the house.

10. Office Building, 1987
Goldman/Firth/Associates;
LA Group and Isabelle Greene, landscape architects
24955 Pacific Coast Highway

The architects have broken up a 20,000-square-foot building into a series of one-, two-, and three-story volumes, so that it reads as a Modernist village. A rectangular grid framework moves up and down at the base; above are occasional metal and glass penthouses.

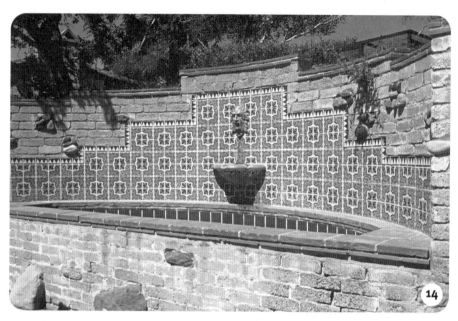

11. Pepperdine University, 1971–73
William Pereira Associates; Armstrong and Sharfman, landscape architects
Seaver Drive, west of Malibu Canyon Road

A vast green lawn with the feeling of a golf course intervenes between the Pacific Coast Highway and the university buildings up the hill. These meticulously maintained lawns, plantings, and trees give you a sense of being in Beverly Hills. The buildings employ the '70s composition of cut-into stucco volumes picturesquely set on a hillside location.

12. Rucker House, 1971
Douglas W. Rucker
Off Malibu Canyon Road at 23704 Harbor Vista Drive

This well-detailed and theatrically situated hillside house can be seen as far away as the Pacific Coast Highway. The architect has borrowed the theme of Schindler's hillside houses from the 1930s.

13. Hodges Castle, 1977–79
Thomas Hodges
23800 Malibu Crest Drive

Dr. Hodges' towered and crenelated castle is poised on a high hill overlooking and guarding the inland approaches to Malibu.

14. Adamson House, 1929
Morgan, Walls, and Clements (Stiles Clements)
Pacific Coast Highway at Serra Road

The Adamson House is now included in Malibu Lagoon State Beach and can be viewed from the beach itself. It is one of the few domestic commissions of Stiles Clements, who is best known for his many commercial and institutional designs either for Morgan, Walls, and Clements, or on his own after 1936. The house is a two-story Andalusian farmhouse that exhibits some splendid examples of metalwork, but its chief glory is in its decorative, highly glazed tiles made by the Malibu Tile Company. Open to the public. Information at (310) 456-8432 or www.adamsonhouse.org.

15. Arch Oboler House,
1940, 1941, 1944, 1946
Frank Lloyd Wright
32436 Mulholland Drive

The grand and spectacular main house, "Eagle Feather," was never built. From the road you can see the gatehouse (1940); below is the small wood-and-stone retreat built in 1941 and added to in 1944 and 1946. The vocabulary that Wright used here is directly related to the 1939 Sturges House in West Los Angeles and the Pauson House (1940) in Paradise Valley north of Phoenix. The Pauson House was badly damaged in a November 1977 fire.

16. Mr. Blanding's Dream House, 1947–48
*Malibu Creek State Park
3800 Solstice Canyon Road
(Malibu Canyon Road, between
Mulholland Highway and
Cold Canyon Road)*

America's post–World War II ideal of a dwelling was built for the popular film *Mr. Blanding Builds His Dream House,* produced by RKO and starring Myrna Loy and Cary Grant. It was built as a stage set on the land owned by movie producer George Hunter, who converted it into his own ranch house. The 2,476-square-foot house is pure Anglo-Colonial Revival (referred to at the time as "Connecticut Colonial").

According to the publicity release for the film, "identical houses" were built across the country, including one in Los Angeles. The house is now used for the offices of the Santa Monica Mountains Conservancy Foundation.

17. Reed House, 1960
John Reed
*21536 W. Rambla Vista
Malibu*

Projecting horizontal-and-vertical volumes in wood create a dramatic hillside composition.

18. Walker House, 1992
Melinda Gray
2935 Las Tunas Canyon Road

The architect described this dwelling as "toys in a playpen connected by an invisible string of timber and glass gridwork." With walls of logs the house appears indeed like a child's plaything. To the right is a curved roof form that houses the living room (with garage below). A high pyramidal roof covers the central house, and to the right is a gable-roofed building with a projecting semicircular bay for sleeping.

19. J. Paul Getty Museum (Old Getty), 1972–73
Langdon and Wilson; Stephen Garrett; Norman Neuerberg, consultant; Emmet L. Wemple and Associates, landscape architects
17985 Pacific Coast Highway

Here is Southern California as it should be—the past as seen through the perceptive eyes of the 1970s, in a landscape that puts the Old World of the Mediterranean to shame. The museum is modeled after an ancient Roman villa, the Villa of the Papyri, which was buried in the eruption of Mount Vesuvius in A.D. 79 and excavated in the eighteenth century by tunneling under the hard lava crust. J. Paul Getty, who commissioned the building, wrote: "What could be more logical than to display it [classical art] in a classical building?" You approach the building through a Roman gate along a Roman road to enter the parking garage, which is under the podium. Ascending to the courtyard, you obtain a view of the Pacific Ocean. Turning around, you face the main museum building across the long reflecting pool. Inside, a cross axis from the central atrium leads to smaller atriums and walled gardens. The classical Greek and Roman sculptures and mosaics all appear at their best in this environment. As the architects planned, the museum and landscaping have mellowed and improved each year.

As of this writing this museum is closed for remodeling. The designers of the new facilities are Salvetti and Machado.

2 • Pacific Palisades, North

The area inland from the coast of Malibu to Santa Monica is rich in important architecture, and fortunately much of it is visible from the streets. If Highland Park was the art center of Los Angeles at the turn of the century, Pacific Palisades took the title from the 1920s through the 1940s. Motion picture figures discovered that it was only a short distance by Pierce-Arrow from Hollywood to the coast, and settled in. Then writers, artists, and musicians—many of them fleeing Nazi Germany—found it a haven for their creativity. And under the leadership of John Entenza, the editor and publisher of *Arts and Architecture,* Pacific Palisades and nearby Santa Monica Canyon attracted the most advanced Modernist taste in architecture.

This community began its architectural life in the late 1860s when Los Angelenos came for the summer breezes off the ocean and pitched their tents just north of where Channel Road now cuts off from the Pacific Coast Highway. It remained a summer beach colony until 1921, when a group of Methodists, sensing a perfect place for Chautauqua and a resting place for their retired ministers, established a colony on the highlands.

Castellammare, which lies to the north of Pacific Palisades, was developed in the 1920s by Alphonzo Bell Sr., who had already profited handsomely from the development of Bel Air. Some Mediterranean villas were built on the hills and cliffs overlooking the Pacific, but like the Methodists to the south, Bell never saw his posh Riviera realized.

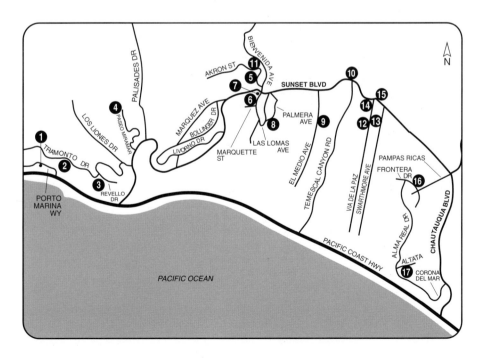

As you travel up the hill on Sunset Boulevard from the Pacific Coast Highway, take note of the "Lake Shrine" at 17190 Sunset Boulevard. Here, in the middle of what looks like an African jungle, is a spring-fed lake (with houseboat), a "Golden Lotus" archway, and domes of gold. This earthly paradise was built by the Self-Realization Fellowship in 1950, under the direction of Paramahanda Yogananda. The fellowship and its instant Eden are pure Southern California.

1. Villa de Leon, 1927
Kenneth MacDonald
17948 Porto Marina Way

A memorable feature of the coast drive as you come down from Santa Barbara is this classical Mediterranean villa perched high on the edge of the cliff overlooking the entrance to the Getty Museum. Much of its splendid landscaping has disappeared in continual landslides, but the house is still sensational, not only from the ocean side but also close-up. Other Spanish and Italian villas of the twenties are situated nearby.

2. House, circa 1935
Mr. Bird
17526 Tramonto Drive

The name of the architect is also a description of the house, quaint beyond dreams of sugarplums. Possibly the Bird in question was George Washington Bird, a midwestern architect who, attracted by the movie industry, moved to the Los Angeles area in 1913.

3. Beagles House, 1963
Pierre Koenig
17446 Revello Drive

A sophisticated and successful assertion of the "less is more" school, '50s and early '60s.

4. Times Demonstration House, 1927–28
Mark Daniels, architect and landscape architect
520 Paseo Miramar

There were a good number of model and demonstration houses built in the Los Angeles area in the 1920s and 1930s. Mark Daniels was a leading exponent of the Mediterranean/Spanish Revival in the 1920s, and he designed a number of houses and gardens in the west Los Angeles area. The *Times* Demonstration House is a romantic hillside Spanish house, two stories to the front, three to the rear. As with all of Daniels' work, he demonstrated an understanding of the language of historicism as well as a wonderful command of forms.

5. House, 1952
Jones and Emmons
16310 Akron Street

A single-level post-and-beam spec house for the Southdown development that was never completely realized. The plan is an open one, with the rooms oriented outward toward terraces and a garden.

6. House, 1952
Jones and Emmons
North of northwest corner of Bienveneda Avenue and Marquette Street

Another variation on the small Southdown development spec housing developed by this firm.

7. Soffer House, 1973
Eric Wright, remodeling
665 Bienveneda Avenue

Austere on the street front and all glass on the garden side, this house has all the good qualities of Wright's grandfather's (Frank Lloyd) Usonian houses and none of the bad ones.

8. House, circa 1935
Attributed to
John Byers and Edla Muir
630 Palmera Avenue

A very quaint Anglo-Norman cottage.

9. 708 House, 1979–82
Eric Owen Moss
708 El Medio Avenue

A major remodeling has produced one of Moss's characteristic buildings. The architecture here is fortunately tinged with a sense of humor. Though radical in form and color, it really fits well on a street of typical California spec ranch houses. The original house (1949; James H. Caughey) was a Modernist version of the California ranch house.

10. Presbyterian Conference Grounds, 1922 and later
North end of Temescal Canyon Road

Once this belonged to the Methodists and was the site of the yearly Chautauqua performances that were so much a part of the cultural "uplift movement" for the common man at the turn of the century. By the time the small cottages were built to service the huge tent shows, the Chautauqua movement was already declining. The Presbyterians took over the grounds and used them as a retreat. Behind it are some beautiful nature trails that may be used by permission of the caretaker at the main gate.

11. St. Matthew's Episcopal Church, 1982–83
Charles W. Moore (Moore, Ruble, Yudell); Campbell and Campbell (Regula Campbell), landscape architects
1030 Bienveneda Avenue

The present church is the third structure on the site. The original Carleton M. Winslow church of 1942 was moved here in the early 1950s and was then remodeled in 1953 by Jones and Emmons. That building burned in 1978 in a hillside fire. The present church by Moore is close to being domestic in scale. It declares its public nature by the barnlike contours and tall campanile, while at the same time snuggling into its site and the excellent landscape scheme of Campbell and Campbell. Internally, the sanctuary has the quality of an informal meeting hall dominated by a pair of wooden arches and an apse that suggest a traditional cruciform plan. North of the church are remnants (including a windmill) of the French-Norman Barnett Estate designed by John Byers and Edla Muir.

Arrangements for visits can be made by calling the church office.

12. Community United Methodist Church, 1929
801 Via de la Paz

The church was organized in 1922, but this structure wasn't started until 1929. Even then the congregation was small, hinting that Methodism would not triumph. The edifice began in the usual Spanish Revival mode, with the bell tower showing the

influence of the Moderne. Much of the original character of the building was covered up by newer facilities in 1972.

13. Palisades Elementary School, 1930
800 Via de la Paz

Spanish Revival again, this school with Moorish tower was slated for destruction after the 1971 earthquake. Even though it suffered no serious damage, the building's construction did not meet contemporary safety standards. A wise citizenry, proud of the architecture of the old building, engaged an architect who showed that gutting the building, reinforcing the walls, and constructing new interiors would not only satisfy the building inspectors but would cost less than building a new structure. As in the case of the Lapiths and the Centaurs, civilization occasionally wins.

14. Santa Monica Land and Water Company, 1924
Clinton Nourse
Southwest corner of Sunset Boulevard and Via de la Paz

A fine Spanish Revival business block. The very name suggests that promoters were early trying to lure buyers to their Riviera.

15. Department of Water and Power Building, 1935
Frederick L. Roehrig
Northeast corner of Sunset Boulevard and Via de la Paz

Did you ever think you would see an example of Regency Moderne? Now you have!

16. House, circa 1929
629 Frontera Drive

This beautifully turned-out Monterey Revival house must be by John Byers. But the real reason

we take you into this area is that we want you to experience the town planning of Olmsted and Olmsted, who also laid out Palos Verdes Estates. The houses are all expensive. Some, like this one, are good. Most date after 1929, which says something about the gravity of the Great Depression for the rich.

17. Harrison House, 1950
Paul Sterling Hoag
14926 Altata Drive

At least from the street, this two-story gable-roofed house has the atmosphere of a contemporary version of California's Monterey tradition. It has a two-story porch, board-and-batten siding, and several walls of adobe brick. The dwelling rests comfortably in a grove of large eucalyptus trees.

3 • Pacific Palisades, South

Santa Monica Canyon initially contained small, quite modest summer beach houses and year-round cottages. In the late 1930s, it began to acquire serious examples of Modern design by Harwell H. Harris, Richard J. Neutra, and others. After 1945, other prime examples of Modernism were built, especially in the area around Chautauqua Boulevard.

The Olmsted brothers, whose father laid out Central Park in New York City, platted a picturesque maze west of Chautauqua Boulevard, where some of the most pleasant houses in the traditional imagery of the twenties and thirties remain. The old canyons attracted a varied coterie, from the Uplifters on Latimer Road to Will Rogers and Thomas Mann in the highlands.

1. Bradbury House, 1922
John Byers
102 Ocean Way

One of the first adobe houses that Byers designed, this was instrumental in establishing his reputation as a Spanish Revivalist.

2. Sten-Frenke House, 1934
Richard J. Neutra
126 Mabery Road, off Ocean Avenue

A classic Neutra with a Streamline Moderne curved-glass bay that overlooks the Pacific. The house, which is nearly impossible to see, lies up the hill behind the street wall and garage. It was sensitively modernized in 1982 by Gwathmey Siegel and Associates.

3. Guerra House, 1992
Melinda Gray
138 Mabery Road

A two-story house composed as an assembly of barrel-vaulted and gable-roofed forms, all very delicately handled. The central gable section, which is perpendicular to the street, centers on a partially enclosed circular court.

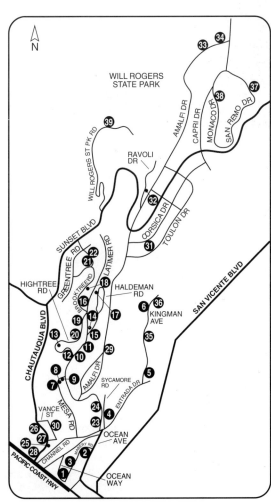

4

4. Clark House, 1997
Melinda Gray
339 Sycamore Road

A house with a lot going on out-side. It provides an interesting puzzle as to what is going on in side and certainly stands out among its conventional neighbors.

5. Pumphrey House, 1939
Harwell H. Harris
615 Kingman Avenue

This horizontal wood-battened house is quite Wrightian and very difficult to see behind fences and foliage.

6. Delores del Rio House, 1929
Douglas Honnold and Cedric Gibbons
757 Kingman Avenue

This impressive example of the early Modern was designed by set designer Cedric Gibbons and architect Douglas Honnold. It has a formal Art Deco quality on the street side, but to the rear it is almost pure doctrinaire International Style in the two-story façade that overlooks Santa Monica Canyon. The gardens were renewed between 1989 and 1993 by the Santa Monica firm of Campbell and Campbell.

7. Entenza House, 1937
Harwell H. Harris
475 Mesa Road

Built for John Entenza, the editor and publisher of *Arts and Architecture,* as a declaration of his commitment to modernity. His curved-wall carport, spiral staircase, and metal railing make it more Streamline Moderne than classical International Style. The Entenza House was Harris's only realized example of Streamline Moderne. It has been renovated and slightly changed by Michael Folonis.

7

8

8. Abell House, 1937
Thornton M. Abell
465 Upper Mesa Road

A gem of the regionalized International Style, this house (depressed on the side of the hill) is barely visible. It consists of a series of stucco volumes stepped down a steep hillside. It is all quite nautical in feeling.

9. Haines House, 1943
Thornton M. Abell
477 Upper Mesa Road

An angled, single-floor, Modernist image (stucco volumes) dwelling set far down the hillside. The garden side of this wood-frame, concrete-block, and fiberglass structure is almost entirely glass, taking advantage of the view. At the base of the hill is a combined studio and garage. This house and Abell's own, just two doors away, are equally difficult to see.

10. Kaplan House, 1973
Michael Leventhal
514 Latimer Road

Parts of old wharfs and houses have been used to construct and decorate this highly expressionistic monument of the late Craftsman movement.

11. House, 1976
Paul Thoryk
528 Latimer Road

A tribute to the enormous popularity of the Moore and Turnbull ideas of the late 1960s, this house is another example of the late Craftsman revival.

12. House, circa 1925
Southwest corner of Latimer and Hightree Roads

Additions have been made to this house, which was once a tiny Hansel and Gretel delight.

13. Gertler House, 1970
Raymond Kappe
14623 Hightree Road

A handsome wedding of the woodsy Craftsman aesthetic of Frank Lloyd Wright and Charles and Henry Greene to the bold angular forms of the International Style. Kappe, whose own house is nearby, has a very personal style well-suited to these ancient groves of eucalyptus and cypress.

14. Uplifters Club, 1923
William J. Dodd
Haldeman and Latimer Roads

The watered-down Spanish Revival of the clubhouse is certainly not as interesting as the club itself. In the early teens the members of a splinter group of the Los Angeles Athletic Club devoted themselves to High Jinx. In the early 1920s, under the leadership of Harry Marston Haldeman, a local executive of the Crane Plumbing Company, the club bought property on Latimer Road (named for one of its members) and set out a sort of retreat, not to be confused with the later settlement of high-minded Methodists on the highlands above. Cottages were built (some log cabins) and, later, more elaborate houses. While not really important individually, as a group they compose a fascinating complex, a significant reflection of the change in taste during the late teens and early 1920s. Although we have not thoroughly researched the architects of each of these houses, it appears from a review of meager records and general observation that the firm of Arthur S. Heineman, whose brother Alfred was the chief designer, was most responsible for the whimsical styles found here.

The log cabins—some of them authentic, some stage sets—are probably of chief interest. The first, at 1 Latimer Road, is the Kley House (1923), a log-faced lodge now almost completely cut off from public view. It is probably by the Heinemans, as are other log-faced cabins at 3 and 18 Latimer Road. Others are on Haldeman Road at 31, 32, and 34. At 36, 37, and 38 are authentically constructed log cabins, of which 38, the Marco Hellman Cabin, is the most interesting.

15. Marco Hellman Cabin, 1923–24
Alfred Heineman
38 Haldeman Road

Tradition has it that this house, as well as those at 36 and 37 Haldeman Road, was part of a movie set transported to the canyon by Hellman, a very rich banker. Alfred Heineman, who designed the Hellman banks in the Los Angeles area under the firm name of his brother Arthur, was responsible for the rustic decor of the interior of Hellman's own cabin. It is probable that Heineman was also responsible for the interiors of the other cabins as well as the interior and exterior design of Heather Hill (1922–23) at 7 Latimer Road, whose shingled roof in imitation of thatch was a trademark of a number of Heineman houses in Pasadena.

16. Abel House, 1978
**Charles W. Moore, Ron Frank, and Robert Yudell
(Urban Innovations Group)**
747 Latimer Road

This elongated house picturesquely rambles over its Rustic Canyon site, but, as in many of Moore's designs, a thin central core holds all of the wings and bays together. The entrance and a walled courtyard are in the fashion of the late-seventeenth-century New England Colonial house. A large chimney and stairs dominate the design both externally and internally.

17. Ruben House, 1936
Richard J. Neutra
50 Haldeman Road

This is a rare case of a Neutra remodeling. The original shingled ranch-style house was built in 1923–24 by Ralph Hamlin, a bicycle manufacturer who had the dubious distinction of owning the first motorcycle west of the Rockies.

We have by no means listed all of the interesting architecture in Rustic Canyon; much of it is well hidden from public view. A case in point is the extensive remodeling (1982) of an older California ranch house by architectural historian Charles Jencks and architect Buzz Yudell. This is a classic example of Postmodernism, but it cannot be seen from the road. The student of lifestyles in the 1920s and 1930s will find many more houses of significance. After

all, Aldous Huxley, Emil Ludwig, Johnnie Weismuller, and other worthies once lived in this area.

18. Emmons House, 1954
Jones and Emmons
661 Brooktree Road

A very neat post-and-beam International Style product that has weathered the years extremely well.

19. Anderson House, 1950
Craig Ellwood
656 Hightree Road

A thin brick wall and aluminum garage door form the austere street façade of this house by one of Los Angeles's most distinguished followers of Mies van der Rohe.

20. Elton House, 1951
Craig Ellwood
635 Hightree Road

If the Anderson House is private, this Miesian house is very open and a strikingly different style from its neighbor.

21. Kappe House, 1968
Raymond Kappe
715 Brooktree Road

A virtual tree house poised over a steep hillside. Glass has been used almost exclusively as the infill between the vertical and horizontal wood frame of the building. Inside, wood bridges and staircases join the principal interior spaces. This house is another example of Kappe's inventive ability to meld the Craftsman aesthetic and the International Style into a very personal style. Other examples of Kappe's work are nearby: the Pregerson House (1966) at 680 Brooktree Road, and the Gates-Dorman House (1961) at 737 Brooktree Road.

22. Harrison House, 1950
Paul Sterling Hoag
728 Brooktree Road

A Modernist dwelling rendered in stone and wood, with some exposed structural members. The stone walls are treated as slabs without any penetration of openings. Designs such as this illustrate how the California Modernists were able to accommodate "warm" traditional materials into their style.

24. Haines House, 1951
Thornton M. Abell
247 Amalfi Drive

A refined pavilion sheathed in horizontal redwood, with a flat roof, brick chimney, and brick terraces.

25. West House, 1948
Rodney A. Walker
199 Chautauqua Boulevard

A romantically sited, single-floor, five-room house sheathed

personal and humane the image of the machine can be in the hands of gifted designers. The interior furnishings were chosen and arranged by both Ray and Charles Eames as an integral part of the design.

27. Entenza House, 1949
Charles Eames and Eero Saarinen
205 Chautauqua Boulevard

The steel-frame and roof design

23. Burns House, 1974
Charles W. Moore
230 Amalfi Drive

A 1970s version of the Spanish Revival of the 1920s. The pink stucco dwelling boasts an array of shed roofs and skylights, along with the basic necessities of Hispanic Los Angeles—a walled and tiled entrance court and a swimming pool. Going inside, an organ dominates the two-story living room.

in striated plywood. This was one of the early Case Study House projects.

26. Eames House and Studio, 1947–49
Charles and Ray Eames
203 Chautauqua Boulevard

One of America's great twentieth-century houses, which is as impressive today as when it was built as part of John Entenza's Case Study House program. The two metal-framed boxes, set against a eucalyptus-covered hillside, dramatically illustrate how

is not as assertive in this Case Study House as in the adjacent Eames House. A single rectangular form contains all of the spaces, including the two-car garage. As with the Eames House, the open interior was most impressive with the furnishings of Saarinen chairs and built-in angular sofa. The house has been considerably altered.

28. Bailey House, 1946–48
Richard J. Neutra,
with later additions by Neutra
219 Chautauqua Boulevard

Esther McCoy has noted the

similarity of this house to Neutra's Nesbitt House of 1942, where he "made a virtue of redwood—even brick." The property is partly enclosed by a serpentine brick wall. A Case Study House.

29. Cernitz House, 1938
Milton J. Black
601 Amalfi Drive

If you look carefully behind the post–World War II remodeling, you will see one of Black's Streamline Moderne delights.

30. Anderson House, 1922
390 Vance Street

Anderson, whose first name seems to have disappeared, was supposed to have been a merchant who brought treasures from all over the world to this tiny house. Most of his travels seem, however, to have been in Mexico. This building, with its magnificent tile, art-glass windows, and mosaic of Mexican dancers in front of a mission arcade, is a real stunner. The house has been extensively rebuilt (from 1986 on) by its present owners, David and Margaret Lederer, who, with architect Finn Kappe, retained the scale of the original in what amounts to a new house.

31. Kenaston House, 1936–37
John Byers, Edla Muir;
remodeled, 1963
Edla Muir
914 Corsica Drive

The Spanish Revival made modern.

32. Case Study House, 1950
Raphael S. Soriano
1080 Ravoli Drive

Almost invisible now, this is the first of the pure steel-frame Case Study Houses sponsored by *Arts*

and Architecture magazine. It has been extensively remodeled.

33. Kingsley Houses, 1946
J. R. Davidson
1620 and 1630 Amalfi Drive

Absolutely simple builders' houses, distinguished only by the name of their architect.

34. House, circa 1925
John Byers (with Edla Muir)
1650 Amalfi Drive

One of the loveliest of Byers's designs. A long, unfenestrated wall in front opens only at a gate, which allows you to see into the central patio of this Spanish Revival house.

35. Ehrlich House, 1988
Steven Ehrlich Architects
624 Kingman Avenue

From the street, the house reads as two separate structures. The wall surface between is recessed and dark in color. The imagery of the woven white surfaces is Modern, via a subtle glance at the 1930s work of R. M. Schindler. To the rear, the dwelling opens up to a terraced hillside garden. There are ocean views from the upper terraces of the house.

36. Gold-Friedman House, 1991
Steven Ehrlich Architects
728 Kingman Avenue

Bold, projecting stucco volumes break up the front façade of the house. The walkway and steps wind their way around a rectangular pattern of retaining walls. As with Ehrlich's own house down the street, this building opens up to a courtyard and terraced garden in the rear. Skylights enhance the vertical space of the interior, making the whole light and airy.

37. Mann House, 1941
J. R. Davidson
1550 San Remo Drive

It is almost impossible to see this stucco-and-glass two-story Modern image house that was built for the great novelist Thomas Mann. It is a pity, since the Manns were so deeply involved with the planning. We list it because of the thrill of knowing it is there.

38. Barclay House, circa 1927
John Byers,
with Edla Muir
1425 Monaco Drive

Monterey Revival.

39. Will Rogers Ranch, 1921 and later
14243 Sunset Boulevard

This is one of those houses that is more important in evoking the spirit of its owner rather than its architecture, though the house does succeed very well in conveying the feeling of early California. It was where Will could occupy himself "messing around doing this and that and not much of either. Get on old 'Soapsuds' and ride off up a little canyon I got here." When the Rogerses moved to the ranch permanently in 1928, they expanded their simple vacation cottage. Again in 1933, when his wife and daughter were in Palestine, Will "raised the roof" of the living room to make room for him to do his rope tricks comfortably. The house, full of curios, is open to the public. See also the barn, whose two bays are actually the halves of an old barn Rogers found in west Los Angeles.

4 • Santa Monica, North

Dubbed the "Zenith City of the Sunset Sea," Santa Monica was open ranch land until Senator John P. Jones of Nevada went into partnership with Colonel Robert S. Baker, the owner of the ranch and laid out a town that he believed would become the port of Los Angeles, given railroad connections. A map of the town, with a grid pattern of streets, was filed with the recorder on July 10, 1875. A few days later, lots went on sale. In nine months, Santa Monica had 1,000 residents and seemed destined to become one of the great ports of America, with the railroad and wharf built by Senator Jones. Though it gained more residents during the land boom of the late 1880s, the idea of a major metropolis was doomed when San Pedro and Wilmington became the ports of Los Angeles.

Santa Monica was, and still is, a beach city. Senator Jones and Mrs. Baker, the widow of the ranch owner, gave the land on top of the palisades to the city as a park. Palisades Park is one of the few places in California where a city has maintained the ocean view for the enjoyment of the people, and the people are there, every day of the week in the summer and on good weekends in the winter, playing cards, sunning, jogging, and chatting in a babble of tongues.

Below the Palisades cliff, between the highway and the beach, the sale of lots meant that the beach became accessible in only a few places. Since the 1940s, the state has bought back many of these properties; but a few houses remain, including several new ones. These beachside locations for dwellings are, needless to say, in great demand.

The town on the highland developed slowly. Third Street (now Santa Monica Mall) became the main commercial street, with residential areas moving northwest, particularly in the 1920s and 1930s. Grand hotels were built. The Arcadia, long gone, was a Queen Anne pile near the pier at Colorado Street. Later, hotels took to the highlands across from Palisades Park. Now, the Miramar (some parts dating from the 1920s) is the only hotel reflecting any part of its former glory, though its gardens have been filled in with a new building. The whole frontage of Ocean Avenue has changed over the past decades, commercial buildings and high-rise apartments taking the place of the old summer homes of wealthy Angelenos. From a distance, the ocean frontage of Santa Monica is beginning to approach the wall-like look we associate with Miami Beach.

Most of Santa Monica's houses of the teens, twenties, and thirties were modest in size, but in and around San Vicente Boulevard the upper-middle-class quality of neighboring Pacific Palisades and Brentwood prevailed. Santa Monica was the home of architect John Byers and has many houses designed by him, often in association with Edla Muir. Byers was self-trained as an architect and developed an interest and sensitivity to the Hispanic architecture tradition. His Spanish, English, French-Norman, and Anglo-American Colonial designs set an example that others followed to good effect, making northern Santa Monica an architectural monument of traditional images of the twenties and thirties.

In the last two decades, Santa Monica has been transformed bit by bit. The modest single-family houses are being replaced by large dwellings, or more often by condominium units. The newest of these condominiums spans a wide range of images, from High Tech to Spanish Revival and Tudor. And in the downtown areas, high-rise office buildings are beginning to line Wilshire Boulevard and other major streets.

Santa Monica found its downtown retail district deteriorating after World War II. The solution was to close several blocks of Third Street and create a pedestrian mall. Like almost all other malls of this type, it was economically and aesthetically a failure. From 1988–89, the mall was redesigned with a partial drive-through section and renamed the "Promenade." This seems to be working, due in part to the creation of Santa Monica Place and the construction of adjoining parking structures. As a design, the Promenade is adequate but not earthshaking. Hardscape dominates the scene.

1. La Mesa Drive
*Enter opposite 19th Street off
San Vicente Boulevard*

No other street in Los Angeles County (not even Prospect Boulevard in Pasadena) is so beautifully landscaped. In this case, Moreton Bay figs, seemingly planted by the pioneers, line the parkways on both sides of the street. The architecture is worthy of the trees. You will have your own favorites, but we begin with the following:

2. Crenshaw House, 1925–26
Gable and Wyant
*1923 La Mesa Drive
Santa Monica*

The romantic ideal of the Spanish house.

3. Thompson House, 1924–25
John Byers
2021 La Mesa Drive

A blend of Spanish, Mexican, and California details.

4. Byers House, 1924
John Byers
2034 La Mesa Drive

The architect chose the balconied Monterey style for his second home in Santa Monica. It was within walking distance of his office.

5. Zimmer House, 1924
John Byers
2101 La Mesa Drive

A single-floor adobe with a high central portal enclosed by end walls. Uncluttered stucco walls and low-pitched tile roofs are the dominant theme.

6. Bundy House, 1925
John Byers
2153 La Mesa Drive

A good example of Byers's personal version of the Hispanic tradition.

7. Tinglof House, 1925–26
John Byers
2210 La Mesa Drive

Hispanic.

8. Nables House, 1949
Lloyd Wright
2323 La Mesa Drive

A low-lying yellow brick house, almost impossible to see.

9. Stothart-Phillips House, 1937–38
J. R. Davidson
2501 La Mesa Drive

You can catch only a glimpse of this elegant 1930s International Style house. The principal front of this house, with extensive glass doors and windows, overlooks the terrace and has a view to the west. The house has been remodeled.

10. Koning Eizenberg House, 1988–89
Koning Eizenberg Architecture
909 – 25th Street

With the growth of trees, all you can see from the street is the second-floor glass pavilion, which looks very woodsy. The base of the glass box exhibits a diamond pattern in its stucco surface, and the corner is cut out to accommodate a small deck off the living room. The major section of the house extends as a two-story hooped roof rectangle to the rear of the lot.

11. Hromadka House, 1937
2320 Carlyle Avenue

Southern California's version of what the eighteenth-century Anglo-Colonial house should have looked like.

12. Offices, 1991
David Lawrence Gray Architects
1546 – 7th Street

A lighthearted interpretation of the International Style framed in yellow. The neighboring palm tree is a welcome contribution to the ensemble.

13. Laidlow House, 1924
John Byers
217 – 17th Street

Byers as a medievalist—in this case French-Norman.

14. Carrillo House, 1925
John Byers
1602 Georgina Avenue, at 16th Street

A monumental California adobe. The house next door at 1628 Georgina Avenue was designed by G. C. McAlister in 1937.

15. Ullman House, 1955
Thornton M. Abell
*800 Woodacres Road
Pacific Palisades
(an extension of 14th Street in Santa Monica)*

This concrete block and vertical wood-batten house in a rationalist version of the post–World War II International Style is just visible through a magnificent grove of trees.

16. Armstrong-Cobb House, 1926
John Byers
1717 San Vicente Boulevard

A large-scale version of a Spanish farmhouse *(cortijo)*. Especially successful is the varied layering of the tile roofs, which conveys a sense that the dwelling has been added to over the years.

17. MacBennel House, 1921–22
John Byers
404 Georgina Avenue, at 4th Street

One of Byers' first real adobes. At this stage in his career, he was a manufacturer of adobe bricks, a builder, and an architectural designer.

18. Jones House, 1907
130 Adelaide Drive

A big wholesome example of the turn-of-the-century Anglo-Colonial Revival.

19. Weaver House, 1910–11
Milwaukee Building Company
(later Meyer and Holler)
142 Adelaide Drive

A gorgeous example of Japanese Craftsman, worthy of Charles and Henry Greene. It was badly damaged in the 1984 earthquake but has been well restored.

20. Milbank House, 1910–11
236 Adelaide Drive

A two-story Craftsman masterpiece, with a strong surge of Asian details, romantically situated in a lovely garden.

21. Gorham-Holliday House, 1923–24
John Byers
326 Adelaide Drive

Certainly one of Byers' most impressive Andalusian houses. A patio occupies the center of the U, and a projecting Monterey balcony overlooks the patio and garden.

22. Gorham House, 1910
Robert Farquhar
*Southwest corner of
Adelaide Drive and 4th Street*

A low stucco house, reminiscent of the Pasadena Culbertson House by the Greenes. The entrance, otherwise classical, is capped by an Asian porch roof.

Across 4th Street (southeast corner) is the Gillis House (1906), a large T-shaped structure set out around a patio. It was designed by Myron Hunt and Elmer Grey during their woodsy Arts-and-Crafts period.

23. Worrel House, 1926
Robert B. Stacy-Judd
710 Adelaide Drive

A Pueblo Revival–Maya fantasy, more fantastic the longer you look at it. The architect wrote of this house, "I was at a loss to designate the type of architecture, but it has come to be known as the 'Zuni' type." The plan of the house is highly rational but, needless to say, the interior and exterior ornament is not. This house was designed shortly after the architect's famous Aztec Hotel in Monrovia.

24. Byers House, 1917
John Byers
*547 – 7th Street, near
Alta Avenue*

Board-and-batten and stucco walls hint more at the hills of Berkeley than the highlands of Santa Monica. This was the first house Byers designed for himself. The Craftsman bungalow (Jones House, circa 1913) at the northeast corner of Alta Avenue and 7th Street is well worth a look, as is the 1925 Boswell House (John Byers) at 624 Alta Avenue.

25. Shorecliff Tower Apartments, 1963
Jones and Emmons
*535 Ocean Avenue, at
Alta Avenue*

A quiet, elegant version of the late International Style of the early 1960s.

26. Witbeck House, 1917
Charles and Henry Greene
226 Palisades Avenue

A two-story faintly Tudor dwelling, sheathed in shingles.

27. Roosevelt School, 1935
Marsh, Smith, and Powell
*801 Montana Avenue and
Lincoln Boulevard*

PWA Streamline Moderne, leaning toward the International Style. Note the wonderful lettering over the major entrance.

28. Sovereign Hotel and Apartments, 1928–29
Meyer Radon
205 Washington Avenue

There was no reticence here on the part of the architect in showing how many Spanish Revival forms and details could be used.

29. Gehry House, 1978
Frank O. Gehry and Associates
*Southeast corner of
Washington Avenue and
22nd Street*

A helpless Dutch Colonial has been maneuvered into one of Gehry's perplexing compositions. A new wall separates the house from the street to the north, and to the rear a courtyard has been created. Fragments of the two-by-four-inch studs of the original house have been revealed, new windows have been added here and there, and of course a swatch of chain-link fence. Inside, notwithstanding the asphalt-driveway floor of the kitchen, the atmosphere is Craftsman. Additions (1992) of concrete retaining walls, gates, planting (by Nancy Powers), a fountain, and even a lap pool dramatically reduce the sharpness of the original design, making the whole more mellow and suburban in nature.

30. Crossroads School

A former concrete warehouse was remodeled to house the school. The principal street façade is horizontally banded, interrupted by a high deep-set entrance—all beautifully proportioned. Facing the alley/plaza are classrooms, an art gallery, and a grand stairway.

Newer buildings have been added:

a. The Peter Boxenbaum Arts Education Center, 1984–89
Moore, Ruble, Yudell
1714 – 21st Street

b. Paul Cummins Library, 1996
Steven Ehrlich

Conservative Postmodern. The greatest attention has been given to the interior.

c. Grisanti Sports Center, 2000
Pica and Sullivan Architects
Northwest corner of 18th and Olympic Streets

The gymnasium is a prefabricated metal building to which a two-story community room in conventional construction was added. The architects have attempted to draw the two parts together by using the same materials on both and by echoing the colors of the community room on the metal gym, though in different patterns. The result is nevertheless two distinct parts. A very pleasant building, but we wonder how it will wear!

31. Claremont Apartments, 1929–30
Max Meltzmann
330 California Avenue

Spanish Revival of the late 1920s, with a splash of colored tile in the forecourt.

32. Voss Apartments, 1937–47
953 – 11th Street, near Washington Avenue

Exuberant Streamline Moderne. There was a surge of multiple housing units built in Santa Monica at the end of the 1930s. The two favored images were the Streamline Moderne and the classically flavored Hollywood Regency.

33. Montana Collection, 1992
Kanner Architects
Northwest corner Montana Avenue and 14th Street

A characteristic approach of the late 1980s and early 1990s to divide a project into a series of separate parts. It has been very well carried out. There are three independent units: a tall white volume with a slanted parapet (which is a stair tower), a corner pavilion with a round vaulted roof, and then a long and low white stucco pavilion held up by tall piers. Parking is on the roof.

34. Villa de Malaga
Townhouse, 1982–83
Miguel Angelo Flores
and Associates
926–930 – 20th Street, near Montana Avenue

Two-story townhouses in the Andalusian mood, organized around a central courtyard. In this instance, the Hispanic of the early 1980s has been carried out with both knowledge and reticence. The long central court of the complex successfully conveys the feeling of a Spanish village street.

35. Bernini House, 1991
Michael McDonough
242 – 17th Street

The building's thin slab roof, corner metal windows, and smooth stucco surface suggest that this might be a modern design of the 1930s. But a closer look at the stepped curves of the entrance wall and other details reveal its more recent vintage. Inside, the angled hood of the double-sided fireplace and the Mayan-like doorways are reminiscent of the

Art Deco and the Mayan Revival of Robert B. Stacy-Judd.

36. Condominiums, 1980
Urban Forms
(Steve Andre and
Alan Tossman)
1319 Harvard Street

Contemporary High Art surface pattern, accompanied by a sense of mechanical technology to suggest that it is all rational.

37. Jacobs Studio, 1984
John Chase and Claudia Carol
303 – 12th Street

An addition to Los Angeles' recent spate of small, two-story, rear-lot studios. This one suggests a Craftsman image that seems to live a strange life of its own, separate from the main building.

38. Gates to Palisades Park,
circa 1912
Sylvanus Marston
Across from the entrance to Idaho Avenue

Craftsman Japanese–inspired gates with tile by Ernest Batchelder of Pasadena.

39. Lawrence Welk Plaza,
1973
General Telephone Building;
Wilshire West Apartments
Daniel, Mann, Johnson, and
Mendenhall
(Cesar Pelli, P. J. Jacobson,
and Dwight Williams);
Wilshire Professional
Building, 1979–80
Gensler Architecture
100 Wilshire Boulevard, at Ocean Avenue

Ocean Avenue facing Palisades Park is still a fascinating blend of new, middle-aged, and old architecture, though the old and middle-aged buildings of modest size are continually being replaced

by modest high-rise buildings. The Lawrence Welk Plaza should have been a major focal point not only for Santa Monica but also for Los Angeles, for here Wilshire Boulevard reaches its western terminus with only the Pacific beyond. The DMJM buildings are dull at best; the newer eleven-story Wilshire Professional Building, with its stepped-back floors and angle to the street, is a better building; but while it is more satisfactory as a design, it still does not really establish the importance of this intersection.

40. Shangri-la Apartments,
1939–40
William E. Foster
Southeast corner of Ocean and Arizona Avenues

An eight-story Streamline Moderne block, with a suggestion of a curved tower dominating the street corner of the building. Next door (for the moment) is a charming Eastlake–Queen Anne house (1890).

41. St. Monica's Roman
Catholic Church, 1925
Albert C. Martin
Northwest corner of California Avenue and 7th Street

A stone-sheathed Romanesque church with an impressive barrel-vaulted interior. The exterior sculpture is by Joseph Conradi. The building presents the case for traditional imagery realized through the modern technology of reinforced concrete.

42. Miles Memorial
Playhouse, 1929
John Byers
In Lincoln Park on Lincoln Boulevard, between Wilshire Boulevard and California Avenue

A public auditorium theater in the guise of an Andalusian building.

43. Santa Monica Post Office, 1937
Neal A. Melick and Robert A. Murray
1248 – 5th Street, at Arizona Avenue

A single-story PWA Moderne building with excellent ornament. The offset of the interior horizontal planking evokes the pioneering nineteenth century of the West. The Art Deco decoration, especially that of the interior chandeliers, hints more at the Native American art of the Southwest than of Paris.

44. Bay City Guaranty Building and Loan Association Building, 1929–30
Walker and Eisen
1225 Santa Monica Mall

For a number of decades, this was Santa Monica's only tall office building. The ground floor has been altered and signage has hidden the corner clock tower, but you can still make out the Art Deco ornament.

45. Keller Block, circa 1890
Northwest corner of Broadway and 3rd Streets

A rare pre-1900 building that still retains its cast-iron street front.

46. Ken Edwards Center for Community Services, 1986–89
Koning Eizenberg Architecture
1527 – 4th Street

The structure is designed as a broken composition of four structures on the street and a fifth

to the rear. Roof forms vary from flat and hipped to a hooped-roof building to the right. Though there is a wide glass entrance, the real way of getting into the building appears to be the wide driveway situated under the

hooped-roof element. On top of the central building is a horizontal louvered screen, which seems reminiscent of the low tower on the nearby City Hall.

47. Santa Monica Place, 1979–81
Frank O. Gehry and Associates
315 Broadway

The downtown enclosed shopping mall has enjoyed popularity throughout America since the late 1970s. Though the multistory mall space is tight, Gehry's design conveys a sense of being rational. His chain-link fencing of the exterior surface of the parking garage creates a strange visual illusion, especially with its signage and palm trees on the south and west façades. In the mall, Gehry

also designed the interior of Bubar's Jewelers.

48. Store and Office Building, 1927
Eugene Durfee
1501–1515 – 4th Street

Los Angeles's own improved version of Spanish and Mexican Churrigueresque.

49. Santa Monica Bus (Transportation) Center, 1982–84
Kappe, Lotery, Boccato
Between Olympic Boulevard, 5th, and 7th Streets, just north of the Santa Monica Freeway

The imagery of the futuristic machine á la Buck Rogers brought up-to-date via science fiction films of the early 1980s.

50. Van Tilburg Office Building, 1979
Johannes van Tilburg and Partners
1101 Broadway

A formal composition of a white stucco box, with cut-in patterns accompanied by projecting volumes.

51. Packard Show Rooms, 1928, Edward James Baume
Southwest corner of Wilshire Boulevard and 17th Street

Spanish Revival with wrought-iron grillwork reminiscent of old Spanish choir screens. This building was badly damaged in a fire. The rebuilding involved some simplification of detail, but it is well done.

52. Frank O. Gehry Offices, 1988
Frank O. Gehry and Associates
1520-B Cloverfield Boulevard

On the building's southeast (alley) side, Gehry has provided a new entrance to his own offices and, using steel beams, has created a strong linear composition along the entire back of this recycled building.

53. Home Savings and Loan Association, 1969
Millard Sheets
Southeast corner of Wilshire Boulevard and 26th Street

Another of Home Savings's attacks on the coldness and dullness of post–World War II Modern. The exterior mosaics are by Nancy Colbath, the stained-glass window by Susan Hertel.

54. The Wave, 1989
Tony DeLapp
Wilshire Boulevard, just northeast of Franklin Street

The artist has created a ceremonial arch as the gateway into Santa Monica. The curved form of this metal arch suggests a wave advancing on the Santa Monica beach. The artist is quoted as saying, "I thought it would be nice to do something that integrated with the automobile."

55. Flint Houses, 1928 John Byers
701, 703 Palisades Beach Road (Highway 1)

Here Byers used the form of a Barcelona urban house oriented around a high-spaced interior court. There are a few other houses still standing on this strand of Pacific Beach Road. Among them is John Byers's Netcher House (1926) at 1020 Pacific Beach Road and Richard J. Neutra's Lewin House (1938) at 512 Ocean Front.

56. Israel House, 1990
Steven Ehrlich Architects
1273 Palisades Beach Road (Highway 1)

A narrow and tall beach house that looks like a small gable-roofed cottage placed on a high base. The walls of the lower podium read as masonry, the upper cottage as a stuccoed box.

57. Koning Eizenberg Office Building, 1999
Koning Eizenberg Architecture
1454 – 25th Street

A conservative statement except that there are strains of nostalgia here. Both husband and wife are native Australians so they have planted eucalyptus bushes and kangaroo paws in their side garden. Besides their own offices, the building contains artists' studios.

58. Sony Music Campus, 1992
Steven Ehrlich Architects
2100 Colorado Avenue

The design themes are many and varied in this complex, ranging from the horizontal strip of band windows and pilotis, which is so closely associated with the International Style, to the curved forms of the Streamline Moderne, countered by sharp angular volumes. The buildings make a nod to traditionalism in their elegant stone cladding. From the public streets, they are viewed through groves of palm trees. Entrance to the buildings is via the automobile court, which is equally well landscaped.

59. Union (originally Bikini) Restaurant, 1991
Brantner Design Associates; Paul Jones, interior designer of present restaurant; Vic Ciannini, water sculpture
1413 – 5th Street, at Santa Monica

Restaurants come and go and the original design is changed every

time there is a new owner. Several restaurants have come and gone here, but the original beautiful space of the street-level dining room and the mezzanine has been retained. A patio for dining is off the second-story bar. Here the exposed brick of the neighboring building rises above the cliché of the nostalgia cult and serves as a nice backdrop for al fresco dining.

60. Colorado Court, 2002
Pugh Scarpa Kodama
502 Colorado Avenue, at 5th Street

The contrast of this essay in picturesque geometry with its older but equally Modernist neighbors is startling. Much has been made of the fact that this is a "green" building because the conspicuous solar panels strongly add to its energy efficiency. The nonresi-

dent onlooker will be impressed with the way the perforated panels add texture to the largely stucco surfaces of the structure. This is a first rate piece of architecture. Oh, yes! A large portion of the stucco *is* painted green.

61. Ralphs Supermarket, 2001
Olympic at Cloverfield

The first impression is that the large volume must be by Charles Moore about the time of his Piazza d'Italia (1978) in New Orleans. The colors, on the other hand, suggest Ricardo Legoretta. But the provenance is local. Not great architecture, but it doesn't take itself seriously, which is a relief. Incidentally, the fountain with sculpture at the corner is by Laddie John Dill and his students at the Santa Monica College of Design.

5 • Santa Monica, South Ocean Park

The section of Santa Monica south of the Santa Monica Freeway has always been mixed in its use—small beach cottages west of Ocean Avenue, then a mixture of residential and commercial buildings reaching up and beyond Lincoln Boulevard. This area, like Venice just to the south, is currently experiencing a growth of multiple housing, ranging from high-rise towers to two- and three-story town houses. Santa Monica's wall of high-rises has continued to work its way south, overlooking the beach. Of these, the Sea Colony at 2910 Nielson Way (1980; Landau Partnership) is unquestionably the best, though it could well be argued that none of these complexes (at least in their present size) should have been built.

1. Santa Monica Pier, 1909–21
City of Santa Monica
Engineering Department;
Carousel Park, 1982–86
Moore Ruble Yudell;
Campbell and Campbell,
landscape architect

West end of
Colorado Avenue
The pier was severely damaged in the heavy storms during the winter of 1982–83, but it is now rebuilt. For decades the pier has been one of the joys of Santa

Monica, rain or shine. On weekends the railings are lined with people fishing or just walking and looking. Restaurants, curio shops, and amusement palaces line the south side of the pier. But the hit architecturally is the merry-go-round.

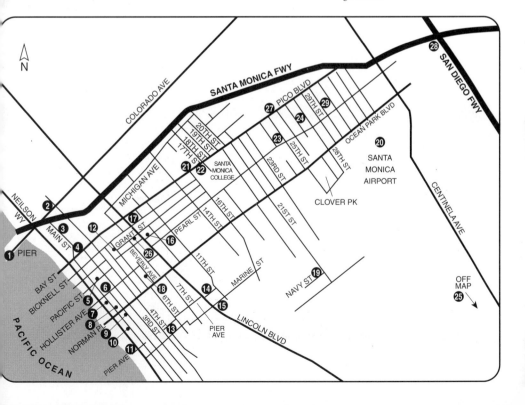

The center of the project is an octagonal entry plaza. At the southern edge of the site is a children's park with a playful but menacing dragon that is about to devour a small Viking ship. A fanciful pair of octagonal carousel towers overlook the volleyball courts. These towers are of metal and read as two-dimensional drawings.

2. Sears, Roebuck and Company Store, 1946–47
Roland H. Crawford
Colorado Avenue, between 3rd and 4th Streets

A classic example of a post–World War II Modern retail store build-

with its beautiful tile entrance, was to have been the central focus of a formal Beaux-Arts grouping of buildings that never took place. In the lobby are two Federal Art Project murals by Stanton McDonald Wright. These were painted in 1939, and the subject is Spanish Revival.

4. Santa Monica Civic Auditorium, 1959
Welton Becket and Associates
North corner of Main Street and Pico Boulevard

This is a perfect period piece of the late 1950s. Its six 72-foot concrete masts that connect with the entrance canopy match in

design conveys that feeling. The design of the building, and especially of the façades, is that of pure architectural patterning along the lines of the machine aesthetic.

6. Horatio West Court, 1919–21
Irving J. Gill
140 Hollister Avenue

As Esther McCoy has pointed out, this four-unit complex is Gill's closest approximation to the later European International Style of the 1920s. The arched entryways and the small patio courts indicate Gill's attachment

ing. The design concept is classical Beaux-Arts; the fenestration and signage are Modern. As with all of the Sears stores, this building was primarily arranged around its parking lot (which was accompanied by its auto service building).

3. Santa Monica City Hall, 1938–39
Donald B. Parkinson and J. M. Estep
1685 Main Street

This PWA Moderne building,

spirit the tail fins of automobiles of these years. The masts play against the entire entrance façade, which is composed of a delicate cast-concrete grille.

5. Condominium Town Houses, 1981–82
Stafford/Binder
116 Pacific Street

The ultimate in high-tech imagery. Though not specifically derived from classical European Modern of the 1920s, the atmosphere of their Constructivist

to the early Mission Revival of California. The buildings have been restored, and though there have been some changes, they do present an excellent sense of Gill's puritanical and abstract approach to design.

7

7. Edgemar Development, 1984–88
Frank O. Gehry and Associates
2415–2437 Main Street

The name of this project comes from the old Edgemar Farms Dairy that occupied this site. (A fragment of the street wall of the dairy remains at the right side.) Included in it are commercial spaces, a museum, and a subterranean garage. This assemblage may be thought of as a mini-mall;

it also harks back to the 1920s in Los Angeles, when a number of theaters were built with fore-courts containing retail shops and restaurants. Gehry leads you into the central courtyard through two passages: one is defined by the curve of the west building, the other by an angled passageway. Instead of a motion picture theater, the major "theater" is the Santa Monica Museum of Art.

Aesthetically, the structures are enlarged pieces of hard-edged sculpture. The enclosed volumes are clothed in sheet metal and stucco; these are countered by pieces of Constructivist sculpture in metal and chain-link fence.

8. Merle Norman Building, 1935–36
George Parr
2525 Main Street

An existing brick building was remodeled and added to, transforming the whole into a Streamline Moderne ship. The south corner of the building suggests an ocean liner with a round tower over an open bridge. The north corner is also streamlined and nautical, in

this case hinting at a streamlined warship of the mid-1930s.

9. First Methodist Episcopal Church, 1875–76
2621 – 2nd Street

Santa Monica's first church building has been moved twice: once in 1893, then again in 1900. It is of architectural interest because it could just as well have been built in Iowa City as on the far reaches of the Pacific Coast.

10. Jones House (now California Heritage Museum), 1894
2620 Main Street

This simply detailed Queen Anne dwelling and its neighbor, the Trask House (1903; Hunt and Eggers), were moved to this site in 1977. Both houses, originally from the 1000 block of Ocean Boulevard, have been restored. Though small, the museum with its changing exhibitions of the decorative arts is an extremely imaginative contribution to the culture of Southern California.

8

11. Parkhurst Building, 1927
Norman F. Marsh
and Company
Northwest corner of
Main Street and Pier Avenue

This Spanish Revival building with its beautiful exposed brickwork might have come out of a Hollywood film on old Seville. It has been restored to its former glory.

12. OP12 Dispersed Affordable Housing, 1986–88
Koning Eisenberg Architecture
2207 – 6th Street

The three-story block facing onto 6th Street has the feel of 1920s housing designed by the Dutch architect Gerrit Rietveld. Six units are encompassed in these two buildings, and garden space is provided between. Another Koning and Eizenberg housing project nearby is their OP12 Dispersed Affordable Housing at 2400 – 5th Street.

Other housing developments by Koning and Eisenberg in this general area are St. John's Hospital Housing, 1314 – 18th Street (1986–88); St. Mary's Housing, 1427 Berkeley Street (1986–88); St. John's Hospital Housing, 2121 Arizona Avenue (1987–88), and the Twenty-two Twenty-Six Town Houses, 2226 Sixth Street (1990–92). All of these examples of group housing have responded in a rational manner to their functional requirements, usually with very modest budgets.

13. Vawter House, 1900
504 Pier Avenue

A shingled Queen Anne dwelling that, with its extensive porches on two sides, suggests the ideal of the seaside resort that Santa Monica was seeking to create at the turn of the century.

14. Condominium Town House, 1981
Janotta-Breska Associates
1016 Pier Avenue

The high-tech image, perhaps in this instance more romantic than other Modernist condominiums of the 1980s and 1990s in Santa Monica and Venice.

15. Condominium Town Houses, 1981
Janotta-Breska Associates
1015 Marine Street

A further continuation of the machine image expressed in the condominiums at 1016 Pier Avenue.

16. Condominium Town Houses, 1979
A Design Group;
David Cooper, Michael W. Folonis, George Blain, and Richard Clemenson
831 Pacific Street

A not-to-be-missed high-tech image that is resplendent with arbitrary forms and surfaces. It gives you the feeling that it belongs in a museum as a model rather than on a city street.

17. Condominium Town Houses, 1981
A Design Group/
Janotta-Breska Associates
821 Bay Street

This stucco-sheathed unit is a little more believable as High Tech and as a place to live than its neighbor at number 831.

18. Beverly House, 1990
Michael W. Folonis
and Associates
2522 Beverly Avenue

Though the present building is technically a remodel, it is in fact an entirely new structure. A fascinating play occurs in this design as a strong expression of structure (especially portions of the exposed steel frame) is countered by stucco-sheathed volumes.

19. Chambers/Folonis House, 1988
Michael W. Folonis
and Associates
735 Navy Street

Though this 1,500-square-foot residence occupies much of its 25-foot-wide lot, it fits in well with the older surrounding dwellings. The architect has accomplished this accommodation via the breaking up of his building into separate volumes. Below, the walls are of concrete block; above is a hooped-roof volume clad in sheets of mahogany plywood. On the second floor, an exterior deck separates the parents' space from that of the children.

20. Typhoon Restaurant, 1991
Grinstein/Daniels Architects
Santa Monica Airport

The show is on the interior, where the architects appear to have intended to evoke the somewhat bland Modernist style of the fifties. But the food is good and the site is terrific, with small planes taxiing right up to your window.

21. Woodlawn Cemetery
Mausoleum, 1924 and later
Pico Boulevard, between 14th and 17th Streets

The 1924 section of this building (which faces toward the south) can be seen from Pico Boulevard and boasts a handsome Plateresque-inspired façade. Note as well the BPOE Monument (circa 1910) to the west. It is an open, round classical temple surrounded by cast-iron elks.

22. Santa Monica City
College: Business Education
and Vocational Building, 1981
Daniel, Mann, Johnson, and
Mendenhall
Pico Boulevard, at 17th Street

A blend of post–World War II International Style Modern with a suggestion of the Streamline Moderne of the 1930s and even a slight nod to recent High Tech. Go to the rear (south side) of the building to see this elevation with its exposed metal stairs.

23. Sun-Tech Town Houses,
1981
Urban Forms;
David Van Hoy and
Steve Andre
2433 – 25th Street

An eighteen-unit condominium, the ultimate in Postmodern High Tech imagery. Though the machine is supposedly rational, High Tech such as this is related to art more than to pragmatic planning. Still, we must admit that it is impressive from the street and from within, especially in the two-story living spaces.

24. Putnam Place Town
House, 1983
2336 – 28th Street

A perfect model of Postmodernism: classical columns, false walls, etc.

25. Condominium Town
Houses, 1980
A Design Group;
Michael Folonis and
David Cooper
Northwest and northeast corners of Barrington and Brookhaven Avenues

Yet another example of Postmodern High Tech. The image in this case is somewhat stronger in nostalgia for the "heroic" period of modern architecture of the 1920s.

26. Condominium Town
Houses, 1981
Tossman/Day
835 Grant Street

A three-story stucco unit whose cut-out forms, shed roofs, and window pattern directly carry on Charles W. Moore's late-1970s vocabulary.

27. Chili Bowl, 1931
Arthur Whizin
12244 W. Pico Boulevard

By 1933 Arthur Whizin, the "Chili Bowl King," had established eighteen of these fast-food stands throughout the Los Angeles area. Only four remain, in varying states of decay.

28. Santa Monica Freeway
Interchange with the
San Diego Freeway, 1961–66
Lammers, Reed, and Reece,
Engineers

The Santa Monica Freeway begins at its western end with a graceful swoop through a curved tunnel, then it proceeds all the way to West Covina to the east. The interchange with the San Diego Freeway is certainly one of the most spectacular interchanges in the world—Norman Bel Geddes's Magic Motorways of 1940 realized in fact. At the freeway's west end are several murals on concrete retaining walls. While these are folksy, they hardly add a positive note to the machine image of the freeway or to its parklike landscaping.

29. 31st Street House,
1992–93
Koning Eizenberg Architecture
1527 – 31st Street

The projecting façade of a charming small Spanish Revival house sits as a Hollywood stage set in front of a Modernist building.

6 • Venice
Marina del Rey

In January 1906, the architect Norman F. Marsh wrote of California's version of Venice: "Like the Aladdin's lamp of nursery days, wealth and labor have been the wand that has transformed an uninviting landscape in the southern part of California into scenes that delight the aesthetic." In a period of twelve months, the architectural firm of Marsh and Russell had (according to Marsh's words) designed "a magic city (built for the generations) with its stately arcades, shimmering lagoons, floating pennants, and glistening minarets.

Venice was the brainchild of Abbot Kinney, who came to California in 1880. His dream was to create an exotic showplace resembling the architecture and waterways of the famous northern Italian city. It would not be an ordinary beach community but one devoted to high culture and equipped with a 3,600-seat auditorium and even a "great university or institute." In 1904 Kinney engaged Norman F. Marsh and his associates to lay out the site plan and to design the first of the community's buildings. The Italian-born sculptor Luigi Peano was engaged to do the sculpture for the bridges and for a number of the buildings.

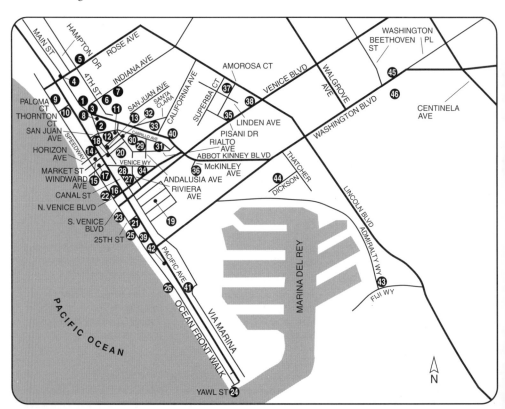

The new city was officially opened by Kinney himself on June 30, 1905. But within a few years, it was evident that it would only succeed if it was oriented to amusements and to the beach. In 1907 a casino was constructed, and other entertainment buildings followed, reaching a high point in the 1912 "Race through the Clouds" roller coaster designed by A. F. Rosenheim. Nevertheless, while tourists came and went, few palaces were built along Venice's canals. A fair number of dwellings were built. They were modest in scale and their image was in the lake or seaside manner of the Craftsman mode. Kinney himself died in 1920, and within a few years any thought of Venice as a cultural center was thrown to the winds. The canals filled with silt and junk; and the gondoliers went home. Oil wells sprouted along a few of the canals, and the center of Venice became increasingly shabby and run down. The final blow came in 1925, when Venice lost its independence and became a part of Los Angeles.

In the 1960s and early 1970s, changes began to occur. To the south, Victor Gruen Associates laid out Marina del Rey (1966–74), a new boat-oriented community checkered by low- and high-rise housing units (located southwest of Lincoln and Washington Boulevards). Marina City (Daniel, Mann, Johnson, Mendenhall; Anthony Lumsden; and Richard L. Tipping) was built in 1971 and other additions followed, including Mariner's Village Apartments (1980; Kamnitzer and Marks). In the end, neither the planning nor the buildings in Marina del Rey are really worth any extended visit.

It was in the 1950s and 1960s that Venice became a Bohemian quarter and began to boast not only artists and their garrets, but also a wide array of public murals. From the late 1970s on, Venice and the southern section of adjoining Santa Monica emerged as the center for self-conscious, avant-garde, Modern architecture—usually in the form of housing and artists' studios. In Venice itself, and to the north in parts of Santa Monica, one will discover a wide array of multiple- and single-family dwellings as well as smaller commercial projects designed by some of Los Angeles's most talented architects of the moment.

1. Commercial Building, 1987
Sam Davis
916 Main Street

The architect has remodeled an existing building, transforming it into a strong but low-keyed composition. A dark band works around the base of the building, and the entrance is marked by a small tower-like form.

2. Chiat-Day-Mojo
Advertising Agency, 1985–91
Frank O. Gehry and Associates;
Claes Oldenburg and
Coosje van Bruggen
Northeast side of Main Street, between Brooks and Clubhouse Avenues

To the northwest, the building begins as an International Style ocean liner that collides with the Oldenburg and van Bruggen binoculars; then to the right, is a third section of the building, that looks like a rusting steel ruin. This adds up to a Programmatic building, but as always, Gehry provides us with an impressive art object, plus a

gentle comment on buildings and society (see page 24).

3. Bright and Associates
Building, 1990
Franklin D. Israel
Design Associates
901 Abbot Kinney Boulevard, on the north corner of Abbot Kinney Boulevard and Hampton Drive

This everyday complex of commercial vernacular buildings had been internally converted in the 1950s, in a very minimal way, into the working studio of Charles and Ray Eames. (They first occupied the building in 1948.) In this, the most recent remodeling of these

4

buildings, Israel has also done very little with their exteriors. The corner gable-roofed building has acquired a metal-sheathed curved vent above the entrance. The parking lot entrance now is covered by a triangular canopy and an entrance with a panel of glass brick. The real transformation is on the interior. The sequence of mysterious space is produced by the way that light is introduced and, above all, by color. The varied experiences along the interior "streets" and in the glass-roofed atrium suggest an updated and forceful abstraction of the worried Surrealism of the 1920s. In this case, the reference seems to be to the wondrous and weird stage sets by Robert Wiene for the 1919 film *The Cabinet of Dr. Caligari.*

4. Renaissance Building, 1989
Johannes Van Tilburg and Partners
Northwest corner of Main Street and Rose Avenue

The inspirations for this three-story block-long complex were the original Venetian buildings laid out in 1904–6 in central Venice (California, of course). A loggia with elaborate Corinthian columns occurs at the street level. Behind this are retail stores; above the stores are two floors of living units. At the corner of Rose Avenue and Main Street is a giant clown designed by the artist Jonathan Borofsky.

5. Store Building, circa 1937
Mid-block on the north side of Rose Avenue, between 4th and 5th Streets

A tiny building with an oversized oval window in the Streamline Moderne idiom.

6. Arnoldi Triplex, 1981
Frank O. Gehry and Associates
322 Indiana Avenue

Everything looks ordinary until you consider the boxlike volume at the corner, which seems to have been tipped on end.

7. Hopper House, 1989
Brian Murphy
326 Indiana Avenue

Next door to the Arnoldi Triplex is the Hopper Studio-House (1989) looking as if it were an addition to the Gehry building.

8. Duplex, 1978–81
Frederick Meyer
(George Mayers, developer and builder)
921–923 Abbot Kinney Boulevard

A late-1970s Victorian Revival via details derived, at least in spirit, from an Eastlake pattern book.

9. House, 1986
Arata Isozaki
16 Paloma Court

A simple elongated stucco box is enriched by fasciated corners of glass and metal roofs.

10. Michich-Small House, 1981
Milica Dedijer-Michich
120 Thornton Court

Viewed from the walkway, its stuccoed angles and curved columns and balconies come from the Modern of the 1920s and 1930s. On the alley side, an angled greenhouse is almost a rationalist image via James Stirling.

11. Apartment Building, circa 1905
Attributed to Marsh and Russell
235 San Juan Avenue

This is one of several of the early designs of Marsh and Russell that reflects the influence of the Midwest work of Louis H. Sullivan and of Frank Lloyd Wright.

12. Caplin House, 1979
Frederick Fisher and Thane Roberts
229 San Juan Avenue

A white stucco box with a partial barrel roof, á la Adolf Loos and Vienna in the early years of the century. The façades, on the other hand, are self-consciously composed of a pattern of rectangular openings and seem to have more to do with art than architecture.

13. Store Building, circa 1937
1332–1380 Main Street, between San Juan and Horizon Avenues

A two-story complex of shops and offices, clothed in the popular Streamline Moderne.

14. Spiller House, 1980
Frank O. Gehry and Associates
39 Horizon Avenue

A three-level town house with roof deck. Most of the building is clad in galvanized corrugated metal, while sticks (two-by-fours) and plywood occur in part of the inner court of the living room.

15

15. Gagosian Art Gallery and Apartments, 1980–81
Studio Works; Hodgetts and Mangurian; with Frank Lupe and Audrey Mitlock
51 Market Street

The gray stucco street elevation and its upper curved studio façade with glass brick suggests the Streamline Moderne of the 1930s. Inside, a circular court interrupts the basic volume of the buildings.

16. Rebecca's Restaurant, 1982–85
Frank O. Gehry and Associates
2025 Pacific Avenue (main entrance on North Venice Boulevard)

Tree trunks help to support the ceiling, and two of Frank Gehry's 18-foot-long crocodiles float from the ceiling and are joined by one of his octopus chandeliers. The tin-collage entrance doors are by Tony Berlant, the window murals are by Ed Moses, and a painting on black velvet is by Peter Alexander.

17. Venice Center, 1904–5
Windward Avenue, between Pacific Avenue and Speedway

The best remaining group of the original buildings are those on the north side of Windward Avenue. At the northeast corner of Windward and Pacific Avenues is the arcaded three-story Hotel St. Mark (architects Marsh and Graham).

18. Speedway Cafe, 1991
Franklin D. Israel Design Associates
Corner of 17th Street and Pacific Avenue

The stuccoed exterior of the café plays between plain and ordinary commercial vernacular and sophisticated European. Inside, sheets of plywood, layered on sections of the walls and ceiling, suggest that we have returned to the Surrealist/Constructivist world of Kurt Schwitters in the 1920s.

19c

19. Venice Canals, 1904–05

A picturesque settlement of houses on a grid of canals is bounded by North Venice Boulevard and Ocean, 28th and Pacific Avenues. In the early 1990s the canals were dredged, a large congregation of resident ducks and geese was removed, and the area was considerably upscaled demographically. Today it has become a much sought-after place to remodel old houses and to build new ones of every description (some of them nondescript). They are often entertaining but not important architecture.

A few exceptions to this generalization must be made. The houses by Mark Mack at (a) 427 Linnie Canal, by Holger Schubert (2001), at (b) 2335 Eastern Court, by Glen Irani (1999), at (c) 419 Howland Canal, and by David Hertz (2000) at (d) 477 Carroll Canal Court are cases in point. They are beautiful evocations of the revival of the International Style—in color.

It must also be said that the water birds have made a comeback. Their raucous conversation does not seem to disturb the residents, but watch your step!

20. Windward Circle, Steven Ehrlich Architects
a. Ace Market, 1989
185 Windward Avenue

b. Windward Circle Art Building, 1988
211 Windward Avenue

c. Race Through the Clouds, 1987
1600 Main Street

The architect was presented with the unique opportunity of designing three of the buildings that define the center of Venice. The first of these buildings, Race Through the Clouds (named after the original roller coaster that was located on the site), captures the spirit of the roller coaster via a neon-edged, galvanized metal track, which goes in and out around the building. The Windward Circle Art Building abstracts the traditional architecture of Venice through a recessed ground-level loggia, accompanied by the suggestion of three towers. The three-story Ace Market displays vertical projecting arms meant to suggest the steam shovels used to dredge the Venice canals.

21. Norton House, 1982–84 Frank O. Gehry and Associates
2509 Ocean Front, at the end of 25th Street

This project is supposedly a remodel, but it is really a new house. Steps lead up from the beach seemingly all the way to the top of the building. Hovering over the single front section of the house is a viewing study, set as a box on a pole. As with so much of Gehry's work, what appears to be arbitrary and capricious turns out, in plan, to be rational.

22. Snipper House ("La Rotonda"), 1988
Miguel Angelo Flores and Associates
2511 Ocean Front Walk

A modular framed box (on a lavender-colored podium) is placed within a light steel box. To the side, one can see portions of the stucco and glass-brick cylinder that forms the core of the house. Contrast it with the Gehry house next door to sense two very different Modernist approaches to design and to a beach house with much public exposure.

23. House, 1990
Steven Ehrlich
2311 Ocean Front Walk

A raised two-story stucco-sheathed volume exhibits a fron-tispiece of banded concrete block. A high loggia occurs at the first floor; above the center of the upper porch is a glass bay. The architect has designed several other residences in Venice that should be mentioned. These include the Ed Moses Studio (1987) at 1233 Palais Boulevard, the Okulick Studio (1989) at 604 S. Hampton Drive, the Ripple House (1989) at 1338 Preston Way, and the Douroux Canal House (1991) at 2570 Grand Canal.

24. Doumani House, 1982
Robert Graham
*Southwest corner of
Ocean Front Walk and
Yawl Street*

The sculptor as architect. A white stucco U-shaped volume. Its step-pattern windows and the sculptured open-metal grill-work at ground level tilt the design toward the Art Deco of the 1920s.

25. Douroux House, 1989–90
Antoine Predock
2315 Ocean Front Walk

Facing the ocean and the public walkway is a cast-in-place rectangular armature, open at the top, filled in with glass below. The most eye-catching feature of this façade is the large, overscaled flipped window. The house extends along the public passageway. The interior is open to view on the beachside walkway.

26. Stone Condominium, 1973
Kahn, Kappe, and Lotery
3815 Ocean Front Walk

Stucco volumes and walls serve as a foil for the west-facing glass and wood sections of the building. The placement of the wood members separating the glass areas creates a strong but unusual horizontal scale.

27. Apartment Building, circa 1910
*Northeast corner of
Venice Boulevard and
Canal Street*

A three-story delight, designed in a kind of parody of Asian Craftsman architecture.

28. Ming-Li Lowe Office Building, 1981
David Ming-Li Lowe
*308 Venice Way, near
Riviera Way*

Architecture realized by the commonplace (materials, structure, methods of assembly, all of steel). You could easily drive by and not notice the building, but once your attention is fixed, the art of design is apparent. There are really two mirrored buildings in this project; a court occurs between these two units.

29. House, circa 1907
*Northwest corner of
Andalusia and Rialto Avenues*

Although altered in recent years, this dwelling still evidences the exotic faraway qualities of Islamic India and the Near East.

30. House, circa 1907
*Cabrillo Avenue and
Market Street*

An arcaded two-story porch with dome suggests Islamic North Africa.

31. Multi-Family Residence, 1989
Ted Tokio Tanaka
1415–1421 Cabrillo Avenue

Behind this dramatic façade of geometric cutouts of squares, triangles, and half circles, four living units are situated. The interior space is divided into six levels, including the sunken parking. The assertiveness of this white stucco building seems to draw more from the traditional architecture of North Africa than from Mediterranean borrowings.

32

33

about in the years before 1945. A barrel roof covers part of the house; the walls are sheathed in smooth plaster and in copper. Internally, the space is organized around a three-story atrium. An upper-level bridge occurs over sections of the atrium.

35. Police and Fire Station of Venice, circa 1930
Northeast corner of Venice Boulevard and Pisani Drive

A two-story PWA Moderne building in exposed concrete, with relief sculptures over the entrance. Next door, to the west, is the former Venice City Hall, a slightly garbled version of the Mission Revival.

36. House, 1996
Syndesis (David Hertz)
2420 McKinley Avenue

An extraordinarily fine house in a pleasant middle-class neighborhood. The architect was obviously influenced by the midwestern Prairie style, but he makes it look modern.

32. University of Arts, 1904–5
Marsh and Russell
1304 Riviera Avenue

One of Abbot Kinney's original buildings, this one intended as part of his cultural institute. The design, like others in Venice, is both Sullivanesque and Wrightian.

33. Electric Art Block, 1989–91
Koning Eizenberg Architecture;
Glenn Robert Erickson
499 Santa Clara Avenue

This 360-foot-long block of twenty artists' lofts is situated on an abandoned electric streetcar right-of-way. Though connected,

the two-story buildings read as separate structures. The two corner buildings facing the streets pose as Modernist false fronts. The interior buildings are sheathed in white stucco, while the end buildings exhibit thin galvanized sheet metal.

34. 411 Venice House, 1991
Michael W. Folonis and Associates
411 Venice Boulevard

Several Modernist themes occur in this three-story dwelling. These range from close looks at early Modern of the 1930s plus a sense of what R. M. Schindler and other California Modernists were

36

37. 2-4-6-8 House, 1979
Morphosis
(Thom Mayne and
Michael Rotondi)
*North side of
Amorosa Court, between
Linden Avenue and
Lincoln Boulevard*

A four-part window as a playful theme, set in front of the pieces of asphalt-shingle siding. Bright colors enhance the dollhouse quality of the design.

Another example of the work of Morphosis is the house at 634¹/₂ Sixth Street, which dates from 1986–87.

38. Brenta Apartments, 1990
Rebecca L. Binder
2207 Brenta Place

The building is a single stucco box that has been articulated by slight projections and recessions to read as a random series of volumes. Another unit nearby by Rebecca L. Binder is the South Venice Apartments (1991) at 438 S. Venice Boulevard.

39. Gardner House, 1992
Rebecca L. Binder
313 – 28th Avenue

This two-story house, composed of independent volumes, opens sections of its interior spaces to decks and courtyards. The design is dominated by a tower-like volume to the rear of the house.

40. Stein Building, 1984
Bill Stein
13323 Abbot Kinney Boulevard

The proliferation of towers, gables, and porches do, indeed, command your attention in this 1980s Queen Anne Revival building.

41. House, circa 1989
*390 Pacific Avenue
Marina del Rey*

A house in the form of a streamline yacht. The bow of the ship, its second-floor bridge, and its slanted mast look out over Pacific Avenue.

42. Stayden Duplex, 1986
Miguel Angelo Flores and
Associates
4112 Pacific Avenue

Particularly from the waterside, this dwelling looks like a grounded houseboat. The dark band at the base effectively separates the building from its site, and the sloped skylight roof hints that this is part of the bridge.

43. Marina Fine Arts Gallery, 1991
John Lautner
*4716 Admiralty Way
Marina del Rey*

Within a conventional retail store space, John Lautner has placed two curved bent surfaces that almost meet. The space between and behind seems entirely open to the gallery, but angled planes of glass do occur in this space, effectively enclosing the interior. A remarkable and inventive solution for a shop front and a strong and wonderful art object in itself.

44. Hampstead House, 1993
Steven Ehrlich Architects
835 Dickson Street

From the street, you experience a composition of cubes that are colored in contrasts of burnt sienna and yellow ocher. The central cube is open and contains within, the segment of a drum (also the entrance). In contrast to the precise rectangular geometry of the building, irregular stone paving leads one up to and into the house.

45. Baldwin Motel, circa 1934
*12823 Washington Boulevard
Culver City*

A small Streamline Moderne motel with a drive-through gate.

46. Mar Vista Houses, 1946–48
Ain, Johnson and Day
(Gregory Ain)
*Beethoven, Moore, and
Meier Streets, south of
Marco Place*

One of Ain's prime interests was low-cost housing. After World War II he designed several small-scale developments of which the Mar Vista Houses were one. Fifty-two single-family houses were initially built in this project, with another fifty-two planned. These houses of 1,050 square feet were planned so that they could take eight different configurations. They were built for the Advanced Development Company. Ain provided internal flexibility, using sliding walls between one of the bedrooms and the living room, and the other two bedrooms could be united or separated by sliding doors. Most of the houses have been remodeled and added to, but one can still get a sense of Ain's view of inexpensive single-family housing.

7 • Los Angeles International Airport, Westchester

Since the 1950s the area directly around the Los Angeles International Airport has developed into an aerospace-related industrial zone, supplemented especially on the east and north by a good supply of hotels and office buildings. North of the airport is Westchester, which is almost exclusively residential housing (with the exceptions of Loyola University and Northrup Institute of Technology). To the west is the beach-oriented community of Playa del Rey, which was substantially reduced in size in the 1960s by the removal of blocks of residences that once existed at the west end of the airport's runways. All that remains now is the picturesque pattern of the streets. The removal of these houses has meant the loss of a number of excellent Spanish Revival, French Norman, English Tudor, and Streamline Moderne houses of the 1920s and 1930s. Two major losses were R. M. Schindler's Zaczek Beach House (1936–38) and Thornton M. Abell's Shonerd House (1935). Within the past twenty years, there has been renewed building activity in what remains of Playa del Rey.

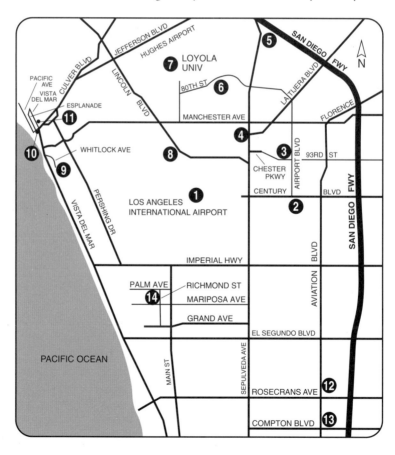

South of the airport is El Segundo (established in 1917), the name of which was derived from the early (1911) oil fields in the area. The section of El Segundo to the west is composed of single-family spec houses—most of which were built just after World War II—while industrial and commercial activity characterize the eastern and northern portions of the community.

1. Los Angeles International Airport, 1925–present
Enter from the east on Century Boulevard

The site of the airport was at first a general flying field established in 1925. In 1928 it became the municipal airport for the city of Los Angeles. Through much of the 1930s the municipal airport was secondary in public use to other fields located in Burbank, Glendale, and Santa Monica. In 1940–41 Sumner Spaulding and John Austin were commissioned to design an extensive new passenger terminal and a number of secondary buildings. In 1941 the airport directors appointed a team of architects—Walker and Eisen, McNeal Swasey, Sumner Spaulding, and H. L. Gogerty—to design the new administration building. Because of the Second World War, this expansion of the public aspects of the airport was put aside.

After the war, various studies and some expansion of runways and buildings took place. But the first phase of the airport came about during the years 1957–61. It was in the mid-1950s that William Pereira, together with Paul R. Williams and Welton Becket, provided a new master plan for the airport, and this was followed later by their designs for a new group of terminals, the administration building, and the central theatrical flying saucer restaurant. Their scheme of a group of terminals built around a central space devoted to parking

worked for a time, though the only visual event of great interest for those using the terminals was the Islamic-like domed spaces that hovered over the escalators and staircases. Externally, the character of the place was established by the landscape design, with its reliance on the palm tree. As to buildings, the Theme Building by Pereira, Williams, and Becket established the space-age theme of the passenger terminal area. Originally, now gone, there was a second minor theme building: the airport Standard Service Station, which was situated east of the theme building. This 1962 station was designed by Charles Luckman, Paul R. Williams, and Welton Becket. Its design repeated the theme of the circle in its wide cantilevered canopy, matched by its small circular drum for an office.

Pereira, Williams, and Becket's scheme for the airport worked well during the 1960s and early 1970s, but eventually the intensity of usage far outstripped what had been planned. Added to this problem was the traffic congestion on Century Boulevard, the short surface street connecting the airport to the San Diego Freeway. Various proposals were made for the airport, including moving it out to the northeastern desert at Palmdale, but nothing came of these proposals. Finally, the impetus of the 1984 Olympic Games prompted an extensive rebuilding of the airport, including a new two-layer road system, new and enlarged terminal buildings, and

an expanded parking system. This new expansion was designed by William Pereira, Daniel Dworsky, Bonito A. Sinclair, and John Williams. When you fly in and out of the airport, look to the south and you will see a group of Spanish Revival buildings of the 1920s. The most important of these is Hangar No. 1, built in 1929, designed by Gable and Wyant (the hangar is located at 5701 W. Imperial Boulevard). This hangar has recently been restored. The design in the 1980s of the multilayered road system, the addition of new buildings, and the remodeling and expansion of the old have somewhat improved the looks of the place, but it is hardly a pleasant visual experience. One exception would be the remodeled Delta Airline terminal, which provides a pleasant, visually calm space oriented around a wide-ramped internal space lined by palms. This was designed in 1987 by Gensler and Associates, with Lawrence Reed Miline Associates, landscape architects.

One of the additions to the architecture of the airport is Siegel Diamond's Airport Traffic Control Tower and Administrative Base Building (1993–95). The architects have aptly described their 257-foot-high tower as an "organic imagery of the high tech tree," and as an "adult tree-house." They have taken the parabolic arches of the Los Angeles Airport theme building and used them as their theme. Flattening the arch form, they used it for the lower building and then as the form to cover the traffic control tower. A system of dramatic extended struts is used to support the extended roofs of these two forms. The visual sense of the new tower is that of an abstracted 1990s version of a World War I airplane with its thin wings and struts.

2. Worldwide Postal Center, 1967
Daniel, Mann, Johnson, and Mendenhall (DMJM) (Cesar Pelli and Anthony Lumsden)
5800 W. Century Boulevard

This building's character is created by the vertical and horizontal units of its two-story frame, left open in parts and filled in others. The exposed concrete frame, thin infills, and rounded corners suggest that the building is some type of fancy machine, housing not postal workers but computers.

3. Hertz Vehicle Maintenance Turnaround Facility, 1982
Daniel, Mann, Johnson, and Mendenhall
9000–9029 Airport Boulevard

A machine object, a two-story curved box with a curved canopy projecting in front of the building.

4. Millron's Department Store Building (now Broadway), 1949
Gruen and Krummeck
Northwest corner of Sepulveda Boulevard and Manchester Avenue

The three-block commercial strip on Sepulveda Boulevard (between Manchester Avenue and Lincoln Boulevard), which serves as the center of Westchester, was developed during the years 1948–52. Like the Miracle Mile section of

Wilshire Boulevard, the stores on Sepulveda Boulevard face toward the street in a traditional manner, while their parking and major entrances are at the rear. The two-story Millron's Department Store Building not only provides parking at the rear but on its roof as well. Millron's itself and most of the adjoining stores employ the usual post–World War II motifs—an angular or curved high pylon sign, curved surfaces, and bands of vertical supports.

5. Wang Tower, Howard Hughes Center, 1986
Barton Myers Associates
6701 Center Drive West, off of Sepulveda Boulevard and Howard Hughes Parkway

Barton Myers did a master plan for the site and then designed this 16-story building as the flagship of the project. The stepped façade of granite terminates in a high round tower, all of which is very visible from the San Diego Freeway.

6. Westchester High School (now Wright Junior High School), 1952
Sumner Spaulding and John Rex
Southwest corner of Cowan Avenue and 80th Street

Miesian pavilions arranged around courtyards.

7. Loyola University, 1865–present
80th Street, between McConnell Avenue and Fordham Road

Loyola University (at first named St. Vincent's College) is one of the oldest academic institutions in California. The Westchester site of the university is open and suburban in character. There are several buildings worth visiting.

These include the following:

a. Sacred Heart Chapel, 1953
M. L. Barker and G. Lawrence Ott

Spanish Revival carried on successfully into the postwar years. The tower and the street façade work well, especially when seen from a distance.

b. Loyola University Theater, 1963
Edward D. Stone

A characteristic Stone Palladian Villa, used in this case for an auditorium, all tinsely and lighthearted.

c. Library, 1977
David C. Martin

A Modernist design with a central skylighted atrium.

d. University Gymnasium, Athletic and Recreational Complex, 1978–80
Kappe, Lotery, Boccato

The graceful concave shape of the roof is a result of the cable-hung suspension system employed.

8. IBM Aerospace Headquarters, 1963
Eliot Noyes; A. Quincy Jones and Frederick E. Emmons
9045 Lincoln Boulevard

An exposed concrete grid clothes a late-1950s International Style box.

We wrote the above in 1993 when this building was still the IBM Aerospace Headquarters, but we did not add that it probably was intended to look like an IBM punch card. In fact it closely resembles the infamous 2000 Florida ballot with some chads still hanging inside the windows. The Otis School of Art and Design remodeled its interiors (Bullock Tice Associates) in 1997

8

and moved in. How anything gets done in it is a great mystery.

Its problems were a factor in causing Otis to expand. According to one of their publications, "Its low ceilings and lack of adequate daylight make it inadequate for a number of functions," so they commissioned Frederick Fisher and Partners to design a new building that would be "full of light and provide space for galleries as well as studios for painting, sculpture, and photography, as well as workshops, classrooms, and faculty offices." The building was finished in 2001.

The Galef Center for Fine Arts and Ben Maltz Gallery is encased in a silver-painted, corrugated aluminum sheathing. Fisher wrote: "We conceived of the Otis studio

building as an *art factory* based on the ethos of art making. . . . It is analagous to industrial lofts favored by artists for studios." It also looks awfully good and heightens the impression that the building next door is extremely funny.

9. House, circa 1938
7540 Whitlock Avenue

The perfect image for a site overlooking the ocean: a Streamline Moderne design equipped with nautical pipe railing, corner windows, glass brick, flat roofs, and white stucco walls.

10. Esplanade del Rey Townhouse, 1982
Convoy Street, between Esplanade and Culver Boulevards

Modern historicism: a block-long row of town houses that seems to hearken back to the 1920s work of J. J. P. Oud in Holland.

11. Duplex, 1977
Eric Owen Moss and James Stafford
6672–6674 Vista del Mar

Except for its light-yellow color and the exposed metal flues, this Streamline design could have been done in the early 1930s by Norman Bel Geddes.

12. Scientific Data System Building (now Xerox), 1966–68
Craig Ellwood and Associates
555 S. Aviation Boulevard

Once you grant the Miesian design principles of Ellwood's work, his buildings are impressive. The symbols of logic and order dominate this three-story post-and-lintel box. The plan is a perfect cruciform with semienclosed courtyards at the north and south. The hand of the designer is evident everywhere.

13. Federal Aviation Agency Building, 1973
Daniel, Mann, Johnson, and Mendenhall
(Anthony Lumsden, Cesar Pelli, P. J. Jacobson, Dwight Wilson)
15000 S. Aviation Boulevard

An early 1970s image of the machine product, on the fragile and breakable side.

14. El Segundo Elementary School, 1936
Northwest corner of Mariposa Avenue and Richmond Street El Segundo

PWA Moderne in exposed concrete.

8 • South Beach Area

The South Beach region comprises the communities of Manhattan Beach, Hermosa Beach, and Redondo Beach (also the district called Hollywood Riviera, which is the western part of Torrance).

Manhattan Beach was laid out in 1897 and slowly developed into a quiet bungalow colony. Hermosa Beach to the south was established in 1901, and by the 1920s it was referred to as a "family resort." Both Manhattan Beach and Hermosa Beach received a continual influx of visitors from Los Angeles during the years 1900–1920 via the Pacific Electric Line. The entire beach strand of both communities is public, though you often have to gain access to the beach by what seem to be small, secret spur streets. The beach is mostly well hidden and does not form a strong element in the townscape.

Redondo Beach, the largest of the beach communities, was founded in 1881 with the hope that it would develop as a major port for Los Angeles. At this time a pier, hotel, and narrow-gauge railroad (completed in 1888) to Los Angeles were built. In 1888 the Santa Fe Railroad constructed a line to the town. But the hoped-for commercial harbor never materialized. In 1938 work did begin on a pleasure marina (King Harbor Marina), which was completed after World War II. Redondo Beach, along with the neighboring section of the Hollywood Riviera, possesses an extensive beach park that runs from Vista del Mar to Torrance Boulevard.

Several large-scale town-house condominium projects were built in the beach communities in the 1970s and early 1980s. In other sections of these communities, density is being substantially increased. Examples of this can be seen on Blanche Road between 30th and 31st Streets in Manhattan Beach, where newer Spanish Revival town houses (1981 and later) now occupy their entire lots. On Myrtle Street in Hermosa Beach, similar intensification of land use can be experienced, only here the occasional image is "Victorian."

1. Marsh House, 1974
John Blanton
469 – 28th Street
Manhattan Beach

Located close to the street is this three-story single dwelling, tied to its site by an extensive pergola. The slope of the shed roof is interrupted by a slot for a balcony.

2. Provost House, 1975
John Blanton
204 Manhattan Avenue
Manhattan Beach

A tall, thin, vertical shed-roof volume with an assertive composition of windows, the whole topped by a projecting chimney. Other works of the 1970s in the area by the same architect are the McNulty House (1975) at 420 Manhattan Avenue and the Shelton Apartments (1974) at 480 Rosecrans Avenue.

3. Shelton Apartments #5, 1988
John Blanton
468 Rosecrans Avenue

A stucco box composed in a variation of Schindler's work of the 1930s.

4. Davidheiser/Kroll House, 1988
John Blanton
120 – 34th Street

A continuation of the Modernist approach of Neutra and Schindler.

5. Roy Condominiums, 1991
John Blanton
106 Manhattan Avenue and
109 Bayview Drive

The architect has looked carefully at late-1920s products of R. M. Schindler, such as his projected Braxton house.

6. House, 1987
Raymond Kappe
1600 The Strand

Mendelsohn-like curved volumes project outward from the concrete frame of the building. The curved forms are elegantly realized in wood and metal-framed bands of glass.

7. Tate House, 1989
Melinda Gray
1920 The Strand

A long narrow residence that makes its way up the hill. A series of circular or semicircular spaces establishes focal points within the dwelling. The largest of these spaces is a "sort of urban Italian courtyard with casement windows opening out onto the void."

8. House, 1983
Morphosis
(Thom Mayne and
Michael Rotundi)
3410 Hermosa Avenue
Hermosa Beach

A borrowing of the Modern image of the thirties with a hint of High Tech, especially in the walls sheathed with galvanized sheet metal.

9. Garmire/Russell House, 1989
John Blanton
406 N. Dianthus Street

A second-floor addition has resulted in the complete transformation of a small stucco house.

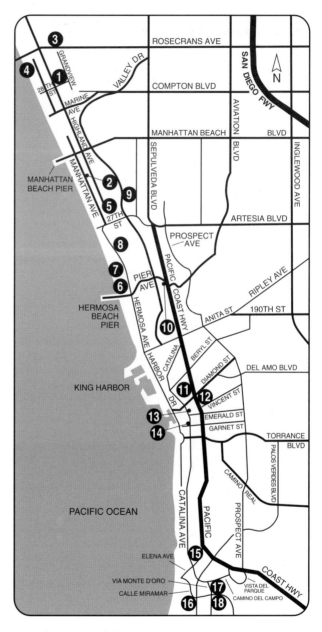

A greenhouse—as half of the gable end of the building—now projects from the second floor of the dwelling.

10. Pier Avenue School, 1939
Marsh, Smith, and Powell
Southwest corner of
Pier Avenue and
Pacific Coast Highway
Hermosa Beach

Classical PWA Moderne; its conventionalized ornament suggests Native American art of the Southwest.

11. Redondo Beach Civic Center, 1962
Victor Gruen Associates
200 Pacific Coast Highway
Redondo Beach

A well-sited and handsomely scaled community center, composed of low boxes connected by freestanding post-and-lintel passages. It is all early 1960s International Style Modern, designed with delicacy. Regrettably, building activities in the 1970s and early 1980s have obscured its civic prominence.

12. Redondo Union High School, 1931 and later
Allison and Allison
Pacific Coast Highway, between
Diamond and Vincent Streets
Redondo Beach

PWA Moderne, with the horizontal pattern of the board forms revealed in the concrete walls. Note the cast-concrete sculpture on the Manual Arts Building extolling the virtues of education and work.

13. Wardrobe Cleaners Building, circa 1950
120 Catalina Avenue
Redondo Beach

An excellent example of a 1950s commercial design with angled piers and plate-glass windows, somewhat held in place by a strong horizontal cornice.

14. Eagles Building, 1949
Northwest corner of
Catalina Avenue and
Garnet Street
Redondo Beach

An almost pure late-1930s Streamline Moderne building, constructed ten years later. Two groups of bands run horizontally across the two façades, connecting all the windows together. The entrances are emphasized by vertical projections that crawl up and over the parapets. Recent remodeling has removed the important horizontal bands.

15. United California Bank Building (now First Interstate Bank), 1970
**Roland E. Coate Jr.,
Stanley Kamebins**
1720 Elena
Redondo Beach

A cutaway passage leads one between two tightly enclosed volumes. One of the volumes rises to form a natural pylon for the sign. Within, warm wood detailing contrasts with the coldness of concrete surfaces.

16. Riviera Methodist Church, 1957–58
Neutra and Alexander
575 Palos Verdes Boulevard
Hollywood Riviera
Torrance

A single, long, rectangular block houses the sanctuary and the Sunday school rooms. An openwork Constructivist post-and-lintel composition of steel and wood emphasizes the entrance to the sanctuary.

17. Reid House, 1928
Mark Daniels
124 Via Monte d'Oro
Hollywood Riviera
Torrance

Daniels was one of California's gifted exponents of the Spanish Revival—in both architecture and landscape gardening. The Reid House clearly illustrates his understanding of Spain's rural Andalusian forms. The house and its siting also indicate how the original concept of the Hollywood Riviera was intended to be composed of large villas, set within ample grounds—something that did not occur.

18. Von Koerber House, 1931–32
R. M. Schindler
408 Via Monte d'Oro
Hollywood Riviera
Torrance

Though little known, the Von Koerber House is one of Schindler's most interesting designs. The interior is composed of a number of levels that open outward onto various decks, terraces, and courtyards. Narrow bands of clerestory windows provide light at the ceiling levels. Because of design restrictions, Schindler was required to use the Spanish Revival image, and he responded with humor and satire to these requirements. Tiles not only cover the roof but also sections of the walls, and are used in an inverted manner around the fireplace.

9 • Palos Verdes, North

In 1913 New York banker Frank A. Vanderlip acquired 16,000 acres comprising almost all of the Palos Verdes Peninsula. He then engaged Olmsted and Olmsted, Howard Shaw, and Myron Hunt to lay out a "Millionaire's Colony." The entire 16,000-acre tract was planned to include a number of large estates, parks, clubs, an elaborate pattern of roads, and three model villages. The intervention of World War I prevented the project from developing. After the war, a pared-down version of the initial scheme was begun. Between 1922 and 1923 Olmsted and Olmsted, together with Charles H. Cheney, laid out a master plan for the 3,200 acres that occupied the northwestern portion of the peninsula. They provided for four commercial centers—Lunda Bay, Valmonte, Miraleste, and Malaga Cove. Of these, only Malaga Cove was built (1922–25).

The Spanish (Mediterranean) architectural tradition was established as the official architectural style, and in 1922 an art jury was formed to review all designs. A number of major Spanish Revival designs were built, including F. L. Olmsted Jr.'s house (1924–25; Myron Hunt and H. C. Chambers), the Buchanan House (1927; Kirkland Cutter), and the Cameron House (1926; Kirkland Cutter). These and other houses are effectively hidden from view today.

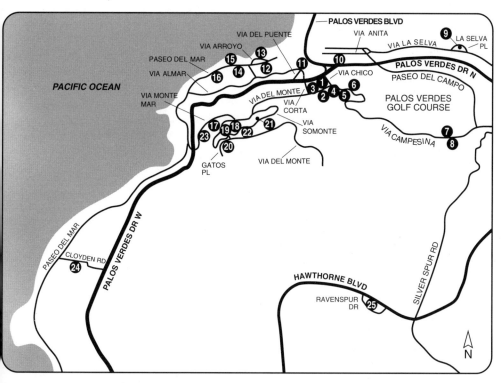

In 1932 the landscape architect A. E. Hanson became the manager of the Palos Verdes Ranch, and it was he who suggested the name Palos Verdes Peninsula to describe the area. The community barely survived the depression, and finally, with the economic recovery of the late 1930s, A. E. Hanson turned his attention to the northern part of the Ranch and began to develop Rolling Hills, whose theme was "own your own dude ranch." Again, as in Palos Verdes, architecture was to utilize two images—in this case the Anglo-Colonial and the California board-and-batten ranch house. A Western-style gate led into handsome, shake-roofed ranch houses (designed by Lutah Maria Riggs) and to Williamsburg Colonial houses (designed by Paul R. Williams). In 1937 Rolling Hills was incorporated, and it has remained a gate-guarded, upper-middle-class enclave to the present day.

The landscape and architectural beauty of Palos Verdes remains, especially in and around Malaga Cove. Palos Verdes Drive (originally laid out by the Olmsteds) was refurbished and replanted (1983). But you can immediately sense the qualitative difference between planning and design in the 1920s and that of the 1970s by comparing the linear shopping center, which has developed just west of Crenshaw Boulevard on Silver Spur Road, with that of Malaga Cove Plaza. Even tile roofs, stucco walls, and some arches (and a Home Savings Bank with its public art) do not redeem the place.

1. Malaga Cove Plaza,
1922 and later
**Olmsted and Olmsted;
Charles H. Cheney;
Webber, Staunton, and
Spaulding**
*Palos Verdes Drive, between
Via Corta and Via Chico*

Each of the four community centers planned for Palos Verdes was to be organized around a plaza and lined with two- and three-story arcaded buildings. The Malaga Cove Plaza was the only one built, and it was not completed as planned. The buildings were all designed in 1924 by Webber, Staunton, and Spaulding, while Cheney and the Olmsteds provided the general plan. Both the plan and the architecture are highly successful, including the "sally port" over Via Chico. Note the fountain (installed in 1930), which is a two-thirds-reduced reproduction of *La Fontana del Nettuno* of 1563 in Bologna.

2. Palos Verdes Public
Library, 1926–30
**Myron Hunt and
H. C. Chambers;
Olmsted and Olmsted,
landscape architects**
*South of Via Campesina at
Via Corta*

One of Hunt's most successful designs, fitted with great care into the steep hillside. Stone walls form the base of the building and extend outward to form terrace walls for the garden. The library is on the second level. Below are an exhibition room and a public meeting room.

3. Garden Apartments, 1937
Attributed to Pierpont Davis
2433 Via Campesina

A 1930s Spanish Revival complex, including a picturesque minaret.

4. Apartment Buildings, 1939
*2508, 2510, 2512
Via Campesina*

A reserved but well-organized International Style group of buildings that step up the hillside away from the road.

5. Stein House, 1928
Kirkland Cutter
2733 Via Campesina

Spanish Revival by a Palos Verdes' major architect of the 1920s, who had practiced for many years in the state of Washington, then transferred his office to Southern California in the 1920s. In addition to designing individual houses, he also designed several of the projected city centers (which were never built). Other designs of his in the Palos Verdes area are the Gilmore House (1927) at 3825 Paseo del Campo, the Paull House (1926) at 3621 Paseo del Campo, the Sisson House (1927) at 1706 Via Montemar, and the Buchanon House (1927) at 700 Via Montemar.

6. Gard House, 1927
Kirkland Cutter
2780 Via Campesina

To be read as Spanish, but in truth, many of its details came from the rural villas of Tuscany.

7. Palos Verdes Golf Course,
1922 and later
Olmsted and Olmsted;
Charles H. Cheney
3301 Via Campesina

You can obtain a good idea of Olmsted's and Cheney's approach to designing in California by driving around the boundaries of the golf course. Today it all looks natural, but the contours of the land were appreciably modified, and almost all of the plant material is non-native. The Spanish Revival Club House, designed by C. E. Howard, has been much altered (and not for the good) over the years.

8. Bowler House, 1963
Lloyd Wright
3456 Via Campesina

The low hovering roof dramatically extends the interior outward onto balconies and terraces.

9. Sias House, 1927
E. Millard
3405 La Selva Place

An Andalusian farmhouse with a separate weaving studio.

10. Goodrich House, 1928
H. Roy Kelley
2416 Via Anita

This modest dwelling was the 1928 model home for the Palos Verdes Estates—Spanish Revival, of course.

11. Gartz House, 1930
Wallace Neff
Northeast corner of
Via Almar and Via del Puente

One of Neff's large villas, more Italian than Spanish.

12. Malaga Cove School, 1926
Allison and Allison;
Olmsted and Olmsted,
landscape architects
North of Via Almar at
Via Arroyo

Mediterranean, with a tower that seems to be derived from late-fifteenth- or early-sixteenth-century Spanish examples.

13. Olmsted House, 1924–25
Myron Hunt and
H. C. Chambers
Northwest corner of
Paseo del Mar and
Via Arroyo, on the ocean side

A rural Spanish-farmhouse complex with a walled garden.

14. Palos Verdes Estates
Project House #2, 1925
W. L. Risley
408 Paseo del Mar

A modest Spanish Revival dwelling, indicating one of the housing types planned for Palos Verdes. Other housing types included connected town houses, garden apartments, and extensive villas and gardens.

15. Haggerty House (now
Neighborhood Church), 1928
Armand Monaco;
Olmsted and Olmsted,
landscape architects
415 Paseo del Mar

An extensive seaside villa, once again more Italian than Spanish. The house is impressively detailed, especially in its ironwork. If Pliny the Younger could have owned this villa and its gardens, we feel he would have been very happy.

16. Moore House, 1965
Lloyd Wright
504 Paseo del Mar

The extensive cantilevered roof ends in a sharp dramatic point, and low horizontal terraces extend the houses outward on its site.

17. Stannard House, 1974
John Blanton
432 Via Monte Mar

A mid-1970s version of the Hispanic tradition, with white stucco walls and balconies.

18. Cheney House, 1924
Charles H. Cheney and
C. E. Howard
657 Via del Monte

Although not easy to see, this is an important Spanish Revival dwelling and garden. It was designed as his own home by one of California's foremost city planners, an advocate of community architectural control. While the house is Spanish, the garden tends toward the Italian.

19. La Venta Inn, 1923
Pierpont Davis;
Olmsted and Olmsted,
landscape architects
736 Via del Monte

When built, it was one of the landmarks of Palos Verdes. The image was that of a whitewashed Mediterranean church set on a steep hillside. Now the planting has grown so high and thick that only the very top of the tower is visible. A pergola encloses one side of the fountained courtyard.

20. Lombardi House, 1965
Lloyd Wright
804 Gatos Place, off
Via del Monte

In this house Lloyd Wright transforms some of the visual excitement of the Los Angeles commercial strip into domestic architecture.

21. Buchanan House, 1927
Kirkland Cutter
700 Via Somonte

Andalusian Spanish, with an outer and an inner court.

22. Schoolcraft House, 1926
Edgar Cline
749 Via Somonte

A rural Tuscan villa with extensive tile work, ironwork, and windows and doors brought from Italy.

23. Beckstrand House, 1940
Richard J. Neutra
1400 Via Monte Mar

America's own domesticated version of the International Style of the late 1930s. Floor-to-ceiling glass visually connects the interior spaces with the surrounding terraces and gardens.

24. Palos Verdes High School, 1961
Neutra and Alexander
600 Cloyden Road

An effective Modernist composition of low-pitched, gabled tile roofs. The buildings are arranged around courts and are connected to one another by low, flat-roofed, open passageways.

25. Ravenspur Condominiums, 1966
Raymond Kappe
5632 Ravenspur Drive, off
Hawthorne Boulevard

Constructivism of the 1960s, composed of vertical and horizontal wood members with an infill of wood surfaces and glass.

10 • Palos Verdes, South

1. Miller House, 1948
Thornton M. Abell
3201 Palos Verdes Drive West

Post–World War II Modern, almost classical in its clarity and reserve.

2. Wayfarer's Chapel,
1949 and later
Lloyd Wright
Portuguese Bend at Abalone Cove, north of Palos Verdes Drive South

This chapel is Lloyd Wright's most widely known and visited building. His concept was to create a sense of place via architecture and landscape architecture. His "Natural Church" was a glass structure hidden in a grove of coastal redwoods. (These did not survive and they were replaced by other trees). Today one sees from the road only the thin, angular, stone-and-concrete tower rising from the forest. Once inside the building you will see how success-

2

ful Lloyd Wright was in creating a sense of a mysterious, almost fairy-tale natural beauty.

3. Ekdale House, 1948
John Rex
3500 Palos Verdes Drive South

A two-story, glass-walled interior looks out from a handsome redwood container.

4. Pray House, 1969
Thornton M. Abell
4500 Palos Verdes Drive South

The 1950s *Arts and Architecture* post-and-lintel vocabulary successfully carried out a decade or so later.

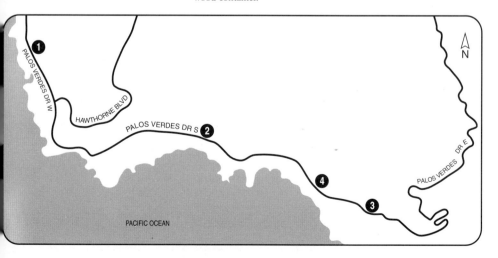

PACIFIC OCEAN

11 • Santa Catalina Island

Santa Catalina Island, the largest of the Channel Islands, was first mentioned by the Spanish explorer Cabrillo in 1540. In the 1820s the Island was granted to Pio Pico, who later deeded it to Nicolas Covarrubias. Later in the nineteenth century it was purchased by James Lick, and it was he who introduced sheep and goats to the island. During the American Civil War a barracks was built on the island. But Catalina's architectural history really began when the shipping interests of William Banning established Avalon (1877) as a summer resort with a Hotel Metropole and a tent city. It was G. Shatto who laid the city out into small lots (in 1885). The hotel is long gone, but evidence of this early city remains in the tiny lots now occupied by cottages just behind the commercial strip along the waterfront.

Further development of Avalon came when William Wrigley Jr. bought the island from the Banning interests in 1919. Wrigley, the owner of the Chicago Cubs, wanted a place for his team to do spring training. Also, like so many businessmen of the time, he hankered after the life of a landed aristocrat. The thousand acres of land provided plenty of subsistence for cattle and horses, as well as for the buffalo imported later for a movie. They can still be seen on the island.

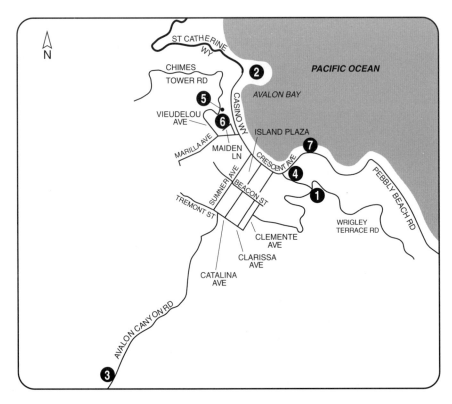

Without attempting to project Catalina as an architectural mecca, we do suggest a number of interesting walks that you can take around the town. There are many old cottages, including a row of Spanish Revival workers' cottages on Fremont Street put up by Wrigley, who further Hispanified the town in 1934–35 by employing commercial artist Otis Shepard to supervise face-lifting the commercial center. It was at this time that controls of signage went into effect, and many of the old wooden fronts were stuccoed and often tiled.

1. Mount Ada, 1921
D. M. Renton;
Albert Conrad,
landscape architect
Wrigley Terrace Road
(from Crescent Avenue, take
Claressa Avenue to Beacon
Street; right one block then
right on Clement Avenue;
Wrigley Terrace Road begins
half a block on the left)

It would be pleasant to report that Mount Ada, the mansion that Wrigley had built by his Pasadena contractor, David Renton, was an architectural pearl. But like their Pasadena house (now headquarters of the

Tournament of Roses), it is more of a curiosity than a work of architecture. It is mildly Anglo-Colonial Revival both inside and out. Its real plus is its wonderful orientation toward magnificent views. One of these, from Wrigley's study, offers an excellent view of the playing field on which the Chicago Cubs worked out. The house is now an expensive bed and breakfast inn. The grounds, designed by Wrigley's head gardener at his Pasadena home, are worth a visit, especially the cactus and succulent gardens.

2. Casino, 1928
Webber and Spaulding
(Sumner Spaulding)
1 Casino Way
(Casino Point,
on the northeast side of
Avalon Bay)

Wrigley employed the architect to design a grand casino featuring moving pictures on the first floor and a ballroom on the second floor. Both of these rooms certainly do evoke the spirit of the 1920s, but it is the theater organ, with its bird calls and automobile horn stops, that seems to thrill the tourists most.

3

The exterior, which looms out of the sea as you approach the island by boat, is a strange mixture of Spanish, Moorish, and Art Deco styles, along with Art Deco murals on the porch. The ground floor (bay side) houses the headquarters and museum of the Catalina Island Museum Society. The wonderful Art Deco nautical murals in the entrance porch are by John Gabriel Beckman. These were intended to be tile mosaics, but only one has been constructed.

3. Wrigley Monument, 1924
Bennett, Parsons, and Frost
Top, west end of
Avalon Canyon Road
(1½ miles from the bay;
train service from
Island Plaza)

Wrigley's family employed this Chicago planning and landscape firm to design a suitable monument to Wrigley. Its grand staircase, with insets of flamboyant Catalina tile, ends in the austerely Goodhuesque Spanish with Art

Deco enrichment mausoleum, which was apparently never used. The view from the monument is indeed handsome. The memorial is approached through a small but fascinating botanical garden (set out by Ralph Roth from 1933 onward). On the way up Avalon Canyon Road you will pass The Bird Cage, an aviary now fallen into ruin but still exhibiting some colorful Catalina tile.

4. Gano House, 1889
Attributed to Dr. Gano
718 Crescent Avenue

"Holly Hill," as the Gano House was called, is a large, picturesque Queen Anne cottage placed on the National Register of Historic Places. It is occasionally opened under the supervision of the Catalina Historical Society, usually for groups by appointment as a fund-raising project.

4

5

5. Wolfe House, 1928
R. M. Schindler
124 Chimes Tower Road

This monument of modern architecture in America in the 1920s was demolished in 2001.

6. Murdock House, 1929
Elmer Grey
*103 Maiden Lane,
on the corner of
Crescent Avenue*

The image of the Murdock House is Spanish Revival, handled in Grey's usual fashion, so that it is restrained and classical rather than picturesque.

7. Cabrillo Mole
Terminal Complex, 1993–94
Campbell and Campbell
*Pebbly Beach Road
Avalon*

For the terminal of the island ferry, the architects designed a small building, promenade, pergolas, and garden.

12 • San Pedro

The open roadstead east of San Pedro was the harbor for the missions of San Gabriel and San Fernando in the late-eighteenth and early-nineteenth centuries. Beginning in the 1820s it continued as the principal shipping point for the growing town of Los Angeles and for the surrounding ranches. A revealing portrait of San Pedro in 1834 and its difficult open harbor is contained in Richard Henry Dana Jr.'s *Two Years Before the Mast* (1840). In the late 1850s, Wilmington, which was established by Phineas Banning at the entrance to the Los Angeles River, emerged as the most-used harbor. In 1909 both San Pedro and Wilmington were incorporated with Los Angeles.

In 1846 a "five-hundred vara square" had been established by the Mexican government as a governmental reserve. This square, which was located on the low cliff in

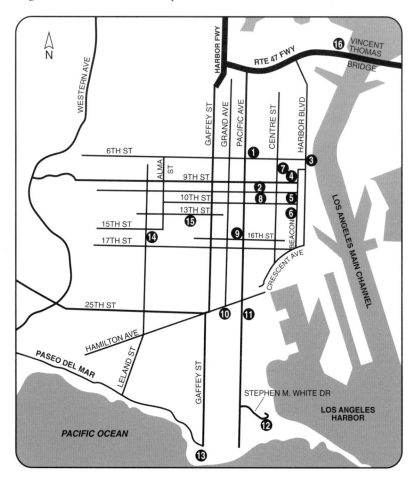

San Pedro overlooking the harbor, was set aside by the U.S. government in 1888 as a military reservation. In 1914 Fort MacArthur was established, comprising not only the "five-hundred vara square" but extensive acreage in and around Point Fermin. Through the 1950s this installation remained as the principal defense for Los Angeles Harbor.

Just before and during the Second World War, a number of Defense Housing projects were built for ship workers and others. These included Banning Homes (1942), Harbor Hills (1939–41), Rancho San Pedro (1942), and Richard J. Neutra's Channel Heights Housing Project (1941–43). Of these the Channel Heights Housing Project was justifiably the most famous, both for its excellent site planning and for the quality of its architecture. There is so little left of this project that it is hardly worth a visit.

Though railroads, freeways, and the high Vincent Thomas Bridge connect San Pedro and Wilmington to Los Angeles and Long Beach, the feeling of both of these communities is that of a small coastal town, certainly not that of a large seaport.

1. Fox-Warner Brothers Theater, 1931
B. Marcus Priteca
478 W. 6th Street

Modest in size, but still an effective example of a Moderne Art Deco theater.

2. YWCA Building, 1918
Julia Morgan
437 W. 9th Street

The Bay tradition of San Francisco brought to San Pedro. A board-and-batten building that has been remodeled on several occasions.

3. Municipal Ferry Building
(City Hall/Harbor Department Building), 1939–41
East end of 6th Street at Harbor Boulevard

A Streamline Moderne Building, the Beaux Arts tradition made Moderne. The low, central tower with its clock face and ladder suggest the nautical origin of the Moderne of the 1930s. The building has been recycled by Pulliam and Matthews to house a Maritime Museum.

4. U.S. Customs House and Post Office, 1935
Northwest corner of Beacon and 9th Streets

A classic PWA Moderne building. Inside is a forty-foot-long mural by Fletcher Martin.

5. McCafferty Studio House, 1979
Coy Howard
1017 Beacon Street

A three-story structure with false gables at each end and a central gabled volume that houses the stairway. The highly complex geometry of the street façade maintains a scale similar to other surrounding structures, but the singular volume does not.

6. Seaman's Center Building, 1954 and 1962
Carleton M. Winslow, Jr., Warren Waltz; Andrew Joncich and William Lusby
Southwest corner of Beacon and 11th Streets

The Modern at the end of the 1950s. Here we have one example that has held up well.

7. House, circa 1898
918–920 Centre Street

A Queen Anne Revival dwelling with an expansive, highly detailed corner bay tower.

8. House, circa 1885
324 W. 10th Street

An early Queen Anne with some Eastlake details. The house has a two-story spindled porch and a corner bay tower whose third stage is open.

9. Commercial Building, circa 1938
Northwest corner of Pacific Avenue and 16th Street

A Streamline Moderne building with a strong commitment to the horizontal. If you continue on down Pacific Avenue you will discover a good number of fragmented remains of the 1930s Moderne.

10. St. Peter's Episcopal Church, 1884
South end of Grand Avenue at 25th Street

A simple, unpretentious Carpenter's Gothic in wood.

11. Fort MacArthur, 1914 and later
East side of Pacific Avenue, between 24th and 27th Streets

Though the fort is not open to the public (it is presently being used by the U.S. Air Force), you can see many of the Mission Revival buildings from Pacific Avenue. These were all constructed between 1916 and 1918. Just barely visible are some of the double NCO Spanish Revival houses that were built in 1933–34. The former Trona Corporation Building at the south end of the fort (built in 1917–18) contains a spectacular timbered interior.

12. Cabrillo Maritime Museum, 1981
Frank O. Gehry and Associates
3730 Stephen M. White Drive

A pipe framework, open in part and covered in other areas by chain-link fencing, provides an introduction to a series of separate enclosed pavilions. Each pavilion is sheathed in corrugated metal and stucco.

13. Point Fermin Lighthouse, 1874
Point Fermin, south end of Gaffey Street

Out of what appears to be a modest Eastlake dwelling emerges a tapered, four-sided lighthouse tower.

14. San Pedro High School, 1935–37
Gordon B. Kaufmann
Leland Street between 15th and 17th Streets

The most impressive aspect of this PWA Moderne building is the curved front auditorium. Its narrow marquee, three louvered openings above, and the relief sculpture are all expressive of Beaux-Arts design principles of the 1930s.

15. Dodson House, circa 1887
859 W. 13th Street

This two-story Eastlake dwelling was first located at the corner of 7th and Beacon Streets. Much of its former lush ornamentation is now gone.

16. Vincent Thomas Bridge, 1961–63
Bridge Division, Division of Highways, State of California
North of the Catalina Terminal (enter from the northeast corner of Gaffey and Oliver Streets)

The Thomas Bridge, which connects San Pedro to Terminal Island and thence to Long Beach, is California's third-largest suspension bridge. There is something stage-set about the Thomas Bridge, for while it does indeed lead somewhere, one is not quite sure why it is there.

13 • Wilmington

Wilmington, first named New San Pedro, was founded in 1858 by Phineas Banning. He started the harbor development by constructing a pier and providing warehouses. In 1869 Wilmington was connected to Los Angeles by rail. Though the community was incorporated in 1872, its independence was lost when it was absorbed into Los Angeles in 1909. Banning Park and the Banning House still form, as they did in the last century, the most important place in the community.

1. Los Angeles Department of Social Service Building,
circa 1925
Southeast corner of Anaheim Street and Broad Avenue

A two-story Spanish Revival building.

2. St. Peter and St. Paul Roman Catholic Church, 1930
Henry C. Newton and Robert Dennis Murray
515 W. Opp Street

Italian Romanesque, the concrete walls with board pattern of the forms exposed.

3. Wilmington Branch Public Library, circa 1926
Marston, Van Pelt, and Maybury
309 W. Opp Street

A T-shaped, single-floor Spanish Revival building. The children's library room leads out onto a pergola and garden.

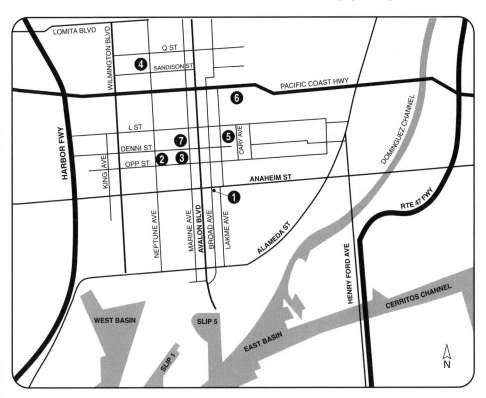

4. St. John's Episcopal Church, 1883
1537 Neptune Avenue

A Queen Anne Revival church building, small in size.

5. Drum Barracks, 1859
1053–1055 Cary Avenue

A two-story try at Greek Revival that really ends up more Federal than Greek. The officers' quarters are all that remain of an extensive group of wooden buildings constructed here in the late 1850s and early 1860s.

6. Banning House, 1864
*Banning Park at
Lakme Avenue and
Pacific Coast Highway*

A luxurious version (at least for California) of the Greek Revival, resplendent with a two-story balconied porch and elegant entrances on both floors. Glass doors with transoms open out onto the entrance porch and the balcony porch above (the Federal-style front door was added in 1910). The Banning House illustrates how the Greek Revival as a style continued into the 1860s, not only in California, but also in many areas of the East and Midwest. A central cupola crowns the eighteen-room house. The present park only hints at what the grounds around the house were like in the 1870s. A long avenue of eucalyptus led to the house, and gardens of flowers and shrubs abounded.

7. Memorial Chapel, Calvary Presbyterian Church, 1870
1160 N. Marine Avenue

A rarity in Southern California— an Italianate church building. The original curved roof of the tower is now missing, and once there were two entrances, one to each side of the projecting tower.

14 • Torrance

The City of Torrance was established in 1911. It was named for its founder, Jared Sidney Torrance, who sought to build an ideal small industrial city. He selected Olmsted and Olmsted to design it. They in turn engaged Lloyd Wright to supervise the landscaping and prevailed upon their client to have Irving J. Gill design the first public, commercial, and residential buildings. They organized the city around a two-and-a-half-block park—El Prado. Symbolically the southwest end of the park was terminated by the high school, while to the northeast the orientation was toward a distant view of Mount San Antonio. A commercial center was placed around the Pacific Electric Station. Beyond this to the north and east the land was laid out for factories and other types of industrial use. The residential areas of the city were placed around El Prado and the high school.

In the mid-1930s a small-scaled civic center was built facing Cravens Street, from El Prado to Post Avenues. The 1930s civic center has now been abandoned for a new one located at the northwest corner of Torrance Boulevard and Maple Avenue. In the 1920s a residential area—the Hollywood Riviera—was developed on the western hills that overlooked the Pacific. In the post–World War II years, there has been a slow infill of the area

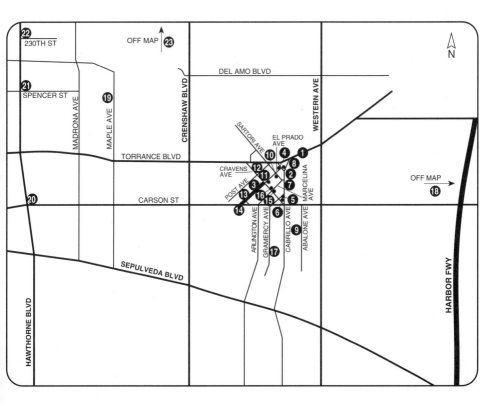

between the Olmsted center of Torrance and the Hollywood Riviera section. This infill is mixed, ranging from office complexes and other commercial uses to single- and multi-family housing.

It must be admitted that most of the Gill buildings in Torrance make for a rather dull scene, especially in their run-down condition. They do not, moreover, relate to each other except in their break with historicism. Gill was not a planner. Often, even in his individual buildings, his proportions are awkward. This cluster is significant because it shows on a fairly large scale what was on his mind.

1. Pacific Electric Railroad Bridge, 1912
Irving J. Gill
Torrance Boulevard, between Western and Cabrillo Avenues

In effect this reinforced concrete, six-arched bridge serves as a ceremonial entrance into Torrance from the east. It was one of Gill's first projects in Torrance.

2. Pacific Electric Railroad Station, 1912
Irving J. Gill
610 S. Main Street, on the west corner of Torrance Boulevard and Cabrillo Avenue

The design of the station originally incorporated a red tile roof and dome, so that it read more effectively as Mission Revival than is currently the case. The two miniature segmented domes on top of the side spur walls illustrate Gill's abstracted use of Mission Revival elements. As with other buildings in Torrance, the structure is of hollow tile and brick, sheathed in stucco.

3. Roi Tan Hotel, 1912
Irving J. Gill
1211 El Prado Avenue

This three-story commercial structure is one of a group of buildings that Gill realized in downtown Torrance. The proportions of the building and of its openings are a hallmark of Gill's approach to design.

Architecturally the building sways between the bland and the aesthetically abstract. Though this building was referred to as being of reinforced concrete, like his other commercial buildings in Torrance, it is of steel, brick, and hollow tile covered with stucco.

4. Murray Hotel, 1912
Irving J. Gill
1210 El Prado Avenue

Similar to the Roi Tan Hotel across the street. The eyebrow of red mission tile at the top has been removed.

5. Colonial Hotel and United Cigar Building, 1912
Irving J. Gill
1601–1605 Cabrillo Avenue, on the south corner of Cabrillo and Gramercy Avenues

A triangular-shaped building with retail uses on much of the ground level and two floors of hotel rooms above. The narrow brick cornice at the top of the building has been removed.

6. Brighton Hotel, 1912
Irving J. Gill
1639 Cabrillo Avenue, on the north corner of Cabrillo and Cravens Avenues

A second triangular building almost identical to the Colonial Hotel, with the usual retail stores on the ground level and hotel rooms and small apartments above.

7. Retail Commercial Building, circa 1928
1420 Cabrillo Avenue

A Spanish Revival design with a highly dramatic entrance.

8. Fuller Shoe Manufacturing Company Building (Casa del Amo), 1912
Irving J. Gill
1860 Torrance Boulevard

The single (false) shed roof and the scale of the symmetrical façade convey more of a domestic than an industrial quality. It has been converted into apartments.

9. Salem Manufacturing Company Building, 1913
Irving J. Gill
1805 Abalone Avenue

A single-story box which, though made of wood, appears to be made of reinforced concrete. Another nearby Gill industrial building is the Rubbercraft Corporation of California Building (1913) at 1800 W. 220th Street. This two-story stucco structure has a pair of false-stepped gable ends.

10. Retail Commercial Building, circa 1916
2266 Sartori Avenue

The Mission Revival image is evident here. Buildings such as this had a much wider popular appeal than most of Irving J. Gill's more puritanical buildings.

11. Torrance City Hall and Municipal Auditorium (now Home Savings Branch Bank), 1936–37
Walker and Eisen
North corner of Cravens and El Prado Avenues

A modest, single-story, PWA Moderne Building.

12. Torrance Public Library, 1936; Walker and Eisen
North corner of Cravens and Post Avenues

PWA Moderne, one of the group of buildings that composed the original 1930s civic center of Torrance.

13. House, circa 1916
1504 Post Avenue

A two-story bungalow improved by references to the Midwest Prairie style.

14. Torrance High School, 1923, 1929, and circa 1935
Farrell and Miller (original High School Building)
Southwest end of El Prado Avenue at Carson Street

The main building, which was axially oriented to El Prado, utilized a Classical and somewhat Beaux-Arts image. The Assembly Hall, with its relief sculpture over its entrance, is an excellent example of the PWA Moderne. Within the foyer of the Assembly Hall is a 1936 Federal Art Project mural by Anna Katharine Skeele. The subject of this mural is Taos Indian Life.

15. Villa Sonora, circa 1922
East corner of Marcelina and Arlington Avenues

A Spanish Revival bungalow court, with single-story units toward the street and a two-story section at the rear of the property.

16. United Methodist Church, circa 1916
Northeast corner of Marcelina and Arlington Avenues

Mildly Midwest Prairie in style, the whole terminated by a wonderful octagonal dome.

17. Worker's Single-Family Housing, 1912; Irving J. Gill
Gramercy Avenue

This street contains several of the concrete (actually hollow tile) bungalows designed by Gill. These are located at 1815, 1819, 1903, 1904, 1907, 1916, 1919, and 1920 Gramercy Avenue. These L-shaped single-floor dwellings have their entrances to the side within the L. A low-pitched roof projects between the two corner parapets. Gill had planned streets of these and double connected bungalows for Torrance, but they were not popular with the workers and their families, who much preferred the more romantic and traditional California bungalow.

18. Child/Family Development Center, 1993
Barton Myers Associates
2181 Normandie Avenue

The plan of the low complex is made up of four nurseries that are grouped around a central court. Each of the nurseries is conceived of as a courtyard house with areas for living, sleeping, etc. These nurseries pose as houses overlooking the inner court. The firm of Sussman/Prejza has provided the graphics and the color.

19. South Bay Industrial Park, 1974
Matlin and Dvoretzky; Emmet Wemple and Associates, landscape architects
300 Maple Avenue

The romantic, picturesque (seemingly natural), landscaped industrial park is what is important here. The unassertive, two-story buildings serve as a backdrop to Wemple's landscape.

20. Ohrbach's Del Amo Fashion Square, 1971
Victor Gruen Associates (Cesar Pelli)
Northeast corner of Carson Street and Hawthorne Boulevard

A fragile-looking blue container looks out onto acres of parked cars.

21. Bill Hopkins Lincoln-Mercury Agency Building, 1966
Daniel L. Dworsky and Associates
20460 Hawthorne Boulevard, at Spencer Street

A well-conceived 1960s Modern design of modular brick walls and steel.

22. Tomanjan Professional Building, 1979–80
Neil Stanton Palmer
Northeast corner of Hawthorne Boulevard and 230th Street

A pyramid in brick and stone.

23. "The Courthouse," 1978–79
Northwest corner of Crenshaw Boulevard and 185th Street, just southwest of the San Diego Freeway

The owner of this building, Dudley Gray, purchased fragments from the 1885 Pottawattamie County Courthouse in Council Bluffs, Iowa, and incorporated them into his own version of a classical courthouse. As a design it works best when seen from a distance.

15 • Long Beach, Downtown and West

The city was founded in 1880 by the Englishman W. E. Willmore, and it was first named the "American Colony." "The project," it was noted in the local press at the time, "includes an ample town site, college grounds, and all the latest improvements." This plan was especially generous in providing a variety of open public spaces. The entire beachfront was to be public, and a number of parks were provided throughout the town site. Shortly after the first sale of land commenced, the city was renamed Willmore City. Though widely advertised, it was not successful. In 1887 it was taken over by the Long Beach Land and Water Company and touted as an ideal seaside resort. A wharf was built and a large wooden resort hotel was constructed on the cliff overlooking the beach. In 1902 the Pacific Electric connected the city with Los Angeles. Four years later, work began on the artificial harbor

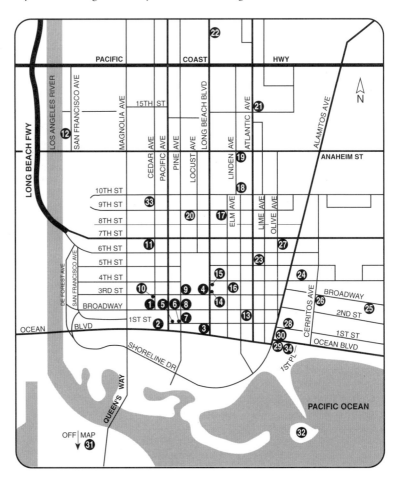

that eventually would transform Long Beach into a major West Coast port. The culmination of all of these efforts was reached in November 1925, when at long last navigation was opened to deep-draft ships.

In the teens and twenties, efforts were made to incorporate a City Beautiful plan for the city. The major axis, Long Beach Boulevard, was to be lined, close to Ocean Beach Boulevard, with classical public buildings. The major result of this scheme was the construction of a Civic Auditorium (1930–32; J. Harold MacDowell of New York and W. Horace Austin of Long Beach) at the south end of Long Beach Boulevard. In the early 1920s a modest City Beautiful City Hall was built on the north side of Lincoln Park (1921; W. Horace Austin). This building was damaged in the March 10, 1933, Long Beach earthquake. City Hall was rebuilt, reflecting the latest Moderne style of the moment (1934; Cecil Shilling and W. Horace Austin). During the 1930s the remodeled City Hall was joined by two other PWA Moderne public buildings: the Municipal Utilities Building (1932; Dedrick and Bobbe), and the Veteran's Memorial Building (1936–37; George Kahrs). This wonderful group of public buildings was demolished in the 1970s as a result of post–World War II urban renewal.

In this case urban renewal happened somewhat later than other cities, in the 1960s and 1970s. In 1981 it was noted, "Major redevelopment surgery has removed six blocks of the city's deteriorated downtown business district to make way for a $100-million mall as part of an investment of more than $1.25 billion in the heart of the city." (*Los Angeles Times,* February 22, 1981, VIII, 1) The results are mixed. The landscaping of Long Beach Boulevard and parts of Ocean Boulevard is unquestionably a step forward. But the new plan for the area ignores what little was realized of the earlier Beaux-Arts plan. The "surgery" within and without the six-block area destroyed a number of good buildings, including the 1930–32 Long Beach Municipal Auditorium with its colorful mosaic by Henry R. Nord, and the group of civic buildings facing Lincoln Park.

The inevitable pedestrian mall ("The Promenade") has been built on the east end of Pine Avenue between Ocean Boulevard and 3rd Street. Its only asset is that it does have a symbolic termination at its north end. Here an arched section of the parking structure exhibits Nord's old Auditorium mosaic, and although the piece was never meant to be seen at eye level and close up, it is still impressive. As with most pedestrian malls, "The Promenade" is not overrun by people.

The high-rise buildings that have been constructed either in or adjacent to the redevelopment area are generally undistinguished. There is an unconvincing attempt at theatrics in the twin fourteen-story, semi-cylindrical glass Arco Center Towers (at 200–300 Oceangate, 1979–82; Luckman Partnership, Inc.). And nothing very positive can be said for the setting or design of the fasciated, glass-sheathed Crocker Plaza office building (at 180 W. Ocean Boulevard, 1980–82; Maxwell Starkman Associates) or the 1974–78 Convention Center (a sad replacement for the Municipal Auditorium). The 1974–75 Queen Surf Condominiums, the 1986–87 World Trade Center Complex, and the 1986–87 Shoreline Square are at best stupid. More in keeping with the character of Long Beach is the glass-sheathed six-story Downtown Plaza at the corner of Ocean Boulevard and Promenade North (1983; Landau Partnership).

Extensive redevelopment of the beachfront took place in the 1980s, but few of the projects had the effect of retrieving the past glories of the city. At the moment, the one saving element of these newer buildings along Ocean Boulevard and on the beach is the mural painted on the walls of "The Arena," Southern California Edison's Redondo Beach Generating Station. This mural of twelve migrating whales was painted in 1991 by the artist Wyland.

concrete pillbox hidden in the ground (á la the Oakland Museum).

3. Downtown Plaza Building, 1981–82
Victor Gruen Associates
Northeast corner of Ocean Boulevard and Promenade North

A fasciated and stepped glass-sheathed building, more suburban than urban.

4. Parking Structure, 1981–82
Victor Gruen Associates
North end of the Promenade at West 3rd Street

As already mentioned, the arched wall of the parking structure that contains the 1930s Federal Arts Project mosaic by Henry Nord and others saves not only the parking structure but the mall as well. The adjacent enclosed City Place shopping mall was to have many of its ground-floor shops open to the adjacent streets, but this has not really worked.

1. California Veteran's Memorial State Office Building, 1981–82
Kenneth S. Wing Sr. and Kenneth S. Wing Jr.
Northwest corner of Cedar Avenue and Broadway

A four-story Constructivist exercise. There is nothing about this design that suggests the civic and public, nor is it even easy to discover the entrance or to find one's way around. Perhaps it is significant that it is now a private office building.

2. Long Beach City Hall and Public Library, 1973–76
Allied Architects;
Hugh Gibbs and Donald Gibbs;
Frank Holmelka and Associates;
Killingsworth, Brady, and Associates;
Kenneth S. Wing Sr. and Kenneth S. Wing Jr.
333 W. Ocean Boulevard

The fourteen-story city hall office tower is a glass box held in place by projecting concrete piers. The library (if you can find it) is a

5. Buffum's Autoport, 1941
J. H. Davis, engineer
North side of 1st Street, between Pine and Pacific Avenues

A classic example—including its signage—of the Streamline Moderne. Horizontal bands terminate in a vertical plane from which project three small, curved balconies. The only change is the open concrete grillwork on the street level.

6. First National Bank (now 115 Pine Building), 1900, 1905–6, 1907
Train and Williams
115 Pine Avenue,
on the northwest corner of
Pine Avenue and 1st Street

A rather severe, six-story Beaux-Arts commercial design. It is saved by the fanciful clock tower added in 1907. The building was restored in 1987 by Lionel Ramirez of Ramirez Design Associates.

7. Security Trust and Savings, 1923–25
Curlett and Beelman
102 Pine Avenue,
on the northeast corner of
Pine Avenue and 1st Street

A fourteen-story Beaux-Arts skyscraper. Large two-story windows occur between the fluted pilasters on the ground floor, and elaborate multicolored relief panels are located above the office tower entrances.

8. Rowan (Bradley) Building, 1930
Northwest corner of
Pine Avenue and Broadway

The ground floor of retail shops has been remodeled, but the second floor displays a wonderfully inventive and colorful array of Art Deco motifs in terra-cotta. Note also the second floor of the adjoining building to the north— another Art Deco Moderne façade in terra-cotta.

9. Farmers and Merchants Bank, 1922
Curlett and Beelman; W. Horace Austin
Northeast corner of
Pine Avenue and 3rd Street

A ten-story, white, terra-cotta-sheathed skyscraper, whose image seems both Beaux Arts and Spanish Renaissance. The vintage interiors are superb.

10. First Congregational Church, 1914
H. M. Patterson
Southwest corner of
Cedar Avenue and 3rd Street

By the mid-teens the northern Italian Romanesque emerged as being appropriate for the image of California as the new,

improved Mediterranean world. Across the street is the Renaissance Revival apartment house called "The Willmore." It was designed by Fisher, Lake and Traver and constructed in 1924.

11. Second Church of Christ, Scientist, 1916–25
Elmer Grey
Southwest corner of Cedar Avenue and 7th Street

Pure Beaux-Arts, except in this instance there is a hint of the Byzantine rather than the Italian. Most impressive are the four large Corinthian columns, which set off the high entrance porch.

12. Southern Pacific Railroad Depot, 1907
1475 San Francisco Avenue (moved here in 1930)

Single-story Mission Revival.

13. Lafayette Hotel Building, 1929
Schilling and Schilling
Southeast corner of Broadway and Linden Avenues

A four-story vertical Art Deco building. Surveying the scene are two large-scaled heads of American Indians looking down from the parapet.

14. Post Office and Federal Building, 1931–32
James A. Wetmore; designed by Hugh R. Davies (Long Beach Architectural Club)
Northeast corner of Long Beach Boulevard and 3rd Street

PWA Moderne, accomplished with restrained and sophisticated taste.

15. Great Western Savings Association Building, 1968
Daniel Dworsky and Associates
350 Long Beach Boulevard

A cut-into box with an exposed concrete frame and an infill of brick. The setback of the building has provided space for planting, brick walks, and walls.

16. Retail Store, 1930
312–316 Elm Avenue

A single-story Art Deco store building with a pattern of metal grillwork above the store windows.

17. Scottish Rite Cathedral, 1926
Parker O. Wright and Francis H. Gentry
Southwest corner of Elm Avenue and 9th Street

A classical Italian Romanesque design, covered with gray mottled terra-cotta that suggests stone.

18. St. Mary's Hospital, 1935, 1937; J. E. Loveless
North end of Linden Avenue at 10th Street

A succession of three-story volumes terminated by a low tower with a hipped roof. A successful Art Deco composition (with strong Beaux-Arts overtones).

19. Hancock Motors, 1929
Schilling and Schilling
Southeast corner of Anaheim Street and Linden Avenue

This single-story Art Deco automobile showroom and repair shop is resplendent with cast relief ornament. Above the corner entrance are a pair of winged rams' heads.

20. York Rite Masonic Temple Building, 1927
Wright and Gentry
829 Locust Avenue

A severe Beaux-Arts block constructed of a steel frame and concrete floors. Plans are to recycle it for loft housing.

21. Long Beach Polytechnic High School,
1932–36 and later
Hugh R. Davies
Northeast corner of Atlantic Avenue and 15th Street

The 1934–36 Industrial Arts Building and the Commercial Arts Building by Davies lean more toward the International Style of the 1930s than the then-popular Streamline Moderne. Note the style of lettering for the buildings. Also, go inside the Industrial Arts Building to see the Federal Arts Project mural by Ivan Bartlet and Jean Swiggett.

22. Pacific Auto Works,
1928–29
Schilling and Schilling
1910 Long Beach Boulevard

Art Deco with both an art and Programmatic intent. The central cartouche suggests a radiator of an automobile, and the double seashell motif to each side creates the needed headlights.

23. Robert Louis Stevenson School, circa 1936
West side of Lime Avenue, between 5th and 6th Streets

PWA Moderne with pre-Columbian touches.

24. Koffee Pot (Hot Cha) Restaurant, 1932
957 – 4th Street

A metal coffee pot for a giant sits on top of the clerestory of a small octagonal building. Abandoned. See it while you can.

25. Apartment Building,
circa 1928
1436 – 3rd Street

A two-story Spanish Revival apartment complex with an open garden court.

26. Ebell Club, 1924
Clark Phillip
Southeast corner of Cerritos Avenue and 3rd Street

A great rectangular box of a building with an exuberant Spanish Plateresque façade. The interior was conceived of as a modern version of the Spanish Renaissance.

27. St. Anthony's Roman Catholic Church, 1952
Barker and Ott
Southeast corner of Olive Avenue and 7th Street

This simple, gable-roofed church was remodeled in 1952. Added to the older building were two fanciful (Gothic?) towers, which now enclose the gable-end mosaic depicting Pope Pius XII watching the Virgin's assumption. Below, a three-part entrance is set in a Gothic screen. Something else!

28

28. Apartment Building, circa 1929
917 – 1st Street

A two-story Streamline Moderne building with all of the needed elements—curved corners, horizontal banded windows, steel railings, and glass bricks.

29. Villa Riviera Apartment, 1928
Richard D. King
800 E. Ocean Boulevard

One of the seashore landmarks of Long Beach. The fourteen-story building contains a one-hundred-car garage, in addition to an "Italian" roof garden. The image—with its dormered, high-pitched, hipped roof and octagonal tower—is French Chateauesque.

30. Tichenor House, 1904
Charles and Henry Greene
852 E. Ocean Boulevard

A much-remodeled, two-story Greene and Greene bungalow. The east façade faces 1st Place and contains a remarkable pattern of brick, wood, and glass.

31. The Queen Mary, 1934
1126 Queen's Way Drive, Pier J
Long Beach Harbor

Another saving element in the harbor area is the great Streamline Moderne 1934 English ocean liner. Unfortunately, another streamline attraction (in this case, the early 1940s), Howard Hughes's airplane the *Spruce Goose,* has departed for the Pacific Northwest, leaving only its hangar intact.

32. Oil Drilling Islands, 1967–68
Herb Goldman;
Linesch and Reynolds,
landscape architects
Long Beach Harbor

A grouping of high, thin, sculptured walls seek to hide the utilitarian equipment of the man-made oil islands from public view on shore. The results are peculiar, though it is a purely Southern California solution.

33. Bungalow, 1913
948 Cedar

Seemingly out of Pasadena, this is a true California bungalow.

34. Bembridge House, 1906
953 Park Circle Drive

A nice late–Queen Anne house now administered as a museum by Long Beach Heritage. The family furniture is still in place.

33

31

16 • Long Beach, East
Naples
Seal Beach

1. Raymond House, 1918
Irving J. Gill
2724 E. Ocean Boulevard

This is one of the few Gill houses in the Los Angeles area that remains intact. It is a concrete and hollow-tile construction. Its proportions and general detailing are similar to the destroyed Dodge House in West Hollywood.

2. Bungalow, circa 1915
2601 – 1st Street

A single-floor bungalow becomes respectable with a front porch displaying classical columns.

3. House, circa 1910
363 Carroll Parkway West

Mission Revival.

4. Bungalow, circa 1909
4341 Broadway

A California bungalow whose concrete columns on the front porch are cast in the form of tree trunks.

5. Gaytonia Apartments, 1930
Reginald Inwood
212 Quincy

Since Inwood's Belmont Theater has been demolished, this apartment house by him will have to

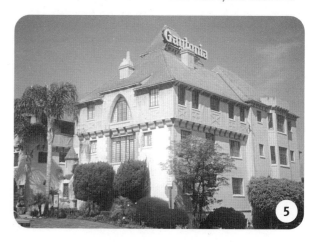

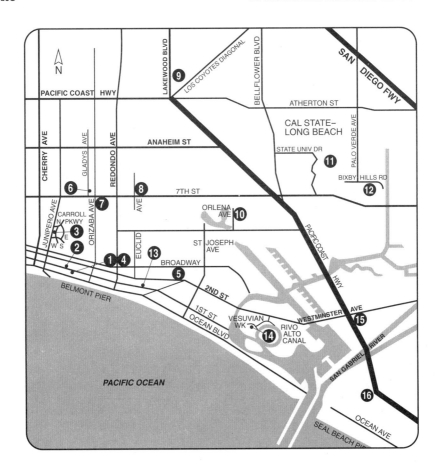

do as an example of his abilities in design. Presumably it was intended to be Chateauesque but the style somehow got away from him.

6. Newton Rummond House, 1932
708 Gladys Avenue

Supposedly this is the narrowest house in the Los Angeles area—10 feet in width. Its image is Hansel and Gretel, but more French than German.

7. Retail Store and Apartments, circa 1927
Southeast corner of Orizaba Avenue and 7th Street

An imaginative crenelated tower stands guard over this complex of remodeled structures. Note the staircase and the entrance to the tower, and also the pink stucco. Style? Perhaps we should think of it as Medieval Spanish.

8. Jefferson Junior High School Building, 1936
Northeast corner of Euclid Avenue and 7th Street

PWA Moderne in exposed concrete. The spiral motif ornamentation of the piers and spandrels is terrific.

9. Duffield Lincoln-Mercury Agency, 1963 Killingsworth, Brady, and Associates
1940 Lakewood Boulevard

A steel-grid frame, mostly infilled with glass, faces the street. The late-1950s Case Study House form enlarged into an elegant auto showroom.

11. California State University, Long Beach,
1949 and later
State University Drive, off Bellflower Boulevard on 7th Street

The architecture of the university can best be described as bland "State College Modern." Though architect Edward Killingsworth has for many years been the master-planning architect for the university, the complex still has not developed much above the ordinary. The best element of the campus is its landscape architecture. The 1966 Sculpture Walk (Killingsworth, Brady, and Associates; Edward Lovell, landscape architect) is a good case in point.

We also recommend the Earl Burns Miller Japanese Garden. Here on a one-acre site is a traditional Japanese garden with a teahouse, stone lanterns, and other elements. It was designed by the landscape architect Edward R. Lovell, in consultation with Dr. Koichi Kawana of UCLA. A recent addition to the campus is the incredible and monstrous athletic facility called "The Pyramid," designed in 1994 by Donald Gibbs, but it lacks camels and their drivers.

10. Kimpson-Nixon House,
1939
Raphael S. Soriano
380 Orlena Avenue

Soriano as an advocate of the purist International Style of the 1930s. Boxy volumes are articulated by horizontal bands of windows on both floors. A beautiful house strongly influenced by Richard Neutra. The house next door was once a wonderful Streamline Moderne bungalow, but it has been mansionized—disastrously!

15. The Market Place, 1976–77
Richard Nagy Martin
*North corner of
Pacific Coast Highway and
Westminster Avenue*

Several major shopping centers have been constructed in and around the intersection of Pacific Coast Highway and Westminster Avenue. Of these, The Market Place is, by far, the most pleasant. The high points are the connected lakes, the traditional large-scale Mexican fountain of Guadalajara Canterra stone, and El Torito Restaurant, a wonderful version of California's Mission Revival.

16. Bay City Center, 1979–80
Irwin and Associates
*Pacific Coast Highway, between
5th and Marina Streets
Seal Beach*

The centerpiece of this commercial development is the central thirty-five-foot-high cupola and dome of copper.

12. La Casa de Rancho Los Alamitos, 1806 and later
6400 E. Bixby Hills Road

This single-floor adobe ranch house is, according to tradition, the oldest domestic building still standing in Southern California. Of equal interest are the gardens laid out over many years by members of the Bixby family. In the twentieth century many of Southern California's major landscape architects were consulted. These include William Hertrich, Allen Chickering, Ed and Paul J. Howard, Charles Gibbs Adams, Florence Yoch, and Lucille Council. Between 1922 and 1936, Yoch and Council laid out the terraces and the geranium, oleander, and jacaranda walks. Open to the public. Check times.

13. Apartment House, 1939
3509 E. 1st Street

This Streamline Moderne building is dazzling on a street of respectable but uninspired dwellings.

Naples

This waterside community was developed between 1903 and 1905 by Arthur Parson. Like Venice, south of Santa Monica, it was planned around a series of canals. The center of the place is an island within Alamitos Bay (itself a fake bay), and it is much more reminiscent of Venice, Italy, than is Santa Monica's Venice. The four romantic concrete bridges over the waterways were designed in 1913 for the Naples Company by Mayberry and Parker.

14. Frank House, 1957
Killingsworth, Brady, and Smith
*5576 Vesuvian Walk
Naples*

Arts and Architecture magazine's Case Study House No. 25. The two-story interior is arranged around a lath-covered interior court. The verticality of space, wall surfaces, and details indicates the course that much of California's Modern followed in the later 1960s.

17 • Long Beach, North

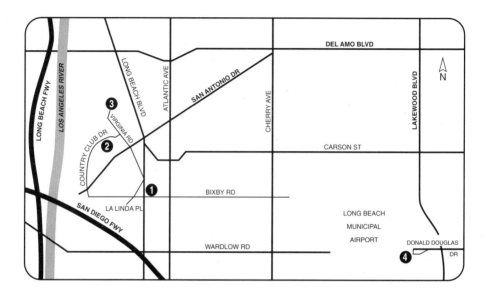

1. Cambridge Investment Inc., 1966
Killingsworth, Brady, and Associates
324 E. Bixby Road

An open post-and-lintel frame building, quite classical in concept.

2. Reeves House, 1904
Charles and Henry Greene
4260 Country Club Drive

A characteristic Greene and Greene two-story house, which was originally built at 306 Cedar Avenue. In 1917 it was moved to 1004 Pine Avenue, and in 1927 it was moved to its present site.

3. Adobe Los Cerritos, 1844
4600 Virginia Road

This large house was built by Don Juan Temple at the center of his extensive ranch located on the banks of the Los Angeles River. It is a U-shaped building enclosing a patio. The center section of the building is surrounded by a two-story wood porch and gallery. Originally the roof was flat and covered with "brea," but after 1866 a hipped shingle roof was added. The Adobe Los Cerritos is one of the finest existing Monterey-style adobes to be found in Southern California. The romantic gardens around the house were restored by Ralph Cornell.

4. Long Beach Airport Terminal, 1940–41
Kenneth S. Wing, W. Horace Austin
West end of Douglas Drive, off Lakewood Boulevard

The late 1930s Streamline Moderne moving toward the bland Modern of the post–World War II years. The site planning, with its dominant axial road leading to a park in front of the two-story terminal building, is characteristic of the Moderne. The park is now gone. The Federal Arts Project murals and mosaics by Grace Clements that once could be seen on the first floor of the terminal have been covered over but the ones on the second floor are still visible.

18 • Inglewood Hawthorne

Inglewood was one of the many boom towns that was established in the late 1880s on the flat plain south of Los Angeles. It was platted in 1887. A large hotel was built, and plans were made for the establishment of the Freeman College of Applied Arts. Then came the bust of 1887–90. The hotel was left standing, but the college never got underway. The town grew very slowly until the late 1930s, when several large tracts of modest spec housing

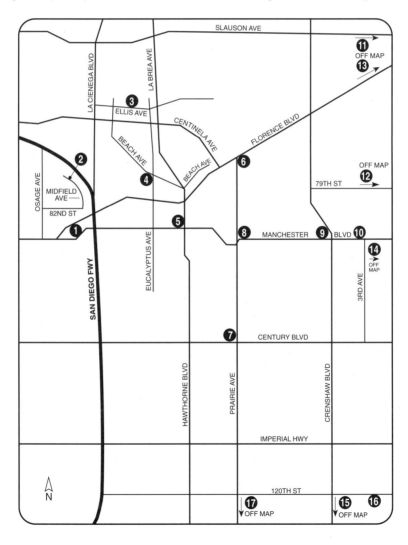

were built, and such streets as Manchester, Crenshaw, and La Cienega began to develop as typical, auto-oriented, retail commercial strips. The city's chief fame for years has been the 1937 Hollywood Turf Club designed by Stiles Clements. Today Inglewood is well supplied with small neighborhood parks and the larger Centinela Park (off Florence and Centinela Avenues). Much of the city lies right in the center of the east jet pattern for the Los Angeles International Airport, but it has somehow managed to survive remarkably well.

Hawthorne, which lies to the south of Inglewood, was founded in 1906. Its system of grid streets basically continues those of Inglewood.

1. Randy's Donuts, 1954
805 W. Manchester Boulevard

A giant doughnut sits atop a tiny, canted-glass, early-Modern fast-food building. The vertical steel supports for the doughnut plunge right through the building below. A classic example of 1950s Programmatic architecture where the sign (the three-dimensional doughnut) is the design, and the building below is merely a base.

2. Centinela Ranch House (Ygnacio Marchado Adobe), after 1844
7636 Midfield Avenue

The Rancho Aguaje de Centinela was granted in 1844, and it is likely that shortly after this date the adobe ranch house was built. The house was added to from time to time, especially in the early 1860s. It is a single-floor adobe with a wood-shingle roof, fireplaces, and deep window reveals.

3. Three Speculative Houses, 1940
Edward Lind (office of R. M. Schindler)
423, 429, 433 Ellis Avenue

Three single-floor spec houses that mirror a number of Schindleresque design motifs. Their garages face toward the street, and the houses open up to enclosed gardens at the sides and rear.

4. Stanford M. Anderson Water Treatment Plant, 1977
Kappe, Lotery, Boccato
Southwest corner of Eucalyptus and Beach Avenues

A two-story Miesian, steel-and-glass box looks out onto a lively world of brightly painted pipes, tanks, and other machine elements. A colorful diagram on the front wall sign explains it all.

5. Inglewood Civic Center, 1973
Charles Luckman Associates; Robert Herrick Carter, landscape architect
Northwest corner of Manchester Avenue and Hawthorne Boulevard

Within this twenty-nine-acre civic center, a nondescript eight-story City Hall has been placed on a two-story base. Set within a separate garden is the two-story library building. Other buildings located within the Civic Center are a police facility, a fire station, and a public health complex. The vegetation is slowly hiding most of the buildings.

6. Los Angeles Railroad, Inglewood Station, 1928
Southeast corner of Prairie and Florence Avenues in Inglewood Park Cemetery

A small Spanish Revival passenger station in the form of an Andalusian church.

7. Hollywood Turf Club, 1937
Stiles O. Clements, with later additions by Frederick Barlow Jr.; Edward Huntsman-Trout, landscape architect
Northwest corner of Century Boulevard and Prairie Avenue

A Streamline Moderne clubhouse and grandstand, easily visible from Century Boulevard. The master plan, which was laid out by Clements and Huntsman-Trout, can best be seen from the window of your jet as you approach the Los Angeles International Airport. Note that in 1937 the architects provided spaces for twenty-two thousand cars.

8. Inglewood Memorial Park,
1905 and later
*Northeast corner of
Manchester Avenue and
Prairie Avenue*

The extensive cemetery is situated in low rolling hills, many of which are covered with tall palm trees. The most important monument are the Mausoleum of the Golden West and other buildings at the north side of the park. These reinforced exposed-concrete buildings were built between 1933 and 1940, and are PWA Moderne in style. They were designed by Walter E. Erkes. If you would rather not bother traveling to Santa Barbara, you can go to the Memorial Park Mausoleum and find the "Santa Barbara Mission Window," designed by the Judson Studios.

9. Academy Theater, 1939
S. Charles Lee
3100 Manchester Boulevard

Notwithstanding recent remodelings, this theater marks a high point of the Streamline Moderne in the United States. Stucco-sheathed cylinders play into one another and culminate in a thin, 125-foot-high tower. The spiral fins of this tower and of the parking sign were originally lighted by blue neon tubes.

10. Brownfield Medical Building, 1938
Gregory Ain
*Northwest corner of
Manchester Boulevard and
Third Avenue*

A small tastefully proportioned "rationalist" design by one of Los Angeles's pioneer Modernists.

11. Milk Bottle (Knudsen's Dairy), circa 1935
1914 W. Slauson Avenue

Appropriately, a good-sized milk bottle sits on top of a dairy building so that the message is clear.

12. Pepperdine College (old campus), 1937
Thomas Cooper;
Katherine Bashford and
Frederick Barlow Jr.,
landscape architects
*West of 79th Street and
South Vermont Avenue*

The college campus contains several excellent examples of the Streamline Moderne, and there are other buildings that come close to being 1930s International Style Modern. The older President's House at 7851 Budlong Avenue and the Pepperdine Center Building on the west side of South Vermont Avenue at West 78th Street are Spanish Revival.

13. Mount Carmel High School Building, 1934
7011 S. Hoover Avenue

An excellent exercise in the more abstracted version of the Spanish Revival of the 1930s.

14. The Teapot, circa 1931
607 W. Manchester Avenue

A little Programmatic restaurant.

15. One-Hundred Fifty-Third Street School, 1957
Ain, Johnson, and Day
*1605 W. 153rd Street, between
Harvard Boulevard and
Denker Avenue*

A 1950s one-story finger-plan school accomplished with Ain's characteristic reticence.

16. Northrop Electronics Division Headquarters, 1982
Daniel L. Dworsky and Associates
2301 W. 120th Street

International Style made fashionable through contemporary High Tech imagery. Many of the glass-walled areas of the building open onto well-landscaped terraces.

17. Richstone Family Center, 1993–94
Siegel Diamond Architects
13620 Cordary Avenue

The architects have broken the building down into a series of small units. The rectangular block-like volumes are countered by those with shed roofs and those with barrel-vaulted roofs.

19 • Gardena

Gardena, which was located at the junction of the Pacific Electric Railroad lines from San Pedro and Redondo Beach, was founded in 1906. The town center of Gardena (located at Gardena Avenue between Western and Normandie Avenues) still conveys a 1920s Spanish image. Newer buildings of the past three decades have somewhat modified the original unity of the place.

At 2501 W. Rosecrans Avenue is the 1952 Gardena Office of Great Western Savings and Loan Association, designed by the San Francisco office of Skidmore, Owings, and Merrill. The architects used the then-fashionable Edward Stone Pavilion mode, except that in this case, they built in massive concrete. The building has been remodeled, but you can still see the architects' original intent. At 2310 El Segundo Boulevard are the Goldwater Apartments designed by Carl Maston in 1964 with the landscape designed by Emmet L. Wemple and Associates. Each of the fourteen two-story units has a private court, and in addition there are larger, more public courts. The imagery is early-1960s *Arts and Architecture,* post-and-beam Modern with an open courtyard created between the stucco-covered boxes and the Constructivist pergolas.

Just east of the San Diego Freeway interchange with Redondo Beach Boulevard is El Camino College (at 16067 S. Crenshaw Boulevard). The administration building and the library were designed in 1951 by Smith, Powell, and Morgridge. These buildings indicate how well the architects of the immediate post–World War II years could apply both the 1930s lesson of the International Style and the popular Moderne to produce a functional and convincing building.

20 • Baldwin Hills Culver City

This section of Los Angeles (county and city) contains the Palms District (laid out in 1886) and Culver City (platted in 1913). Palms, which was established alongside the Santa Monica Railroad, was planned as a grain shipping center, and until the early 1900s was an agriculture-based community.

Culver City, founded in 1913 by Nebraska real estate promoter Harry Hazel Culver, has long been famed for the major film studios, which began to locate there from the late teens on into the 1920s. Land use in the area now varies considerably. Light industry occurs here and there, extensive commercial strips abound (Venice, Washington, Culver, and Jefferson Boulevards). For the vernacular commercial-strip fancier, a long leisurely drive along Pico Boulevard or Washington Boulevard from Santa Monica to downtown Los Angeles is a must. If your interest is in middle-class suburbia and its planning, then visit a development such as Monte Mar Vista, a 130-acre development south of Rancho Park (north off the Santa Monica Freeway, east of Overland Avenue, west of Robertson Boulevard). This development was laid out in 1924 by Cook, Hill, and Cornell. In Palms, on Overland Avenue between National and Venice Boulevards, is Westside Village, a spec development of small single-family houses that was built between 1939 and 1941. The small clapboard houses with their shuttered windows evoke the then-popular Anglo-Colonial Revival. During the past two decades Culver City has emerged as a major center of Postmodern architecture in the Los Angeles area, thanks particularly to Eric Owen Moss.

1. Petal House, 1982
Eric Owen Moss
2828 Midvale Avenue

This complex of buildings (it is in part a remodeling) displays the architect's inventive ability to carry pedestrian architecture over into the world of high art. The commonest of materials coupled with the most common of architectural forms produces a very uncommon composition. Though the design, including its strong colors, is assertive, it fits with ease into a neighborhood of typical, modest, post–World War II spec houses. And the forms and details of this house convey a sense of charm and delight. See the house close-up from the street, and also observe how it works from the Santa Monica Freeway.

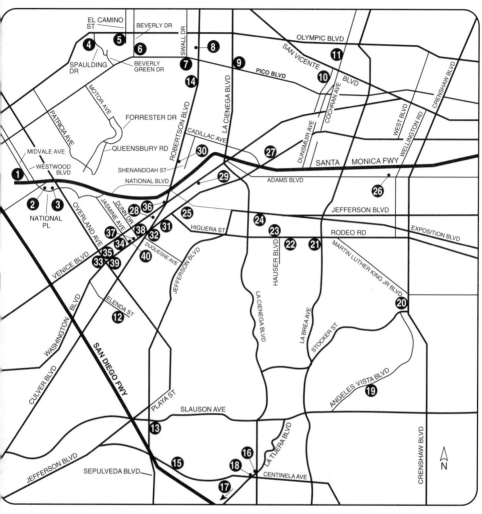

Photo of Petal House (left) by David Gebhard; courtesy of the University of California Art Department, Santa Barbara.

2. Garden Apartments, 1955
Carl Maston
10567 National Boulevard

A series of volumes that step down the hillside to the street, with garages at the street level. Above, each of the units has its own small, enclosed courtyard garden. The building is sheathed in vertical redwood. Glass in horizontal bands occurs between the top of the redwood walls and the thin-fascia flat roofs.

3. National Boulevard Apartments, 1954
Raymond Kappe
10565 National Boulevard

This building provides a good neighbor for Carl L. Maston's apartments next door. The design concept is similar, except that here Kappe's detailing is more delicate, and in places there is a hint of his later wood Constructivism.

4. Karaski House, 1960
Lloyd Wright
436 Spalding Drive
Beverly Hills

Lloyd Wright at his best; a wonderful essay in stucco, concrete open grillwork, and stone. The grillwork encloses courts and parts of balconies. The two-story rear of the house has the appearance of the bridge of a ship.

5. Beverly-Landau Apartment Building, 1949
Alvin Lustig
Southwest corner of Olympic Boulevard and El Camino Drive

These two rectangular volumes, set at right angles to each other, have façades that are divided into repeated modules. One strongly senses the hand and heart of a careful designer.

6. Liberty Building, 1966
Kurt Meyer and Associates
1180 S. Beverly Drive

A Los Angeles version of the 1960s New Brutalism. Its awkwardly proportioned seven-story form is a reminder of how rapidly architectural fashions come and go.

7. B'Nai David Synagogue and School Building, circa 1929
South side of Pico Boulevard at Swall Drive

The pattern of the board forms has been left exposed in this Art Deco concrete structure. The tower is mildly reminiscent of several of the buildings at the 1925 Paris Exposition of Decorative Arts.

8. Ellwood Office Building, 1965–66
Craig Ellwood & Associates
1107–1111 S. Robertson Boulevard

A close-to-magical transformation of two fifty-year-old buildings into one of Ellwood's thin refined versions of the post-and-beam Miesian grids.

9. Supermarket Building, circa 1940
Attributed to Stiles Clements
Northeast corner of Pico and La Cienega Boulevards

The Streamline Moderne street façade of this building culminates

in two thin, vertical fin signs that turn out to be relief sculpture of a Hugh Ferriss skyscraper from his 1929 *Metropolis of Tomorrow.*

10. Dunsmuir Apartments, 1937
Gregory Ain
1281 S. Dunsmuir Avenue

A mid-1930s classic of Modernism, often illustrated during those years in magazines and books on housing. It was this building, presented through the revealing photographs of Julius Shulman that established Gregory Ain's national reputation. The building is composed of four two-story units stepped back up the low hillside with a narrow entrance walkway on one side and a small terrace and garden for each unit on the other side. Each

12

of the second-floor bedrooms of the units opens onto an upper pergola-covered deck.

11. Mackey Apartments, 1939
R. M. Schindler
1137–1141 S. Cochran Avenue

Each of the building's elevations is composed of projecting and cut-into volumes, articulated by a carefully designed pattern of windows and doors. Some of the interior spaces are two stories in height.

12. Robert Lee Frost Auditorium, Culver City High School and Middle School, 1964
Flewelling and Moody
South corner of Elenda Street and Franklin Avenue

The drama of concrete that so excited architects in the 1950s and 1960s is realized in this structure. A singular curved leg of reinforced concrete joins a curved, partial dome and folded-roof structure. In the center, below the concrete forms, is a circular drum that houses the stage and other rooms. This firmdesigned a number of schoobuildings in the years after 1945, all of which employed some version of the Modern.

13. Fox Hills Shopping Mall, 1973-76
Gruen Associates (Cesar Pelli)
Southeast corner of Sepulveda and Slauson Boulevards, below the freeway

A form seemingly designed to make an impression from the freeway interchange. The landscaping and buildings do not work as well close up.

14

14. Robertson Branch Library, 1997
Steven Ehrlich
1719 S. Robertson Boulevard

This certainly is not Pasadena! The building is almost lewd. Postmodern in the extreme! Expressionism in excelsis! A library?

15. Hillside Memorial Park
Centinela Avenue, just southeast of Bristol Parkway

Visible from the San Diego Freeway is the Al Jolson Memorial, designed in 1951 by Paul R. Williams. The memorial is an impressive abstracted version of an open classical temple that is oriented toward a water cascade.

16. Ladera Center, 1983
Urban Innovations Group
Corner of La Cienega and La Tijera Boulevards and Centinela Avenue

A small older shopping center brought up-to-date by a new stage-set façade, which looks to the classical tradition (in a strange way). A successful revamping, utilizing the symbols of Postmodernism.

17. St. Anselm Church, 1956–57
J. Earl Trudeau
Southwest corner Van Ness Avenue and 70th Street

One of the many Roman Catholic churches built in Los Angeles that continued the Spanish tradition, in this case based upon Renaissance examples. The building, its tall tower, and central dome are of reinforced concrete. All of the exterior and interior ornament of cast concrete are sharp angled and highly simplified.

18. Pann's Restaurant, 1958
Armet and Davis
Northwest corner of La Tijera and La Cienega Boulevards and Centinela Avenue

A classic 1950s Los Angeles coffee shop designed by the firm that built many of Los Angeles's restaurants and coffee shops in the post–World War II years. The restaurant was restored in 1991 and is now an official Los Angeles landmark. Towering over the pitched gable-roofed restaurant is an enormous animated sign. The interior space (with its open kitchen) has been returned to its original colors, red and white, with

touches of yellow and orange. The low-pitched gravel-covered roof is once again lighted, and the original exotic plant material—phapis palms, hibiscus, giant birds of paradise—surrounds the restaurant.

19. California Military Academy (now Foundation for the Blind), 1934–36
Richard J. Neutra
5300 Angeles Vista Boulevard

A single-floor L-plan building constructed of a metal frame and sheathing. Each of the classrooms opens to its own outdoor space through sliding glass walls. Skylights balance the light in the classrooms and the interior corridors. (Note that Neutra's buildings lie to the rear of the site.)

20. Crenshaw Shopping Plaza, 1947–48
Crenshaw Boulevard, between Martin Luther King Boulevard and Stocker Road

This was one of the first large suburban shopping malls to be built in Los Angeles after World War II. It took the lesson learned from the large department stores along Wilshire Boulevard and applied it to a suburban situation. The first increment of the complex was the May Company Crenshaw Department Store. This three-story, reinforced-concrete, department store building is situated on the northwest corner of Crenshaw Boulevard and Martin Luther King Boulevard. It was designed by Albert C. Martin and Associates and was built in 1946–47. As with the pre–World War II May Company on Wilshire, the architects employed a dramatic curved corner, except that in this case, it was a curved showcase on the ground level and then three balconies above.

25g

Though there were doors to the street, the real entrance was at the rear where 750 parking spaces were provided. Albert C. Martin is quoted as saying about this design that an important "consideration of design is that of simplicity. Without simplicity in mass and color treatment, the sole purpose of designing housing for merchandising is lost." (*Southwest Builder and Contractor*, Nov. 28, 1947).

A year later across the street (Martin Luther King Boulevard), architect Albert B. Gardner designed the Broadway-Crenshaw Department Store. This, too, was Modern in architectural design and also faced onto its parking lot to the west. Other stores were provided with the department store, including a Vons Super Market, designed by Stiles Clements in 1947–48.

21. Baldwin Hills Shopping Center, 1954
Robert E. Alexander
Southwest corner of La Brea Avenue and Rodeo Road

A small, neighborhood shopping center directed primarily to the residences of nearby Baldwin

Hills Village. Changes in shop fronts and signage have tended to destroy its unity of design.

22. Baldwin Hills Village, 1940–41
Reginald D. Johnson, Wilson and Merrill, Robert E. Alexander; Clarence S. Stein, consultant and site planner; Fred Barlow and Fred Edmunson, landscape architects
5300 Rodeo Road

At the time it was built and in the years that have followed, Baldwin Hills Village has continually been mentioned as a successful example of multiple medium-density housing. Two-story units are arranged around open well-landscaped spaces that lead into the central village green. In addition, each of the units has its own small walled courtyard, which helps to separate the buildings even further from the more public open spaces. Parking and garage courts were laid out on the edge of the site, and near the center are the clubhouse and the offices. The buildings' low-pitched hipped roofs are neutral

in design, and it is the trees, shrubs, grass, and flowers that dominate. Recently the project has been turned into a condominium, with individual ownership of each unit.

23. University Elementary School, 1948, 1950
Robert E. Alexander
Northwest corner of Rodeo Road and Hauser Boulevard

Post-and-beam Modern of the 1950s. A good example of the indoor/outdoor classroom building.

24. 8522 National Building, 1986–90
Eric Owen Moss
8522 National Boulevard

The architect has remodeled a group of warehouse buildings into an office complex that centers on an interior covered street that meanders through the buildings. The entrance is emphasized by a semicircular open court. Games of high-tech—as structure with materials—occur throughout the project.

25. Air Rights City
Eric Owen Moss

a. Samitauer Building, 1989–96
3457 S. La Cienega (in an alley off La Cienega)

b. 8522 National Building, 1986–90
8522 National Boulevard, at Hayden Avenue

c. Paramount Laundry Building, 1987–89
3960 Ince Boulevard

d. Lindblade Tower, 1987–89
3962 Ince Boulevard

e. Gary Group Office Building, 1988–90
9046 Lindblade Street

f. The Box, 1994;
The Beehive, 2000
8520 National Boulevard

g. Stealth Building, 2001
3528 Hayden Avenue

Actually these are only a few of a number of old factories and warehouses that Moss has redesigned for Frederick and Laurie Smith. They can be seen by starting from the corner of Washington Boulevard and Higuera Street. Go southeast on Higuera, with its miniature roundabouts, to Hayden and then east on Hayden to National, and with a few short detours, you will have seen them all except for the Samitauer Building, which is not far away.

We find it impossible to describe these buildings adequately. They are surrealist jokes that probably are intended to be taken seriously—we are not sure! Also problematical is their expected longevity; things go so quickly in Los Angeles. Like the Pop Architecture of the twenties and thirties (to which they are remotely related), they should probably have been spread around town in order to shock the viewer with the strange. But here they are in concentrated

form—and they are *exceeding* strange!

h. Pterodactyl Building, 2001
*3528 Hayden Avenue
(courtyard behind the
Stealth Building)*

26. Two Retail Commercial Buildings, circa 1934
*4500 block of
West Adams Boulevard,
north of Wellington Road*

Two Moderne commercial buildings, more Art Deco than Streamline Moderne. Each has a corner tower and splendid cast-concrete Moderne ornament.

27. Kings Tropical Inn Restaurant Building, 1925
5879 Washington Boulevard

A domed Islamic building that was intended to signify the exotic and faraway lands of the tropics.

28. Tisch/Avnet Building,
1991
Franklin D. Israel Design Associates
3815 Hughes Avenue

A steel-and-glass canopy entrance leads into the frame of an existing four-story building. From the entry, one comes into an interior

street (defined by a long curved wall). At the center of this street is an oculus. At right angles to the main street is a secondary passage that leads into a three-story conference room. Certainly one of the most impressive studies in spatial sequences to be designed in recent years.

29. Helms Bakery, 1930
E. L. Bruner
8800 Venice Boulevard

The vocabulary of the PWA Moderne realized in an extensive two-story building. Now missing is the regimented row of precisely trimmed shrubs in front of the building and the central rooftop sign advertising Helms Olympic Bread.

30. La Casa de Rocha, 1865
2400 Shenandoah Street

This story-and-a-half adobe ranch house is surrounded on three sides by a covered corridor. The upper walls of the building are sheathed in shiplap siding.

31. Thomas Ince Studio, 1915
9336 W. Washington Boulevard

The offices of a motion picture company pose as a stage set—in this case an Anglo-Colonial Revival southern plantation house. The colonnaded two-story porch remains as a freestanding screen in front of a newer building. This was the first major studio building to be constructed in Culver City.

32. Culver Theater, circa 1950
*Southeast corner of
West Washington Boulevard
and Duquesne Avenue*

A post–World War II theater where the façade is all sign. Its design is both Moderne and Baroque.

25h

33. Ship's Culver City Restaurant, 1957
Martin Stern Jr.
Northwest corner of Washington Boulevard and Overland Avenue

Another still-standing Los Angeles coffeehouse of the 1950s. The usual low-pitched, hovering, hipped roof shelters the building below. A composition of wood, stone, and gravel roof. Ship's sign, contained within a circular disk, is accompanied by an angled V, suggesting that a rocket has started its flight.

34. Murphy Buick Showroom and Garage, circa 1949
A. Quincy Jones
9099 Washington Boulevard

This lively late-1940s Moderne assemblage remains intact, including its wonderful signage. A surprising, but very well carried out, popular image by one of Los Angeles's exponents of High Art Modernism.

35. Citizen Publishing and Printing Company, 1929
9355 Washington Boulevard

The pylon-like entrance façade (as an impressive stage set) contains a deep arched opening accompanied by classic Art Deco ornamentation.

36. Los Angeles Pacific Railroad Company, Ivy Park Substation (later Pacific Electric Culver Substation), 1907
Northwest corner of Venice and Culver Boulevards

The Mission Revival image for a small single-story substation. The substation has now been restored (1992), and a small park has been laid out around it.

37. Sony Pictures Entertainment, Child Care Center, 1993–94
3845 Clarington Avenue

Sony Pictures Entertainment, Digital Production Building, 1993–94
Steven Ehrlich Architects; Campbell and Campbell, landscape architects
10101 Washington Boulevard

For the Child Care Center the architect has developed a curved masonry wall that supports the exposed glue-laminated (glue lam) timber beams. The undulating roof establishes the scale and character of the building. The design is such that, most of the time, the building can be cooled by natural ventilation. Next door, the Digital Production Building poses as a miniature castle with corner towers. It, too, uses curved glue-lam beams for the roof. A large monitor unit on the roof seems almost to be a distant building. Both the Digital Production Building and the Child Care Center are entered through gateways that bring one into protected inner courts.

38. Garden Court, circa 1925
3819–3825 Dunn Drive

A Medieval fairy-tale world of Hansel and Gretel cottages in a witch-infested jungle with pools

of water. It is unbelievable that it is still with us, only a block from the center of Culver City.

39. MGM Studios, 1938–39
Claude Beelman
East corner of Washington Boulevard and Overland Avenue

The Beaux-Arts in the guise of the monumental PWA Moderne. Rounded corners and decorative panels of concrete make it as official as any governmental building. The studios were established at this location in 1923, and there are both pre- and post-1938 buildings on the site. The 1923 building is an impressive, classical, columned structure just northeast of the corner of Washington Boulevard and Overland Avenue.

40. St. Augustine's Roman Catholic Church, 1956–57
J. Earl Trudeau
Northeast corner of Washington Boulevard and Jasmine Avenue

A Gothic revival church in revealed concrete with horizontal board patterns as a surface. All the details are treated in a highly simplified manner. Inside, reinforced-concrete ribs rise from the floor to support the gabled roof.

38

21 • Brentwood

Originally part of the Rancho San Vicente y Santa Monica, modern Brentwood began when the Western Pacific Development Company acquired the land in the early 1900s and named it Brentwood Park. In 1906 the company platted the lots and streets in a manner consciously modeled on the plan of Golden Gate Park in San Francisco. The area—bounded on the east by 26th Street, on the west by Cliffwood Avenue, on the south by San Vicente Boulevard, and on the north by the Santa Monica Mountains—was intended, from the first, to be the home of the upper crust of society. It was determinedly residential, with thirty-four traffic circles interrupting the flow of rapid transit. All but seven of the circles have been eliminated by progress.

Our listing includes the area east to the San Diego Freeway. Originally this was part of the Bel Air District developed in the same period by Alphonzo Bell Sr., an early alumnus of Occidental College. For some reason, he decided to separate his historically coeducational college into men's and women's divisions. The women were to remain in Eagle Rock, and the men moved to Bel Air, not far from where UCLA was soon to settle. The old grads and students were generally disgusted with Bell's idea, and nothing came of it except the name "Tigertail Road" in honor of the Oxy Tigers. His real estate, on both sides of the present freeway, sold well. Like Brentwood Park, it was bought by the upper-middle to upper-upper classes. By and large, the former class hired the better architects.

1. Sawtelle Veterans Hospital
Wilshire Boulevard and Sawtelle Avenue

Technically, this is not in Brentwood, but it is so near that it makes a good starting point. It was founded in the 1880s—one of the first veterans' hospitals opened after the Civil War. Unfortunately the old buildings, called Domiciliaries, have been destroyed. They were excellent examples of Shingle-style resort architecture. Little remains of the old hospital. The picturesque wooden Chapel (1900) is easily seen from Wilshire. Its architect, J. Lee Burton, mixed the Colonial Revival with Gothicism. The same architect designed a tiny Streetcar Station (circa 1900) at the corner of Dewey and Pershing, north of the chapel. The station, all arches and posts, is not really Eastlake, but the feeling is.

2. World Savings Center Building, 1982
Maxwell Starkman and Associates
Northwest corner of Wilshire and San Vicente Boulevards

A tall, late example of Corporate International Style Modern of no great distinction, but it is so big that you will wonder about it.

3. Four Apartment Units, 1966
J. R. Davidson
955 Westgate Avenue, at Darlington Avenue

Naturally stained, diagonal flush boards mark this assemblage.

4. Abell Office, 1954
T. M. Abell
654 S. Saltair Avenue

This building, though visible, makes its statement from the interior court rather than the street façade. Offices and drafting rooms open into a garden.

5. Shairer House, 1949
Ain, Johnson, and Day
11750 Chenault Street

Very Neutraesque. The members of the Los Angeles school constantly exchanged ideas, making the subject of influences often beside the point.

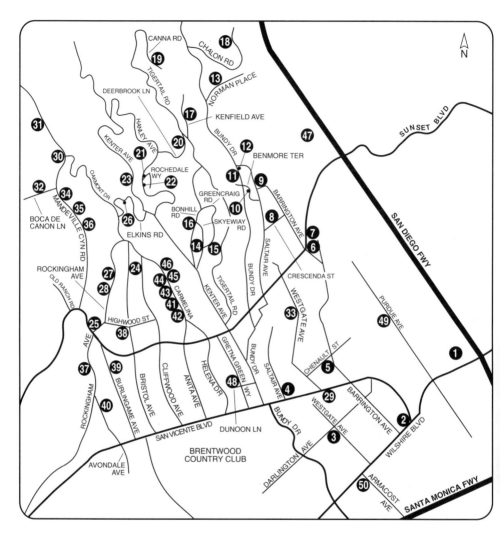

6. Shopping Center, circa 1935
*Barrington Avenue and
Sunset Boulevard*

Mainly Spanish Revival and dominated by a huge service station
with tower. Many a Pierce-Arrow
tanked up here on the way to the
Hollywood studios.

7. Eastern Star Home, 1931–33
William Mooser and Company
11725 Sunset Boulevard

You can see a few pieces here and
there of this firm's somewhat earlier Santa Barbara Courthouse,
but it lacks the finesse of its
northern relative. The huge concrete corbels are grained and
painted to resemble wood.

8. Goss House, 1950
Milton H. Caughey
11731 Crescenda Street

Understated vertical board-and-
batten with the ends of the roof
beams projecting.

9. House, circa 1928
Northeast corner of
Saltair and Barrington Avenues

Obviously a work of one of the better architects, this Spanish Revival house dominates its neighborhood.

10. Evans House, 1936
Lloyd Wright
12036 Benmore Terrace

Big but less ornamented than most of Wright's work, this house can be seen from 554 N. Bundy Drive below and from its entrance on Benmore.

11. Samuel House, 1934
Lloyd Wright
579 N. Bundy Drive

The Bundy façade is saved from austerity by lush foliage. Strangely, the eaves at the side, which are carried into a sort of trellis, do not hold vines.

12. Leslie House, 1950
Thornton M. Abell
525 N. Saltair Avenue

As usual, the garage is the street façade, and the International Style house is set below street level.

13. Wyle Guest House, 1983
Tedesco Architects
(Lorenzo C. Tedesco)
1043 Norman Place

A contemporary version of the traditional Japanese farm and teahouse, handsomely realized.

14. Sturges House, 1939
Frank Lloyd Wright
449 Skyewiay Road

Cantilevered from the hill, this house seems windowless from the street side, although all the major rooms open through glass doors to the balcony deck. It is, of course, one of Wright's monu-ments. The house is really quite small, some 1,200 square feet, but its open plan and bank of glass doors that lead onto the twenty-one-foot-wide extended deck make it seem large. A roof terrace occurs at the top of the house and, as with most Wright houses of these years, a carport occurs at the rear (which is the entrance to the house).

15. House, 1973–74
Lomax-Mills Associates
548 Greencraig Road

The stucco volume has been dra-matically cut into by deep rectan-gular openings.

16. Herman House, 1948
Carl Louis Maston
650 Bonhill Road

A good International Style house.

17. Bernheim House, 1961
Raymond Kappe
1000 Kenfield Avenue

A fine essay in fragile wood and glass.

18. Mount St. Mary's College,
1930–31
Mark Daniels;
1939–40 and later
**M. L. Barker and
G. Lawrence Ott**
12001 Chalon Road
The design theme of these buildings is Hispanic. Bardy Hall, designed during 1930–31 by Mark Daniels, has the feeling

of a small Spanish palace, and it fits beautifully into its hillside site. In 1939 Barker and Ott designed a chapel and faculty building that was of Spanish Gothic design. It is lovely.

19. Gould House, 1969
Raymond Kappe
12256 Canna Road

Again, glass and wood prevail in this house with stylistic affinities to Schindler's now-demolished Wolfe House on Santa Catalina Island.

18

20. Shoor House, 1952
William S. Beckett
12336 Deerbrook Lane
Trim International Style Modern.

21. Mutual Housing
Association Community,
1947–50
**Whitney Smith,
A. Quincy Jones, and
Edgardo Contini;
James Charlton,
Wayne R. Williams
and Associates;
Garrett Eckbo,
landscape architect**
*Hanley Avenue at
Rochedale Way*

The community comprises a number of houses, some now remodeled. We picked out 717, 727, 738, and 743 Hanley Avenue and 12404, 12408, 12414, and 12428 Rochedale Way as exemplary and visible. There are others on Broom Way and Bramble Way. The grouping remains a remarkable social, planning, and architectural development by three of Los Angeles's most important architectural figures. The informal siting and the woodsy detail suggest the Bay tradition and Frank Lloyd Wright.

22. Lotery House, 1962
Rex Lotery
1007 Hanley Avenue

This house effectively presents a composition of thin volumes of glass and wood, over which has been delicately placed a thin roof slab, which terminates in an open sunscreen. On the garden side of the house, a broad glass wall opens onto a wood-sheathed balcony.

23. Rodes House, 1978–79
Moore, Ruble, and Yudell
*1406 N. Kenter Avenue,
north end of pavement*

Moore says that this stucco box was based on ideas the architects had in their minds of "modernized eighteenth-century houses in the south of France," i.e., Moore's version of the Hollywood Regency. It has a two-story convex façade that acts as a stage set for the owner's amateur theatrical productions.

24. Epstein House, 1949
Craig Ellwood
N. Cliffwood Avenue

A redwood façade by an architect who was soon to turn to glass, steel, and brick.

25. House, circa 1972
*Northwest corner of
Rockingham and
Burlingame Avenues*

A house with huge wooden shafts pointing skyward. It must be very dramatic inside.

26. Rich House, 1968
T. M. Abell
689 Elkins Road

Unfenestrated stucco walls, broken only by a simple door. Pure architecture.

27. Avery House, 1934–37
Lloyd Wright
365 N. Rockingham Avenue
A pyramid!

28. Temple House, 1935–36
**John Byers (with Edla Muir);
Benjamin Morton Purdy,
landscape architect**
231 N. Rockingham Avenue

This mixture of English and Norman farmhouse is a real delight. There is a fair view of it from the entrance gate and a view of an amusing fragment from Sunset Boulevard below. Shirley Temple lived here.

29. Kaufman Branch Library
Arthur Erickson
11820 San Vicente Boulevard

It almost seems as if this Canadian architect was trying to create a modernist version of an

old Carnegie Library. The low dome is the giveaway. It is pleasant to see Erickson do a relatively small building, though his fame rests on his large ones.

30. Rex House #1, 1949
**John Rex, Edla Muir;
Edward Huntsman-Trout,
landscape architect**
1888 Mandeville Canyon Road

The feeling is that of an updated Craftsman dwelling, somewhat in the same fashion as you would find in the architecture of San Francisco Bay tradition during the 1940s and 1950s. The motor court is especially handsome.

31. Rex House #2, 1955
John Rex
1900 Mandeville Canyon Road

Asia seen through the eye of an International Style architect.

32. Lassoff House, 1989
Rex Lotery
13151 Boca de Canon Lane

As in other designs by this architect, the layered effect of roofs is achieved via assertive fascias. In this house he has countered this horizontality by tall V-shaped skylights and by a metal-and-glass Constructivism that faces onto the garden at an upper level. From the street one can see how the architect has made dramatic the series of stepped volumes that work their way up the hillside.

33. Lawson/Westen House, 1993
Eric Owen Moss
167 S. Westgate

A real stunner made of concrete, but more Postmodern than Brutalist. A prow juts out into the sea breeze. Very cool!

34. Sperry House, 1953
Wurster, Bernardi, and Emmons
2090 Mandeville Canyon Road

A rational post-and-beam house, rather Los Angeles in spirit, though by a Bay Area firm.

35. Siple House, 1949–59
Allen Siple
2669 Mandeville Canyon Road

This dressed-stone house, obviously a labor of love, was constructed by the architect and his wife, aided by neighbors.

36. Seidel House, 1960
Pierre Koenig
2727 Mandeville Canyon Road

Two small Miesian pavilions, delicately articulated, compose this Case Study House.

37. Johnson House, 1919
Harry Johnson, assisted by John Byers; Edward Huntsman-Trout, landscape architect
201 S. Rockingham Avenue

Byers, Harry Johnson's cousin, employed Mexican laborers to make the adobe bricks for the walls of this Spanish Revival house. It was landscaped with

native plants, which have all but obscured the view.

38. Siskin House, 1966
Thornton M. Abell
12822 Highwood Street

Set far back from one of the original Brentwood circles, this International Style house contrasts with its wooded environment.

39. Newfield House, 1961
Thornton M. Abell
250 S. Burlingame Avenue

Buff-colored Roman-laid brick. We thought that the art of the mason went out with the coming of the International Style, but here it is in wonderful shape.

40. Nesbitt House, 1942
Richard J. Neutra
414 Avondale Avenue

The Nesbitt house marks an early excursion by Neutra into warm nonmachine materials: wood and brick. Unfortunately for the architecture buff, few of its features can be seen from the street.

Carmelina Avenue:

There is a series of fascinating houses on Carmelina Avenue just below its intersection with Anita, continuing south to San Vicente Boulevard. The best have been selected for listing here.

41. Greenberg House
Ricardo Legoretta
223 N. Carmelina Avenue

Legoretta's usual large intersecting blocks, brightly colored and extremely dramatic in the Southern California sunlight. The palms are certainly important to the effect.

42. Hamilton House, 1931–33
John Byers,
with Edla Muir
193 N. Carmelina Avenue

Monterey Revival.

43. Stedman House, 1935–36
John Byers,
with Edla Muir
363 N. Carmelina Avenue

A path leads from a typical Byers gate through carefully clipped boxwood hedges to the Colonial Revival front door.

44. Zimmerman House, 1950
Craig Ellwood
400 N. Carmelina Avenue

An interruption in the Byers boutique. A stark brick wall faces the street—the beginning of an L-shaped house that immediately breaks into glass and steel.

45. Kerr House, 1930
John Byers,
with Edla Muir
428 N. Carmelina Avenue

A very different version of the Monterey Revival when compared with the Hamilton House.

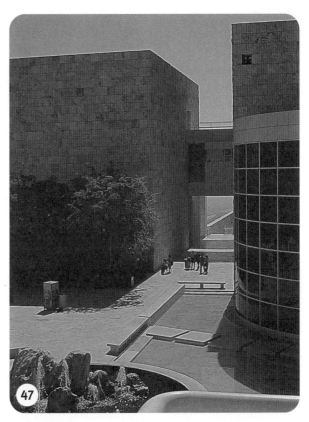

47

46. Murray House, circa 1935
John Byers,
with Edla Muir
436 N. Carmelina Avenue

Colonial Revival.

47. The J. Paul Getty Center
for the Arts, 1984-97
Richard Meier
*Get off the
San Diego Freeway on
Sepulveda Boulevard at
Getty Center Drive;
follow signs to the parking
area and entrance.*

This complex of buildings set high on a hill overlooking the San Diego Freeway (and UCLA and the Pacific Ocean) has elicited an extraordinary amount of critical comment pro and con that can be summed up with observations that the buildings are okay, with moments of great beauty; the art is mostly mediocre, with some exceptions (e.g., five *real* Rembrandts); and the view (including Magic Johnson's estate) is sensational, especially toward evening when the sun sets over Santa Monica Bay. A number of critics have found it too far from the city, an Italian hill town gone astray. Others have noted its similarity in intention to Disneyland ("a theme park run by librarians," *Wall Street Journal*, October 6, 2000), which can also be approached by a space-age railway. In our last guide, published before the buildings were finished, David Gebhard wrote: "This all adds up to the classic environmental arrogance which one associates with so much of the International Style of this century." (David could be so cruel!)

There is some truth in all these estimates, but few visitors will come away from this place without feeling that they have had a great experience. It was pure inspiration to have left the impression of fossils showing on the tan marble walls that contrast strongly with Meier's beloved white surfaces. In fact, ironic contrast is one key to your feelings about the Getty scene. The central garden designed by the artist Robert Irwin, who had never done a garden before, clashes with the sharp neo-International Style lines of Meier's architecture, a point not lost on Meier, who was furious over the result. John Walsh, the director when the museum was built, got Thierry W. Despont to finish the interior galleries, some of whose walls he covered with damask. It is fun to pop out of these sedate old-fashioned rooms into Meier's white corridors and onto his staircases that seem to have been crafted for an ocean liner.

Among the exhibits, the *pièce de la resistance* is an eighteenth-century four-poster bed (Getty loved the decorative arts) that has ostrich plumes bunched at the top of the posts. At one of the grand openings of the museum, one of the Getty employees, on encountering this absurdity, turned to me and said, "Remember, this was created in the Age of Reason!"

The Getty Center is not just a museum. There are separate quarters for a Conservation Institute, an art history information program, a center for education in the arts, and a film center, as well as a library, a lecture hall, and two restaurants. Criticism that the Getty Foundation, with its billions of dollars in endowment, was not doing enough for the culture of Los Angeles led to a grant program that supports initial studies of projects in historical preservation, education, and other worthy causes.

Some say that the Getty has lost its buzz, but not as far as I am concerned.

For information or parking reservations (required on weekdays but not on Saturday or Sunday and after 4 P.M. on weekdays), call (310) 440-7300 or visit www.getty.edu.

48. Drucker Apartments, 1940
J. R. Davidson
Northwest corner of Gretna Green Way and Dunoon Lane

A curious blending of Schindler and Gill, though the greatest influence was the International Style.

49. "Gerb in California" Houses, 1990
David Ming-Li Lowe
1955 Purdue Avenue

Two steel-frame structures are floated on specially designed isolated bases to resist earthquakes. This technology was developed in Germany and was applied to American buildings by "Gerb in California."

50. Armacost Duplex, 1989–90
Rebecca L. Binder
1224 Armacost Avenue

The architect has fitted two 1,500-square-foot units onto a narrow 25-foot lot. The design makes it possible for the living areas of the two units to face an internal patio/deck. The various volumes of the building assert their independence via different materials—split block below, then stucco and fiberboard siding.

22 • Bel Air

This hilly area above UCLA was developed by Alphonzo Bell in the teens and obviously sold well in the 1920s. It is the last word in respectability, having its own security patrol years before other highbrow enclaves felt the need. It is a gorgeously landscaped area. The entrance to Bel Air is through imposing gates at Bel Air, Stone Canyon, and Bellagio Roads. Much of the planning during the 1920s was by architect Mark Daniels (Elmer Grey Associates), who also designed the Administration Building (circa 1928) on Stone Canyon Road just north of the intersection with Bellagio. It is a handsome building of white walls and red tile roofs, whose plan focuses on two patios.

The large and small estates exude wealth, not by the imposing façades (most of which cannot be seen), but by beautifully trimmed plantings, literally inundating the sumptuous dwellings. Foliage hides residences by George Washington Smith (his only one in west Los Angeles), Gordon B. Kaufmann, Wallace Neff, Roy Selden Price, Palmer Sabin, Douglas Honnold, George Vernon Russell, Paul R. Williams, and Paul Laszlo. The following list only hints at what is hidden away.

1. Nordlinger House, 1948
A. Quincy Jones
11492 Thurston Circle

Very much under the influence of Frank Lloyd Wright.

2. Winans Apartments (now Bel Air Gardens), 1948
A. Quincy Jones
850 Moraga Drive

The jutting roofs are very dramatic.

3. Zeigler House, 1952
Paul Sterling Hoag
1060 Acanto Street

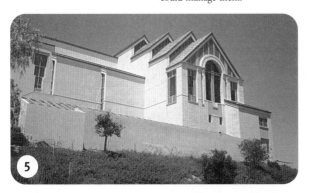

5

A graceful post–World War II California ranch house. A low-pitched hipped roof shelters the redwood walls below. Nature, by way of large sycamore trees, dominates the site and house.

4. Leo Baeck Temple, 1962
Victor Gruen Associates
1300 N. Sepulveda Boulevard

A series of apparently thick walls of varying shapes and a great hood of a roof enclose the space of the

sanctuary. It all reads well, especially from the San Diego Freeway.

5. Bel Air Presbyterian Church, 1991
Moore, Ruble, and Yudell
16221 Mulholland Drive, west of the San Diego Freeway

Presbyterians are not supposed to have cathedrals, but this church ranks close to what the Catholics and Episcopalians have produced. Romanesque and Gothic elements have been woven together with some spectacular structural effects as only Charles Moore could manage them.

6. Mirman School, 1972–73
Brent, Goldman, Robbins, and Brown
16180 Mulholland Drive, west of the San Diego Freeway, just beyond Mulholland Place

A good-looking group of stucco buildings obviously influenced by Charles Moore—a good influence.

7. Steven S. Wise Temple, Chapel, and School Facilities, 1975
Sidney Eisenstadt
North corner of Mulholland Drive and Casiano Road, east of the San Diego Freeway

Very impressive Expressionism with great leaning roofs.

8a. Skirball Museum and Cultural Center, 1996

8b. Ahmanson Performing Arts Complex, 2002
Moshe Safdie and Associates
2701 N. Sepulveda Boulevard, at the intersection of the 405 Freeway and Mulholland Drive

8b

The museum is not at all reminiscent of Safdie's Habitat at the Montreal World's Fair. It is, indeed, aesthetically forbidding while at the same time performing excellent service in exhibiting and promoting Jewish culture. The Ahmanson Center, while in a different style, is not better architecture. Too bad because the site is wonderful. For information, call (310) 440-4500.

9. Rabinowitz House, 1960
J. R. Davidson
2262 Stradella Road

A major design by one of Los Angeles's most important modern architects. Most of this architect's houses are either well hidden from public view or have been remodeled. What a pleasure to actually be able to see an International Style house by this architect.

10. Chappellett House, circa 1925
H. Roy Kelley
848 Stradella Road

A beautiful Monterey Revival dwelling in a style of which Kelley was a master.

11. Beck House, 1955
Thornton M. Abell
952 Roscomare Road

With flush, horizontal wood boards, this house still looks brand new.

12. Brown House, 1955
Richard J. Neutra;
Dion Neutra
10801 Chalon Road

A steep hillside house of stucco and redwood, just barely visible from the road.

13. Anderson House, 1951
Honnold and Rex
621 Perugia Way

International Style with a Las Vegas stone base.

14. Healy House, 1949–52
Lloyd Wright
565 Perugia Way

The Usonian House updated as a California ranch house with a little Asian influence.

15. Norcross House, 1927
Roland E. Coate
673 Siena Way

A beautiful Monterey Revival dwelling that opens onto a high-walled auto court.

16. Japanese Garden, 1961
Nagao Sakurai, designer, assisted by Dudley Fridgett; Kazuo Nakamura, construction
Bellagio Road, west of the intersection with Stone Canyon Road

The original garden was designed and laid out by A. E. Hanson for Harry Calendar in 1923. At that time it was picturesque Spanish, not Japanese. It was transformed into a Japanese garden in 1961. This beautiful hillside was given to UCLA in 1965. Call the UCLA Visitors Center for information: (310) 825-4574.

17. Miller House, 1932
Wallace Neff
10615 Bellagio Road

An enlarged two-story English cottage with some references to Charles F. A. Voysey's turn-of-the-century work in England.

18. Nilsson House, 1977
Eugene Kupper
*10549 Rocca Place
(can only be seen from the end of Somma Way)*

An elongated, two-story sky-lighted spine serves as the core of this dwelling. Although the spaces and their relation to one another are complex, the general atmosphere of the house is Classical and Mediterranean. The garden walls and terraces beautifully integrate the house to its hillside site.

19. Kranz House, 1989–91
Barton Phelps and Associates
245 Estrada Corta

A 1950s California ranch house was removed and replaced by the present dwelling, which uses the old foundation. A garage was projected to the street, helping to enclose a motor court. As in the original house, an angled living room acts as a hinge between the two wings of the house. Simple surfaces and geometry dominate the design. A focal point of this geometry is the tall canted chimney behind the glass courtyard entrance.

20. Curtis-Noyes House, 1950
Raphael S. Soriano
111 Stone Canyon Road

One of Soriano's largest commissions. About all that can be seen are the grid-motif garages.

21. Case Study House #16, 1951
Craig Ellwood
1811 Bel Air Road

A steel-frame Miesian exercise based upon eight-foot modules. The infills are of Palos Verdes stone, wood siding, and glass.

22. Gordon B. Kaufmann House, circa 1929
Gordon B. Kaufmann; Florence Yoch, landscape architect
245 Carolwood Drive

Mediterranean (Italian) style with Spanish Colonial aspects, this is much warmer than most of Kaufmann's houses. The house is close to the street and beautifully landscaped. Just below at 230 Carolwood Drive is the Lohman House (1925), also by Kaufmann, in a version of the Tudor style.

23. Colbert House, 1935
Lloyd Wright
615 N. Faring Road

Here Lloyd Wright brings together the Moderne and the Anglo-Colonial Revival.

24. Broughton House, 1950
Craig Ellwood
909 N. Beverly Glen Boulevard

Modular design, midway between traditional post-and-beam and the insistent Miesian steel beam.

25. Bernatti House, 1947
Rodney Walker
1025 N. Beverly Glen Boulevard

A simple frame structure. You can see the garage best.

26. Lohrie House, 1940
Rodney Walker
1648 Beverly Glen Boulevard

The traditional California ranch house emerging as a Moderne product with corner windows, sliding glass doors, and extending and overlapping horizontal planes.

27. Phelps-Simonson House, 1981–85
Barton Phelps and Associates
10256 Lelia Lane

One of those creative Los Angeles designs for what would appear to be an impossible site. An arroyo runs through the center of the site, so the house simply bridges over it. The house has a slight feeling of historicism, in this case, what has been labeled Caribbean Colonial. The fenestration is reserved and Classical in spirit; the parapeted gable ends and round windows put it into what one could think of as mild-mannered Postmodernism. Internally, the centerpiece is the platformed staircase that takes you to the top of the house.

28. Johnson House, 1949
Harwell H. Harris
10261 Chrysanthemum Lane

Here Harris simplifies and opens up the woodsy style of Charles and Henry Greene to terraces and gardens.

29. Sommer House, 1941
Rodney Walker
2252 Beverly Glen Place

Related to the 1930s San Francisco Bay tradition designs of William W. Wurster, Gardner Dailey, and others.

30. Singleton House, 1973
Wallace Neff
384 Delfern Drive, corner of Faring Road

A French Norman house.

31. House, circa 1926
Northeast corner of Sunset Boulevard and Stone Canyon Road

A splendid Moorish/Spanish house with an abundance of colorful tile work and an impressive, cusped arch loggia looking to the south. The garden, with its terraces, fountains, and watercourse, is Moorish as well. From time to time in its existence, this house has been visible from Sunset Boulevard; on other occasions little could be seen.

23 • Westwood, West

Westwood was developed by the Janss Investment Company during the early 1920s. The business center of Westwood was designed in 1928 by Leon Deming Tilton, the West Coast representative of the firm of Harland Bartholomew of St. Louis. The Janss firm had successfully lobbied with the University of California to relocate its southern branch—UCLA—just north of the business center.

As with many of the new communities established in the 1920s in California, the design of the buildings was reviewed by an art jury. In an article on the village published in the *Architect and Engineer* in 1930, it was noted that "The founders of Westwood Village did not permit, and still do not permit, the erection of any building of any kind

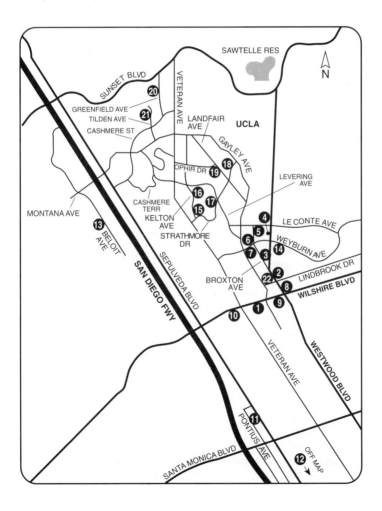

whatsoever that does not fit into the picture. The new city is almost entirely constructed of the best type of Mediterranean architecture."

By the end of the decade, the area was composed of upper-middle-class single-family residences, with streets laid out to conform to the irregular pattern of the hilly terrain. In the center was the new UCLA campus, and to the south around Wilshire and Westwood Boulevards was Westwood Village. Many houses employed one or another of the historic images—Spanish Revival, Mediterranean, Monterey Revival, English and Norman Medieval, Colonial, and Regency. Since the late 1940s, a smattering of modern housing of one variety or another has been built. Multiple housing developed around the area, along Wilshire Boulevard and to the east of the UCLA campus (around Landfair Avenue and Strathmore Drive). The quality of these historic-styled houses and apartments is remarkably high, and the buildings, coupled with the quality of the landscaping, make this section one of the most pleasant in Los Angeles.

Before the advent of high-rises around Westwood Village, it was one of Southern California's most successful regional suburban shopping centers. The Mediterranean image continued to be used (with some instances of Regency and Streamline Moderne) through the early 1940s. Later remodelings, modernizations, and replacements have compromised its original character. Among the greatest losses have been the several Mediterranean-image service stations with their high towers and illuminated signs.

Beginning in the early 1960s, the scale of Westwood Village was destroyed by the construction, one after another, of high-rise buildings along Wilshire Boulevard. The earliest of these was designed by such well-known Southern California architects as Claude Beelman, while some of the latest have been projected or built by Eastern name-brand firms.

These include:

1. 10940 Wilshire Tower, 1988
Murphy/Jahn Architects
10940 Wilshire Boulevard

Center West, 1989–90,
Mitchell/Giurgola Architect,
with DMJM and
Edgardo Cantini
10877 Wilshire Boulevard

Ashton Towers, 1989
Robbins and Brown, Inc.,
Architects
10930 S. Ashton Avenue

All of these have contributed to the destruction of the scale of the village (and of the residential areas to the northeast), and none have turned out to be particularly distinguished buildings. There are to be no more high-rises added to this area (the 23-story Center West Building supposedly being the last), but the urban damage has been done.

2. Ralph's Grocery Store,
1929
Russell Collins
1150 Westwood Boulevard

Colonnades extending along the two streets culminate in a low corner round tower into which has been placed an impressive pedimented entrance. The entablature of the tower has a band of corbeled arches, and a small lantern tops the conical roof of the tower. The walls were built in imitation of stone, but they have now been stuccoed over. In style the building is Spanish, both Romanesque and Renaissance.

3. Janss Investment Company Offices ("The Dome"), 1929
Allison and Allison
1099 Westwood Boulevard

This domed octagonal building still remains as the dominant structure within the village itself. Though the building is on the dry side, the dome with its Islamic (Zigzag) retrieves it all. In 1999 the interior was remodeled by Michael Chow.

4. Holmby Hall, 1929
Gordon B. Kaufmann, John and Donald Parkinson
West side of Westwood Boulevard, between Weyburn and LeConte Avenues

A Spanish Revival streetscape of six stores. The corner building at Weyburn Avenue once had a pinnacled tower with four clock faces.

5. Bruin Theater
S. Charles Lee
925 Broxton Avenue

A 1930s Moderne theater whose semicircular façade above the marquee housed a lighted sign to advertise the theater.

6. Fox Westwood Village Theater, 1931
P. O. Lewis
961 Broxton Avenue

Like "The Dome," the Fox Theater and its tower turn the axis of Broxton Avenue toward the northeast. The theater is essentially Spanish Revival with a touch of Moderne. The shaft of the tower rises to support projecting single columns and entablatures. On top, a Fox sign is surrounded by Art Deco patterns in metal.

7. Weyburn/Gayley Building, 1990–91
Kanner Associates
950 Gayley Avenue

A Postmodern design that fits in with the older buildings of the village. A little too classical in its detailing, but the scale works very well.

8. Armand Hammer Museum of Art and Culture, 1989–90
Edward Larabee Barnes; John M. Y. Lee and Partners, with Gruen Associates
10899 Wilshire Boulevard, at Westwood Boulevard

Barnes has produced a handsome but unassertive building. The walls are banded in dark and light Carrara marble, which effectively shuts out the busy external world. A segmented arch on the Lindbrook Drive façade of the building emphasizes a second entrance and also provides a view of the upper-level courtyard. As in Barnes' design for the Walker Art Center in Minneapolis, the gallery spaces inside work well for exhibition purposes, being well proportioned and well lighted by natural and artificial light. The building is supposed to get a new entrance and a remodeling of its central court by architect Michael Maltzan.

9. Wilshire West Plaza, 1971
Charles Luckman Associates
10880 Wilshire Boulevard

Perhaps adequate as an urban high-rise complex, it is devastating in what it and the other high-rises in the area have done to destroy the scale of Westwood Village.

10. U.S. Federal Office, 1970
Charles Luckman Associates
11000 Wilshire Boulevard

An immense file cabinet that one can't miss. As depressing a comment on architecture of the 1970s as it is a condemnation of the bureaucracy of our society.

11. Siskin Companies Office, 1972
Thornton M. Abell
1617 S. Pontius Avenue

A modest, very-well handled late version of the *Arts and Architecture* aesthetic.

12. Distribution Station #28, Department of Water and Power, 1945–46
G. E. Benker, engineer
Southeast corner of Cotner Street and Missouri Avenue

If we did not know better, we would assume that this water and power station, which is plainly visible from the San Diego Freeway, was built in the 1930s. Its exposed reinforced-concrete structure is pure PWA Moderne, with strong references to the Classical tradition and the Art Deco. The rows of piers are part of the adjoining wall surfaces, and ornament occurs only around the entrance.

13. Plywood Model Experimental House, 1936
Richard J. Neutra
427 S. Beloit Avenue

This plywood panel house was designed so that it could easily be transported—and so far, it has been moved twice. In the late 1930s, plywood was just coming into its own. The material conveyed modernity and the image of the machine. Neutra's use of it here fulfills these ideals.

14. Westwood Center, 1999
Michael Walden;
Nadel Partnership
1100 Glendon
Westwood

This large high-rise is a reconstruction and addition to an old building. It is not great architecture, but it is infinitely superior to any of the other tall buildings in Westwood—or in Central Los Angeles for that matter.

Incidentally the restaurant on the first floor is quite good.

15. Kelton Apartments, 1942
Richard J. Neutra
646–648 Kelton Avenue

Five apartments are grouped into two buildings. Each apartment is provided with its own outdoor terrace. The fenestration of the building is less insistently International Style than one experiences in Neutra's earlier nearby Landfair Apartments (1938).

16. Elkay Apartments, 1948
Richard J. Neutra
638–642 Kelton Avenue

A post–World War II extension of his earlier Kelton Apartments next door. The Elkay units are more woodsy and less committed to the image of the machine than the 1942 Kelton units.

17. Strathmore Apartments, 1937
Richard J. Neutra
11005 W. Strathmore Drive

In these apartments Neutra updated the Bungalow Court, providing it with a new image (the Modern), more light and air, and more extensive greenery. These four buildings contain eight apartments that, in part, face out onto the central garden and toward UCLA.

18. Sheets (L'Horizon) Apartments, 1949
John Lautner
10901–10919 W. Strathmore Drive

An eight-unit apartment building (image on page 24) that suggests the futuristic Modern of the twenty-first century. Visually this building is as fresh today as when it was built. Functionally it is a beautiful solution for multiple housing, with each apartment completely separated from the others, and each with its own terraces, decks, and outdoor garden space—all indicative of Lautner's understanding of how people will respond to the Modern as well as the environment of Los Angeles.

19. Landfair Apartments, 1937
Richard J. Neutra
Southwest corner of Landfair Avenue and Ophir Drive

The Landfair Apartments are one of Neutra's most International Style designs of the decade of the 1930s. This impressive exercise with its roof terrace is composed of patterned surfaces of stucco, metal, and glass bands.

21. Galli Curci House, 1938
Wallace Neff;
Florence Yoch and
Lucille Council,
landscape architects
201 Tilden Avenue

Neff took the theme of the informal rambling Andalusian farmhouse and produced a stunning composition of white stucco volumes terminated by a tile roof. The result, accompanied by one of his tall picturesque chimneys, illustrates the vigor of the Hispanic tradition in the late 1930s.

20. Tischler House, 1949
R. M. Schindler
175 Greenfield Avenue

Schindler set a 3-D de Stijl composition as a frontispiece for a stucco gable-roofed volume. The roof of the house was originally made of corrugated fiberglass, which was to have been shaded by parallel rows of eucalyptus planted along each side of the house.

22. In-N-Out Burger, 1997
Stephen Kanner Architects
922 Gayley Avenue
Westwood

Pop Art touched with Postmodernism—you can't miss this. It's a far cry from the old respectable Westwood. Some people will like the sign; others will wonder at the crossed palm trees.

24 • Westwood, South and East

1. Kaufmann House, 1937
Richard J. Neutra
234 S. Hilgard Avenue

A beautiful example of Neutra's version of the International Style. In this case, the building works not only as a symbol of the machine but also as an excellent "machine for living." The house takes advantage of its site, with the principal public spaces opening toward the garden, away from the street. The bedrooms on the second floor have glass doors leading onto a roof deck. Glass, brick, stainless steel, and interior mirrors add a Moderne note.

2. St. Alban's Episcopal Church, 1940 and later
P. P. Lewis
Northeast corner of South Hilgard and Westholme Avenues

This early 1940s chapel illustrates how strong and vigorous traditional imagery was in this decade—in this case Romanesque (both Italian and French) in brick, rough mortar, and stone trim. The post–1945 parts of the building do not convey any of the strength of the original. The narthex window was produced by the Judson Studios.

3. Doheny Memorial Dormitory for Girls (now YWCA), 1931
Stanton, Reed, and Hibbard
Hilgard Avenue

If only the smaller buildings on the UCLA campus could have followed the Monterey tradition expressed in this building, well sited on its hillside lot; the land-scaping works with the irregular form of the building to create its own world away from the very busy street.

4. Van Cleff House, 1942
Richard J. Neutra
651 Warner Avenue

All of the hallmarks of Neutra's Modern image are present in this single-story dwelling, though

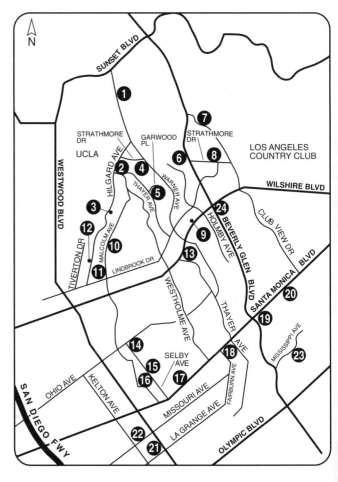

the roof form and the wood detailing help it to fit in with its neighbors.

5. Greenberg House, 1949
Richard J. Neutra
10525 Garwood Place

During the late 1940s Neutra designed several houses with low-pitched shed roofs and walls of stucco and redwood. The Greenberg House exhibits these elements on its hillside site.

6. Dean McHenry House, 1940
Harwell H. Harris
624 Holmby Avenue

A two-story stucco dwelling hidden behind a walled enclosure that provides privacy from the street and creates small, enclosed garden spaces within. As with many of Harris's dwellings where the garden and the house are really one, we are asked to read the dwelling as a series of separate fragments (as with a traditional Japanese house).

7. Mudd House, 1969
Roland E. Coate Jr.
420 Club View Drive

A formal wood-sheathed group of pavilions set inside a concrete wall and base with Corbu overtones. The interior spaces and the way in which they extend themselves to the outdoors is axial and Beaux-Arts.

8. Maslon House, 1970
Thornton M. Abell
10345 Strathmore Drive

A U-shaped stucco volume faces the street. To the rear and sides, the interior opens out through glass walls and doors to various terraces and gardens. The atmosphere, though Modern in image, is in fact quite classical.

9. Westwood-Ambassador Apartments, 1940
Milton J. Black
10427 Wilshire Boulevard

A textbook image of the Streamline Moderne before the Second World War, this two- and three-story, U-shaped stucco apartment building has horizontal groupings of windows going around the corners, along with curved bays and terraced walls. This architect designed many of Los Angeles's Streamline Moderne apartment buildings of the 1930s.

10. House, circa 1929
862 Malcolm Avenue

The avenues (not, it should be noted, streets) of Westwood curve in and out of the low hills both east and west of the UCLA campus. They are filled with excellent, well-designed, Period Revival houses of the 1920s and 1930s, all beautifully taken care of, including their grounds. In the 1920s the preference was for Spanish/Mediterranean, English Tudor, and French Norman; in the 1930s it was the Monterey and then the Anglo-Colonial Revival. All of these are present in the eastern section of the Westwood district. These houses illustrate how well the architects of that time could work with traditional images (in this case, English Tudor) and at the same time produce a functional house for an upper-middle-class family.

11. Garden Apartment Building, circa 1936
1001–1009 Malcolm Avenue

Streamline Moderne in a mild manner.

12. Monterey Garden Apartment Building,
circa 1930
James N. Conway
10840 Hilgard Avenue

A two-story garden apartment in the Monterey style, built around a central court. Another garden-apartment building is located at 10830 Hilgard Avenue. This one is mildly Spanish Revival (also circa 1930). South of Wilshire Boulevard at the northeast corner of Westwood Boulevard and Wilkins Avenue is a combined garden apartment and retail shop, designed in the Spanish Revival style (circa 1931; J. E. Dolena).

13. Ten-Five-Sixty Wilshire Boulevard, 1980–82
Maxwell Starkman and Associates
10560 Wilshire Boulevard

Wilshire Boulevard between the Los Angeles Country Club to the east and the San Diego Freeway to the west has, since the early 1960s, developed as a high-rise double-wall corridor of expensive condominium apartment buildings and office towers. It looks great from the air, but its effect on the nearby single-family houses and on Westwood Village itself is devastating. None of the tall apartment buildings or the office towers are outstanding in design, but several of them are so visually aggressive that it is difficult to ignore them. A case in point is this 108-unit, 22-story apartment building. The eight-cornered tower with its crowd of curved balconies does succeed in conveying a sense of transient luxury.

14. Church of St. Paul the Apostle, 1930–31
Newton and Murray
Southeast corner of Ohio and Selby Avenues

A classically reserved design, which the architects say they based on late eighteenth-century Spanish architecture. It is constructed of reinforced concrete with the exposed surfaces (inside and out) revealing the wood pattern of the forms.

15. Ralph Waldo Emerson Junior High School, 1937
Richard J. Neutra
1650 Selby Avenue

This is a project that you should walk around and through in order to get an idea of what was

going on in the 1930s in school design in California, and how Neutra responded to the California tradition of the open-air school. Though Neutra's design is out-and-out International Style, the plan of the building and of the site is really quite traditional (especially for California). Behind the two-story section of the complex are classrooms that open out to their own individual gardens through sliding glass doors.

16. Moore/Rogger/Hofflander Condominium Building, 1969–75
Charles W. Moore and Richard Chylinski
1725 Selby Avenue

A version of a Spanish Revival auto court. A ground-level fountain provides the entry theme of this remarkable building. From the street, one sees a cascading roof to the north interrupted by stepped dormers. To the south, one can see a curved grouping of windows (forming a pattern like spokes of a wheel) that ends in another roof dormer. It is close to impossible to know what is going on inside, which is part of the romance of this design. In fact, it is difficult to know that there are

three units in this building. Each of the units faces out to the west, away from the street, and each has walled terraces and balconies.

17. The Los Angeles Temple of The Church of Jesus Christ of Latter-day Saints (Mormon), 1955
Edward O. Anderson
10741 Santa Monica Boulevard

Described by one High Art observer as "Cocktail Lounge Moderne," it is on a scale that

would put any Sunset Boulevard lounge to shame. The design, in fact, could best be described as modernized Classical. A gold-leaf statue of the angel Moroni graces the summit of the building. The hilltop site is beautifully landscaped with a precisely manicured lawn and low shrubs. The building and its site form a completely unified composition. The Temple is best seen from the San Diego Freeway.

18. Psychoanalytic Building, 1968–69
Charles W. Moore and William Turnbull
1800 Fairburn Avenue

Driving along Little Santa Monica Boulevard, one can easily miss this gem, for its stucco volumes set behind the trees appear right at home in Los Angeles. A complex stage-set gateway composed of a single plane of stucco wall leads into an interior courtyard. Double walls make you wonder what is building and what is screen.

19. Bungalow Court ("The Grove"), 1932, 1940
Allen Siple, Edla Muir
10500 Santa Monica Boulevard

The front group of bungalows was designed by Allen Siple, while the rear two bungalows were designed in 1940 by Edla Muir. A romantic group of English cottages, actually situated in a thick grove of trees—easily missed if you sail by at thirty-five miles an hour.

20. The Barn, 1955
A. Quincy Jones; restored, 1996
Frederick Fisher and Partners
10300 Santa Monica Boulevard

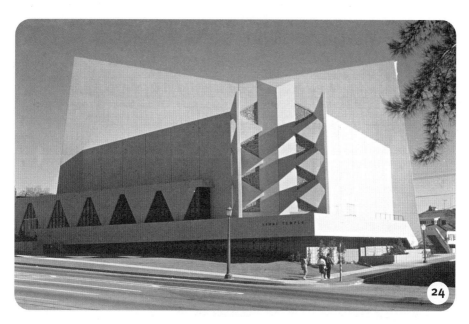

Quincy Jones's two-and-a-half-story "Barn" served as a place of work, of entertaining, and of living. It is a remodeled structure, though you would not know it once you were inside and able to experience the wonderful central space of the building. As with the best of Quincy Jones's work, it is not openly assertive. But its sense of proportions and detailing make it wear very well.

21. Westwood Hills Congregational Church, 1928
Northwest corner of Westwood Boulevard and LaGrange Avenue

A small Spanish Revival church coupled with some suggestions in detailing of the Art Deco.

22. Kelton-Missouri Townhouses, 1980
Mutlow-Dimster Partnership
10925 Missouri Avenue

The basic forms of this building look back to the Dutch and German International Style housing of the 1920s. But there are other features, such as the stepped-window patterns and the greenhouse elements, which are pure late 1970s and early 1980s.

23. Feitler House, 1993–94
Siegal Diamond Architects
10346 Mississippi Avenue

From the street, the visual impact of this dwelling is that of a late 1920s International Style box that has been split open in the middle by a heavy angled wall and an attached segment of a glass bowl with canted sides. The stucco wall to the left of the entrance exhibits a vertical irregular cut to emphasize even more the split nature of the design. The angled space created by this central wall is a living hall that projects through the whole house and terminates in a private rear terrace.

24. Sinai Temple, 1956
Sidney Eisenstadt
10400 Wilshire Boulevard, at Beverly Glen Westwood

Eisenstadt was a student of Frank Lloyd Wright. This is clear when you look at the entrance to this building, but Eisenstadt makes his own statement. The interior is impressive with superb stained-glass windows.

The recent (1999) addition of a school and dining facilities by Mehrdad Yazdani with Dworsky Associates is a kind of compromise between the Wrightian aesthetic and Postmodernism. Although well done, it does make you question compromises in architecture—also the relevance of Frank Lloyd Wright to contemporary architecture.

25 • University of California, Los Angeles (UCLA)

The University of California, Los Angeles, was established as a State Normal School in 1881 on a five-acre site in downtown Los Angeles, where the Central Los Angeles Public Library is now situated. In 1919 it became a two-year southern campus of UC, and in 1924 it became a four-year school and was named UCLA. The institution's second location, a site at Vermont and Heliotrope Avenues, was felt to be far too small for the projected major institution. In 1925 the site in Westwood was selected, and the cities of Los Angeles, Beverly Hills, Santa Monica, and Venice voted bonds to purchase the land. The new campus then became an element in the Janss Corporation development of Westwood. It was to be surrounded by single-family residences (with some multiple housing) on the east, north, and west sides and was to adjoin the commercial district of Westwood Village to the south.

San Francisco architect George W. Kelham was engaged in 1925 to prepare a master plan for the Westwood campus. For this hilly site, Kelham developed a dramatic cross-axial Beaux-Arts scheme. The main axis ran east/west from Hilgard to Westwood Boulevard. The hilly irregular site provided the drama of terraces and steps leading down the west side of the hill to Westwood Boulevard. To the east a small arroyo created a contrasting English Romantic garden element, and over this, Kelham placed a bridge (this bridge was the first structure erected on the UCLA Campus; it now lies buried between the north and south sections of the filled-in Dickinson Plaza). A circle on Westwood Boulevard created the major north/south axis.

The architect's initial plan called for forty buildings, and he and the Regents "chose red brick Romanesque architecture of Milan and Genoa because Westwood's rolling hills and gentle climate were reminiscent of northern Italy." The selection of Northern Italian Romanesque for the Westwood campus was not, as the quote would seem to imply, based upon a careful look into appropriate styles. Italian Romanesque in brick was a fashionable style for educational buildings in all of California during the teens and 1920s. Also, it was the style that had been used in the teens by Allison and Allison for the Vermont Avenue campus of the university. By 1932 ten buildings (in addition to the bridge) had been completed at the Westwood campus.

To help create the Italian image, John W. Greg, a well-known Bay Area landscape architect and professor of landscape architecture at Berkeley, was engaged to work with Kelham. He presented his plan in 1928, and this was followed through the mid-1930s.

During the depression years of the 1930s, only a few buildings were built. Kelham remained as supervising architect until his death in 1935 when he was replaced by Allison and Allison (David C. Allison). After World War II, David C. Allison and landscape architect Ralph D. Cornell prepared a revision of the Kelham plan. Retaining its essential ingredients, they still argued for low-rise buildings. They did, though, suggest the filling-in of the arroyo in 1947, which in part now includes Dickson Court and Plaza, so as to obtain additional building sites. Their most far-reaching recommendation was to locate the Health Science (Medical School) on the Westwood campus, rather than to separate it, as UC Berkeley had done. This decision and the ideal of having a 25,000-plus student campus eventually led to immense buildings and the commitment to moderate high-rise.

In 1948 the firm of Wurdeman and Becket was appointed as supervising architects (the title was changed to consulting architects). After the death of William Wurdeman, Welton Becket and Associates continued as consulting architects through 1968. It was during the immediate post–World War II years that the decision was made to abandon the commitment to the historicism of the Northern Italian Romanesque and to embrace the "Modern." At first the Modern was approached in a general but skillful fashion through the style we associate with the designs of Eliel Saarinen. This approach can be seen in such buildings as the first Dickson Art Building (now the School of Architecture and Urban Planning, 1952; Paul Robinson Hunter). Later, variations of the 1950s International Style were employed. Today it is very difficult to discover anything positive to say about these buildings. The pileup of buildings comprising the Court of Sciences and the Medical Center is as depressing a grouping as you can find (and it becomes more so with age). To the west on the hillside above the athletic field is a group of four high-rise dormitories (1959–64; Welton Becket and Associates), which go far in marring this side of the campus and the adjacent residential district north of Sunset Boulevard.

The principal saving grace of the old campus is the landscaping. In 1937 landscape architect Ralph D. Cornell was appointed. He and his firm continued to develop the campus until his death in 1972. Cornell's firm—Cornell, Bridgers, Troller, and Hazlett—has continued to work on campus landscaping since 1972 with Jere H. Hazlett as the official landscape architect. While all the landscaping efforts have not been able to hide the tragedies of unfortunate planning and buildings, they have been able to create, throughout the campus, pockets of space that are pleasant, visible, and in many instances, beautiful.

Since the mid-1970s, a new group of good buildings has appeared, including Frank O. Gehry and Associates' Student Placement and Career Planning Center (1976–77); Daniel L. Dworsky and Associates' UCLA Parking Structure (1979–80); Venturi, Scott-Brown & Associates' (with Payette Associates') Gordon and Virginia MacDonald Medical Research Laboratories (1991–92), and others. Beginning in the 1980s, a number of the older buildings on the campus were subjected to seismic retrofitting. These include Royce Hall, Powell Library, Moore Hall, Haines Hall, Kerckoff Hall, and others.

With the grouping of newer buildings toward the southwest section of the campus and the closing of Westwood Boulevard, it was evident that a new entrance should be provided. In 1991 the firm of Hodgetts + Fung Design Associates did a master plan for the new UCLA Gateway and then instituted its first phase. This consisted of entrance kiosks and a pavilion, a pool, plus soft and hard landscaping. This new entrance leads off of Westwood Boulevard and Le Conte Avenue.

To a large degree the present renaissance of architecture at UCLA is due to the campus architect, Charles Warner Oakley. Through his efforts the current architectural scene at UCLA is encouraging, both in the general overall quality of the new buildings and exterior spaces and the sensitivity to the difficult task of retrofitting and revamping the older buildings. We hope that the new campus architect, Natalie Shivers, will continue this good work.

Obtain a map at the entrance kiosk:

1. Royce Hall, 1928–29
Allison and Allison
(David Allison)

Royce Hall set the stage for the adaptation of the Lombardian Romanesque style for the campus. The design of this building was inspired by the Church of St. Ambrosio in Milan, with side glances at other northern Italian churches: details gathered from the Cathedral of SS Pietro e Paolo, the Church of Il Santissimo Crocifisso, the Church of St. Sepolcro, and others. It was noted in 1930 that Royce Hall "shows an almost complete symposium of the Romanesque-Italian school of architecture."

The open loggias to each side were originally intended to connect with adjoining buildings. The siting of this building by Kelham and Allison and Allison

illustrated how these architects were seeking to convey the image of UCLA as a Lombardian hilltop town. The court between Royce Hall and the Library Building to the south, along with the terraces and stairs leading down to Westwood Boulevard, convey an attempt to combine the picturesqueness of an Italian city with Beaux-Arts axial planning. In 1983–84 Royce Hall was restored and seismically retrofitted by John Carl Warnecke and Associates. After the 1994 earthquake it had to be restored again by Barton Phelps and Associates and Anshen and Allen.

2. The Powell Undergraduate Library, 1927–29
George W. Kelham

Italian Romanesque realized in reinforced concrete and steel with a skin of brick and terra-cotta (manufactured by Gladding

McBean and Company). As with Royce Hall, specific northern Italian Romanesque buildings inspired portions of the design: the central dome was derived from San Ambrosio, while the Church of St. Sepolcro was a source for parts of the interior. The library contains one of the best interiors in the style. Much of the interior was decorated by Julian Ellsworth Garnsey. Especially impressive is the interior of the dome of the main reading room.

In 1947 Earl T. Heitschmidt and Charles O. Matcham added a three-story wing at the southeast corner of the building. Though somewhat simplified, this new wing essentially carried on the style of the existing building. Eleven years later, in 1958, Modernism triumphed over traditionalism in an infill stucco box that was inserted between the two south wings by Albert C. Martin and Associates. The library has undergone seismic retrofitting and restoration by Moore, Ruble and Yudell. Notable is the renewal of the main reading room.

3. Haines Hall, 1928
George W. Kelham

A continuation of the Italian Romanesque image.

4. Physics-Biology Building, 1928–29
Allison and Allison

A version of modernized Romanesque, more picturesque than Kelham's usual approach to this style.

5. Moore Hall of Education, 1930
George W. Kelham

Italian Romanesque with major emphasis placed on the east and south doorways. One of what were a pair of auditoriums on the south side of the building (room 100) has been restored as part of the seismic retrofitting. You can now see its wood-paneled walls and its stenciled, beamed, and gabled ceiling. The firm of Brenda Levin was the historic architectural consultant for the restoration.

6. Kerckoff Hall, 1930
Allison and Allison
(Austin Whittlesey)

A lone Gothic building designed in this style, partly because of the donor's insistence, partly because Berkeley's Student Union (1923; John Galen Howard) was Gothic in style. For a long time UCLA fell in the shadow of Berkeley.

7. Ackerman Union Building, 1959–60
Welton Becket and Associates

A late 1950s modular Modernist box equipped with sun grilles. In case you may have missed the thoughtful contextual relationship between the old and the new, the building was (according to an article of the time) "carefully related to its predecessor [Kerckoff Hall] through the use of related materials." In 1996 Rebecca Binder designed an addition, which not only adds space to the existing building but more sensitively reorganizes its presence on Westwood Plaza.

8. University Residence (Chancellor's House), 1930
Reginald D. Johnson

A northern Italian Villa, exhibiting Johnson's customary sophistication and reserve.

9. Mira Hershey Residence Hall, 1930
Douglas McLelland

Spanish Revival rather than the usual brick Italian Romanesque. This complex, with its courtyards, low scale, and planting, is one of the most successful buildings on the campus.

10. Men's Gymnasium, 1932
George W. Kelham

This building and the Women's Gymnasium to the south form the lower terrace grouping for Kelham's main axis.

11. Anderson Graduate School of Management, 1994
Pei Cobb Freed and Partners (Henry Cobb);
Leidenfrost Horowitz Associates

Big and solid, as a business school should be, this continues the Corporate Moderne image of the Pei firm. It is enlivened by a monumental central court.

12. Business Administration and Economics Building, 1948
John C. Austin

One of the last efforts in the use of the Italian Romanesque style on the campus. As with the earlier buildings, it is sheathed in patterns of brick with limestone trim. The corner tower was designed to contain the mechanical and boiler facilities of the building. In 1992, a new addition to this building had been completed, returning in this instance to the imagery of the Italian Romanesque style.

13. Dickson Art Building (now School of Architecture and Urban Planning Building), 1952
Paul Robinson Hunter

This building attempts to play the game of being twentieth-century Modern and Classical at the same time. It works reasonably well to the south, but the rest tends to be bland, especially the original interiors. The influence of Eliel Saarinen is clear in this and other buildings, such as the following one.

14. Schoenberg Hall, 1955
Welton Becket and Associates

Schoenberg Hall mirrors the influence of Eliel Saarinen. Above the exterior foyer of the building is a 164-foot mosaic mural by Richard Haines. In sixteen panels he depicts the history of music through the ages.

15. East Building: Corinne A. Seeds University Elementary School, 1990–93
Barton Phelps and Associates

Neutra and Alexander's 1957–59 building has been replaced by this new complex. It is situated behind and up the hillside next to one of Ralph Cornell's gardens (1954). The two-story building is slightly curved and is broken in the center by a wide passageway and waiting area. It is dug into the hill so that the upper level is on ground level. The buildings are of concrete block, steel, and glass, designed so as to maintain a sense of intimacy for the users and for the site.

16. Faculty Center, 1959
Hutchinson and Hutchinson

A woodsy California ranch house. The interiors are pleasant, as are the gardens around the building, but it has none of the vigor of a Cliff May design.

17. Bunche Hall, 1964
Maynard Lyndon

The size of the structure and its walk-through scale are poorly related to the adjacent older buildings. Both in fact and symbolically, the design of the building consciously separates the students and the faculty by putting lecture and discussion facilities in a separate structure. When the faculty members get on the elevators to go to their offices, they divorce themselves from their teaching function. Mary Holmes, a former member of the faculty, aptly called the building "death on little pig's feet."

18. Bradley International
Center, 1997
Ricardo Legoretta

This building stands out from the mediocre to ugly dormitories near it, partly because of its good design and also because of its striking dusty pink color.

19. University Research
Library, 1967
Jones and Emmons

A modest nonassertive Modernist building that is very pleasant to work in.

20. Sunset Canyon
Recreation Facility, 1964
Smith and Williams

This building climbs up its steep hillside site to create an impression of a child's elaborate tree house

21. Northwest Campus
Housing and Commons, 1992
Barton Myers Associates;
Antoine Predock Architects;
Esherick, Homsey,
Dodge and Davis;
Gensler Architecture

The Commons Building and the adjacent housing unit were designed by the Myers firm; Predock's housing units, organized around a triangular courtyard are to the west; and the Esherick, Homsey, Dodge and Davis section lies to the north. The Commons Building makes very direct references to the Classical tradition; the housing

is all mildly Modernist but very reserved. The Esherick units are the most domestic in their scale and detailing. The site design of the complex responds well to the terrain and to the scale needed in student housing.

22. UCLA Childcare Center
1987
Charles and Elizabeth Lee
Southeast corner
Sunset Boulevard and
Veteran Avenue

Though these low, one-story structures were prefabricated off-site, they illustrate how such buildings, with great care in design, can turn out very well. Within the modular post-and-beam system, the architects have placed window units, doors, and solid panels.

23. Chiller/Cogeneration
Plant, 1994
Holt Hinshaw Pfau Jones
(Wes Jones)

The Machine Image, naturally; this is also very colorful and certainly not hidden away.

24. Murphy Sculpture Court,
1969
**Cornell, Bridgers, and Troller,
landscape architects**

Perhaps the landscaping will
eventually block out the adjacent
buildings so that this space will
really have the sense of a court in
which are placed freestanding
sculptures. Major pieces are by
Henry Moore, Jacques Lipschitz,
Louis H. Sullivan, and many
other important sculptors.

25. Student Placement and
Career Planning Center,
1976–77
Frank O. Gehry and Associates

This small-scaled, long low box
is loosely International Style.
Gehry's delight in exposing the
equipment and structure harkens
back to the Smithsons and the
English New Brutalists of the
mid-1950s. The suggestion of a
building as a machine also ties
the design into Los Angeles's own
version of the High Tech image
of the late 1970s and early
1980s. The building is well snug-
gled into its landscaped site, and
the interior spaces have a comfortable easy-going scale.

26. UCLA Hospital Parking
Structure, 1979–80
**Daniel Dworsky
and Associates**

Certain parts of this reinforced
concrete parking structure are
pure Brutalism—quite impressive as sculpture, especially the
top roof deck's layer effect.
Other sections of the structure
are, as John Dreyfuss of the *Los
Angeles Times* noted, "tediously
fortress-like."

27. Gordon and Virginia
MacDonald Medical Research
Laboratories, 1991–92
**Venturi, Scott-Brown
& Associates;
Payette Associates**

Venturi described this six-story
structure as a loft space "wrapped
with a brick skin." It is similar in
design approach to the firm's earlier Lewis Thomas Laboratories at
Princeton University. On the
northwest side, a primitive Doric
column holds the figure of a
cutout bear. Behind this column,
stairs and a ramp for the handi-

capped ascend to the building's
forecourt. The south side of the
forecourt is contained by a pergola, reminiscent in many ways
of the design of Joseph Hoffman
at the turn of the century in
Vienna. On the west side of
the forecourt Venturi and Scott-
Brown (with Lee Burkhart Liu)
have designed and built an
equally handsome Gonda
(Goldschmied) Neuroscience
and Genetics Research Building
(1998).

A new hospital by the Pei partnership is projected for 2004.

26 • Beverly Hills, North

Beverly Hills, entirely surrounded by the city and county of Los Angeles, lies on the land known in the early nineteenth century as the Rancho Rodeo de las Aguas, the "gathering of waters" from present-day Benedict, Coldwater, and other canyons near the site of what is now the Beverly Hills Hotel. In the 1850s and 1860s, the Yankees—with Benjamin Wilson, Henry Hancock, William Workman, James Whitworth, and Edson A. Benedict in the lead—took over land development and speculation. Several attempts to found a city were made. A German colony was planned in the 1860s, the only remnant of which is Los Angeles Avenue, now Wilshire Boulevard. Until the 1880s the area's chief contribution to

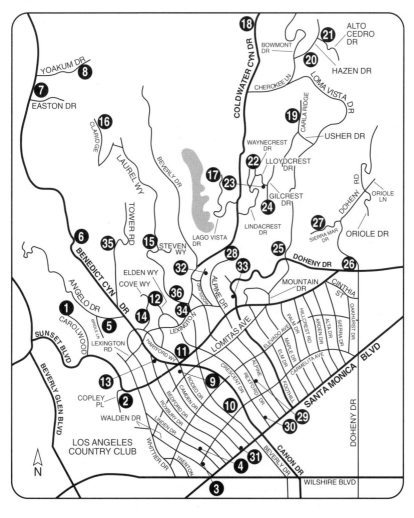

civilization was lima beans.

In the 1887 land boom, the town of Morocco was platted, but with the economic collapse the next year, the real estate promoters' dream fizzled. The founding finally occurred in 1906 when the Rodeo Land and Water Company, under the leadership of Burton E. Green, conceived of a city for the swells, very much the way Beverly Hills has developed. Landscape architect and planner Wilbur Cook (assisted by architect Myron Hunt) planned the present business area with a grid running at forty-five-degree angles north from Wilshire Boulevard. He laid out the gently curving streets between Santa Monica and Sunset Boulevards. In the hills north of Sunset, the Olmsted Brothers set out streets that undulated picturesquely with equally undulating streets crossing them. The result of this plan is that driving, especially at the six-way intersection of Canon Drive, Beverly Drive, and Lomitas Avenue, can be very interesting.

In 1912 the extremely fashionable Beverly Hills Hotel was built on Sunset Boulevard just above this intersection, and fine houses, most of them on surprisingly small lots, were soon appearing all around. It is usually assumed that these houses were built by the motion-picture crowd, since so many stars live in them now. Actually, the first owners were usually lawyers, doctors, oil men, or wealthy retired people from the frigid zones. It is remarkable how few of these houses, most of them in the varied styles of the 1920s, have strong architectural or landscape distinction. They are pleasant and highly visible, but not outstanding. It is only when you get into the radically winding streets in the hills that you will discover distinguished buildings and gardens—some the Modernist work of Neutra, Schindler, Ain, and Harris, and an array of talented architects who employed period revival images.

The commercial section in the city below Santa Monica Boulevard was originally the strong mixture of Spanish Revival and Art Deco that you would expect. Some dazzlers still remain. But the business section has, since the mid-1960s, literally been transformed by high-rise. Some of it, particularly the most recent, has real artistic merit.

As with other upper-middle-class enclaves in Southern California, it is the landscape architecture that makes the place. The impressive rows of palms and other trees along the wide curved streets are mainly due to the efforts of landscape architect, Raymond E. Page, who was involved in planting them from 1919 through the early 1950s.

1. Frederick Weisman Collection ("Art Pavilion"), 1991
Franklin D. Israel Design Associates
275 N. Carolwood Drive

A classic (in proportions and scale) almost Japanese-like pavilion sits atop a masonry wall and is surrounded by terraces on three sides. There are episodes, such as the large corner windows, that are related to the work of Frank Lloyd Wright and R. M. Schindler in Los Angeles in the 1920s. The main floor of the building is a single gallery space, 28-feet high, with the wood timber trusses of the roof left exposed. A fanciful boat-like balcony projects off the garden side of the building.

2. Helms House, 1933
Gordon B. Kaufmann
135 Copley Place

A beautifully and carefully proportioned Spanish dwelling, accompanied by terraces, pools, and a summer house.

3. Spadena House, 1921
Henry Oliver
Southeast corner of Carmelita Avenue and Walden Drive

Originally designed in Culver City as a movie set and office for Irvin V. Willst Productions, this masterpiece of the Hansel and Gretel mode was moved to a respectable neighborhood and set in an unconventional garden that matches it beautifully. Apparently it has always been occupied by people who understand and respect its overwhelming madness.

4. Menzies House, 1926
William Cameron
604 N. Linden Drive

Tudor with flamboyant stucco enrichment in the gable.

5. Gate House ("Doll's House"), circa 1925
1808 Angelo Drive

A medieval cottage too sweet for words.

6. Heidemann House, 1972
Pulliam, Matthews, and Associates
1236 Benedict Canyon Drive

An award-winning example of the cut-into box. Almost monumental.

7. Vorkapich Garden House, 1938; Gregory Ain
2100 Benedict Canyon Drive, just north of Easton Drive

A small modular plywood house. Here Ain was exploring the idea of prefabricated structure, though it should be noted that the statement of the house as prefabricated architecture is more symbolic than real.

8. Hale House, 1949
Craig Ellwood & Associates
9618 Yoakum Drive

A single-story Miesian box on stilts.

9. O'Neill House and Pavilion, 1978–84
Santa Monica Architectural Group (Tom Oswald)
507 N. Rodeo Drive

The most dramatic structure of this complex is the pavilion that can be seen from the alley behind 507 N. Rodeo Drive. Eighty years too late, but here is Los Angeles's first real Art Nouveau building—Gaudiesque in the extreme.

10. Forrest House, 1930–31
Roland E. Coate
612 N. Beverly Drive

The columned porch suggests both the nineteenth-century one-story Monterey house and the later California ranch house. As befitting its location in Beverly Hills, the Forrest House signals respectability.

11. Beverly Hills Hotel, 1911–12
Elmer Grey
9600 Sunset Boulevard

Old photographs reveal a rambling version of the then-popular version of the Mission style. Aesthetically, a great deal has been lost in remodelings and additions, but the building and its lovely garden setting still evoke genteel hospitality. The first extensive additions to the hotel were designed in 1946–47 by Leonard Schultze and Associates of New York and Earl T. Heitschmidt and Charles O. Matcham of Los Angeles. In 1959 Paul R. William and Associates remodeled portions of the building, adding a new elegance to it.

12. Robinson House and Garden, 1911, 1924
Nathaniel Dryden; Charles Gibbs Adams, landscape architect
1008 Elden Way

While the Beaux-Arts Classical house is impressive, the 1924 pavilion is the most elegant building on the site. The real glory of the place is in the gardens laid out by Pasadena landscape architect Charles Gibbs Adams, who provided an axis that aligned the house, lawn, pool, and pavilion. The rest of the six-acre estate is arranged in a more informal fashion. The estate was willed by Virgina Robinson to Los Angeles County as a botanical garden. It is open by appointment only: (310) 276-5367.

13. Anthony House, 1909
Charles and Henry Greene
*910 Bedford Drive, at
Benedict Canyon Drive*

It is significant that Earle C. Anthony, who monopolized the Packard agencies in California, would employ Bernard Maybeck to do his showrooms in San Francisco and Oakland and get the Greenes to design the interiors of his showroom (demolished) in Los Angeles and his first house, which once stood at the corner of Wilshire and Berendo. When relationships changed (Charles Greene sold his Packard and bought a Hudson), Anthony got Maybeck to design a castle for him near Griffith Park and a large addition to his showroom (also demolished). The Greene and Greene house has been conscientiously restored by the owners, and is worthy of comparison with its contemporaries, the Gamble and Blacker-Hill houses in Pasadena. The Kerrys, who moved the house to its present site, got Henry Greene to design walls and garden appointments in 1925. A real surprise in an area mainly developed in the revivals of the 1920s.

14. Familian House, 1971
John Lautner
1011 Cove Way

A huge house of stone cairns and wood, just as startling (in a different way) as the Greenes' Anthony House, not far away.

15. Quen House, 1959
Ladd and Kelsey
1211 Laurel Way

Except for the fact that it is all white, this house would pass for the Craftsman style.

16. Epstein House, 1988–89
Barton Phelps and Associates
1462 Claridge Drive

The architect wrote of this house that it "takes a middle route between sculptural fragmentation and the traditional unified exterior envelope." There is a suggestion of Schindler and of Soriano in this design. The entrance is under the house (by the garage) into a garden. Grand steps lead up to the main floor of the house; above are bedrooms and a study.

17. English House, 1950
Harwell H. Harris
1261 Lago Vista Drive

A large house whose architect was inspired by Frank Lloyd Wright—in this case almost as if the Hollyhock House had been divested of ornament. The effect is stunning.

18. Three Houses, 1976
Tom Roberts
*2433, 2439, 2445
Coldwater Canyon Drive*

A 1970s version of High Tech. All was once painted a pristine white. Walls and fences have been added.

19. Model House for the Trousdale Development Company, 1965
Rex Lotery
1875 Carla Ridge

A glass horizontal wood-and-stucco dwelling built as a model house for this section of Beverly Hills. The high volume of the major living space is countered at right angles by the much lower service wing and accompanying carports. In the instance of this house, Modernism takes on an elegance of materials and detailing that is associated with Beverly Hills.

20. Rourke House, 1949
Richard J. Neutra
9228 Hazen Drive, off Coldwater Canyon Drive onto Cherokee Lane, then Bowmont Drive, then Hazen Drive

Post-and-beam, stucco with wood trim. Neutra's famous spider-legs (bents) arch the entrance corridor.

21. Rodakiewicz House, 1937
R. M. Schindler
9121 Alto Cedro Drive (beyond Rourke House, right on Alto Cedro Drive; view obtained above on Alto Cedro Drive if you go beyond the house, now obscured by a tennis court)

Here, with plenty of money to spend, Schindler unleashed all the powers of his romantic vision of De Stijl. This is a classic. It was once set in a tropical rain forest, but the present tennis court pretty much wiped that out.

22. Grossman House, 1949
Greta Magnusson Grossman
1659 Waynecrest Drive

A simple Modern brown box sheathed in vertical board-and-batten.

23. Schulitz House, 1977
Helmut Schulitz
(Urban Innovations Group)
9356 Lloydcrest Drive, near the southwest corner of Gilcrest Drive

Another spin-off from Charles Eames's Case Study House in Santa Monica Canyon. The aesthetic of scarcity can go no further.

24. Miller House, 1948
Ain, Johnson, and Day
1634 Gilcrest Drive

Very expressionistic for Ain, the roof angles just every which way. A really handsome house, easy to see.

25. Doheny House ("Greystone"), 1925–28
Gordon B. Kaufmann;
Paul Thiene,
landscape architect
905 Loma Vista Drive Greystone Park

Tudor and Jacobean on the grandest possible scale. The house is no longer open except on rare occasions, but the glorious gardens are open every day, 10:00 A.M.–5:00 P.M.

Farther up Loma Vista Drive is the housing development, much of it on formerly Doheny land, called Trousdale Estates. It is essentially spec housing for the rich. Although there seems to be a strong predilection for the Neoclassical, all styles exist here. Everything is so wrong it forms a kind of unity.

26. Commercial Building,
circa 1935
9169 Sunset Boulevard

Rather elegant Streamline Moderne.

27. Sierra Mar House, 1991
Michael W. Folonis
and Associates
9443 Sierra Mar Drive

This remodeled building is composed of two parts: the lower floor covered by a low-pitched shed roof and the upper floor whose curved forms suggest the bridge of an ocean liner. Though the new upper level has a strong

visual presence, it certainly fulfilled the architects' goal of acknowledging "the character of the existing structure in scale and style." The new second floor was made possible by a steel frame that was inserted into the existing wood-frame dwelling.

28. Parker House, 1951
Paul Sterling Hoag
959 N. Alpine Drive

A house sheathed in stone and wood, in an abstract way reminiscent of Pennsylvania Dutch houses of the eighteenth century.

29. Hawthorne School, 1929
Ralph C. Flewelling
624 N. Rexford Drive

This exposed concrete building, with the impression of the board forms retained, is Spanish Revival. The tower, capped with a dome of glazed colored tiles, and the two-story entrance portico off the courtyard are the focal points.

30. Howland House, 1933–34
Lloyd Wright
502 Crescent Drive

This house is a radical remodeling

of a simple stucco box. The exterior is as restrained as the interior is flamboyant.

31. All Saints Episcopal Church, 1925
Roland E. Coate
Northeast corner of Santa Monica Boulevard and Camden Drive

The extensive areas of plain uninterrupted walls and the restrained historical detail of this church show how close some aspects of the Spanish Revival were to the "new" architecture then developing in Europe and America.

32. Kritzer House, 1966
Rex Lotery
1030 Woodland Drive

Looking up from the road you see the low hovering roof of the house, below which is the white stucco face of a projecting balcony deck. The aesthetic feel of the house is Frank Lloyd Wright abstracted, including the tent-like ceiling of the living room.

33. Schacker House, 1956
Rex Lotery
917 N. Foothill Drive

The centerpiece of this dwelling is a story-and-a-half glass volume that houses the entrance and principal living space. Off of this project the secondary wings of the house, including the garage. The recent remodeling by the architect (1992–93) has both changed and brought the house back to its original condition. Walls have now been stuccoed, and a low wall separates the dwelling from the street.

34. Pendleton House, 1942
John Woolf
1032 Beverly Drive

A mansard-roofed Regency Moderne house with urns in niches at each side of the colonnaded entrance, this is a fine example of what John Chase calls "exterior decoration."

35. Imerman House, 1936
Wallace Neff
1143 Tower Road

Like so many houses in Beverly Hills and Bel Air, the Imerman house is not easy to see from the public road, but it is a Neff gem. The impression of the house is that a drawing from a children's storybook of the 1920s has been enlarged and made real. An immense hipped roof bears down on thin low walls, and small dormers pop out of the roof surface. At the entrance, the dominant images are two of Neff's very tall trademark chimneys.

36. House, 1983–84
Kamran Khauakani
1081 Laurel Way

Paired Ionic columns grace this enormous testimony to the fact that Beverly Hills will always remain the same—too much!

27 • Beverly Hills, South

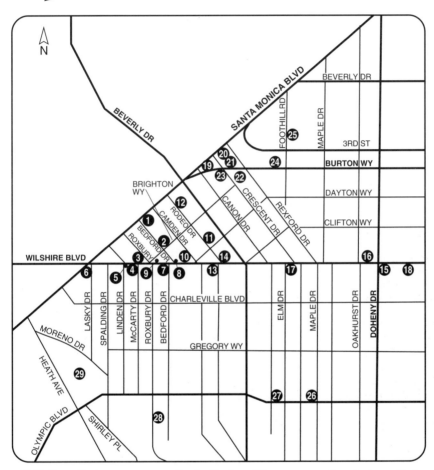

1. Wells Fargo Bank, 1973
Sidney Eisenstadt
9600 Little Santa Monica Boulevard

The architect's unusual way with glass creates the illusion that each floor of his multistory building is cantilevered over the one below. Note also the entrance court with fountain supporting Jack Zajac's Swan IV (1971–73).

2. Barclay Bank and Shops, 1973
Kahn, Kappe, and Lotery
Northeast corner of Brighton Way and Bedford Drive

It is fascinating to find Kappe's ideas, usually seen in domestic building, applied to downtown architecture. The result is a pleasant relief from the usually bland Modernism of the late International Style.

3. Manufacturers Bank, 1973
Daniel, Mann, Johnson, and Mendenhall
Northwest corner of Wilshire Boulevard and Roxbury Drive

A very large building encased in a curtain of black glass undulates around the corner. It has won much applause from people whose taste was jaded by the dry International Style tradition.

4. Perpetual Savings Bank,
1962
Edward D. Stone
Southwest corner of
Wilshire Boulevard and
McCarty Drive

A steel-caged high-rise encased in a shell of vaguely Moorish arches. The result, with window-boxes trailing real vines, is best described as "Venetian Modern."

5. Nieman-Marcus Store, 1981
John Carl Warnecke Associates
9700 Wilshire Boulevard

Both the travertine monolith exterior and the spatially elegant interior completely express the essence of the Beverly Hills grand manner—and by a Frisco firm at that.

6. Creative Artist Agency,
1989
Pei, Cobb Freed and Partners (I. M. Pei);
Langdon and Wilson,
associate architects
Southeast corner of
Santa Monica Boulevard and
Lasky Drive

Three separate Modernist fragments confront viewers as they drive by on Santa Monica Boulevard. The focal point of Pei's design is the impressive semicircular glass-roofed atrium. Both inside and outside the detailing is elegant and expensive. It all adds up to the excessively precious. The most lively element is a huge mural by Roy Lichtenstein, which dominates the 57-foot-high travertine wall of the atrium.

7. I. Magnin and Company
Store, 1939
Myron Hunt and
H. C. Chambers

Southwest corner of
Wilshire Boulevard and
Bedford Drive

Classical Moderne, very refined.

8. Security Pacific Place, 1969
Craig Ellwood & Associates
Northeast corner of
Wilshire Boulevard and
Bedford Drive

Black Miesian austerity softened somewhat by a plaza and sculpture. The small matching State Savings Bank (1972–73) is also by Ellwood.

9. Saks Fifth Avenue Store,
circa 1936–37
John and Donald B. Parkinson;
Paul R. Williams
9600 Wilshire Boulevard

Elegant Hollywood Regency with enough curved surface to suggest that the 1930s Streamline Moderne could be elegant.

10. Frank Perls Gallery,
circa 1948
Alvin Lustig
350 N. Camden Drive

The International Style given Beverly Hills classiness by a talented designer of the postwar years.

11. Anderton Court, 1953–54
Frank Lloyd Wright
328 Rodeo Drive

Said not to have been carried out precisely according to Wright's plans. It is as if the Guggenheim ramp had been zigzagged and shops put along it. This building by The Master has received little publicity, probably because it is one of his zaniest productions. The ramp winds its way around a central metal mast; somewhat nautical and Streamline Moderne are the groupings of round windows.

12. Rodeo Collection, 1980–82
Le Sopha
Group/Environmetrics, Inc.
(Olivier Vidal)
421 N. Rodeo Drive

A collection of stores perhaps more notable for its opulence than good taste. Tall arches and oversized round windows face Rodeo Drive. The shops are arranged around a sunken courtyard. The architectural theme seems to wander from Classicism to the Art Deco and the Modern, richly incoherent.

13. Beverly-Wilshire Hotel,
1926
Walker and Eisen
Southwest corner of
Rodeo Drive and
Wilshire Boulevard

The Italian Renaissance strained through Beaux-Arts ideas by a very productive Los Angeles firm. The hotel is very grand. In 1990 it received new interiors by Glen Texierra Project Associates.

14. Two Rodeo Drive, 1989–90
Kaplin, McLaughlin and Diaz
Northeast corner of
Rodeo Drive and
Wilshire Boulevard

You need not go all the way to London to experience a British retail street. The curved street of Two Rodeo Drive, lined by twenty-six two- and three-story buildings, provides visitors with a much-improved version of what they would encounter in England. Each of the stores is different, intending to reflect not only different styles but also different moments of the past. The curved street rises abruptly from Rodeo Drive. Underneath is an extensive parking garage. At the Wilshire end of the street, formal steps lead down to a fountain.

Proponents of serious architecture have called it a theme park in the manner of Disneyland.

15. Coast Savings Office Building, 1987
Wilshire Boulevard
Southeast corner of Wilshire Boulevard and Doheny Drive

Perhaps late-fifteenth-century buildings of the Florentine Renaissance were on the architect's mind when he designed this building. All of these historic fragments have been wonderfully enlarged and marvelously misconstrued.

16. Kate Mantilini Restaurant, 1985
Morphosis
(Thom Mayne and Michael Rotondi)
9101 Wilshire Boulevard

Mostly light gray with darker gray accents, this well-proportioned pavilion seems to be a parody (of sorts) on Mies. The interior plays a wonderful and lighthearted game of High Tech. The interior and the façade is the result of a remodel.

17. Columbia Savings and Loan (I), 1987
Skidmore, Owings and Merrill/Los Angeles
(Richard Keating)
Southeast corner of Wilshire Boulevard and Elm Drive

This three-story building is an elegant modernist stage set. Richard Keating, who designed the building, commented that it and the La Peer Drive Building up the way on Wilshire ". . . are meant to read scenographically, as floating façades, skin-deep movie-set 'flats' over which the eye may slide in passing."

18. Columbia Savings and Loan (II), 1987
Skidmore, Owings and Merrill/Los Angeles
(Richard Keating)
8942 Wilshire Boulevard

Another elegant Modernist stage set. The façade is organized around a group of three metal drums that suggest a space station. Beyond the drums is a courtyard that exhibits an excess of over-refined, machine-like detailing.

19. Beverly Hills Post Office, 1932–33
Ralph C. Flewelling; Allison and Allison
Southeast corner of Canon Drive and Santa Monica Boulevard

Although the building was much admired when completed, some civic leaders felt that it was too domestic and not public and monumental enough. A beautiful rendition of the Italian Renaissance in terra-cotta and brick. Inside the post office are mural lunette paintings by the artist Charles Kassler II (1935–36). These depict the *Pony Express* in one mural and *Air Mail* in another.

20. Beverly Hills City Hall, 1932
William J. Gage
East side of Crescent Drive, between Santa Monica and Little Santa Monica Boulevards

Spanish Renaissance magnificence built significantly at the beginning of the depression when the people in this vicinity felt little pain. The scheme of the building—that of a low classical base (symbolizing government) surmounted by a tower—was frequently employed for public buildings in the United States from the teens through the 1930s.

21. Beverly Hills Civic Center, 1981–92
Charles Moore/ Urban Innovations; Albert Martin Associates; Campbell and Campbell, landscape architects
North of Burton Way, between Crescent and Rexford Drives

In 1981 a competition was announced by the city council for an expansion of the Civic Center. Five architectural firms were selected to present architectural plans: Frank O. Gehry and Associates, Arthur Erickson Architects, Gwathmey Siegel and Associates, Moshe Safdie and Associates, and Charles Moore/Urban Innovations Group.

Moore's winning design has a Spanish flavor, enriched by references to the Art Deco. It carries the Art Deco one or two steps further, making it the dominant theme. The buildings are organized around a public promenade that slices diagonally through the project, with the existing City Hall forming part of the northside promenade terminating to the northeast at the parking garage. While a number of features of the landscape design were eliminated, the planting that was carried out is already bringing all the elements together. The crown of the project is the wonderful library, especially the children's section with its row of arches converging at the reception desk.

22. Music Corporation of America, 1940, 1968–72
Paul R. Williams;
Phil Shipley and Associates, landscape architects
South of Burton Way, between Crescent and Rexford Drives

The former Music Corporation of America building, with its gardens, marks a high point of traditional image architecture in Los Angeles. It is a formal, but still somewhat rambling, version of the work of the late-eighteenth-century English Neoclassical tradition. (Robert Adams et al. Adams, an architect, was an influence on Williams' design.) The building's architect, Paul R. Williams, maneuvered it so that it read traditional, modern, and California. Note not only the two-story porticoed entrance to the northeast, but also the garden (Phil Shipley) facing southwest.

23. Parking Structure for Litton Industries, 1968–72
Paul R. Williams and Associate
South corner of Crescent Drive and Burton Way

To tie the parking structure into the existing building across the street, Williams clothed it in Georgian garb.

24. Burton-Hill Town Houses, 1974
Widon-Wein and Associates
9323 Burton Way

Twenty-four units, extremely sophisticated and understated Modern in wood and brick.

25. Virgin Records, 1991
Franklin D. Israel Design Associates
338 N. Foothill Road

A beautifully proportioned bright red wall gently curves into the canopied entrance. On entering, you are in a miniature city with streets and buildings inside of buildings.

26. Volkswagen Showroom, circa 1937
Northwest corner of Maple Drive and Olympic Boulevard

Here it is again. Los Angeles would seem to have more monuments to the Streamline Moderne than any other city in the United States.

27. Canon Court, 1930
J. Raymond
9379 Olympic Boulevard, at the northeast corner of Canon Drive

This lovely Spanish garden-court apartment house seems out of place on this now-noisy street.

28. Wosk House, 1981–84
Frank O. Gehry and Associates
440 S. Roxbury Drive

Gehry took an existing four-story apartment building and transformed its top floor into what amounts to a new series of spaces and forms. His approach to the new fourth floor was to "rebuild [it] as a series of objects set back from the existing building's perimeter. The dense rooftop composition of "appropriated" forms is suggestive of a miniature city and evokes the scale, details, and eclecticism of its surroundings." At the request of the client, the lower portions of the building were refinished in pink stucco.

29. Swimming Pool Building, Beverly Hills High School, circa 1937
Stiles O. Clements
Between Heath Avenue and Moreno Drive, above Olympic Boulevard

This elliptical-façaded building with its barrel-vaulted skylighted interior contrasts with the knife-sharp Yamasaki towers behind it in Century City. The single-story entrance pavilion with rounded corners and rows of deep horizontal bands makes the building Streamline Moderne.

28 • Century City

In what, to an easterner, would seem easy walking distance of the Beverly Hills business district is Century City, built on what used to be the Twentieth Century-Fox movie lot. This is a totally new complex of high- and medium-rise buildings, some by distinguished name-brand American architects. There is, however, none of the intimacy and human scale that characterize the buildings of Beverly Hills. In fact, the governing idea seems to have been to inspire awe of corporate America via wide avenues and over-scaled architecture. If you accept the effort to impress, then the attempt, even at this stage, has been successful. But there are problems. Except around the Century Plaza Hotel and a few theaters doing business, the place is pretty spooky on weekdays and downright frightening on Sundays. There is no on-street parking. In fact, there are few crosswalks. Pedestrians are forced to go under streets. You have the strange feeling that this city was planned not for people but for architectural photography. We have included only the buildings that we feel cannot be ignored, either because of their size or, in a few instances, because of their architectural importance.

1. Century City Medical Plaza,
1969
Daniel, Mann, Johnson,
and Mendenhall
(Lumsden and Pelli;
P. J. Jacobson)
Northeast corner of
Olympic Boulevard and
Century Park East

These architects have since gone off into attacks on the International Style. This complex, a seventeen-story office tower and a ten-story hospital, stands at the turning point in their reaction.

2. Fox Plaza, 1985–87
Johnson, Fain, Pereire
Associates;
Robert Herrick Carter
Association,
landscape architects
2121 Avenue of the Stars

This pink-and-gray thirty-four-story behemoth with its six-story parking structure is most notable for its size. H. G. Wells might have loved it.

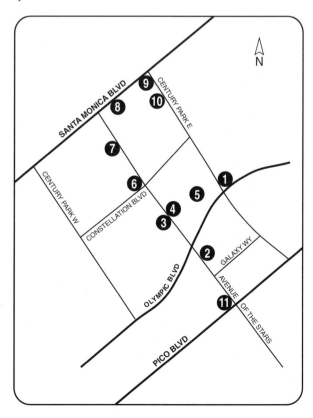

3. Century Plaza Hotel, 1966
Minoru Yamasaki;
Robert Herrick Carter,
landscape architect
2025 Avenue of the Stars

A huge high-rise ellipse enlivened by delicate detail.

4. ABC Entertainment Center,
1972
Henry George Greene
2040 Avenue of the Stars

Big and dull—mildly Brutal below, crisper above.

5. Century Plaza Towers,
1969–75
Minoru Yamasaki;
Robert Herrick Carter,
landscape architect
East of ABC Entertainment Center

These two soaring towers, identical in height and triangular floor plan, are the focal point of Century City. They are truly stunning when viewed nearby and play strange optical tricks from the distant Santa Monica Freeway.

6. First Los Angeles Bank,
1975
Maxwell Starkman and
Associates
Northwest corner of
Avenue of the Stars and
Constellation Boulevard

An extraordinarily fine building of brown brick and black glass tilted to give the effect of the skylight in an artist's studio.

7. 1900 Avenue of the Stars,
1969
Albert C. Martin and
Associates
1900 Avenue of the Stars

A twenty-seven-story building of aluminum and tinted glass.

8. ABI Tower, 1971
Skidmore, Owings, and Merrill
(E. Charles Bassett)
10100 Santa Monica Boulevard

A twenty-six-story building of light aluminum and black glass.

9. San Diego Savings and
Loan Association, 1972
Daniel, Mann, Johnson,
and Mendenhall
(Lumsden; P. J. Jacobson)
Southwest corner of
Santa Monica Boulevard and
Century Park East

A squarish twenty-story building set at a diagonal to the corner. The mitered corners that line up with the street indicate that the designer was perhaps trying to make some sort of statement. Or was he simply being playful? The building nevertheless seems askew and unrelated to anything else.

10. Northrop Complex,
1982–83
Welton Becket and Associates
1800 Century Park East

A nineteen-story corporate International Style tower. An equally dull twenty-three-story tower sits beside it.

11. Fox Network Center, 2002
HLW International
(Michael White)
Northwest corner of Avenue of
the Stars and Pico Boulevard

Many new and generally dreary high-rises have been built since the last *Guide* was published. An exception to the prevailing dullness of the place is the Fox Network Center (2002), situated at the northwest corner of Avenue of the Stars and Pico Boulevard. A little farther west and just off Pico is a refurbished movie set of pseudo-Victorian storefronts.

29 • Carthay Circle

Carthay Circle was planned in 1921 by landscape architects Cook and Hill. The area is bounded by Fairfax Avenue to the east, Olympic Boulevard to the south, and Wilshire Boulevard to the north. It is bisected by San Vicente Boulevard. The founder of the 136-acre, mainly Spanish Revival community was developer J. Harvey McCarthy. It had been planned around a shopping center. Originally the main buildings and many of the lesser ones were designed by Alfred W. Eichler and H. W. Bishop. Several of the spec houses were designed by Irving J. Gill while he was working for Bishop. The chief feature of Carthay Circle was the theater, now long gone. No major monuments remain—only a pleasanter-than-usual community.

30 • South Carthay

This area just southeast of Beverly Hills and bounded by Olympic, Crescent Heights, Pico, and La Cienega Boulevards was developed in the 1930s by a builder named Ponti. It is really all of one piece, mainly Spanish Revival, but it also exhibits the other Period Revivals as well as the Moderne. It is mostly single-family dwellings, all in the same scale, except for the fringes on Olympic and Crescent Heights where small apartment houses in the same 1930s styles appear. There are very few intrusions from the succeeding decades, and where they do appear they are not liked. The sense of an organic community of period architecture caused the Los Angeles Cultural Heritage Board to recommend to the Planning Commission and the City Council that South Carthay be recognized as a cultural-historic district, or, in officialese, a Historic Preservation Overlay Zone remarkable for its consistent good design.

31 • West Hollywood

For many years West Hollywood was unincorporated, i.e., located in the county, not in the city of Los Angeles. This had tax advantages and is one reason that it attracted small businesses such as interior design. It also drew a group of unusual human beings, some of them of great significance, who ended up living in the area: writers Theodore Dreiser and Aldous Huxley, architect R. M. Schindler, and patent-medicine czar Walter Dodge, who in 1916 commissioned Irving J. Gill to design a house that came to be considered one of the great monuments of modern architecture. In fact, the loose organization of government in the unincorporated area without many ordinances, especially in historic preservation, helped to make it possible for a developer to destroy the famed Dodge House and replace it with hideous condominiums.

Since that time, West Hollywood has become a city with a strong historic preservation ordinance and a real sense of place. The preservationists have helped to restore Schindler's own house on Kings Road and have protected many other monuments such as Lloyd Wright's house on Doheny Drive.

The Grand Palais for interior designers has been the Pacific Design Center at the corner of San Vicente Boulevard and Melrose Avenue—"The Blue Whale"—that houses the most prestigious wholesalers. But small shops, the mainstay of an earlier day, still abound. And not far from them are acres of bungalows, many being literally transformed by their designers-owners into miniature villas in a congeries of taste that stretches the imagination to the point that John Chase has written a book about them—*Exterior Decoration* (Los Angeles, 1982).

The notorious part of Sunset Boulevard that is called "The Strip" is also in the area, as are some wonderful garden apartments of the 1920s and 1930s. The hills above Sunset Boulevard are in Los Angeles proper and are full of excellent Period Revival houses as well as outstanding avant-garde work by Carl Maston, Raphael Soriano, Richard J. Neutra, John Lautner, Gregory Ain, Pierre Koenig, and R. M. Schindler. This is a wonderful part of the world.

We have taken the liberty of extending West Hollywood into these hills to the north and have pushed its southern boundary to Olympic Boulevard. At the same time we have observed the conventional western and eastern boundaries at Doheny Drive and Fairfax Avenue.

1. Sunrise Plaza Apartment,
1982
John Siebel Associates
1201 Larrabee Street

High Tech with all of its clichés.

2. Sunset Plaza, 1934–36
Charles Selkirk
Honnold and Russell
8578–8623 Sunset Boulevard

Clustered near the intersection with Sunset Plaza Drive, most of these shops were designed by Charles Selkirk. Some are now being restored and rebuilt in their original Neoclassical, Regency, and Colonial Revival styles. Advanced respectability on the Sunset Strip! The crown jewel of them all is the shimmering white Ionic temple (1936) at 8619 Sunset Boulevard.

3. Muller House, 1990
Allyn E. Morris
2221 Sunset Plaza Drive

A carrying-onward of Schindler's Modernist work of the late 1930s. The theme of layered horizontality asserts itself in a strong fashion, especially on the south elevation of the house. Numerous decks, some open, some covered, provide outdoor living space on a steep hillside lot.

4. Lomax House, 1970–71
Lomax/Mills Associates
1995 Sunset Plaza Drive

An elegant cut-into stucco box, a reminder in the Modernist tradition that architecture can be minimalist sculpture on a grand scale.

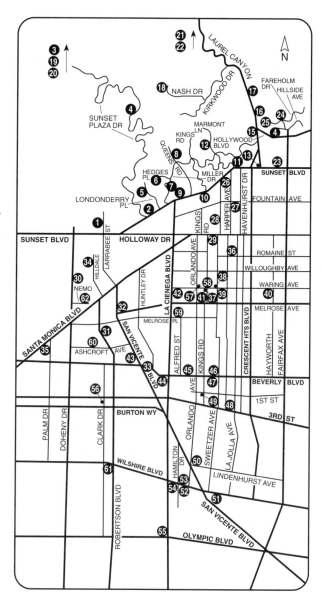

5. Wayne House, 1950
Alvin Lustig
1365 Londonderry Place

You can catch only a glimpse of this International Style house.

6. Wolff House, 1963
John Lautner
8530 Hedges Place

This steep hillside house is a characteristically dramatic statement of its architect. It is made of dressed boulders, concrete, and jutting glass. Its most salient feature from the street is the greatly extended lip of the carport.

7. Reis House, 1950
R. M. Schindler
1404 Miller Drive

In this single-floor dwelling Schindler suspended a thin roof plane over a set of quite fragile stucco planes. As in all of his work, and especially in his post–1945 designs, there are many ideas going on in this small dwelling. But here the roof planes hold everything together.

8. Polito House, 1939
Raphael S. Soriano
1650 Queens Road

A two-story Modernist box characterized by the abstract composition of stucco walls, horizontal banks of windows, and cantilevered balconies.

9. Carney's Restaurant
8361 Sunset Boulevard

A Union Pacific dining car brought to the site in the 1970s.

10. Sunset Tower Apartments,
1929–31
Leland A. Bryant
18358 Sunset Boulevard at Kings Road

The lower part of the tower is a first-class monument of the

Zigzag Moderne while the upper portion anticipates the 1930s Streamline Moderne. The building has long been as much an emblem of Hollywood as the Hollywood Sign. Drive to the rear and note the stylized automobile radiator grills incorporated into the decoration of the garage.

11. Chateau Marmont, 1928
Arnold Weitzman
8225 Marmont Lane near Sunset Boulevard

Perhaps more important historically than architecturally, this Norman pile was a favorite of the screen stars . . . still is.

12. Maston House, 1948
Carl Louis Maston
1657 Marmont Lane

Rather surprising to find this partisan of the "less-is-more" aesthetic practicing here in what would seem to be a late Craftsman technique—lots of wood.

13. Store and Office Building,
circa 1925
Morgan, Walls, and Clements
Northwest corner of Laurel Canyon and Sunset Boulevards

Somewhat defaced but still recognizable as these architects' brand of the Churrigueresque, realized in cast concrete.

14. Mace House, 1958
Lloyd Wright
8292 Hollywood Boulevard

The façade right on the street is very private looking.

15. Storer House, 1923
Frank Lloyd Wright
Lloyd Wright,
landscape architect
8161 Hollywood Boulevard

Wright's romantic creation of

decorated concrete block, wonderfully fitted into the hillside. The interior space of this house is dominated by a central two-story living room that opens onto front and rear terraces. The house was purchased by producer Joel Silver and was partially restored in the 1970s by Lloyd Wright. More extensive renovation has taken place recently under the direction of Eric Wright, Martin Eli Weil, and Linda Marder.

16. House, circa 1925
1808 Laurel Canyon Boulevard (actually a spur that veers off about 100 yards above Hollywood Boulevard)

A beautiful tribute to the Spanish Revival.

17. House, circa 1910
Paul Arnold Needham
2044 Laurel Canyon Boulevard (spur)

A horizontal one-story house raised above the street level by the garage below. It is an example of the West Coast adaptation of the Prairie School aesthetic.

18. Jones House and Studio,
1938
A. Quincy Jones
8661 Nash Drive (Laurel Canyon Boulevard, then left on Kirkwood Drive, right on Ridpath Drive to Nash Drive)

The influence in these buildings with broad eaves is Wright filtered through the San Francisco Bay tradition of the 1930s.

A little farther up Laurel Canyon Boulevard, again jutting off to the left (west), is Lookout Mountain Avenue, which you will recognize by a suitable log cabin at the entrance. Lookout Mountain Avenue leads to some important houses.

19. Janson House, 1949
R. M. Schindler
*8704 Skyline Drive
(Lookout Mountain Avenue to
Wonderland Avenue to
Greenvalley to Skyline Drive)*

A house on a scanty budget. It looks as if it were made of sticks. It is amazing to return to this house after many years and discover that, where in the 1950s it could easily be photographed, now it is almost invisible amid foliage and new neighbors. A number of changes also have been made to the house in recent years. If you look closely at this dwelling and then at the 1980s designs of Frank O. Gehry, you will see a connection.

20. Case Study House #21, 1958
Pierre Koenig
*9038 Wonderland Park Avenue
(Lookout Mountain Avenue to
Wonderland Avenue to
Wonderland Park Avenue.
House on left, just above
Burroughs)*

Koenig carried the elegance of the metal post-and-beam aesthetic to the point that it almost seems related to the popular Hollywood Regency of the 1930s. Another example of this refined approach can be seen in his Case Study House #22 (1959), located at 1635 Woods Drive. In #22 the idea of the glass pavilion is fully realized. This elegant, precisely detailed Modernist house of vertical wood panels is still very smart.

21. De Bretteville-Simon Houses, 1976
Peter de Bretteville
*8067–8071 Willow Glen Road
off Laurel Canyon Road*

Image of the twentieth-century dwelling as a machine. A spin-off from Charles Eames's own house in Santa Monica Canyon.

22. Ain House, 1941
Gregory Ain
7964 Willow Glen Road

A narrow room-in-a-line plan with all the major spaces opening toward a terrace and the view, the whole covered with a low-pitched hipped roof.

23. Sunset Car Wash, 1972
Robert Barnett
7955 Sunset Boulevard

A monumental, almost Egyptian, object in concrete.

24. Kun Houses, 1938 and 1950
Richard J. Neutra; Gregory Ain, collaborator
7947 Fareholm Drive

Two adjoining, machine-image, International Style houses on a precipitous hillside. The 1938 stucco-and-steel-windows dwelling was advertised as an "all-electric house." From the street you see only the top level. The rear elevation reveals that it is actually three levels.

25. Tucker House, 1950
R. M. Schindler
8010 Fareholm Drive

A two-story stucco frame design whose planes project and recede in a complex pattern.

26. Garden Apartments
Mainly on north/south streets between Sunset Boulevard and Fountain Avenue

Usually, as the name suggests, these are two- or three-story apartments arranged around a garden, often elaborately landscaped with palms and other tall trees. A swimming pool is not usually a part of the ensemble, although it may exist on some other part of the property or may have been added more recently. The apartments are at their best in the Spanish Revival mode and are generally charming if not great architecture. A visitor from Canada was heard to say, "Why don't all the people in Los Angeles live this way?" For a discussion of these garden apartments, see Stefanos Polyzoides, Roger Sherwood, James Tice, and Julius Shulman, *Courtyard Housing in Los Angeles* (Berkeley, 1982).

Here is a group of apartments that are within easy walking distance of each other:

a. Patio del Moro, 1925
Arthur B. and Nina W. Zwebell
8225 Fountain Avenue

Although not the first designer/builder to hit upon the garden court, Zwebell was certainly a very active pioneer. This Spanish design has a gorgeous entrance and an interesting garden.

b. The Ronda, 1927
Arthur B. and Nina W. Zwebell
1400 Havenhurst Drive

From the street all you can see is the three-story façade with a garage entrance to the side and a small garden entrance to the north. Within this complex are two courtyard gardens.

c. The Andalusia, 1927
Arthur B. and Nina W. Zwebell
1475 Havenhurst Drive

Two garage buildings to each side form a forecourt beyond which a large arch leads into the inner court. Cantilevered balconies, a round tower, and a loggia complete the composition.

d. The Romanesque Villa Apartments, 1928
Leland Bryant
1301–1309 N. Harper Avenue

This three- and four-story garden-courtyard apartment was produced by Leland Bryant, who also designed the Moderne Sunset Towers. His image in this case was Spanish Churrigueresque, notwithstanding its name, "Romanesque." Note the Spanish galleon weather vane, which tops the square and octagonal tower at the northeast corner.

e. Villa Sevilla, 1931
Elwood Houseman
1338 N. Harper

An Andalusian village scene set on the hillside. A narrow interior garden court contains the entrances and stairways.

f. Villa d'Este, 1928
Pierpont and Walter S. Davis
1355 Laurel Avenue

Vaguely modeled on the Villa d'Este on Lake Maggiore, not on the famous one at Tivoli. This apartment house with garage as a forecourt on the street is surely the most beautiful of these wonderful garden courtyard apartments of the 1920s. Beyond the entrance and pool lies the main courtyard. Each of the two-story units has a private patio.

Actually, to have settled on the garden apartment house may seem perverse. Look around at the other delightful apartments in this area. The nearby Chateau Marmont is only the most conspicuous of these.

27. Villa de Malaga Apartments, 1988
Miguel Angelo Flores and Associates
8228 Fountain Avenue (southeast corner of Fountain Avenue and Harper Avenue)

A seven-unit apartment building, well carried out in the Andalusian mode. This architect also designed the Spanish-inspired 1982–83 Villa de Malaga town houses in Santa Monica.

28. Coral Gables Bungalow Court, circa 1932
1233–1239 Sweetzer Avenue

A two-story Spanish Revival complex.

29. West Hollywood City Hall, 1995
Mehrdad Yazdani and Ellerbe Becket
8300 Santa Monica Boulevard at Sweetzer

A remodeling of an old building, the City Hall sets a tone of razzle-dazzle that the newly incorporated city evokes. Perhaps form follows function here, but the conglomeration of shapes and colors does not read that way.

30. Wright House, 1928
Lloyd Wright
858 N. Doheny Drive

The house is of stuccoed frame with elaborate precast concrete-block decoration within and without, suggested by the Joshua tree. It is easily missed under its pine tree, which acts as an insulating device. No more romantic scene could be imagined than when Mr. Wright lighted a fire on the hearth of the "great hall" and opened the canvas drapery that separates the room from the small patio over which the huge tree sprawls.

31. Office and Showroom, 1982
Tom Roberts Associates
638–642 N. Robertson Boulevard

Three low towers identify this small wood-and-stucco complex. The towers are open frame, and the two to the side are placed at forty-five-degree angles to their buildings. A Postmodern building that does not employ the usual language of the mode.

32. Pacific Design Center ("Blue Whale"), 1975, 1985–88
Victor Gruen Associates (Cesar Pelli)
Northeast corner of Melrose Avenue and San Vicente Boulevard

Controversial to say the least. Some critics have damned "The Blue Whale," usually because it obviously contradicts the scale of the area, which is mainly small shops and houses. Others have praised it for its break with high-rise. The Center is vast and, on its San Vicente side, reminds you of London's Crystal Palace in its roofline. With the exception of the top floor, its interiors are just big spaces, possibly because the architect expected them to be filled with color and people by the designer tenants. A grand exception is the Sunar Showroom (#206) designed by Michael Graves in 1981.

A decade after the original building was built, Cesar Pelli was commissioned to do two more structures and a plaza. For the first building he chose green glass as an exterior finish. The other, a kind of wedge, was to be colored maroon but has still not been constructed. When completed, they and the "Blue Whale" will stand, in Pelli's words, "as separate overscaled fragments in strong contrasting colors."

33. Herman Miller Showroom, 1949
Charles Eames
8806 Beverly Boulevard

Although no longer used by Herman Miller, the glass street façade of this small building still looks as delicate, crisp, and bright as when it was built.

34. Margo Leavin Gallery, 1989
David Serrurier; Claes Oldenburg and Coosje van Bruggen, sculptors
817 N. Hilldale Avenue

The apartments of Merle Oberon and Norma Talmadge have been recycled! A six-by-twelve-foot stainless-steel knife blade cuts down through the parapet of a nondescript stucco-sheathed building. The stroke of the knife cuts into the center of the façade with such force that the adjoining plaster surfaces are curled back.

35. Rapid Transit District Bus Maintenance Facility, 1982
Ralph Parsons Company (Engineering)
Santa Monica Boulevard at Palm Drive

About as Brutalist as we go in Southern California.

32

36. Duplexes, 1922
R. M. Schindler
Northeast corner of
Harper Avenue and
Romaine Street;
northwest corner of
La Jolla Avenue and
Romaine Street

These two identical low-budget structures were built as spec investments. Their style is close to Art Deco.

37. Schindler Studio House,
1921–22
R. M. Schindler
833 N. Kings Road

Actually a double house, with guest quarters and a common kitchen, built for the Schindlers and R. M.'s engineer colleague Clyde Chase and his wife. In this studio house, Schindler experimented with tilt-slab concrete walls, the vertical space between each slab being filled with glass. In a sense, the house follows historic precedent. The interiors are in the woodsy do-it-yourself Craftsman style. The plan, which opens all rooms to courtyards, suggests both the Hispanic and Japanese traditions. It is a classic in modern architecture—and we use the word sparingly. God preserve it! Call Schindler House for hours (323) 651-1510.

38. Apartment Building, circa
1925
Carl Kay
Northwest corner of
Sweetzer and Waring Avenues

An Islamic Revival complex, beautiful to behold.

39. Duplex, 1936
William P. Kesling
754–756 Harper Avenue

Splendid Streamline, coming close to International Style.

40. El Greco Apartment
Building, 1929
Pierpont and Walter S. Davis
West side of Hayworth Avenue,
north of Melrose Avenue

You enter this 1920s garden apartment building through an arched opening. The central courtyard has a pool and is furnished with potted plants. A projecting second-floor balcony overlooks the courtyard of this Andalusian design. This apartment building was originally located at 1028 Tiverton in Westwood. It was moved in 1986 by the architectural firm of De Bretteville and Polyzoides.

41. Gemini Studio Building,
1976
Frank O. Gehry and Associates
8365 W. Melrose Avenue

A remodeling and addition to an older single-story commercial structure, this is so understated that you do not notice the subtle relationship of the new façade and the huge sign on its roof.

42. Gerwin-Ostrow Office
Building, 1960
Craig Ellwood & Associates
Southeast corner of La Cienega
Boulevard and Waring Avenue

Less glass than usual, the building still shows the influence of Mies.

43. Tail-O-The-Pup, 1938
Milton Black
329 N. San Vicente Boulevard,
just north of
Beverly Boulevard

A Programmatic hot dog stand in the shape of a hot dog in a bun. The structure was moved from its former location on the northwest corner of La Cienega and Beverly Boulevards. Incidentally, the prices have gone up since the photo was taken.

44. Beverly Center, 1982
Welton Becket Associates
8500 Beverly Boulevard

Just behind the Tail-O-the-Pup, so to speak, this monstrous shopping center with its department stores and shops is a sort of unintended joke on the Pompidou Center in Paris.

45. Los Angeles Free Clinic,
1989–90
**Morphosis
(Thom Mayne and
Michael Rotundi)**
8405 Beverly Boulevard

A steel-frame box provides the
entrance to this three-story clinic
building. Juxtaposition of volumes is the game with this
structure. Forms at the base are
of concrete block (including
bands of split-faced block) that
are stucco sheathed above. The
building houses the nation's
oldest no-cost health clinic.

46. Janus Gallery, circa 1928
*Northwest corner of
Beverly Boulevard and
Sweetzer Avenue*

Art Deco.

47. Carson-Roberts Building,
1958–60
Craig Ellwood
8322 Beverly Boulevard

This building stands on stilts,
providing a garage below. The
front is made of glass panels
extended beyond the real walls.
These give extra privacy from
the busy street.

48. Crescent Professional
Building, 1959
Richard J. Neutra
8105 W. 3rd Street

White marble, unfenestrated on
the street side, the architecture
is asserted by a stainless-steel
canopy extended over the
side walls.

49. Apartment Building,
circa 1940
*Southwest corner of
1st Street and
South Kings Road*

A late version of the Streamline
Moderne.

50. Marshall House, 1948
**Konrad Wachsmann and
Walter Gropius**
*6643 Lindenhurst Avenue
(rear)*

You cannot easily see it from the
street, but we had to put it in
because the prefabricated "panel
houses" by these famous architects are rarities.

51. Century Bank, 1972
**Daniel, Mann, Johnson, and
Mendenhall (A. Lumsden)**
6420 Wilshire Boulevard

A well-designed medium-rise
with much attention toward a
break with 1960s Modern, but it
does inspire us to feel like spank-
ing whoever it was that invented
black glass.

52. Fox Wilshire Theater, 1929
S. Charles Lee
8440 Wilshire Boulevard

A wonderful creation in Art
Deco.

53. Shopping Center,
circa 1928
*Northeast corner of
Wilshire Boulevard and
Hamilton Drive*

A specimen of Spanish Revival
architecture. Corner L-shaped
shopping centers of this vintage
are rapidly fading from the scene.
It is good to find one in this area.

54. Great Western Savings
Center Building, 1972
William Pereira Associates
*Southeast corner of
Wilshire and
La Cienega Boulevards*

This huge black-glass building
with an oval floor plan certainly
makes a break with International
Style sermonizing.

55. Beverly Hills Water
Department Building
(now Center for Motion
Picture Study), 1927
**Salisbury, Bradshaw, and
Taylor (Arthur Taylor)**
*Northwest corner of
Olympic and
La Cienega Boulevards*

You will at first think that this
huge poured-concrete structure
with Romanesque detail and
reasonably accurate facsimile of
"La Giralda" is a cathedral. And
so it is in Los Angeles County
where water is sacred. In 1988
the building was taken over by

the Academy of Motion Picture Arts and Sciences. In the hands of architect Francis Offenhauser, the existing building was extensively remodeled and a new wing, sympathetic in character to the original building, was added.

56. Temple Emmanuel and School, 1954
Sidney Eisenstadt
300 N. Clark Drive

The temple is not as dramatic as much of Eisenstadt's work, but it contains a mural by Joseph Young, who designed the Triforium in downtown Los Angeles. The school, comprised of very low arches with brick and glass above, reminds us of the Frank Lloyd Wright civic building at San Raphael.

57. Orlando/Waring Condominiums, 1974
Kenneth Dillon
8380 Waring Avenue, at Orlando Avenue

A large complex in the cut-into box idiom. Not great architecture, but the planting around it is magnificent.

58. Senior Citizens Housing Project, 1978–80
Bobrow, Thomas and Associates;
Charles W. Moore/
Urban Innovation Group
Northwest and northeast corners of Kings Road at Waring Avenue

These 106 one- to three-story units in stucco and tile spell Spanish. Several existing Spanish Revival houses of the 1920s have been incorporated in the project and help to tie the present to the past. The new buildings have been scaled and sited so as to continue the low residential character of Kings Road before the advent of apartment houses in the 1960s.

59. Woolf Studio, 1946–47
John Woolf
8450 Melrose Place

A one-story building, its outsize Pullman-door surround has been greatly admired by the interior designers in West Hollywood.

60. House Remodeling, 1961
Lawrence Limolti
8937 Ashcroft Avenue

Originally Spanish Revival, this tiny bungalow has been entirely rejuvenated with mansard roof, complete with bust in the tower and topiary work in the front yard.

61. Owl Drug Store, circa 1930
Southwest corner of Wilshire and Robertson Boulevards

A version of the Art Deco. Between fluted engaged columns on the upper floor are small highly decorated columns and spandrels and rich relief ornamentation.

62. Click Agency, 1991–92
Hodgetts + Fung Design Associates
9057 Nemo Street

Modernist rectilinear geometry is handsomely realized in a series of three contrasting volumes that compose this small office building. These volumes are in turn countered by a gentle curved wall of the mezzanine and by the segment of an oval volume that brings up the rear.

32 • Central Hollywood

Since everything about Central Hollywood is supposed to be fabulous, it is worth noting that the name may have been chosen by the developers, Mr. and Mrs. Horace Wilcox of Topeka, because Father Junipero Serra may have once said the Mass of the Holy Wood of the Cross near the site. Unfortunately, a much more prosaic explanation of the derivation is probable. But it is significant that the Wilcoxes were determined when they platted the community in the late 1880s that it would be a center of high culture and morality, however contradictory these might be. They offered a free lot to any church that would build there. Their high tone was evidently contagious, for when movies were first developed in New York, they were banned in Hollywood, as were liquor and other forms of sin.

This happy condition did not last very far into the twentieth century. Whatever its present resemblance to Sodom and Gomorrah, Hollywood is conspicuously a city of churches, the First Presbyterian being the largest of that denomination in the world. But the movies came seeking the sun like everything else that came to California. The result may still be noted on the map in the form of large areas devoted to movie studios that, incidentally, may be converted eventually to new uses, as in Universal City to the north and Century City to the west. Also, the city acquired some of the most spectacular moving picture palaces that were built anywhere in the world in the 1920s and 1930s. Grauman's (now Mann's) Chinese is the most famous, but the Hollywood Pantages is the most magnificent.

The effect of movie madness on domestic architecture, or perhaps on the world of the interior designer, can be seen in many remodels in the West Hollywood area. John Chase aptly labeled this approach "exterior decoration," the turning of nondescript small bungalows into miniature renditions of Versailles. In the earlier decades the taste of the stars and moguls, whatever their quest for opulence, was generally channeled into Spanish, Tudor, and Anglo-Colonial. Nevertheless, the imaginative atmosphere did encourage a taste for the exotic in some citizens—the Egyptian, Islamic, Hansel and Gretel, Medieval, and Mayan traditions finding much favor. On the other hand, the same atmosphere seems to have encouraged other residents to employ some of the early Modernists—Gregory Ain, Richard J. Neutra, R. M. Schindler, Harwell H. Harris, Raphael S. Soriano, Pierre Koenig, and the Wrights, father and son. As a matter of fact, Hollywood Hills, though full of commonplace architecture, is an area that no student of twentieth-century traditional or avant-garde architecture can ignore.

If you are such a student, be sure to have your car and your patience in prime condition. We have done our best to make the maps accurate, but they can forecast only a few of the steep, tortuous roads and barely suggest the many opportunities to get lost. Persevere! Civilization is always nearby.

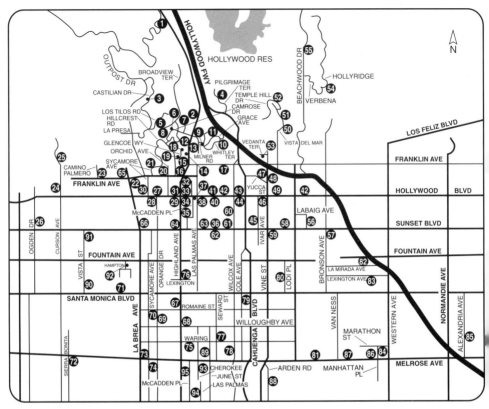

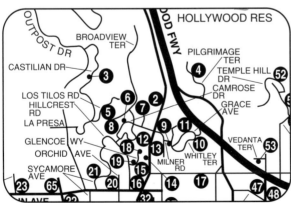

1. Maston Architectural Office Building, 1967
Carl Maston
2811 Cahuenga Boulevard (west side of the Hollywood Freeway)

An ideal Modern design. An austere horizontal brick wall as an abstract plane is all that meets the eye from the street. Behind this wall is the glass façade of the building.

2. Hollywood Bowl,
1924 to present
2301 N. Highland Avenue

The first performance in the originally natural amphitheater was in 1922. In 1924 it was decided to improve the carrying power of the sound by building a shell, and Lloyd Wright was chosen as the designer. The result was a wood shell that was successful both visually and acoustically. In 1928 Wright was again employed to design a second shell that was elliptical in shape. In 1931 the Allied Architects of Los Angeles replaced that shell with a more pretentious one in concrete that never worked, in spite of almost continual remodeling. The latest shell (1982) is by Frank O. Gehry and Associates. Now the complaint is about the quality of the amplification system. The best thing at the Bowl is the gate on Highland Avenue. Three Federal Arts Project sculptures representing music, drama, and dance were sculpted by George Stanley (circa 1935). Very inspirational, especially at night when lighted.

3. Goldberg/Bean House, 1991 Franklin D. Israel Design Associates
2029 Castilian Drive

If you look closely, you can make out that the building we now see is a remodeling of a California ranch house. The architect has tied the existing dwelling to the new via red-and-yellow-colored stucco and natural wood walls. The new addition plays with both volumes and structure. Added to the exterior sheathing of wood and stucco are walls of concrete block and others covered with galvanized metal.

4. House, circa 1928
2403 Pilgrimage Terrace
At first this seems to be a Queen Anne house, but closer inspection suggests a later date, perhaps even later than our guess.

5. Myers House, 1928, 1985 Barton Myers Associates
6900 Los Tilos Road

The architect acquired a modest but spectacularly sited Spanish Revival dwelling of the late 1920s and added elements that bring this revival up-to-date. A small tower is now situated at the entrance, and Moorish-inspired tile walls enclose a new Franklin fireplace.

6. Hollywood Duplex, 1990 Koning Eisenberg Architecture
6947–6949 Camrose Drive

These units appear from the street as two very separate towers, placed over their ground-level garages. In plan each is L-shaped; between the Ls are small terraces. The street fronts are rectangular stucco boxes, while the rear wing is covered by a low-pitched barrel roof and cut-out sections, which in fact are the stud structure of the buildings.

7. The High Tower, circa 1920
North end of High Tower Road

A bit of whimsy, a small-scale version of the extravagances at Bologna. Unfortunately the elevator no longer works. The two flanking Moderne houses are by Carl Kay (circa 1937).

8. Otto Bollman House, 1922 Lloyd Wright
2200 Broadview Terrace

Architectural expressionism at its height. This stuccoed frame house has pyramidal roofs once covered by a pattern of horizontal and vertical boards. It is almost unreachable by footpath, and you can see very little when you get up there.

9. House, circa 1928
Southwest corner of Milner Road and Las Palmas Avenue

A charming Hansel and Gretel in a storybook area.

10. Pike House, 1952 George Vernon Russell
6675 Whitley Terrace

A characteristic, rather-delicate version of post–World War II Moderne, now painted brown. You can see this better than most of Russell's domestic work.

11. Lingenbrink House, 1930 Jock Peters
2000 Grace Avenue

Like other Los Angeles designers, Jock Peters used both Moderne and International Style images. They are here in this house. In fact, Lingenbrink published several small books on both styles. Later in the 1930s he was a major patron of R. M. Schindler.

12. The Roman Gardens, 1926 Pierpont and Walter S. Davis
2000 N. Highland Avenue

The tower that you see does not look Roman (it could be from Spain or North Africa), but this is one of the most elaborate of Los Angeles's garden court apartment houses.

13. American Legion Headquarters Building, 1929
Weston and Weston (Eugene Weston Jr.)
2035 Highland Avenue

Goodhue's Los Angeles Public Library certainly was on the architect's mind when he designed this modern Classical spectacle; its glittering tile ornamentation is still very fresh. The building is of reinforced concrete with the board pattern of the forms left exposed.

14. Shrader House, circa 1915
Mead and Requa
1927 Highland Avenue

Spanish Revival (via Irving J. Gill) by an important San Diego firm. It is amazing that it still exists.

15. Duplex for De Keysor, 1935
R. M. Schindler
1911 Highland Avenue

The walls and sloped roofs of this hillside house are covered with roll roofing material in a manner similar to the original condition of the now-demolished Packard House (1924) in Pasadena.

16. First United Methodist Church, 1929
Thomas P. Barber
Northwest corner of Highland and Franklin Avenues

English Gothic in revealed reinforced concrete; it is a marvelous focal point at the curve of

Highland Avenue. Nearby at the southeast corner of Selma Avenue and Las Palmas Avenue is the First Baptist Church (1935; Douglas McLellan and Allen McGill), which illustrates the broad popularity of the Anglo-Colonial Revival of the 1930s.

17. Montecito Apartment Building, 1931
Marcus Miller
6650 Franklin Avenue

The architect looked to the Art Deco skyscraper when he produced this ten-story apartment building. As with most Art Deco structures, the windows are arranged in vertical bands, and classic Art Deco ornament enriches the base and the top of the building. In 1987 the building was carefully restored for use as moderate-rent apartments.

18. Koosis House, 1940
Raphael S. Soriano
1941 Glencoe Way

A delightful building because it does not seem to take the International Style too seriously.

19. Freeman House, 1924
Frank Lloyd Wright
1962 Glencoe Way

Another of Wright's concrete "knit-block" houses that seems to begin Mayan and end Islamic. To have seen the Freeman House above the Methodist Church is to have reached Mecca! Much of the built-in and freestanding furniture was designed by R. M. Schindler in 1927. While Wright's other concrete block houses of the 1920s in Los Angeles are larger, the Freeman house is the most picturesque in its siting. It was terribly damaged in the 1994 earthquake.

20. Lane House
(now Magic Castle), 1909
Dennis and Farwell
7001 Franklin Avenue, at Orchid Avenue

This French Chateau has been transformed into a private club for magicians. Lucky you are if you get a chance to hear invisible Irma at her magic piano.

21. Bernheimer Bungalow
(now Yamashiro Restaurant), 1913
Franklin M. Small;
Walter Webber
1999 N. Sycamore Avenue

A stunning Japanese mountain palace and garden (with a real 600-year-old pagoda), built by two importers of oriental art, Adolphe L. and Eugene Bernheimer. The food is average.

22. Crippled Children's
Society Regional Office, 1969
Ladd and Kelsey
Southeast corner of Franklin and La Brea Avenues

A sleek brick edifice in the late International Style.

23. Fuller House, 1924
Arthur S. Heineman
(Alfred Heineman, designer)
Northeast corner of Franklin Avenue and Camino Palmero

A strange mixture of Anglo-Colonial Revival and Italianate forms.

24. Erlik House, 1952
R. M. Schindler
1757 N. Curson Avenue

One of Schindler's last houses—an essay on how to use the typical Los Angeles stucco box. The interior of this single-floor house contains mirrored halls and much built-in furniture.

25. Wattles House and
Gardens, 1905
Myron Hunt and Elmer Grey
1824 N. Curson Avenue

This large Mission Revival house was one of several designed by this Pasadena partnership. A pair of two-story wings encloses a three-arch arcade, which looks out over the valley. To the rear, adjoining the garden is a two-story porch. Originally the house was entered via the south arcaded porch; later a new entrance with a porte cochere was added to the west. The detailing of the house hints both at the aesthetic of the late nineteenth century and the then-popular Craftsman movement. Originally it was almost entirely furnished in Craftsman fumed oak furniture.

The fame of the house rests on its terraced gardens to the rear and the plantings and winding pergola that ascend the steep hillside. The gardens were frequently published in the architectural journals and shelter magazines of the times. Originally the gardens extended down to Hollywood Boulevard. The lower section is now used for the community's small garden plots. The gardens around the house were continually changed and enlarged over the years. In 1911 Elmer Grey added walls and new handrails to the garden as well as a two-story reinforced-concrete garage. The house and the garden are owned by the City of Hollywood. The house and the lower portions of the garden are administered by Hollywood Heritage. This organization has extensively restored both the house and its garden, which are open by appointment through Hollywood Heritage by calling (323) 874-4005.

26. Henry Bollman House, 1922
Lloyd Wright
1530 N. Ogden Drive

An early use of textured "knit-block" construction combined with a wood-stud frame covered with stucco. Lloyd Wright maintained that this was the first actual use of the concrete block "knit-block" system, which his father was to use in such later Los Angeles designs as the Storer House (1923), the Freeman House (1924), and the Ennis House (1924).

27. Grauman's Chinese Theater (now Mann's), 1927
Meyer and Holler
6925 Hollywood Boulevard

This giant tourist attraction surely must be familiar to everyone. Fortunately, nobody has tried to modernize it.

28. Hollywood Masonic Temple, 1922
Austin, Field, and Fry
Intersection of Hollywood Boulevard and Orchid Avenue

A magnificent Classical pile pushed up against the wildly Churrigueresque Paramount Theater.

29. El Capitan Theater (now Paramount), 1926
Morgan, Walls, and Clements;
G. Albert Lansburgh, theater designer
6834 Hollywood Boulevard

At first a combination furniture store and theater, the store (six stories) has pulled out, leaving the theater to make ends meet. The South Sea interior by Lansburgh was removed years ago, but it has been re-created.

Extensive restoration was completed in 1991 under the direction of Fields and Devereaux Architects.

30. El Cadiz Apartment Building, 1936
Milton J. Black
1731 Sycamore Avenue

A large Spanish Revival garden apartment with nice tile trim and art glass. Notice that the garage is in the basement. A much smaller Hispanic charmer is El Cabrillo (1928; Arthur and Nina Zwebell), 1832 Grace Avenue at the corner of Franklin.

31. Hollywood and Highland Retail Center, 2001
Trizec Hahn, developer
Hollywood Boulevard at Highland Avenue

A great many shops fitted into a rabbit warren that also houses a dull subway station. The tedium is relieved only by a large court that has details from D.W. Griffith's famous set for *Intolerance* splashed around. Unfortunately some rearing elephants and an Assyrian gate do not raise the building out of the cheap and tawdry.

a large building, but because of its scale, style, and the good taste of its architects, it fits into its neighborhood beautifully.

33. Los Angeles First National Bank (now Security Pacific), 1927
Meyer and Holler
6777 Hollywood Boulevard

A strange but effective Gothic and Spanish Revival goulash.

34. Bank of America, 1914
Ellet Parcher;
Classical façade added, 1920s;
remodeling, 1935
Morgan, Walls, and Clements
6870 Hollywood Boulevard

This originally was a four-story building. It was cut down to its present one-story size by MWC, who added the tile roof. At present it has gone garish.

35. Max Factor Building, 1931
S. Charles Lee, remodeling
1659–1666 Highland Avenue

Lee was a fashionable theater designer (e.g., the Los Angeles Theater in downtown Los Angeles). He chose Regency Moderne (with side-glances at the Art Deco) to clothe this old warehouse, giving it delicate and sophisticated cosmetic richness with the use of pink and white marble. Take a look inside. The building now houses the Max Factor Museum of Beauty.

36. 6565 Sunset Boulevard, 2001
Shimoda Design Group (Joey Shimoda)
6565 Sunset Boulevard

This is yet another facelift of an old building. The façade is a sheer curtain wall of glass reminiscent of Willis Polk's Hallidie

32. Linn House AIDS Hospice,
1996
Cavaedium
1001 Martel Avenue

Late International Style, but it also looks Spanish, particularly with all the bougainvillaea and other luxuriant growth. This is

36

39. Kress and Company (now Frederick's), 1935
Edward F. Sibbert
6606–6612 Hollywood Boulevard

It is very tempting to leave out this lavender-and-purple horror, but behind the recent color scheme is a good late–Art Deco building by the New York–based architect who designed Kress stores across the country. Note the setbacks; try to ignore the window displays.

40. J. J. Newberry Company, 1928
Newberry Company
6600–6604 Hollywood Boulevard

The most lively Art Deco on Hollywood Boulevard, but it is upstaged by Frederick's next door.

41. Baine Building (now U.T.B.), 1926
Gogerty and Weyl
6601–6609 Hollywood Boulevard

Very lovely Spanish Revival above the "modernized" first floor.

Building (1917) in San Francisco—without the ornament. A cornice or hood tops the building. Two giant palms, reflected in the glass, complete the experience.

37. Egyptian Theater, 1922
Meyer and Holler
6712 Hollywood Boulevard

Pure architecture of entertainment, this building was altered over the years and then let fall apart. Several attempts were made to put it together again during the several efforts to revive Hollywood, but the theater, like the city, continued to deteriorate until 1993 when angels of mercy

descended from heaven and hired Hodgetts and Fung to restore the Egyptian's lost glory. It isn't exactly what it was originally, but is enough to make you feel that the 1920s have been reborn.

38. Shane Building (now Hollywood Center), 1930
**S. Norton;
F. Wallis**
6652–6654 Hollywood Boulevard, on the southwest corner of Cherokee Avenue

A marvelous Art Deco marquee on Cherokee Avenue calls attention to an equally distinguished lobby, almost completely intact.

37

42. Janes House, 1903
Dennis and Farwell
6541 Hollywood Boulevard

By a miracle this late–Queen Anne house remains on this otherwise commercial boulevard. Farwell worked in the New York office of McKim, Mead, and White before he came to California.

43. Warner Theater (now Pacific Hollywood), 1926–27
G. Albert Lansburgh
6423–6445 Hollywood Boulevard

Somehow the architect combined Renaissance, Rococo, Moorish, and Art Deco ornamentation to produce a very effective piece of architecture.

44. Owl Drug Company, 1934
Morgan, Walls, and Clements
6380–6384 Hollywood Boulevard, on the southwest corner of Cahuenga Boulevard

Surely this must be one of the crowning achievements of the Streamline Moderne, to be rated in the same class as Robert Derrah's Coca-Cola Bottling Plant.

45. Francis Howard Regional Branch Library, 1985
Frank O. Gehry and Associates
1623 Ivar Avenue

The old Hollywood Public Library burned in 1982 and was replaced by this present Gehry building. Internally, it is a pleasant and functional building, although the single, small circular staircase is inadequate for public traffic. What is really disturbing is the exterior, which has no presence at all. From a distance, this structure could be a small office building; close up, the stairs lead-ing down to the confining small forecourt hardly hint that this is a public building. A few classic palms might have at least hinted at its function.

46. Corner of Hollywood Boulevard and Vine Street
a. Taft Building, 1923
Walker and Eisen
6290 Hollywood Boulevard

b. B. H. Dyas Company, 1927
6300 Hollywood Boulevard

c. Hollywood Equitable Building, 1929
Aleck Curlett
6253 Hollywood Boulevard

These buildings are not great or even outstanding architecture. But for their time they were notable for their height—150 feet, the limit in the 1920s. Therefore, they represented a visible center for Hollywood. The Dyas (Broadway) Building is closed. Ironically, two lower buildings on the northwest corner were more notable—the Laemmle Building (1933) by Richard J. Neutra and Sardi's Restaurant Building (1932–34) by R. M. Schindler. Because of extravagant remodeling, neither has a sign of its architect's style.

47. Yucca-Vine Tower, circa 1928
Gogerty and Weyl
Northwest corner of Yucca and Vine Streets

French curvilinear ornament mixed with Art Deco.

48. Capitol Records Tower, 1954–56
Welton Becket Associates
1750 Vine Street

Symbolic architecture. What could be more appropriate for the headquarters of a recording com-

pany than for the building to look like a stack of records! The twelve-story tower is constructed of reinforced concrete. Across the street at 1735 Vine Street is the old Hollywood Playhouse (later refurbished as The Hollywood Palace), a Churrigueresque dream designed (1926) by Gogerty and Weyl.

49. Pantages Theater, 1929
B. Marcus Priteca
6233 Hollywood Boulevard

On the exterior this theater building does not have the sensational quality of Mann's Chinese theater down the street, but go inside. It is one of the most dramatic Baroque statements ever made.

50. Krotona Court, 1912–13
Mead and Requa
2130 Vista del Mar Avenue

Originally built for the Theosophical Society, this complex is properly exotic, although its exoticism is played off against the purity of Irving J. Gill (Mead had been a partner of Gill in San Diego for a few years). The aura of the mystical East is suggested in the Islamic domes, horseshoe, and cusped arches.

51. Hansel and Gretel Cottages, circa 1925
2234, 2244 Vista del Mar Avenue

Two cottages look to the medieval rural English cottage. The double cottage with its central drive-through and folk paintings on its exterior walls, which is located at 6114–6116 Scenic Avenue, hints at the French rural cottage. Across the street, at 6111 Scenic Avenue, is a delightful French Norman cottage with a small tower attached to the hillside garage.

52. House, circa 1920
6147 Temple Hill Drive

Islamic, with dome and all. A smaller Islamic cottage is situated nearby at 6106 Temple Hill Drive.

53. Vedanta Temple, 1938
1946 Vedanta Terrace

The onion dome of this Islamic complex is visible from various points of the eastern Hollywood Hills.

54. Mosk House, 1933
Richard J. Neutra
2742 Hollyridge Drive

The Mosk House is intended to be machine-repeatable, the first of a colony of Neutra houses. The living room serves as a focal point for the lower wings at each side.

55. Hollywoodland Gates, Hollywood Sign, 1923
The gates are located on Beachwood Drive at Westshire Drive (the sign is situated off Mount Lee Drive)

The tall, picturesque, somewhat-Gothic fairy-tale sandstone gates were built on the lowest slopes of Mount Lee to tell you that you were entering a very prestigious part of Hollywood. The subdivision was advertised by the famous Hollywood Sign still standing high on Mount Lee. When constructed, the sign read "Hollywoodland," and it was a grand lighted billboard for that most time-honored activity in Los Angeles, the sale of real estate. The letters forming "land" were dropped off in 1945. The sign has been restored and restored, a reminder that beneath the façade of materialism, Los Angeles hides a strain of sentiment. Both the gate and the sign are official Cultural-Historic Monuments of the city. The last major restoration of the fifty-foot-long sign, lighted by more than 4,000 bulbs, took place in 1979. The suburban

56. Courtyard Apartments, 1952
Craig Ellwood
1570 Labaig Avenue

A Miesian complex in a strange area for "less is more" architecture to appear.

57. Warner Brothers West Coast Studios, 1922
Southeast corner of Sunset Boulevard and Bronson Avenue

A long low building that salutes the street with a magnificent set of Doric columns.

58. Columbia Broadcasting System Building, 1937–38
William Lescaze and E. T. Heitschmidt
6121 Sunset Boulevard

area above the gates is fascinating for the student of Period Revivals. Note the tiny English cottage on the north side of Beachwood Drive at Ledgewood Drive. This was originally the real estate office for the development.

A classic well-publicized example of the early (for America) International Style, now badly remodeled. You can still sense Lescaze's design if you erase the present walls behind the pilotis.

59. Sunset-Vine Tower, 1964
Honnold, Reibsamen, and Rex
*Corner of Sunset and
Vine Streets*

Thin, late International Style emphasizing the vertical.

60. U.S. Post Office,
Hollywood Branch, 1937
Claude Beelman;
Allison and Allison
1615 Wilcox Avenue

A small but impressive expression of the Classical PWA Moderne.

61. Commercial Building,
circa 1928
6607 Sunset Boulevard

Lively Churrigueresque ornament around the entrance. We wonder how long such romantic buildings will last.

62. Hollywood Chamber of
Commerce, 1925
Morgan, Walls, and Clements
*Just west of Hudson Street on
Sunset Boulevard*

These architects always seem to treat their cast-stone Churrigueresque ornament in a lighthearted manner. The building was more charming, however, when large pepper trees once stood in front.

63. Crossroads of the World,
1936
Robert V. Derrah
6671 Sunset Boulevard

The theme is set by a Streamline Moderne ship sailing into Sunset Boulevard with a tall open tower (supporting a lighted globe) on its prow. Go to the stern and you will find shops in the Spanish Revival, Tudor, and French Provincial modes. The architect has carried the concept of the 1920s pedestrian mall into the new streamline age of the mid-1930s. It is perhaps significant that Derrah is one of the few architects to have two of his buildings declared cultural-historic landmarks by the

Los Angeles Cultural Heritage Board (now Commission). The other is the equally remarkable Coca-Cola Bottling Plant near downtown Los Angeles.

64. Hollywood High School
Science Building, 1934–35
Marsh, Smith, and Powell
*Northwest corner of
Sunset Boulevard and
Highland Avenue*

Monumental Streamline Moderne given juice by high-minded slogans at appropriate places and a characteristic Federal Arts Project bas-relief by Bartolo Mako over the door. In the school library is a mural, *Education*, by Haldine Douglas. This was painted in 1934.

65. Franklin/La Brea Family
Housing, 1994
Adele Naude Santos
*Northwest corner of
La Brea and Franklin Avenue*

About all you can see of this large

group of "affordable" housing units are its barrel-vaulted roofs, but it is by an important architect, a professor of architecture at Berkeley. Maybe it will be on a tour someday.

66. Carolina Motel, 1959
Armet and Davis
East side of La Brea Avenue, just north of Sunset Boulevard

A pure Southern California project of the 1950s, designed by a firm that produced a wide array of popular automobile-oriented restaurants and other buildings. With the exception of the lobby, a two-story perforated metal screen covers the entire front of the building. Behind this linear surface is the two-story motel, with underground garage and, of course, a pool-patio area.

67. Toberman Storage Warehouse, 1925
Morgan, Walls, and Clements
1025 N. Highland Avenue

This is an illustration of how a small skyscraper could be clothed in the Spanish Revival mode and at the same time appear as an excellent example of the 1920s "American Vertical style." The building has lost some of its zest in remodeling.

68. Community Laundry Building, 1927
W. J. Saunders
Northeast corner of Highland and Willoughby Avenues

The piers of this Spanish Revival building are covered with shields. When the sun rakes over them about midday, the effect is that of the Casa de las Conchas in Salamanca. We never exaggerate.

69. Aaron Brothers Building, circa 1928
East side of Orange Drive, between Romaine Street and Willoughby Avenue

Spanish Revival with some good ornament. But its salient feature is its present unearthly color.

70. Producers Film Center, circa 1928
Southeast corner of Romaine Street and Sycamore Avenue

A little gem of the Art Deco.

71. Plummer Park Community Center, 2001
Koning Eizenberg Architecture
7377 Santa Monica Boulevard West Hollywood

The visible architecture in this building is the offbeat street façade that somewhat resembles a Ships Restaurant of the 1950s. It is a redo and extension of an older building, and houses a motley crew of senior citizens, kids, and cross-dressers. The park also includes a 1930s theater and game area. It is a pleasant surprise.

72. Claudia Grau Building, 1990
South side of Melrose Boulevard, east of Sierra Bonita Avenue

A wonderful shop front in tile (including the sign), inspired by the turn-of-the-century designs of Antonio Gaudi in Barcelona.

73. Danziger Studio, 1965
Frank O. Gehry and Associates
7001 Melrose at Sycamore Avenue

This small studio building was one of Frank Gehry's first buildings to be widely published. Though restrained compared to his current work, the Danziger Studio building indicates how he was moving from the world of traditional architecture to sculpture as architecture. Minimal architecture at its best.

74. Telesound Studio, circa 1945
6926 Melrose Avenue

The architect of this late Streamline Moderne building

71

curved the corners into the entrance, leaving a single column in the middle. This one, with its glass brick, is certainly not minimal!

75. Propaganda Films, 1988
Franklin D. Israel Design Associates
Corner of Waring and Mansfield Avenues

The nonassertive stucco façade of this 10,000-square-foot warehouse building hides inside a Constructivist village. In the center is a boat-shaped enclosure of rooms. Independent "houses" define the other side of the streets as they wander around the lozenge-shaped centerpiece.

76. Limelight Productions, 1991
Franklin D. Israel Design Associates
Corner of Highland and Lexington Avenues

Like the Propaganda Films design, this is a small village within a wood-roofed warehouse building. The principal "street" plays with different inexpensive materials, deep colors, and natural and artificial light. With some of the enclosures, the structure of the walls are revealed; in others, a painted skin of plywood and other materials establishes either planes or entire volumes.

77. EVCO Film Library, 1968
Leroy B. Miller
838 Seward Street

Minimal Modern architecture in brick.

78. Apartment Building, 1926
J. M. Close
747 N. Wilcox Avenue

It is amusing to speculate upon what on earth was in this developer-builder-architect's mind when he conceived of buildings such as this, only one of several essays in the Egyptian Revival that he erected around Hollywood and elsewhere. J. M. Close designed, built, and then marketed many of these apartment buildings. In his advertisements, he encouraged prospective buyers to "pyramid your dollars." But that which is Egyptian is only the pylon and colonnaded frontispiece. The rest is pure Los Angeles stucco box.

79. Film Exchange, Inc., Building, circa 1928
Southeast corner of Santa Monica Boulevard and Cole Avenue

A tiny relic of the Regency Moderne. There is a key on top of the tower that may someday release something.

80. Hollywood Studio Club, 1925–26
Julia Morgan
1215 Lodi Place

A mildly Italian Renaissance design; the second-floor loggia and the painted and decorated walls are carried out with delicacy.

81a. Hollywood Cemetery, 1900 and later
Morgan, Walls and Clements, and others
5950 Santa Monica Boulevard

With its mausoleums and ornate sculpture, not to mention the quantity of famous people buried here, this cemetery seems to be an annex of the Paramount Studio at the other end of the block. Probably the most distinguished architecture is the Classical mausoleum of William Andrews Clark designed (1922) by Robert Farquhar. Egypt and other exotic sources are present in other monuments and mausoleums. A more recent addition to the major monuments of the cemetery is the tombstone of Carl Morgan Bigsby (1959) that confronts us with a tall rocket ready to take us quickly to heaven.

81b. Paramount Studio Lot
5500 Melrose Avenue

Off-limits to the public, but the main attraction is the old iron gate (circa 1928) at the end of Bronson Avenue at Marathon Street. Here a Spanish Renaissance gate is placed between two white-stucco, tile-roofed Hispanic buildings. The script sign "Paramount Pictures" is as much a delightful period piece as the gate.

82. Karnak Apartment Building, 1925
J. M. Close
5617 La Mirada Avenue

Since there is another Egyptian Revival apartment house just a block from here, we suggest that urban renewalists investigate the possibility of building a pyramid in honor of J. M. Close. They could do (and have done) worse.

83. Ahmed Apartment Building, 1925
J. M. Close
5616 Lexington Avenue

Almost a duplicate of the Karnak, this apartment house has been refitted with the original murals, which have been restored with considerable verve.

84

85. House, 1939
Edward Richard Lind
822 Alexandria Avenue

Lind was in Schindler's office in
the mid-1930s. Here you can see
how creatively he applied the lessons of the master to a small one-
story stucco dwelling.

86. Service Station,
circa 1928
5125 Melrose Avenue

Art Deco.

87. Hollywood-Wilshire
Health Center, 1968
Honnold, Reibsamen, and Rex
5505 Melrose Avenue

Some may write off this low concrete building as 1960s Brutalist.
We think it has class.

88. Morgan House, 1917
Irving J. Gill
626 N. Arden Road

A variation by Gill of his small
prototype, single-family dwelling.
As with most of his buildings, its
walls are of hollow tile covered
with stucco. The building has
been carefully restored by Roy
McMakin and Andie Zelnio. For
those interested in Gill's architecture, this building is a must.

89. House, circa 1925
717 June Street

A tiny mosque.

90. Four Apartment
Buildings, circa 1928
*1128–1144 S. Vista Street, just
above Santa Monica Boulevard*

A whole row of Andalusian
treasures.

84. Jardinette Apartments,
1927
Richard J. Neutra
*5128 W. Marathon Street,
at the southeast corner of
Manhattan Place*

This project began as a joint
Schindler-Neutra venture, with
Neutra finally doing it as an
independent commission. Neutra
provided bands of black (now
painted over) between the windows that gave the illusion that
this concrete building was composed of strongly contrasting horizontal bands of glass and
projecting balconies. In his classic
volume written with Philip
Johnson (*The International Style,
Architecture Since 1922*, New
York, 1932), Henry Russell
Hitchcock asserted that this col-
oristic effect of banding was "dis-
honest" and that it compromised
the design of the building.

85

91. Bungalow, circa 1920
1127–1129 Vista Street

A modest bungalow as a miniature Egyptian temple.

92. Normandie Towers, 1924
7219 Hampton Avenue

An apartment complex of twenty-three units that is designed to suggest a fragment of a French Norman village. Towers, turrets, and balconies are enshrouded within a heavily planted garden.

93. Lamy/Newton House, 1988
Franklin D. Israel Design Associates
620 N. Cherokee Avenue

An addition to an existing house. This pavilion comes close to being a cube, clothed in deep colors—maroon, mustard, and blue. It seems to float on a thin wood shelf extended over the pool.

94. Gabriel Duque House, 1932
Paul R. Williams
340 N. Las Palmas Avenue

Paul Williams's version of the French Provincial dwelling became increasingly delicate in its detailing and at the same time more classical. This house and #95 are still Country French, but they seem to have more to do with the then-popular Anglo Colonial Revival.

95. Banning House #1, 1929
Paul R. Williams
425 N. McCadden Place

This Banning house is a version of the French Provincial, in this case, stucco; the design is intimate in scale and well adapted to its suburban siting.

33 • Hollywood Hills

Although the roads were laid out in the 1920s, the summit of this section of
the Santa Monica Mountains did not begin to be developed until the 1930s. Schindler's
Fitzpatrick House (1936), which is so prominent when you finally twist to the top of
Laurel Canyon Boulevard, was built as a real estate come-on to attract buyers to the area.
The development of the summit before and after World War II is a dramatic illustration
of how a landscape, even a rugged one, can be transformed by energy and water. Indeed,
the vegetation is now far more significant than most of the housing.

There are a remarkable number of important houses located in the Hollywood
Hills. Sadly enough, only a dozen or so are really visible from a distance or from a public
road. Even these are often difficult to find because of the bewildering pattern of meandering streets. These are all indicated on our map, but it might be advisable to plan your
journey beforehand with a Thomas map in hand. We have set this section apart from
central Hollywood simply because when you are up this high, you might as well stay up.
Incidentally, there are other things on and just off Mulholland Drive, a road that sticks
with determination to the top of the hills almost as far as the ocean, many miles to
the west.

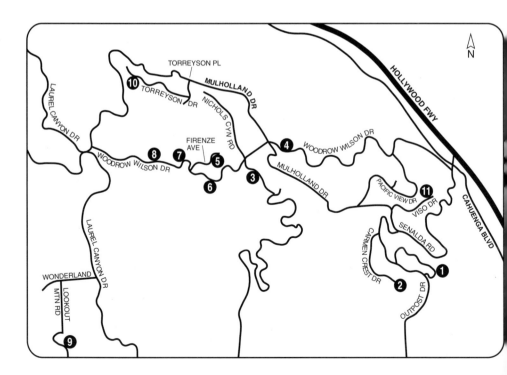

1. Johnson House, 1963
Lloyd Wright
7017 Senalda Drive

Ancient Mayan made Moderne. If the lavender hue isn't original, it should be.

2. Wolff House, 1960
Ladd and Kelsey
2400 Carmen Crest Drive

A sheer stucco wall and metal door seal this purist house from the curious.

3. General Panel House, 1950
Konrad Wachsmann and
Walter Gropius
2861 Nichols Canyon Road

Of the four such houses by these famous architects in the Los Angeles area, this is the most easily seen. This single-story design projects both logic and dullness.

4. Bell House, 1940
John Lautner
7714 Woodrow Wilson Drive

Set far from Woodrow Wilson Drive on a very private road, the house can nevertheless be seen from certain points to the east. Like Lautner's own house in the Silver Lake district, the pre–World War II Bell House shares stylistic similarities with the works of Harris, Ain, and Wurster.

5. House, 1937–39
Barcume and King
7777 Firenze Avenue

A mixture of Monterey and Moderne.

6. Shulman House and
Studio, 1950
Raphael S. Soriano
7875 Woodrow Wilson Drive

The distinguished architectural photographer's studio is connected to the main house by a small pergola and courtyard. He has landscaped the grounds so

magnificently (including a Redwood grove!) that you cannot see the house from the street.

7. Granstedt House, 1938
Harwell H. Harris
7922 Woodrow Wilson Drive

We are pleased that this beautiful house can easily be seen. A drive-through garage runs parallel to the street. Also, here you can see how Harris worked with his roof to create clerestory and other high sources of lighting.

8. Fitzpatrick House, 1936
R. M. Schindler
8078 Woodrow Wilson Drive

The de Stijl composition of overlaid volumes of horizontal stucco surfaces can best be seen from below on Laurel Canyon before it joins Mulholland and Woodrow Wilson. The front has been altered, but the southwest façade and the sunken garden to the west are still intact.

9. Margaret Shelby Fillmore House (Edward A. Bailey), 1929
Roy Selden Price;
Benjamin Morton Purdy, landscape architect
8818 Lookout Mountain Avenue

Price was one of the most gifted of Los Angeles Period Revival architects of the 1920s. He really understood what the "picturesque" meant for his Los Angeles clients. His most famous residence, the extensive Spanish Revival house in Beverly Hills for the film director Thomas H. Ince, is now gone. Though small by comparison to the Ince House, the Margaret Fillmore House is one of the city's gems of traditionalist architecture. When it was completed, the editors of *Arts and Decoration* wrote of its style, "Though rural in effect, there is a suggestion of Medieval Italy in the doorway and wrought-

iron stair rails." In fact, its image has much more to do with the provincial cottage architecture of England and France. Countering this cultivated provincial style (in the manner of Edwin Lutyens) is an expansive Classical main entrance with pilasters supporting a pair of broken volutes, which serve as a porch roof. The play between the Medieval and the Classical continues on the interior. The rooms of the Fillmore house are oriented around an inner court, while to the rear looking over a view of the city and far distant ocean is a large, pillared, circular garden structure with a fireplace.

10. Leonard J. Malin House ("Chemosphere"), 1960
John Lautner
7776 Torreyson Drive

At first it seems to be a flying saucer, but then you see that it is on a pedestal firmly riveted to the hill. The house is at the end of a private drive, but there are many places to view it on Torreyson Drive and Woodrow Wilson Drive. The owner/builder of the house commented that "there are a great number of very normal, intelligent people who do not specially enjoy doing yard work on Saturday afternoon. I am one of these. I will be very happy, sitting, looking down at the tops of trees, which do not have to be mowed."

11. Viso House, 1989
Hodgetts + Fung Design Associates
2911 Viso Drive

The vernacular tradition of Schindler is taken into the late 1980s in this stucco-sheathed hillside dwelling. The design centers on an internal cylinder, which is sliced through by an angled axis. To the rear you can experience the play of the layered volumes.

34 • East Hollywood Los Feliz Griffith Park

We have let the Hollywood Freeway (Highway 101) act as a dividing line between central Hollywood, east Hollywood, and the Los Feliz district. To the north, Griffith Park provides a hilly backdrop to the area. The 3,015-acre park was given to the city in 1896 by Col. Griffith J. Griffith, though its development for public use had to wait until the twentieth century.

The meandering array of streets that makes up east Hollywood (including Griffith Park and the Los Feliz district) was annexed to the City of Los Angeles in 1910. Through the early 1920s a number of large houses and estates were built in the Los Feliz area. The only one of these still standing is the Earl C. Anthony house, designed by Bernard Maybeck. In the teens, 1920s, and later, middle- and upper-middle-class houses were built in the hilly section north of Los Feliz Boulevard. Below Los Feliz Boulevard, reaching down to Hollywood Boulevard, land use was more mixed. Single-family housing (dating from the turn of the century on through the early 1940s) was, generally, more modest in size, and there were a good number of duplexes and apartments built. Strip commercial development

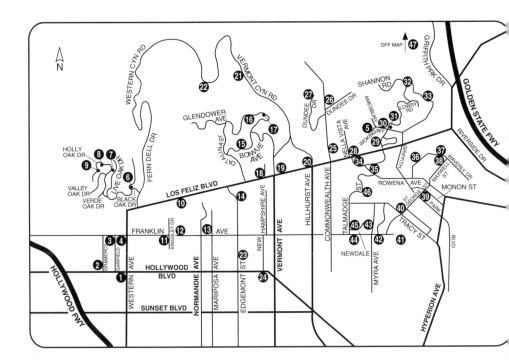

occurred along several of the north/south streets, and along portions of Franklin Avenue and Hollywood Boulevard.

The original Griffith Park consisted of 3,015 acres of hilly terrain. This was slowly increased to its present area of 4,063.87 acres. Thus, in size it is in the league of New York's Central Park, Philadelphia's Fairmount Park, or San Francisco's Golden Gate Park. But, for a variety of reasons, this great park functions not as an urban park but more like a distant regional park. Its rough landscape does not readily lend itself to the easygoing pleasures that Frederick Law Olmsted had in mind when he laid out Central Park in New York or Prospect Park in Brooklyn. Added to this limitation is the fact that the park really has no meaningful connection to the city proper. Its one major connection to the city is via Vermont Canyon Road, but even though this is a handsome winding boulevard, it creates the feeling of upper-middle-class suburbia, not the entrance to the city's major park. Griffith Park has had to battle off the believers in hardscape—ranging from the incursion of freeways to the location of buildings constructed within it.

1. MPA Office Building, 1928
S. Charles Lee
Southwest corner of
Hollywood Boulevard and
Western Avenue

Art Deco, but the great effect is in the high-relief sculpture on the balcony fronts.

2. Hollywood Christian Church, 1922
Robert H. Orr
1717 N. Gramercy Place

A great Ionic pile.

Kleihauer Memorial Chapel, 1967
Carleton M. Winslow Jr. and Warren Waltz
Austerely exotic, this building has no relationship to the older building.

3. Garfield Court Apartments, 1927
A. J. Waid
1833 Garfield Place

A really grand Spanish court with beautiful trees. Even the fire escapes are beautifully designed and crafted. The twenty units of this two- and three-story, garden-court apartment building are organized around a large court-yard. Below parts of the complex is an underground garage.

4. Security Pacific Bank, 1972–73
Craig Ellwood & Associates
1811 N. Western Avenue

"Less is more" at a 45-degree angle to the street.

5. Walt Disney House, 1932
F. Scott Crowhurst
4053 Woking Way

This house is an enlarged Hansel and Gretel cottage. A large, squat round tower with a high-pitched conical roof houses the entrance.

6. Taggart House, 1922–24
Lloyd Wright
5423 Live Oak Drive

One of Lloyd Wright's simplest and most picturesque stucco-and-wood buildings, carefully related to the hill to which it clings. Incidentally, Ferndell Park just below the house is one of the loveliest parks in Los Angeles.

7

7. Samuels-Navarro House, 1926–28
Lloyd Wright
5609 Valley Oak Drive

Here Lloyd Wright translates the textured pre-cast-concrete Mayanesque block into pressed metal. The result hints at pre-Columbian Revival and Art Deco composition. The main (top) floor is cross-axial, with one arm terminating in an open court with swimming pool. In 1990–91 Schweitzer BIM (Josh Schweitzer) provided a sophisticated remodeling of the interior spaces. This sort of remodel of a major historic monument always creates an inherent conflict between preservation and the desire of new owners to express themselves. The Schweitzer firm has sought to play a close game between their new work and a respect for Lloyd Wright's design, an approach that in this case is probably for the best.

8. Ernest House, 1937
Gregory Ain
5670 Holly Oak Drive

Using large areas of glass in this house, Ain emphasizes the relationship between indoors and out. Some details of the house indicate his admiration for Schindler's designs of the late 1920s and early 1930s.

9. Edwards House, 1936
Gregory Ain
5642 Holly Oak Drive

This single-story house comprises a series of walled enclosures that give each space complete privacy.

10. Vinmont House, 1926
Roland E. Coate
5136 Los Feliz Boulevard

A characteristic Mediterranean/Spanish Revival two-story house by an architect who specialized in this mode, but who also did equally well in the Tudor and Anglo-Colonial Revival styles.

11. The Casa Laguna, 1928
Arthur B. and Nina W. Zwebell
Southwest corner of Franklin Avenue and Kingsley Drive

A twelve-unit Spanish Andalusian garden-court apartment by the pair who designed many of the most successful examples in Los Angeles. Behind a pair of palm trees is the balconied two-story building. Entrances to the individual apartments are off the large central courtyard. The courtyard contains a large fountain and an outdoor fireplace. To the rear, a sunken row of garages supports a south-facing terrace.

12. Sowden House, 1926
Lloyd Wright
5121 Franklin Avenue

Built around an inner court that originally contained an elaborate fountain and Mayan-inspired stele, the building is entered through a door at the lower level, almost hidden under a huge cave-like window framed in decorative concrete blocks. Brendan Gill called this "a kind of pre-Jaws jaws." It has recently been restored and updated by Xorin Balbes, whose flourishes seem to be appropriate.

13. Apartment Building, circa 1938
Carl Kay
1941–43 Mariposa Avenue

A two-story Streamline Moderne composition.

14. House, circa 1925
David J. Witmer
2020 Edgemont Street

An unusual example of a reinforced concrete house with the wide board marks of the forms strongly showing. Its image and detailing are Tudor.

15. Moore House, 1964
Craig Ellwood & Associates
4791 Bonvue Avenue

Here Ellwood applies his personal Miesian aesthetic to a structure that exhibits even more wood than the Kubly House, which he was building in Pasadena at the same time.

16. Skolnik House, 1952
R. M. Schindler
2567 Glendower Avenue

In several of his late works Schindler concentrated on simple stucco-covered volumes, roofs extending over clerestory windows, and thin linear wood members. All are present in the Skolnik House. Later additions were made by Gregory Ain (1960).

17. Ennis House, 1924
Frank Lloyd Wright
2607 Glendower Avenue

Variously called a mausoleum, a Mayan temple, and a palace, this is without a doubt the most monumental of Wright's experiments with "knit-block" construction. It was damaged in the 1994 earthquake.

18. House, circa 1924
Northwest corner of Los Feliz Boulevard and New Hampshire Avenue

A striking openly revealed concrete house best viewed from New Hampshire Avenue.

19. Los Feliz Manor Apartment Building, 1929
Jack Grundfor
4643 Los Feliz Boulevard

One of Los Angeles's very effective examples of the Art Deco. It still retains the contrast of white surfaces and green trim.

20. Barcelona and Coruna Apartments, 1932
George Fosayke
Northwest corner of Los Feliz Boulevard and Hillhurst Avenue

A pair of Spanish apartments share a common interior court. Each has an arched entrance for the driveway, and both boast cantilevered wood balconies.

21. Greek Theater, 1913, 1929–30
S. Tilden Norton and F. H. Wallis;
Heath and Gore of Tacoma, Washington;
Department of Parks
Vermont Canyon Road

Heath and Gore were brought into the planning of the theater because they were considered experts on Greek theaters. A flat Doric façade masks an open-air theater seating four thousand people. It isn't much as architecture, but you will certainly notice it on the way up Vermont Canyon.

22. Griffith Park Observatory and Planetarium, 1935
John C. Austin and F. M. Ashley;
obelisk and bas-reliefs, (*Galileo, Copernicus,* etc.), 1934
Archibald Garner;
interior murals, 1935
Hugo Ballin
Western Canyon Road

PWA Classical Moderne in exposed reinforced concrete. A fine achievement of the depression years. High on the hill, it is a very romantic object, completing many vistas in Los Angeles like a huge eighteenth-century English garden. Its siting and entrance are pure axial Beaux-Arts. Closed until 2006.

23. Thirteenth Church of Christ, Scientist, 1930
Allison and Allison
1750 N. Edgemont Street

A very sophisticated Italian Renaissance ensemble.

24. Barnsdall Park
Entrance on Hollywood Boulevard, about 100 yards west of intersection with Vermont Avenue

a. Barnsdall ("Hollyhock") House, 1917–20
Frank Lloyd Wright

As of January 2003, the house is closed for earthquake repairs.

b. Studio-Residence A, 1920
R. M. Schindler, under Wright's supervision

c. Garden Wall and Landscaping, 1924
R. M. Schindler

d. Wading Pool and Pergola, 1925
R. M. Schindler and Richard J. Neutra

e. Junior Arts Center, 1967
Paul Hunter, Walter Benedict, Herbert Kahn, Edward Tarrell

f. Municipal Art Gallery, 1971
Wehmueller and Stephens

Aline Barnsdall, like another oil millionaire, Gaylord Wilshire, toyed with Marxist ideas. She envisioned a veritable "people's park" when she gave her estate to the city. In the years that have followed, the fringes of her estate

on Vermont and Sunset have been inundated with commercial buildings and a medical complex that do nothing for the spirit of the place. But go up the drive and you are almost out of this skulchpile. The first important building that you see is Studio-Residence A, now called the Arts and Crafts Center. This was to be the first of several such artists' residences in the manner of the MacDowell Colony in New Hampshire. Even though designed by Schindler, the building is very beholden to the Prairie style of Frank Lloyd Wright, for whom Schindler acted as supervisor of the main house construction while the Master was in Japan.

Studio-Residence B was razed in the 1950s. The main Barnsdall House, with its pre-Columbian air and stylized hollyhock orna-

24a

mentation, was badly damaged in the 1994 earthquake and is being restored. Even with time's changes, the interior—particularly in the entrance, living room, and dining areas—displays Frank Lloyd Wright's magical spatial concepts. All is drama. The principal interior spaces have been restored, and several pieces of Wright's original furniture for the house have been reproduced.

Wright constructed a temporary gallery between the main house and the pre-Colombian-style dog kennels in 1956. This gallery was intended to house a major showing of his drawings, and was used as the municipal art gallery until the late 1960s, when a new gallery was designed and constructed by another firm and the old gallery was torn down. No loss, except that Wright had several interesting designs for a new museum. Suffice to say that the present building, while not great architecture, has exhibition spaces that, though small, are better adapted to the viewing of art than those found in several other public museums around town.

The Junior Art Center is a much-needed facility in a light Wrightian manner. The garden structures were designed by Schindler and Neutra.

25. House, 1924
Alfred Heineman
2234 Commonwealth Avenue

Important because, with its roof swooping into the eaves and with its Hansel and Gretel ornament, it demonstrates a tendency of the Arts and Crafts movement toward sentimentality.

26. Schrage House, 1951
Raphael S. Soriano
2648 Commonwealth Avenue

A one-story International Style design in plywood, glass, and steel. Soriano at his best.

27. Lovell House, 1929
Richard J. Neutra
4616 Dundee Drive

Without question, this house and Schindler's house for the same clients in Newport Beach are the greatest monuments of the early International Style in Southern California. The Lovell House, with its open free-flowing plan, its modern machine-age materials, and its structural form, firmly established Neutra's world reputation. Today, more than seventy years after its construction and in spite of slight alterations, the Lovell House looks new—the highest compliment.

28. Apartment House, 1935
Northeast corner of Los Feliz Boulevard and Nella Vista Avenue

Regency Moderne.

29. Johnstone House, 1935
W. P. Kesling
3311 Lowry Road

Streamline Moderne. We emphasize this style because it took an act of moderate courage to flout the conventions of the time.

30. Ulm House, 1937
Milton Black
3606 Amesbury Road

We are sounding one note. Just the same, this Streamline Moderne two-story house, with its dramatic curved staircase encased in glass brick, simply stands out.

31. Cole House, 1948
Ain, Johnson, and Day
3642 Lowry Road

A regional version of International Style in stucco and wood.

32. House, circa 1928
End of Lowry Road at Shannon Road

Ye olde English cottage.

33. Griffith Park Girl's Camp, 1949
Smith, Jones, and Contini
North end of Griffith Park Boulevard

A wood post-and-beam structure that is more of an open shelter than a building.

34. Farrell House, 1926
Lloyd Wright
3209 Lowry Road

An ordinary Spanish Revival bungalow of the 1920s becomes pre-Columbian with a facing of textured concrete blocks.

35. Carr House, 1925
Lloyd Wright
Southeast corner of Lowry
Road and Rowena Avenue

Originally, this still-unusual
house had a tent room at the side
(overlooking Rowena) and a bent
pattern of fine canvas awnings,
which provided privacy and kept
the west sun off the side of the
house. Portions of the exterior
stucco walls were stenciled to
suggest an ornamented concrete-
block pattern.

36. Anthony House, 1927
Bernard Maybeck;
Mark Daniels,
landscape architect;
1956–66
Lutah M. Riggs
3431 Waverly Drive

Now a Roman Catholic retreat,
this is almost impossible to see
unless you want to retreat, which
might be a good idea. We include
it because it is the only well-
authenticated building by
Maybeck in the Los Angeles area.
It is one of the architect's most
romantic houses, which is saying a
lot. The general effect is Medieval,
but of course Maybeck thought
nothing of bringing in elements of
other styles in order to get desired
effects. It is fascinating to compare
Maybeck's spatial explosions with
Frank Lloyd Wright's equally dramatic but more integrated volumes. Between 1956 and 1966
impressive formal gardens and
walled terraces were laid out by
Lutah M. Riggs (she also added a
Studio Building in 1967). These
landscape additions represent the
most extensive formal gardens
realized in Southern California in
the post–World War II years.

37. McAlmon House, 1935–36
R. M. Schindler
2721 Waverly Drive

The house is a piece of architectural sculpture embracing the
complete range of Schindler's
de Stijl aesthetic. Actually you
get two for the price of one. The
house, with garage at street level,
is an old bungalow that Schindler
moved down the hill and clothed
in modern dress.

38. Schapiro House, 1949
J. R. Davidson
Northwest corner of
Waverly Drive and
Maxwell Street

Almost all of Davidson's houses
are hard to see, but here, enough
of the jutting roof is visible to
make your trip worthwhile.

39. Bungalow Court,
circa 1925
2906–2912 Griffith Park
Boulevard

Each of these eight units is a
miniature Norman cottage.
A matching tower stands at
the rear to give visual focus.
Certainly this is one of the
outstanding bungalow courts
in the Los Angeles area!

40. John Marshall High School, 1930–31
George M. Lindsey
Northeast corner of Tracy and St. George Streets

Collegiate Gothic. After the 1971 earthquake the School Board said that it had to come down. But the neighborhood, after a fine battle, convinced the board that the shell could be stabilized and the interior remodeled.

41. Franklin Avenue ("Shakespeare") Bridge, 1926
J. C. Wright
for City Engineer's Office
Built over Monon Street, between St. George Street and Myra Avenue

A great open spandrel arch is laced by long Gothic arches. At both ends of the bridge are pairs of Gothic aedicules that cry out for sculptured saints.

42. Apartment Building for Dr. F. Haight, circa 1937
Wesley Eager
4116 Franklin Avenue

The lines of this Streamline Moderne complex are muted in comparison to those of the spectacular bridge next to it.

43. Schlesinger House, 1952
R. M. Schindler
1901 Myra Avenue

From the street this dwelling is a deceptively plain design for Schindler, yet the interiors and his method of providing natural lighting for them are as successful and complex as the interiors of any of his other houses.

44. Apartment House, 1939
J. Knauer
4230–4234 Franklin Avenue

Part of the fine effect of this Streamline Moderne building is the result of its being sited on the crest of a hill.

45. Elliot House, 1930
R. M. Schindler
4237 Newdale Drive

Schindler set the house far back on the site in order to allow a view of the valley. On the street level is a garage and entrance, both covered by a pergola. The house is also partially covered by a second level that opens to front and rear terraces.

46. Gogol House, 1938–39
Raphael S. Soriano
2190 Talmadge Street

Only a single floor is visible on the Talmadge Street side of the house. A deck and patio face toward the view. The style: purist International.

47. The Gene Autry Western Heritage Museum, 1987–89
Widom, Wein and Cohen
(Charles A. Widom and Michael Heinrich)
Zoo Drive
Griffith Park

A mild-mannered version of Postmodern architecture. The banded tower with its tile roof and the various courtyards and other details suggest, but do not directly re-create, California's Hispanic architectural tradition. While you are in the eastern reaches of the park you might also wish to visit the Los Angeles World Zoo, which was designed in 1963 by Charles Luckman, with Robert Herrick Carter and Associates as landscape architects.

While you are now well around the northeast side of the park and are adjacent to Burbank, you can continue to the Griffith Park Equestrian Center (located north of the Ventura Freeway off of Victoria Boulevard). George Vernon Russell and Associates designed this complex in 1963, and the image is woodsy California ranch—carried out with sophistication.

35 • Silver Lake

For so small a district, the Silver Lake area has a high concentration of first-rate architecture, making it one of the most important places to visit in the city. The most interesting work is by the best Los Angeles Modernists: Schindler, Neutra, Ain, Soriano, Harris, Lautner. These works stand side by side with houses designed in the Period Revivals of the 1920s and 1930s. It is essentially this latter work that gives Silver Lake its special character. In fact, looking from Schindler's ingenious Walker House down over the flood of tile roofs to the lake below reminds you, well, of the Los Angeles version of Urbino. Obviously the view (of hills and the reservoir) was the attraction, and the architects have played up to it. Along the eastern section of Sunset Boulevard running through the area is a sprinkling of Spanish and Moderne commercial relics. There are also a few exotics. For example, at 933 Parkman Avenue is a two-story garden apartment (circa 1920) that declares its allegiance to Islam through its minarets, dome, and arches. Here are our choices of the most representative architectural finds in Silver Lake:

1. Holy Virgin Mary Russian Orthodox Cathedral, 1928
650 Micheltorena Street

A lovely Russian village church, the cathedral is even more attractive inside. It reflects the taste of the émigrés from the Revolution—Russian intellectuals of the Count Tolstoy school. Great simplicity with patches of opulence.

2. McIntosh House, 1939
Richard J. Neutra
1317 Maltman Avenue

One of the earliest of Neutra's wood-sheathed houses. The narrow plan with the garage, sleeping, and service areas in front and living area to the rear takes full advantage of the narrow lot and view over the city.

3. Landa Apartments, 1966
A. E. Morris
Southeast corner of Griffith Park Boulevard and Landa Street

A stepped design of connected stucco boxes certainly inspired by the earlier work of R. M. Schindler. This architect is even more Expressionistic than Schindler.

4. Bubeshko Apartments, 1938, 1941
R. M. Schindler
Southeast corner of Griffith Park Boulevard and Lyric Avenue

A dramatic setback of each level allows the building to hug the hillside and at the same time to continue internal spaces of each apartment outward to roof terraces and patios.

5. CDLT 1, 2 House, 1987–92
Michael Rotondi
1955 Cedar Lodge Terrace

The architect has written of this house, "No working drawings were made for this project. Sketches were made for the contractor to work from each

morning. At the end of the day the contractor would leave lights pointed at the areas that needed to be resolved by the following morning." Though, as the architect has said, "The element of surprise was a major component of this house," its design turns out to be composed—composed to be sure of discordant elements, but then this is the language that he has employed in this design. The resulting house is certainly one of Los Angeles's most important buildings of the early 1990s.

6. Falk Apartments, 1939
R. M. Schindler
Northeast corner of Lucile and Carnation Avenues

Working with an extremely difficult hillside site, Schindler twists and turns the building so that each living unit has a garden and roof terrace.

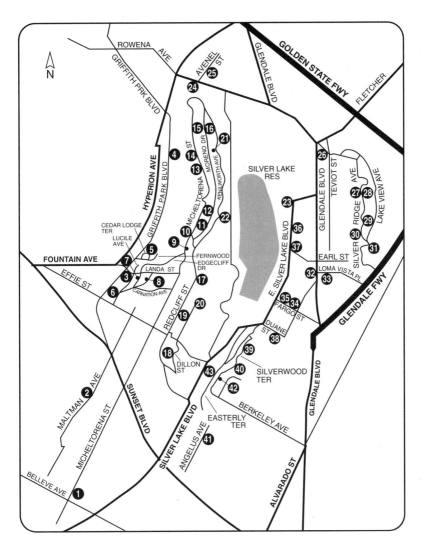

7. Manola Court (Sachs) Apartment Building, 1926–40
R. M. Schindler
1811–1813 Edgecliff Drive

These apartments, designed for the artist/designer Herman Sachs, are examples of the studied abstraction that Schindler was beginning to develop. They are designed as steps leading from the lower street up the steep hillside to the next.

8. Westby House, 1938
R. M. Schindler
1805 Maltman Avenue

Schindler's late de Stijl aesthetic at work in a two-story house.

9. Daniels House, 1939
Gregory Ain
1856 Micheltorena Street

The stucco box as a fragile container, masterfully detailed and imaginatively planned. The

architect angled the house on a steep hillside in order to allow for a private patio and garden.

10. Lautner House, 1939
John Lautner
2007 Micheltorena Street

After World War II, Lautner became one of the leading Expressionist architects in the country. Here we see him working in a subdued, controlled manner with redwood and concrete.

11. "Silvertop" House and Garden, 1957
John Lautner
2138 Micheltorena Street

Here's what we have just been talking about! This structure gets a high grade for exotic form. The total design includes the canti-levered driveway and swimming pool, the house, and, of course, the landscaping. Actually it can be seen better from a rear entrance near 2134 Redcliff Street and best (with binoculars) from across the lake on East Silver Lake Boulevard.

12. Olive House, 1933
R. M. Schindler
2236 Micheltorena Street

A house full of Schindler's won-derful contradictions. The house seems flat-roof International Style from the street, but it is all shed and gable roofs on the gar-den and view side. As a result, the interior is a syncopation of ceiling heights and changing axes. The living room, with its built-in furniture, is one of Schindler's most handsome.

13. Alexander House, 1941
Harwell H. Harris
2265 Micheltorena Street

Harris had learned a great deal from Frank Lloyd Wright about composition. Here he simplified Wright's Usonian concept. The low hipped roof and simple walls seem to have as much to do with the traditional California ranch house as they do with Wright.

14. Tierman House, 1938–39
Gregory Ain;
Visscher Boyd, collaborator
2323 Micheltorena Street

A very ingenious house on two levels, pivoting around a central core lighted by a skylight. Essentially, the Tierman House is a stucco box with an attached garage, one-story on the street, two-stories on the garden side.

15. Orans House, 1941
Gregory Ain
2404 Micheltorena Street

The living room is covered by a gently sloping shed roof that floats above bands of glass.

16. Van Patten House, 1934–35
R. M. Schindler
2320 Moreno Drive

This dramatic hillside house has been fenced in and the garages with their overlapping shed roofs have been converted to living space, but basically, Schindler's ideas have been maintained.

17. Wilson House, 1938
R. M. Schindler
2090 Redcliff Street

Here, in another of his hillside houses, Schindler cantilevered three floors of projecting and receding boxes out to the rear and then connected them with pro-jecting balconies at the side.

18. Hopmans House, 1951
Harwell H. Harris
1727 N. Dillon Street

A subtle touch revealed in a wood pavilion, the house has been modified a bit since it was built.

19. Lipetz House, 1935
Raphael S. Soriano
1843 Dillon Street

The living room is in the form of a Streamline Moderne ship's bridge. Bands of horizontal steel windows and metal railings extend the nautical theme, now somewhat altered.

20. House, circa 1930
1824 San Jacinto Street, beyond the turn of Dillon Street

A dollhouse of a mosque with flashing tiles on its lovely tower.

21. Droste House, 1940
R. M. Schindler
2025 Kenilworth Avenue

As this house was being finished, Schindler asked the owners to sit where their dining table would be on the second floor so he could adjust the lintel of the picture win-dow so that the owners wouldn't miss anything in the view.

22. Walker House, 1936
R. M. Schindler
2100 Kenilworth Avenue

The closed-in street façade reveals nothing of the glass and project-ing, balconied, three-level drama to the rear.

23. Hansen House, 1951
Harwell H. Harris
2305 W. Silver Lake Boulevard

This stucco-and-wood beauty is rather surprising amid the rela-tively conventional suburbia on this street.

24. Kenngott-Brossmer Design Studio, 1968
Carl Maston
2840 Rowena Avenue

A gray brick street façade almost hides a court beautifully articu-lated with much use of wood.

25. Avenel Housing, 1948
Ain, Johnson, and Day; Katharine Bashford and Fred Barlow Jr., landscape architects
2839 Avenel Street

This is now painted pink, but the raking angle of the roof marks it as early Los Angeles International Style mixed with Los Angeles's tradition of the common stucco box and enclosed gardens.

26. Conrad's Drive-In (now Astro's), 1958
Louis Armet and Eldon Davis
Southeast corner of Glendale Boulevard and Fletcher Drive

A striking example of People's Moderne of the 1950s with its angled roof. Other examples of the designs of Armet and Davis are Romeo's, Times Square (1955; now Johnie's), at the corner of Fairfax Avenue and Wilshire Boulevard; Pann's (1956), at the corner of La Cienega Boulevard, Centinela Avenue, and La Tijera Boulevard in Inglewood; and Norm's (1957), at the corner of Overhill Drive and Slauson Avenue.

27. Hawk House, 1939
Harwell H. Harris
2421 Silver Ridge Avenue

Although very close to the road, this house is easy to miss. It is in dense foliage, but you can still see enough of this horizontal board house with its low hovering roof to recognize the work of a consummate artist. The serene Japanese-influenced interior has always been beautifully maintained.

28. Howe House, 1925
R. M. Schindler
2422 Silver Ridge Avenue

The exterior is horizontal board-and-batten and concrete, very boxy. The house was originally flat-roofed. The interior is a tour de force in interlocking spaces. Incidentally Eads Howe was known as the "King of the Hoboes." The floor of the house below street level was, according to legend, a sort of dormitory for tramps who would come up from the railroad below. We cannot vouch for this, but it should be true.

29. Duplexes, 1958–62
A. E. Morris
2378–2390 Silver Ridge Avenue

Morris is sort of a Schindler undisciplined by Loos, who was a great disciplinarian. These two-story buildings shoot out blocky stucco volumes with apparent

abandon. Number 2390 is Morris's own Studio Building (1957). The studio has a Wrightian flavor, realized in steel, glass, and brick. Equally theatrical is Morris's Murakami House (1962) at 2378 Silver Ridge.

30. Sabsay House, 1940
J. R. Davidson
2351 Silver Ridge Avenue

Rather quiet and bulky looking from the street, this is one of the few works by Davidson that you can actually see, and it is not one of his best.

31. Duplexes, 1964
A. E. Morris
2330–2350 Silver Ridge Avenue

Another group of Morris's stucco box duplexes, similar to those nearby.

32. Bungalow Court, circa 1926
Glendale Boulevard at Loma Vista Place

A lovely grouping of Hansel and Gretel bungalows.

33. House, circa 1965
2384 Loma Vista Place

One of the most conscious imitations of Antonio Gaudí in America. It is most strange to see the Barcelona architect's special style coupled with louvered windows.

34. Eltinge House, 1921
Pierpont and Walter Davis;
Charles G. Adams,
landscape architect
2327 Fargo Street, reached from Apex Street

A Spanish Revival garage plus garden walls are about all you can see of this extensive Mediterranean villa and its terraced Italian gardens. The Eltinge House was one of Los Angeles's first major essays in the Mediterranean style.

35. Presley House, 1946
Gordon Drake
2114 Fargo Street

Drake was one of California's gifted young architects in the immediate post–World War II years. Unfortunately there are few of his houses in existence, and none of them remains unaltered. This is one of the least changed.

36. Neutra House, 1964
Richard J. Neutra and
Dion Neutra (principal)
2300 E. Silver Lake Boulevard

The original pure International Style Research house built in 1933 was partially burned in 1963. The present structure, though far from having the experimental quality of the first, is late romantic Neutra. It steps away from Silver Lake in three stages, and each stage has its own tiny rooftop lake.

37. Colony of Neutra Houses
Richard J. Neutra, Dion Neutra
Intersection of Earl Street with Silver Lake Boulevard and Argent Place

It is rare that you have the chance to survey the work of a major Modernist in such a concentrated form, particularly in Los Angeles.

a. Yew House, 1957
2226 E. Silver Lake Boulevard

b. Kambara House, 1960
2232 E. Silver Lake Boulevard

c. Inadomi House, 1960
2238 E. Silver Lake Boulevard

d. Sokol House, 1948
2242 E. Silver Lake Boulevard

e. Treweek House, 1948
2250 E. Silver Lake Boulevard

f. Reunion House,
1949, 1966 and later;
remodeled,
Dion Neutra
2240 Earl Street

g. Flavin House, 1958
2218 Neutra Place

h. Ohara House, 1961
2210 Neutra Place

i. Akai House, 1961
2200 Neutra Place

35

37a

38. Silverview Condominiums, 1983
EDC, Inc. Architects
(Walter Abronson and
Ko Kiyohara)
2330 Duane Street

A suitable neighbor for the Neutras.

39. Koblick House, 1937
Richard J. Neutra
1816–1818 Silverwood Terrace

A three-story beautifully sited house with windows ranked around the third-floor living room, which has a sensational view of the lake and mountains.

40. Walther House, 1937
Harwell H. Harris
1742 Silverwood Terrace

It is very interesting to see the two very different design philosophies of Neutra (the dwelling as an art-object machine) and of Harris (the dwelling as a romantic shelter) on the same street.

41. Meyers House, circa 1939
Raphael Soriano
1607 Angelus Avenue

The façade is mainly bands of windows. The setback of the second story makes the house almost classically composed.

42. Silverwood Duplex, 1965
A. E. Morris
1611 Silverwood Terrace

Nice, white, with Schindleresque interlocking volumes and details.

43. Three Houses, 1935–38
William Kesling
1530–1536 Easterly Terrace
2808 W. Effie Street

Balanced somewhere between High Art Modern and Streamline Moderne. Kesling designed other Streamline Moderne houses in this area, but they have been altered.

36 • Angelino Heights
Echo Park
Elysian Park

This area is now cut off by freeway from the Silver Lake area to which it is atmospherically related. The northern part has some funky things as well as High Art. The district around Echo Park is much older. In fact, the 1300 block of Carroll Avenue in Angelino Heights has the highest concentration of Victorian houses still remaining in Los Angeles—not many in comparison with San Francisco, but very choice—including two by Joseph Cather Newsom.

Don't miss the lake in Echo Park (1894), reminiscent of the Public Garden in Boston, with peddle boats for rent and the most magnificent lotus plants you will find anywhere.

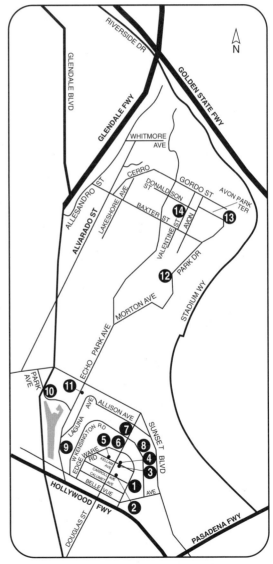

1. Betsford House, circa 1890
801 E. Edgeware Road

The mansard tower, with original iron balustrade, deserves mention.

2. Carroll Avenue

This was once an esteemed residential district with a nice view of the city, previously reached by

time with pronounced Stick-style features.

c. Heim House, 1887–88
1320 Carroll Avenue

This time Queen Anne combines with Italianate brackets in the cornice and a wonderful round tower.

g. Foy House, 1873
1325 Carroll Avenue

The Foy House was moved in 1993 from its original location at 633 S. Witmer Avenue. As with many other California cities and towns, Los Angeles once had a tremendous number of late Italianate houses built during

2k,l

streetcar. It has been coming back, due mainly to attempts by its proud residents to improve the surroundings. Three Victorian houses have even been moved in to take the place of ones demolished long ago. We begin at the east end of the block.

a. Philips House, 1887
1300 Carroll Avenue

Almost pure Queen Anne with just a little Eastlake decoration here and there.

b. Russell House, 1887–88
1316 Carroll Avenue

Again, Queen Anne, but this

d. Scheerer House, 1887–88
1324 Carroll Avenue

A Queen Anne cottage.

e. House, circa 1887
1321 Carroll Avenue

Both this house and the next, number 1325, were once on Court Street—1145 and 1123 respectively. They were moved to Carroll Avenue in 1981. Both are late Eastlake, working into the Queen Anne.

f. House, circa 1887
1325 Carroll Avenue

Eastlake/Queen Anne.

the years 1865 through the early 1880s. Only a few of these houses still remain in the Los Angeles area. This one exhibits the usual high entablature accompanied by extended paired brackets. The restoration was under the direction of Jai Pol Vhalsa; the preservation consultant was Lawrence E. Winans.

h. Sessions House, 1888
Joseph Cather Newsom
1330 Carroll Avenue

A fine Newsom creation recognized as such by the architect, who illustrated and described it in his *Picturesque and Artistic*

Homes and Buildings of California (No. 3), (San Francisco, 1890). The predominant Queen Anne theme of Carroll Avenue is here sustained and embellished by Moorish and Chinese detail, including "Moongate" openings on the second-floor porch.

i. Innes House, 1887–88
1329 Carroll Avenue

Built for a shoe store magnate, this house illustrates the peculiar California wedding of Queen Anne and Eastlake styles.

j. Haskin House, circa 1888
1344 Carroll Avenue

Some authorities have dated this house in the 1890s, but it is such a pure example of Queen Anne expansiveness (much spool-work and no Eastlake ornament) that we suspect it was done about the same time as the other houses (if not earlier). It is immaculately maintained and constantly being used as a subject for painters and a backdrop for TV commercials.

k. Sanders House, 1887
1345 Carroll Avenue

Good Queen Anne with wrought-iron railing still crowning the roof.

l. Pinney House, 1887
1355 Carroll Avenue

Similar in style and scale to the Sanders House next door, this house is still in the Pinney family. It seems to be in its original colors.

m. Cohn House, circa 1887
1443 Carroll Avenue

A two-story Queen Anne house with an unusual corner bay tower.

n. Cottage, 1889
Joseph Cather Newsom
1407 Carroll Avenue

This story-and-a-half cottage falls basically into the Queen Anne style, though some portions, such as the angled bay and the roof, have an Eastlake quality. This was one of several spec houses built from Newsom's published "El Capitan" plan.

Other houses on Carroll Avenue are worthy of preservation and restoration. In fact, the whole of Angelino Heights is a delight to anyone who can, in the mind's eye, see these houses and their gardens restored to their original condition.

3. House, circa 1890
1334 Kelham Avenue

A very late Queen Anne/Colonial Revival cottage.

4. Houses, 1890
1347, 1343, 1341 Kelham Avenue

Obviously designed by the same Queen Anne–inspired architect. Number 1341 has the most ornament.

5. House, circa 1905
1405 Kelham Avenue

A large Mission Revival dwelling. This suggests that the Angelino Heights area is important for other styles besides the Victorian ones.

6. House, circa 1887
917 Douglas Street

A rare, almost pure, example of the Eastlake style.

7. House, circa 1896
1101 Douglas Street

A merging of Queen Anne and Colonial Revival.

8. Weller House, 1887
824 Kensington Road

Certainly this Queen Anne gem is worthy of its neighbors on Carroll Avenue. The spindly porches and open belvedere tower add to its fairy-tale quality.

9. Lacey Duplex, 1922
R. M. Schindler
830–832 Laguna Avenue

A remodeling of an older house, Schindler's design suggests both the Spanish Revival and the early Moderne.

10. Angelus Temple, 1925
A. F. Leicht
Northeast corner of Glendale Boulevard and Park Avenue

The architect of this concrete, classical-styled temple must have been inspired by the Mormon Tabernacle in Salt Lake City. Strange, since the egg shape is hardly symbolic of the Four Square Gospel once preached by the Temple's Aimee Semple McPherson.

11. Apartment, circa 1928
1650 Echo Park Avenue

A four-story Art Deco structure further enlivened by a vivid floral motif.

10

12. Southhall House, 1938
R. M. Schindler
1855 Park Drive

The garage is right on the street with the house secluded behind it. The plan of the house is a large rectangle from which three bayed spaces project. The whole is sheathed in plywood.

13. Atwater Bungalows,
1931 and later
Robert Stacy-Judd
1431, 1433 Avon Park Terrace

Northwest corner of Park Drive and Avon Park Terrace (best following northerly route along Park Drive as indicated).

This architect, who was best known for his advocacy of the pre-Columbian Revival, here shows himself equally the master of the Pueblo Revival in a most romantic rendering.

14. Ross House, 1938
Raphael S. Soriano
2123 Valentine Street

Again, a garage stands almost in front of one of Soriano's handsome early International Style designs. The two-story glass and stucco house is one of Soriano's best works.

37 • Wilshire Boulevard District Hancock Park

As the map and dates of the following buildings suggest, Wilshire Boulevard, named for an oil millionaire who was also a Marxist, has had several spurts of growth. In the 1920s it had already started its march west to Santa Monica and the Pacific, the complete apotheosis of the linear city. It was commercial about as far as Western Avenue. Beyond that, a great region of bungalows proliferated. Still farther, starting near Crenshaw Boulevard, the rich took up their abodes north and south of Wilshire with a little commercial building here and there. The buildings on Wilshire Boulevard itself gradually began rising in height and ostentation until the beginning of the "Miracle Mile" at Hauser Avenue, where ten-story or so office buildings and luxury shops were built at the end of the 1920s and on into the 1930s, and where a great deal of building has occurred since World War II. To the north and south of Wilshire Boulevard are multiple housing units and an array of upper-middle-class suburban housing. In the area around Hancock Park there are larger apartment buildings, then fourplexes and duplexes, and finally single-family housing. Most of this housing was built before 1942, and thus it provides a wonderful look at architectural styles from the early 1920s through the late 1930s. Drive north on Cochran, Cloverdale, or Detroit Avenues to see how successful this housing was. You will also note how intrusive and unfortunate most of the multiple housing developments in this area have been.

In fact, it is greatly fascinating to drive the length from Number One Wilshire in downtown Los Angeles to the sea in an open car. In its own way it is as overwhelming as a similar drive along the length of Park Avenue in New York. Strangely, if you go off Wilshire on the streets above and below it, you will still find residential areas sometimes only a block away.

1. CBS Television City, 1952
Pereira and Luckman;
major addition, 1976
Gin Wong Associates
Southeast corner of
Beverly Boulevard and
Fairfax Avenue

A low modern cube, big and bland but not without distinction. The addition is in exactly the style of the original.

2. Farmer's Market,
1934–37 and later
Northeast corner of
Fairfax Avenue and 3rd Street

Built by Roger Dahljolm to show off Southern California's

ability to grow magnificent fruits and vegetables, this complex of buildings is more an institution than it is architecture. Its only pretension is the somewhat Colonial Revival tower that replaced a wonderful windmill advertising the name of the building on a blade. The place was Colonialized (Anglo, that is) even more in 1941 with additions and changes by Beverly Hills architect J. E. Dolena.

Behind the Farmers' Market on Gilmore Lane (cuts between 3rd Street and Beverly Boulevard) is the Gilmore Adobe that Antonio Jose Rocha built on the Rancho La Brea in 1828–30.

This L-shaped adobe (the present south and west wings) originally had a flat tar-covered roof. In the 1920s it was remodeled by John Byers and Edla Muir. They added the north wing and built a low second story over a portion of the original adobe. They also added pitched gable roofs covered with tile. As we see the adobe today, it reflects the 1920s ideal more than what it actually looked like in 1830.

In 2002 Koning Eizenberg Architecture added four more buildings and another clock tower to the market. See if you can tell the new from the old.

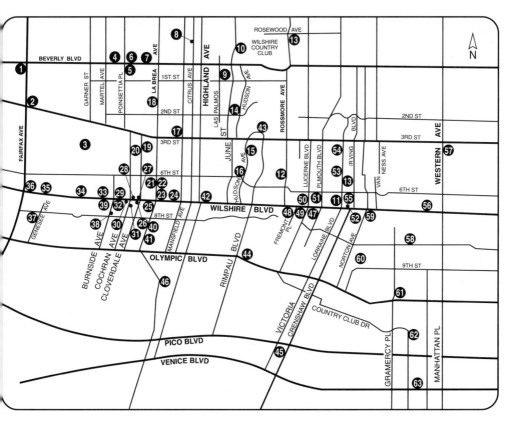

3. Park La Brea Housing (Metropolitan Life Housing Development), 1941–42; towers, 1948–49
Leonard Schultze and Son and E. T. Heitschmidt; Tommy Tomson, landscape architect; tower complex, Leonard Schultze and Associates of New York, and by J. E. Stanton and Gordon Kaufmann; landscape design, 1948 Thomas Church
A 10½-acre development bounded by 3rd Street, Cochran Avenue, 6th Street, and Fairfax Avenue

The first thing that strikes your eye from a distance is that Carcassonne has been transported to Los Angeles—the 1948 towers merge to appear to be a medieval wall. From a shorter range the most interesting features are the early two-story housing units that are in a sort of stripped Regency Moderne mode.

4. A. J. Heinsbergen Decorating Company, 1925
Claude Beelman, with A. B. Heinsbergen; Willard White, details
7415–7421 Beverly Boulevard

The general impression of this brick building is English Medieval with a little Baroque added here and there. Very picturesque and Old World in a strange area for that to happen.

5. Commercial Building, 1930
J. R. Horns
Southeast corner of Poinsettia Place and Beverly Boulevard

Art Deco.

6. Commercial Building, 1929
L. Mulgreen
7223 Beverly Boulevard

Art Deco.

7. Service Station, circa 1925
7201 Beverly Boulevard

Mission Revival with a dome!

8. Beckman House, 1938
Gregory Ain
357 N. Citrus Avenue

An immaculately maintained Los Angeles conception of the International Style. In plan the house is narrow, and the principal rooms open to small terraces and enclosed courts.

9. Churchill House, 1928, 1982
Pierpont and Walter S. Davis; Tedesco Architects (Lorenzo C. Tedesco)
108 N. Las Palmas Drive

One of Davis's excellent examples of the Mediterranean type. Low-pitched tile roofs, which are thinly detailed at the eaves, carefully shelter fenestrated stucco walls. The Tedesco firm added a new contextual wing and remodeled portions of the existing house.

10. Meade House ("La Casa de las Campanas"), circa 1927
Lester Scherer
350 June Street

Needless to say, you are among the swells. This immense Mediterranean-style house on this gently winding street has real distinction. The Meade House and the now-destroyed Ince House were the two most lively versions of the Mediterranean style to be built in the 1920s in the Los Angeles area. Note the impressive formal entrance, the ironwork in the entrance gates, and the projecting wood balcony at the north end of the house.

11. Leistikow House, 1923
Paul R. Williams
554 S. Lorraine Boulevard

The first full year of independent practice for Paul Williams was 1923. The Leistikow house is an English Cottage design, realized in brick. Note the large stair window to the left of the entrance. Nearby is the Collins House, also by Paul Williams, at 601 S. Lorraine Boulevard.

12. Rothman House, 1926
Paul R. Williams
541 Rossmore Avenue

This brick and half-timber English-type dwelling reads as a story-and-a-half house. A pair of tall picturesque English chimneys hold the house to its site. A low-walled formal garden lies to the west.

13. Apartment Building, circa 1928
Southeast corner of Rossmore and Rosewood Avenues

This huge, somewhat Spanish pile, the Ravenwood (an Art Deco Moderne structure with Assyrian inclinations at 570 Rossmore Avenue), and a few rather nondescript lesser monsters nearby are among the few large Los Angeles apartment complexes that would compare in size to those of the apartment house craze in New York during the same period.

14. Smith House, 1929–30
J. C. Smale
Northwest corner of 2nd Street and Hudson Avenue

A rare concrete Art Deco house. It is very elegant in an extremely elegant neighborhood. Paris would be proud of it.

15. Bowen House, 1925
Elmer Grey; Florence Yoch, landscape architect
336 Hudson Avenue

Grey, in an English mood. As the editors of *Southwest Building and Contractor* commented late in 1925 in reference to this house, "English types of residence architecture fit beautifully into many California settings, and just now they are very much in vogue." This large Tudor house has a lower floor of brick and then a variety of half-timber gable-roofed bays on the second floor. As befitted a house of this size, "a garage with space for four machines" was included. Florence Yoch provided a formal garden, enclosed in part behind a blue brick wall. Note that this block contains a number of splendid examples of the English Tudor mode.

16. Sisson House, 1926
Robert B. Stacy-Judd
Northwest corner of 6th Street and Hudson Avenue

Although we generally associate Stacy-Judd with the pre-Columbian Revival, he designed a number of Medieval French and English houses in Southern California. An article in the magazine *Arts and Decoration* (April 1928), which illustrated this design, stated "how delightful the English Norman architecture suits these same flower-covered lands and vivid Sky [of Los Angeles]." As with all of this architect's designs, there are many odd moments to be encountered in this house.

17. Apartment Building,
circa 1928
*Northwest corner of
3rd Street and
Mansfield Avenue*

This two-story Art Deco building is a typical Los Angeles flat.

18. Retail Shop, circa 1930
153 La Brea Avenue

La Brea was once a rich feast for the connoisseur of the Moderne in its various ramifications and permutations. Today almost all the shops in this mode have been demolished or refaced. This one seems pretty well tuckered out.

19. Apartment Building, 1930
J. C. Smale
364 S. Cloverdale Avenue

Another Art Deco flat.

20. Apartment Building, 1938
Milton J. Black and R. Borman
462 S. Cochran Avenue

A two-story Streamline Moderne structure. Black, who designed well in the Mediterranean Style in the 1920s, has here kept up with the times.

21. Automobile Showroom,
circa 1927
Morgan, Walls, and Clements
611 La Brea Avenue

Probably intended to be Moorish, this tiny building must have been very swanky in its day.

22. Courtyard Retail and
Office Building, circa 1926
Roy Selden Price
624 La Brea Avenue

A U-shaped Spanish building with Moorish arches.

23. Campanile Restaurant,
1988
Schweitzer BIM
624 S. La Brea Avenue

A rather bland rendering of Postmodernism in front, the interior mixes the modern with the archaic in the first room but retains the Spanish arches of Charlie Chaplain's studio in the rear. The food is terrific and the attached bakery is outstanding.

24. Security First National
Bank of Los Angeles, 1929
Morgan, Walls, and Clements
5209 Wilshire Boulevard

A single-story, glazed, black-and-gold, terra-cotta-sheathed building similar to this firm's famous Richfield Building, which was destroyed in 1968.

25. The Dark Room, 1935
Marcus P. Miller
5370 Wilshire Boulevard

A Programmatic building clothed in black vitrolite with silver trim. Streamline Moderne, the conventional nautical porthole in this case is placed in the middle of a plateglass window and thus becomes the lens of a camera. The new tenant has maintained the Streamline Moderne image but not, of course, the sign.

26. Dominguez-Wilshire Building, 1930
Morgan, Walls, and Clements
5410 Wilshire Boulevard

An eight-story Art Deco tower placed on a two-story base. The detail is sharp and brittle.

27. Chandler's Shoe Store, circa 1938
Marcus P. Miller
Northwest corner of Wilshire Boulevard and Cloverdale Avenue

One of the busiest buildings ever done in the Streamline Moderne idiom, this building is actually a remodeling of a Spanish Revival structure of the 1920s.

28. Roman's Food Mart, circa 1935
5413 Wilshire Boulevard

Streamline Moderne with a matching small tower at one end.

29. El Rey Theater, circa 1928
W. Cliff Balch
5519 Wilshire Boulevard

A small, angular Art Deco gem with marvelous box office and original signage, a king's head etched in neon.

30. Commercial Building, 1927
Frank M. Tyler
5464 Wilshire Boulevard

Art Deco framed by two small, and quite mad, towers.

31. Cochran Avenue Court, circa 1928
Charles Gault
Just south of Wilshire Boulevard on Cochran Avenue

Small Spanish court covered with dense foliage.

34

32. Desmonds Department Store Building, 1928–29
Gilbert Stanley Underwood
5514 Wilshire Boulevard

Art Deco with flamboyant ornament; an eight-story tower placed on a two-story base with enormous rounded corners.

33. Ralph's Supermarket Building, 1927–28
Morgan, Walls, and Clements
5623 Wilshire Boulevard

Once this was typical of the firm's work—a simulated cut-stone façade with Spanish Gothic arches and Churrigueresque ornament. It has been almost completely ruined by modernization, but its proud tower still stands above the mess.

34. Prudential Building, 1948
Wurdeman and Becket;
Ruth Shellhorn, landscape architect
5757 Wilshire Boulevard

A large office and commercial building in the International Style, affected more by Gropius than by Mies. It thus shows its age stylistically but well.

35. Hancock Park
Wilshire Boulevard at Genesee Avenue Hancock Park

a. Los Angeles County Museum of Art, 1964, 1982–83
Pereira and Associates; Hardy, Holzman and Pfeiffer

The original 1964 complex was a group of three pavilions, set on a podium in a park. The buildings were reflected in a surrounding moat of water and fountains—all very 1960s modern. The architecture was dull. This has all been lost behind the more recent entrance building (the Robert O. Anderson Building), which brings the complex right up to the street. As with much of H.H.& P.'s work the theme is a multistory, glass-and-metal shopping-mall atrium. The façade facing Wilshire Boulevard tries to be urbane, but fails—the feeling is again that of an upscale shopping mall. According to plans (2002), all of these buildings will be demolished and replaced by a huge one by Rem Koolhaas.

Off to the side, hovering over the park's famed tar pits is the Pavilion for Japanese Art (The

35a

Price Museum of Oriental Art), designed by Bruce Goff before his death in 1982. Goff started the design in 1978, and the building was completed in 1988 under the direction of the New Mexico architect Bart Prince. The quality of the interior space with its ramps and open lighting is very successful. This will be saved.

b. A Discovery of La Brea Museum, 1976
Thornton and Fagan Associates

36

Hancock Park gets its name from the family that bought the Rancho La Brea (essentially our Wilshire District) in 1860, and, after having tapped it for almost all of its crude oil (brea), gave the tar pits to the city and sold off the rest to rich people. In drilling for oil, Major Henry Hancock began digging up large

bones but thought little of it until in 1906 Professor J. C. Merriman of the University of California recognized that these pits had trapped large numbers of prehistoric animals. Many of their skeletons can now be seen at the County Museum of Natural History in Exposition

Park. The new museum, a sort of mound, celebrates this major scientific discovery, but we are sorry to say that in spite of the planners' good intentions, it makes further inroads on valuable open space.

37. Buck House, 1934
R. M. Schindler
*Southwest corner of
8th Street and Genesee Avenue*

All privacy on the exterior with just a touch of Streamline Moderne. The interior spaces open through great panels of glass into the south garden area. One of Schindler's finest houses.

36. May Company
Department Store Building,
1940
Albert C. Martin and
S. A. Marx
*Northeast corner of
Fairfax Avenue and
Wilshire Boulevard*

Streamline Moderne. The corner gold tower (really a sort of elegant perfume bottle) with its sign is the architecture of the building, especially when lighted at night. This also marks an entrance, but the main entrance is characteristically at the parking lot connected to the building. The adjoining multi-level parking structure was designed by Albert C. Martin and Associates in 1953. The May Company left the building at the end of the 1980s, and for some time its future was in doubt. Miracles do happen. The County Museum bought the building and thus acquired more gallery space. This also will remain in the new construction of the County Museum

38. The Monterey Apartments, 1925
C. K. Smithley
754 Burnside Avenue

Extremely austere and absolutely impregnable Mediterranean-style garden apartments.

39. Craft and Folk Art Museum, circa 1950; remodeling and addition, 1994; Hodgetts + Fung; remodeling of next door building, 2002
5800 Wilshire Boulevard

The old building in Anglo-Colonial Revival, the Hodgetts + Fung Postmodern, of course. The recent remodeling of another building next to it is hard to place stylistically except that it seems to be related to the zombies across the street. Is this contextualization?

40. Firestone Garage, 1937
R. E. Ward, engineer
800 S. La Brea Avenue

Difficult to describe! A huge streamlined shell cantilevered over the corner.

41. Cedu Foundation Building, circa 1928
842 La Brea Avenue

A very lovely Spanish Revival assemblage that has survived the changes on La Brea.

42. AVCO Savings Building (now Imperial Savings), 1973
Burke, Kober, Nicolais, and Archuleta
4929 Wilshire Boulevard

This ten-story building is one great cube of bronze-hued glass. At least it's bronze and not black.

46

43. Reynolds House, 1958
John Woolf
200 Rimpau Boulevard, on the cul-de-sac north of 3rd Street

A tall arched door, looking very much like a paper clip, cuts through a high mansard roof—one of Woolf's most imitated designs.

44. Memorial Library, 1930
Austin and Ashley
4625 W. Olympic Boulevard

Submerged in vines is this Tudor and Gothic branch library obviously intended to go with the old Collegiate Gothic Los Angeles High School, now replaced by repressed Brutalism. The fine art glass window with heraldic emblems on it was fashioned by the Judson Studios.

45. Paul R. Williams House, 1951
Paul R. Williams and Associates
1690 S. Victoria Avenue

When completed the house was described as California Modern. Its design entails traditional proportions coupled with Modernist devices such as cantilevered balconies, thin hovering roofs, and a dominant semicircular bay. The principal interior space is a lanai that opens out to an enclosed courtyard/garden. Leaping deer in brass line the brass railing of the circular staircase. The informality of the lanai is countered by the formality of the dining room and the living room with its fireplace in green Swedish marble.

Quite Romanesque on the exterior, this exposed reinforced concrete church turns Gothic inside. To top that, it has another of those free interpretations of the "La Giralda" that were so popular, whether in New York or in Florida or in Southern California.

which produced a wide array of concrete, stone-like products. Unfortunately Fremont Place is a private street. Within this enclave Martyn Haenke designed a number of classical-inspired residences (1911), including three for members of the Janss family.

51

46. St. Elmo's Village, 1994
Alex Istanbullu and
John Kaliski
4830 St. Elmo Drive, off of La Brea

This is a revitalization of a twenties bungalow court with some additions in buildings and color. A charming way for artists to live. The planting is dramatic.

47. Wilshire United Methodist Church, 1924
Allison and Allison
4350 Wilshire Boulevard

48. Fremont Place Entrance Gates, 1911
Martyn Haenke
South corner of Wilshire Boulevard and Fremont Place

This pair of cast-stone entrance gates was one of several built along the Hancock Park section of Wilshire Boulevard. You have to look twice to know that these classical design pylons flanked by colonnades are in fact concrete made to look like stone. They were made by the California Ornamental Stone Company,

49. Ebell Club, 1924
Hunt and Burns
4400 Wilshire Boulevard

The club building, auditorium, and garden are very sedate and respectable versions of Beaux-Arts classicism mixed with Spanish details.

50. Verbeck Mansion, circa 1897
637 Lucerne Boulevard

A huge 2$^{1/2}$-story Queen Anne Revival house with Colonial Revival touches. It was moved here in the 1920s.

51. Gless House, 1913
Arthur S. Heineman
(Alfred Heineman, associate)
Southwest corner of
Plymouth Boulevard and
6th Street

The Tudor exterior shows traces of Frank Lloyd Wright, and the magnificent interiors of teak reflect the ideas of Charles Greene. The art glass, designed by Alfred and carried out by the Judson Studios, is especially fine. Incidentally, it was moved to this area in the 1930s, though it looks as if it has always been on this corner. It is one of the Heinemans' most important structures outside Pasadena.

52. Lytton Building, 1968
William Pereira and Associate
4333 Wilshire Boulevard

Cleaned up Brutalism, there is a cocked-hat attitude to the roof.

53. Donovan House
("Sunshine Hill"), circa 1910
Theodore Eisen
419 S. Lorraine Boulevard

A Classical giant portico disguises a house that is strongly Adamesque inside.

54. Van Nuys House,
1898
Frederick L. Roehrig
357 S. Lorraine Boulevard

A fine example of the emergence of the Colonial Revival Shingle style from the earlier Queen Anne style.

55. House, circa 1915
Southwest corner of
Irving Boulevard and 6th Street

This is a Tudor effort. In fact, this entire area is very strongly Tudor.

56. St. James Episcopal
Church, 1925
Benjamin G. McDougall
Northwest corner of
Wilshire Boulevard and
St. Andrew's Place

Wilshire is lined with churches and synagogues dating from the twenties—a sign that not all Angelenos were sinners in those days. This one is good old Episcopalian Gothic on the outside. The interior is even better with a floor of tiles manufactured by the Mueller Mosaic Company (Trenton, New Jersey) and stained-glass windows designed by the Judson Studios (Highland Park, Los Angeles) over many decades.

57. Commercial Building,
circa 1928
356 S. Western Avenue

Art Deco with a tall tower and urn.

58. Apartment House,
circa 1935
3919 W. 8th Street

This three-story-plus-penthouse Streamline Moderne structure with a large parking area in the basement is premonitory of present systems.

59. INA-PEG Building, 1960
Charles Luckman and
Associates
Southeast corner of
Wilshire Boulevard and
Norton Avenue

This building, except for a little unnecessary detail, would pass for a Skidmore, Owings, and Merrill interpretation of Mies.

60. Weber House, 1921
Lloyd Wright
3923 W. 9th Street, at
4th Avenue

Lloyd Wright's first realized building in Los Angeles. It is a two-story, modified Prairie-style building, including art glass in geometrical patterns resembling those developed by his father.

61. House, circa 1915
965 Gramercy Place

This has to be the supreme act of misunderstood Japonicism in America. Gable after gable protrudes, shaming the Greene brothers into insignificance.

62. House, circa 1910
G. Lawrence Stimson
3340 Country Club Drive

Mission style mixed with Beaux-Arts details.

63. Apartment Building, 1936
Earl D. Stonerod
1554–1560 S. St. Andrews
Place

A symmetrical Streamline Moderne building.

38 • MacArthur Park, West

This section of the city, west of downtown, developed early as a desirable place for middle-class dwellings. At first it was the modestly hilly area just west of the present Harbor Freeway that became a fashionable neighborhood. The grouping of houses on South Bonnie Brae Street and on Alvarado Terrace provides a glimpse of what this section of Los Angeles was like in the 1890s and early 1900s. The single-family residential nature of the area continued throughout the First World War, but the 1920s introduced a strong pattern of auto-oriented strip commercialism along such streets as Venice, Pico, Washington, and Olympic Boulevards, and along Western Avenue and other north/south streets. Multiple housing also became more frequent—at first bungalow courts, and two- and three-story apartment buildings. Later, in the 1920s, a number of six- to eight-story apartment buildings were built. Generally, the mixed use of the region—retail, commercial, and single and multiple housing—has continued right on down to the present day. Since the 1950s, high-rise buildings from downtown have slowly spread into the area.

Two major public spaces occur along this part of Wilshire Boulevard. MacArthur Park (originally named Westlake Park) with its small picturesque lake provides thirty-two acres. Lafayette Park to the west has eleven acres donated to the city in 1899. MacArthur Park was laid out in the 1880s. Wilshire Boulevard, which formerly went around MacArthur Park, was rerouted to slice through the middle of it in 1934, an advantage for the auto and the boulevard, but hardly for the park.

The glory of the area has been and is Wilshire Boulevard, the "Champs Elysees of Los Angeles," as it was characterized in the 1920s. Beginning in the 1920s, major churches, retail stores, and office buildings were built along it. Since the early 1950s new and even higher office towers have been added, so Wilshire Boulevard is the image of the prototype linear city.

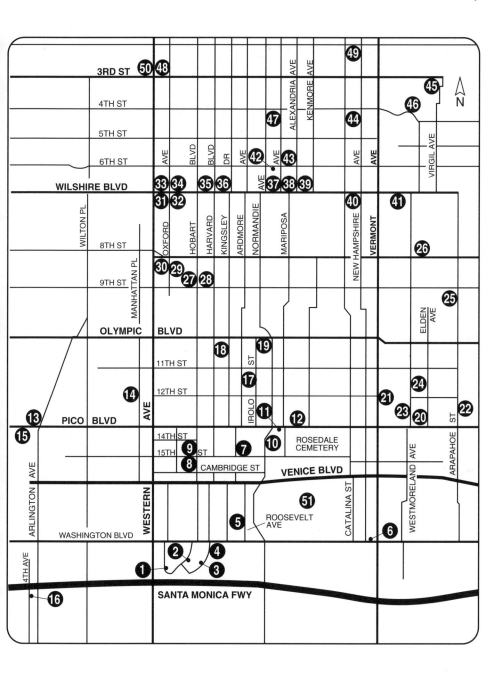

1. United Church of Christ, 1945
South end of Oxford Avenue, just north of the Santa Monica Freeway

A small but impressive Spanish Revival church building, whose tower is visible from the Santa Monica Freeway. The Hispanic borrowings on the design are varied. The tower is from the Mission Revival, the entrance of cast stone suggests the Churrigueresque, and the central rose window relates to the late Gothic in Spain. All of this mixture of sources has been carried out well. Originally the building was located where the freeway now stands, but was moved to its present site in 1963.

2. House, circa 1905
2068 Hobart Boulevard

Mission Revival with a wonderful entrance porch supported by stout, primitive cylindrical columns.

3. House, 1908
2091 Harvard Boulevard

A commodious box becomes picturesque and Mission by the addition of parapeted end-wall gables, quatrefoil windows, and a delightful second-floor arcade with its cusped Moorish arches.

4. Scott House, circa 1906
Frank M. Tyler
1910 S. Harvard Boulevard

When built it was described as "an Italian design with the qualities of Moorish architecture incorporated." This all adds up to Southern California Mission Revival with an Islamic touch.

5. Apartment Building, circa 1925
1817–1819½ Roosevelt Avenue

Spanish Revival with a peculiar entrance.

6. Boulevard Theater, 1925
Albert C. Martin
1615 W. Washington Boulevard

Spanish Revival with a penthouse on top.

7. Pacific Telephone Company Building, circa 1926
Northeast corner of Ardmore Avenue and 15th Street

A Churrigueresque dress for a utilitarian building.

8. Wheeler House, 1905
Charles and Henry Greene
2175 Cambridge Street

A modest, two-story Craftsman bungalow. The broad cantilevered roof projects its rafter ends. The low attic gable is entirely vented, and sticklike posts and rails articulate the entrance porch.

9. Bungalow, circa 1910
Henry L. Wilson
Southwest corner of Hobart Boulevard and 14th Street

A classic California bungalow, which was published in Wilson's *Bungalow Magazine.* Note the front door that goes right through the middle of the chimney.

10. St. Sophia's Greek Orthodox Cathedral, 1948
Gus Kalionzes, Charles A. Klingerman, and Albert R. Walker
1324 S. Normandie Avenue

Anyone who has seen a Byzantine church in Greece will come away from this building wondering where all of these inventive ideas came from. Even though pendentives supporting crystal chande-

liers are where columns should be, the design does manage to read as Byzantine.

11. St. Thomas the Apostle Roman Catholic Church, 1905
Maginnis, Walsh, and Sullivan
1321 W. Pico Boulevard

This church illustrates the inventiveness of these Boston architects who employed the Mission Revival image. The building conveys a strong primitive quality, and its towers and upper roofed arcade never occurred in this manner in original Mission architecture of the late-eighteenth/early-nineteenth centuries.

12. Retail Store/Apartment Building, circa 1925
2713 W. Pico Boulevard

A three-story apartment block and store has been taken out of the ordinary by being clothed in a rectangular pattern of glazed and unglazed tile.

13. Arlington Avenue Christian Church, 1926
Harold Cross and A. F. Wicker
Northwest corner of Pico Boulevard and Arlington Avenue

A concrete church that employs detailing derived from the Spanish Renaissance. The gable roof has been highly simplified, with the tile pulled out to the edges of the walls. The tower is undecorated up to the belfry, where cast-concrete ornament provides decorative relief.

14. Wilshire Ward Chapel, The Church of Jesus Christ of Latter-day Saints (Mormon), 1928
Harold W. Burton
1209 S. Manhattan Place

A Goodhuesque abstraction of

Medieval architecture—a little Gothic mixed with Byzantine and Romanesque. The dome's octagonal tower is impressive. The structure is of reinforced concrete with the form-board pattern exposed.

15. Forum Theater Building (now a church), 1921–24
Edward J. Borgmeyer
Southwest corner of Pico Boulevard and Norton Avenue (6th Street)

The most refined example of a Beaux-Arts theater still standing in Los Angeles. Two pedimented porticoes enclose a six-columned entrance porch. The fluted Corinthian columns, the cornices, entablatures, and the engaged piers are all richly decorated.

16. Alice Lynch House, 1922–23
Harwood Hewitt
2414 - 4th Avenue South

The Lynch House was one of those early 1920s dwellings that firmly established the popularity of the Spanish Revival in Southern California. The style of the house is derived from Andalusian farm houses of south-ern Spain. Facing the street is a story-and-a-half wing that houses the living room; the rest of the house behind is arranged around a small patio. The house is of adobe construction, with the adobe bricks being made on the site. The architect was a major figure in the Mediterranean/ Hispanic revival of the 1920s.

17. Bungalow Court, circa 1920
1038–1044 S. Ardmore Avenue

A narrow single-story bungalow court in the guise of Islam. A sloped and painted archway leads from the street into the narrow

entrance court. To the side, pairs of small towers adorn each of the two wings.

18. Apartment Building, circa 1922
1020 S. Kingsley Drive

A typical Los Angeles stucco box apartment with an Egyptian Revival street façade.

19. VIP Palace Restaurant Building, circa 1973
Southeast corner of Olympic Boulevard and Irolo Street

A return to the romanticism of Asia. Not, of course, the real Asia, but one that must exist some-where in a storybook.

20. House, circa 1912
1223 S. Elden Avenue

One-and-a-half-story, shingle-and-stone, Anglo-Colonial Revival house.

21. American National Red Cross Chapter Building, 1939
Spaulding and Rex
1200 S. Vermont Avenue

A late-1930s, flat-roofed, California Modern house some-what enlarged to serve as an office building set in a garden. The atmosphere is woodsy and suburban.

22. Double House, circa 1900
Attributed to Joseph Cather Newsom
1214 S. Arapahoe Street

A central driveway entrance goes right through the 1 1/2-story double bungalow. The main gable and the front dormers, which are now enclosed, were originally open sleeping porches.

23. House, circa 1910
1229 S. Westmoreland Avenue

A large number of upper-middle-class suburban houses built in Los Angeles between 1900 and 1917 are clothed in respectable English Tudor, as is this one.

24. Apartment Building, 1936
1146–1152 S. Westmoreland Avenue

Streamline Moderne with the usual strong nod to the nautical with portholes and steel railings.

25. House, circa 1900
Attributed to Joseph Cather Newsom
957 S. Arapahoe Street

Since Newsom invented terms to indicate style, he would most likely have labeled this stucco, wood-detailed, and high-pitched-roof dwelling as "Rhenish."

26. First Unitarian Church, 1930
Allison and Allison
2936 W. 8th Street

You have a feeling that the archi-tects had cast a quick glance at northern Italian churches of the early sixteenth century when they designed this exposed-concrete church. They also included a small pointed dome on the tower, which seems somewhat Islamic. The sanctuary and the cloisters enclose a charming courtyard.

27. Apartment Building, 1936
Milton J. Black
Northwest corner of Hobart Boulevard and 9th Street

A Streamline Moderne apart-ment building of four units, designed by one of Los Angeles's masters of the style. A horizontal bay once boasting a row of fins dominates the street façade. Unfortunately, the fins have been removed.

28

28. Harvard Apartments,
1992–93
**Kanner Architects
(Stephen Kanner)**
*9th Street at
Harvard Boulevard*

At first glance this three-story stucco apartment house (it contains thirteen one-bedroom units) appears as an updating of a late 1920s European International Style building. Insistent horizontal bands of windows are carried around the corners, with round windows suggesting the nautical. But a second look reveals that this International Style stage set projects from a "Swiss Cheese" section (in bright yellow stucco), which in turn backs up to a long red-painted volume. The round windows (some real, some not) give the feeling of being casually placed here and there on the building. In contrast, the rear red volume has square windows, some on edge, others not.

29. Val d'Amour Apartments,
1928
G. W. Powers
854 S. Oxford Avenue

Art Deco. At the street entrance, kneeling male figures somehow manage to hold up the five concrete stories above. Cast-concrete figures stand guard along the parapet and alternate with Moderne relief ornament.

30. Parking Garage,
circa 1926
824 Western Avenue

The plan is that of an L-shaped structure with a drive-in entrance, open on three sides, facing onto Western Avenue. This automobile entrance is surrounded by a rich array of cast-concrete Churrigueresque ornament. It all adds up to a remarkable composition in reinforced concrete. Note the stepped pattern of the walls, like the garage's ramp. Do not miss the building (circa 1939)

directly to the south. It is a sophisticated exercise in the Art Deco.

31. Warner Brothers Western Theater; Pellissier Building (now Wiltern Theater),
1930–31
Morgan, Walls, and Clements; G. A. Lansburgh; Anthony B. Heinsbergen
Southeast corner of Wilshire Boulevard and Western Avenue

An intact Art Deco theater and office tower building. The narrowness of the vertical recessed band windows and spandrels removes any reference to scale, so that from a distance you would think you were looking at a large skyscraper (in reality it is only twelve stories high). In 1985 the extraordinary auditorium, vandalized in the 1970s, and the exterior were restored by Brenda Levin Associates for developer Wayne Ratkovitch.

32. Beneficial Plaza, 1967
Skidmore, Owings, and Merrill
3700 Wilshire Boulevard

An eleven-story ice-cube tray set on end (it must have been cut out of graph paper), situated in a late-1960s nonpedestrian plaza.

33. McKinley Building, 1923
Morgan, Walls, and Clements
Northwest corner of Wilshire Boulevard and Oxford Avenue

Morgan, Walls, and Clements developed their own version of the Spanish Churrigueresque, of which this is one example. The upper portion of the corner tower is encrusted with cast-concrete ornament. Although the building has been modified over the years, the original courtyard remains.

34. Ahmanson Center, 1970
Edward D. Stone Associates
3701 Wilshire Boulevard

Ten floors plus a penthouse, this building is rather neutral Modern in spite of the curves.

35. Wilshire Boulevard Temple, 1922–29
Abraham A. Adelman, S. Tilden Norton, and David C. Allison
Northeast corner of Wilshire and Hobart Boulevards

The mystery and the opulence of the Near East are suggested in this luxurious Byzantine-inspired edifice. Black marble, inlaid gold, brilliant multicolored mosaics, and rare woods were used throughout the interior. Hugo Ballin's murals add the final touch of richness.

36. St. Basil's Roman Catholic Church, 1974
Albert C. Martin and Associates; Emmet L. Wemple and Associates, landscape architects
Northwest corner of Wilshire Boulevard and Kingsley Drive

A forest of vertical concrete volumes creates an illusion through fuzzy dark glass of Sir Basil Spence's Coventry Cathedral. Herb Goldman did the interior sculpture of the Stations of the

Cross as well as other sculpture in the side altars.

37. Wilshire Boulevard Christian Church, 1922–23
Robert H. Orr
Northeast corner of Wilshire Boulevard and Normandie Avenue

Northern Italian Romanesque, which was popular in Southern California in the teens and twenties, was used for this church. The campanile and other features of the church are Italian, while the great rose window is French. The building is of reinforced concrete with the pattern of the form boards revealed.

38. Office Building, 1936
Walker and Eisen
Northwest corner of Wilshire Boulevard and Alexandria Avenue

Behind all sorts of odds and ends on the street level you will find an excellent version of a four-story Art Deco office building. Wide fluted piers encase a row of double narrow piers. Above, double spirals provide the needed ornament.

39. Tishman Building, 1956
Victor Gruen and Associates
3325 Wilshire Boulevard

A characteristic mid-1950s Corporate International Style building—dull and dry. Now it is a real period piece of its time. Perhaps we will eventually come to respond to it in a positive fashion.

40. One Park Plaza, 1971–72
Daniel, Mann, Johnson, and Mendenhall
(Anthony J. Lumsden)
3250 Wilshire Boulevard

A twenty-two-story skyscraper clad in a thin, fragile glass skin set with a light metal frame. The form of the building, with the secondary towers projecting from each of the corners, suggests the shape of a Richardsonian Romanesque tower.

41. Bullocks-Wilshire Department Store, 1928
John and Donald Parkinson;
Feil and Paradice;
Jock Peters
3050 Wilshire Boulevard

Bullocks-Wilshire is a remarkable building, a treasure trove of late-1920s Moderne design. The store's management engaged some of the most notable Los Angeles artists of the time to design the interior of the building. The principal figure involved with the interior was the architect-designer Jock Peters. His hand can be seen most forcibly in the sportswear shop as well as in the center foyer at ground level. Art abounds. If you go through the parking lot entrance, you will pass through Art Deco gates. On the ceiling of the porte cochere is a mural by Herman Sachs expressing the theme "Times Fly." A relief sculpture, *The Spirit of Sports,* by Gjura Stojano adorns the walls of the sports shop. Other decorations are by Mayer Krieg, David Colins, George De Winter, and John Weaver. This store was one of the first on Wilshire Boulevard to provide front and rear main entrances, one (traditional) on

the street (for advertising purposes) and the other facing on the extensive well-landscaped parking lot to the rear (this is, of course, the real entrance to the store). The building is sheathed in light tan terra-cotta and trimmed with brown copper now turned green. We see it today as five floors plus the tower, but it was to have been the first phase of a ten-story structure. What is remarkable about the building is that so much of its original Art Deco interior design remains and is so beautifully maintained.

The building was damaged in the 1992 riots, but was restored. It has been recycled as a library for the Southwestern School of Law.

42. Commercial Garage, 1927
Robert H. Orr
South side of 6th Street, between Normandie and Mariposa Avenues

The design concept for this five-story reinforced-concrete garage structure was to disguise its use. When the garage opened, it was noted that "The site is in a high class district, amid residences, hotels and apartments, yet so unobtrusively does it blend into the surrounding buildings that it is often mistaken for a residential structure of some sort." In style it is Mediterranean, detailed in a crisp abstract fashion that we associate with the Postmodernist mode of the 1980s. The client/owners of the garage were the Chapman Brothers, who also commissioned Chapman Park Market down 6th Street.

43. Chapman Park Market,
1928–29
Morgan, Walls, and Clements
Northwest corner of
West 6th Street and
Alexandria Avenue

A Spanish Revival shopping center that occupies the entire block between Alexandria and Kenmore Avenues. The central court was an auto park with the surrounding retail stores facing both onto the parking lot and onto the adjoining streets. Across Alexandria Avenue at the northwest corner of West 6th Street is the Chapman Building (1928; Morgan, Walls, and Clements), a two-story Spanish Revival retail store and office building. In 1991 the complex was restored by Brenda Levin Associates.

44. Temple Sinai East
(now Korean Royal Church),
1926
S. Tilden Norton
407 S. New Hampshire Avenue

A mixture from the Eastern Mediterranean area—Byzantine, Islamic, plus other odds and ends. A central dome dominates both the interior and the exterior, and hand-cut bricks of varied colors create a rich tactile surface.

45. Virgil Apartments, 1950
Carl L. Maston
315 S. Virgil Avenue

A two-story building whose image is light post–World War II Modern. Each of the living units opens onto an enclosed small patio.

46. Shatto Recreation Center,
1991
Steven Ehrlich Architects
3191 W. 4th Street

The intent of the architect was to suggest the curved form of

a Pacific wave in his building. For the vertical surface of the wave, Ehrlich and the artist Ed Moses created a broken-up abstract pattern of sandstone-colored, split-faced concrete blocks, along with red clay bricks. Similar geometric patterns occur on the inside walls of the large gymnasium.

47. Ninth Church of Christ,
Scientist, 1924–27
Robert H. Orr
433 S. Normandie Avenue

This Classical English brick building lightly suggests the turn-of-the-century work of Sir Edwin Lutyens. In contrast, drive over to South Alvarado Street and see Elmer Grey's handling of the Romanesque in a highly traditional but vigorous manner in his 1912 First Church of Christ, Scientist.

48. Kentucky Fried Chicken,
1990
Grinstein/Daniels Architects
340 N. Western Avenue

Hardly a normal image for a fast-food establishment. The building ranges from a suggestion of the Programmatic, in the chicken-bucket-like form of the main section of the building, to the suggestion of the commonplace turned into high art in walls of corrugated metal. Above all of this is a white cube with the face of the Colonel on four sides.

49. Automotive Garage,
circa 1926
248 S. Berendo Street

A single-story Spanish Revival automobile garage, luxurious enough in its ornate cast-concrete façade to accommodate Franklins, Packards, and Pierce Arrows.

50. Selig Retail Store
(now Crocker-Citizens
National Bank Branch
Offices), 1931
Arthur E. Harvey
Northwest corner of
Western Avenue and
West 3rd Street

Though modest in size, this is one of Los Angeles's most vigorous examples of the use of glazed terra-cotta tile of the late 1920s/early 1930s. The gold ornament is dramatically set off against the rich black-tile background, and is pure Art Deco. The sheathing of this building will give you some indication of what the famous Richfield Building in downtown Los Angeles looked like.

51. Rosedale Cemetery
West Venice Boulevard,
between Normandie Avenue
and Catalina Street

Rosedale Cemetery exhibits a number of monuments and buildings well worth a visit. One of the most interesting of these is the Chapel of the Pines, 1903. The chapel itself is a low, domed, round building. It is approached through a classical Greek Doric temple front, the proportions of which are quite "correct." Another major monument is the Emma and Lewis Grigsby Mausoleum, in the form of a miniature Egyptian pyramid, sheathed in smooth black slate.

39 • MacArthur Park, North

1. Bungalows, circa 1910–25
Arthur Heineman
(Alfred Heineman, Associate)
South Ardmore Avenue

The Heinemans designed a number of bungalows in the northern part of the MacArthur Park district, including a group on South Ardmore Avenue. Those that are authenticated are situated at 110, 179, 201, and 228. The bungalow at 228 S. Ardmore Avenue is also Asian, while the one at number 201 is Colonial Revival with a sandstone base and columns.

2. Studio Court, circa 1925
4350 Beverly Boulevard

The French Norman mode was particularly popular in Los Angeles in the 1920s for small cottage-like commercial complexes and bungalow courts. With the continual intensification of land use in the west Los Angeles region, most of these have unfortunately disappeared. Here is a good remaining example in fairy-tale proportions.

3. Mount Vernon Office, Pacific Savings, 1960
Rick Farver Associates
270 N. Vermont Avenue

This lighthearted version of George Washington's Mount Vernon was originally built at 400 N. Vermont Avenue where one could readily see it from the Hollywood Freeway. It has now been moved down the street where you will have to search it out.

4. KFL (KEHE) Radio Station, 1936
Morgan, Walls, and Clements
133–141 N. Vermont Avenue

Though altered, this radio station building is still one of Los Angeles's forceful examples of the 1930s Streamline Moderne. The central pylon tower, designed for the display of the station's call letters, was originally topped by an open, metal, vertical tower 475 feet high.

5. Multipurpose and Classroom Building, Commonwealth Avenue Elementary School, 1992–93
Siegel Diamond Architects
(Katherine Diamond)
215 S. Commonwealth Avenue

The architect mentioned that this addition to an older school building was "based on children's building blocks, playfully breaking down the scale of the building through colors and materials." Some of the boxes are of wire and mesh, making them light and airy and also permitting you to see into the various staircases. The building encompasses multipurpose/auditorium, a food service area, six classrooms, and three kindergarten rooms with their adjacent play areas.

6. American Storage Company, 1928–29
Arthur E. Harvey
3639 Beverly Boulevard

A fourteen-story (supposedly ten stories to meet the restriction on height) Los Angeles landmark. The thin verticality of the tower creates the illusion of great soaring height. In contrast to the Art Deco tower, the base of the building exhibits a rich vocabulary of the Spanish Revival.

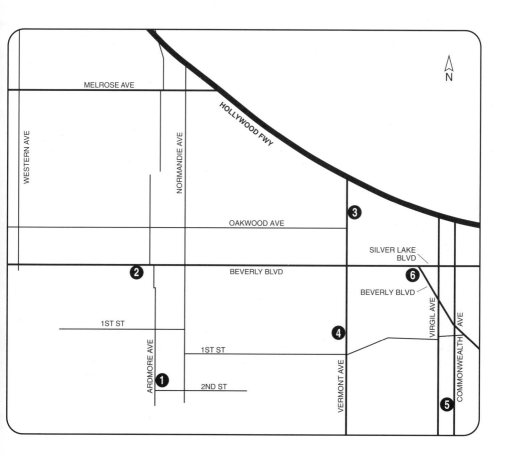

40 • MacArthur Park, East

1. Ponce de Leon Apartments, circa 1905
1136 S. Alvarado Street

The building is pure Beaux-Arts and exhibits an elaborate columned entrance that provides the appropriate formal entry.

2. Cottage, circa 1895
1805 - 12th Place

A small Queen Anne cottage.

3. Dora Apartments, 1906
1600 W. Pico Boulevard

Between 1900 and 1915 a good number of three-story Mission Revival apartment buildings were built in the area west and south of downtown. In the Dora Apartment Building a corner bay emerges above the tile roof as a low octagonal tower. Gabled parapets, arched openings, and stucco walls help to create the needed Mission image. Apartment buildings with retail stores on the ground level, such as this one, were common.

4. Pico Union Villa Building, 1980
John Mutlow
1200 S. Union Avenue

A three-story multiple-housing building for the elderly, in the form of a square with an interior courtyard. A diagonal passage pierces through the two opposite corners of the complex. Free-

standing pylons in the courtyard and at the entrance are, one assumes, usually to contradict the square and its diagonals. The idea of the interior courtyard comes from the traditional courts found in the Mediterranean tradition—though in this case its design suggests a prison exercise yard.

5. Alvarado Terrace Houses
Southeast of the intersection of Pico Boulevard and Alvarado Street

Alvarado Terrace, laid out as a gentle, curved, upper-middle-class residential street, was planned in the early 1900s by Pomery Powers, who was president of the Los Angeles City Council at the time. The development was at first called Windmill Links—named after the landmark of a nearby windmill and tank. The seven remaining houses on the north side of the street provide us with a good glimpse of Los Angeles's suburban streets from about 1900 through the mid-teens. These houses indicate the variety of images employed by architects and clients.

a. Barmore House, circa 1902
1317 Alvarado Terrace

English and Germanic Medieval styles establish the character of this suburban house.

b. Cohan House, circa 1902
Hudson and Munsell
1325 Alvarado Terrace

Late Queen Anne in concept but simplified and made more classical with references to the Shingle Colonial Revival.

c. Gilbert House, circa 1902
1333 Alvarado Terrace

A late–Queen Anne Shingle house with the usual hint of the Anglo-Colonial Revival. The building with the round corner bay tower is sheathed in Santa Barbara sandstone below and shingles above. There is an abundance of ornament, both inside and out.

d. Powers House, 1903
A. L. Haley
1345 Alvarado Terrace

This is the house that the developer of Alvarado Terrace chose for himself—an exuberant Mission Revival piece (one of the best examples still standing in Los Angeles). The house was designed by A. L. Haley, whose extensive practice was primarily in the realm of spec apartments and other commercial buildings. The front porch of the Powers House exhibits an arcade supported by short, thick, fat columns, and the roof presents a picturesque assembly of open and closed towers, scalloped parapets, and quatrefoil windows.

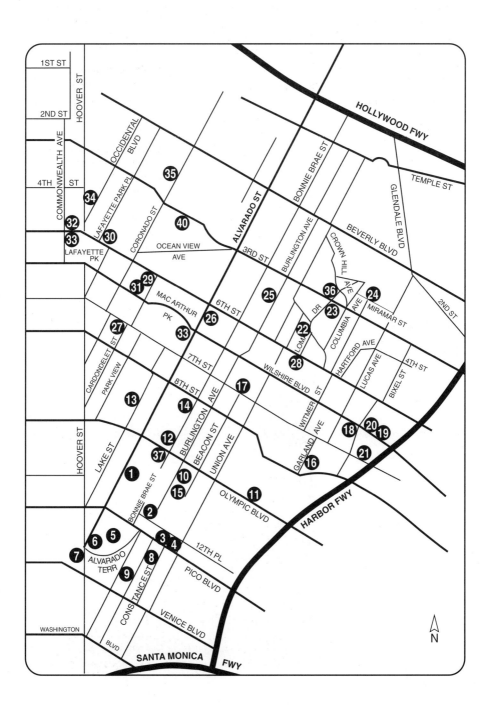

e. Raphael House, circa 1902
Hunt and Eager
1353 Alvarado Terrace

A good-sized, two-story English Tudor dwelling. Note the beautiful entrance with its windows of beveled glass.

f. Evanardy-Kinney House, 1902
Hunt and Eager
1401 Alvarado Terrace

Late Queen Anne modified by Colonial Revival details. The house is sheathed in sandstone and stucco below, and in shingles above.

g. House, circa 1905
1406 Alvarado Terrace

A good example of Los Angeles turn-of-the-century attachment to Anglo fashions, here in a Colonial Revival dwelling.

h. Milner Apartment Building, circa 1925
1415 Alvarado Terrace

A multiple-housing unit intrudes in this single-family enclave. This apartment building utilizes an elaborate English Gothic image.

6. First Church of Christ, Scientist, 1912
Elmer Grey
1366 S. Alvarado Street

Northern Italian Romanesque as a source, but strongly abstracted. A high, semicircular temple porch with Corinthian columns looks out toward the street intersection. Another more delicately detailed porch faces east, and the tower has been reduced to a single rectangular volume with a grouping of three vertical windows on each of its surfaces.

7. House, circa 1900
1515 S. Hoover Street

Another late–Queen Anne dwelling, this time modified with classical Anglo-Colonial Revival detailing.

8. House, circa 1900
1346 W. Constance Street

This imaginative composition, using seemingly all of the current imagery of the period, could well be labeled as the Bavarian Hunting Lodge style.

9. Bungalow Court, 1925
Edwin W. Willit
1428 S. Bonnie Brae Street

A miniaturized pylon gateway with relief sculpture establishes the Egyptian theme for this single-story, double-row bungalow court (the Hollywood film set brought into the world of "real" architecture).

10. House, circa 1898
1030 Burlington Avenue

An unbelievable array of Islamic details cover this simple wood building.

11. Loyola University Law School, 1981–84 and later
Frank O. Gehry and Associates
1441 W. Olympic Boulevard

One of Los Angeles's really important commissions of the early 1980s. Here we can see

Gehry and his associates at their best, in both planning and design. The main building is broken in the middle by a greenhouse-like gabled-roof temple, which is approached from below by a long narrow staircase. The smaller single-story buildings in the court in front of the large building are rendered as small, abstracted classical temples. A number of other buildings have been added to the complex over the years. They were all designed by Gehry when he was skeptical of about the ability of Los Angeles workmen to carry out elegant details. His attitude has changed.

12. Houses
South Bonnie Brae Street

Bonnie Brae Street was one of a series of fashionable suburban streets situated west of downtown Los Angeles. Most of the single-family upper-middle-class dwellings that lined these north/south streets were built between 1890 and 1910. As one would expect, much has been lost. Still enough remains so that we can gain a sense of suburban Los Angeles at the turn of the century.

a. House, circa 1897
1026 S. Bonnie Brae Street

"Palladian" (perhaps). Really a Queen Anne design with Anglo-Colonial Revival frosting.

11

b. House, circa 1896
1032 S. Bonnie Brae Street

An additional example of the late–Queen Anne open plan, with much Anglo-Colonial Revival references.

c. House, circa 1898
1035 S. Bonnie Brae Street

Shingled, late Queen Anne/Colonial Revival.

d. House, circa 1895
1036–1038 S. Bonnie Brae Street

One of the remaining architectural gems of the area, this dwelling is French Chateauesque accomplished in wood, with small corner turrets and a low balcony between.

e. House, circa 1897
1047 S. Bonnie Brae Street

A two-story, simplified, late–Queen Anne house.

f. House, circa 1905
1053 S. Bonnie Brae Street

A boxy Colonial Revival dwelling with some imaginative touches, including a small Gothic window set in a frame with tiny columns, and a Romanesque window placed below. Fluted pilasters terminate the corners of the building.

13. Marlinex Apartment Building, circa 1930
938 S. Lake Street

A seven-story Art Deco (Zigzag) Moderne apartment building. Perhaps its most impressive detail is the Modernistic lettering.

14. Wright-Mooers House, 1894
818 S. Bonnie Brae Street

This house is one that is often illustrated in discussions of West

Coast Victorian architecture. The open plan and the overall general design of the building are Queen Anne. The arched street entrance (in wood) with its two pairs of small columns is Richardsonian Romanesque, while the tower with its elongated domed roof and ogee dormers appears Islamic. And there are other suggestions, as well, of the French Chateauesque and of the Anglo-Colonial Revival. Note especially the stair hall-landing window on the north side of the house.

15. House, circa 1902
Attributed to
Joseph Cather Newsom
1011 Beacon Street

Newsom employed a combination of images in all of his work in Los Angeles and elsewhere. He would probably have labeled this dwelling as an example of the Bavarian Hunting Lodge style. This meant a combination of a Queen Anne floor plan with medieval vernacular detailing from central Europe.

16. Dennis House, 1910
Dennis and Farwell
767 S. Garland Avenue

The architectural firm of Oliver P. Dennis and Lyman Farwell was one of Los Angeles's most productive offices from around 1896 through the mid-teens. A good number of their designs tend toward the Beaux-Arts Classical and to the Anglo-Colonial Revival. (Farwell had worked in the New York office of McKim, Mead, and White.) Here in Dennis's own house we can see a Colonial Revival dwelling with a few leftovers from the earlier Queen Anne.

17. Young's Market
(now Andrews Hardware and
Metal Company), 1924

Charles F. Plummer
1010 W. 7th Street

A Maybeckian romantic version of the Beaux-Arts tradition. A row of classical columns supports the upper arcade. Between them is a "life-size frieze of genuine della Robbia style." The interior is decorated in a Pompeiian fashion with marble and antique mosaics. The market was damaged in the 1992 riots, but it now has been restored and is open to the public.

18. Wilshire Financial
Building, 1985–86
Albert C. Martin
and Associates
*Southwest corner of
Wilshire Boulevard and
Bixel Street*

The opinion that the downtown core should leap over the Harbor Freeway to the west has long been in the minds of planners and business interests. The thirty-eight-story Wilshire Financial Building was conceived as an important step in that westward march of high-rises. Although it is on Wilshire Boulevard, it does not make itself an element within the Wilshire corridor. It, like most urban downtown buildings, exists in and of itself. The unique aspect of its design is that the building becomes a triangle above its twelfth story.

19. Office Tower for the
Signal Oil Company, 1958
Pereira and Luckman;
remodeled, 1973–74
Craig Ellwood & Associates
1010 Wilshire Boulevard

Ellwood resheathed a rather dull, 1950s Modern tower of seventeen floors into his own version of the Miesian aesthetic.

20. Woodbury College, 1937
Claude Beelman
1027 Wilshire Boulevard

A monumental Streamline Moderne building. The grand entrance and the basic symmetrical façade suggest the dignity of an institution.

21. Arco Center, 1988–89
Gin Wong Associates
1055 W. 7th Street

Another high-rise, like the Wilshire Financial Building, which hopes to establish the downtown connections of the "West Bank," i.e., west of the Harbor Freeway. There is not much to say about this dark thirty-three-story high-rise other than its form is reserved.

22. Loma Court, circa 1925
380–388 Loma Drive

One of Los Angeles's many Mediterranean-style bungalow courts.

23. Mary Andrews Clark
Memorial Home (YWCA),
1912–13
Arthur B. Benton
306 Loma Drive

The master of the Mission Revival here turned his hand to the French Chateauesque. The building seems most satisfactory from a distance, where the towers and high roofs emerge out of the surrounding trees. Inside, the more public spaces exhibit exotic woods and some splendid leaded and colored art glass.

24. Lewis House, 1889
Attributed to
Joseph Cather Newsom
1425 Miramar Street

The Newsom brothers, Samuel and Joseph Cather Newsom, best known for their often-illustrated Carson House in Eureka, California, produced some of the wonderful, inventive, if not slightly "mad," Victorian houses in Los Angeles during the Great Boom of the 1880s. It is a shame that most of these houses have disappeared over the years. The Lewis House is a delightful but subdued example of one of their Queen Anne designs whose effectiveness would be more apparent if the second-floor porch above the entrance were not enclosed.

25. Bungalow Court,
circa 1937
428–432 S. Burlington Avenue

A Streamline Moderne bungalow court. Other nearby courts are to be found at 445 S. Burlington Avenue (Mission Revival, circa 1914) and at 470–478 S. Burlington Avenue (a bit of Dutch Cottage imagery, circa 1922).

26. Westlake Theater, 1926
Richard M. Bates Jr.
638 S. Alvarado Street

The interior was originally Adamesque, but both the interior and the exterior have continually been updated over the years. The interior is still worth a visit.

27. Hite Building, 1923–24
Morgan, Walls, and Clements
Southwest corner of
Carondelet and
West 7th Streets

The firm of Morgan, Walls, and Clements designed well over a dozen small retail/commercial buildings in the MacArthur Park

area. They employed a Spanish image, but maneuvered it into something that always read as a pure 1920s design. Ornament inspired by Spain and Mexico (the Plateresque, the Churrigueresque, and the Renaissance) was placed as accent marks on simple stucco volumes. In the Hite Building the street elevation of the single-story section boasts a composition of a six-columned arcade balanced on each side by entrances with cast-concrete ornamented panels above. Two other Morgan, Walls, and Clements buildings nearby are the Thorpe Building (1924) at the northwest corner of Parkview and West 7th Streets and the Studio and Shop Building (1924) for Mrs. Olive J. Cobb at 2861 W. 7th Street.

28. Carl's Supermarket Building, 1933
Morgan, Walls, and Clements
1530–1536 W. 6th Street

An early supermarket building. Its image is transitional between the Art Deco and the then-emerging Streamline Moderne. Note the composition of the pylons to each side, which

sprout three layers of plant-like spirals at their tops.

29. The Elks Building,
1923–24
Curlett and Beelman
607 S. Park View Street

A monumental Goodhuesque composition with its prime reference being to the early Romanesque. The glory of the building externally lies in the groupings of large-scale sculptured figures at the upper ends of each of the wings of the building and the eight larger-than-life-size figures near the parapet of the high central section of the building. The interiors were decorated by Anthony Heinsbergen.

30. Granada Building, 1927
Franklin Harper
627 S. Lafayette Park Place

A full block of retail stores, offices, and studio apartments designed as a single Spanish village. Inner paseos, balconies, and courts create a series of pleasing small-scaled spaces.

31. The Town House, 1928
Norman W. Alpaugh
1600 Wilshire Boulevard

A thirteen-story, brick-and-stone-trimmed Beaux-Arts hotel of the twenties. Designs such as this were common across the country, but there were never a great number built in Los Angeles in the teens and twenties. This hotel makes its nod to the Southland in its garden enclosed within the L of the building. In the spring of 1993 it was declared a Cultural/Historic Monument by the city.

32. First Congregational
Church, 1930–32
Allison and Allison
(Austin Whittlesey)
Northeast corner of Commonwealth Avenue and West 6th Street

A concrete structure with revealed horizontal form-board patterns on its wall surfaces. One assumes that the design was derived from late English Gothic, especially the central tower.

33. CNA Building, 1972
Langdon and Wilson;
Emmet L. Wemple
and Associates,
landscape architects
Southeast corner of Commonwealth Avenue and West 6th Street

A mirrored glass cube works well as long as there is something around worth reflecting, such as the Congregational church across the street.

34. Church of the Precious
Blood, circa 1932
Henry C. Newton and
Robert D. Murray
North of the intersection of Hoover Street and Occidental Boulevard

Italian Romanesque in reinforced concrete, beautifully sited in relation to the joining of two major streets.

35. Hill House, circa 1911
Walker and Vawter
201 S. Coronado Street

This Craftsman dwelling was frequently illustrated as the typical Los Angeles bungalow. The principal rooms open through glass doors to a terrace surrounded by a clinker-brick wall. Long heavy shingles cover the walls, and the Japanese exposed roof beams lend an Asian feeling.

36. Bungalow Court,
circa 1925
West corner of Loma Drive and Crown Hill Avenue

Hillsides were often used to advantage throughout Los Angeles for stepped patterns of bungalow courts. This example displays a Spanish Revival image.

37. House, circa 1900
Southwest corner of Bonnie Brae Street and West Olympic Boulevard

A Chateauesque dwelling with the characteristic dominant round tower surmounted by a conical roof.

41 • Downtown

The present-day central city lies southeast of the fabled multilevel interchange of the Hollywood, Santa Ana, Pasadena, and Harbor Freeways. The northern section of this area, occupying what remains of Bunker Hill, is devoted to public buildings and spaces—symbolic, cultural, and bureaucratic. The remainder of Bunker Hill and south into the flatlands is given over to commerce (with some more recent high-density housing).

Downtown Los Angeles is the product of three major building booms. The first was in the years 1900–1917; the second was from the early 1920s through 1931; and the last started in the late 1960s. The first two booms employed the imagery of the Classical Beaux-Arts, and it is amazing how many ten- to twelve-story office buildings were built, especially on South Broadway and on South Spring Street. The second expansion moved toward the west from South Broadway to South Flower Street and was clothed in variations of the Art Deco and the PWA Moderne.

In the late 1930s a few Streamline Moderne buildings were constructed and a number of street-level frontages were remodeled. Little building activity occurred from 1945 through the early 1960s, so there are only a few examples of post–World War II Modern buildings. The high-rise buildings constructed since the late 1960s are much more varied in form, running the gamut from smooth-skin Modernism to outright Postmodernism. Many, even the Modernist buildings, convey a Postmodernist stance, clothing the building in skins of stone rather than in the usual metal-and-glass sheathing that we associate with Modernist products.

Since the early 1920s, downtown Los Angeles has been a disappointment for those who feel that a city should have a primary high-density urban core with the necessary cityscape of skyscrapers. Even today, downtown Los Angeles finds itself doing battle with other urban cores and strips.

During the 1930s the view that downtown should only be one among many urban centers was officially codified in the regional plan for the Los Angeles Basin. It was in the late 1930s that the freeway system was planned, and as soon as World War II was over, work commenced on completing the Hollywood Freeway. A short time later, the Santa Ana and Harbor Freeways were built. In the 1950s these freeways and the pre–World War II Pasadena Freeway (1934–41) were connected by the famous multilevel interchange known as "The Stack."

So far, downtown Los Angeles has followed the classic approach to urban renewal, namely bulldozing the past and starting anew. The greatest losses were the Victorian residences on Bunker Hill that were swept away in Charles Luckman's plan for the area. Many of the buildings that were situated on Bunker Hill could have been revamped and reused, but they are all gone now. With the exception of several restored nineteenth-century buildings near the Plaza (and of course the Bradbury Building at Broadway and Third Street), little or no evidence of nineteenth-century Victorianism remains in downtown Los Angeles. The number of major buildings lost in the last fifty years is impressive. Included among the major lost monuments are the great black-and-gold 1928 Richfield Building (Morgan, Walls, and Clements), the 1935 Sunkist Building (Walker and Eisen) with its roof gardens and abundance of sculpture and paintings, and more recently the Sullivanesque Philharmonic Auditorium Building by Charles F. Whittlesey. We have also lost through remodeling the wonderful Moderne-style Clifton's Cafeteria, and more recently have seen the demolition of St. Paul's Cathedral, the Hotel Cordova, the Abbey Building, the Bath Building, the Municipal Water and Power Building, and others.

Through urban renewal, the houses of Bunker Hill were bulldozed and replaced bit by bit with the big-city illusion of high-rise towers. On the whole these towers are competent exercises, but they in no way address the specifics of Bunker Hill as a hill or the climate and geography of Los Angeles. The streets adjacent to these high-rises are for the automobile, and they are not a pleasant experience for pedestrians, notwithstanding a few very handsome ground-level plazas.

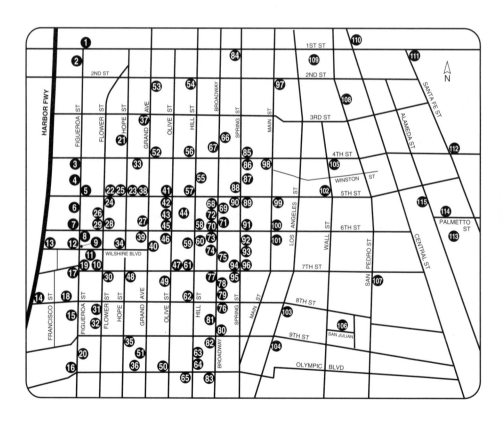

1. Bunker Hill Towers, 1968
Robert E. Alexander
*Northeast corner of
Figueroa and West 1st Streets*

Three high-rise towers that were supposed to introduce residential living into downtown. In style and concept they are marginally respectable.

2. Promenade Towers, 1985
Kamnitzer and Cotton;
Abraham Shapiro;
Fong and Associates,
landscape architects
*West side of
Figueroa Street, between
1st and 2nd Streets*

The idea of providing downtown living accommodations is fine, but the buildings are bland. The garden between them with palms and exotic planting is the best part of the project.

3. Sheraton Grande Hotel
(now the Downtown Marriott),
1978–83
Archsystems
*Southwest corner of
Figueroa and West 4th Streets*

A fifteen-story structure that plays off curvilinear and angular shapes. Like the Bonaventure Hotel, it is best when experienced from the freeway. The thick planting of palms at the entrance is the high point of the design.

4. Union Bank, 1968
Albert C. Martin and
Associates
*Figueroa Street, between
West 4th and West 5th Streets*

A typical example of the late–1960s International Style, here is a vertical box set on a low podium. It is notable for being the first high-rise in central Los Angeles since the 1920s.

5. Bonaventure Hotel,
1974–76
John Portman and Associates
*Northeast corner of
Figueroa and West 5th Streets*

The science-fiction world of Buck Rogers and the twenty-first century have not left us. Five bronze-clad glass towers rise from their podium base, just like one of the 1940s drawings by Frank R. Paul for *Amazing Stories*. As a contribution to downtown Los Angeles, they work best when seen from one of the freeways. Portman was quoted as saying of Los Angeles and his hotel, "Put cars in their place, put people on their feet, and put the city in order" (1973). Obviously his view of putting people on their feet meant inside of his building, not on the adjoining streets. The streetscape of the Bonaventure is grim; the public sidewalk alongside the adjoining streets is not for pedestrians, an attitude reinforced by four pedestrian bridges that connect the upper level of the Bonaventure Hotel with adjoining buildings. These are dull, both for their users and as objects within the streetscape. The atrium space within Portman's hotel is visually exciting, but maddening when you try to find your way around. As a partial answer to the criticism that the hotel ignored the street, an entrance was added on Flower Street (1985–86; John Portman and Associates). This change helps the hotel and the street, but this section of Flower represents the world of the automobile, not the pedestrian.

6. Manulife Plaza, 1981–82
Albert C. Martin and Associates
515 S. Figueroa Street

Another vertical reflective box, in this case blue-green glass with a step-back façade. A suggestion of luxury is added to this twenty-story skyscraper by the use of green granite both externally and in the lobby. Below the shaft of the building are four levels of parking. The usual stage-set plaza is provided, adorned by a sculpture of a family of bears fishing for salmon, the work of Christopher Keene.

7. Jonathan Club, 1924
Schultze and Weaver
545 S. Figueroa Street

A restrained low-rise building realized in a Beaux-Arts version of early-sixteenth-century Italian Renaissance architecture.

8. Linder Plaza, 1973–74
Honnold, Reibsamen, and Rex
888 W. 6th Street, at Figueroa Street

A fifteen-story triangular skyscraper whose fragile skin is sheathed in silver-and-gray steel and glass. The fine and expensive machine-image detailing of the building is impressive.

9. Engine Company #28 Building, 1912
John Parkinson
644 S. Figueroa Street

This three-story brick-and-stone-trimmed firehouse was restored in 1989 by the architectural firm of Altoon and Porter. It is now a restaurant—a good one!

10. Fine Arts Building, 1925
Walker and Eisen
811 W. 7th Street

The street façade of this twelve-story building displays a highly original use of Romanesque (the Cathedral at Lucca comes to mind). Twisted columns, sculptured corbeling, heavy arched windows, and elongated columns were all employed. The tripartite division of the façade has taken into account how the building is viewed; it is subtle close up at the street level, large and bold at the top so that it will make an impact from a distance. The tour-de-force of the building (and a must to see) is the two-story, arcaded main lobby with its rich surfaces and ornament produced by the tile-maker Ernest Batchelder.

11. Office Building, 1978–80
Skidmore, Owings, and Merrill (Chicago Office)
911 Wilshire Boulevard

One more horizontal-grid sky-scraper, twenty-three stories high. This is a familiar type unfortunately found in urban environments across the U.S. Not surprisingly, it has attracted substantial government tenancy.

12. Sanwa Bank Plaza (name to be changed), 1986–89
Albert C. Martin and Associates
Northwest corner of Figueroa Street and Wilshire Boulevard

The architect's design is that of a 760-foot-high, fifty-story sky-scraper that exhibits slightly layered setbacks and clipped corners. Its principal walls are of coral-colored granite contrasted with bronze panels and green glazing. On the first floor is an impressive 75-foot-high atrium. Before you glance at this high-rise, bear in mind that, until a number of years ago, this was the site of St. Paul's Episcopal Cathedral, a major Los Angeles landmark.

13. 1000 Wilshire Building, 1984–87
Kohn Peterson Fox
Wilshire Boulevard, just east of the Harbor Freeway

The 1000 Wilshire Building is downtown Los Angeles's most assertive Postmodern building. Though by no means as tall as other downtown skyscrapers (it contains twenty-one stories), it really stands out when viewed from the Harbor Freeway. The building exhibits gabled ends, enlarged/overscaled windows, contrasting banding, and frequent references to Art Deco

13

designs of the late 1920s. The best way to experience the building is from the south at 7th Street; you go up formal stair-cases, through a gateway onto a plaza, and then into the building. At the north side you enter through a 34-foot-high gate-house. There is no question that as long as it is around, this building will dominate the western sections of downtown Los Angeles.

14. Harbor Freeway Murals, 1991–93
Kent Twitchell, artist
8th Street and the Harbor Freeway (on the Citicorp Plaza Parking Structure facing the Harbor Freeway)

Players of the Los Angeles Chamber Orchestra greet you as you go by on the freeway. Twitchell really understands how large-scale public murals can function. Often they are far more important than the buildings around them. Other downtown examples of this artist's public murals are *Ed Ruscha Monument,* (1978–87) on the exterior of the Job Center Building, 1031 S. Hill Street; and *The Bride and Groom,* (1972–76) on the exterior of Victor Clothing Company Building, 240 S. Broadway. Twitchell's best known public mural is *The Freeway Lady,* located on the exterior of the Prince Hotel at 1255 W. Temple Street (visible from the Hollywood Freeway). This work was painted in 1974; in 1981 a new building was constructed that partially obscured the mural, and then in 1986 it was painted over. A legal settlement was made between the owner of the property and the artist (1992), and it has now been repainted (with a few changes and extensions).

15. 865 South Figueroa Tower, 1985–87
Albert C. Martin and Associates
865 S. Figueroa

A thirty-six-story skyscraper rendered in polished red granite with bronze windows. The building's surfaces are layered as in skyscrapers of the late 1920s and early 1930s.

16. Hotel Figueroa, 1925
Stanton, Reed, and Hibbard
939 S. Figueroa Street

A learned Beaux-Arts interpretation of northern Italian Renaissance town houses. The lobby and pool area do not seem to have been redecorated since the twenties and are definitely worth some time.

17. Citicorp Plaza 777 Tower, 1988–90
Cesar Pelli and Associates; Langdon Wilson Mumper
Southwest corner of Figueroa and 7th Streets

A reflective-skinned fifty-three-story tower, its form a layered series of cylinders. The structure, and especially the lobby, reveal the sophisticated detailing one associates with Pelli's work.

18. Seventh Market Place, 1985–86
Skidmore, Owings and Merrill (Chicago Office)
925 W. 8th Street

Essentially this is a posh shopping center arranged around a sunken court that boasts plenty of exposed ironwork, fountains, and trees. The project is colorful in its use of a varied scheme of mauve, peach, light blue, and celadon. Robinson's May (formerly Bullocks) itself has the feel that its designer was inspired by one of Otto Wagner's metal-frame-and-paneled railroad stations in Vienna. It all seems light and festive; good for shopping.

19. Home Savings of America Tower, 1988–89
Albert C. Martin and Associates (Tim Vreeland)
Northeast corner of Figueroa and 7th Streets

Another odd Postmodernist highrise. Tim Vreeland, who was responsible for the design of this twenty-eight-story building, noted that he looked to the turn-of-the-century New York versions of the French Chateauesque style. The most dramatic space in the building is the domed and barrel-vaulted sixth-floor "Sky Lobby." While the reference to the Chateauesque mode is apparent,

the proportions and detailing needed to carry out this historic mode are only partially apparent in the building.

20. Variety Arts Building, 1923–24
Allison and Allison
938–940 S. Figueroa Street

A Beaux-Arts formula; in this instance there seems to be a suggestion of Byzantine or Romanesque.

21. Security Pacific Plaza, 1973–74
Albert C. Martin and Associates
333 S. Hope

The return of the Beaux-Arts: the tower is fifty-five stories high and its façades are accentuated by thirty-six vertical piers sheathed in light gray granite from Ponteverde in Spain. The gardens and their fountains are quite formal. A large arched sculpture in steel (painted red) by Alexander Calder is placed near the entrance to the tower. Across Flower Street to the west is the full-block World Trade Center (1974–76; Conrad Associates), which, notwithstanding its twin eight-story towers, comes across as an urban non-space.

22. Wells Fargo Building (444 Plaza Building), 1979
Albert C. Martin and Associates
Northeast corner of South Flower and West 5th Streets

When one considers that this forty-eight-story skyscraper replaced the handsome Sunkist Building (1935; Walker and Eisen), the demand for a building whose design would be far above the normal was to be expected. The emphasized horizontality of its stepped-back rectangular volume is well carried out, but hardly distinguished. The plaza with its palm trees heads in the right direction, but it does not save the composition. Equally mixed is the sense of meaningful public sculpture by Michael Hiezer, Bruce Nauman, Robert Rauschenberg, Frank Stella, and Mark di Suvero.

23. Library Tower, 1988–90
I. M. Pei and Partners
North side of 5th Street, west of Grand Avenue

A round high-rise that, in a slab-like fashion, reduces its diameter as it nears the top. This tower comes off as one of the best of the newer downtown Los Angeles skyscrapers.

24. Los Angeles Public Library, 1922–26
Bertram G. Goodhue and Carleton M. Winslow
Southeast corner of South Flower and West 5th Streets

This building and the Nebraska State Capitol at Lincoln are Goodhue's two most significant works and also two of his most influential designs. In both, Goodhue sought to bring the past and present together in a single readable image. From the past he borrowed from Egypt, Rome, Byzantium, and Islam. He also continued the tradition of monumental construction and the extensive use of sculpture, painting, and mosaics. He implied the new age of the twentieth century in his hint at the skyscraper (modern business), his utilitarian planning, the expression of undecorated surfaces, and the use of twentieth-century materials, here reinforced concrete.

As with several of his impor-

tant designs, Goodhue's early sketches show a rather elaborate building, with domes and much ornament in the Spanish Revival style, one which he himself had done so much to popularize at the 1915 San Diego Exposition. He simplified and abstracted his original design to produce a design that was "modified Spanish Colonial style." As in his design for the Nebraska State Capitol Building, Goodhue created an abbreviated skyscraper as the exterior focal point of his design, but inside he retained his traditional dome, vaulting, and arches.

Operating within a Beaux-Arts tradition, he introduced a wide array of art: exterior sculpture by Lee Lawrie, the twelve murals in the second floor of the rotunda

by Dean Cornwall, the thirteen murals in the History Room by Albert Herter. In the Children's Room, the fresco *Stampeding Buffalo* was by Charles M. Kassler, and the scenes by Julian Garnsey and A. W. Parsons convey episodes from Sir Walter Scott's novels. "Sculpture here," wrote Lee Lawrie, "is not sculpture, but a branch grafted on to the architectural trunk; forms that portray animated life, emerge from blocks of stone and terminate in historical expression." As with the Nebraska State Capitol Building, Goodhue and Lawrie worked closely with philosopher Hartley B. Alexander in drawing up the ideological program of decoration for the library. Their theme was "centered in the illuminated book, symbolized by the torch of knowledge which is handed on from one age to another by the great literary figures of all ages."

The design of the landscape provided by Goodhue and Winslow was to pass on historic symbols (in the plants used and the design of the landscape) and to see that they were regenerated and made meaningful for the present. The east garden pointed to the informality of the English Picturesque tradition; the west garden looked to the ancient Mediterranean world and the Islamic gardens of Near Persia. His view that the library was a building in a park was integral to his design. When in the post–World War II era it became clear that room for more books was needed, the first idea was to demolish the building and sell the site to a developer. A new library would be erected where there was more space—perhaps the San Fernando Valley.

As if to hurry on that event, an arsonist (who has never been found to this day) set the building on fire in 1986. A second fire occurred a few years later, augmented by damage suffered in the 1987 earthquake. Earlier, in 1983, the city had finally decided that the approach to the library should be a complicated affair of restoration, expansion of the building to the east, granting of air rights to surrounding development, etc. This led to the development of the Library Square project, with the library building being surrounded and dwarfed by a ring of high-rise towers. The Los Angeles office of the New York firm of Hardy, Holzman and Pfeiffer was selected to guide the renovation and design the additions. The architects initially

proposed a new wing, which was to dominate the Goodhue building. After much public review, this design was modified to be lower than the massing of the original building. In the meantime, Brenda Levin and Associates was engaged to supervise the restoration, and Lawrence Halprin together with Campbell and Campbell were brought in to redesign the remaining parkland around the building.

In mid-1993 all of this work was finished. What of the results? On the good side is the wonderful and sensitive restoration of the old building, particularly its great interior public spaces. Another asset is the relandscaping of the west garden, though this has some problems with the injection of new structures and an underground parking garage. But it has been replanted, even overplanted, an approach perhaps needed in the world of the surrounding hardscape of streets, sidewalks, and buildings. A number of new works of art have entered the building and its landscape, including sculptures and inscriptions by Jud Fine for the *Spine,* which leads up to the building's west entrance. On the negative side is the loss of the charmingly scaled Children's Wing and the east park. Hardy, Holzman and Pfeiffer's addition may work functionally, but aesthetically it is unfortunate. They have reverted to their theme of a central skylighted atrium. The verticality of the eight-story atrium space suggests Gothic, whereas Goodhue's design is fully within the tradition of horizontality associated with Classical architecture. Externally, their efforts in massing and detailing to mimic Goodhue has little substance to it.

25. Bunker Hill Steps, 1989–90
Lawrence Halprin

Across from the north entrance to the library, Los Angeles's own version of Rome's Spanish Steps meanders up the hillside from 5th Street to Hope Street, 103 steps in all. The steps are divided by a raised water channel whose watercourse suggests a natural rock-bedded stream. Terraced planting occurs on each side. At the top of the stairs and watercourse is a pretty, small-scaled, sculptured figure by Robert Graham (1992).

26. Atlantic Richfield Plaza, 1972
Albert C. Martin
and Associates
*West side of
South Flower Street, between
West 5th and West 6th Streets*

These two, thin, fifty-two-story towers replace one of Los Angeles's major monuments, the 1928–29 Art Deco, black-and-gold, terra-cotta Richfield Building (Morgan, Walls, and Clements). The dark polished-stone-sheathed twin towers of the new buildings are formal, dignified, and reticent. The plaza between the towers contains a fountain sculpture, *Double Ascension* (1973), by Herbert Bayer. Below the plaza are two levels of an underground mall, which in color and design is more self-consciously fashionable than the towers (Bielski and Associates, design consultants for the mall).

27. Checkers Hotel, 1927
Charles F. Whittlesey
535 S. Grand Avenue

A small hotel built in the Spanish mode. Its elaborate façade contains sculptures of gargoyles and ships (including the *Santa Maria* and the *Mayflower*). In 1989 the building was remodeled and restored by Holtsmark Architects, Kaplan/McLaughlin/Diaz.

28. The California Club, 1929–30
Robert D. Farquhar
538 S. Flower Street

The classical tradition via the Beaux-Arts in an eight-story

structure. The architect carried out his instructions "to use the best materials without elaboration and to provide an atmosphere of the finest type of American Club life." The exterior is of warm brown Roman brick with a thin tufa trim. The interior, available only to club members and their guests, has a fine display of the work of the California school of plein air painters.

29. Security Pacific Building, 1973
William L. Pereira Associates
Southwest corner of South Flower and West 6th Streets

The picturesque aspects of Louis Kahn's Richards Medical Towers at the University of Pennsylvania are applied to a seventeen-story office tower, all a bit thin and of a decorative nature.

30. MCI Plaza, 1972–73
Charles Luckman and Associates
Southeast corner of South Flower and West 7th Streets

This square block project contains the Hyatt Regency Hotel with its round revolving restaurant on top, a thirty-two-story office tower, the downtown Macy's Department Store, and the open-atrium Plaza Galleria. The two-story Galleria is pleasant, but the ground floor level of the building creates a grim experience for both pedestrians and passengers in cars.

31. 801 Tower, 1991
Architects Collaborative (John Hayes)
801 S. Flower Street

The high-rise tower sits somewhere between early 1970s

Modern and the Postmodernism of the mid-1980s. The best aspect of this project is the Zanja Madre Plaza to the west of the building. It was designed by Andrew Leicester working closely with the architect. Though somewhat on the hefty side as far as hardscape is concerned, it makes wonderful use of water and metal, tile, and stone abstraction of plant forms.

32. Southern Counties Gas Company Building, 1939–40
Robert V. Derrah
820 S. Flower Street

Forget the ground floor of the building. It has been hopelessly remodeled. But the five floors above indicate how well Derrah (who designed the Coca-Cola Building and the Crossroads of the World) could work with the Streamline Moderne. The slightly recessed center is of glass, and the two concrete side sections curve into the center.

33. Mellon Bank, 1982
Welton Becket Associates (Robert Taylor);
The SWA Group, landscape architects
South side of 4th Street, between South Hope Street and South Grand Avenue

A twenty-six-story tower of six sides, sheathed horizontally in alternating bands of tinted reflective glass and polished brown granite. The tower is set at an angle on its site, and at ground level there is an ample plaza with a double row of sixty-eight Italian cypress trees. The lobby of the tower is composed of a fifty-foot-high greenhouse. The building's most distinguished feature from afar is its thirty-degree slope roof, suggesting that it is either a minimal piece of sculpture or that solar panels are in use.

34. 707 Building, 1973
Charles Luckman and
Associates
Northwest corner of
South Hope Street and
Wilshire Boulevard

A nondescript vertical shaft, sixty-two-stories high; characteristic not only of the work of this firm, but of American high-rise architecture of the late 1960s to early 1970s.

35. Grand Hope Park, 1989–93
Lawrence Halprin
Southeast corner of
South Hope Street and
9th Street

This small 2¹/₂-acre site was set aside for a park in 1975, whose theme of the park was described as "bringing functional art and nature to an urban setting." On this tiny piece of land Halprin has imposed a fifty-three-foot-high yellow and red clock tower (somewhat Postmodernist in design), a pair of fountains, and pergolas, but even with this amount of hardscape, nature will probably win out. The planting is rich, with the introduction of good-sized palms, sycamores, California oaks, Italian cypresses, and ficus trees. The snake fountain was designed by Raul Guerrero; Halprin and Lita Albuquerque designed the other fountain. Added late in the project is an eight-foot-high wrought-iron fence with seven gates; this addition has provoked extensive controversy.

36. Standard Oil Company
Office Building, 1923–24
George W. Kelham
605 W. Olympic Boulevard,
between South Hope Street
and South Grand Avenue

San Francisco architect George W. Kelham utilized a rusticated, late-fifteenth-century, northern Italian "Palazzo" scheme for this urbane eight-story building. The Los Angeles building is similar to the 1921 office building, which he designed for Standard Oil in San Francisco.

37. Wells Fargo Tower,
1982–83
Skidmore, Owings, and Merrill
Southwest corner of
South Grand Avenue and
West 3rd Street

Two 760-foot-high prismatic towers of polished brown granite and tinted glass. In the space between the two towers is a glass-atrium garden court with an exotic garden designed by Lawrence Halprin. In it are pieces of sculpture by Jean Dubuffet, Robert Graham, Juan Miro, and Louise Nevelson.

38. Southern California
Edison, 1930–31
Allison and Allison
(Austin Whittlesey)
Northwest corner of
South Grand Avenue and
West 5th Street

The slope of the two streets made it logical to place the main entrance of this twelve-story Art Deco office building at the corner. Over the entrance are three relief panels by Merrell Gage: *Hydro Electric Energy, Light,* and *Power.* Once in the formal entrance, go on to the elevators, and there you will find a mural, *Apotheosis of Power,* by Hugo Ballin. The tower portion of the building is basically classical and massive, but the deep-cut vertical window/spandrel units create a strong vertical pattern.

39. National Oil Building,
1925
Walker and Eisen
603 S. Grand Avenue

Another example of the wide range of images used within the Beaux-Arts tradition in downtown Los Angeles, in this case a thirteen-story office block imprints a Romanesque image on a classical frame. The building is sheathed in Granitex, a terracotta surfacing that reads as stone. Cast iron was used for the arched openings of the first floor.

40. One Wilshire Building,
1964
Skidmore, Owings, and Merrill
(San Francisco)
East side of
South Grand Avenue at
Wilshire Boulevard

A big bulky box with a stamped-out façade. Renovations have helped its look.

41. The Gas Company Towers,
1988–91
Skidmore, Owings and Merrill
(Los Angeles Office,
Richard Keating)
555 W. 5th Street,
on the northwest corner of
Olive and 5th Streets

A fifty-two-story high-rise with an impressive 300-foot abstract mural by Frank Stella at its base. The towers seem to refer back to SOM's classical Modernist work of the late 1950s/early 1960s (modular and thin-skinned), coupled with the concept of layered slabs associated with Rockefeller Center in New York.

42. Biltmore Hotel, 1922–23
and 1928
Schultze and Weaver
Southwest corner of South
Olive and West 5th Streets

Designed by the New York firm that in the teens and twenties produced many of America's major hotels. Its composition and much of its detailing are faithful Beaux-Arts, called Renaissance at the time. But if you look closely, you will find that much of the brickwork and terra-cotta detailing are sixteenth-century Italian.

Internally, a variety of moods are created, including the Spanish Churrigueresque. The two interior spaces that should attract your attention are the old lobby, with its dramatic staircase, and the interior shopping street, labeled El Camino. Many of the ceilings were painted by Giovanni Smeraldi, who also did the designed plasterwork and sculpture. After Smeraldi's death the work was finished by Anthony B. Heinsbergen. In the mid-1970s the hotel was renovated and handsomely restored (Gene Summers and Phyllis Lambert). The building was remodeled once again in late 1986 by Barnett and Schorr, and the painted ceilings were restored by Anthony T. Heinsbergen, the son of Anthony B. Heinsbergen.

43. Biltmore Place, 1985–87 Landau Partnership
Olive Street, on the south side of the Biltmore Hotel

A twenty-four-story copper-roofed office tower that is, at least on the surface, contextual to the adjoining hotel. The scale of the upper stories and the vertical bays are badly overscaled in relation to the original hotel.

44. Pershing Square (formerly La Plaza Abaja, Public Square, and Central Park), 1991–93 Ricardo Legorreta
Between South Olive, South Hill, West 5th, and West 6th Streets

This five-acre park was part of the original public land of the Pueblo of Los Angeles. It was set aside as a park in 1866. Over the decades it fell into disuse several times, and each time was rescued. The most successful of these revampings was the 1910 scheme of Parkinson and Bergstrom. They introduced a grand-scaled central fountain and four entrances provided with balustrades. They also replanted the park with lush foliage and introduced underground toilets.

Up until the early 1950s the park was best known for its vegetation, which included a wide variety of palm trees. All of this went out when Stiles Clements (1950–51) dug it all up to provide an underground parking garage in the manner of Union Square in San Francisco. The idea of a multilayered parking structure under a park is an attractive one. Seemingly it is the best of both worlds, a park and a place for autos. But the difficulty is always how to get the cars in and out; it always results in reducing the size of the park and then destroying the pedestrian perimeter of the park.

In 1985–86 a competition was held for a new design for the park. This was won by SITE of New York (the jury was chaired by Charles W. Moore). For a variety of reasons, the SITE scheme (titled The Magic Carpet) was put aside in the next few years and a new team was selected. This team consisted of Mexican architect Ricardo Legorreta and landscape architect Laurie Olin.

The theme of their approach was to provide a symbolic bridge between Los Angeles's Hispanic and Anglo communities; in fact the design almost divides the park in half, each section supposedly addressing one of these constituencies. The dominant note in this design is a 120-foot-high purple-colored campanile and what seems like acres of hard-surface pavement, low walls, and other structures, including restaurants. The overall effect is that of a miniature city realized primarily in hardscape. The Olmstedian idea that an urban park should provide a natural oasis within a city is obviously thrown aside in this design. Olmsted wanted us to experience nature so that we could collect and calm ourselves. Legorreta and Olin's design of this park projects the staccato liveliness one associates with Magic Mountain or Knott's Berry Farm.

45. Pacific Mutual Building, 1912, 1922, 1926, 1937, 1974
523 West 6th and South Olive Streets

The original Pacific Mutual Building was a close-to-unbelievable, six-story, glazed, white terra-cotta Corinthian temple (1908; John Parkinson and Edwin Bergstrom). In 1922 a new twelve-story building was constructed next door (designed by Dodd and Richards). In 1926 a three-story parking garage was added, and in 1937 Parkinson and Parkinson remodeled their Corinthian temple into a lukewarm Moderne building. Dodd and Richards's 1922 twelve-story building is a typical example, well done, of a Beaux-Arts office tower. The H-plan building has an arcaded base that embraces three stories, then a seven-story shaft, and finally two floors hidden behind a colonnade and capped by a heavily bracketed overhanging roof. The vaulted ceiling and engaged piers that line the walls of the ground-floor elevator lobby are more impressive. The building was restored in 1974 by Wendell Mounce and Associates using Bond and Steward as design consultants.

46. Oviatt Building, 1927–28
Walker and Eisen
617 S. Olive Street

Though the building's design is essentially Italian Romanesque, it is the Art Deco details of the building that attracted attention when it was built; it was described as "Ultra Modern." Extensive use was made of Lalique glass in the external store front, marquee, interior lobby, and salesroom that, according to publications of the time, were designed and produced in France and were then shipped to Los Angeles accompanied by five French engineers and architects who had "come over especially to supervise the installation of the fixtures." It was also noted at the time that "Mr. Oviatt had built a bungalow on the roof for his use." The two-story bungalow was no bungalow at all, but a sophisticated Art Deco apartment with "Modern" French furniture and decorative arts. The building has been restored and recycled as a restaurant and office building by Brenda Levin Associates.

47. Los Angeles Athletic Club, 1911–12
John Parkinson and Edwin Bergstrom
Northeast corner of South Olive and West 7th Streets

This steel-frame twelve-story building is certainly a model

of Beaux-Arts principles of design. The exterior of the building is pressed brick with terra-cotta trim and a projecting iron cornice.

48. Clifton's Silver Spoon Cafeteria (now Brock and Company Jewelry Store), 1922
Dodd and Richards
515 W. 7th Street

A small four-story building with a theatrical parapet, almost Sullivanesque in feeling. The three upper floors of the building are treated as a picture within a frame.

49. Los Angeles Pacific Telephone Company Building, 1911
Morgan and Walls
716 S. Olive Street

This is one instance where a recent renovation has enhanced an earlier design. The circa 1930 remodeling of this building by Morgan, Walls, and Clements produced a good, but textbook, example of the Art Deco. Timothy Walker and Associates brightened it all up in 1979 so that its façade is more forcefully Art Deco today than it was in 1930.

50. Los Angeles Branch, Federal Reserve Bank of San Francisco, 1930
John and Donald Parkinson
Northwest corner of South Olive Street and West Olympic Boulevard

Based on the belief that a Federal Reserve Bank should look like a cold impersonal fortress, the Parkinsons provided what was asked for. The severe exterior is Moderne Beaux-Arts. Over the entrance is a relief sculpture composed of a spread-wing eagle

placed between two kneeling figures (by Edgar Walter). To the rear of the building is a vault-like door opening to a ramp that winds down to the basement level so that armored cars can safely enter the building.

51. Los Angeles Branch, Federal Reserve Bank of San Francisco, 1985–87
Dworsky Associates
950 S. Grand Avenue

The newer building is situated adjacent to the 1930 structure, so you can compare the 1980s effort to the older building. The Dworsky building is an office building in a park (it is only five and six stories high) and does not seem urban. The design is composed of two parts, a formal granite-clad structure toward the front and a layered glass-wall structure behind. The bowed entrance with its high doorway suggests the monumental and public use. Through the entrance, a four-story atrium lighted by a glass skylight meets the eye. The walls of the lobby are of granite and marble. The present owners intend to convert it to residential lofts.

52. California Plaza and Two California Plaza, 1983
Arthur Erickson Architects; Kamnitzer and Cotton; Gruen Associates
Northeast corner of Grand Avenue and 4th Street

A pair of metal-and-glass-clad buildings, with the southwest corner rounded off in each tower.

53. Museum of Contemporary Art (MOCA), 1983–87
Arata Isozaki; Gruen Associates
Southeast corner of Grand Avenue and Kosciuszko Way

MOCA is unquestionably one of the most beautiful buildings erected in Los Angeles during the past four or five decades. Its wonderful surface of red Indian stone clothes a grouping of forms that is both Modernist and traditional. Nevertheless, the layout of the museum seems a bit strange. The public galleries are approached down a flight of stairs that lead into the south pavilion. From the street, these stairs are hardly apparent. It almost seems as if the architect wished to make the museum embody a religious ritual. Do not overlook the Moorish/Spanish garden on the eastern side of the museum, which seems much in keeping with the building. It was designed by Arthur Erickson Architects.

The north structure contains offices and the museum shop. The galleries are housed in the southern building under an elegant barrel-vaulted roof.

To the north of the museum at 200 S. Grand is the Colborn School of Performing Arts (1998) designed by Hardy, Holzman and Pfeiffer to harmonize with Isozaki's masterpiece. It was a nice try, but the result is bland. It does, however, contain Jascha Heifetz' studio rescued from his house designed by Lloyd Wright in 1946.

For permission to enter the building and studio, call (213) 621-2200.

54. Angelus Plaza, 1981
Daniel Dworsky
and Associates
*Southwest corner of
South Hill and
West 2nd Streets*

A group of three sixteen-story, concrete, medium-rise apartment units for the elderly, with an accompanying parking structure to the east.

55. Subway Terminal
Building, 1924–26
Schultze and Weaver
417 S. Hill Street

According to the architects, this large twelve-story building was based upon a sixteenth-century Italian prototype. From the street the four-bay division of the building makes it appear as four individual buildings. Rusticated masonry is used on the lower two floors, and the upper portion of the building is treated as a two-story Palazzo. Far below the ground level, five subway tracks entered the building, from such faraway destinations as Santa Monica and San Fernando in the valley. The subway tunnel, which was a mile in length, brought trains in from the west. It was in operation from 1925 through 1955. The columned entrance lobby of the building was restored in the early 1980s by Bernard Judge. In 1986 Brenda Levin designed a trompe l'oeil for the side wall of the building; you have to look twice to know that the windows, pilaster, and cornice of her painting are not real. Vacant for most of the past twenty years, it is proposed for residential conversion in 2003.

56. Angels Flight, 1900
*Northwest corner of
Hill and 4th Streets*

This funicular railroad was built in 1900 to carry passengers from Hill Street up to Olive Street, then a fashionable residential district of Bunker Hill. It continued in operation until 1969 when it was purchased by the Community Redevelopment Agency, with a promise that it would be rebuilt in the near future. In 1993, funds were appropriated by the CRA. It was restored but an accident has closed it.

57. Title Guarantee Building, 1929–31
John and Donald Parkinson
*Northwest corner of
South Hill and West 5th Streets*

A twelve-story Art Deco skyscraper, sheathed in light buff terra-cotta with a granite base. A suggestion of the Gothic is conveyed in the upper reaches of the building with its tower and flying buttresses. The building's verticality was accentuated at night by dramatic exterior lighting. In the lobby is a mural, *The Treaty of Cahuenga,* by Hugo Ballin.

58. International Jewelry Center, 1979–81
Skidmore, Owings, and Merrill (Los Angeles)
*Northeast corner of
South Hill and West 6th Streets*

A horizontal, ribbon-windowed, sixteen-story building with a faceted Sienna-granite and reflective-glass façade. The building occupies approximately half of the east side of Pershing Square,

and though its façade is broken up above its lower street level (a serrated design allowance for more natural north light—important for jewelers), it is somewhat overbearing for the scale of the park. If you look to the west side of the square at the Biltmore Hotel and the Pacific Mutual Building (on South Olive Street), you can sense how much more satisfactory their contribution is to the public space of the park.

59. William Fox Building, circa 1929
S. Tilden Norton
608 S. Hill Street

A mild Art Deco office tower converted to jewelry use, with ground-floor jewelry booths and an excellent black-and-gold vestibule and lobby.

60. Bankers Building (now International Center), 1930
Claude Beelman
629 S. Hill Street

The late 1920s Moderne, leaning toward the verticality of the Gothic. Unfortunately, the Moderne marquee has been removed, but the entrance/elevator lobby retains its Moderne elegance. It is now used by jewelers.

61. Warner Brothers Downtown Building and Pantages Theater, 1920
B. Marcus Priteca
*Northwest corner of
South Hill and West 7th Streets*

A Beaux-Arts composition of the late teens, much more French than the typical designs of American architects of the 1920s. Heavy piers accent the corners and divide the two street façades into three vertical window bays.

The corner of the building is rounded, forming an impressive bay surmounted by a Baroque dome. The ground-floor theater area is now jewelry booths; the upper floor is also in jewelry industry use.

62. Garfield Building, 1928–30
Claude Beelman
*408 W. 8th Street,
on the northwest corner of
South Hill Street*

The exterior is bland, but the Art Deco entrance/elevator lobby is a gem with its dark marble walls and detailing in German silver and gold leaf.

63. Mayan Theater, 1926–27
Morgan, Walls, and Clements
1040 S. Hill Street

Seven "Mayan" warrior-priests look down on you as you enter the theater, and going inside you are a participant in a 1920s Hollywood film re-creating a pre-Columbian world. The cast-concrete sculptured façade of the building (by Francisco Comeja) has been brightly painted (originally it was left a light gray concrete color that suggested an aged quality).

64. Belasco Theater, 1926
Morgan, Walls, and Clements
1050 S. Hill Street

Morgan, Walls, and Clements going forward at full steam, with the Spanish Churrigueresque realized in concrete. The ground level of the street façade has been remodeled, so concentrate your gaze above. The ceiling of the theater and the asbestos curtain were painted by Anthony B. Heinsbergen.

65. White Log Coffee Shop, 1932
Kenneth Bemis
1061 S. Hill Street

Here, the best of the past and present are combined: the time-honored American theme of the rustic nonurban world of the log cabin coupled with its white steel frame and concrete logs that signify the hygienic present as well as the Colonial past. By the end of the 1930s Kenneth Bemis had created sixty-two imitation log cabins on the Pacific Coast. The building is now painted brown, and the original roof sign (of steel) in imitation of logs has been replaced by an excellent sign typical of the late 1950s.

66. Bradbury Building, 1893
Sumner Hunt;
finished by George H. Wyman
304 S. Broadway

You would hardly believe that this dull exterior (mildly Romanesque) hides one of the most beautiful interior spaces to be found in Los Angeles. The iron and glass-skylighted court contains open balconies, staircases, and elevators. The lacy quality of the metalwork in the inner court plays off against its glazed brick walls.

The building was restored in 1991 by Brenda Levin Associates. Levin also added a new south entrance to the building that connects the building to Biddy Mason Park (Burton and Spitz) and to the Broadway/Spring Center Parking garage.

66

67. Million Dollar Theater, 1918
Albert C. Martin;
William L. Woollett
307 S. Broadway

A lush Churrigueresque exterior is complemented by an equally sumptuous and rather mysterious Baroque interior (now much simplified) designed by William L. Woollett. Symbolism abounds in Woollett's sculptured and painted decoration. What is needed is a Nancy Drew to figure it all out. The lobby has been altered, but the Baroque auditorium remains pretty much as built. This building, together with the nearby Grand Central Market Building, the Homer Laughlin Building, and the Lyons Building, has been recycled in the early 1990s for housing and office use. This renovation, named Grand Central Square, was carried out in 1994 by private developers (led by Ira Yellin) and the city's Community Development Agency.

68. Roxie Theater, 1932
John M. Cooper
518 S. Broadway

Here the Art Deco eases over into the Streamline Moderne. This was the last major theater to be built in the downtown theater district.

69. Reed Jewelers, circa 1929
533 S. Broadway

Art Deco with an impressive bas-relief on the front. Don't miss Hartfells next door, which is equally committed to the Moderne.

70. Pantages Theater, 1911
Morgan and Walls
534 S. Broadway

An early Beaux-Arts theater building.

71. Broadway Arcade Building, 1922–23
MacDonald and Couchot
542 S. Broadway

The lower three floors of this twelve-story building are whole-heartedly Spanish Renaissance while the upper nine floors are Beaux-Arts. An open skylighted shopping arcade runs through the building from Broadway to Spring Street. The upper floors, vacant for decades, are scheduled for residential conversion in 2003.

72. Clunes Broadway Theater (now Cameo Theater), 1910
Alfred F. Rosenheim
528 S. Broadway

A nickelodeon with its interior fully intact, including the silk canopy under the auditorium ceiling.

73. Story Building and Garage, 1916 and 1934
Morgan, Walls, and Clements
Southwest corner of South Broadway at West 6th Street

The often-repeated Beaux-Arts formula of stacking one horizontal volume on top of another, here successfully realized in white terra-cotta. The upper zone uses arcaded openings, an attic story, and a heavy projecting cornice to terminate the composition effectively. On West 6th Street is a garage whose entrance was designed in 1934 by Stiles Clements. This entrance with its gates represents a high point of the Moderne in Los Angeles. In the late 1980s this building was converted to jewelry industry use, with the ground floor later converted to jewelry booths.

74. Los Angeles Theater, 1931
S. Charles Lee
615 S. Broadway

A Baroque motion-picture palace. Twin Corinthian columns frame the central notched arch. Above, a varied skyscraper is provided with pinnacles and other sculptured forms. The interior grand staircases and rich decoration is as French Second Empire as the street façade. Probably the finest theater building in Los Angeles.

75. Orpheum Theater and Office Building (now Palace Theater), 1911
G. Albert Landsburgh
630 S. Broadway

A French Second Empire theater, reserved on the outside and exuberant on the inside (with sculpture by Domingo Mora). Note the use of multicolored terra-cotta decoration throughout the building. The San Francisco architect G. Albert Landsburgh was the principal designer of theaters' on the West Coast during the decades 1900 through 1930. In 1927 two wall panels were added to the auditorium, painted by Anthony B. Heinsbergen.

76. Tower Theater, 1925–26
S. Charles Lee
Southeast corner of South Broadway and West 8th Street

A Spanish composition with Romanesque and Moorish details. The small but highly effective tower that rises from the corner of the building is quite Goodhuesque. This was one of the earliest theater designs by S. Charles Lee, who was to emerge in the 1930s and 1940s as Los Angeles's principal designer of motion-picture theaters. The present marquee was added after the end of World War II.

77. State Theater, 1921
Weeks and Day
703 S. Broadway

One can assume that the Beaux-Arts-educated Charles P. Weeks of San Francisco was thinking of the Mediterranean when he designed this building.

78. Globe Theater, 1921
Morgan and Walls
744 S. Broadway

A classical Beaux-Arts design. The interior reflects the influence of nineteenth-century Paris.

79. Charles E. Chapman Building, circa 1923
756 S. Broadway

A twelve-story Beaux-Arts office block, large Ionic columns gracing the ground-floor level.

80. Ninth and Broadway Building, 1929
Claude Beelman
850 S. Broadway

A thirteen-story Art Deco (Zigzag) Moderne office block with an emphasis on the vertical. The lobby is especially worth a visit.

81. The Eastern Columbia Building, 1929
Claude Beelman
849 S. Broadway

In this stepped-back design, vertical piers and shafts extend close to the top of the tower, which houses four faces of a neon-lighted clock. The exterior terra-cotta sheathing is in gold and blue-green. The building originally housed two retail stores: Columbia and Eastern Outfitting. An L-shaped arcade, with entrances on South Broadway and West 8th Street, separated the two stores. Above the entrances are pierced grilles forming a sunburst pattern, and these are stippled in gold.

82. Texaco/United Artists Building, 1927
Walker and Eisen; C. Howard Crane
929 S. Broadway

It is surprising that in Los Angeles the 1920s rage for Spanish (and Mediterranean architecture in general) was not employed frequently for commercial building. As this building indicates, it is a shame that the style was not used more often. Terra-cotta and cast stone readily lend themselves to the style, and its richness can be fully expressed. In this building the style is Spanish Gothic. The lobby is modeled after the nave of a Spanish church, richly decorated with vaulting and murals.

83. Women's Athletic Club, 1924
Allison and Allison
1031 S. Broadway

Described when built as an example of Italian Renaissance architecture. The most interesting aspect of the design is the court-

81

yard roof garden, with its plantings, loggia, and stairs.

84. Times-Mirror Building, 1931–35
Gordon B. Kaufmann
Southwest corner of South Spring and West 1st Streets

American newspapers have a fondness for assuming official governmental garb and, whenever possible, locating themselves so as to imply that they and the government are one. The *Los Angeles Times* building fulfills this image very well. The original building is monumental PWA Moderne, and its siting, just across the street from the buildings of the Civic Center, makes it seem as if it belongs. There are some wonderful spaces inside the Kaufmann

building, if you can arrange to get inside. Above all, see the rotunda with Hugo Ballin's mural *Newspaper.* In 1948 Rowland H. Crawford designed a ten-story addition at the northwest corner of South Spring and West 3rd Streets. It too is PWA Moderne, but in this case the classical monumentality has been mellowed quite a bit. Nevertheless the sculpture at the central parapet still helps the building to read with authority. To the west of the older building, William L. Pereira and Associates added a six-story addition (1970–73) consisting of two horizontal boxes hovering over various vertical boxes below. The marriage of the old and new is not a happy one, but then it seldom is in the hands of a "Modern" architect.

85. Hellman Building (now Banco Popular Center), 1903
Alfred F. Rosenheim
Northeast corner of South Spring and West 4th Streets

A Beaux-Arts office building, similar to others erected across the country.

86. Braly Block (later Hibernian Building), 1904
John Parkinson
Southeast corner of South Spring and West 4th Streets

This building has often been cited as Los Angeles's first skyscraper. It is a twelve-story Beaux-Arts office block that has an elaborately decorated attic with a colonnade in the Corinthian order. It has been converted to residential use as part of Gilmore's "Old Bank District."

87. Stowell Hotel, 1913
Frederick Noonan
416 S. Spring Street

A sort of Neo-Gothic treatment of the façade, including extensive cantilevered canopies. The walls, sheathed in glazed green brick, contrast with the light tan cast-stone ornament.

88. Title Insurance and Trust Company, 1928
Walker and Eisen
433 S. Spring Street

Lightly Art Deco. There are mosaic panels above the entrance and murals by Hugo Ballin. The lobby was decorated by Herman Sachs. Note the elevator doors.

89. Security Trust and Savings Bank Building, 1907
John Parkinson and Edwin Bergstrom;
Security National Bank Building, 1916
John Parkinson
Southeast corner of South Spring and West 5th Streets

Two fine contributions to the cityscape. The office building is textbook Beaux-Arts with a pronounced cornice. The two-story bank is quite elegant, with its four pairs of Ionic columns behind which are windows that light the main banking room. From 1982 to 1985 the bank building was converted into the Los Angeles Theater Center by John Sergio Fisher. To the side of the old bank façade, which was left intact, a new deep-set entrance has been created. This leads into Modernist 35-foot-high skylighted space. Off this central lobby are four theaters.

90. Alexandria Hotel, 1906
John Parkinson
Southwest corner of South Spring and West 5th Streets

What counts in this building is the interior palm court with its stained-glass ceiling. The palm court was refurbished in 1967–70 when the Baroque lobby was drastically remodeled in order to look Victorian.

91. Merchants National Bank Building, 1915
William Curlett and Son
Northeast corner of South Spring and West 6th Streets

Another squarish but well-designed Beaux-Arts office block.

92. Pacific Coast Stock Exchange, 1929–30
Samuel E. Lunden; John and Donald Parkinson, consulting architects
618 S. Spring Street

Monumental PWA Moderne (in somber gray granite) as an appropriately solid fortress. Four large-scaled fluted pilasters articulate the street elevation. Under the flat entablature are three panels symbolizing modern industry (by Salvatore Cartaino Scarpitta). Inside is sculpture from the Wilson studio and murals by Julian Ellsworth Garnsey. Next door at 626 S. Spring Street is a handsome six-story Beaux-Arts building with the space between the engaged piers now filled with glass.

93. Banks-Huntly Building, 1929–31
John and Donald Parkinson
632 S. Spring Street

A vertical Art Deco twelve-story building with its upper façade treated as a tower with vertical panels of chevrons.

94. Union Oil Building, circa 1911
John Parkinson and Edwin Bergstrom
Northwest corner of South Spring and West 7th Streets

An eleven-story Beaux-Arts office block in white terra-cotta.

95. I. N. Van Nuys Building, 1910–11
Morgan and Walls
Southwest corner of South Spring and West 7th Streets

Another eleven-story, white terra-cotta exercise in the Beaux-Arts tradition, with engaged Ionic columns at the street level. It was converted in the late 1970s to senior housing. Next door at number 719 is a four-story Beaux-Arts Annex (designed by Morgan, Walls, and Clements, 1929–30) with an office space in the center and a garage door to each side. The north garage entrance retains its original classical metal gates.

96. Hellman Commercial Trust and Savings Bank Building (now Bank of America), 1924
Schultze and Weaver
*Northeast corner of
South Spring and
West 7th Streets*

Four two-story Ionic columns bring dignity to the ground floor of this Beaux-Arts office block.

97. Formerly St. Vibiana's Cathedral, 1871–76
Ezra F. Kysor;
W. J. Mathews
114 E. 2nd Street

This cruciform-plan church was supposedly modeled after the church of San Miguel del Mar in Barcelona. In 1922 John C. Austin added the present "more correct" entrance façade in stone. The rear elevation and the interior are, in spite of heavy remodeling, basically mid-nineteenth-century Italianate. It will be converted to a performing arts center.

98. Van Nuys Hotel (now Barclay Hotel Building), 1896
Morgan and Walls
103 W. 4th Street

A six-story Beaux-Arts composition of repeated bays separated by four-story-high pilasters.

99. Charnock Block, 1888
*Southeast corner of
South Main and
West 5th Streets*

A rare late-nineteenth-century commercial building. As usual, forget the remodeled first floor and look at the second floor of this brick building. Five classical decorated oriel bays and a corner bay tower punctuate the façade.

100. Kerkhoff Building (now Santa Fe Building), 1907, 1911
Morgan and Walls
*Northeast corner of
South Main and
East 6th Streets*

A ten-story Beaux-Arts office block that is now partially artist lofts.

101. Pacific Electric Building, 1903–5
Thornton Fitzhugh
610 S. Main Street

A turn-of-the-century combination of Richardsonian Romanesque and the Beaux-Arts. In this case huge pilasters with exaggerated Ionic capitals separate the major bays, while small arched bays occur within. A pergola garden with wonderful views was placed on top of this ten-story building.

102. Fire Station No. 29, 1910
Hudson and Munsell
225 E. 5th Street

Small mild classicism in concrete. Located along east Fifth Street—skid row.

103. Gray Company Building, 1928
Morgan, Walls, and Clements
824 S. Los Angeles Street

Stiles Clements convincingly demonstrated in this five-story building how well the Spanish Revival vocabulary could be used for a commercial structure. Here he used thin vertical piers that terminated in an entablature of cast-concrete ornament.

104. Gerry Building, 1947
Maurice Fleischman
910 S. Los Angeles Street

A 1930s Streamline Moderne design built in the years immediately after the Second World War. The center of the façade, which is almost entirely of glass, curves inward on each side.

105. Wolfer Printing Company Building, 1929
Edward Cray Taylor and Ellis Wing Taylor
416 Wall Street

A Tudor Revival commercial building.

106. Simone Hotel, 1989
Koning Eizenberg Architecture
520 San Julian Street

This five-story, 123-room hotel was designed to provide inexpensive single rooms. Each room is equipped with a sink, closet, small refrigerator, desk, and bed. Common bathrooms are located on each floor. The rooms, though small, enjoy good-sized windows. Externally, the building looks to some of the turn-of-the-century designs in Vienna of Adolf Loos and Otto Wagner. The trademark of this firm's work is the curved parapet of the building.

107. Commercial Block, circa 1889
740–748 S. San Pedro Street

A two-story brick Queen Anne commercial building with a cast-iron street front.

108. Japanese American Cultural and Community Center
San Pedro Street, between Azusa and East 3rd Streets

This area of Little Tokyo experienced considerable building activity in the late 1970s and 1980s. Note should be made of the theme tower of wood (1978; David Hyun) and Isamu Noguchi's stone sculpture *To Issei* (1983) placed in the Plaza of the Center. Close by is the Japan American Theater (244 S. San Pedro; 1982; Kajima Associates, George Shinno), a gracefully curve-façaded building that looks out onto the plaza. There is also a lovely Japanese garden next to the Center building, accessible by taking the elevator to the basement. (The James Irvine Garden received the National Landscape Award in 1981).

The Japanese American National Museum at the northwest corner of Central Avenue and 1st Street is a remodeling by Knusu Joint Venture Architects (James R. McElwain) of an Egyptian Revival Theater building (1925; Edgar Kline) that had served as a Buddhist Temple. In the 1970s it was turned into a museum with exhibits highlighting the contribution of Japanese Americans to the American culture. In 1999 it was spruced up by Hellmuth Obata Kassebaum (HOK). At the same time, Gyo Obata designed the Resource Center and Galleries across the small plaza in the Corporate Moderne style.

109. Weller Court, 1982
Kajima Associates, George Shinno
123 Weller Street

The ground-level section of this building with its flat and curved volumes, together with the plaza and its fountain and planting, provide a pleasant Modernist pedestrian space (but more planting and less hard surfaces would have helped).

110. The Geffen Contemporary, Los Angeles Museum of Contemporary Art, 1982–83
Frank O. Gehry and Associates
134–152 Central Avenue

An extensive warehouse complex (partially of wood and partially of concrete) that has been remodeled to serve as an extra exhibition space for the Museum of Contemporary Art on Bunker Hill. The interior spaces work well.

111. 1st Street Bridge, 1928
H. P. Cortelyou, engineer
East 1st Street, east of
Santa Fe Avenue

Concrete homage to the classical
tradition of Rome.

112. 4th Street Bridge,
1930–31
Louis L. Hunt, architect;
Merrill Butler, engineer
East of Santa Fe Avenue

Mildly Medieval forms in concrete.

113. 6th Street Bridge
(Whittier Boulevard Bridge),
1932
Louis Blume and
Merrill Butler, engineers
Between Alameda and
Soto Streets

The Art Deco is the dominant
theme in the 3,446-foot-long
6th Street bridge. It was the
largest concrete bridge built in
California before World War II.

Three other bridges to the

south that also cross over the
railroad yards and the river
are the 7th Street Bridge, the
Olympic Boulevard Bridge,
and the Washington Boulevard
Bridge, which boasts a colorful
frieze depicting various bridge-
building activities.

**114. Palmetto Construction
Headquarters, Department of
Water and Power,** 1991–92
**Neil Stanton Palmer Architects
(Walter Scott Perry)**
Palmetto Street, east of
Alameda Street

A high-tech steel-framed and
sheathed object, somewhat reminiscent of the Streamline
Moderne of the 1930s. The bent
curved-metal sheathing is white,
while the glazed window-walls
are Postmodern green.

115. Florence Hotel, 1911, 1986
**Urban Innovations
(Rex Lotery)**
310 E. 5th Street

This is one of a series of renovations of small older hotels that
provide living spaces for the
homeless. Urban Innovations'
work on this 1911 three-story
hotel was essentially to refurbish
the interior, to add bathrooms,
and to bring the building up to
current seismic codes. Urban
Innovation has also revamped
a number of other small hotels,
including the Carleton Hotel
(1924), located at 47 Wall
Street. Their work on the
Carleton Hotel was completed
in 1992.

110

42 • Downtown, Civic Center

As early as 1900 there were discussions of creating a "City Beautiful" Civic Center for the City and County of Los Angeles. In 1905 a Municipal Arts Commission was appointed, and this group in turn engaged the pioneer city planner Charles Mulford Robinson to prepare a plan, which it published in 1909. Robinson's report did suggest the loose grouping of civic buildings but not really a characteristic City Beautiful Civic Center. The task of carrying forward the then highly popular idea of a City Beautiful Civic Center fell into the hands of a newly formed City Planning Association, formed in 1913. The Southern California Chapter of the A.I.A. advocated that a national competition should be held to select an architect/planner to design a civic center for the city.

The first comprehensive proposal for a City Beautiful Civic Center was made early in 1917 by landscape architect and engineer J. S. Rankin, who argued for the present site of the center. Immediately after World War I in 1919, a Civic Center Plan Committee, chaired by engineer William Mulholland (builder of the Los Angeles Aqueduct), was appointed to develop the plan. But while several different schemes were offered in the course of years, real action did not occur until after World War II, when the planning and construction of the Civic Center became closely involved with urban renewal, and the razing of the historic buildings on Bunker Hill took place. Construction also was begun on the depressed Santa Ana Freeway, which divided the Civic Center complex from the old Plaza area. At first it was proposed that this six-block section of the freeway be completely covered by both parkland and buildings, but this was abandoned for the much more economical scheme of simply bridging over the north/south city streets.

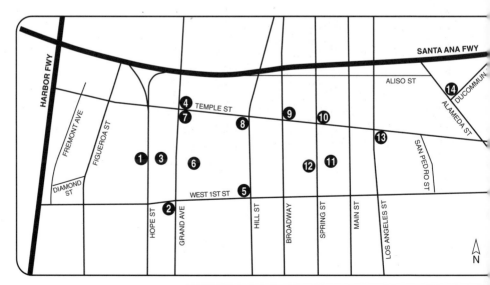

What developed was a modified Beaux-Arts plan proposed as early as 1923. An east/west axis runs from the Water and Power Building at the west end to the City Hall on the east. Lining the axis are the buildings of the Music Center; then, to the north, the Hall of Administration, the Hall of Records, and the Criminal Court Building; to the south, the Courthouse, Law Library, and State Building. The City Hall was to have been the termination of this major axis and to have been the center of a north/south axis. The latter idea never was achieved. Somewhat off-center, the Department of Water and Power building forms a sort-of termination of the major east/west axis. By the end of the 1960s the formal portion of the terraced mall with its underground parking garages was completed (designed by Ralph Cornell and his associates).

The major planning addition to the Civic Center in the 1970s was the Los Angeles Mall Shopping Center between City Hall South and the Los Angeles Children's Museum to the north. This mall (1974–75) combined space for retail stores, plus a park well planted in palms. A bridge over Temple Street connected the two sections of the mall. William Stockwell and landscape architects Cornell, Bridgers and Troller (Howard Troller) designed it.

The grand City Beautiful vision that continued to underlie the development of the Civic Center (see below), even as late as the 1960s, has bit by bit been abandoned in recent years. Public buildings continue to be built, particularly at the east end of the Civic Center from Los Angeles Street to Alameda Street. But they are not in any way sited to contribute to, or become part of, the Civic Center. These buildings and their surrounding spaces pose as commercial buildings casually lining the streets. Frank O. Gehry's new Walt Disney Concert Hall adds a major jewel to the Civic Center, but much more will be needed to make it distinguished.

1. Los Angeles Department of Water and Power Building, 1963–64
Albert C. Martin and Associates
South Hope, between Temple and West 1st Streets

Best seen at night from the Harbor Freeway to the north with all of its lights on. After dark the solidity of the building melts, and all that is left are thin vertical and horizontal lines of support, the floors, and the sunscreen. Note the forest of fountains around its base; they may be on or off depending on the availability of water.

2. Walt Disney Concert Hall, 1988–2003
Frank O. Gehry and Associates
Southwest corner of Grand Avenue and 1st Street

The four finalists announced in 1988 to be considered for designing the Disney Concert Hall were Gottfried Bohm of Germany, Hans Hollein of Austria, James Stirling of England, and Frank O. Gehry. Gehry's submission was selected and was seen as a symbolic garden placed in front of a series of oddly placed, layered boxes. Numerous changes were made in this initial design, and in truth it has become more adventuresome as it has gone along, especially the exterior of the building. It should not be surprising that Gehry's design provoked praise, criticism, and bewilderment. Some writers to the *Los Angeles Times* called it "space trash,"others thought it indicated that the "whole world has gone mad."

3. Los Angeles Performing Arts Center, 1964–69
Welton Becket and Associates; Cornell, Bridges and Troller, landscape architects
North of West 1st Street, between South Hope and South Grand Streets

The building located within a seven-acre park faces onto an east/west plaza with a central pool dominated by a 1969 Jacques Lipschitz sculpture. A new addition to the plaza at the head of the east stairs (from Grand Avenue) is Robert Graham's sculpture, *Dance Door.* To the south is the largest of the three buildings, the Dorothy Chandler Pavilion; to the north, enclosed by a freestanding colonnade, is the circular Mark Taper Forum (see above) and the Ahmanson Center (Theater).

Under all of this is the essential multilayered parking garage. Aesthetically, the most forceful of these buildings is the circular Mark Taper Forum. It rises from a pool of water, and the walls are composed of an abstract 378-foot-long, cast-concrete, low-relief panel. These three buildings and their siting characterize the accommodations then being made between Modernism and the continuing Beaux Arts–Classical tradition. The whole composition is light, fragile, but elegant. However, it should be noted that, like most 1960s Modern designs, it is not growing better with age. Functionally, it appears to be working very well.

4. The Cathedral of Our Lady of the Angels, 2002
José Rafael Moneo;
Robert Graham,
sculptured doors;
John Nava, tapestries;
Lita Albuquerque, fountain;
Max De Moss, tabernacle;
Campbell and Campbell,
landscape architects
Northeast corner of
Temple Street and
Grand Avenue

As noted in the introduction to this guide, the exterior of this building is quite forbidding from the freeway, but once inside, you are in one of the most beautiful spaces in Los Angeles (I almost said "the world."–R.W.). As the famous architectural photographer, Julius Shulman, has said, there are also great individual moments everywhere that you move in the space. It is true that the chandeliers interfere

with your experience. The tapestries, although beautifully designed and crafted, are really not necessary. These and other loving details seem added on. But the space, flooded with mysterious light from windows made from thin sheets of alabaster, inspires the souls even of non-believers. Praise God.

5. Los Angeles County Courthouse, 1958
J. E. Stanton;
Paul R. Williams;
Adrian Wilson;
Austin, Field and Fry
Northwest corner of
Hill and 1st Streets

In 1944 a competition was announced for the new courts building. A consortium of architects was finally selected to provide the design. The result was a late-1950s Modern design making at least a half-hearted effort to be classical and public. The building does go public with some sculpture. Note the higher portion of the building to the north that exhibits a clock face, and the east façade that is windowless and divided into squares and has an overlay of relief sculpture.

6. Paseo de los Pobladores, 1961
J. E. Stanton;
W. F. Stockwell;
Adrian Wilson;
Austin, Field, and Fry
East of Grand Avenue, between
the County Courthouse and the
Hall of Administration

A series of terraces, pools, and steps lead up the hill from Broadway to Grand Avenue.

Though formal, but with Modernist tricks, the design is somewhat heavy in the realm of hardscape.

7. Hall of Administration, 1956–61
Stanton; Stockwell; Williams and Wilson;
Austin, Field and Fry
Southeast corner of
Grand Avenue and
Temple Street

The best section of this eight-story building is the west façade that somewhat carries on the PWA Moderne of the 1930s. The best we can say about the design of this building is that it is reticent.

8. Hall of Records, 1961–62
Richard J. Neutra and Robert Alexander;
Honnold and Rex;
Herman Charles Light and James Friend
320 West Temple Street

A rare, realized Neutra high-rise. Functionally it seems to fulfill its task, but its design seems confused, and it ends up neither a distinguished example of Modernism nor making any strong contribution to the Civic Center. Note the large eighty-foot glass mosaic mural *Water Sources in Los Angeles County* by Joseph Young (1962).

9. Hall of Justice, 1925
Allied Architects of Los Angeles
Northeast corner of
South Broadway and
West Temple Street

This fourteen-story building in the Italian style indicates what the Allied Architects had in

mind for the buildings of the Civic Center—pure Beaux-Arts classicism of the early 1920s. There are plans to restore and recycle it.

10. Federal Building and Post Office (now U.S. Federal Courthouse), 1938–40
Louis A. Simon;
Gilbert Stanley Underwood
*Northeast corner of
South Spring and
West Temple Streets*

PWA Moderne of the late 1930s, beautifully and convincingly carried out. When the *Architectural Record* in 1940 asked a number of Los Angeles citizens to pick their favorite buildings, the then-new Federal Building was one of them. Though seventeen stories high on South Spring Street, the building manages to remain snugly within the classical tradition, albeit in an abstracted manner. Within, luxury and formalism are evident, ranging from rose marble and Sienna travertine to James L. Hauser's

larger-than-life-size sculpture *The Young Lincoln,* to Archibald Garner's eight-foot-high sculpture in stone, *Law.*

11. Los Angeles City Hall, 1926–28
John C. Austin, John and Donald Parkinson, and Albert C. Martin;
Austin Whittlesey, interiors
*Block bounded by
Spring, Temple, Main, and
1st Streets*

The approach that the architects took was Goodhuesque, combining the traditional classical temple as a base with the symbol of a skyscraper, commenting on the prowess of American business. In its presentation of the design, the consortium of architects noted that "the first story of the City Hall would be of monumental character," and that the skyscraper tower "was necessary to cut the skyline." The tower, with its sloping walls, turned out to be monumental as well, and the top

of the tower seems to be a 1920s interpretation of what the ancient Mausoleum at Halicarnassus should have looked like. Following in the footsteps of Goodhue, Hartley Burr Alexander of the University of Nebraska furnished the inscriptions for the building. ("The city came into being to preserve life; it exists for the good life."

In the interior public spaces, especially in the central rotunda, the mood is Byzantine, with the floor, wall, and ceiling decoration by Austin Whittlesey, who worked closely with Herman Sachs and Anthony Heinsbergen. It was fitting that when the building was dedicated in April of 1928, the three-day affair was under the direction of Sid Grauman, the moving-picture-palace tycoon.

Until the 1950s the twenty-eight-story tower was the only structure allowed to exceed the 150-foot height limitation. Now it is only one among many.

From 1989 to 2001 the City Hall, both inside and out, has been restored, including much of its decoration, artwork, and furnishings.

12. Los Angeles Mall, 1973–74
Stanton and Stockwell;
Cornell, Bridgers, Troller and
Hazlett, landscape architects
East side of
South Spring Street,
between West 1st and
Aliso Streets

This civic addition consists of a six-level mall, a four-level underground garage, and two buildings: City Hall East and a small Children's Museum. The skyway, which connects the mall to the original City Hall, is as dull as the other buildings. The two objects that make a noble, but vain, attempt to lift all of this out of the mundane is Millard Sheet's wonderful mural at the Spring Street entrance to City Hall East (1973–74; Stanton and Stockwell) and Joseph Young's Triforium (1975), a sixty-foot fountain of light and music. The landscaping is well carried out, but now thirty years after it was finished, it is all beginning to look a bit tired. Even the fountains run only intermittently.

13. Parker Center, 1955
Welton Becket and Associates
(J. E. Stanton)
Southeast corner of
Temple Street and
Los Angeles Street

As with most Corporate Modern buildings of the 1950s and 1960s, this building has not aged well. When built, it was a good example of where Modernism was taking us.

11

14. Los Angeles Department of Water and Power Central District Headquarters, Phase II, 1988–92
Barton Phelps and Associates;
Clements and Clements/
Benito A. Sinclair
and Associates
444 E. Ducommun Street,
on the corner of
Alameda and
East Ducommun Streets

A handsome addition to the group of public buildings erected at the east end of the Civic Center. Groups of four rectangular volumes arise from a horizontal base. Phelps described his design approach as "mantel over a base." The upper section of the building is sheathed in white and light green metal panels while the lower section is of concrete.

Other recent buildings in the area are the Federal Building at the northeast corner of Temple and Los Angeles Streets, as well as the Federal Center and the Metropolitan Detention Center, both behind (to the east) of the Federal Center. (Go into the courtyard behind the Federal Building to see the curved pergola and its sculpture, designed by Tom Otterness, 1992–93). At the northwest corner of Temple Street and Alameda Street is the V.A. Outpatient Clinic, a well-scaled cornerpiece for this end of the Civic Center.

43 • Downtown, Plaza and Northeast

The section around the Old Plaza and east toward the present course of the Los Angeles River was the center of Los Angeles from 1781 through the mid-nineteenth century. The first public plaza, which lay to the northeast near Sunset Boulevard, was gradually filled in by early settlers. The present plaza, which was essentially the church/government plaza, has continued to remain open and public, though some of the buildings to the north have extended into the public space (especially after it was "improved" in the 1840s). In 1862 the plaza was replanned and replanted, this time with topiary work.

By the 1870s the business center of Los Angeles had moved south, and the Plaza area remained a low-density backwash. In the early 1900s, the area was somewhat rejuvenated by a renewed interest in things Hispanic, and during the 1920s Olvera Street and several of its adjoining buildings were restored. The plaza area has just missed extinction on two occasions: in the early 1920s it was proposed that the area be incorporated into the projected civic center, and in 1949–50 the plaza was almost devoured by the construction of the Santa Ana Freeway. Since the 1950s, and especially since it was made a state park, the plaza area has increasingly become a tourist spot amid restored historic buildings.

Chinatown originally developed in the 1870s where the Union Passenger Terminal now stands. New Chinatown lies in and around North Broadway and Alpine Street, and was built after 1933 when clearing was begun for the terminal.

1. Fort Moore Pioneer Memorial, 1949–57
Kazumi Adachi and Dike Nagano;
Albert Stewart, art advisor;
Department of Water and Power
North side of Hill Street, between the Santa Ana Freeway and Sunset Boulevard

A Los Angeles extravaganza dedicated to the importation of water, which made modern Los Angeles possible. This block-long concrete memorial contains (when it is running) a 77-foot-long, 50-foot-high sheet of water. When it was built, it was noted that it was "probably the most spectacular man-made waterfall in the United States," and it probably still is. The inscription on the glazed ceramic wall reads, "May those who live in our naturally arid land be thankful for the vision and good works of the pioneer leaders of Los Angeles, and may all in their time ever provide for its citizens water and power for life and energy."

2. The Church of Our Lady, Queen of the Angels,
1818–22, 1861–62, 1875, 1912, 1923
535 N. Main Street

The simple, gable-roofed adobe church was rebuilt and received a new façade in 1861. A bell tower was added in 1875. In 1912 the church was once more restored and enlarged, making it more "Mission" Spanish than it had been before. In 1923 a tile roof replaced the late-nineteenth-century shingle roof. As originally built, the façade of the church had a single arched entrance placed within a molded rectangle. Above was a single window that lighted the choir and nave. Above a horizontal molding that followed the parapet molding of the sides of the building was a single *espadaña* (belfry wall). To the south of the façade was a *campanario* (bell tower), which had a single opening (not a double opening as we now see it). The church was at first flat-roofed.

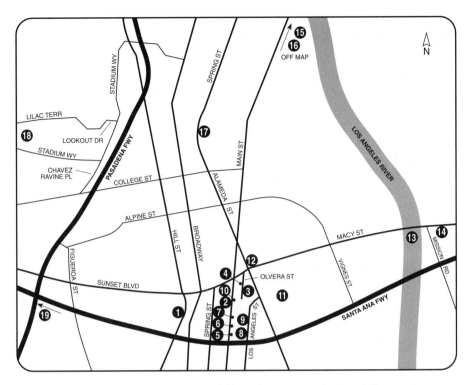

Thus, what we see today is a parish church that essentially dates from 1861 onward—especially onward.

3. Avila Adobe, circa 1818
10 Olvera Street

This once was the oldest original dwelling standing in Los Angeles. As with most late-eighteenth/early-nineteenth-century adobes it is not clear what it originally looked like. By the 1830s the dwelling consisted of a traditional double row of rooms, one set facing a porch looking out on the street; to the rear was a second porch facing toward the court. The house is now covered with a tile roof, but it is unlikely this was part of the original building. The adobe was damaged in an earthquake in 1971, and it has now been rebuilt in concrete.

4. La Casa Pelanconi, 1855
33–35 Olvera Street

This two-story house was the first brick dwelling in Los Angeles. A winery occupied the ground floor; the living quarters were above. Note the wood balcony and the main fireplace on the ground level. Although not strong in character, the house is basically very late Greek Revival in style.

5. Masonic Temple, 1858
Attributed to Ezra F. Kysor
416 N. Main Street

A cast-iron balcony hovers over the triple-arched street opening below. The Italianate style shows up in the widely projecting cornice.

6. Merced Theater, 1870
Attributed to Ezra F. Kysor
420–422 N. Main Street

A three-story masonry building, Italianate in style. The second and third floors boast arched openings inset between simple pilasters. A cast-iron balcony projects off the third floor. The ground level was planned as a retail store, the second floor as a 400-seat theater, and the third floor as an apartment.

7. Pico House, 1869–70
Ezra F. Kysor
430 N. Main Street

This Italianate hotel was the first three-story masonry building constructed in Los Angeles. The openings are all arched and set between vertical pilasters and projecting horizontal cornices. The street elevations of the building were stuccoed over and then painted to imitate light blue granite. The building has been completely rebuilt and has awaited use for a number of years.

8. Garnier Block, 1890
415 N. Los Angeles Street

What we now see of this restored building is only half of the original block. The south half went in 1950 when the Santa Ana Freeway was built. The building is a two-story brick-and-stone structure, mildly Romanesque in style.

9. Old Plaza Firehouse, 1884
*Southwest corner of
Old Plaza and
North Los Angeles Street*

A two-story brick building with an Eastlake balcony over the high entrance.

10. Sepulveda House, 1887
624 N. Main Street

This two-story redbrick building was constructed as a hotel and a restaurant. The upper bay-window balconies suggest the Eastlake style.

11. Union Passenger Terminal, 1934–39
**John and Donald B. Parkinson;
J. H. Christie, H. L. Gilman,
R. J. Wirth;
Herman Sachs,
color consultant;
Tommy Tomson,
landscape architect**
*East side of
North Alameda Street, between
Aliso and Macy Streets*

The last of the large metropolitan passenger depots to be built in the United States. The terminal provided for sixteen tracks and for extensive parking (120 cars underground and 400 in front of the building). Landscaped grounds and courtyards convey

an indoor-outdoor sense of space seldom encountered in large-scale public buildings. The design successfully merged the Streamline Moderne and the Spanish. The 135-foot-high observation and clock tower, the principal interior spaces, and the patios manage to convey both modernity and tradition.

12. Terminal Annex Post Office, 1937–38
*Northeast corner of
Macy and Alameda Streets*

A late version of the Spanish Revival, realized in exposed concrete. Note the two drums and domes that dominate the building.

13. Macy Street Viaduct, 1926
*Macy Street, between
Keller Street and Mission Road*

The most northern of the series of bridges that were built to cross over railroad tracks and the Los Angeles River. The reinforced-concrete Macy Street Viaduct is Spanish Renaissance with Ionic and Doric columns.

14. Macy Street Residence,
circa 1890
1030 Macy Street

A brick Queen Anne dwelling.

15. Carlson-Reges House,
1996
**Ro To Architects
(Michael Rotondi)**
*698 Moulton Avenue, north of
Main Street*

An old warehouse has been given
new life by adding great sails and
panels in metal. Some people
might call this "deconstruction,"
others might see it as "construction with a vengeance," but it
seems to fit right in to this part
of town that is pretty funky. In
fact its neighbor "The Brewery,"
technically located at 642
Moulton, is actually a congeries
of warehouses and factories and
seemingly gerry-built dwellings
stretched out over several acres
near the I-15 freeway. Here
artists have created their homes
and workplaces in a manner that
suggests complete freedom of
expression, with bougainvillaea
climbing over wrecked cars and
unfinished buildings and with a
horde of cats enjoying the urban
ambience. The residents are
awfully nice and seem to want
you to enjoy their utterly mad
surroundings.

16. Fuller Paint Company
Warehouse, 1924–25
Morgan, Walls, and Clements
290 San Fernando Road

Creative exercises in the Spanish
Revival by Morgan, Walls,
and Clements for a five-story
reinforced-concrete warehouse
building. The façade is a classical
tripartite division, the base is
decorated with low relief cast
in stone (with a wonderful three-
unit entry), above is a row of piers

15

for three floors, and then there is
an attic with perforated openings.

17. Capital Mill, 1884
1231 N. Spring Street

The Capital Mill was the oldest
flour mill in the city, until closed
in the 1990s. The utilitarian
building is of brick. Sections of it
are as high as four stories. The
1884 building incorporates parts
of an even earlier brick building,
constructed circa 1855. Now
vacant, a remodeling for retail
space and artists' lofts is planned.

18. U.S. Naval and Marine
Corps Armory, 1939–40
Stiles Clements
*North side of Stadium Way,
southeast of Lilac Terrace*

Late PWA Moderne terra-cotta-

sheathed design with engaged
fluted piers and panels of relief
sculpture. The Armory is a little-
known late-1930s Los Angeles
monument. Do not miss the
wonderful eagles.

19. Bank Americard Building
**(Bank of America Computer
Center),** 1979
Skidmore, Owings, and Merrill
*Beaudry Avenue, between
West Temple and
Mignonette Streets*

An eleven-story box, easily
visible from the freeway interchange. It seems purposely to
be a nonbuilding that con-
tributes nothing to one's
experience, either from the
freeway or close up.

44 • Downtown, South

1. Los Angeles Herald-Examiner Building, 1912
Julia Morgan
1111 S. Broadway

The Mission-revival image of the Los Angeles Herald-Examiner Building with its central square drum and dome certainly looks back to A. Page Brown's California Building at the 1893 World Columbian Exposition in Chicago. The Mission theme had been used in a number of Julia Morgan's early works, and she was to use it again in her Las Milpitas (1932–36), the ranch house adjacent to the Mission San Antonio for William Randolph Hearst. One gathers from the pages of the *Los Angeles Herald-Examiner* that the urge to use the Mission style was one shared by both architect and client. Morgan is quoted as commenting on the design of the building in the December 22, 1914, issue of the *Herald-Examiner:* "There has been so much wasted architectural opportunity in this South Land, when public and commercial buildings might well be a part with their environment, and where the rich colors and contrasts and rich shadows could be allowed to play such an invaluable part in the design."

At the time it was built, the local Los Angeles press (including the *Herald-Examiner*) did not refer to the design as Mission, but as an example of the Spanish Renaissance style. The *Herald-Examiner* Building is certainly one of California's distinguished Hispanic-inspired buildings, with its colorful domes, tile roofs, white walls, and base with a row of arched openings. The richly decorated lobby with its staircases is really a domestic baronial hall, not what one would ever expect as an entrance to a commercial newspaper plant. This luxurious, almost Baroque space is one that we can be quite certain no Mission father would recognize as being like anything else in Alta California. Morgan made some alterations in the building in 1921, and more alterations and an annex were built from her 1930–31 designs. As you look at the building today, the one appreciable external change has been the removal of the windows between the ground-level arches and the closing in of these spaces. It was through the windows of this arcade that one could see the great printing presses at work. The building is now vacant, but there are plans to restore and recycle it.

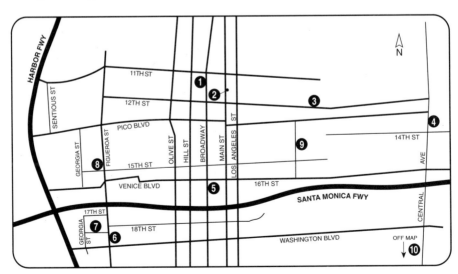

2. Morgenstern Warehouse,
1978
Moss and Stafford
1140–1146 S. Main Street

This is an instance where even
strong exuberant architecture is
having a difficult time maintain-
ing itself against use, in this case
the need for signage. The low
stucco boxes with their cylinder
ends adjacent to the street are
now on the tawdry side. Still it is
a delightful, if somewhat self-
indulgent, design.

3. Cohn-Goldwater Building,
1909
525 E. 12th Street

This was supposedly the first
Modern "Class A" steel-
reinforced concrete building
erected in the city.

4. Coca-Cola Bottling Company, 1936–37
Robert V. Derrah
1334 S. Central Avenue

The Streamline Moderne as ocean liner is one of the most frequently illustrated buildings in the Los Angeles area. This reinforced concrete structure is equipped with a ship's bridge, metal railings of a nautical feeling, porthole windows, ship doors, and suggestions of metal rivets. "What, therefore, could more aptly express the bottling method of the Coca-Cola Company than a ship motif . . ." The interiors were originally as nautical as the exterior of the stucco and concrete flagship. The suggestion of a ship is still present internally, but not the way it used to be. The two-story ship is, in fact, a remodeling and addition to several older structures that were on the site.

Across the street is Fire Station #30 (right), once abandoned but now refurbished by Edward H. Fickett as a museum and monument to Los Angeles's firefighters.

5. Illing of California, 1946–47
Paul Laszlo
1600 S. Broadway

Most of Laszlo's work was domestic. Here you can see how the master of the Moderne created a classic statement.

6. Patriotic Hall, 1926
Allied Architects
1816 S. Figueroa Street

The impressive Beaux-Arts façade works equally well from the street or from the Harbor or Santa Monica Freeways. The west street elevation of the ten-story concrete building is Italian Renaissance. The sides and back are nondescript.

7. Forthmann House, circa 1887
Burgess J. Reeve
629 W. 18th Street

This elegant Victorian house boasts Eastlake details with Italianate brackets, plus a mansard-roofed tower.

8. Los Angeles Convention Center,
1972, 1980, 1993
Charles Luckman Associates;
Pei Cobb Freed & Partners
(James Ingo Freed);
Gruen Associates
(Ki Suh Park)
1201 S. Figueroa Street

A classic and example of a Los Angeles building geared to the auto and the freeway. The original formal building sits on a podium with its parking structure situated across Sentous Street to the west. The new addition more than doubles the size of the original building. Like other buildings by the Pei firm, it turns its back on the old and proceeds to reflect the latest in fashion—in this instance, glass roofs and exposed structure. Though Freed is quoted as saying he wished to create a major architectural statement for downtown Los Angeles, the result, like his Holocaust Museum in Washington, D.C., is reasonable but hardly brilliant. Strangely, even though the structure is large, it does not establish any presence when seen from the freeways.

Next door is the Staples Center (2000; NBBJ Architects, Ron Turner) in the same Corporate Moderne image as its neighbor but with even less exuberance.

9. Central Distribution Center, Department of Water and Power, 1988–89
Ellerbe Becket
(Mehrdad Yazdani);
Fong and Associates,
landscape architects
Maple Avenue, between
Pico Boulevard and 15th Street

A group of rectangular volumes are attached to, or project above, a twelve-foot-high concrete-block security wall. This may not sound like an impressive composition of buildings, but it is. The dominant focus of the design is the projecting semicircular bay with the building's entrance to the side and a glass-sheathed volumetric box on top (the box houses an assembly room).

10. Second Baptist Church (First A.M.E. Church), 1924
Paul R. Williams;
Norman F. Marsh
2412 Griffith Avenue,
on the corner of
24th Street and
Griffith Avenue

This church was the young architect's first major public commission (he also designed several public schools at this time), and it was also one of his few commissions for the African American community. In design the building reflects the then very popular northern Italian Romanesque. Entrances occur to each side of the principal gabled façade, and a high Lombardian tower is situated to the right. The building is of ruffled-face brick along with cast-stone trim.

45 • Boyle Heights

By the late 1880s Boyle Heights, which lies just east of the Los Angeles River, was connected with downtown Los Angeles by two street railroads that crossed the river on the East First Street and the East Aliso Street Bridges. Boyle Heights itself is centered around Hollenbeck Park (acquired in 1892) and its lake, while Brooklyn Heights to the north has a similar center in and around the oval form of Prospect Park. By the time of the First World War, the area had declined as a home for artisans and the middle class. In the 1950s four freeways cut huge swaths through the area; the worst and most unbelievably thoughtless was the Golden State Freeway, placed adjacent to the once-quiet Hollenbeck Park. The past twenty years present a mixed picture of decay, restoration, well-kept yards and gardens, high, protective chain-link fences, and formidable watchdogs.

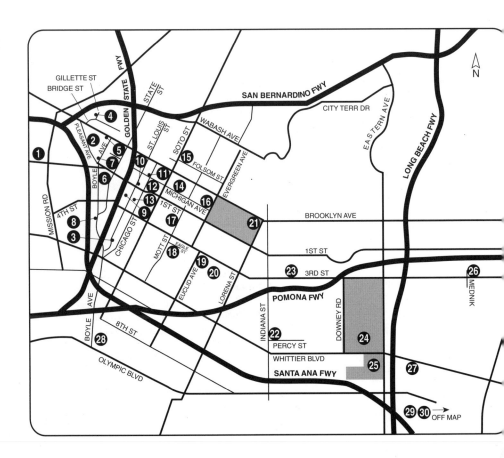

East Los Angeles in the late 1960s and through much of the 1970s was famous for its ever-changing street murals. A number of these can be seen on Whittier Boulevard from Soto Street east to Atlantic Boulevard. Others are situated on First Street between Lorena and Indiana Streets, on Brooklyn Avenue at Gage Avenue. Some of these murals are by professional artists, others are by self-taught painters and children.

1. Public Housing Projects, 1941–42

Several of these housing projects were started as low-cost developments of the later Great Depression years, and then with the approach of the Second World War they became War Housing Projects.

a. Aliso Village, 1941–53
George G. Adams, Walter S. Davis, Ralph C. Flewelling; Eugene Weston Jr., Lewis E. Weston, Lloyd Wright; Katherine Bashford and Fred Barlow Jr., landscape architects
Northwest corner of 1st and Mission Streets

This housing project consists of thirty-three two-story, masonry/stucco/wood-framed, flat-roofed boxes. It was planned to house 2,975 persons on the 34.3-acre site. As is true of many public projects in Los Angeles, the site plan and the landscape design emerged as being far more imaginative than the architecture.

b. Rosehill Courts Public Housing, 1942
W. F. Ruck and Claude Beelman
Rose Hill Drive and Amethyst Street (go northeast on Huntington Drive to Esmeralda)

A small World War II housing project of one hundred living units contained in fifteen two-story frame and stucco-sheathed buildings. Existing eucalyptus trees were retained.

c. William Mead Homes, 1941–42
T. A. Elisen; A. R. Walker, Norman R. Marsh, David D. Smith, Herbert J. Powell, and Armand Monaco
1300 N. Cardinal Street (take North Main Street to Elmyra Street, east on Elmyra Street to Cardinal Street)

These 449 living units were built on a site of 15.2 acres. Corner windows, horizontal balconies, and other details slightly suggest the late 1930s Moderne.

d. Pico Gardens Public Housing, 1941–42
John C. Austin, Sumner Spaulding, Earl Heitschmidt, and Henry C. Newton
500 S. Pecan Street (south on Pecan Street, off East 1st Street)

This project contains 250 living units in thirty-seven two-story buildings.

2. Mount Pleasant Bakery Building, circa 1885
1418 Pleasant Avenue

This small, false-fronted wooden building is supposedly the oldest bakery building still standing in Los Angeles. It is essentially Queen Anne in style with some older elements of the Italianate. It has been stuccoed, but it is still there! Don't miss the bandstand and mariachi vendors at the intersection of Pleasant and Boyle Avenues.

3. House, circa 1900
706 S. Chicago Street

What appears to be a late–Queen Anne two-story dwelling moves on to suggest either the Richardsonian Romanesque or, more likely, the Mission Revival. Note the two rows of cobblestone arches.

4. House, circa 1905
603 Gillette Street

A boxy, hip-roofed, turn-of-the-century Colonial Revival dwelling is yanked from the normal by the injection of a pointed Gothic window in the center of the street façade. And this feature is "balanced" on one side by an oversized round window.

5. Cottage, circa 1885
914 E. Michigan Avenue

A rare (for Los Angeles) surviving example of a Second Empire mansard-roofed cottage. It exhibits a traditional street elevation that includes a small porch placed between two bay windows.

6. Cottage, circa 1889
327 S. State Street

A story-and-a-half Queen Anne cottage with original chimney still present (which in Los Angeles is rare because of frequent earthquakes). Sunburst patterns occur in the gable ends, and jigsaw work is present on the entrance porch.

7. House (now a neighborhood center), circa 1895
358 S. Boyle Avenue

A two-story Queen Anne/Colonial Revival dwelling with both first- and second-floor porches sporting an abundance of turned woodwork.

8. Hollenbeck Home for the Aged, 1896, 1908, 1923
Morgan and Walls;
Morgan, Walls, and Clements
573 S. Boyle Avenue

Pure Mission Revival, though many design elements, proportions, and details came directly from the Richardsonian Romanesque style of the 1880s. One can see this in the entrance arcade, in the corbeling below the extended eaves, and in the engaged columns employed around openings.

9. Cottage, circa 1885
2018 E. 2nd Street

Compared to cities of the East and Midwest, there were few Eastlake houses and cottages built in and around Los Angeles. And of these, very few remain. This one displays a wide array of wood surfaces and sawed work that we associate with this style. The exterior surfaces include forty-

five-degree shiplap, tongue-and-groove horizontal boards, and a small bit of fish-scale shingles.

10. Grace Methodist Episcopal Church, 1906
John C. Austin
200 N. Saint Louis Avenue

A shingled Craftsman Gothic church building with leaded-glass windows. A picturesque composition with two miniature towers over the side entrance.

11. First Hebrew Christian Church, 1905
Northeast corner of North Chicago Street and East Michigan Avenue

Here you will find a New Yorker's idea of architecture in Los Angeles: a stucco Austrian Secessionist/Islamic façade (with a corner dome) placed in front of a plain clapboard box. The

culmination of the design is a large roof sign in the form of an open Near Eastern scroll.

12. Hollenbeck Presbyterian Church, 1884
East side of North Chicago Street, south of Michigan Avenue

A wood Craftsman church building with both Gothic and Romanesque details. The design displays an assortment of different window shapes, including pointed Gothic windows. We are not certain whether we are to respond to the entrance porch as Richardsonian Romanesque or Mission. The tower is almost worthy of the Episcopalian Ernest Coxhead. It is one of the oldest church buildings remaining near central Los Angeles, and it is still imposing, even behind its chain-link fence.

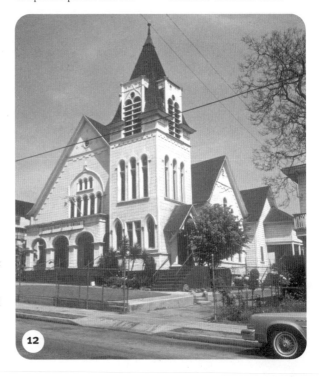
12

Incidentally, it is the place where Occidental College was founded in 1887.

13. House, circa 1887
2123 E. 2nd Street

Shingled arches are supported by turned wood columns on the entrance porch of this Queen Anne cottage. Across the street at number 2126 is another larger cottage (circa 1890) that represents more of the typical Los Angeles builder's spec cottage (Queen Anne in style).

14. Los Angeles Jewish Community Center, 1937
Raphael S. Soriano
2317 E. Michigan Avenue

Pre–World War II International Style. A stucco-sheathed rectangular box with a strong emphasis placed on horizontality via bands of windows, the usual thin roof fascia, and then the horizontal bands of the stucco itself.

15. Apartment Building,
circa 1925
East side of
North Soto Street, north of
East Folsom Street

A common man's do-it-yourself version of Austrian Secessionism just emerging into the 1920s Art Deco Moderne.

16. Cottage, circa 1890
2533 E. Michigan Avenue

A many-gabled Queen Anne cottage. It could be right out of any number of late-nineteenth-century architectural pattern books.

17. House, circa 1895
South side of
East 2nd Street, west of
Mott Street

A two-story Queen Anne/ Colonial Revival dwelling. A round corner bay tower is covered with a conical domed roof.

18. House, circa 1895
2700 East Eagle Street

Another Queen Anne dwelling with the traditional corner bay tower.

19. House, circa 1890
2922 Euclid Avenue

A two-story Queen Anne dwelling with emphatic projecting boxed windows.

20. Cottage, circa 1887
3407 E. 4th Street

A picturesque tower roof projects above the bay and porch of this Eastlake/Queen Anne cottage.

21. Evergreen Cemetery, 1877
Southwest corner of
Brooklyn Avenue and
Lorena Street

Evergreen Cemetery is one of the oldest cemeteries in the city of Los Angeles, and it contains some interesting nineteenth-century tombs and sculpture. Architecturally, the important object within the cemetery is Ivy Chapel, designed by Arthur B. Benton in 1903. The chapel is a medieval stone structure with a handsome front composed of four pointed windows along with a long narrow porch.

22. Bungalow, circa 1910
3672 E. Percy Street

The porch of this modest bungalow establishes it as something almost regal. Four flat arches with stuccoed brackets are supported by thick primitive columns. Above the eave a curved pediment marks the principal entrance.

23. Our Lady of Lourdes Roman Catholic Church, 1930
L. R. Scherer
3773 E. 3rd Street

An imaginative and forceful mixture of Art Deco Moderne and the Spanish Revival of the 1920s (plus hints of the Mission Revival and the Gothic). All of this imagery has been realized in a reinforced-concrete church building.

24.

24. New Calvary Cemetery, 1923
4201 E. Whittier Boulevard

Ross Montgomery's design for the main Mausoleum (1927–29) is a concrete building in the same league as the Los Angeles Public Library and the Los Angeles City Hall. It is a major but little-known monument. The architect has beautifully succeeded in creating a picturesque and memorable building by combing the past and choosing references to Babylon, to the Hindu architecture of India, to the Mausoleum at Halicarnassus, to Italian and Spanish architecture, and to

the then-developing Art Deco Moderne of the late 1920s. Inside the mausoleum are paintings of California scenes and a great deal of art glass fabricated by the Judson Studios. The entrance gates off Whittier Boulevard were designed in 1923 by Albert C. Martin.

25. Home of Peace Cemetery, 1931
4334 Whittier Boulevard

The chapel is somewhat Byzantine in feeling, enriched by what appear to be a pair of Islamic minarets. The major monument of the place is the

1931 Hamburger Mausoleum, which is a fine example of the monumental Art Deco.

26. David Wark Griffith Junior High School, 1978
Fernando Juarez
4765 E. 3rd Street, at Mednik Avenue

The architect has been able to suggest the atmosphere of a northern Mexico adobe church through a wonderful grouping of the arched bays that project from the entrance front of the building.

27. Boulevard Theater, circa 1937
Balch and Stanberry
4549 E. Whittier Boulevard

A Moderne motion-picture theater, more angular than streamlined. The nine letters of "Boulevard" project separately off the horizontally lighted tower.

28. Wyvern Wood Housing Project, 1938–39
David J. Wetmore and Loyal Watson
Between East 8th Street and East Olympic Boulevard, south of South Soto Street and South Grande Vista Avenue

The first low-cost public-housing project to be built in Los Angeles (built with private, not public, funds). The seventy-acre site was designed with curved streets and open courts. It includes retail stores that face Olympic Boulevard and Soto Street and a school and playground that adjoin Grande Vista Avenue. The loosely Monterey Style buildings are two-story stucco, some with projecting balconies.

**29. Samson Tyre and
Rubber Company Building
(The Citadel),** 1929–30
Morgan, Walls, and Clements
*5675 Telegraph Road
City of Commerce
(take the Santa Ana Freeway
to the South Washington
Boulevard exit, then northeast
on Telegraph Road)*

An architectural wonder of
Los Angeles, and a startling
experience as you travel up or
down the Santa Ana Freeway.
This industrial office and manufacturing plant was built as a
walled Assyrian city, right out
of a 1920s Hollywood movie set.
After carefully consulting the
published archaeological reports,
architects modeled the building
after the famous ziggurats and
fortified walls of the ancient city
of Khorsabad, to which they
added features from other ancient
Assyrian and Babylonian cities.
Priest-kings and other creatures
adorning the walls added prestige

to the production of automobile
tires. The name Samson is associated with Babylon—improved
upon here in Los Angeles.

The factory closed in 1978,
and the buildings remained
vacant for a decade. In 1990–91
the site was transformed into a
shopping center (The Citadel
Outlet Center). The metal factory
buildings were removed, and the
stage set of the 1,700-foot
Assyrian wall was left. New buildings were grouped around a central allée that runs through the
wall. The glory of the place is the
new landscape, especially the new
forest of palm trees. The master
plan for the site was developed
by landscape architect Martha
Schwartz of San Francisco
(Schwartz/Smith/Meyer). The
specific design of the project was
by Sussman/Prejza Inc., and by
Peridian Irving.

**30. Lever Brothers Office and
Soap Company,** 1951
Welton Becket and Associates
*6300 Sheila Street
City of Commerce
(take the Santa Ana Freeway to
East Washington Boulevard
exit, then to Sheila Street)*

A period piece of the 1950s
Modern, very well done. The
most assertive element of the
design is the glass penthouse
placed on top of the principal
building.

46 • Exposition Park, West Leimert Park

Before and after the turn of the century, the northeast part of this section of Los Angeles was a prestigious residential area. This was especially true of the district around Chester Place and St. James Park. The great residential street of the 1900s was West Adams Boulevard, extending from South Figueroa Street to South Arlington Avenue. Though individual enclaves of upper-middle-class exclusiveness were laid out in the 1920s, much of the eastern section in and around Adams Boulevard began to decay.

South of Adams Boulevard a number of subdivisions were laid out in the 1920s. One of the most successful of these was Leimert Park, planned in 1927 by Olmsted and Olmsted. Their centerpiece for the community was Leimert Plaza (at the junction of Leimert Parkway, Crenshaw Boulevard, and Vernon Avenue). They connected the plaza with a narrow park strip extending up Leimert Parkway to the northeast, and to the south on Crenshaw Boulevard as far as 60th Street. The hilly area southwest of the plaza exhibits the usual winding streets that one associates with upper-middle-class enclaves.

It has in part become commercialized or has been turned into various types of multiple housing. The extensive flat plain south of Exposition Boulevard developed in the usual strip commercial fashion along major thoroughfares (South Western and South Vermont Avenues, South Figueroa Street), with an infill primarily made of modest artisan bungalows and some small-scale multiple housing.

Though Exposition Park and adjacent USC to the north provided open space, those two enterprises really had very little to do with residential neighbors nearby. The 1960s redevelopment has torn down a number of blocks of houses and stores west of USC and replaced them with new commercial buildings (oriented around the auto), and now multiple housing. The streets north of USC once had many examples of late-nineteenth- and early-twentieth-century residential architecture, ranging from Queen Anne through Mission Revival and adaptations of English Medieval, but now there are few examples left.

A number of the late-nineteenth-century Victorian houses around USC have been renovated and a handful of others have been moved—even as far away as Pasadena. Probably the greatest loss has occurred and is occurring along West Adams Boulevard. One of Los Angeles's great formal Italian gardens with a hillside water staircase used to surround the Beaux-Arts classical Murphy House (circa 1906; Hudson and Munsell) at 2079 W. Adams (landscaped, revised, and enlarged in 1931 by A. E. Hanson and Lutah Maria Riggs), but only a few of the larger trees now remain. More recently, the Anglo-Colonial Revival Childs House at 3100 W. Adams Boulevard was demolished.

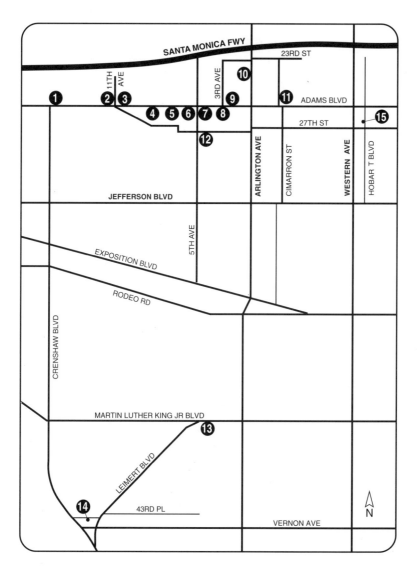

1. Church of the Advent, 1925
Arthur B. Benton
4976 W. Adams Boulevard

This was one of Benton's last major commissions (he died in 1927). It follows the form of the rural English Gothic churches that he had so often used (with wonderful results) from the 1890s on throughout Southern

California. He designed several important houses on West Adams Boulevard, but these are all now demolished.

2. McCarty Memorial Christian Church, 1931
4101 W. Adams Boulevard, on the northwest corner of West Adams Boulevard and 1st Avenue

An excellent example of one of Los Angeles's reinforced-concrete churches of the late 1920s. The style in this instance is Gothic, partially English and partially French.

3. Apartment Building,
circa 1955
4025 W. Adams Boulevard

A post–World War II Los Angeles stucco box that emerges as something exotic because of its Japanesque roof details.

4. Louise Denkin House, 1912
B. Cooper Corbett
3820 W. Adams Boulevard

By 1910 there were over half a dozen Beaux-Arts villas on West Adams. This one, somewhat eighteenth-century French, is one of the few still remaining.

5. Mary L. Briggs House, 1912
Hudson and Munsell
3734 W. Adams Boulevard

The firm of Hudson and Munsell produced a number of houses on West Adams Boulevard. Few are left. Their architectural vocabulary went the rounds from Beaux-Arts classicism to Tudor/Craftsman dwellings such as this. Somewhat more in the Craftsman vogue is the nearby MacGowan House (1912) at 3726 Adams Boulevard.

6. Gusti Villa (Busby Berkeley Estate), 1910
Hudson and Munsell
3500 W. Adams Boulevard

One of the few examples of this firm's work in the Beaux-Arts classical imagery. This one has the atmosphere of a late-eighteenth-century French country house.

7. Lindsay House, 1908
Charles F. Whittlesey
3424 W. Adams Boulevard

This massive stone house comes close in spirit to Secessionist work from Vienna, though its arches and other elements help it to read as Mission as well. Two balls balance on projecting pinnacles at

each side of the west front dormer. A heavy arcaded balcony projects over the entrance porch. The house, which is of hollow terra-cotta tile, was built by the Western Art Tile Works of Los Angeles.

Whittlesey was one of Los Angeles's gifted architects at the turn of the century. He, along with Irving J. Gill, was one of many Southern California architects who were fascinated with the possibilities of reinforced concrete for small as well as large buildings. Most of Whittlesey's work has been demolished or defaced.

8. Walker House (now Seventh-Day Adventist Building), 1905–6
Charles F. Whittlesey
3300 W. Adams Boulevard

Whittlesey's designs were always original, and the Walker House is no exception. Half-timbering suggests the Medieval, but basically the stucco volumes and tile roofs are Mission Revival. Generous terraces face toward the street and the rear (south), overlooking the hillside and garden.

9. Fitzgerald House, 1903
Joseph Cather Newsom
3115 W. Adams Boulevard

Whatever Newsom touched, he transformed. This design is as inventively outrageous as any of his earlier Queen Anne or Eastlake designs. If you wonder what style it is, the architect labeled it Italian Gothic. While it is Medieval in spirit, none of the details are handled traditionally. The tour de force is the elaborate entrance and large clinker-brick chimney with an arched window punctured through it. Fortunately, the house has been restored.

10. House, circa 1902
2301 W. 24th Street

"Tahitian Tudor"—a little bit of the Medieval coupled with the Colonial Revival and even a little Queen Anne.

11. William Andrews Clark Memorial Library (UCLA), 1924–26
Robert Farquhar;
Ralph D. Cornell,
landscape architect
2520 S. Cimarron Street

According to the literature, this building was "designed in the style of the Italian Renaissance." A more obvious source was Wren's addition to Hampton Court Palace, though for some reason Farquhar omitted the oranges from Wren's symbolic decoration and substituted yellow brick for his lovely pink. At the time the library was built, landscape architect Ralph Cornell introduced the more formal garden that we now see. The villa (library) was undoubtedly more successful when the walled and hedged formal gardens that surround the building were well planted and maintained. The interior is "correct" and elegant. The rooms are decorated with a number of murals painted by Allyn Cox.

In addition to the library building, the only remains of the former estate is the service building at the northwest corner of the property. In 1989–90 architect Barton Phelps and Associates was commissioned to design buildings at the north side of the property. This narrow band of a building, named North Range, was designed to house a variety of needs ranging from offices to conference rooms. Phelps's approach was to keep it all

10

low-key modern, but in sympathy with the main building. His design consists of a series of brick-sheathed boxes attached by a single brick wall. A metal pergola stands in front, and eventually will provide a screen in front of the structure.

Arrangements to visit can be made by calling the library at (213-731-8529).

12. Lukens House, 1940
Raphael S. Soriano
3425 W. 27th Street

The single-floor dwelling is arranged around an enclosed patio in a design much less insistently International Style than most of Soriano's pre–World War II plans.

13. Touriel Medical Building, 1950
Raphael S. Soriano
2608–2610 W. Martin Luther King Jr. Boulevard

A steel-frame post-and-beam building with a small entrance courtyard that carries the Arts and Architecture Case Study House aesthetic into the commercial realm (it all seems interchangeable).

14. Leimert Theater (now Jehovah's Witness Hall), 1931–32
Morgan, Walls, and Clements
3300 - 43rd Place

Except for the ornamental open-work oil derrick tower and signage, this Art Deco theater

building is a direct result of the Paris Exposition of 1925. The interior ceiling of the oval-shaped auditorium still retains its Moderne patterns. Also, note the murals in the lobby. The theater, which faces onto Leimert Park, was a major element in this Los Angeles suburban development.

15. Fire Engine House No. 18, 1904
John Parkinson
2616 S. Hobart Boulevard

A small, delightful, twin-towered Mission Revival building.

47 • Exposition Park, East

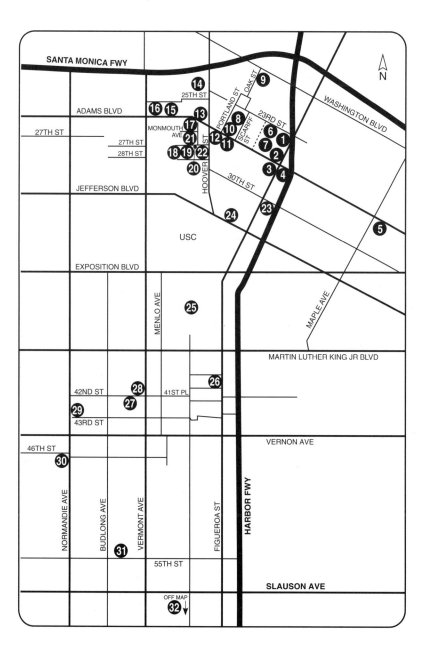

1. Stimson House, 1891
Carroll H. Brown
2421 S. Figueroa Street

The Richardsonian Romanesque in stone never enjoyed as great a popularity in California for residences as it did throughout the United States. The Stimson House was one of the largest and most elaborate examples built in Los Angeles. In plan, with its great living hall, it is really Queen Anne. Externally the four-story octagonal tower with crenelated battlements is picturesque.

2

foot-diameter dome. The interior ceiling decoration is by John B. Smeraldi.

3. Automobile Club of Southern California, 1921–23
Hunt and Burns;
Roland E. Coate;
Aurele Vermeulen, landscape architect
2601 S. Figueroa Street

The corner of this building, with its octagonal tower surmounted by a domed cupola, and the Baroque entrance screen are forceful elements of the Spanish Revival. Equally impressive is the interior, especially the public entrance and lobby space.

4. St. John's Episcopal Church, 1922–23
Pierpont and Walter S. Davis
514 W. Adams Boulevard

The design for this church was the result of a competition juried by Ernest Coxhead of San Francisco, William Templeton Johnson of San Diego, and the Rev. George A. Davidson of Los Angeles. The historic source for the design was northern Italian Romanesque. The interior ceiling was modeled after the Church of San Miniato in Florence. The bas-reliefs around the rose window were designed by S. Cartaino Scarpitta. The surfaces of this reinforced-concrete church reveal the horizontal board pattern of the forms.

2. St. Vincent de Paul Roman Catholic Church, 1923–25
Albert C. Martin
Northwest corner of South Figueroa Street and West Adams Boulevard

Certainly one of the principal landmarks of Los Angeles and of the Spanish Revival in California. The Spanish Churrigueresque of Mexico was used as a design source for this church, certainly inspired by Bertram G. Goodhue's California Building at the 1915 San Diego Exposition. A richly decorated screen made of Indiana limestone dominates the entrance, and brightly colored tile covers the forty-five-

5. House, circa 1900
426–428 E. Adams Boulevard

Medieval imagery of a sort, with a remarkable composition of connected dormers.

6. Severance House, 1904
Joseph Cather Newsom
650 W. 23rd Street

Joseph Cather Newsom designed a number of Mission Revival buildings during his second period of active practice in Los Angeles. Of these, the story-and-a-half Severance House was one of the most frequently illustrated. While for a Newsom design it looks reasonably calm from the street, it is anything but sedate behind and inside.

7. Chester Place
Between West 23rd Street and West Adams Boulevard, west of South Figueroa Street

Chester Place was a private enclave of twenty acres that originally contained thirteen large dwellings. It was laid out as a residential park in 1895. The various houses in the park were built just before and after 1900. Of the houses that still remain, the two most interesting are the Doheny House at number 8 and the Wilson House across the street at number 7. The Wilson House was designed by Dennis and Farwell in 1916 and is Mission/Islamic in style. Its cast ornament was certainly inspired by the work of Louis H. Sullivan. The Doheny (originally Posey) House was built in 1898–1900 and was designed by Theodore A. Eisen and Sumner P. Hunt. Externally, the house is Chateauesque. Internally, its most famous space is the Pompeiian Room, designed by Alfred F. Rosenheim and built in 1906. Other additions and alterations (including the main entrance) were also made by Alfred F. Rosenheim in 1913. Much of the interior was remodeled in the French rococo style in 1933–34.

8. Apartment House,
circa 1905
2342 Scarff Street

An authoritative Beaux-Arts frontispiece set in front of a conventional apartment house.

9. Odd Fellows Temple, 1924
Morgan, Walls, and Clements
1828–1834 Oak Street

A reinforced concrete building with cast-concrete ornament, in this instance more Spanish Renaissance than Churrigueresque.

10. House, circa 1875–79
2624 Portland Street

One of the modest Italianate dwellings that formerly lined many Los Angeles streets from the late 1860s through the early 1880s.

**11. Casa de Rosas
(Froebel Institute),** 1894
Sumner P. Hunt
950 W. Adams Boulevard

Charles F. Lummis labeled this as
Mission and so it must be. It was
stuccoed and had an arcade supported by short Tuscan columns.
And above all it had a patio.
Historically it was important as
one of the very early instances of
the self-conscious cultivation of
the myth of the Mission in a new
building.

**12. Second Church of Christ,
Scientist,** 1905–10
Alfred F. Rosenheim
948 W. Adams Boulevard

This Beaux-Arts classical design
was inspired by the Mother
Church in Boston. The concrete
dome is sheathed in copper.
An authoritative bank of six
Corinthian columns faces
Adams Boulevard.

13. House, 1892
1140 W. Adams Boulevard

A two-story Queen Anne
dwelling.

14. Rindge House, 1900
Frederick L. Roehrig
2263 S. Harvard Boulevard

An imposing Chateauesque
dwelling with fat corner towers
between which is a Richardsonian
Romanesque porch.

15. Kerckhoff House, 1900
1325 W. Adams Boulevard

A shingled Queen Anne/Colonial
Revival dwelling.

16. Cottage, circa 1889
1308 W. 25th Street

This small wood cottage was
moved in 1981 and handsomely
restored. In style it exhibits both
Eastlake and Queen Anne features.

17. Adlai E. Stevenson House,
1895
2639 S. Monmouth Avenue

A late, simplified Queen Anne
dwelling, characteristic of many
built in the Exposition Park area.

18. Kiefer House, 1895
**Sumner P. Hunt and
Theodore A. Eisen**
1204 W. 27th Street

Queen Anne in concept, but with
a turn-of-the-century nod to the
Anglo-Colonial Revival.

19. House, 1904–5
John C. Austin
1194 W. 27th Street

A Craftsman dwelling given
Tudor roots and respectability.

20. House, circa 1890
1160 W. 27th Street

A Queen Anne dwelling. Of special interest are the long horizontal windows in the gable ends.

21. House, 1890
Bradbeer and Ferris
1163 W. 27th Street

A Queen Anne with a touch of
the Colonial Revival. Its com-
manding feature is the third-floor
tower set on the thin posts of the
second-floor porch.

22. House, 1891
Bradbeer and Ferris
2703 S. Hoover Street

Queen Anne with an extensive,
curved, wraparound veranda, plus
the obligatory palm trees.

23. Bungalow Court,
circa 1920
627 W. 30th Street

A late-Craftsman bungalow court.
A group of clapboard bungalows
faces onto a long, narrow, open
court.

**24. Shrine Auditorium
(Al Malaikah Temple),**
1920–26
**John C. Austin, A. M. Edelman,
G. Albert Lansburgh**
665 W. Jefferson Boulevard

Islamic imagery from somewhere
(Hollywood stage sets, perhaps?)
was employed externally and
internally. The pair of domed
cupolas and balcony loggia are
the strongest features of the
design. The auditorium seats
6,400. A large ballroom pavilion
adjoins at the north.

25. Exposition Park
*Between Menlo Avenue,
South Figueroa Street,
Exposition and Martin Luther
King Jr. Boulevards*

This site was established in 1872
as a privately operated fair-
grounds and racetrack. The
Southern District Agricultural
Society that owned the park went
bankrupt in 1880. In 1898 the
land was purchased jointly by the
state, county, and city. The fanati-
cally Beaux-Arts Los Angeles
County Historical and Art
Museum, now a small part of the
County Museum of Natural
History, was designed in 1910 by
Hudson and Munsell and opened
in 1913. It was thought of as
being an example of Spanish
Renaissance architecture. In 1911
landscape architect Wilbur D.
Cook Jr. laid out the grounds of
the park.

The Memorial Coliseum was
designed in 1921–23 by John and
Donald B. Parkinson. This was the
central sports facility for the 1932
Olympic Games in Los Angeles.
One of the high points of the park
is the seven acres of sunken Rose
Gardens that run parallel to
Exposition Boulevard and to the
east of the Natural History

28. Manual Arts High School, 1934–35
John and Donald B. Parkinson
*Northwest corner of
South Vermont Avenue and
West 42nd Street*

A two-story, exposed-concrete, Streamline Moderne building. Don't miss the relief sculpture over the entrance to the auditorium, and of course the dramatically rounded corners of this building.

29. St. Cecilia's Roman Catholic Church, 1927
Ross Montgomery
*Northeast corner of
South Normandie Avenue and
West 43rd Street*

An impressive version of the Italian Romanesque. A low, highly effective tower dominates the crossing. Sections of the exposed-concrete walls were originally tinted in reds, yellows, and tans.

30. Pilgrim Congregational Church, circa 1905
*West side of
South Normandie Avenue, at
West 46th Street*

A shingled Craftsman church with some Gothic detailing.

31. Two Bungalows, circa 1910
1102 and 1156 W. 55th Street

Two characteristic Los Angeles Craftsman bungalows. Nearby on West 54th Street, east of South Normandie Avenue, are other spec Craftsman bungalows.

32. Mount Carmel High School, 1934
7011 S. Hoover Street

Here, in a mid-1930s building, one can sense how the Spanish Revival tradition was being continually and creatively modified.

Museum. A late addition to the buildings in Exposition Park is the California Aerospace Museum (1982–84; Frank O. Gehry and Associates; see above). This complex design, resplendent with references to technology, flight, and high art, contains spaces that enhance and dramatize the objects on exhibition. Two other buildings are the Museum of Afro-American History (1983–84; Jack Haywood and Vincent J. Proby) and the Multicultural Center (1983–84; Barton Myers). For the 1984 Olympic Games, sculptor Robert Graham designed the Olympic Gateway composed of two bronze piers supporting two figures, one male and the other female, both headless and nude. The most current addition for the park is a new California Museum of Science and Industry building (1993) located south of the Rose Garden and for which the Zimmer Gunsul Frasca Partnership has provided a play between space frame elements and thin enclosed volumes.

26. Van de Kamp Building, circa 1930
*Northwest corner of
South Figueroa Street and
41st Place*

A windmill tower, sadly lacking its blades, brings attention to this corner. The suggestion of shingles with their V-shaped forms hints at the Art Deco.

27. Apartment Buildings, circa 1915
*1016–1018, 1020–1022,
1040–1042 W. 42nd Street*

A group of typical Los Angeles Craftsman apartment houses.

48 • University of Southern California (USC)

The University of Southern California was established in 1880 on an eighteen-acre site located adjacent to Exposition Park. In 1910 the architectural firm of Train and Williams prepared a general plan for the campus, followed in 1920 by a strong axial plan prepared by John Parkinson, who projected the major axis—University Avenue—as being lined with three- and four-story, northern Italian Romanesque buildings. The avenue itself was to be bridged at various points by Venice-like footbridges. During the 1920s a number of these buildings were constructed along University Avenue.

At the end of the 1930s, the strict adherence to the vocabulary of the northern Italian Romanesque was modified and modernized in the Hancock Foundation Building and in the Harris Hall/Fisher Gallery. After World War II, Marsh, Smith, and Powell prepared a revised master plan in 1949–50, but this was never really carried out. In 1961 William L. Pereira and Associates was engaged to provide still another master plan with additional changes in 1966. One result of this last plan was the gradual closing off of all the streets that cut through the campus, replacing them with pedestrian walkways. Another element was to intensify the density of the campus by introducing high-rise buildings.

From the early 1950s to the present, the tendency has been to fill the campus's older green spaces with new buildings, and also to slowly expand the campus into the residential area to the north. The newer high-rise buildings—some of which are up to fourteen stories high, do not fit in very well with the older buildings, and there is not much open green space left (although some of the more recent landscaping has been handsomely carried out). USC's architectural image since 1945 has been self-consciously Modern, and, as is true in the case of most of America's academic architecture after World War II, the structures built during these years are, as a group, hardly distinguished. During this time the University has engaged an impressive array of national and regional name-brand architects and architectural firms, including I. M. Pei, Albert C. Martin and Associates, Stanton and Stockwell, Robert E. Alexander, and others. But on the whole, the overall results have been disappointing.

We wish that the situation had improved since we last wrote about the campus, but such has not been the case. The fourteen-story Webb Tower and the adjacent eleven-story Flour Tower are as mindless as the earlier high-rise designs. Competent but disappointing are such buildings as the Pertusati Bookstore (1987; Grillias Pirc Rosier) and the Law Center Addition (1987; Albert C. Martin Associates). Several smaller projects have turned out to be quite successful. These include the Helen Topping Architecture and Fine Arts Library Addition (1989) by Ellerbe Becket (Graeme Morland), where the task was to introduce natural light into a basement structure; and The Forthman House, which is an 1880s house that was moved to the campus from the site of the Los Angeles Convention Center. The renovation of the house took place in 1988 by De Bretteville and Polyzoides. It is possible, as has been the case at the UCLA campus, that a distinguished landscape architectural program might rescue it all, but this will be a formidable task to carry out.

Obtain a map at the entrance kiosk:

1. Widney Hall (Alumni House), 1880 Attributed to Ezra F. Kysor and Octavius Morgan

This two-story wood structure reads as an early example of the Anglo-Colonial Revival, though it was in fact an Italianate dwelling when it was originally built. It was moved to its present site in 1958 and transformed into a Colonial Revival dwelling by Lawrence Test, who added green shutters and a widow's walk on the roof.

2. George Finley Bovard Administration Building, 1920–21 John and Donald Parkinson

The first of this architect's brick northern Italian Romanesque designs to be built on the campus. It is interesting to note that the reactions to the building's architectural images varied. In the 1920s it was described as a fine example of the Spanish Renaissance, while others labeled it Lombardian. The building's large square tower, which was built as a bell tower with eight heroic sculptured figures at each corner by Casper Gruenfeld, who also did the sculpture on the south front, was meant to dominate the new center of the campus. If you compare USC's version of the northern Italian Romanesque with that of UCLA's, it is apparent that

Parkinson and others produced a group of buildings that were more inventive, playful, and lively. Even the most distinguished of the northern Italian Romanesque designs at UCLA, Royce Hall, cannot be compared in quality of design and detailing to the Wilson Student Union Building, the Doheny Library, or the Mudd Hall of Philosophy at USC.

By the southeast corner of Bovard Administration building is the sculpture *Tommy Trojan.* This eight-foot-high warrior is supposed to look war-like; instead it is delightful camp. It was designed by Roger Noble Burnham and was dedicated in 1930.

3. Elizabeth Von KleinSmid Hall (now Student Administrative Services Building), 1925 William Lee Woollett

A low brick complex that meanders over its site, similar in feeling to an English medieval collegiate building.

4. Law School Building (now School of Social Work), 1926 John and Donald Parkinson

Northern Italian Romanesque, with some excellent cast-stone detailing around the windows and the main entrance.

5. Gwynn Wilson Student Union Building, 1927–28 John and Donald Parkinson

This version of the northern Italian Romanesque exhibits a

first floor treated as an enclosed loggia and two upper floors that are rich in cast-stone ornament. The southeast and southwest corners of the building are particularly successful in their imaginative use of cast-stone ornament and low- and high-relief sculpture.

6. Physical Education Building, 1928 John and Donald Parkinson

The centerpiece of this northern Italian Romanesque design is the west entrance, with its single large arch and extensive use of cast-stone detailing.

7. Bridge Hall, 1928 John and Donald Parkinson

A four-story interpretation of the nave of a northern Italian Romanesque church.

8. Science Building, 1928 John and Donald Parkinson

A deep entrance passageway from the east leads through a pair of wrought-iron gates to a ceramic tile panel by Jean Goodman (1937), depicting four figures captivated by the world of science.

9. Colonel Seeley Wintersmith Mudd Memorial Hall of Philosophy, 1928–29 Ralph C. Flewelling

The high campanile of this complex was the dominant vertical element of the campus until it was supplanted in 1966 by the Carillon Tower of the Von KleinSmid Center. Though the Parkinson buildings are very good

9

examples of the northern Italian Romanesque, they do not come up to the quality of the Lombardy Romanesque entailed in this design. Its high point is the cloister at the south side of the building.

10. Methodist Episcopal University Church (now United University Church), 1931
C. Raimond Johnson

Another important, but often neglected, monument of the campus. One enters this northern Italian Romanesque church through a partial cloister situated on the southeast side of the build-

ing. The building's picturesque skyline is enlivened by a pair of buttress towers surmounted by twisted cast-stone roofs.

11. Edward L. Doheny Jr. Memorial Library, 1932
Cram and Ferguson (Ralph Adams Cram); Samuel Lunden

The Doheny Library is certainly the most luxuriant of the northern Italian Romanesque buildings on the USC campus. Cram modeled its design closely on the buildings that he and Bertram G. Goodhue had designed in 1910

for Rice University in Houston. The centerpiece of the building is the two-story-plus square entrance hall with stained-glass windows. Other interior spaces are impressive, especially the reading rooms. The Library Building to the east and Bovard Hall to the west create the central open space of the campus with its fountain and planting of sycamores.

North of the Doheny Library is the Thomas and Dorothy Leavey Library, completed in the late fall of 1993.

12. Harris Hall of Architecture and Fine Arts (including the Fisher Art Gallery), 1939
Ralph C. Flewelling

The architect sought to modernize both the vocabulary of the Italian Romanesque and that of the Beaux-Arts, and he succeeded admirably. The brick and cast-stone walls and the scale of the building closely match his earlier Mudd Hall of Philosophy to the east. And the rambling character of the building is admirably played against the more formal classical elements, such as the two splendid entrances on the south side of the building.

13. Alan Hancock Foundation and Memorial Museum, 1940
Cram and Ferguson; C. Raimond Johnson; Samuel E. Lunden

Although its scale is compatible with the older 1920s northern Italian Romanesque buildings around it, the four-story Hancock Building is in reality a version of the classical PWA Moderne. An abstracted portico is presented at the center of the west façade. The sculpture (by Merrell Gage) used around the building consists of figures that float out in front of the wall surface. Do not miss the delightful group of animals and other forms (dominated by an elephant) cast into the exposed-concrete wall of the auditorium on the north side of the building. Also see Alan Hitchcock's yacht sculptured above the south entrance door.

The Museum houses rooms and furnishings from the no-longer-standing Hancock House of 1907 that stood on the corner of Wilshire Boulevard and Vermont Avenue. In addition, there are four rooms and their furnishings rescued from Emperor Maximilian's Palace in Mexico City (which was demolished in 1936).

14. Faculty Center, 1960 Jones and Emmons

A modest nonassertive design by one of Los Angeles's important early Modernist firms.

15. Ahmanson Center for Biological Research, 1964 William L. Pereira and Associates

The dominant note of these connected, box-like, five- and six-story buildings is a surface pattern of cast-concrete hooded windows—the same on the north as well as on the south.

16. Registration Building, 1964 Ladd and Kelsey

A delicate pavilion set on a low podium that employs the Miesian post-and-beam system.

17. Von KleinSmid Center of International and Public Affairs, 1966 Edward D. Stone Associates

The block of the campus that contains the Von KleinSmid

Center to the north, the Social Science Building in the center, and the Phillips Hall of Education (all by Edward D. Stone Associates) is the finest of the post–World War II group of buildings on the USC campus. The U-shaped Von KleinSmid Center is composed of three low, rectangular volumes placed on a podium and surmounted by a projecting roof. A four-sided, concave-surfaced Carillon Tower is situated to one side of the courtyard. The brickwork and the general exterior detailing enhance the polished feeling of the design.

18. Social Science Building, 1968 Edward D. Stone Associates

The square Social Science Building has been carefully sited and designed to be related to the Von KleinSmid Center to the south and the tower of the Phillips Hall of Education to the north. The façade of the Social Science Building is arcaded, and the building looks out to the west upon a sunken courtyard with a central fountain.

19. Waite Phillips Hall of Education, 1968 Edward D. Stone Associates

The architect has articulated the four façades of his tower into thin, vertical brick piers with narrow intervening spandrels and windows. The building rises from a freestanding arcaded brick wall.

20. Ray and Nadine Watt Hall of Architecture and Fine Arts, 1973 Killingsworth, Brady, and Associates; Sam T. Hurst

A heavy exposed-concrete savings and loan pavilion that does battle with the 1939 Harris Hall to the

west (note that Harris Hall easily wins). The interior public areas of Watt Hall convey a funereal atmosphere—a rather strange environment in which to educate future architects and artists.

21. Charlotte S. and Davre Davidson Conference Center, 1975 Edward D. Stone, Inc.

A characteristic Stone pavilion, with the east and west façades centering on a recessed three-arch loggia. The building stands on a podium, its brick walls held in place by a thinly detailed projection roof. There is a handsome sunken garden to the south of the building.

22. Arnold Schoenberg Institute, 1978 Adrian Wilson and Associates

The Institute is unquestionably an impressive piece of complex angular sculpture of exposed-concrete walls and metal-and-glass windows and roofs. The whole composition is set above a really fine garden of ferns and trees.

23. Cinema-Television Center, 1983 A. Quincy Jones and Associates

Not one of A. Quincy Jones firm's great buildings; the well-developed landscape helps it.

24. Zohrab A. Kaprielian Hall, 1989 Abbott Marshall Partners

Postmodern enters the USC campus.

49
• **Vernon**
Commerce
Huntington Park
South Gate
Bell
Maywood
Watts

The southern section of the Los Angeles plain west of the Los Angeles River was the scene of extensive speculation during the great land boom of the 1880s. Some residential and commercial growth took place in the late 1880s and early 1890s, but basically the area was devoted to agriculture. The development of the communities of Vernon, Huntington Park, Maywood, Bell, and South Gate came after 1900. Huntington Park was incorporated in 1903, Vernon in 1905, and South Gate as late as 1923. In the teens and later, this section of Los Angeles County emerged as the industrial region of the basin, though it should be noted that the industrialization was accompanied by quite a bit of spec single-family housing. There are a few examples of turn-of-the-century housing to be found in Huntington Park, but almost all of the houses to be found today date from after 1920. These communities do contain several of Los Angeles's major architectural monuments—the murals of Farmer Johns, the Watts Towers, and several wonderful 1930s Streamline Moderne office and industrial buildings.

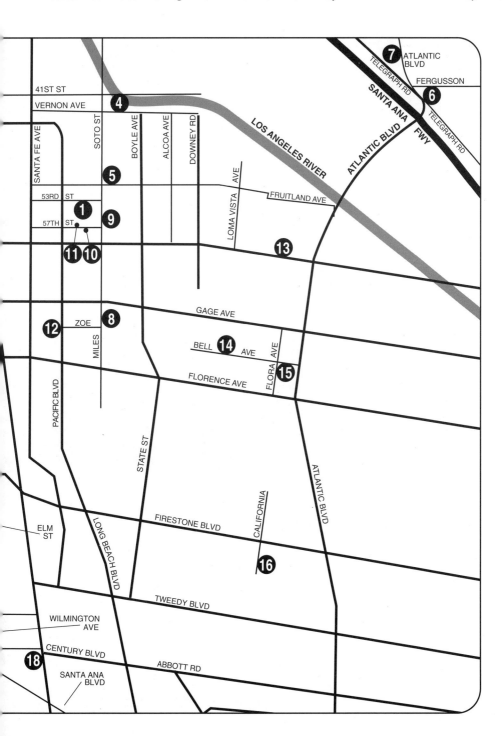

1. Pueblo del Rio Public Housing, 1941–42
Paul R. Williams, chief architect; Adrian Wilson, Gordon B. Kaufmann, Wurdeman and Becket, Richard J. Neutra; Ralph Cornell, landscape architect
1801 E. 53rd Street
Vernon

Pueblo del Rio still stands as a beautiful oasis within this section of Los Angeles. The grounds are well kept, as are the buildings. This project consisted of fifty-seven two-story units placed on a 17.5-acre site. These brick and reinforced-concrete buildings, with their horizontal banding of windows, walls, and roofs, are mildly Modern in style. As part of the project, individual garden plots and fruit trees were provided.

2. Avalon Gardens, 1941–42
Carleton M. Winslow, chief architect; Roland E. Coate; Samuel Lunden, Katherine Bashford and Fred Barlow, landscape architects
Avalon Boulevard at 88th Place, to the south of Manchester Avenue

Another of the city's well-preserved war-time housing projects. The successful approach to planning was stated in a 1942 article in the *Architect and Engineer:* "By planning the site as a whole there will be dwellings for one hundred and sixty families in sixty-two buildings, each placed at the proper angle to obtain the best exposure to the sun and each surrounded by generous open space of attractively landscaped gardens and recreation areas for children and adults."

Although the site is not large (14.9 acres), its design does realize these goals. Fourteen of these wood-frame buildings are two stories; the rest are California ranch houses.

3. Hacienda Village, 1941–42
Paul R. Williams, chief architect; Adrian Wilson, Richard J. Neutra, Walter Wurdeman and Welton Becket
1515 E. 105th Street
(103rd Street at Compton Boulevard)

Hacienda Village is in excellent condition, notwithstanding over a half century of use. It is the most suburban of the public housing projects of these years. The site of 17.63 acres has 72 one-story buildings that contain 184 units, conveying the feeling of modest California ranch houses of the late 1930s.

4. Farmer John's (Cloughtan Packing Company), 1953 and later
3049 E. Vernon Avenue
Vernon

Farmer John's expresses a high point in the use of painted illusionism to create its own world, despite what goes on within. Here you will find little pigs right out of an illustrated children's storybook romping along with nineteenth-century Tom Sawyer farm boys. The painted scenes continue along the fences, along the street walls of the buildings, and here and there the pigs become three-dimensional and climb onto or over the roofs. If you drive along Vernon Boulevard at 35 mph, the small boulevard trees become a part of the scene. The fences and walls were painted in this public-scaled trompe l'oeil by Leslie A. Grimes, and since his death (he fell from a scaffold while painting), they have been repainted by the Arco Sign Company.

5. Owens-Illinois Pacific Building, 1937
H. H. Brunnier
Northeast corner of East Fruitland Avenue and South Soto Street
Vernon

As you would expect from this company, this is an ode to the

glory of glass brick. Best of all is the Streamline Moderne corner bay. As with well-designed glass-brick walls, those on this building work well both day and night.

6. East Los Angeles Union Pacific Railroad Passenger Station, 1928
Gilbert Stanley Underwood
Southeast corner of Atlantic Boulevard and Ferguson Drive

Architect Gilbert Stanley Underwood designed a number of stations for the Union Pacific Railroad. The East Los Angeles Station was one of his late designs using the Spanish Revival style. The dual frontispieces of this hollow tile building were the two entrances, one facing the parking lot, the other the train platform. These convey in their cast-stone ornament a strong Churrigueresque feeling. Heavy ornate ironwork was used for window and door grilles. Inside,

the exposed wood-beam ceiling was sumptuously stenciled and painted. At present the station is abandoned, but we hope that it will be preserved and restored.

7. Lees Market Building,
circa 1929
1247 Atlantic Boulevard

This narrow-fronted two-story commercial building plays at being much larger by suggesting that it is composed of two side pavilions enclosing a recessed center. Vertical pilasters climb up the front of the building, and then project beyond the parapet as finials.

8. Huntington Park Civic Center, 1945–51
Hugh R. Davies
East corner of Miles and Zoe Avenues

Planning for the Civic Center started in 1939, but the coming of the Second World War stopped any activity. In 1947 Hugh R. Davies prepared a Spanish Revival

scheme that organized the buildings around a courtyard. The principal point of interest in this plan was a large auditorium to the rear of the courtyard and a high-domed Spanish tower to the south. Modifications of this scheme were made. The first unit built was the City Hall, which was dedicated in December 1947. Other buildings were added to the complex, including the 1951 Justice Building. Davies' tower in the courtyard was joined by an even larger tower placed to the front at the north end of the enclosing arched corridor. Other buildings were added, following the architect's original scheme. The most important of these was the 1951 Justice Building. In 1970 the firm of Williamson and Norris turned, with only marginal success, to the imagery of late Modern for the Regional Library Building.

9

9. Lane-Wells Company, 1938–39
William E. Myer
*5610 S. Soto Street
Huntington Park*

This and the adjoining buildings to the north (now W. W. Henry Company) represent one among Los Angeles's really impressive Streamline Moderne buildings. "Rounded corners and three large continuous glass areas give the building a strong horizontal feeling, but the tall pylons provide interesting contrasts at the entrances," wrote the architect shortly after this reinforced-concrete building was completed. Essentially, the buildings were placed in a park-like setting "so that when one enters the plant nothing reminds him of manufacturing, for beautiful flowers and shrubs, well-kept grounds and distinctive buildings have removed the stigma of the old-fashioned factory."

10. Apartment Building, circa 1925
*2802 E. 57th Street
Huntington Park*

A near-perfect solution (especially with the budget in mind) to bring history and fashion into a Los Angeles stucco box: Place a stucco-relief mission bell within a panel and then give a slight indication of Spanish at the entrance with columns and an entablature. By magic it all becomes Mission Revival.

11. Cottage, circa 1889
*2735 E. 57th Street
Huntington Park*

A spec Queen Anne cottage. Farther west on 57th Street at the southwest corner of Malabar Street, the bungalow court devotee will discover one that is attired in a Mission Revival design.

12. Warner Brothers Theater, 1930
B. Marcus Priteca
*6714 S. Pacific Boulevard
Huntington Park*

An Art Deco motion picture theater. The auditorium is still intact and has a multilayered ceiling and hidden lights.

13. Maywood City Hall, 1938
Wilson, Merrill, and Alexander
*4319 E. Slauson Avenue
Maywood*

A two-story Streamline Moderne public building. If you look closely as you drive along Slauson Boulevard from Maywood west to Baldwin Hills, you will find the remains of a good number of late 1930s Streamline Moderne buildings.

14. Bell Avenue School (Corona School), 1935
Richard J. Neutra
3835 Bell Avenue
Bell

Neutra continued the early California tradition of the open-air school in this building. Each of the classrooms opens through sliding glass walls to an enclosed outdoor court. An open exterior corridor runs along the other side, and high clerestory windows balance the interior light of the classrooms. This stucco and wood-frame building is an excellent example of pre–World War II Modern.

15. Bell High School, 1935
Robert F. Train
Southeast corner of
Bell and Flora Avenues

This building, and especially its central section, is a characteristic example of the PWA Moderne in reinforced concrete.

16. South Gate Civic Center, 1941–42
William Allen and
W. George Lutzi
Southeast corner of
California and
Ardmore Avenues

Rather than use the prevailing Spanish style or that of the Art Deco, the architects and the community settled on a version of the Anglo-Colonial Revival. When the building was dedicated, the editors of the *Southwest Builder and Contractor* wrote, "The architectural style is a modified Georgian with a pitched roof, an imposing pediment at the main entrance and a graceful cupola surmounting the main section." The structure is of reinforced concrete, the surface treated

with a buff color. In the lobby are two murals by Frank Bowers. They depict the history of South Gate. In the porticoed entrance of the Civic Center Community Building (formerly the City Library) is a tile mosaic by Stanton McDonald Wright (1938), produced through the Federal Art Project. The subject is *Evolution of Writing.*

17. Watts Towers, 1921–55
Simon Rodia
1765 E. 107th Street
Watts

Los Angeles's most notable contribution to the architecture of folk fantasy, accomplished on a grand scale that fits the image

of Los Angeles and Southern California. Broken tile, china, soda pop bottles, plaster, concrete, steel, and iron form the colorful lacework of these towers. Rodia, an Italian emigrant turned tile-setter for the telephone company, said that he wanted to do something big for Los Angeles, "so I did." The towers have recently been restored.

Be sure to get instructions on times of touring from Los Angeles City Hall. An easy way to get to them if you don't have a car is to take the interurban Blue Line from the 7th Street Station and get off at the Watts Station. You can spot the Towers from the train platform.

17

18. Dominguez Ranch House, 1826
18127 S. Alameda Street
Compton

The front of this house, as we see it today, is pure Mission Revival, circa 1910. The long open corridor with its simple, square wood posts and Greek Revival double-hung windows is characteristic of Spanish-Anglo adobes from the mid-1830s on.

19. Bethlehem Baptist Church, 1944
R. M. Schindler
4900 S. Compton Avenue
Los Angeles

This is Schindler's only built church, and it is a must see, although it is not in the best condition. The street front on busy Compton Avenue is composed of a series of wide overlapping stucco bands, closing off the main building effectively from the street and its noises. The principal natural light for the auditorium is introduced by skylights placed at the base of the cruciform tower.

20. Thomas Jefferson High School, 1936
Stiles O. Clements
319 E. 41st Street
Los Angeles

Here is monumental Streamline Moderne at its best. Horizontality asserts itself everywhere via moldings, bands of windows, and horizontal fins. The tour de force is the concave wall of the entrance with its band of dramatic lettering.

21. Root Beer Barrel Restaurant, circa 1932
1000 E. Slauson Avenue

A drive-in restaurant in the form of the container of its product.

50 • Highland Park

This community, still discernible in spite of merging with Los Angeles, was once one of the famous "suburbs in search of a city." Situated on the road to Pasadena (Figueroa Street in this area was once Pasadena Avenue), it was perhaps the first of the suburbs. By the turn of the century it had many fine houses and exhibited a high cultural tone—Charles Fletcher Lummis, William Lees Judson, Clyde Browne, Mary Austin, and other luminaries lived there. It was the home of Occidental College until 1914. It must also be noted that near what is now Sycamore Grove Park was one of the most notorious red-light districts in Los Angeles County.

No more! The Sycamore Grove area, once the site of many dalliances, is now quite respectable. Occidental College flourishes today in nearby Eagle Rock. Most of the artists are gone (many younger ones are on Mount Washington nearby), as are most of the Victorian houses (one of them moved across the Arroyo Seco to Heritage Square). A sad note: the pre-Columbian Revival buildings that once composed Luther Burbank Junior High School have been leveled.

But do not despair. Much fascinating material remains.

1. Robert Williams House (now Hathaway Home for Children), circa 1905
Train and Williams
840 Avenue 66

A huge, boulder-based Craftsman piece, now painted but having some good interiors, including a stair-hall with a large panel of stained glass designed by Judson Studios. Train and Williams's work was featured in the one and only issue of the *Arroyo Craftsman* (October 1909).

2. McClure House, 1889
James H. Bradbeer
432 Avenue 66

Queen Anne, Eastlake, and Italianate styles have been merged here. The house has been altered but it still shows what the architect intended.

3. Bungalow, circa 1905
201 N. Avenue 66

This is a true California bungalow, with strong Swiss Chalet influence and even a little of Japan in its slightly upswept eaves. The vertical board-and-batten siding suggests the early date.

4. Judson Studios, 1901
200 Avenue 66

Originally, before the roof burned off in 1910, this was a three-story building in Islamic Revival style. It was the home of the Los Angeles College of Fine Arts founded by William Lees Judson, a prominent regional painter who

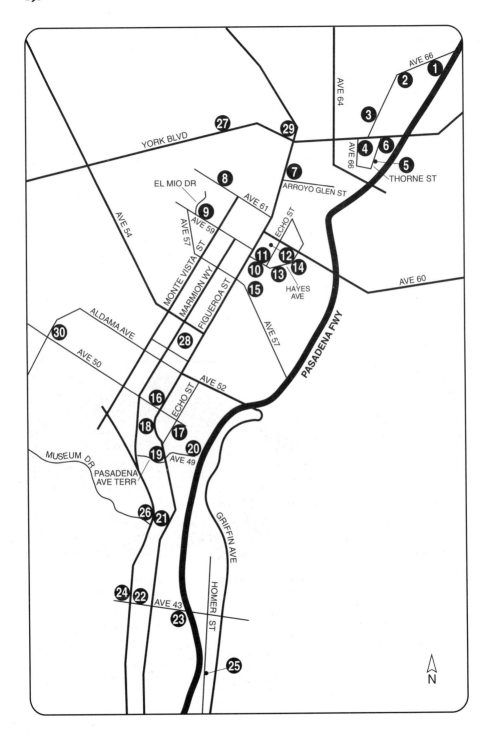

4

came to the area in 1893. When the college became a part of the University of Southern California, the building was converted into a Guild Hall for the Arroyo Guild of Fellow Craftsmen, a group of workers inspired by Judson and George Wharton James, an editor of *The Craftsman,* to emulate William Morris and Gustav Stickley. Note the logo of the Guild, an arm and hammer and the motto "We Can" over the entrance. Still later it became the Judson Studios, the "Tiffany of the West," fabricating fine art glass—as it still does. It is on the National Register of Historic Places.

5. Judson House,
circa 1895
William Lees Judson
216 Thorne Street

Judson's interpretation of the Shingle style is a real curiosity.

4

7

6. Fargo House, 1908
Harry Grey
206 Thorne Street

The elevation is remarkably similar to a number of designs by the Greenes. The house is most picturesque viewed from the Pasadena Freeway behind it.

7. Abbey San Encino, 1909–25
Clyde Browne
6211 Arroyo Glen Street

A miniaturized stone abbey that reads as a child's medieval castle. Browne was a printer who, like his hero William Morris, collected the literati of the area in his living room. The house begins with Mission Revival and ends with regionalized Spanish. Browne's grandson, Jackson Browne, the singer, once lived here.

8. Bungalow Court, circa 1915
337 Avenue 61

Big independent units along the court with a two-story duplex at the end. A Craftsman ensemble with Japanese flourishes.

9. House, 1890
5905 El Mio Drive, at Avenue 59

A Queen Anne mansion with a great view in every direction.

10. Yoakum House, circa 1900
140–145 Avenue 59

Rather rare Tudor Revival.

11. House, circa 1905
5903 Echo Street, at the northwest corner of Avenue 59

Spanish Revival.

12. House, circa 1910
5915 Echo Street

Spanish Revival again, but this time made Californian with Islamic arches!

13. Duplex, circa 1900
5960–5962 Hayes Avenue

Mission Revival with holly leaves in leaded glass.

14. House, circa 1895
6028 Hayes Avenue

A one-story Queen Anne reminiscent of some of the simpler Southern plantation houses.

15. Ebell Club, 1912
Sumner Hunt and Silas Burns
127 Avenue 57

Ever since this building was constructed, it has been the civic, educational, and social center of Highland Park. The style is Mission Revival with Italianate brackets, but the broad overhanging eaves suggest the midwestern Prairie style.

16. Hall of Letters, 1904–5
G. A. Howard Jr.
Old Campus
Occidental College
(northwest corner of Figueroa
Street and Avenue 50)

In this redbrick, now non-descript but once vaguely French Renaissance building, Robinson Jeffers studied English literature. Incidentally, the architect was the son of the chairman of the Occidental Board of Trustees.

17. Three Duplexes, circa 1900
Echo Street at the southeast
corner of Avenue 50

Exactly alike, the adjoining buildings resemble Neoclassical city houses of 1870s London.

18. Professor's Row, 1911–12
Milwaukee Building Company
(Meyer and Holler)
4967–4985 Figueroa Street

Originally there were five of these excellent Craftsman houses in the manner Gustav Stickley would have approved (there are now only three left). They were all supposedly built for professors at the nearby old campus of Occidental College.

19. Hiner House and
Sousa Nook, 1922
Archibald Dixon Pechey
4757 Figueroa Street at
Pasadena Avenue Terrace

This was the house of Edwin M. Hiner, the director of the most popular brass band in the Los Angeles area. He founded the music department at the old Los Angeles Normal School, now UCLA. The Tudor house done in boulders is unusual. The nook is more conventional Craftsman bungalow style, but John Philip Sousa slept here (according to legend)!

20. Bent House, circa 1909
Hunt, Eager, and Burns
End of Avenue 49, next to the
Pasadena Freeway

Another (but very different) flat-roofed Craftsman/Tudor house whose picturesque oak and boul-der-strewn garden once wandered down into the Arroyo Seco.

21. "Casa de Adobe," 1917
Theodore Eisen
4603 N. Figueroa Street

An interesting effort (because it is

early) to re-create an authentic hacienda of the Spanish-Mexican period. It is, in spite of a few mod-ernisms, completely successful. It houses a museum of materials from the late-Mexican and early-Anglo periods in Los Angeles history and is administered by the Southwest Museum on the hill above it.

22. Mount Washington
Cable Car Station, 1909
Fred R. Dorn
200 W. Avenue 43

A small Mission Revival building that housed a waiting room for people riding the funicular rail-way to their homes on Mount Washington. The operation was closed down in 1919, apparently a victim of the automobile.

23. Lummis House
("El Alisal"), 1895–1910
Sumner Hunt and
Theodore Eisen;
Charles F. Lummis
200 E. Avenue 43

Lummis, a Harvard student who had taken courses from Charles Eliot Norton (an authority on the Greek culture, a friend of Ruskin, and first president of the Boston Society of Arts and Crafts) built this house of boulders from the Arroyo and named it for the huge sycamore in the patio. Little of the original furniture exists, but there is a great deal about the place that evokes the presence of this amazing man whom his friend Charles Keeler called "William Morris turned into a Mexican Indian." Lummis was the founder of the Southwest Museum, one of the important repositories of Native American art in the United States. You can see Lummis's admiration of the Indian culture in the beautiful

19

23

pottery that was left after the 1971 earthquake dashed most of his personal collection to pieces and also in the lantern slides fixed in one window showing Indian dances. The doors and some built-in furniture were designed by Maynard Dixon, as was the magnificent hardware on the main door on the garden side. And there is even an Art Nouveau fireplace designed by Charles Walter Stetson, a prominent painter and an important figure in the local Arts & Crafts movement. Be sure to notice the Mission-style gable on the dining room wing, with a bell given to Lummis by the king of Spain. This reminds us that, among his many other contribu-

tions to the culture of Southern California, Lummis founded the California Landmarks Club in 1894 that, in its efforts to save the California missions, was one of the first preservation organizations in the United States.

24. Elmer and Marion Cavanaugh Wachtel House and Studio, 1906
Elmer Wachtel
315 W. Avenue 43

A pleasant Arts & Crafts cottage that is remarkable because it was the home of two excellent plein air painters. The interior, all paneled in wood, is very fine.

25. Heritage Square
End of Homer Street, south of Avenue 43
(Pasadena Freeway off-ramp)

Whatever you may think of such projects, it is quite clear that none of the buildings moved here in the last two decades would exist if some enterprising people had not decided to do something about retaining these disjointed shards of the Victorian culture. Ruskinian purists in preservation do not like to see buildings moved from sites to which they were meant to relate (in some cases). But what do you do when buildings of this quality are being vandalized and would otherwise be demolished? The obvious solution: move them. And it may be significant for the image of Los Angeles that two of these buildings had been moved before—one of them twice! The site has been described as "a freeway-isolated arroyo littoral" (Nathan Weinberg, *Preservation in American Towns and Cities*, p. 63). It is not ideal, but with landscaping the problems of the site are being diminished. And then it has the advantage that you can take it all in as you travel on the Pasadena Freeway.

Listed from north to south:

a. Palms Railroad Station, circa 1886

An Eastlake building brought from Palms near Century City.

b. Perry House ("Mount Pleasant"), 1876
Ezra F. Kysor

An Italian villa that probably was the finest house in Los Angeles when it was built by William Hayes Perry in Boyle Heights.

c. Hale ("C. M.") House, circa 1885
W. F. Norton

Queen Anne proportions with Eastlake and Queen Anne details. Restoration is almost complete inside and outside. Although named for the Hale family that was its longest resident, high in the front gable are the letters "C. M." carved in a shield, the initials of Charles Morgan, the original owner.

d. Shaw ("Valley Knudson Memorial") House, circa 1877

A French Second Empire (Mansard) cottage built originally for Richard E. Shaw in East Los Angeles. The restoration has been liberally endowed by the Bel Air Garden Club of which Mrs. Knudsen was a founder and president.

e. Ford ("Beaudry Street") House, circa 1885

Queen Anne, Eastlake, and Italianate mixed. But the style is not so important as the elaborate decoration on such a small house. The first owner, John J. Ford, was a wood-carver of extraordinary imagination and talent. The house was moved from Beaudry Street where the Bank of America computer center now stands.

f. Lincoln Avenue Methodist Church, 1898–99
George W. Kramer; W. A. Benshoff, supervising architect

Moved from Pasadena to make way for a new and strikingly hideous post office, this is a good Eastlake Gothic building that will make a good meeting place at the Square. The door, with its pilasters and pediment, is at the corner, suggesting that the inte-rior is laid out on the famous Methodist "Akron Plan"—the pulpit at the opposite corner with the pews in arcs around it.

g. Longfellow-Hastings ("Octagon") House, 1893

Before being moved to Heritage Square, this house was situated on South Allen Avenue in Pasadena (where it had been moved from a previous site). The Longfellow-Hastings House is closely modeled after the octagonal designs published in the mid-nineteenth century by the phrenologist O. S. Fowler in his often reprinted *A Home for All or the Gravel Wall and Octagon Mode of Building*. The nationwide rage for the octagonal house was in the 1850s and early 1860s. California came late on the scene and only a few were built in the north and south. The Longfellow-Hastings House is the only example still standing in Southern California. Its interior with the central staircase lighted by the cupola is fascinating. The house is currently under restoration, and the surrounding porches and other details will be returned to their original locations.

26. Southwest Museum, 1910–14 and later
Sumner Hunt and Silas R. Burns
Northwest corner of Museum Drive and Marmion Way

A monument of the Mission

SOUTHWEST MUSEUM

26

27

Revival with definite references to the siting and exterior of the Alhambra and its hilltop site. This building houses a fine collection of Native American art. Its specialty is, of course, Southwestern, but there are some excellent Plains and Alaskan things. One of the thrills of visiting the museum is to enter through the 1919 Mayan Entrance (Hunt and Burns) at the base of the hill, and then proceed through a 240-foot-long tunnel lined with dioramas to an elevator, which after 108 feet brings you to the building on the hilltop. Nowadays, you drive up the steep road to the top of the hill.

27. Northeast Police Station, 1925
City of Los Angeles Building Department
6045 York Boulevard

A buff-colored brick building in the Beaux-Arts style, too sophisticated, perhaps, for its surroundings.

28. Morrell House, 1906
Charles E. Shattuck
215 N. Avenue 53

A handsome brick Arts & Crafts bungalow. It was illustrated and discussed in *The Craftsman* magazine in 1909.

29. Arroyo Seco Bank Building, 1926
Austin and Ashley
6301 N. Figueroa Street

A rather odd interpretation of Beaux-Arts classicism, with an elegant Churrigueresque entrance situated at the corner.

30. Aldama Apartments, 1961
A. E. Morris
5030–5038 Aldama Avenue, near Avenue 50

These stepped stucco boxes clinging to the hill evoke the spirit of Schindler's apartment houses of the 1920s and 1930s but are more openly mannered than their ancestors.

51 • Mount Washington

Artists' nests abound in this area above Highland Park and the real world. When you get to the top of San Rafael Avenue, you realize that Mount Washington was invaded in the early twentieth century and people have been building there ever since. It is said that Mount Washington is above the smog. Not true. But it does, in spite of the winding streets, give a sense of neighborhood as few places in Southern California do.

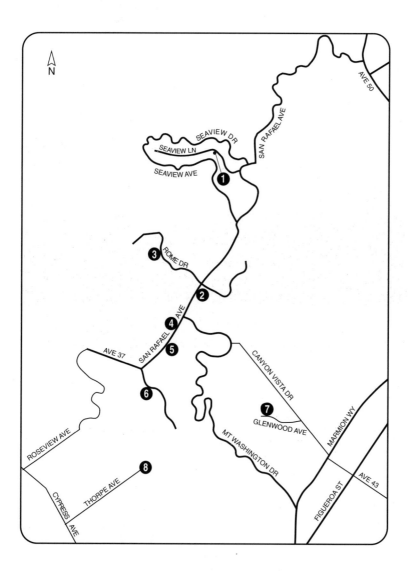

1. Birtcher-Share House, 1942
Harwell H. Harris
4234 Seaview Lane,
between Seaview Drive and
Seaview Avenue

Influenced by Wright's Usonian
houses, Harris nevertheless seems
to straighten the Master out. This
large one-story wood house is one
of his masterpieces. Another small
view of it can be obtained from
Seaview Avenue unless the bushes
have grown too high.

Subdued for this architect, the
derivation from Frank Lloyd
Wright's Usonian houses of the
1930s is clear.

4. House, circa 1910
3855 San Rafael Avenue

A great Mission Revival structure
with massive columns. While
here you will want to look at the
large house across the street now
owned by the Vedanta Society.
Although big, it is not distinguished architecture.

6. Byler House, 1937
Gregory Ain
914 Avenue 37

Vertical boards stained brown and
looking very Craftsman. It is
amazing how many Ain houses
have weathered the years and
come out looking as if they were
brand new. The architect must
have satisfied the owners.

7. Williams House, 1948
Smith and Williams
4211 Glenwood Avenue

2. Hinds House, 1947
Richard J. Neutra
3941 San Rafael Avenue

Yes, you can see the house if you
get out of your car. The number
is on the lower part of the small
cliff. It is one of Neutra's few
wood-sheathed houses.

3. Mauer House, 1949
John Lautner
932 Rome Drive

5. House, circa 1925
3820 San Rafael Avenue

An adobe structure with adobe
wall and gate. In spite of its late
date it is much more convincing
than most of the nineteenth-
century adobes. Across the street
is a good Craftsman house often
mistakenly attributed to the
Greenes.

From the street this house is a
simple box with huge protruding
eaves.

8. Jeffries House, circa 1905
End of Thorpe Avenue, east of
Cypress Avenue

It is significant that Jim Jeffries,
the famous pugilist, would build
a refined Classical Revival house
as his ideal in life. Ah, that someone would see his intelligence and
restore it!

52 • Eagle Rock

When Occidental College moved from Highland Park to Eagle Rock in 1914, the town was a crossroads whose only other real ornament was a huge rock with a naturally formed image of a spread-winged eagle on its face. The rock and the area around it had been a significant Indian site at the beginning of the nineteenth century and earlier. Later it was a favorite picnic site for city folk who rode the old trolley line out Figueroa Street.

In the 1920s the town grew, as is evidenced by the thousands of bungalows that cover the land between Glendale and Pasadena. Few of these small dwellings have claims to aesthetic significance, but as a whole they signify a pleasant and respectable way of life

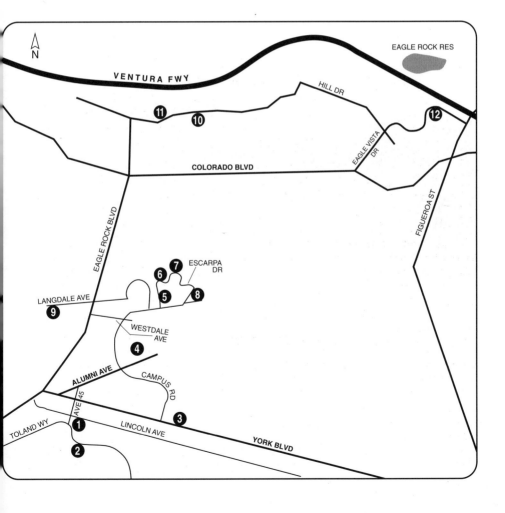

in the American tradition of single-family housing. More expensive houses were erected on the hills, but again the architectural talent displayed is not outstanding. Two Schindler houses, the Lowe House #1 (1923) and the Lowe House #2 (1937) were demolished when the Ventura Freeway was constructed. The old buildings that stood at the corners of Colorado and Eagle Rock Boulevards, and once gave a kind of Midwestern charm to the place, have been demolished or remodeled beyond recognition. Eagle Rock Boulevard has somehow managed to become even more ghastly than it was when our first architectural guide came out.

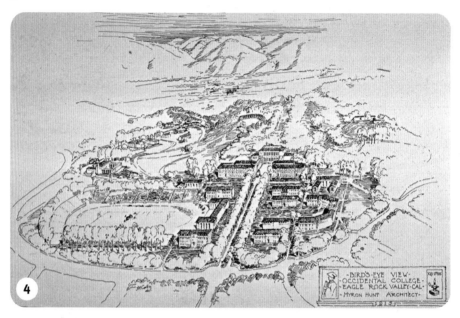

1. Sparkletts Drinking Water Corporation, 1925–29
Attributed to a "Mr. King"
4500 Lincoln Avenue

A mosque of the first water. Unfortunately the 1971 earthquake so shook its minarets that they had to be removed.

2. Kapin House, 1935
George Kapin
4512 Toland Way

Situated above the Sparkletts plant, this house seems to be related to it.

3. Motels R Us, 1983
4855 York Boulevard

This building defies all canons of taste and must be mentioned for its sheer horror, impossible to experience in black and white.

4. Occidental College
Myron Hunt;
Beatrix Farrand,
landscape architect
1600 Campus Road

The architecture of the college contrasts sharply with that of the community. It seems, in spite of its many tile-roofed buildings, to have been transplanted from New England, so orderly and understated is its campus style, a kind of regionalized Palladianism. Jarring intrusions, such as the chapel, are all the more irritating because of the overall unity throughout the campus that was achieved by hiring Myron Hunt and H. C. Chambers to design almost all the buildings right up to the mid-1930s.

We have listed only the most interesting buildings:

4a

a. Swan, Johnson, and Fowler Halls, 1914
Myron Hunt

These buildings were the college until a flurry of building in the 1920s transformed the campus. Indeed, they set the tone for future building. Hunt originally designed a columned hall to connect Johnson (see above) and Fowler, but this part of his plan was never carried out. In 1968 the Coons Administrative Center, designed by William Pereira Associates, was placed where Hunt envisioned a colonnade. Most of the building is invisible

but not quite underground. The second level is almost entirely sheathed in glass so that it has, perhaps unkindly, been dubbed "the Chrysler Showroom."

b. Clapp Library, 1924
Myron Hunt and
H. C. Chambers

Extensions at each side of the original tiny Mediterranean-style building doubled its size in 1954. Then in 1969 an addition in "State College Modern" was made by Neptune and Thomas, again

doubling the size of the building. Except for the fact that the old book stacks are separated from the new ones, the entire building functions well.

c. Herrick Chapel, 1964
Ladd and Kelsey

Distinguished by its slip-form concrete construction (marvelous to view when construction was underway but unremarkable when finished) and its magnificent stained-glass windows by Perli Pelzig.

d. Johnson Student Center (Freeman Union), 1928
Myron Hunt and
H. C. Chambers

The charming, double-arcaded entrance patio is good for dancing. In 1956 Chambers and Hubbard added a large extension to the old building. It never worked out functionally, and it was dull aesthetically. In 1996 the college commissioned Brenda Levin Associates to devise a plan for the remodeling of the extension. Again, the problems with the building could not be resolved so it was torn down and a new one was constructed that was harmonious with the Old Union but not a reproduction of its design. At the same time the Old Union by Hunt and Chambers was refurbished and slightly modified. The result is admirable. Levin also restored Myron Hunt's Art Barn (originally the Women's Gymnasium) as an annex of the student union.

4e

e. Thorne Hall (Auditorium), 1938
Myron Hunt and H. C. Chambers

The last of Hunt's major designs for Occidental. The incidents surrounding its construction figure prominently in Aldous Huxley's *After Many a Summer Dies the Swan*, in which Occidental is "Tarzana College." The firm of Brenda Levin Associates has extensively refurbished this building, continuing an Occidental tradition of revamping and reusing the twenty-two original Myron Hunt buildings rather than destroying them.

f. Booth Music-Speech Center, 1929
Myron Hunt and H. C. Chambers

The old building comprises studios and a small recital hall around an arcaded court. A large classroom, office, and theater addition was made by Charles Luckman Associates in 1960.

Brenda Levin remodeled this building to house the Education Department and a new Music Library.

g. Orr Hall (now Weingart Center for the Arts), 1925
Myron Hunt and H. C. Chambers

Originally built as the first women's dormitory on the campus, it is also one of the loveliest of Hunt's buildings. Unfortunately it was discovered to have serious seismic problems. It was completely gutted and its walls were reinforced (under the supervision of the architectural firm of Neptune and Thomas). It now houses the Art Department and the offices of the Core Curriculum.

h. Erdman Hall, 1927
Myron Hunt and H. C. Chambers

Another example of civilized student housing.

i. Admissions Office (originally President's House), 1922
Myron Hunt and H. C. Chambers

Anglo-Colonial Revival at its best.

j. Dean of Students' House (now Day Care Center), 1951
Smith and Williams

Unassuming rationality with a hint of the Japanese taste.

k. Comptroller's House (now Public Policy Center), 1932
Myron Hunt and H. C. Chambers

Monterey style. Well planned for entertaining.

l. Dean of the Faculty House (now President's House), 1932
Myron Hunt and H. C. Chambers

Monterey Revival again, bigger than the Dean's House but not so well planned—or seen.

m. Bird Hillside Theater, 1925
Myron Hunt and
H. C. Chambers

Very Greek, this amphitheater is used for commencement exercises, recreation, and excellent summer drama. A beautiful place to watch the sun set through eucalyptus trees.

over the volume of the auditorium—red tile roof and all. If you think that the exterior is too Brutal, go inside. The architect has treated the theater as a rococo hall worthy of staging a Mozart opera. It all cost a great deal of money and even agony to build, but it is simply a lovely place,

5. Chambers House, 1923
2068 Escarpa Drive

The Chambers were enthusiasts for American Indian designs and thus had their house built in the style of the Pueblo Revival. A Hopi symbol for happiness is used again and again in details as well as in the floor plan.

n. Norris Residence Hall, 1966
Pereira and Associates

Bay Area style plastered on Harvard-inspired clustered apartments around stairs. The scale is too small for active students.

o. Keck Theater, 1987–88
Kamnitzer and Cotton

After experimenting with the Modernist movement in the 1950s, 1960s, and 1970s the college, like many institutions, adopted the contextual approach in the 1980s. Kamnitzer has made a strong statement by placing the apse of a Spanish church

without doubt acoustically and aesthetically one of the finest modern theaters in the city.

p. Mullin Sculpture Studio and Gallery, 1996
Brenda Levin and Associates, in collaboration with Hodgetts + Fung

An industrial image building erected to take the place of the old Art Barn, now the Samuelson Pavilion. It is a kind of memorial to George Baker, an Occidental College graduate, professor, and well-known sculptor, whose courses were an inspiration to many students, art majors, and amateurs alike.

6. Martin House, 1966
Donald Martin
2039 Escarpa Drive

Designed by the architect for his parents, this house shows the influence of Richard J. Neutra.

7. Three Houses, 1962–68
Oakley Norton
*2003, 2009, 2026
Escarpa Drive*

These neo-Craftsman houses cling to the hill for a view of Mount Verdugo and, though they didn't ask for it, the Ventura Freeway.

8. Paxson House, 1971
**Buff and Hensman
(Conrad Buff)**
1911 Campus Road

The Craftsman tradition revived.

9. Mason House, 1916
2434 Langdale Avenue

This house has often been attributed to Irving J. Gill, although few of the details suggest his work.

10. House, circa 1925
2403 Hill Drive

Hill Drive has some very good Spanish Revival houses. This is one of the best.

11. Brauch House, 1923
**Egasse and Brauch
(J. L. Egasse)**
2327 Hill Drive

The general impression is medieval (of some sort) until you see the drooping swags of stucco at the point of the front gable. Hansel and Gretel appear. The architect said of his house that "In this particular instance, Norman lines, such as were left by the descendants of the Vikings, following their peregrination of an ante-medieval period, were the main source of inspiration" (*California Southland*, December 1923). A double stone archway (one for people, one for autos) provides entrance to the garden. As you ascend the hill, you pass through a series of arches leading to the front terrace.

12. Eagle Rock Playground Clubhouse, 1953
**Richard J. Neutra and Associates
(Dion Neutra)**
1100 Eagle Vista Drive

A Neutra house enlarged, an International Style building unexpected in this area.

53 • Lincoln Heights

Northeast Los Angeles is now bisected by the east/west San Bernardino Freeway and the north/south Golden State Freeway. The section west of the Golden State Freeway is industrial/railroad with some modest residential sections to the north. There is a smattering of modest late-nineteenth-century Queen Anne cottages and houses still standing in and around Workman and Griffin Streets. Equally nineteenth century in feeling is Lincoln Park with its small lake. Lincoln Park (then East Lake Park) contains a conservatory building designed in 1913 by Franklin M. Small of New York, with Walter Webber being the resident architect. The major visible monument in the Mission Road area is the Los Angeles County Hospital, but the real architectural landmark is Ernest Coxhead's Epiphany Chapel of 1888–89.

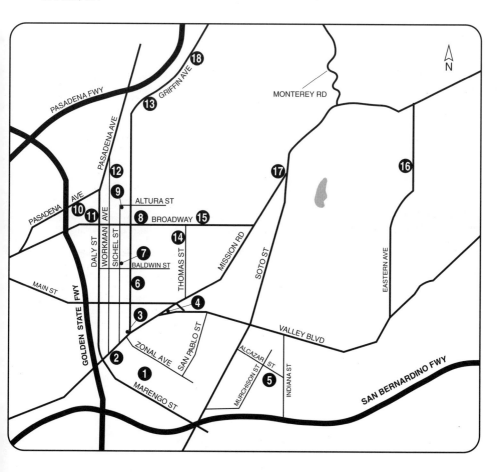

1. Los Angeles County/ USC Medical Center,
1928–33 and later
Allied Architects of Los Angeles: Edwin Bergstom, Myron Hunt, Pierpont Davis, Sumner P. Hunt, and William Richards
1200 N. State Street

The twenty-story central con-crete-and-steel unit of the hospi-tal has remained as the landmark in eastern Los Angeles. Its basic form is PWA Monumental Moderne—with more than a slight hint of the influence of Bertram G. Goodhue. Its design of sculptural volumes and heavy arches slightly suggests early Romanesque. High-relief sculp-ture on a grand scale adorns the major entrance from the west. This entrance, which is still par-tially preserved, has an axial walkway and garden leading up to the building. Not much can be said of the many later addi-tions to the building except that they look as if they were put up quickly and cheaply (which they probably were not).

2. Administration Building, Los Angeles County Hospital,
circa 1912
1100 N. Mission Road

An Austrian/German Secessionist design in the classical manner. The center of the building exhibits a low dome.

3. University of Southern California School of Medicine, Administration Building, circa 1920
Northwest corner of Mission Road and Griffin Avenue

The rows of arches, stucco walls, and Mission bells leave no one in doubt that this is a Mission Revival building, though when we look closer we will find that the low tower is in fact Spanish Revival. The arcade to the north of the building (with Mission bells) is a freestanding wall—really a screen that encloses a small garden.

4. Lincoln Park (formerly East Lake Park),
1874
East corner of Mission Road and Valley Boulevard

This forty-five-acre park contains a picturesque lake (man-made, of course) and once housed a won-derful carousel (which burned). In the late nineteenth century and through the early years of the twentieth century, the park was widely known for its exotic plant-ing, its ostrich farm, and its alli-gator farm. Alas, it is all quite tame nowadays.

5. Ramona Gardens Public Housing, 1940–41
George G. Adams, Walter S. Davis, Ralph C. Flewelling, Eugene Weston Jr., Lewis Eugene Weston, and Lloyd Wright; Katherine Bashford and Fred Barlow Jr., landscape architects
Between Alcazar, Murchison, and Indiana Streets

In this public housing project, 102 concrete units of two stories provide 610 living units on a thirty-two-acre site. The hilly location of the project with its meandering streets seems well planned. The housing units themselves are simple and straightforward with a minimal sense of architecture about them. The wall murals that have been painted on a number of the housing units may perhaps be ideologically satisfying, but they add little to the home-like atmosphere of the project.

6. House, circa 1890
2054 Griffin Avenue

A modest two-story Queen Anne (most likely spec) dwelling.

7. Sacred Heart Roman Catholic Church, circa 1900
2210 Sichel Street

A late–Victorian Gothic brick church with a traditional square corner tower but without its original high spire.

8. Federal Bank Building, 1910
Otto Neher and C. F. Skilling
2201 N. Broadway

A V-shaped building with a semi-circular pavilion where the angled streets come together. The public banking room is covered by a delightful, quite small glass dome.

9. Epiphany Chapel, 1888–89
Ernest Coxhead
2808 Altura Street,
on the southeast corner of
Sichel and Altura Streets

The small gable-roofed chapel to the left is a really fine, small Coxhead design. Low stone walls support a slightly projecting single gable with an overscaled round window. Coxhead maneuvers the shingles across the surface in an original fashion. The building has been restored. The rest of the church complex, including the Sanctuary (now much remodeled), was designed by Arthur B. Benton in 1913.

10. Engine Company No. 1 Fire Station, 1940
2230 Pasadena Avenue

A Streamline Moderne design. The street elevation of this two-story building comes close to being pure two-dimensional design, with the windows and entrance door as an L-shaped form articulated in the lower section with horizontal fins, the lettering treated as a horizontal line, and then the two fire truck entrances as two deep rectangles.

11. Department of Water and Power Building, circa 1937
S. Charles Lee
2417 Daly Street

Regency Moderne. The slightly convex façade of glass suggests the product that this public department sells. The marquee with its projecting letters can be seen best at night when the glass behind it is lighted.

12. Cottage, circa 1889
2652 Workman Avenue

A well-preserved Queen Anne cottage. The gable end over the front bay and the entrance porch are decorated with sawed relief work.

13. House, circa 1890
Attributed to Joseph Cather Newsom
3537 Griffin Avenue

A two-story Queen Anne dwelling with a number of sharp angular Eastlake details in wood. Especially unusual is the double-gabled dormer on the third floor.

14. Sturgis House, 1889–90
Ernest Coxhead
2345 Thomas Street

Probably this design was supposed to evoke the feeling of the Anglo-Colonial Revival. As with a good number of Coxhead's designs of the 1890s, the Sturgis House seems to be a composition of architectural fragments, each of which strongly stands on its own. The street elevation of the entrance porch sits as a screen with its paired columns and independent entablature. Above, the arched opening of the small second-floor porch contrasts with the pair of high, vertical, transomed windows to the side.

15. Abraham Lincoln High School, 1937–38
Albert C. Martin
3501 N. Broadway

A formal axis leads up from the street. The concrete buildings fit within the PWA Moderne, but in their scale, and some of their details, they point to the Spanish Revival.

16. Farmdale School Building, 1889
2839 N. Eastern Avenue,
at the rear of the school
grounds

An unusually elaborate Queen Anne Revival–style schoolhouse with a large, open, square bell tower.

17. Lunch Pail Restaurant Building, circa 1930
4067 Mission Road

A small fast-food restaurant that suggests a pail with perhaps a milk bottle on top.

18. Group of Spec Bungalows, circa 1910
4000 block of Griffin Avenue

This group of spec Craftsman bungalows provides an excellent glimpse of what many of the residential streets of Los Angeles looked like by the mid-teens.

54 • Alhambra

One of the oldest suburbs of Los Angeles, this town was set out (1873) in five-to ten-acre lots by Benjamin D. Wilson (who later became mayor of Los Angeles) between the Arroyo San Pasqual and the Old Mill Wash. He called it Alhambra because his wife was rather belatedly reading Washington Irving's *The Alhambra* (1832). The shrewd land speculator had found a theme and named the streets after incidents and characters in the romance. The present Main Street was, for instance, called Boabdil for the last king of Granada, who wept as he surveyed his beloved city seized from him by Ferdinand and Isabella in 1492. The name was soon changed because the residents found it impossible to pronounce. Unfortunately, almost every evidence of the world of Don Benito has been erased, some fairly recently. As usual, most of the old buildings were situated in the town center where urban renewal, early and late, got them.

The main commercial street dates from the 1950s with a little decoration from the 1920s interspersed. The local urban conservationists have wisely decided to restore each building to its original state, even if it has the 1950s blahs. A strong element in the design of the entrances to these buildings is often a terrazzo floor (see below), sometimes elaborately designed in pastels. Alhambra has other good things, some on the outskirts. Unfortunately, one of Alhambra's gems, the 1907 Chinese Cajal house, has been demolished.

1. Descanso Court, circa 1915
509 Atlantic Boulevard

Eight Asian bungalow units.

2. Alhambra Women's Club,
circa 1910
204 S. Second Street

A good Craftsman building with interiors intact.

3. House, circa 1937
Southeast corner of Second Street and Linda Vista Avenue

A Streamline Moderne structure—a ship's bridge sailing into Second Street.

Terrazzo floor, located in an entrance to one of the restored buildings on Alhambra's main commercial street

4. Service Station, circa 1938
Northwest corner of Valley Boulevard and Garfield Avenue

This is bigger than the last entry, but the inspiration is the same Streamline Moderne.

**5. "Crawford's Corner"
Shopping Center,** circa 1965
Northwest corner of Valley and Atlantic Boulevards

Victoriana again raises its head.

6. Mark Keppel High School,
1939
Marston and Maybury
501 E. Hellman Avenue

A huge Streamline Moderne structure. The brick base is

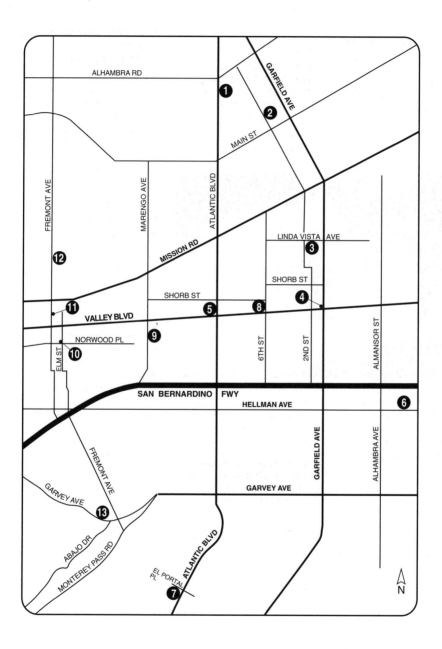

vaguely pre-Columbian while still being Moderne. The high point of the design is the monolithic curved corner auditorium that contains two stainless-steel and enamel murals by Millard Sheets. One panel depicts the early history of California; the other contains a map of California.

7. Cascades Park, circa 1928
**Cook, Hill, and Cornell
(Ralph D. Cornell),
landscape architects**
*Atlantic Boulevard and
El Portal Place
Monterey Park
(south of Alhambra)*

Here is a real estate developer's dream if there ever was one! At the west end of El Portal Place a small hill rises on which has been constructed an elaborate tile fountain with cascade. At the other end is a Spanish Revival building with the original "El Encanto" sign in place, apparently once a restaurant and offices. It faces El Mercado, a commercial district that never developed. Across the street from El Encanto is an adobe bungalow court that looks early.

The whole area was finally built up in the 1950s.

**8. Fire Station and City
Administration Building,**
circa 1938
*Sixth Street, north of
Valley Boulevard*

The complex is extremely picturesque, but the most attention has been given to the fire station. The buildings are sheathed in pink brick, painted white, and allowed to weather.

**9. Church of Sts. Simon
and Jude (Episcopal Home
for the Aged),** 1926
Reginald D. Johnson
1428 Marengo Avenue

Spanish Revival on an almost medieval dollhouse scale by the son of the Episcopal Bishop of Los Angeles.

10. Fire Station No. 4,
circa 1938
*Northwest corner of
Norwood Place and
Elm Street, near
Fremont Avenue*

A Spanish Gothic surprise.

11. C. F. Braun and Company,
circa 1929–37
Marston and Maybury
1000 S. Fremont Avenue

We mean no sneer when we say that these buildings are comparable to the best work of Albert Speer in the Germany of the 1930s. Austere red brick with almost peep-hole fenestration, they owe nothing to the International Style.

12. Sears Complex, 1971
**Albert C. Martin
and Associates**
900 S. Fremont Avenue

This group of buildings set within a landscaped site is dominated by a great mirrored glass box.

**13. St. Steven's Serbian
Orthodox Cathedral,** 1949–52
*North side of Garvey Avenue,
west of the intersection with
Abajo Drive*
Serbian Romanesque with two glistening tile domes, the church is done in California's favorite ecclesiastical material—concrete with the impression of the forms still showing.

55 • Montebello
Pico Rivera

The Italian name Montebello was once applied to a large section of the Repetto Ranch that the Anglo pioneer Harrison Newmark purchased in 1887. When he subdivided a portion of the ranch and established a town, he, of course, called it "Newmark." In 1920 the town's name was changed to Montebello. Notwithstanding its poetic name, Montebello and the regions to the south and west are now basically industrial, spawned by the discovery of oil shortly after 1900. As a commercial retail strip Whittier Boulevard deserves a cruise

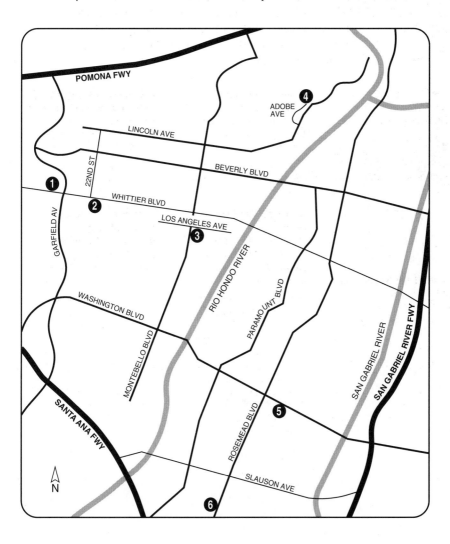

(though note that it is often closed at night to automobiles because of drag racing and other social problems). The façades of many of the one-story (and a few two-story) commercial buildings along Whittier Boulevard exhibit a number of variations on the late-1930s Streamline Moderne, plus a sprinkling of other exotic images.

Montebello Park, south of Whittier Boulevard between Gerhart and Vail Avenues, was laid out in 1925 by the planning and landscape architectural firm of Cook and Hill. On paper the plan looks fine, but in actuality there is little of great inspiration to be found in either the landscaping or the modest houses that line the streets. Montebello marks the beginning of what is a great industrial park (the City of Industry sprawls nearby). Huge complexes of factories and warehouses are erected in an anonymous architecture that might best be called Computer Moderne, a style that is even more salient in the Irvine area.

Pico Rivera, which lies to the east of Montebello between the Rio Hondo and San Gabriel Rivers, is a fairly recent creation (1958), when the towns of Pico and Rivera were combined. Like Montebello, it is an industrial city whose principal architectural glory is the commercial strip of Whittier Boulevard.

1. The Tamale, 1928
6420 Whittier Boulevard
East Los Angeles

An often-illustrated example of California's Programmatic architecture, this is a small roadside restaurant in the form of one of its products—a tamale. The poor little structure is now pressed in by buildings on both sides, and it is no longer painted or signed as it was when built, but we should be happy that it is still with us.

2. Marcel and Jeanne French Café, circa 1930
Southeast corner of
Whittier Boulevard and
22nd Street
Montebello

A dollhouse-scaled French Norman cottage right out of a children's storybook. Do not miss the final mark of France—a small version of the Eiffel Tower as the restaurant's sign.

3. House, circa 1915
Southeast corner of
Montebello Boulevard and
Los Angeles Avenue
Montebello

A clapboard dwelling of modest size that almost succeeds in being Moorish.

4. Juan Matias Sanchez Adobe,
1845, mid–1850s, and later
945 N. Adobe Avenue, off
Lincoln Boulevard
Montebello

Here on the west bank of the Rio Hondo River is an impressive story-and-a-half adobe. The oldest section runs parallel to the river, while the mid-1880s wing was extended at a right angle to the original house. . The wide hipped roof with dormer windows and much of the woodwork are twentieth century. Nonetheless, the adobe and its site do an excellent job of conveying what Southern California was like in the 1840s and 1850s. It is now used as a museum by the City of Montebello.

5. Santa Fe Passenger Station (now Pico Rivera Chamber of Commerce), circa 1880
9122 E. Washington Boulevard
Pico Rivera

This early Eastlake-style railroad station has been moved, restored, and converted into offices.

6. United Auto Workers Union Building, 1961
Neutra and Alexander (Dion Neutra)
8503 S. Rosemead Boulevard
Pico Rivera

A Neutra Modern machine image, indoors and out, with courtyards, pools, plantings, and covered walkways. When you walk in and out and through a building of this quality, you sense how unusual it was in the era of the 1960s, which produced little really good commercial design.

56 • Whittier

A Quaker organization, the Pickering Land and Water Company, founded the community of Whittier in 1887. A college was founded in 1887 but succumbed in the bust of 1888 and was reorganized as the Whittier Academy in 1891. Though the extensive orange, lemon, avocado, and walnut orchards are now gone, the city still retains a pleasant small-town atmosphere, quite separate from the rest of the valley to the south and west. The community has done reasonably well at preserving its historic buildings. The two unfortunate losses in the last few years are David S. Bushnell's 1928 Whittier Theater, which combined a motion picture theater with a forecourt of shops, and the rather mad Harvey Apartments of 1913.

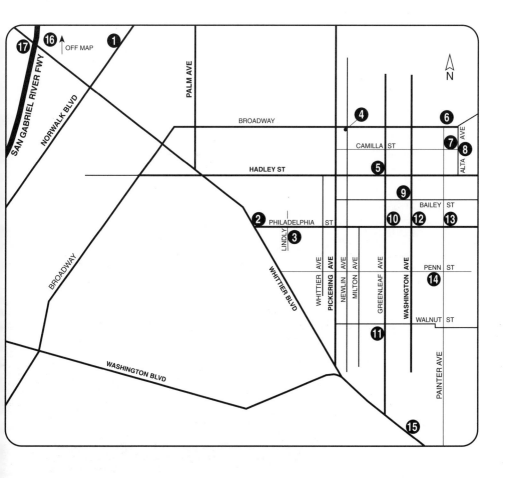

1. El Rancho High School, 1954–55
William H. Harrison
*West corner of
Norwalk Boulevard and
Orange Grove Avenue*

The post–World War II years
experienced a renaissance in public school construction across
California. The El Rancho High
School won an Award of Merit in
a 1955 awards program of the
A.I.A. and the American
Association of School
Administrators. The plan is that
of a characteristic finger scheme
of one- and two-story buildings,
with exterior corridors. These are
carefully arranged over the thirty-
nine-acre site.

2. Whittier Union High School, 1939–40
William H. Harrison
*Northeast corner of
Philadelphia Street and
Whittier Avenue*

PWA Moderne structures, the
best of which is the auditorium
with its lettering high on each
corner and its undulating façade,
which comes close to the then-
popular Hollywood Regency.

3. Santa Fe Railroad Passenger Station, circa 1889
*South of the corner of
Philadelphia Street and
Lindley Avenue*

This wooden Eastlake-style
station has been temporarily
moved to this site. It will eventually be relocated and restored.

4. Lincoln School, circa 1935
**Attributed to
William H. Harrison**
*Southwest corner of
Broadway and Newlin Avenue*

PWA Moderne, more classically
monumental than the nearby

high school building. One wall of
the kindergarten classroom wing
folds aside to combine garden
with classroom.

5. First Christian Church, 1923
*Northwest corner of
Greenleaf Avenue and
Hadley Street*

A nice minor effort in Beaux-Arts
Neoclassicism.

6. C. W. Harvey House, 1888
*Northeast corner of
Painter Avenue and
Beverly Boulevard*

This two-story Queen Anne
dwelling was one of the first
substantial houses built in the
community. It is picturesquely
located on a hillside, and it has
been carefully restored.

7. Bailey House (The Old Ranch House), 1887
*North side of Camilla Street,
between Painter and
Haviland Avenues*

A one-story, gable-roofed, wood
ranch house with a porch across
the front.

8. Lou Henry Hoover School, 1938
William H. Harrison
*East end of Camilla Street at
Alta Avenue*

The severity of this Regency
Moderne building is lightened by
the concave central bay with
a handsome Wedgewood-like,
curved relief panel depicting
the *Pageant of Education* by
Bartolo Mako.

9. Whittier Post Office, 1935
Louis A. Simon
*Northwest corner of
Washington Avenue and
Bailey Street*

A single-story, rather mild PWA
Moderne building that fits well
into the streetscape of downtown Whittier.

10. National Trust and Savings Building, circa 1935
William H. Harrison
*Northeast corner of
Philadelphia Street and
Greenleaf Avenue*

An impressive example of the
PWA Moderne. Bunched fluted
pilasters to each side of the
entrance terminate in four large,
highly stylized NRA eagles.

11. Wardman Theater, 1932
David Bushnell
7038 Greenleaf Avenue

An Art Deco theater accompanied by seven adjoining stores.
The building was damaged in
the 1987 earthquake. The

exterior façade and the lobby of the theater have since been restored.

12. Charles House, 1893
6537 S. Washington Avenue

A simple, well-maintained, two-story Queen Anne.

13. Whittier College (founded as Whittier Academy in 1887)
Corner of Philadelphia Street and Painter Avenue

The college has been situated on its present site since 1896. Much of the building activities took place in the 1920s, resulting in a group of white-walled, red-tile-roofed Spanish Revival buildings. A 1990 Postmodern version of the Spanish Revival is the Ruth Shannon Center designed by Albert C. Martin Associates. The traditional Hispanic details are scattered as fragments throughout the project—it is almost a ruin, or perhaps a catalogue of parts.

14. Whittier Civic Center, 1955–59
William H. Harrison
13230 Penn Street

a. City Hall, 1955

In this building the architect looked at the Modern through the eyes of Eliel Saarinen. A tower with a stone base sur-mounted by two cylinders dominates the north side of the building. The editors of the *Southwest Builder and Contractor* (1959) wrote that "the Kaibab stone-faced tower at the entrance of the city hall is topped by a beacon symbolizing enlightened good government, and terminates in an illuminated super-structure of concrete and aluminum which can be seen many miles away." Next to the tower is the two-story

lobby, equipped with a floating concrete stairway. The lobby has glass walls at both ends; those to the south open out onto a terrace and garden. To the west of City Hall is the 1988 Centennial Garden (celebrating Whittier's one-hundredth birthday), which is a miniature English garden. In the garden, sitting on a rock by the pool, is Tita Hupp's 1988 sculpture *The Barefoot Boy*, derived from the poem by John Greenleaf Whittier.

b. Whittier Public Library, 1959

The architect has in this building turned to the pavilion forms we associate with Edward D. Stone in the 1950s and 1960s. A curved concrete ramp leads up to the glass entrance, which is covered by a cantilevered thin slab roof. The design (very well carried out) also boasts precast open concrete grilles.

15. Krause House, 1950–52
Raphael S. Soriano
*8513 La Sierra Avenue
(take Whittier Boulevard to Catalina Avenue, left on Mar Vista Street, right to Sierra Vista Avenue, then right)*

A large, single-story, steel-modular post-and-beam house, with most of the walls being infilled with glass, masonry, and corrugated fiberglass. The front wall facing the auto court has a narrow band of windows carried just below the roof. The precise geometry of the house contrasts with the luxuriant planting of the grounds.

16. Skyrose Chapel, 1998
Fay Jones
*Rose Hills Cemetery
(off Workman Mill Road, just north of Mission Mill Road)*

A neglected masterpiece designed by an Arkansan who was a student of Frank Lloyd Wright, the chapel's façade resembles a Stealth bomber taking off. Inside, Jones's familiar ceiling pattern of wooden braces tieing together the walls in an almost Gothic pattern is accomplished here with narrow steel rods giving almost the same effect.

17. Governor Pio Pico Adobe, 1842, 1882; restored, 1913, 1946
Pioneer and Whittier Boulevards, just west of San Gabriel River Freeway (Whittier Boulevard off-ramp)

According to some accounts, this adobe was once two stories in height and contained thirty-three rooms. Hard to believe, but Pio Pico, the last of the Mexican governors of California, was a very successful manager of real estate until financial problems in the 1880s forced him into bankruptcy. The house was flooded in 1867 and rebuilt on a more modest scale, then restored three more times! Nevertheless it remains one of the most credible of the adobes because the present curators have kept the early Victorian furnishings good but sparse, as they probably were in Pico's day. It is a state historic park and is normally open to the public, but it should be noted that the adobe was damaged in the 1987 earthquake and is closed at the moment. Its exterior can be seen, but it will be some time before the building is restored and open to the public.

57 • Santa Fe Springs

This community was founded in 1873 when J. E. Fulton established the Fulton Sulfur Springs and Health Resort. The town was renamed Santa Fe Springs in 1886 and it remained agricultural until oil wells were brought in during the early 1920s. The city was incorporated in 1957, and the basic impression one has is that it is all quite new. While there are a number of recent office and commercial buildings located around Telegraph Road, the real point of architectural interest is the handsome, small-scaled, Santa Fe Springs Town Center.

The site is the northern portion of the Clarke Estate, the lower section of which contains the Clarke House designed by Irving J. Gill. In a beautifully landscaped park are located a group of one-story, concrete-block public buildings. While none of these buildings is architecturally assertive, they do seem to work well with one another and within the context of the park.

1. Santa Fe Springs Town Center and Clarke House
South side of Telegraph Road, between Alburtis Street and Pioneer Boulevard

a. Fire Station, 1959
Marson and Varner
(Marion J. Varner)

This redbrick, "warm" Modernist building was the first in the civic center, and it does reflect a somewhat different architectural image from the others. But because of its scale and the planting around it, it seems compatible with the other structures.

b. City Hall, 1967
William L. Pereira and Associates

In a traditional California fashion, the covered walkway around the building is in fact the corridor for the interior spaces.

c. Library, 1976
Anthony and Langford

A very pleasant building on the interior. Stop and see the ceramic mural by Raul Esparza at the entrance. It depicts events in the history of the community.

d. Town Center Hall, 1971
William L. Pereira and Associates

Another of the Civic Center's small-scaled Modernist buildings.

e. Santa Fe Springs Post Office Building, 1969
William L. Pereira and Associates

Like the other structures in the Civic Center, this building is of concrete block, and is well sited in its landscape.

1f

f. Marie and Chauncey Clarke House (1919–22)
Gill and Pearson (Irving J. Gill)

The sixty-two-acre site of the Clarke House was purchased by the Clarkes in 1914, and they planted it in orange groves. In 1919 they engaged Gill to design this large two-story country house. But with the discovery of oil on the land, they abandoned the idea of using the house as a country retreat.

It is organized around a central patio. The pavement of the patio contains a pattern of Maya hieroglyphs, and several wall planters exhibit pre-Columbian motifs. On the second floor, miniaturized Italian balconies look out over the patio. Sections of the exterior walls contain the imprint of various species of leaves, and somewhere along in its existence, fake *vigas* were added to the upper reaches of

the building. One suspects that the pre-Columbian elements, as well as the leaf patterns, reflect the interests of Marie Rankin Clarke. She was intensely interested in plants and landscape gardening, and was one of those responsible for the development of the Hollywood Bowl.

The Clarke House is not only the largest of Gill's houses that is still standing, but also matches in its quality of design his famous Scripps House at La Jolla (now extensively remodeled) and the destroyed Dodge House in Hollywood. After its purchase by the City of Santa Fe Springs, the house was extensively restored. It is open to the public by making arrangements with the Recreation Services Division of the Department of Community Services, City of Santa Fe Springs.

2. Heritage Park
12100 Mora Drive

Opened in 1987, this park recreates portions of the historic horticulturist ranch of Harvey Hawkins (which dated from the 1880s). You can see the ruins of the ranch house and its accompanying English-style gardens. The Carriage Barn (which houses a museum of local history) and the tank house/windmill have been rebuilt. The beautiful grounds contain an aviary, Tongva/Gabrielino exhibits, and a restored Santa Fe steam locomotive and station. Also try the sandwich shop. For information, call (562) 946-6476.

58 • Downey

Although the city was subdivided as early as 1865 by Governor John G. Downey, like the neighboring communities, it is essentially a product of the post–World War II years. At the southwest corner of Lakewood Boulevard and Florence Avenue is a monument of roadside architecture, America's first McDonald's drive-in restaurant (1953), established before the chain itself developed. It preceded by one year the McDonald's at 563 E. Foothill Boulevard in Azusa, and it was also earlier than the one often mentioned in the Midwest. The design consists of two neon-lighted elliptical arches, which plunge through the typical 1950s shed-roofed restaurant building. Architecturally, this design, in contrast to the later classic McDonald's restaurant buildings, stands midway between popular and serious architecture. Also take note (as if you could miss it) of the impressive well-lighted sign at the corner. It is part and parcel of the entire composition of sign, parking lot, and building.

59 • Norwalk

Norwalk was founded in 1877, and two years later a post office was established. The early commercial center of the community was laid out around Front Street, which parallels the Southern Pacific tracks. A few of the older commercial buildings, including a turn-of-the-century Beaux-Arts bank building, still remain on Front Street, although most of these have been remodeled over the years. At the northwest corner of Pioneer Boulevard and Rosecrans Avenue is one of Southern California's greatest freestanding signs, which announces the Norwalk Square Shopping Center. The very high sign is composed of an inverted, open metal triangle topped by an open metal rectangle (upon which the letters are placed), and finally a series of four upward-reaching loops—it is similar in feeling to the spaceship restaurant at the Los Angeles International Airport. This extravaganza was designed and built between 1951 and 1954 by Stiles Clements for the Pacific Mutual Life Insurance Company, which sponsored the shopping center as an investment. Farther to the north on the northeast corner of San Antonio Drive and Sproul Street is an excellent Art Deco former auto showroom (now used for the sale of auto parts). The building is designed around a low, squat square tower, and it is ornamented (in cast concrete) with horizontal bands of connected chevrons. It dates from about 1930. In Norwalk Park (at Sproul Street and Norwalk Avenue) you will find the Gilbert Sproul House, an Eastlake cottage (circa 1889). The city now maintains it as a house museum.

60 • Artesia

This town, located south of Norwalk, was set out in the 1870s by the Artesian Water Company, although nothing remains from these early years. The character of the community is primarily post–World War II, both in its commercial buildings and in its housing. Like Bellflower to the northeast, the town is located on the Southern Pacific Railroad tracks and is adjacent to the San Gabriel River. The architectural gem of Artesia is the former First National Bank Building (1925) on the northwest corner of Pioneer Boulevard and 187th Street, designed by Los Angeles architect Henry Withey. This Mediterranean building is a simple rectangular box with an elegant three-arched loggia resplendent with doubled twisted Saracenic columns. The community has also done much better than most with its Post Office Building (1970–71; Donald M. Forker), located at the northeast corner of 183rd Street and Alburtus Avenue. It is a low slumpstone building with deeply splayed recessed windows, a low-pitched tile roof, and a wide portal.

61 • San Fernando Valley

Charles Lummis wrote that the Franciscans "unerringly chose from the California wilderness the garden spots, and a hundred years of experiment have failed to find anything better than their first judgment." Early pictures show the San Fernando Mission in pasture land, dependent on the winter rains for life. But the Franciscans dammed the springs near the mission (the dam is its oldest fragment) and then the Los Angeles River. The fertile land bloomed.

San Fernando Mission, Convento

Heavy settlement waited for the Yankees, who carved up the former Mexican holdings. In the early 1870s a Bavarian emigrant, Isaac Lankershim, and his friend, I. N. Van Nuys, both large landholders in northern California, set out the southern part of the valley to sheep ranches and to dry farming in wheat. Charles Maclay, a Methodist minister turned land speculator, bought the northern valley a few years later, thanks to a loan of $60,000 from Leland Stanford, who seems to have trusted Methodists.

Stanford sustained his interest. He made San Fernando the southern terminus of his Southern Pacific Railroad and shipped some railroad equipment there to make the designation look realistic. In fact, Maclay's deal determined the route of the line that broke through the mountains in 1876 and linked San Francisco and Los Angeles, leaving San Fernando a way station between two great cities.

The railroad brought more people to the balley. They settled in old towns such as Calabasas and Chatsworth, both of which had been stagecoach stations, and, of course, San Fernando. But there were new settlements at Zelzah (now Northridge), Reseda, Pacoima, Roscoe (now Stonehurst), Sunland, Lankershim, Burbank, and Glendale. These towns, like the railroad, serviced a magnificent agricultural area, made more magnificent by the completion in 1913 of Mulholland's aqueduct, bringing what at that time seemed unlimited water from the High Sierra 250 miles to the north.

Then, gradually at first, landscape was transformed from wheat and citrus planting to what has been called "Los Angeles's bedroom." Hollywood spread across the Santa Monica Mountains to form North Hollywood. Glendale oozed northwest. Although the scent of orange blossoms filled the air until World War II and even after, the rural idyll was then approaching a metamorphosis into miles of dull tract housing and streets of apartment buildings, shopping centers, and commercial strips that mark it today. Ventura Boulevard was the great commercial strip to the south and the beginning of the main inland route to Ventura and Santa Barbara until the Ventura Freeway took its place in the mid-1960s. The immediate effect of the freeway was to further disintegrate the community, but the long-term effect has been to renew it, especially at Sherman Oaks and Encino, where mediocre high-rise is beginning to obscure the mountains.

The valley became super-respectable in places. In fact, it has been denounced too often. The stately rows of trees on east/west streets such as Sherman Way and the dry winds that sweep through them near sunset evoke a quieter past.

62 • Glendale

Long inhabited by Mexican rancheros, the huge Rancho San Rafael was, before the Yankees came, mainly grazing land interspersed with a few farms that raised wheat, corn, beans, and hay. After the Gringo conquest, the land was subdivided, the southern half comprising what is now Glendale as well as Eagle Rock and part of Pasadena.

With the extension of the Southern Pacific Railroad north in 1873, the town (originally called Riverdale) was planned. Then in 1876, when the railroad was completed to San Francisco, and with Los Angeles County thus open to transcontinental immigration, the community now called Glendale began to grow. It was supposed to grow wildly in the land boom of the 1880s. The obligatory extravagant hotel designed by Joseph Cather Newsom was built, but when the boom collapsed in 1888, the hotel stood finished but empty. After serving as a girls' school and then a tuberculosis sanitarium, it was demolished in the 1920s.

Significantly, it is very difficult to find anything left of Glendale's Victorian past. Its real history begins with the early twentieth century when the Pacific Electric Railroad (interurban) extended its tracks from Central Los Angeles to Glendale (1904). The city is thus well-bungalowed, and in its upper reaches and along main street (Brand Boulevard) it is well-stocked with the architecture of the 1920s that is either being spruced up or demolished, and in some cases replaced with architecture that looks as if it came from the 1920s or wished it had. Most of the newest buildings are clichés derived from old issues of *Progressive Architecture*—banal hives in concrete, or glass aviaries punctured with angular extrusions à la James Stirling. These, along with pretentious street lights at corners and brick pedestrian walkways across streets, make Glendale super-Mod. Oh yes, it has a galleria (shopping mall), which is so successful that it appears that it eventually will consume the entire business district. During the late 1980s a rash of high-rises with their accompanying huge parking garages were built in and around the freeway and upper Brand Avenue. As with most groupings of high-rise buildings, these work best at night.

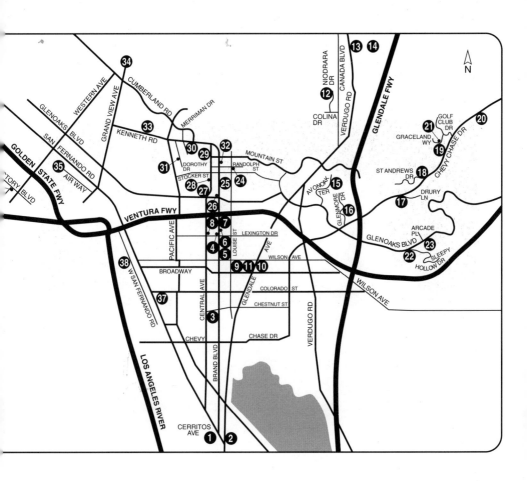

1. Southern Pacific Railroad Station, circa 1922
MacDonald and Couchot
Southwest end of Cerritos Avenue at Railroad Avenue

If there ever was a stage set, this is it! The Spanish Revival appears here at its most cloying. But it still works. It has been beautifully restored.

of misshapen monuments . . . a place where lovers new and old shall love to stroll." In other words, Forest Lawn was calculated to be something more than an architectural experience.

But architecture resides here. Behind the Tudor Administration Building (1918 and later), designed by Charles Kyson and

at Rottingdean. It isn't.

Everyone, we assume, will want to see the enormous painting *Calvary* by the Polish artist Jan Styka, with its accompanying light show and music from Wagner's *Parsifal*. It is housed in the Cathedral/Auditorium designed in 1950 by Roy W. Donlay, with David S. Allison

2. Forest Lawn Memorial Park, 1917–present
Frederick A. Hansen, landscape architect
Entrance just north of the intersection of San Fernando Road and Glendale Boulevard.

Map of grounds available at the Information Booth near the entrance and an art guide at the Administration Building near the Information Booth.

The man behind this famed Southern California inspiration was Dr. Hubert L. Eaton, who planned it as "a great park, devoid

given ornamental enrichment by Austin Whittlesey (who also designed the Kerckhoff Monument), is the Church of the Flowers, adapted (1918) by A. Patterson Ross from the church at Stoke Poges, about whose cemetery Thomas Gray composed his "Elegy." It is the best piece of architecture at Forest Lawn and is often missed. F. A. Hansen's inexact copy of the Wee Kirk of the Heather is here, as is Paul O. Davis's Church of the Recessional, which is supposed to be an exact copy of Rudyard Kipling's home church

as consulting architect.

The main program here is, of course, sculptural, with more copies of Michelangelo's work than exist anywhere else on earth. Also an awful lot of modern Italian stuff, the most arresting being E. Gazzeri's *The Mystery of Life* in the Court of Memory. Just as interesting for other reasons is *The Dream of Peace* by Gutzon Borglum in his Art Nouveau phase.

We could go on, but will add only that in spite of all the generally execrable art, Forest Lawn does preserve a lot of open space.

3. Glendale Chamber of Commerce (now Sons of the American Revolution Genealogical Library and Patio Gallery), circa 1925
600 Central Avenue, at southeast corner of Chestnut Street

A one-story Spanish Revival building whose walls preserve their original burnt umber coloring.

4. Glendale Federal Savings, 1959
Bank Building and Equipment Company
Northwest corner of Brand Boulevard and Lexington Drive

When this office building was erected, it was the biggest, tallest structure on Brand Boulevard—pure 1950s razzle-dazzle. Now look north and you encounter nothing but mediocre to ugly behemoths that are an insult to the magnificent site at the foot of the mountains.

5. Alex Theater, 1924–25
Arthur G. Lindley and Charles R. Selkirk; front added, 1939
268 N. Brand Boulevard

An Art Deco piece that puts the more recent architecture on Brand Boulevard to shame. The central pylon erupting out of curved forms gives dramatic emphasis to the fact that the silver screen is inside. Probably the most salient feature of the building is its lobby, which combines Greek Doric columns with chandeliers that resemble giant heliotrope blossoms.

6. The American Savings Bank, 1986
Skidmore, Owings, and Merrill
Northwest corner of Brand Avenue and Milford Street

The white marble walls and red window trim of this high-rise assault the eye with awful intensity.

7. 550 N. Brand Building, 1987
Hellmuth, Obata and Kassebaum
550 N. Brand Avenue

Postmodern of a sort; a white marble whopper crowned with a gigantic Palladian arch.

8. First American Title Company of Los Angeles, 1987
Leason/Pomeroy Associates
520 Central Avenue

In some lights this high-rise appears to be greenish, in others violet, with blue glass trim around the edges of the windows.

9. Glendale Post Office, 1933–34
George M. Lindsay; J. A. Wetmore
313 E. Broadway

Italian Renaissance with a good interior.

10. Glendale City Hall, 1940–42
Albert E. Hansen
Northwest corner of Broadway and Howard Street

Crisp Classical Moderne with a clock tower.

11. Glendale Municipal Services, 1965
Albert C. Martin and Associates (Merrill W. Baird)
Northwest corner of Broadway and Glendale

Toned-down concrete Brutalism hovering on stilts over a plaza with fountain.

12. Rodriguez House, 1941
R. M. Schindler
1845 Niodrara Drive

The angled roof with its wooden projections protects the rectangular de Stijl composition below. The extraordinary structural gymnastics of the house can be seen fairly well from the street.

13. Paietta House, 1928
Southeast corner of Verdugo Road and Sparr Boulevard

A hillside Spanish Revival extravaganza thrown together by a builder with a lot of money and even more spirit.

14. Leavitt House, 1948
A. Quincy Jones and Frederick E. Emmons
1919 Bayberry Drive

A woodsy late-Craftsman bungalow all on one floor. Variations on the same theme are to be seen at 3068 Chevy Chase Drive and at 1709 Golf Club Drive (see entry #20).

15. House, 1980
950 Avonoak Terrace, north of Glenoaks Boulevard

It is encouraging to see that fantasy is still with us. A small castle.

16. House, circa 1920
680 Glenmore Drive, off Chevy Chase Drive

The stone façade of the house and the garden layout are similar to those at Tujunga, which is one of Southern California's meccas of boulder architecture.

17. House, 1929
*2322 Drury Lane, at
Chevy Chase Drive*

Unsophisticated but very
romantic Spanish Revival,
almost Hansel and Gretel.
Quantities of such houses
abound in Glendale, especially
in the area above the Ventura
Freeway.

18. Derby House, 1926
Lloyd Wright
*2535 Chevy Chase Drive, at
Saint Andrew's Drive*

Built mainly in what Wright's
father, Frank Lloyd Wright, called
his "textile block" construction,
Lloyd claimed it as his own
invention. The design of the concrete blocks was inspired by pre-
Columbian ornament, but the
general effect of the house is
Islamic. Since the road has been
widened practically to the front
door, there is no problem seeing
the house.

19. Calori House, 1926
Lloyd Wright
3021 Chevy Chase Drive

An abstract arrangement of shed
and gable roofs hovers incongru-
ously over the volumes below,
while two massive brackets supporting a small enclosed balcony
create a cave-like entrance to the
house. A very free interpretation
of the Spanish Revival.

20. Fuller House, 1948–49
**A. Quincy Jones and
Frederick E. Emmons**
3068 Chevy Chase Drive

As noted in entry number 14,
this house was a variation on a
theme established by the architects for several houses. Nearby at
1709 Golf Club Drive, the Kett
House (1948–49) preserves its
woodsy Craftsman exterior.

21. Lewis House, 1926
Lloyd Wright
2948 Graceland Way

This stucco structure has been
modified, but the south elevation
is similar to the strong vertical
components of the Millard
House by Wright's father. (Lloyd
was just finishing the studio for
Mrs. Millard at this time.)

22. House, circa 1927
*2414 E. Glenoaks Boulevard, at
Sleepy Hollow Terrace*

A rare use of the Zigzag Moderne
in domestic architecture.

23. Bauer House, 1938
Harwell H. Harris
*2528 E. Glenoaks Boulevard, at
Arcade Place*

A fence screens this house from
the street, but what can be seen
is good late Craftsman in style.

24. House, circa 1905
*Southwest corner of
Randolph and Louise Streets*

A Mission Revival house that
once was a famous Mexican
restaurant, Casa Verdugo, at the
end of the Pacific Electric Line.

**25. St. Mark's Episcopal
Church,** 1948
**Carleton M. Winslow;
Louis A. Thomas**
1020 N. Brand Boulevard

Poured-concrete construction
with the wooden forms indented
in the exterior surface, this
large Gothic-image building
shows the strength of the
Episcopalians in Glendale.
This church was the last one
designed by Winslow before
his death. It was completed
by Louis A. Thomas. Take
note of the Nativity window
and the triple lancet window,
The Te Deum, designed in
1949 for the church by Judson
Studios.

26. Church of the Incarnation,
1951
*Northwest corner of
Brand and
Glenoaks Boulevards*

Both inside and out, this is a
superb period piece of late
Classical Moderne. This building
and its adjacent school, along
with the Methodist church
down the block and the Mormon
church nearby (next two entries),
form a shrine for the Moderne
enthusiast.

**27. North Glendale Methodist
Church,** 1941
Harry W. Pierce
*Northwest corner of
Glenoaks Boulevard and
Central Avenue*

Gothic Moderne. One of the
parishioners said she liked it
because it wasn't "this far-
out stuff."

**28. Glendale Second Ward,
The Church of Jesus Christ of
Latter-day Saints (Mormon),**
1937
Georgius Y. Cannon
*Northwest corner of
Dryden Street and
Central Avenue*

Rather dry and somewhat academic but still a good example
of abstracted Art Deco of
the 1930s.

29. House, circa 1927
*Southwest corner of
Central Avenue and
Spencer Street*

A fairy-tale castle with a lovely
tile band wrapped around
the tower.

30. House, circa 1905
*Southeast corner of
Merriman Drive and
Kenneth Road*

A two-story tribute to the eastern
Colonial tradition.

31. Adobe San Rafael, 1865;
restored, 1932
1330 Dorothy Drive

A one-story beautifully maintained structure with Monterey-
style porch. It is notable that such
buildings evoke New England as
much as they do the West. The
house and gardens are open to
the public at posted hours.

**32. First Church of Christ,
Scientist,** 1989
**Moore, Ruble and Yudell
(Charles W. Moore)**
1320 N. Brand Boulevard

Here, as in his St. Matthew's
Episcopal Church in Pacific
Palisades, Moore catches the
spirit of the denomination—
in this case a kind of Christian
Science smile. When you go
into the pristine white sanctuary, you have a feeling that no
problems really exist. Although
the complex is raised up above
the boulevard and is fenced,
it seems that all is open
and inviting.

33. Senator Madison Jones House, 1902

727 Kenneth Road

A two-story Ionic portico with Adamesque front door is the pride of this house. Tradition has it that Senator Jones's brother was the architect.

34. Brand House ("El Miradero"), 1902–4
Nathaniel Dryden

1601 W. Mountain Street, at the north end of Grandview Avenue

Certainly worth a trip to Glendale. This Islamic folly is supposed to have been inspired by the East Indian Pavilion at the World's Columbian Exposition in Chicago in 1893. It was the home of Leslie C. Brand, the Glendale booster who brought the Pacific Electric to Glendale in 1904. He gave his estate to the city on the condition that it be a public library and park, and so it is. In 1955 "Brand Castle" was converted into a library by

Raymond Jones. This firm also added a harmonious addition in 1969 (Jones and Walton). It is currently used as an art library and cultural center. The grounds are beautiful. The Queen Anne "Doctor's House" (circa 1887), formerly at Wilson Avenue and Belmont Street, has been moved into the park.

35. Grand Central Air Terminal, 1928
Henry L. Gogerty

1310 Air Way

A surviving Spanish Revival curiosity, since the airport has disappeared and has been replaced by factories and warehouses.

36. Two Bungalows, 1935

246, 248 Jesse Avenue, at Victory Boulevard

Tiny treasures of the Streamline Moderne with glass brick and portholes.

37. Joy Company, 1972–73
Craig Ellwood & Associates

4565 Colorado Street

One Miesian box cantilevered over another, this fine example of Ellwood's taste can be viewed best from the Golden State Freeway across the Los Angeles River channel (paved, of course). Traveling north on the freeway in this area you will also get a good view of public art of a sort: huge cat faces that have been painted around drainage ducts emptying into the river.

38. Aeroscopic Building, circa 1935

5245 W. San Fernando Road

A dynamic version of the Streamline Modern, with special pizazz over the main entrance.

63 • Burbank

Contrary to popular assumption, this city was not named for Luther Burbank, the horticulturist, but for a typical Angeleno, Dr. David Burbank, a dentist who was one of the happy subdividers in 1887. Too much fun has been made of "beautiful downtown Burbank." It has a shopping mall that seems to work, i.e., where you see people. It is amusing that almost everything worth seeing is on or just off Olive Avenue, a street that cuts diagonally southwest through the conventional grid that lines up on the Los Angeles River, of all things.

We begin, however, in the northwest, near the very busy Burbank Airport:

1. Memorial Rotunda, 1927
Kenneth MacDonald Jr.
End of Valhalla Drive, just off Hollywood Way, south of the main runway of the airport

One of Los Angeles's extravagant gems; an open-domed temple richly embellished with cast-concrete ornament almost worthy of Berkeley's Bernard Maybeck. This was to have been the entrance to a sumptuous memorial park.

2. Public Service Department Building, 1945
Daniel A. Elliot
Northeast corner of Magnolia Boulevard and Lake Street

If your interest is in Modernist architecture after World War II, then this building is worth a visit. Bland, not assertive, but it was read as Modern in the late 1940s.

3. Adolph's Office Building, 1951–53
Raphael S. Soriano
1800 Magnolia Boulevard, at Parish Place

The post-and-lintel modular system taken to the point where it almost becomes an anonymous building.

4. Bungalow, circa 1920
Southwest corner of Olive Avenue and 9th Street

One of the handsomest and most characteristic "airplane" bungalows in the region.

5. Two bungalows, circa 1920
Northeast corner of Olive Avenue and 9th Street

Indigenous boulder architecture.

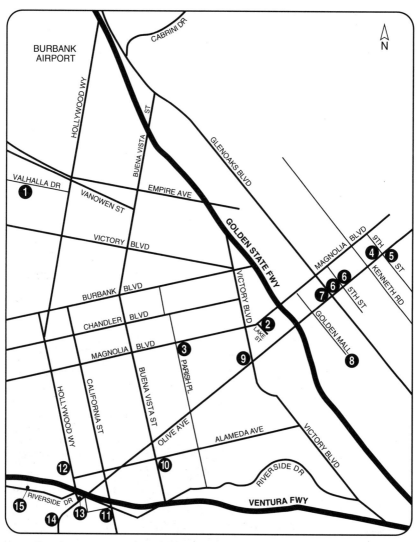

6. St. Robert Bellarmine Complex

Northwest and southwest corners of Olive Avenue and 5th Street

Monsignor Martin Cody Keating, the priest who envisioned this, deserves some kind of medal. Next to God, his hero was Thomas Jefferson. The Jefferson-Bellarmine Elementary School, a rebuilding in the 1930s of the old Holy Trinity Church, is thus partly Neoclassical, supposedly based on Jefferson's stables at Monticello, and partly Moderne. It was designed by Paul Kingsford. The nearby St. Robert Bellarmine Church (1939; George Adams), at the southeast corner of Fifth Street and Orange Grove, is similarly Neoclassical with its portico modeled on the south front of Monticello. Then back on Olive Avenue is the Jefferson-Bellarmine High School (1945; Barker and Ott), a facsimile of Independence Hall with a splendid facsimile of the Liberty Bell in the entrance hall under the tower. All this is followed by a Classical Roman auditorium (1952; Barker and

Ott), inspired by Jefferson's library at the University of Virginia. Three cheers for the architect(s) and the priest who conceived of (and for the church who endorsed) this Fourth of July celebration.

7. Burbank City Hall, 1940–41
William Allen and
George Lutzi
Southwest corner of
Olive Avenue and 3rd Street

A reinforced concrete classic of the PWA Moderne with matching fountain decorated with WPA bas-relief (by Bartolo Mako) on the Third Street side, the whole carried out with great delicacy. The lobby has retained all of its original pizazz. In the two-story lobby (at the stair landing) and in the council chambers are large murals by Hugo Ballin.

8. The Golden Mall, 1967
Simon Eisener and
Lyle Stewart
San Fernando Road, from San
Jose Avenue to Tujunga Avenue

Eisener and Stewart were major figures in the planning world of Southern California in the years after 1945. In this instance they created a wonderful tree-lined pedestrian way.

9. Grist Mill Restaurant,
circa 1950
Southwest corner of
Olive Avenue and
Victory Boulevard

A skirted windmill whose slats, edged with lights, actually twirl and make you nostalgic for those old blue Van de Kamp's bake shops of the 1920s and 1930s.

10. Disney Studio Buildings
Southeast corner of
Buena Vista Street and
Alameda Avenue

a. Studio Buildings, 1939–40
Kem Weber

The original set of buildings: their interiors, including Walt Disney's own offices and bedroom suite, and much of their furnishings were designed by one of America's leading industrial designers of the 1920s and 1930s, Kem Weber. His buildings were reticent, somewhat of a play between a Modernism and industrial architecture. The only outright playful elements were things such as street signs with one or another of Disney's characters on them. Unfortunately, one can see these buildings only from a distance and behind a high fence, but they are there.

b. Disney Studio Office
Building, 1992
Michael Graves

Graves has provided one of his classical-inspired buildings, and it is terribly ponderous. He has sought to make it Programmatic and playful by using the seven dwarfs from Snow White as caryatid figures to support its low gable roof. We wish that somehow this design had succeeded in restoring what Freud called "the lost laughter of innocence," but such was not its fate. Equally pretentious is the formal plaza in front of the building. As with the Weber buildings, the Graves building must be viewed from the street behind a metal fence.

11. Warner Brothers Records
Building, 1975
A. Quincy Jones Associates
South side of Riverside Drive,
at the junction of
Warner Boulevard and
California Street

Natural wood framed in metal

softens the International Style building.

12. Bungalows, circa 1930
300 Block of Hollywood Way

A block-long row of tiny, terribly quaint, Hansel and Gretel cottages with some "intrusions."

13. Warner/Elektra/Atlantic
Corporation Building, 1981
Gibbs and Gibbs
Northwest corner of
Olive Avenue and
Hollywood Way

The building appears to be a vast assemblage of huge Tinkertoy beams, perhaps as a comment on the early Craftsman movement.

14. Warner Brothers Office
Building, 1979
Charles Luckman Partnership
Northeast corner of
Olive Avenue and Maple Street

A Postmodern and very conscious revival of the Streamline Moderne of the 1930s by the firm whose head once ironically participated in the design of New York's International Style Lever House that pioneered the Miesian aesthetic in post–World War II America. In every way the new building is monumental!

15. Bob's Big Boy Restaurant,
1949
Wayne McAllister
4211 Riverside Drive

The design of a fast-food restaurant as a sign, in this case thirty-five feet high. This Big Boy was one of the first group of six built in the Los Angeles area; the others have been torn down. In 1992, over the objection of its owner, the building was recommended for historic designation by the State of California.

64 • Universal City

Tucked in below Toluca Lake, Los Angeles River to the north, and the Hollywood Freeway to the south at the intersection of Cahuenga and Lankershim Boulevards is the old lot of Universal Studios, now turned into an amusement park, with a fringe on Lankershim Boulevard of elegant office buildings by Skidmore, Owings, and Merrill (1970–present). It all began with a black-glass tower and three lower volumes, also black-glass boxes. Then, as if the architects had changed their minds, huge horizontal, brown, travertine marble slabs began appearing as if fragments of a long-lost Schindler design had developed elephantiasis. There is also a new tower, the headquarters (1984) of the Getty Oil Company Building (Skidmore, Owings, and Merrill). One of the most recent additions to Universal City is the Ivan Reitman Productions Building (1993) at 100 Universal City Plaza, designed by Barton Myers Associates. As with a number of contemporary Modernist buildings, this one creates a small townscape within its large open space. From the entrance, a long curved wall leads you through the space. Externally, the building strongly expresses its modular steel-frame construction.

Oh yes, we should mention the restaurants. The Victoria Station (1980; Swinerton and Walberg Company) and Fung Lum's (1981; Tracey Price) are architecturally the most sensational.

An addition to entertainment shopping is Universal City's City Walk, designed in 1992 by Jerde Partnership. It is located off Lankershim Boulevard on Universal Terrace Parkway. This is the cleaned-up retail strip as it should be. It is excellent stage-set architecture, lively and well carried out. In City Walk are a few assertions that read as "real" buildings. One of these is the Panasonic Building (1991) by Hodgetts + Fung Design Associates. This small-scaled building provides the visitor with a good case study of what many contemporary Los Angeles architects were about a decade ago. It is a classic Postmodernist design: the theme of "logical" Modernism asserted and then countered by seemingly irrational elements. The whole of City Walk stands somewhere between the shopping area of Disneyland in Anaheim and Two Rodeo Drive in Beverly Hills. While some critics have reservations about the antiseptic nature of the place, it does work well.

65 • North Hollywood

North Hollywood, the sister of the Hollywood over the hill, owes its existence to the film industry that found the valley photogenic and less hazy than the Los Angeles Basin. Not the faintest trace of Isaac Lankershim's wheat barony remains except for his name attached to a street that has the gall to cut diagonally across a grid firmly based on north/south, east/west axes. North Hollywood had an unusual number of parks and other spaces, but the freeway engineers have taken advantage of almost all of them in order to put through their great works easily. So much for parks.

Not much really exotic or monumental architecture exists in the acre upon acre of tract housing, apartments, and condominiums. But North Hollywood is far from a total loss:

1. North Hollywood Pump Station, Department of Water and Power, 1989–92
Barton Phelps and Associates
11803 Vanowen Street

The street façade of this long concrete building acts as a billboard, containing an abstract map of California and the three aqueducts that feed Los Angeles. A low arched window at the ground provides a view into the station so that one can see the pumps at work. A long, low, glass-and-metal clerestory projects out over the concrete box below.

2. St. Charles Boromeo Roman Catholic Church, 1959
J. Earl Trudeau
Parish Hall, 1938
Laurence Viole
Southwest corner of Moorpark Street and Lankershim Boulevard

The original church was designed in 1938 by M. L. Barker and G. L. Ott. This complex is impressive when viewed from the Ventura Freeway, but the Spanish Revival church itself is not as bold when closely inspected. The ascetic Mission Revival Parish Hall adjoining it is more impressive architecturally.

3. La Caña Restaurant Building, circa 1935
Near the northeast corner of Lankershim Boulevard and Vineland Avenue

An enlarged root beer barrel, a Programmatic image that enlivens an otherwise dreadful area.

4. DWP Building, 1939
Attributed to S. Charles Lee
5108 Lankershim Boulevard

A tasteful exposition of the fragile Streamline Moderne.

5. Methodist Church, 1949
*Northeast corner of
Riverside Drive and
Tujunga Avenue*

A Spanish Revival building with a sort of Mudejar tower ending in two stages that might have been designed by Asher Benjamin.

6. Masonic Temple, 1946–51
Robert B. Stacy-Judd;
J. Aleck Murrey
5122 Tujunga Avenue

Egypto-Mayan with a small dose of 1930s Moderne by California's most passionate pre-Columbian exponent. This structure maintains the tradition of off-beat architecture established by the Freemasons in early California.

7. Los Angeles County Regional Branch Library,
circa 1929
Weston and Weston
*Near the northwest corner of
Magnolia Boulevard and
Tujunga Avenue*

Spanish Revival with a strange nonfunctional porch.

8. DWP, Distribution Headquarters, 1992
Ellerbe Becket
(Mehrdad Yazdani)
*11847 Vose Street, off of
Laurel Canyon Boulevard*

What a strange place to find a piece of good architecture! But the DWP historically has done well over the decades in the building's arts. Note the pumping station next door. Not great, but it tries.

9. *The Great Wall* (murals), 1974–83
Judy Baca
*Northwest corner of
Coldwater Canyon Avenue and
Burbank Boulevard*

In 1972 the Army Corps of Engineers was inspired to commission Judy Baca, a professor of art at U.C. Irvine, to supervise the painting of a mural on the history of California that would cover the west concrete wall of the Tujunga Wash. She began the project by sketching out plans that members of street gangs would carry out in a series of panels. These were then touched up by trained artists. The murals strike a note of celebration in an otherwise lackluster area.

66 • Toluca Lake

This lovely residential section, roughly bordered by the Ventura Freeway, the Los Angeles River, Cahuenga Boulevard, and Burbank, is a real surprise in the valley. The drawing card for the well-heeled gentry coming in the 1930s and later was the lake and the country club. The winding tree-lined streets are up to Pasadena standards. Yet, very little noteworthy architecture exists in the shade of the trees.

The mildly International Style MacFadden House (1948) at 10152 Toluca Lake Avenue near the intersection with Tolofa Avenue was designed by J. R. Davidson as a foil for its "traditional" neighbors. The Elliott House (1951) at 10443 Woodbridge Street, near Strohm Avenue, is one of Harwell H. Harris's late-Craftsman masterpieces. Rather unexpectedly at 4217 Navajo Street, near the corner of Valley Spring Lane, you will find a large Streamline Moderne house whose roof is adorned with a huge antenna obviously tuned to "Buck Rogers in the Twenty-fifth Century." The house was designed by Kenneth Worthen Sr. in 1935. A more recent addition to Toluca Lake's small trove of outstanding architecture is Frank O. Gehry and Associates' World Savings Building (1982) at 10064 Riverside Drive (intersection with Mariota Avenue). It is definitely Postmodern with its false walls, including fenestration. The King's Castle Restaurant (circa 1986) at the northeast corner of Riverside Drive and Valley Street contrasts with the dullness of its neighbors.

67 • Studio City

It is difficult to distinguish Studio City from North Hollywood except that its heart (the word seems inappropriate) is south of the Los Angeles River and along Ventura Boulevard, which begins here. In fact, this section of Ventura marks one of the earliest (1930s) commercial strips in the valley. Its remains can still be seen.

Also, Studio City is blessed with a considerable amount of good to excellent architecture, some of it by R. M. Schindler.

1. Condominiums, 1975
Tom Roberts
12024 Kling Street

Originally this High Tech–image multiple-housing unit, with the second floor served by exterior spiral staircases, was painted white. Appropriately, solar panels now occupy the roof.

2. Ward House, 1939
Richard J. Neutra
3156 Lake Hollywood Drive

Low, sleek, private, its inner complexities are masked by an International Style façade.

3. Hay House, 1939
Gregory Ain
3432 Oakcrest Drive

This modular box, done mainly in wood, looks as if it had just been finished. The International Style at its most beautiful.

4. Showboat Restaurant, 1968
Cahuenga Boulevard near Bennett Drive at the Hollywood Freeway ramp

Well, part of a Mississippi showboat with its pair of metal smokestacks appropriately situated near the Los Angeles River.

5. Centrum Office Building, 1982
Johannes Van Tilburg and Partners
3575 Cahuenga Boulevard, near Multiview Drive

Described as "futuristic," this vast hulk seems somewhat old-fashioned—brutal at the bottom moving into Stirling-like tipped-glass panels at the top. Nevertheless, it acts as a nice foil for the "less-is-more" of Universal City directly across the freeway.

6

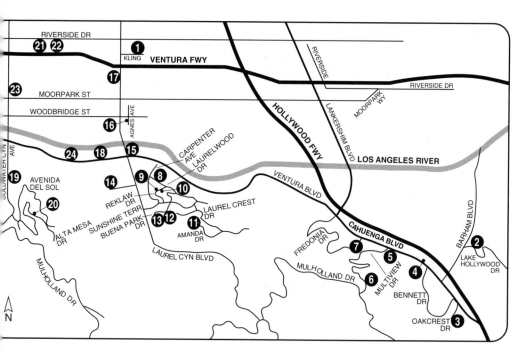

6. Kallis House, 1947
R. M. Schindler
3580 Multiview Drive

This angular cliff-hanger, now sequestered in foliage, is one of Schindler's most dramatic houses.

7. Fredonia Apartment Building, 1964
Raymond L. Kappe
3625 Fredonia Drive, off Ventura Boulevard

An ellipse of glass and stucco set into the hill, this small but luxurious building commands a magnificent view of the valley.

8. Laurelwood Apartment Building, 1948
R. M. Schindler
11833–11837 Laurelwood Drive

Two rows of simple stucco-box de Stijl designs step up the small rise of land. At the time of this writing they are somewhat the worse for wear, but we should rejoice in the fact that at least they are still here.

9. Goodwin House, 1940
R. M. Schindler
3807 Reklaw Drive

Not much can be seen of this small-scaled de Stijl composition from the street.

10. Gold House, 1945
R. M. Schindler
3758 Reklaw Drive

From the gate you will get a good view of Schindler's imaginative maneuvering, both vertically and horizontally, of light stucco volumes.

11. Lechner House, 1948
R. M. Schindler
11606 Amanda Drive

Actually, the best view is from Laurelvale Drive below. Schindler gives conventional builders' forms the stamp of his genius in this tent-like structure. The house was extensively remodeled in 1985 by Paul Sterling Hoag.

12. Waxman House, 1964
J. Barry Moffat
3644 Buena Park Drive

A theatrical essay in vertical and horizontal thrusts.

13. Roth House, 1945
R. M. Schindler
3624 Buena Park Drive

Another "builder's house" whose flaring porch at the curve of the road is a major exterior feature.

14. Rodgers House, 1937
Arthur S. Herbergon Jr.
12045 Maxwellton Road

A handsome brown clapboard Anglo-Colonial Revival dwelling. It is difficult to photograph because of the close-up trees, but it can be seen easily if you walk past it.

15. Home Savings and Loan Building, 1968
Millard Sheets
*Northeast corner of
Ventura and
Laurel Canyon Boulevards*

Sheets' huge mosaic over the door adds zest to an area that needs it.

16. Presburger House, 1945
R. M. Schindler
4255 Agnes Avenue

Not much can be seen, but this house with its high clerestory window running full length was imitated many times by contractors in the Los Angeles area.

17. Campbell Hall School, 1951
Jones and Emmons
4533 Laurel Canyon Boulevard

Modest International Style on a small shaded campus.

18. Medical Arts Building, 1945
R. M. Schindler
12307 Ventura Boulevard

Very chaste, this structure remains almost exactly as Schindler designed it.

19. Saint Savior's Chapel, Harvard School, 1914
Reginald D. Johnson
3700 Coldwater Canyon Avenue

In 1937 this building was moved from the old campus at Venice Boulevard and Western Avenue in Central Los Angeles. It is mildly Gothic inside—supposedly based on a chapel at Rugby. The exterior suggests rural Spanish models. Just across the road from it is a Neo-International Style Art Center (1998) by Michael Maltzan.

20. Stevens House, 1941
Rodney Walker
3642 Altamesa Drive

All you can see are some Mexican pots hanging from a pergola, but this view is suggestive of Walker's romanticism.

21. Dorman/Winthrop Clothiers Building, 1966
**Pulliam, Zimmerman, and Matthews
(Bernard Zimmerman)**
12640 Riverside Drive

A glistening, International Style glass box pushed up against the Ventura Freeway; its street front is almost a classical temple.

22. Riverside Law Building, 1972
**Goldman/Brandt
(Ron Goldman)**
12650 Riverside Drive

Brownstone and wood, this two-story office building is designed around a small court. It looks fine and the lawyers say that it works.

23. Office Building, 1983
Ebbe Videriksen
4400 Coldwater Canyon Avenue

Twenty-eight thousand square feet of English Queen Anne.

24. Kinsey Office Building, 1978
Pulliam, Matthews, and Associates
12345 Ventura Boulevard

A beautifully articulated, brick cut-into box with the front covered in plates of glass set behind metal columns.

68 • Sherman Oaks

A residential development of the 1930s with a commercial strip along Ventura Boulevard, Sherman Oaks was changed by the intersection here of the Ventura and San Diego Freeways in the early 1960s. Sherman Oaks is now exposed to medium high-rise, all of it boring. The process has continued to the present with the same results. Nowhere is the aphorism "change and decay" more apt. In the last few years Smith and Williams' Goldman Medical Building (1948) has been demolished and an awful thing put in its place. The "dazzling scraffito work" on the Fiore d'Italia Restaurant has been painted over, though the façade remains. The best here is elderly.

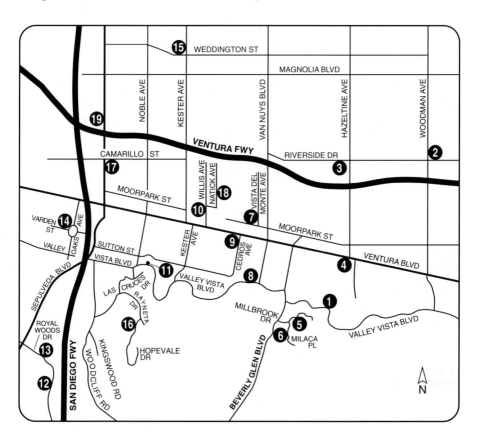

1. Model House, 1935
H. Roy Kelley,
Edgar F. Bissantz, and
H. G. Spielman
14211 Valley Vista Boulevard

This Model House was erected at the first housing exhibition held at the Pan Pacific Auditorium in West Los Angeles. The house was raffled off and moved to this hillside site in the San Fernando Valley. It is essentially a California ranch house that has been brought up-to-date by elements (such as portholes), which we associate with the Streamline Moderne. There have been a few changes to the dwelling, but its original design is still apparent.

2. Notre Dame High School Building, circa 1938
Northeast corner of
Woodman Avenue and
Riverside Drive

Mission style of the 1930s for the building facing Woodman Avenue and Riverside Drive. It is difficult to say what the model was for the depression-period Churrigueresque-style gymnasium that makes a diagonal behind the corner.

3. Sunkist Headquarters Building, 1969
Albert C. Martin
and Associates
14130 Riverside Drive

A huge four-square wine crate on stilts, all in concrete; it works well from the freeway.

4. Bungalow Court, circa 1930
South side of
Ventura Boulevard, just west of
Hazeltine Avenue

A conversion of the Craftsman staple of the Southern California diet to a restaurant and shops. Well done.

5. Schwenck House, 1940
Harwell H. Harris
14239 Millbrook Drive

A barely-visible "Brown and Brown" clinging to the hillside.

6. Dyer House, 1980
Paul Sterling Hoag
4009 Milaca Place

With a steep-gabled roof, this redwood house has the fenestration playing between the vertical and the horizontal. The living room is two stories high with a small balcony library.

7. Bungalow, circa 1935
Northwest corner of
Moorpark Street and
Vista del Monte Avenue

A tiny stucco cottage exhibiting a good checklist of all elements of Streamline Moderne.

8. Mesner House,
1951 and later
Gregory Ain
(Ain, Johnson, and Day)
14571 Valley Vista Boulevard

Everything but the jutting roof is swamped in foliage.

9. La Reina Theater, 1939
S. Charles Lee
Southwest corner of
Ventura Boulevard and
Cedros Avenue

A small Moderne structure with multisided marquee supporting a crown. A little of the etched glass is left in the otherwise disappointing interior.

10. Esplanade Apartment Building, 1967
Kamnitzer, Marks, and Vreeland
4617 Willis Avenue

International Style with a bit of color.

11. Bernstein House, 1985
Rebecca Binder
15119 Valley Vista Boulevard

A highly inventive and imaginative remodeling of a post–World War II ranch house.

12. Barsha House, 1959
Raymond Kappe
3515 Royal Woods Drive

A Modernist version of the Craftsman aesthetics. Note the three stepped-up clerestories on the roof.

13. Handman House, 1963
Raymond Kappe
3872 Royal Woods Drive

A late–Constructivist Craftsman piece lost in foliage.

14. Smith House, 1948
Rodney Walker
15435 Varden Street

Designed in International Style simplicity before the architect developed his strong tendency toward romanticism.

15. Kester Avenue Elementary School, 1951
Richard J. Neutra;
addition, 1957
Dion Neutra
Northwest corner of
Kester Avenue and
Weddington Street

A refinement of the finger-plan open-air school for which Neutra is famous.

16. Willheim House, 1978–79
Charles W. Moore
(Urban Innovations Group),
with Elias Torres and
John Ruble
3944 Hopevale Drive

A plaster-and-wood castle clinging to a hillside.

17. Sherman Oaks Galleria,
1980
Albert C. Martin
and Associates;
Charles Kober Associates,
interior wall
*Southeast corner of
Sepulveda Boulevard and
Camarillo Street*

A vast assemblage of white,
late–International Style forms
stretching for a long city block.

18. Zimbalist Apartment
Building, 1973
B. H. Bosworth
4520 Natick Avenue

This Los Angeles Postmodern
endeavor consists of a large
ellipse of classical columns
and pediments.

19. Castle Miniature Golf
Course
*5000 Block of
Sepulveda Boulevard*

Begun in the late 1960s,
this elaborate development
of Hansel and Gretel forms
and fantasy fountains is a nice
stage set for the off-ramp from
the Ventura Freeway to the
San Diego Freeway.

69 • Encino

The Portola Expedition (1769) referred to what we now call the San Fernando Valley as "Santa Catalina de Bononia de los Encinos" for the many great oaks found in the area. The development of Encino, beginning with the introduction of an alternate route of the Southern Pacific Railroad in 1890, did not banish the oaks, many of which still exist. Significantly, one of the oldest oaks (1,000 years) in the state is on Louise Avenue just below Ventura Boulevard.

If you continue on Louise Avenue and then turn west on Rancho Street, you will have a pleasant drive back to Ventura Boulevard, where at 16661 you will see the Travelers Insurance Building (1966) designed by Howard Lane in a Neo-Streamline Moderne mode. Not far away and just off Ventura Boulevard (turn north on Petit Avenue) at 16756 Moorpark Street is the two-story masonry Greek Revival house (1849) of the Rancho de los Encinos, a state monument of California, open 1:00–4:00 p.m., Wednesday through Sunday. The southern hillside of Encino contains a number of large country houses, almost all of which cannot be seen from a public road. It is possible to catch a few brief glances at Welbourne House at 17128 Rancho Street. This house, including a freestanding mirador tower plus other outbuildings, was designed in 1940–41 by Myron Hunt and H. C. Chambers, who produced, in this complex, one of their really elegant versions of the Spanish Revival, abstracted to a marked degree. Back on Ventura Boulevard at the northwest corner of Genesta Avenue is an intriguing row of Tudor shops that seems to hail from the 1920s.

When you drive on either the Ventura Freeway west of its interchange with the San Diego Freeway or on the San Diego Freeway north of the Ventura Freeway, you will see the spillway of the Sepulveda Flood Control Dam off to the northwest. This rock-faced dam was built between the years 1939 and 1941 as a flood-control point on the Los Angeles River. The dam was designed by the U.S. District Engineer, War Department, in Los Angeles. The total length of the earth-fill dam is 15,444 feet. The spillway and outlet works are an impressive 550 feet long and 50 feet high. The central concrete floodgates and tower are one of the most impressive examples of the PWA Moderne to be found in the Los Angeles Basin. As with so many of the dams and similar utilitarian constructions of the 1930s, the spillway section of the dam was designed through the eyes of the Streamline Moderne—beautiful curved surfaces for the water channels and even round porthole windows for the concrete control tower. In order to reach the dam you must park at its north end, just off Burbank Boulevard, north of Sepulveda Boulevard, and then put on your jogging shorts and prepare for a long run to the spillway and tower that are off limits. You can wander around in the basin and below the basin to obtain a close view of its design.

Since the basin is a vast area of open land, proposals have been and are continually being made as to how it might be further developed. Fortunately, most of these proposals have not taken place, since the area after all is a flood-control basin. One project that adds much to the area is the Donald C. Tillman Japanese Gardens, designed in 1983 by Koichi Kawana of UCLA. The theme is traditional Japanese, yes, but the resultant landscape has a strong Modernist tinge. These gardens are located at 6100 Woodley Avenue. They are not always open to the public, so you had better inquire beforehand about their hours.

Adjacent to the Japanese Gardens is the 1984 Sepulveda Flood Control Basin Reclamation Building (actually a sewage disposal plant), designed by Anthony Lumsden. While this is a strong Modernist assertion, somewhat on the futuristic side in its design, its beautiful scale and detailing relate it to the Japanese Garden, which flows in and around it.

70 • Tarzana
Woodland Hills

There is really no distinguishing these bedroom communities along the Ventura strip. Tarzana has the more colorful name given it by express permission of Edgar Rice Burroughs, whose ranch covered much of the area. Two Modernist buildings of the 1970s worth a visit are the Barclays Bank Building (1971) by Honnold, Reibsamen, and Rex at 18321 Ventura Boulevard, and the Medical Center of Tarzana (1973) just north of it (via Etiwanda Avenue and Clark Street) by Rochlin and Baran and Associates.

Tarzana

1. Fleetwood Center, 1987
Martin and Dovretzky
19611 Ventura Boulevard
A continuation into the 1980s of Los Angeles's tradition of Programmatic architecture. In this instance a huge pink automobile-radiator front with double headlights. We suppose that it is Postmodern?

2. Wilbur Medical Plaza, 1986
Albert C. Martin Associates
5620 Wilbur Avenue

It's nice to see that Tarzana is really getting with it. This Postmodernism is a study in lavender and white. We especially like the planting of palm trees.

3. Shopping Center, 1987
18711–18743 Ventura Boulevard

Very nifty version of the Spanish Revival with plenty of room to park in the central courtyard. Everything is right except the scale.

4. Wall Street Plaza, circa 1988
Robert and Lillian Wall (the owners)
A lot of gables suggest the Tudor was on the minds of the designers, but where is the black-and-white work? As a matter of fact the predominant color is a sort of turquoise and is very unnerving. Will this building weather well?

5. Apartment House, 1976
Tom Roberts
6350 Reseda Boulevard

Though this is perhaps not Roberts' best work, this mildly High Tech assemblage stands for quality on a street of the tackiest apartments you have ever seen. Incidentally, if you have a taste for tract housing of the 1950s, try the streets east and west of Reseda Boulevard.

Woodland Hills

R. M. Schindler's Van Dekker House (1940) may be viewed from a distance at 5230 Penfield Avenue. It is sited on the slope of a small hill. A dramatic shed roof corners the living room and is intersected by layers of low horizontal roofs; the walls are made of wood, stucco, and stone.

An exotic addition in 1984 to the Woodland Hills landscape is the Struckus House (1982–84) just northwest of the corner of Saltillo Street and Canoga Avenue (see right). It plays off several quite different images—that of a delightful eighteenth-century birdcage strung between four oak trees, while its round windows have the feeling of Captain Nemo's submarine. It was designed by Bruce Goff (his only house in Southern California) just before his death in 1983.

The Griffith ranch house (1936) by Lloyd Wright is almost invisible at 4900 Dunman Avenue. In this dwelling, Wright took the theme of the late 1930s California ranch house and imposed a Prairie cruciform plan upon it.

As the Ventura Freeway (Highway 101 West) ascends the hill west of Winnetka Avenue, one is treated to a characteristic varied world of Southern California's architectural images.

To the east on the hillside at the northwest corner of Ventura Boulevard and Del Moreno Drive is a three-story Spanish Revival Office Building (1983). From the Ventura Freeway its large round tower, tile roofs, and white walls look romantic; unfortunately it is not as impressive close up. Then as you proceed up the hill,

Struckus House,
1982–84,
Woodland Hills;
Bruce Goff

Versailles suddenly comes into view via the Château Office Building. This 1985 building located at 20501 Ventura Boulevard was designed by Siegel, Skarek and Diamond. It is a grand Hollywood stage set that visually works best from a distance. Rows of Corinthian columns are matched by classical pediments and balustrades. It looks best at night when it is brilliantly lighted. Still farther along to the west on the Ventura Freeway you see yet another architectural image, in this case what appears to be a half-timbered Medieval building. This structure, located behind 20631 Ventura Boulevard, was an addition to what was a small two-story restaurant building (circa 1970). The restaurant is now an accounting office, and the new building to the rear (circa 1980) contains a ground-level garage and two floors of additional offices. Next door to the east is one of the Victoria Station Restaurants—in the form of a railroad car.

71 • Calabasas
Malibu Canyon Area
Westlake Village

Calabasas

One of the oldest settlements in the valley, Calabasas was a stagecoach stop on the Camino Real route from Santa Barbara to Los Angeles. Only a few simple brick buildings remain from the late-nineteenth-century commercial district and these have been "Disneyized" to create an image of the Wild West that will amuse if not edify. A touch of reality at 23400 Calabasas Road is the beautifully restored two-story Leonis Adobe (circa 1850) with its wooden Queen Anne gingerbread added by Miguel Leonis when he moved there in the 1870s. The back lawn, shaded by one of California's greatest oaks, helps to create a nineteenth-century atmosphere even with the freeway only a hundred yards away. Thanks to the late Catharine S. Beachey and her family, this may be one of the best endowed house museums in the country.

About a mile southwest of Calabasas (via Calabasas Road and Park Granada Boulevard) is a subdivision called Calabasas Park. The landscape of the lake area was designed in 1972 by Julian George. The Country Club (1972) was laid out by Robert Trent Jones. The surrounding condominiums and town houses (1974 and later) were designed by Dorman/Munselle Associates, who chose the Spanish Revival image. Along with the provision of a multitude of trees, the whole enterprise fits well into the landscape.

Almost directly south of Calabasas (Mulholland Drive, then Val Mar Road to Bluebird Drive) are the remnants of the Park Moderne, conceived by Los Angles's early patron of the Moderne and Modern, William Lingenbrink, in 1929 (see Lingenbrink Shops, Studio City) for "Lovers of Modernistic Art," meaning both the de Stijl and Art Deco phases of that passion. He employed European-educated R. M. Schindler and Jock Peters to design houses "along Modern lines." Due to the depression, few of these houses were built. We don't want to encourage you to make a desperate effort to see what is left (for there is little left today) but thought it our duty to record the facts:

1. House, 1931
Jock Peters
*Northeast corner of
Bluebird Drive and
Meadowlark Drive*

Art Deco transformed by later
hands into an English Cottage.

2. Community Building (now a private residence), 1931
Jock Peters
23031 Bluebird Drive

Close to European Modern of
the 1920s with a strong contrast
between the horizontal corner
windows and the vertical fins
and piers.

3. Fountain, 1930
Jock Peters
*South side of
Blackbird Way, south of
Meadowlark Drive*

Art Deco in concrete.

4. House, circa 1931
*South side of
Blackbird Way, south of
Meadowlark Drive*

Remodeled Art Deco.

5. House, 1929
R. M. Schindler
3978 Blackbird Way

Of the three houses Schindler
designed for Lingenbrink at
Park Moderne, one remained a
project and a second was built
and subsequently demolished.
Only this one remains. In scale
it is a single-floor cabin dominated by strong horizontals,
projecting flat roofs and narrow
bands of clerestory windows.

6. Well-house, 1931
Attributed to Jock Peters
*Opposite to
22959 Hummingbird Way*

Angular Art Deco in cast
concrete.

7. Andy Anderson House, 1937–38
Andy Anderson
22912 Bluebird Way

The best-preserved house of this
early period, and Pueblo Revival
to boot. Except for the Southern
California vegetation, it seems to
be in Santa Fe. It was designed
and built by its owner, craftsman
Andy Anderson. Because of the
building codes of the time, it
employed wood-frame construction to imitate adobe.

Malibu Canyon Area

1. King C. Gillette Ranch (presently Soka University), 1929
Wallace Neff
*26812 W. Mulholland Highway, just off of
Las Virgenes Road*

This ranch complex represents one of the high points of the Spanish Revival. In this house, Neff fully captured the spirit of a rural Cortijo that you might come across in southern Spain. You enter the complex through a ceremonial arch into the auto court. Constructed of adobe, the house itself is centered around a central fountained courtyard. Over the years there have been some insensitive remodelings and additions, but the strength of Neff's abstraction of the Hispanic remains.

2. Sree Venkateswara Temple, 1982–88
S. M. Ganapathi
East side Las Virgenes Road, north of its junction with Mulholland Highway

Towered Hindu temples peer out from the trees and shrubs of a small Southern California canyon. The temples with their stepped towers were built by Hindu craftsmen from India. The structures are of concrete and brick, and are covered with carvings of elephants, lions, dragons, and lotus flowers. Their white surfaces gleam in the sunlight.

Westlake Village

In the classic relationship of freeways and suburban development, a number of communities began to develop in western Los Angeles County as Highway 101 was transformed from a two-lane affair to the present six and eight lanes. Hidden Hills, a horse-oriented community, was laid out after World War II by landscape architect/developer A. E. Hanson (California ranch houses, rail fences, horse corrals, and guarded gates). The most impressive single development was Westlake Village, "A new city in the country." The American-Hawaiian Land Company purchased the 12,000-acre Albertson Ranch and engaged Bechtel Corp. to draw up the initial master plan in 1966. This plan was revised the following year by Albert C. Martin and Associates, and once again revised in 1967 by Jack Bevash. The planning ideal of Westlake Village was that it would not be a bedroom suburb; rather it would be a small city within which most of its inhabitants would work, live, shop, and have their own recreational activities.

While there was no strong aesthetic style laid down, the general guidelines looked to Spanish and specifically to variations on the California ranch house. These were later loosened up to include some modern and some other traditional styles. Now after almost forty years (the city officially opened in 1966), you can see the results. It is upper-middle-class, pleasant, and it seems to work well, but it does not project a strong personality. The best aspect of the project is the landscape architecture; the trees and other plants have really taken over, and everything is very well maintained.

While Westlake Village has continued to maintain its stucco/tile-roof Hispanic image in a loose way, there are some inroads. There is a Frank Gehry house in the hills (unfortunately not visible from a public road), and then for those enamored of the Anglo-Colonial tradition, there is the Sherwood Country Club (1991–92) at 320 W. Stafford Road, Thousand Oaks. (This is a gated community, but you can see some of the buildings from the public road.) In the way of public visibility, certainly the most interesting building in Westlake Village is the Prudential Building designed by Albert C. Martin and Associates (1978–80). This late-Modernist building angles itself between two knolls, so that all you see from the freeway is a series of three horizontal bands looking out over a typical landscape of wild grassland studded with native California oaks. The heavy eyebrows over the strip windows do function, for this side faces to the south and west. To the northeast you can see the multistoried atrium space of the building. The Prudential Building is located north of Highway 101 on Thousand Oaks Boulevard, between Lindero Canyon Road and Westlake Boulevard.

As long as you have gone as far as Westlake Village, you might be interested in traveling a few minutes more on Highway 101 to Thousand Oaks—to see a modern "monument," the Thousand Oaks Art and Civic Center (1994) designed by Antoine Predock and located north of Highway 101, off Thousand Oaks Boulevard.

72 • Simi Valley

1. Ulmar House,
1939 and later
Terry Ulmar
4986 Cochran Street

One of Southern California's
folk follies. The owner/builder
has wrought his composition
out of concrete block to create
something that at one moment
is medieval, the next pre-
Columbian.

**2. Grandma Prisbrey's Bottle
Village,** 1959–74
Tressa Prisbrey
4595 Cochran Street

When the Walker Art Center of
Minneapolis organized its exhibition "Natives and Visionaries" in
1974, the Bottle Village was
selected as an important national
example of America's folk tradition (see Esther McCoy's chapter
on Grandma Prisbrey's Bottle
Village in the catalogue for this
exhibition). It's a miniature Simi
Valley folk village, with buildings
of glass bottle walls, dolls (whole
and parts), automobile headlights,
a fountain of old fluorescent
tubes, and so on. The buildings
include a schoolhouse, a chapel,
a thatched house, the "Leaning
Tower of Pisa," and "Cleopatra's
Bedroom." We wonder how long
they will be with us. Needless to
say, this is a folk monument like
Simon Rodia's Watts Towers,
which should be preserved for
future generations to enjoy.

73 • Canoga Park

The early seat of the Orcutts and the Workmans, this area is really "Valley"—meaning that it is given over to tract housing that was the subject of cartoons in the 1950s. If you wish to view this phenomenon, it is best to take the north/south streets off the main boulevards—Roscoe, Saticoy, Sherman Way (magnificent lines of Imperial palms), and Vanowen. You should also see these same areas from the air, for the glint of the sun off the unused swimming pools is quite charming. Some good things on the ground:

1. Canoga Mission Gallery,
1934–36
Francis Lederer
23130 Sherman Way

Lederer, the famous cinema idol of yesteryear, designed this building as stables in the simple, very late Mission mode. But when the city decided to cut through his estate to extend Sherman Way, the road led right past the stable. Mrs. Lederer, sensing an opportunity, remodeled the stables to serve as a gift shop selling Mexican and Californian crafts. In fact, it also serves as a kind of social hall for this part of the valley.

2. W. W. Orcutt House
("Rancho Sombra del Roble"), circa 1930
23555 Justice Street

Orcutt was an early oil baron who bought this property that had years before provided the timber used in firing the kilns producing bricks for the San Fernando Mission. His Spanish Revival house is rarely open to the public and is barely visible from the street.

3. Workman House ("Shadow Ranch"), 1869–72; remodeled, 1935–36
Lawrence Test;
Charles Gibbs Adams, landscape architect
22633 Vanowen Street

The original board-and-batten two-story ranch house was the center of a 23,000-acre ranch. At the time of its mid-1930s remodeling, the site had been reduced to ten acres. Lawrence Test retained much of the informal quality of the original building. But he did add to and revamp the exterior, moving the old carriage house and attaching it to the main house with a long, low garage and dogtrot. The radical changes came about inside where (with the exception of the "Adobe Room") all looked to the Anglo-Colonial Revival of these years. Eighteenth-century wide floorboards were shipped from Connecticut, and the eighteenth-century fireplace in the dining room came from a house in Fredericksburg, Virginia.

In 1961 the house and its site were acquired by the City of Los Angeles, and the grounds were somewhat altered for public use by landscape architect Arthur

G. Barton. The house is really lovely, set in a public park with some of the oldest eucalyptus groves in the state.

4. Great Western Savings Building, 1966
Kurt Meyer and Associates
6601 Topanga Canyon Boulevard

A huge Neo-Brutalist temple in exposed concrete and glass. The projecting roof is supported on both sides of the entrance by two sets of double columns.

5. Bullock's Woodland Hills, 1972–73
Welton Becket and Associates
Promenade Shopping Center, 6000 block of Topanga Canyon Boulevard Canoga Park

The sparingly fenestrated, white slumpstone façade evokes the image of the walls of a Mexican village—on a very large scale, to be sure.

6. Canoga Park Post Office, 1938
Louis A. Simon, supervising architect
Northwest corner of Sherman Way and Jordan Avenue

The building is simple Spanish Revival with Moderne tendencies. Inside is a fine Federal Arts Project (WPA) mural, *Palomino Ponies,* painted by Maynard Dixon in 1942.

7. Crippled Children Society ("Rancho del Valle"), Main Building, 1979
John Lautner
6530 Winnetka Avenue

A wing of this radially planned one-story building has been erected. It has all the drama that we have come to expect of Lautner designs.

8. Platt Office Building, 1981
T. W. Layman
19725 Sherman Way, just west of Corbin Avenue

Parts of buildings formerly on Bunker Hill have been assembled here to give us something more than a new Victorian (Queen Anne) commercial building. This is a bona fide and very welcome folly.

74 • Chatsworth

In an earlier *Guide* we noted that "This old town has, in spite of growth, managed to avoid being submerged." Well, the deluge has made horrible inroads since then, mainly in the form of vast tasteless "mansions" that are a monument to our self-centered culture.

Chatsworth began its Anglo life as a small settlement at the southeast end of the Santa Susana Pass, where it was a stop on the inland stagecoach route opened in 1861 between San Francisco and provincial Los Angeles. The trail down the pass (parts are still visible) was so steep that the wheels of the coaches were locked and timbers hauled behind in order to control the descent. Harried travelers were relieved when the stagecoach line was relocated (1874) along the Camino Real (see Calabasas), but the trail was used by travelers to and from the Simi Valley until the railroad tunnels were built in 1904. Now a freeway to the north of the town communicates with Simi.

The great outcrop of rock known as Stoney Point has often been used as a backdrop for Wild West movies. Earlier it marked the site of Indian settlements. The very active Chatsworth Historical Society is an excellent source of information on Indian lore. It is also the agency chiefly responsible for moving the picturesque Eastlake-Gothic Methodist Church (1904) to the Oakland Cemetery (10000 block of Valley Circle Boulevard) when the church was threatened by progress.

75 • Northridge

First named Zelzah (in 1908), the settlement's current respectable name was suggested in 1935 by Carl S. Dentzel, a founding member of the Los Angeles Cultural Board. Immediately after World War II this part of the valley was sparsely settled agricultural land planted with orange groves and truck crops. In the 1950s a little Modern tract housing (1954; Smith and Williams) was tried near Reseda Boulevard. The block, bounded by Chase Street, Darby Avenue, and Rathburn Avenue, contains the highest proportion of original, relatively unremodeled examples. Obviously, builders' tract housing took off from there.

Also, in the early 1960s Northridge became the seat of San Fernando Valley State College ("Valley State") that in a few years raised itself to a university (California State University, Northridge) that is roughly bounded by Reseda Boulevard, Lassen Street, Zelzah Avenue, and Nordhoff Street (where there is a little visitor parking). Architect Richard Neutra (with Robert E. Alexander)—whose nearby Streamline landship, the Von Sternberg House (1935), now destroyed, may have suggested him to the trustees—designed the Fine Arts Building (1959). The architects of several other buildings tried to imitate his design featuring elongated sunshades, but they succeeded only in reproducing State College Modern dullness. Many of these were badly damaged by the 1994 earthquake and have been removed.

In places, Reseda Boulevard retains memories of its strip development in the 1930s. In fact, just off Reseda Boulevard at 18448 Saticoy Street is a Streamline Moderne diner, Brown's Burger Bar (circa 1940). North of Saticoy Street are several stucco-box apartments. The variety of images possible in this medium is suggested by 7923 Reseda Boulevard, which is Polynesian (circa 1958), and the one at the northwest corner of Reseda Boulevard and Strathern Street, where a large corner mosaic of a winged bull proclaims its Assyrian heritage (circa 1960).

Farther west, on and off Tampa Avenue, are some equally interesting developments. Bullock's Northridge (1972), designed by Welton Becket and Associates, is in the Northridge Plaza near the southwest corner of Plummer Street and Tampa Avenue. It is all roof with its two ends resembling sawed-off pyramids. Southwest of it at 190601 Nordhoff Street (northeast corner of Corbin Avenue) is the black sophisticated Teledyne Systems Company (1968) that Cesar Pelli designed for Daniel, Mann, Johnson, and Mendenhall before Postmodern tendencies struck him. At the Corbin Avenue corner is a tiny grove of orange trees, and across the street is a large wood lot with green fields behind it. South on Tampa Avenue at the west end of Cantara Street there is actually a large barn. But this arcadian bliss is passing, as the large Northridge Hospital (1968 and later) by Rochlin and Baran and Associates attests. This complex, just east of the intersection of Roscoe and Reseda Boulevards, is superficially a spin-off from Louis Kahn's Richards Medical Center in Philadelphia.

76 • Granada Hills Mission Hills

This area of the northern San Fernando Valley began its residential development in the late 1950s, and the newer tracts reach right up to the Santa Susana Mountains. Its green space has been enhanced by golf courses and parks in a manner very uncharacteristic of the normal tendencies in Southern California. To be sure, some of these spaces are cemeteries.

Most of the housing is conventional middle-class stuff, a better-than-average tract being reached by driving north on Balboa Boulevard to Westbury Drive and then west to Jimeno Avenue. Joseph Eichler developed Jimeno Avenue, Lisette Street, Nanette Street, and Darla Avenue. The housing was designed by Jones and Emmons (1963–64) around courtyards.

Mission Hills has as its great claim to fame a Victorian Queen Anne house (1887) moved there from Pacoima. It was designed by Joseph Cather Newsom as one of a group of spec houses. The house, moved to 17410 Meyerling Street (between Shoshone and Andasol Avenues), has a two-story, side-hall plan and exhibits an array of Newsom's ornament in sawed and turned wood.

77 • Van Nuys
Panorama City
Sepulveda

The name Van Nuys is the only thing that memorializes the great wheat rancher. The area has not seen wheat for years. It is dignified by having a branch of the Los Angeles City Hall around which some urban renewal has appeared. Otherwise, there is not much to distinguish it from its neighbors, Panorama City and Sepulveda, to the north. Thus, if you get off the freeway here, you might as well see them all.

1. Post Office, circa 1926
14540 Sylvan Street
Van Nuys

Modest Spanish Revival, but worth protecting against urban renewal. Next door at 14550 is one of those charming Moderne gas stations (Richfield) of the 1930s and next to it is a small, dumpy Classical Revival office building. An imaginative urban designer could give great interest to this group.

2. Valley Municipal Building, 1932
Peter K. Schabarum
14410 Sylvan Street

An eight-story Art Deco office building that certainly stands out in this area of the San Fernando Valley.

3. U.S. General Services Administration, 1974
Lyman Kipp
Southeast corner of Van Nuys Boulevard and Erwin Street

This long, sleek, four-story example of modern classicism in white brick and concrete is ultra-sophisticated for the valley. In case there is a misunderstanding of the relationship between architecture and art, the building's cornerstone bears the following: "Federal Art in Architecture Program."

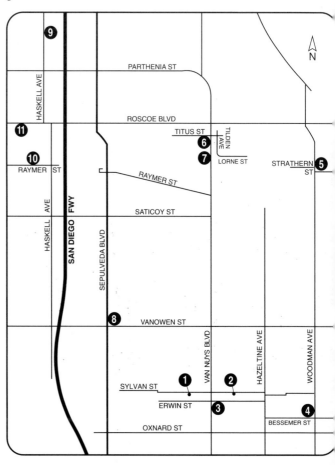

4. House, 1935
*Just behind the apartments
at the northwest corner of
Woodman Avenue and
Bessemer Street*

At least the extremely picturesque Spanish Revival house
was preserved when the front
yard was taken over by progress.
Incidentally, George Brent once
lived here—before progress.

5. The Taos West Apartments,
1972
7924 Woodman Avenue

Pueblo Revival that no resident
of Taos would recognize as home,
but which gets some points for
its outrageous parody of folk
architecture.

6. Great Western Savings
Bank, circa 1970
*Northwest corner of
Van Nuys Boulevard and
Titus Street
Panorama City*

We admire bankers who have the
nerve to go so deeply into the
architecture of fantasy. This is not
great architecture, but it certainly
pokes convention in the nose. Its
spaceship image would not seem
to inspire confidence in banking.

7. Carnation Research
Building, 1952–53
*8015 Van Nuys Boulevard, at
Lorne Street*

An understated, post–World
War II Streamline Moderne
building, if such is possible.

8. Valley Presbyterian
Hospital, 1983–84
Thomas, Bobrow,
and Associates
*Northeast corner of
Sepulveda Boulevard and
Vanowen Street*

The nondescript 1950s buildings
have been included in a new site
plan of Bobrow and Thomas. The
first phase of their plan provided
a new entrance at the center of
the complex that joins two of the
older buildings together. Also,
parking facilities were added. The
entrance and the other additions
express a reserved sophisticated
version of the late Modern mode,
realized in exposed concrete
and glass.

9. Greer House, 1940
Lloyd Wright
9200 Haskell Avenue

Some touches of Streamline
Moderne (portholes) adorn this
building, now easily accessible
since it has been incorporated
with the church next door.

10. Ninety-fourth Aero
Squadron Headquarters
Restaurant, 1973
Lynne, Paxton, Paxton, and
Cole
16320 Raymer Street

French Provincial with a
vengeance, this large farmhouse
at the Van Nuys Airport even has
bales of hay apparently ready to
be pulled into the loft. The only
thing that is missing is the pile
of manure that would give this
marvelous creation complete
authenticity.

11. The Torrington
Manufacturing Company,
1953
Marcel Breuer
(Craig Ellwood,
supervising architect)
16300 Roscoe Boulevard

Incredibly close (a few blocks)
to the previous entry, this long
two-story monument to Bauhaus
modularism stands (perhaps as it
should, considering its attack on
history) in a visual wasteland.
In spite of its age, it looks just
fine—one of the things that
should slow you up on your
way to Bakersfield.

78 • Mission San Fernando Rey de España

The mission was founded by Padre Fermin Lasuen in 1797. Nothing architectural remains from this period except the ruins of the dam that provided a water supply for the acres of wheat and corn. The church looks and is new. The earthquake of 1971 shook the old building so badly that it had to be demolished. The 1974 building, while in concrete, is faithful to the former one, but it must be noted that the previous church was in its turn a rather imaginative reconstruction (1935) by M. R. Harrington of the original. With few hints as to the details of the first building, Harrington set out to investigate the decoration of other missions and imitated what he found in order to give romantic appeal to the new church, an appeal that the good fathers have attempted to render in the 1974 building.

The Convento (1810–22), the first thing that you see when you approach the entrance, is old. It used to look old until the 1974 restoration, which spread from the church to the outbuildings. Stucco was swished over everything (especially exposed adobe bricks) and painted so that the Mission complex looks brand new.

The cemetery, containing the graves of Indian converts and early white settlers, is just north of the church. Across the street from the Convento is a lovely park that, with its fountain, gardens, and statue of Father Junipero Serra, almost makes you forget the follies of contemporary restoration projects.

By jogging south on Columbus, just west of the mission, you will encounter, amid a trailer court and other skulch, the Andres Pico Adobe. Its address is 10940 Sepulveda, well marked. The house was the home of the Mexican who in 1845 leased the entire San Fernando Valley and began its development. In 1873, after the American occupation, Pico decided to remodel the adobe (begun in 1834) in American style, adding Yankee sash, a second story, and other fashionable details. The house has been remodeled and enlarged many times, particularly by Dr. M. R. Harrington in the 1930s when the Spanish porch was added. It is, in the mess of the valley, an oasis of civilization.

Iglesia, 1974
(based on the church
of 1804–6)
15151 San Fernando Mission
Boulevard, just east of
Sepulveda Boulevard and the
Golden State Freeway

A map of the mission complex is available when you buy your ticket to the grounds.

79 • San Fernando

This town is the oldest in the valley. It was settled northeast of the mission that, by a fluke of politicking, is in Los Angeles and not in separately incorporated San Fernando. Its short boom began in 1874 when it was reached by the Southern Pacific Railroad, coming up from the south. The one remaining shred of this Victorian period is the Geronimo Lopez Adobe (1878) at the northwest corner of Pico Street and Maclay Avenue. It is two-story Monterey style with some pretty Queen Anne sawed gingerbread across the gallery. Otherwise all signs of the old town have disappeared, except for the railroad.

Some attempts to invent a Spanish Revival past have been made in the new buildings by the use of stucco walls and tile roofs, but the effect is not as successful as the similar effort at Santa Barbara. An exception is St. Ferdinand's Roman Catholic Church (1949) just across Maclay Avenue from the Lopez Adobe. The church takes its sculptural forms from the simple mission churches, even going as far away as Taos, New Mexico, for its inspiration. It may have been designed by Ross Montgomery.

A typical stone house of the 1920s, so evocative of the picturesque image of the valley, appears on the northeast side of Laurel Canyon Boulevard near Brand Boulevard. The Municipal Light, Water, and Power Building (circa 1937) at 313 S. Brand Boulevard near the corner of Pico Street is a semiprecious gem of the Streamline Moderne. But don't go out of your way to see the oldest town in the valley.

St. Ferdinand's Roman Catholic Church

80 • Newhall
Saugus
Valencia

In your eagerness either to enter or to leave Los Angeles, you may forget that a good deal of history, mainly transportation and engineering, took place in this area. Beside you on the Golden State Freeway is "The Cascade" that in 1913 marked the termination of William Mulholland's Los Angeles Aqueduct, which brought water from the Owens River Valley so that Los Angelenos would never be thirsty—or so it seemed at the time. Near this place is an off-ramp marked "The Old Road," meaning the famous Ridge Route that was opened in 1915 and that, in spite of its curves, cut off many miles between Los Angeles and San Francisco. Much of the concrete is still there, but the roadhouses and gas stations are all gone.

By turning northeast on the Antelope Valley Freeway, you will soon come to the Placerita Canyon State Park and Nature Study Center. Here you can see the "Oak of the Golden Dream" under which Francisco Lopez discovered in 1842 the first gold to be found in California in commercial quantities. Architecturally, the award-winning Nature Center (1973), a collection of low hipped-roof buildings designed by Richard L. Dorman and Associates, is more rewarding.

Turn back (west) on the Sierra Highway, then north on San Fernando Road. In a few hundred yards you will see a State Landmark sign directing you to the first commercial oil refinery (1876) in California, a plausibly restored group of buildings in a strangely picturesque setting. Continue north on San Fernando Road to the William S. Hart Park, once the estate of the famous cowboy movie star. The original ranch house (circa 1910) is a log cabin, but by climbing the hill you will come upon the mansion (1925; Arthur Kelly), which will delight followers of the Spanish Revival.

Back to San Fernando Road and north again at Drayton Street you will come to the site of the bracketed Southern Pacific Railroad Station (circa 1900) that unfortunately burned a few years ago. This site should remind you that in 1876, about ten miles east of this place, the last section of track was completed on the railroad link between Los Angeles and San Francisco, thus joining with the transcontinental railroad to bring thousands of people to Southern California, eventually transforming Los Angeles from a sleepy village into questionable urbanity.

Heading north again on San Fernando Road, you will almost immediately see Magic Mountain Parkway. Turn left on it and then left again on Valencia Boulevard and then again on Newhall Avenue, which becomes McBean Parkway. To the south of this road is the community of Valencia, which you may wish to visit because it was planned

(1966) by Thomas L. Sutton Jr. and Victor Gruen Associates as a new town (like Westlake Village and Irvine). It was to be, according to the descriptive literature, "a semi-contained urban element" with its own industry as well as retail centers and housing. The promoters expect a town of 150,000 people by the year 2020. The housing (designed by Barry Berkus, Maxwell Starkman and Associates, Edward C. Malon, and others) ranges from garden apartments to single-family dwellings and, in spite of its essential dullness, works out better than most project housing because of excellent planning and landscaping.

Near the intersection of the McBean Parkway with the Golden State Freeway, you will see the entrance to the California Institute of the Arts, whose main buildings were designed by Ladd and Kelsey (1969–70) in brown slumpstone and concrete. One would expect better architecture considering the competence of the architects and the wherewithal of the Walt Disney estate that is behind it financially, but the architecture is only a cut above that of the tract housing nearby.

After looking around Valencia, cross under the Golden State Freeway (Highway 5) to Magic Mountain Parkway. Go to the end (west), and you will arrive at the Magic Mountain Amusement Park (now Six Flags Magic Mountain) designed in 1970 by Thomas L. Sutton for the Newhall Land and Farming Company, the developer of Valencia. After establishing clearly where you have parked your car in relation to the "auto gate," go on to the ticket counter and entrance. Until 1982 you entered through the gates of a French chateau and moved ahead into a formal garden with a fountain and geometrical planting. Visually this arrangement helped to bring a sense of order before you plunged into the exuberance of the park. Unfortunately this has all been changed. An entrance designed in serious High Tech provides no joy or tone of fantasy.

The same seriousness pervades the High Tech image of the Texas Instruments Computer Discovery Center (1982). Notwithstanding these recent movements away from the original lightheartedness of Magic Mountain, its glory remains in landscaping designed by Emmet Wemple and Associates, who also designed the old French forecourt. The architecture runs the full range from the Asian (perhaps it is Japanese, but who can be sure) to German, Swiss, and English Medieval to American Colonial and Victorian. And California's own tradition of the Mission Revival can be seen in the Forecourt of the Revolution. The Monterey style is featured in the Holiday Bazaar. Magic Mountain is far more informal and easygoing than the organized environment of Disneyland, its rival to the south.

81 • Palmdale
     Lancaster

This country is hardly an architectural oasis. Lancaster's Western Hotel (1874), a plain two-story building with columned porch at 557 W. Lancaster Boulevard, is a remnant of pioneer days. There are several PWA Moderne public buildings in Lancaster, including the Post Office Building (1940; Louis A. Simon; Neal A. Melick) at 567 W. Lancaster Boulevard, and the former School Building (circa 1937) now used as offices for the Lincoln School District. The Post Office Building, together with the other mildly PWA Moderne civic buildings, has been placed (1993) on the National Register of Historic Places. The school is located on Cedar Street, between New Grove Street and Lancaster Boulevard. Beyond Palmdale, about fifteen miles along Avenue O, you will come to Avenue 170 East. Go north on it and then west on Avenue M. Almost immediately you will come upon the Antelope Valley Indian Museum (1928), a simple wooden building intended by its creator, H. Arden Edwards, to embody elements of Indian design, but tending to look more like a Swiss chalet than any example we know of Native American architecture. The collection of Indian artifacts, particularly southwestern rugs, is excellent. The Kachina Hall will attract the Craftsman enthusiast.

82 • La Crescenta Valley

If you have visited Newhall, Valencia, and Magic Mountain and wish to return to Los Angeles by a different route, exit from the Golden State Freeway (Highway 5) onto the Foothill Freeway (Highway 210) (Pasadena signs!). You thus skirt the eastern side of San Fernando and eventually, after some beautiful, lonely, and almost desert landscape, enter Sunland, from which you can make an amusing diversion south on Sunland Boulevard to Sun Valley.

Actually, Sun Valley is closer to the Golden State Freeway, so you can make your choice between it and the Foothill Freeway. If you choose the former, exit at Sunland Boulevard and go north to the city of Sunland. Thereafter, you should probably stay on Foothill Boulevard visiting the towns as we have listed them. You will come out at Pasadena, as you will if you take the Foothill Freeway. A general map of the area will make all this clear and also, we believe, make you sympathize with our problems of establishing a rational plan for visiting the Los Angeles area.

If you want to get the feel of working-class Southern California in the 1920s and 1930s, you cannot get it anymore in Hollywood. The epicenter of "Old Wide-Open Southern California" is in the Sunland-Tujunga area. It is hot, dusty, and occasionally smog-ridden, but with exceptions that you must learn to cancel out (especially along Foothill Boulevard), here are almost the last of the freewheeling communities with close ties to nature, golden hills, and monuments to dreams. For instance, the Villa Rotunda (circa 1955) at 8618 La Tuna Canyon Road. What is it? Why is it round?

The delight of the area is the quantity of its boulder architecture. The house (circa 1922) at 8642 Sunland Boulevard near Olinda Street is a good introduction. But the mecca for boulder enthusiasts is the old town of Roscoe (now Stonehurst). Here forty or so boulder bungalows were built, according to the story, for $100 apiece, some say by Indian labor. You can see that we are hedging on facts. There is disagreement about them as there is about the English colony that is supposed to have lived here and the movie stars that are supposed to have vacationed in Roscoe with the idea of "roughing it." Stick to what you see along Stonehurst Avenue and Sheldon, Thelma, Allegheny, and Wicks Streets.

AN ARCHITECTURAL GUIDEBOOK TO LOS ANGELES •

Going east along Sunland and Foothill Boulevards you will encounter more delights, although, we are sorry to say, a great many have disappeared in recent years. But venture into the side streets. Try going north on Orovista Avenue to Hillrose Circle. The whole area is delightful, but it is simply preparing you for Tujunga.

One major relic remains in the area. The Old Vienna Gardens (now the Villa Cinzano Restaurant), located at 9955 Sunland Boulevard, is an unexpected Hansel and Gretel house in this seeming wasteland. It was built over a period from 1928 to 1937. Also notice the August Furst Castle, situated high above the restaurant (at 9983 Johanna Avenue). The one major public monument of La Crescenta Valley area is the Hansen Dam and its flood basin, behind which is a large park-like recreation area. The dam was designed by the U.S. Engineering Department, and was constructed between 1938 and 1940. At the time it was built, the compacted earth structure was the "largest of its type in the world." The centerpiece of the dam is the handsome streamline spillway and outlet works. This monolithic concrete structure of spillway, gates, and tower is 285 feet in length. From a purely aesthetic point of view this dam and the nearby Sepulveda Dam are two of the most impressive structures in the valley. To reach Hansen Dam and its spillway, take the Osbourne Street off-ramp and proceed southwest to the parking and picnic area. Then prepare yourself for an enjoyable long hike along the top of the dam to the spillway.

83 • Tujunga

Parts of the Tejunga and La Cañada ranchos were subdivided in the boom of the 1880s, and it was thought that the picturesque acreage that now constitutes Sunland and Tujunga would take off economically. Soon, however, most of the town plots were "sold for taxes." Another try at building came in 1907 when M. V. Hartranft, whose family had speculated in land in other parts of Los Angeles County, attracted a little group of Socialists with his slogan, "A Little Land and a Lot of Living," thus settling "La Ciudad de los Terrenitos," or the "Little Landers." Their boulder clubhouse, whose cornerstone was laid on April 12, 1913, is still at 10116 Commerce Avenue and has been restored. The boulder houses, which until the 1971 earthquake made the town very picturesque, date from the 1920s. Some remain, along with their wonderful boulder retaining walls. Several of them are spectacular. We have tried to list the best, but we have undoubtedly missed some. The town is best seen by walking along Commerce, Samoa, Pinewood, and Fairgrove Avenues. It is easily as funky as Venice West. But see it soon; slummy apartment houses are rapidly taking the place of stone follies. The end of camp ambience is near.

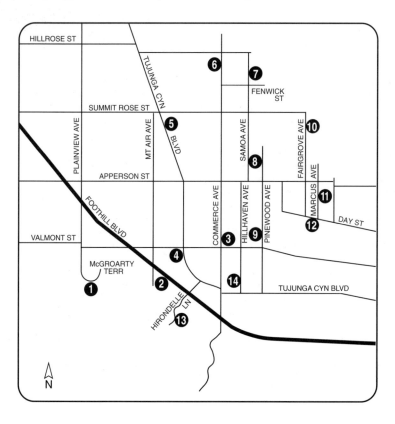

3

1. McGroarty House, 1923
Arthur B. Benton
7570 McGroarty Terrace,
south of Foothill Boulevard
at the end of
Plainview Avenue

The architecture is not much,
even with the leaded art-glass
windows given to John Steven
McGroarty, once Poet Laureate
of California, by Frank Miller,
the host of the Mission Inn at
Riverside where McGroarty
wrote his once-famous *Mission
Play* (the inspiration, incidentally, for the building of the
Mission Playhouse in San
Gabriel). This house took the
place of an earlier dwelling that
burned. The original furniture
that survived is as delightfully
bombastic as the play.

2. Harris House, circa 1910
George Harris
7320 Foothill Boulevard,
east of Mount Air Avenue

Perched just below street level,
this bungalow is remarkable for
still existing on a street that has
gone honky-tonk commercial.
Harris came west as a representative of an eastern publishing
house. He doffed his Prince
Albert, donned corduroy vest and
knickers, and began making curious garden furniture in what
must be called the "Rustic
Baroque" style. A suggestion of
this is the concrete railing along
the walk (bridge) to his house.
His most important piece of
architecture is the next entry.

3. Bolton Hall (now known as
Tujunga City Hall), 1913
George Harris
10116 Commerce Avenue

If you think that the exterior
of this boulder Mission-style-
influenced building is extraordinary, you should see the
wood-beamed interior! It was
originally the clubhouse for the
"Little Landers" and was called
Bolton Hall for the New York
Socialist of the same name.

4. "Blarney Castle,"
circa 1925
10217 Tujunga Canyon Road,
at the southwest corner of
Valmont Street

A stucco two-story house with
a round tower that now guards
the parking lot of a large shopping center.

5. House, circa 1925
10428 Tujunga Canyon Boulevard, south of Summitrose Street

A long, low boulder house enhanced by new boulder walls in the front.

6. Weatherwolde Castle, 1928
Dumas
10633 Commerce Avenue, near the southwest corner of Hillrose Street

A stucco suggestion of Normandy.

7. Reavis House, 1923
10620 Samoa Avenue, north off Fenwick Street

A boulder gem built for a blind man who was attracted to Tujunga by McGroarty's *Mission Play.*

8. House, circa 1925
10142 Samoa Avenue

A fine boulder house in the Craftsman tradition.

9. Tujunga American Legion Hall, circa 1928
10039 Pinewood Avenue

Egyptoid and Art Deco combined. A real surprise in bungalow-land.

10. House, circa 1925
10420 Fairgrove Avenue

A very tidy Craftsman boulder structure.

11. House, circa 1925
10226 Marcus Avenue

This towered boulder house with its matching garage is really delightful; apparently it was originally a schoolhouse.

12. House, circa 1915
6915 Day Street

Not one of the best boulders (upper clapboard story added) but interesting because it is supposed to have been a Wells Fargo station. Hard to believe, but it's part of local lore.

**13. Park House
("The Rock of Ages House"),**
circa 1925
D. M. Denton
9920 Hirondelle Lane

Self-explanatory; very nicely designed.

**14. Newcomb House
("El Roble"),** 1910, 1922
**J. J. Blick;
The Postle Company**
9725 Hillhaven Avenue

A good Craftsman house beautifully sited on a hillside.

84 • La Crescenta

This community, settled in the 1880s, is still unincorporated. It continues the commercial strip along Foothill Boulevard, with fine residential areas on each side. Try Briggs Avenue and the streets east of it. Orange Cove Avenue with its shingle and boulder Craftsman architecture (numbers 2301, 2321, and 2346) is good.

La Crescenta also has an extremely picturesque boulder church—St. Luke's of the Mountains (1924; S. Seymour Thomas)—at the northeast corner of Foothill Boulevard and Rosemont Avenue. La Crescenta's high-toned ruggedness is nowhere better asserted than in this church, all done up in boulders. Significantly, the idea for it was sketched by plein air painter S. Seymour Thomas, and then in 1924 the plans were drawn by architect Harry Peters. The effect of the building, even today when much of the area has become suburbanized, is a picture-postcard evocation of the rural idyll.

St. Luke's of the Mountains, 1924; S. Seymour Thomas

85 • La Cañada–Flintridge

Flintridge and La Cañada, both subdivided in 1920, were joined and became incorporated as a city in 1976. Both parts are very upper-middle-class. Montrose to the south is a step lower on the social ladder.

1. House, circa 1927
*2143 Montrose Avenue, at
Rincon Avenue*

The Craftsman house is all right but the tile is better.

**2. Wallace House
("El Nido")** 1911
Arthur B. Benton
End of Castle Knoll Road

A vaguely Medieval Venetian folly built as a summer home for a lieutenant governor. It is known locally as the "Pink Castle."

3. Lewin House, 1962
Gregory Ain
15310 Jessen Drive

Very simple International Style, barely visible from the street.

**4. Lutheran Church
in the Foothills,** 1965
Culver Heaton
*Foothill Boulevard,
on the southeast corner of
El Camino Corto*

It is the campanile rather than the church that is visually striking. The bland shaft is topped by a huge sculpture by Perle Pelzig, characterizing the people looking toward the foothills.

5. House, 1927
*Southeast corner of
Alta Canyada Boulevard and
Hacienda Drive*

This splendid Spanish Revival house has the quality of a John Byers design, though it is not by him. There is a splendid Byers

house, the Robbins House, at 717 Hillcrest Avenue (1931), but it is very difficult to see from the road. Note the fine garden. In fact, almost all of Alta Canyada is beautifully landscaped.

**6. Lanterman House
("El Retiro"),** 1915
Arthur L. Haley
4420 Encinas Drive

Lanterman was a distinguished

California legislator whose family home was a period-revival affair on West Adams near central Los Angeles. The Lantermans apparently built this Craftsman house in the extreme suburbs as a retreat from the city. Eventually they moved their refined furniture to their country residence. Almost all of it, Chippendale and other revivals, has been retained and contrasts wildly with the

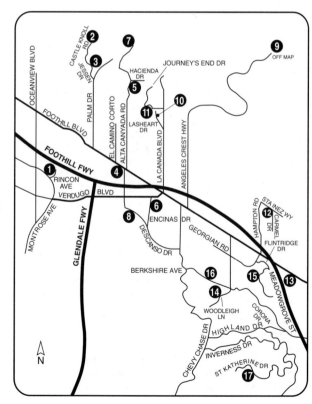

woodsy Craftsman interiors.

The house is open to the public. Call (818) 790-1421 for times.

7. Degnan House, 1927
Paul R. Williams
5200 Alta Canyada Road

The Degnan House is one of Paul R. William's really fine versions of the Mediterranean—part Spanish, part Italian. The main block of the house is quite formal, though modest in scale. This formality is countered by the picturesque siting of the building on the hillside and by low pergolas and walls to each side. For those interested in California's Spanish Revival of the 1920s, this house is a must.

8. Descanso Gardens,
1937, 1941 and later
1418 Descanso Drive

In 1937, E. Manchester Boddy, editor of the old *Los Angeles Daily News,* bought the 165 acres on which the gardens are now situated and began setting out camellias in a forest of live oaks. When Japanese-American nurserymen and their families were sent to relocation camps in 1941, Boddy was able to acquire thousands of camellias and azaleas. The county bought the gardens in 1953, and they are now a branch of the county arboretum. In 1966 the Descanso Guild commissioned Whitney Smith and Wayne Williams to design a Japanese-inspired teahouse. Here you may sip tea while you take in the natural beauty and listen to the mockingbirds sing their hearts out. Open year round during the day.

9. Mount Wilson
Observatory, 1913
Daniel H. Burnham
and Company
*Mount Wilson Road, off
Angeles Crest Highway*

One of the last buildings designed by Burnham, completed after his death.

10. House, 1945–48
J. R. Davidson
4756 Lasheart Drive

The Moderne lamps on the gateposts are about all that you can see.

11. Gainsburg House, 1946
Lloyd Wright
1210 Journey's End Drive

A variation on the Usonian houses, but more theatrical than his father's work.

12. Cottage, circa 1925
*Southwest corner of
Santa Inez Way and
Carmel Road*

A rustic hunting lodge gone bungalow. Notice the magnificent planting. In fact, the streets in this area have been planted with a variety of trees, all of which have flourished. The houses, mostly small, have a great deal of charm.

13. Flintridge Country Club
(now St. Francis High
School), 1921
Myron Hunt and
H. C. Chambers
*Just east of the Foothill
Freeway off-ramp at the inter-
section with Daleridge Road*

The hacienda section, more Mexican than Spanish, of the club still exists with its long portal.

14. La Cañada Thursday Club,
circa 1930
Henry Newton and
Robert Murray
4440 Woodleigh Lane

Beautifully scaled Spanish Revival.

15. House, 1928
Myron Hunt and
H. C. Chambers
535 Meadow Grove Street

Georgian Revival and livelier than most of Hunt's work. Important houses by Hunt, Paul Williams, Wallace Neff, and the rest of the Pasadena crowd are in this section of town but, as in Bel Air, they have been landscaped out of sight.

16. Mitchell House, 1924
Paul R. Williams
640 Berkshire Avenue

Paul R. Williams designed a number of the houses built in the early 1920s in Flintridge-La Cañada. He employed three different images for these houses: the English Tudor, the Spanish, and the Anglo-Colonial. The Mitchell House is Anglo-Colonial, a white clapboard dwelling picturesquely situated on a gentle hill looking to the north.

17. The Flintridge Biltmore
(now Flintridge Sacred Heart
High School), 1927
Myron Hunt and
H. C. Chambers
*St. Katharine Drive
(take Corona Drive off
Highland Drive and
follow the signs)*

More impressive from the valley of the Arroyo Seco than up close, this is an ample but dry building in Hunt's usual Spanish manner. The Biltmore saw a few good years. Then the Great Depression and the building's remoteness from anything did it in, but not before the management had commissioned two huge pictures (1929) for the lobby by George Fisher and Desmund Rushton. One is rather strange (considering the context): a group of Plains Indians on horseback. The other depicts a highly diverse procession of people in their national costumes, moving toward the then-new Los Angeles City Hall.

86 • A Note on Route 66—San Gabriel Valley

The "Main Street of America" of old still plies its way east along Colorado Boulevard through Pasadena and Arcadia, connecting with Huntington Drive, which becomes Route 66 until Huntington suddenly becomes Foothill Boulevard just west of Azusa, when it then joins Alosta Avenue. When Alosta runs into the City of San Dimas, it becomes Foothill Boulevard again and with that name continues to Claremont and on through Cucamonga, beyond the Los Angeles County line.

For many years the camp ambience of roadhouses, gas stations, and motels seemed to have passed, but the nearby Foothill Freeway that should have been the final blow to America's Main Street has ironically brought Route 66 back, not as a highway but as an access road. Almost every single building dating from as far back as the 1920s has been spruced up and in some cases recycled. In fact, it is fun to try to pick out the old places from the cheap modern horror that surrounds them.

Significantly, it is at San Dimas that you easily begin to pick up the once-forlorn monuments to the early days of transcontinental driving. This area was decaying, but it is now coming back with new motels and restaurants lined along the right-of-way of the old road.

San Gabriel Valley

The San Gabriel Valley is roughly bounded by the San Gabriel Mountains to the north, the desert to the east, the Whittier Hills to the south, and the Arroyo Seco to the west. Not all of it is covered here because the Los Angeles County line cuts down the middle of it. It is an area of many towns, a large number founded by land speculators attached to the Southern Pacific and Santa Fe Railroads. Some towns still show their nineteenth-century origins in their display of Victorian architecture, but instead of the citrus groves and vineyards that once surrounded them, you see acres and acres of tract housing, most of it tedious. It has come to resemble the San Fernando Valley except that you see few trees outside the boundaries of the old towns. Also, sadly, the San Gabriel Valley, particularly the eastern side, often gets the worst smog in the county.

87 • Pasadena

It is said that Pasadena means "Crown of the Valley" in the language of the Chippewas, an Indian tribe that never set foot in the area. The land on which the city was built was first occupied by Gabrielino Indians and then by the Spanish and the Mexicans who built several adobes. (One, Adobe Flores, still exists in South Pasadena.) The history of Yankee settlement really began in 1874 when the San Gabriel Orange Grove Association acquired most of the land of the old Rancho San Pasqual, east of the Arroyo Seco to the present Fair Oaks Avenue, and sold it to prospective citrus growers.

The Indiana Colony, as it was called, was actually a group of land speculators, most of whom never came to Pasadena, but the town flourished in the gently rolling land dotted with clumps of oaks and sycamores and later orange and olive groves. But the surge of growth came in the 1880s and 1890s when the Southern Pacific and Santa Fe Railroads entered the town, and, with the aid of local boosters, the farming community turned into a fashionable winter resort with large hotels on the scale of those at Atlantic City, Miami, and the White Mountains of New Hampshire. The grandest hotel was the Raymond, situated on a small hill just inside the South Pasadena boundary. But the Green Hotel near the Santa Fe Station, whose location was not as picturesque, was so popular that it had to be enlarged three times, the second time to a site on the other side of the street and connected to the older building by a picturesque "Bridge of Sighs." The Maryland, the Wentworth (now Ritz Carlton–Huntington), and the Vista del Arroyo were other hotels patronized into the 1920s and beyond. The Huntington is still a very popular Pasadena institution.

The resort atmosphere was of great significance for Pasadena's architectural history. It drew conservative and often very rich immigrants, some of whom eventually decided to become permanent residents of a city that could provide plenty of sun and a cog-railway up past the Echo Mountain House to Mount Lowe. A local legend has it that in 1900 there were fifteen millionaires on Orange Grove Avenue (now Boulevard). Naturally these people desired mansions in the latest eastern styles and especially those that easterners thought most suitable for the West. Architects such as Harry Ridgeway, A. B. Parkes, and Frederick L. Roehrig made sure that supply kept up with demand. Lawrence Test, an architect who grew up in this environment of building, answered when he was asked how he happened to go into architecture: "Why, there was never any other thought in my mind about my profession. With so much building going on, how could I think of anything else but architecture?" And he added slyly, "I wonder what would have become of me if I had been raised in Glendale or Monrovia!"

From the beginning, Pasadenans were partisans of cultural uplift. The Orange Grove crowd was drawn to the Valley Hunt Club, from which they set out to catch more coyotes than foxes. They founded that excessively famous Pasadena institution, the Tournament of Roses, whose parade once ended with a chariot race à la Ben Hur rather than the present football game. Another group, highly educated and usually residents of the area around the picturesque Arroyo Seco, created the Coleman Chamber Music Association (1904) and the Pasadena Playhouse Association (1917), two pillars of Pasadena culture.

The abundance of money meant that Pasadenans would have expensive homes. What is just as interesting is that on Orange Grove these people would engage in an elaborate Victorian Baroque street planning with traffic circles at major intersections and a parkway in the center in the shape of two giant lozenges linked together. Apparently part of this 1874 plan was carried out. The pattern east of Orange Grove was the usual grid with the business center at Fair Oaks Avenue and Colorado Boulevard. By the 1990s the commercial district was already moving east along Colorado with an array of business blocks designed in Victorian styles whose boldness should shame the fainthearted efforts of modern architects. In the 1920s Colorado Boulevard was widened and all of these buildings lost their fanciful façades. Most were then refaced with Art Deco and Spanish fronts, so that Colorado as far as Euclid Avenue, in spite of recent encroachments, still has 1920s-era fronts and Victorian red brick in the alleys to the rear.

In the old residential districts, many Queen Anne cottages remain. The grand Victorians on Orange Grove have almost been completely eliminated and replaced by garden apartments, now mainly condominiums. Elsewhere a few pretentious gingerbreads have stood up against change. But, in spite of the fact that Barney Williams's "Hillmont" has one of the finest ensembles of nineteenth-century interiors in America, Pasadena is not strong in Victoriana. Its great treasury of building (and great it is!) comes from the period 1900 to 1940, the first years dominated by the woodsy Arts and Crafts aesthetic so much appreciated by Gustav Stickley in *The Craftsman* magazine (1901–1916), and the later years devoted to the period revivals. The Arts and Crafts, or Craftsman style, a kind of amalgam of Swiss Chalet, Tudor, and Asian forms, can best be savored on the eastern side of the Arroyo Seco. There, just north of the Ventura Freeway, the greatest concentration of work by now-famous architects Charles and Henry Greene still stands. South of the freeway important houses by less familiar names such as Louis B. Easton, Arthur and Alfred Heineman, G. Lawrence Stimson, and Jeffrey, Van Trees, and Millar, provide the finest collection of Craftsman architecture outside of Berkeley.

Pasadena's architectural heritage of the 1920s and 1930s, on the other hand, parallels the accomplishments of Santa Barbara. In fact, the two cities often used the same architects. Besides Bertram G. Goodhue, George Washington Smith, and J. Wilmer Hershey, all of whom worked in both places, Pasadena residents employed Roland E. Coate, Reginald D. Johnson, Garrett Van Pelt, Gordon B. Kaufmann, and Wallace Neff—the last coming closest to Smith in originality and assurance within the forms of the Spanish Revival. Their work is most magnificent on the western edge of the Arroyo Seco and best viewed from Arroyo Boulevard on the eastern side. Smaller but still ambitious Period Revival architecture is more easily seen in the Oak Knoll district. Lombardy Road is particularly rich.

As in most of Los Angeles County, the greatest amount of fine architecture is domestic, but Pasadena is ahead of most of her neighbors in public architecture. The Civic Center is one of the few successes of the "City Beautiful" movement. The 1923 general plan was designed by the Chicago firm of Bennett, Parsons, Frost, and Thomas. The same year a competition was announced for the design of the main buildings. The winners were Myron Hunt for the Library, Edwin Bergstrom of the firm of Bennett and Haskell for the Auditorium, and Bakewell and Brown (San Francisco) for the City Hall whose proposed façade was an incredible enlargement of the campanario of the San Gabriel Mission. This design was eventually discarded in favor of the present, more respectable triumphal arch and dome. The imagery of all three of these buildings was Classical Mediterranean.

The result of this planning is magnificent. The major axis running along Holly Street toward City Hall begins with the YMCA designed by the important Pasadena firm of Marston and Maybury, and the YWCA by Julia Morgan. Neither is among these architects' best buildings, but both illustrate Pasadena's historic mission to wed ethics and aesthetics. Bakewell and Brown's City Hall is a wonderful stage set, or better, a wedding cake, less elaborate than the same firm's San Francisco City Hall, but much more entertaining. In front of it runs Garfield Street, the minor axis of the Beaux-Arts plan. At its north end is Hunt and Chamber's Public Library. The south end of the axis is closed by Bergstrom's Civic Auditorium on Green Street. The grand plan of the Civic Center is still evident and effective, especially since it stands aside from Colorado Boulevard, the main commercial artery, and thus does not interfere with traffic and business. It is in every sense a triumph of California's own version of Beaux-Arts ideas.

The skyline of the city should be viewed from the steps of the Norton Simon Museum or, even better, from the campus of Ambassador College to the south. Besides the dome of City Hall, church spires appear at just the right places. Unfortunately, the cityscape is marred by the tasteless out-of-scale Parsons Tower and outbuildings, which cannot be landscaped out of sight. It is sad to say that even greater blemishes were erected in the 1980s, particularly along Lake Avenue.

Like most California cities, Pasadena has not invested in many parks. Its high moral tone has never interfered with real-estate values. Partial compensation for the paucity of open spaces is the very large park in the valley of the Arroyo Seco that runs in a southerly direction through the western part of the city. When visiting the site in 1911 Teddy Roosevelt is supposed to have said, "The Arroyo would make one of the greatest parks in the world."

The northern valley of the Arroyo is broad and includes a golf course and an exhibition area as well as the famous Rose Bowl, which is used more often for flea markets than for athletic endeavors. At a narrowing of the gorge is a freeway bridge modeled as closely as possible on the lines of the old Colorado Street Bridge (1912–13) alongside it. The huge concrete arches of both bridges are spectacular, especially when seen from Arroyo Boulevard that cuts through them. Unfortunately the streambed has been paved with a concrete channel, but the palisades on both sides are covered with trees and are very picturesque.

Nature and architects were, until the 1950s, very good to Pasadena. Modern architecture has not fared so well. Certainly the city continues the tradition of rearing and attracting excellent architects, but their work tends to be elsewhere. Single-family dwellings of distinction are now rarely built and, needless to say, the quality of most apartment houses and condominiums is undistinguished. Naturally there are exceptions to these observations, and we have tried to include them.

88 • Pasadena—Upper Arroyo Seco

This area north of the Ventura Freeway is one of the richest architectural districts in the West. The Linda Vista Avenue (western) side is hilly, exclusive, and well guarded. Some beautiful architecture is there, but it can best be viewed in the pages of the sumptuous *Architectural Digest* of the 1920s and 1930s. The east side is even richer in art if not in banknotes. It contains two monuments of American architecture—the Millard House ("La Miniatura") by Frank Lloyd Wright, and the Gamble House by Pasadena architects Charles and Henry Greene. In fact, one whole street, Arroyo Terrace, was designed by the Greenes and another, Grand Avenue, has works by them, by Myron Hunt, and by other architects of equal talent.

The entire Arroyo Seco should be declared a national monument. The architecture is as important as that of Charleston, South Carolina, and the scenery is much better.

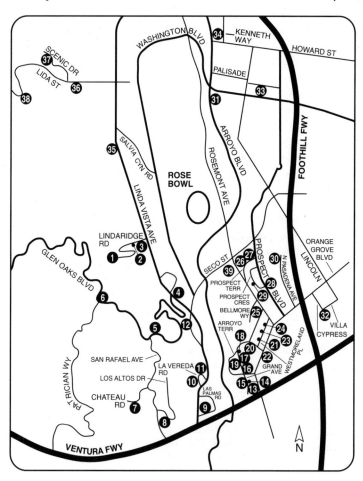

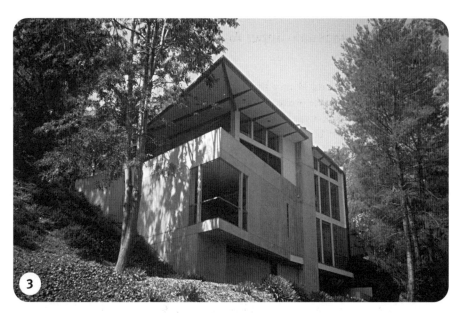

1. Matthews House, 1966
**Mortimer Matthews
(Pulliam, Matthews,
and Associates)**
1435 Lindaridge Road

The arresting roofline of this
house can best be seen from the
curve below it.

2. Ralphs House, 1950
**Ain, Johnson, and Day
(C. Raimond Johnson)**
1350 Lindaridge Road

One of Ain's largest houses, it
has been well maintained over
the years.

3. Dumbacher House, 1996
Hagy Belzberg
*1234 Linda Ridge Road, off
Linda Vista*

Not really Postmodern but certainly a loosening of the International Style tradition, this
house, flaunting a dominant
prow, juts out into space and
has a magnificent view of the
Arroyo Seco and the mountains
beyond.

But what is really striking is that
the house is one of the few recent
examples of Modernist residential
architecture in Pasadena.

4. Schonbach House, 1946
Leland Evison
701 Linda Vista Avenue

A modular post-and-beam system
in which the frames are made of
asbestos; concrete panels exposed.

5. Ladd Studio, 1950
Thornton Ladd
1085 Glen Oaks Boulevard

Pasadena's own version of the
house as a glass box. The house
(actually a studio for the architect's own use) is an elegant 900-
square-foot enclosure of steel
frame, glass, and sliding canvas
sunscreens. It perches at the edge
of a cliff, with an extensive garden to the rear. The studio building won an A.I.A. Award of
Honor. You catch a glimpse of
this International Style building
from the street below. This small
studio, is without doubt, one of

the great classics of post–World
War II Modern architecture in
Southern California. It is a pity
that Ladd never had the opportu-
nity to design one of the *Arts and
Architecture* Case Study houses.

6. Ladd House, 1956
Thornton Ladd
*1280 Glen Oaks Boulevard, at
Patrician Way*

Not as imposing as the studio
listed above.

7. Kelsey House, 1961
Ladd and Kelsey (John Kelsey)
1160 Chateau Road

The architect's own house is a
beautifully articulated Miesian
structure. This is all accomplished via wood and glass. The
house is very private on the
street side. Perched just below
the crest of a hill, this low-lying
modular structure is as handsome as when it was built.

8. Wilbur House, 1928
Gordon B. Kaufmann
25 Los Altos Drive

This Mediterranean-style house peers through trees at the Annandale Golf Club. It is on a private road but can be seen from San Rafael Avenue.

9. Fowler House, 1927
Edward W. Fowler
825 Las Palmas Road

Apparently Fowler got his ideas from magazine illustrations. This Andalusian house, the Basque house around the corner on El Circulo Drive, and the Majorcan house at 95 El Circulo were all designed by him and certainly seem to have come out of a picture book, all the more incredible since now the enormous arches of the freeway bridge tower over this quaint assemblage.

10. Smith House, 1929
David A. Ogilvie
181 La Vereda Road

A Tudor villa on a pleasant street.

11. Kubly House, 1964
Craig Ellwood & Associates
215 La Vereda Road

Ellwood at his most Miesian. An elegantly detailed house, gaining strength of character from its exposed timber framing.

12. Two Houses, circa 1924
Train and Williams
373, 405 Mira Vista Terrace

Both are Bavarian hunting lodges, especially significant because they were designed by the only architectural firm to be directly affiliated with the Arroyo Guild of Fellow Craftsmen.

13. Halsted House, 1905
Charles and Henry Greene
90 N. Grand Avenue

The Greenes were just finding their way here, but this is a fine Craftsman house in spite of frequent alterations during the 1910s and 1920s.

14. Park House, 1904
130 N. Grand Avenue

An awkward but fascinating example of turn-of-the-century Anglo-Colonial Federal Revival.

15. Newcomb House, 1910, 1922
141 N. Grand Avenue

A Tudor mansion complete with necessary gatehouse and servants' quarters. Just around the corner is 200–236, a group of condominiums designed (1980) by Buff and Hensman. We mention them because they are good examples of the fashionable Neo-Craftsman mode.

16. Myron Hunt House, 1905
Myron Hunt
200 N. Grand Avenue

Simplified Doric columns mark the entrance of this otherwise Craftsman house, very much in the same style Hunt employed in Chicago.

17. House, circa 1887
202 N. Grand Avenue

A Queen Anne pearl that was moved from the site (across the street) of the present Culbertson House. This must have been one of the first houses in this area. Notice the original carriage house in the rear.

18. Van Rossem House, 1904
Charles and Henry Greene
210 N. Grand Avenue

Josephine Van Rossem, a real estate speculator, built this brown, barn-like Craftsman house just after having built another Greene and Greene around the corner on Arroyo Terrace.

19. Speirs House, 1904
Hunt and Grey
230 N. Grand Avenue

A good early example of the Dutch Colonial Revival.

20. A Colony of Charles and Henry Greene Houses:

a. Duncan-Irwin House, 1900, 1906
240 N. Grand Avenue

One of the largest and finest houses by Greene and Greene, this house began its history as a single-story bungalow that was incorporated in the Irwins' 1906 extension that we see today. The composition of the façade is more beautiful than the elegant Gamble House.

b. James A. Culbertson House, 1902
235 N. Grand Avenue

Little of the original very important house is left. Only the bay window, the front door with its Tiffany glass, and the magnificent pergola and wall along Grand were designed by the Greenes. These items would also have been demolished except for the protests of architects Smith and Williams, who remodeled the house in 1953.

c. Charles Sumner Greene House, 1901, 1906, 1912, 1914
368 Arroyo Terrace

Charles was mainly responsible for the design of this house and its additions. It is not as richly appointed as the nearby Gamble House, but its Craftsman details are just as fine.

d. White Sisters House, 1903
370 Arroyo Terrace

Charles Greene's sisters-in-law lived in this once completely shingled house. Notice the crescendo of the retaining wall made of clinker brick and Arroyo Seco boulders.

e. Van Rossem–Neill House, 1903, 1906
400 Arroyo Terrace

Carefully restored, this shingled house looks very much as it did when it was pictured in *The Craftsman* magazine in 1915.

f. Hawks House, 1906
408 Arroyo Terrace

Almost identical to the contemporaneous Bentz House on Prospect Boulevard.

g. Willet House, 1905
424 Arroyo Terrace

A Craftsman house completely remodeled on the exterior by another architect who chose the Spanish Revival mode.

h. Ranney House, 1907
440 Arroyo Terrace

Another Oriental Craftsman two-story house, recently beautifully restored. This completes the row of Greene and Greene houses but, of course, there are many more nearby. Across the street from the cluster:

21. Neighborhood Church, 1972
Whitney R. Smith
1 Westmoreland Place

Modern Shingle style evoking memories of the old Neighborhood Church on California Street. The pines and other trees are beginning to give the area the park-like atmosphere that the architect had in mind.

22. Fenyes House, 1906
Robert Farquhar
170 N. Orange Grove Boulevard

Neoclassical, expensive, but not Farquhar at his best (see Clark Library on West Adams and the California Club in Central Los Angeles). This design nevertheless suggests the high style of living that once characterized Orange Grove Avenue. It can be visited courtesy of the Pasadena Museum of History whose headquarters are on the grounds. Call (626) 577-1660 for visiting hours. The Fenyes House is a half-block from the Green's Gamble House. Both houses were built about the same time, but they offer contrasting

tastes and should be seen together on the same day.

23. Cole House, 1906
Charles and Henry Greene
2 Westmoreland Place

The Greenes hit their stride here. The interior has been remodeled for use as church parlors, but the exterior is almost precisely as the Greenes designed it. Notice the monumental boulder chimney to the south, which emerges from the ground like a tree trunk.

24. Gamble House, 1908
Charles and Henry Greene
4 Westmoreland Place

Certainly this is the masterpiece of these master architects, not because of its façade or its plan (which is conservative even by late-Victorian standards) but for the rich interiors, unmatched for loving attention to detail. Like most architects, the Greenes were happiest when they had a rich client who gave them an open purse. But what is remarkable is that the intricate teak interiors that they designed could be carried out with such incredible

craftsmanship, forget the price. Containing almost all of the original Greene-designed furniture, this is probably one of the five finest house museums in America. Thanks to the Gamble family, and to the City of Pasadena and the University of Southern California who jointly administer it, this house is open to the public. For tour hours and admission fees for the Gamble House, call (626) 793-3334 or (213) 681-6427.

Note as well, the stone gateposts and wrought-iron gates (1913) at the Rosemont Avenue entrance to Westmoreland Place.

25. Dickinson House, 1941
**Lawrence Test
(Woodbridge Dickinson, associate)**
429 Bellmore Way

An understated dark-wood house in the Craftsman tradition. This is the best house on a street of good houses built during and just after World War II.

26. McMurran House, 1911
Frederick L. Roehrig
499 Prospect Terrace

Roehrig could and did design in
every style. This house shows him
expansive in the Mission style.

27. Hindry House, 1909
Arthur S. Heineman
(Alfred Heineman, associate)
781 Prospect Boulevard

A huge Mission-style mansion
overlooking the Arroyo Seco.
Arthur Heineman saw the clients
and worked out the floor plans.
His brother Alfred, who had just
joined the firm, had a hand in
designing the details, as he continued to do until the firm broke
up in the 1930s. The leaded glass
in the dining room was carried
out to Alfred's designs by the
Judson Studios. The fireplace in
the hall may have been designed
by Charles Greene.

28. Bentz House, 1906
Charles and Henry Greene
657 Prospect Boulevard

The architects at their most
restrained. The house is perfectly
maintained.

Prospect Boulevard deserves
special praise. The houses on it
are comfortable and some are of
high quality. But the real attraction is the cork oak, camphor,
and small palm trees that line
it—one of the loveliest sights
in Pasadena.

29. Millard House
("La Miniatura"), 1923
Frank Lloyd Wright
645 Prospect Crescent

The first of Wright's "textile
block" constructions, La
Miniatura has the feeling of a
Mayan ruin set in a jungle ravine.
The famous view of it is from a
gate on Rosemont. The studio at
the west side of the pond is by
Lloyd Wright (1926). While the
studio is related to the house in
scale and materials, it does reveal
the differences of approach
between father and son. The
house and its garden play a fascinating environmental game. It all

appears natural, but the ravine (arroyo) is in fact filled in, and of course most of the shrubs and trees are not native to the place. The house is being restored by the firm of Marmol Radziner & Associates.

30. Gartz Court, 1910
architect unknown;
De Bretteville and Polyzoides, restoration architects
745 N. Pasadena Avenue

These six half-timber and stucco bungalows (actually four and a duplex) were moved from Madison Avenue near central Pasadena. The restoration is immaculate. De Bretteville and

31. Franks House, 1932
Palmer Sabin
1260 N. Arroyo Boulevard

A well-turned Monterey Revival house overlooking the Arroyo Seco.

32. Charlotte Perkins Gilman House, circa 1900
Architect unknown
Southeast corner of Villa Street and Cyprus Avenue

A turn-of-the-century Colonial Revival house of no great architectural distinction, but it was the home of the great American feminist, the author of *Yellow Wallpaper* and many other books. It was moved into this neighbor-

34. Byles and Weston House, 1950
H. Douglas Byles and Eugene Weston III
1611 Kenneth Way

An understated vertical batten house.

35. Wadsworth House, 1925
1145 Linda Vista Avenue

The supreme Craftsman statement—a two-story log cabin.

36. House, circa 1887
1360 Lida Street

This Queen Anne cottage is a relic of the tiny hamlet of Linda Vista.

Polyzoides also designed complementary garages and rear patios that you would swear were original. More than that, the court looks better here than it did on Madison Avenue; so good, in fact, that in spite of being moved, it was kept on the National Register.

hood from near Caltech and has been restored.

33. Grover Cleveland Elementary School, 1934
Robert H. Ainsworth
524 Palisade Street

PWA Moderne with a direct message bas-relief of a child reading.

37. Hernly House, 1949
Lawrence Test
1475 Scenic Drive

The siding is three-quarter-inch plywood with the inside face exposed in rooms. The skilled workmanship is an echo of the Craftsman era. The use of unusual materials is representative of the experimental work that was done just before and after World War II.

38. Art Center College of Design, 1977
Craig Ellwood & Associates
1700 Lida Street

Every follower of Mies must have wanted to design a bridge that was also a building. Here Ellwood had his opportunity. This is a very striking building, and yet notice how it is sited so as to avoid spoiling the natural landscape. The mess of equipment on the roof was not designed by the architect. Recent additions are the Alyce de Roulet Williamson Gallery (1992; Frederick Fisher) and the Garden Pavilion (2000; Hodgetts + Fung). Both are fine complements to Ellwood's strongly assertive architecture.

39. Kidspace Children's Museum, 2003
Michael Maltzan
Architecture, Inc.
In the park, just southeast of the Rose Bowl

A Neo-International Style building linking three old buildings, this is a beautiful addition to Pasadena's history of architectural excellence by a Los Angeles firm. The firm has won positive critical comment for its remodeling of an old factory in Queens, New York, as temporary gallery space for the Museum of Modern Art in New York City.

89 • Pasadena—Lower Arroyo Seco, North

On a map, the Lower Arroyo seems to be cut off from the upper by the freeway, but in reality Arroyo Boulevard connects the two areas as it always has. It is a lovely drive and is favored by bicyclists, joggers, and people who like to stroll. In fact, it is one of the few residential sections in Southern California where you see people walking because there is something to experience—lovely scenery and interesting-to-distinguished architecture set in well-kept gardens.

In the nineteenth century, the edges of the Arroyo were not considered desirable places to build. Too many vapors! The Arroyo was used as a woodlot by the millionaires on Orange Grove Boulevard and also for picnics and the collecting of wildflowers. The western bank pitched abruptly into the streambed, but the eastern side was moderated by two natural terraces before it too dropped into the valley. This land provided the locale for elaborate gardens, the most extensive being that of Adolphus Busch, the beer tycoon. The Busch Gardens, in fact, ran into the Arroyo. They were open to the public until they were subdivided in the late 1930s.

As the gardens disappeared, so did most of the Orange Grove mansions that were eventually replaced by pleasant but unremarkable garden apartments. But beginning around 1900, the lower slopes had become attractive to people of moderate means and often of intellectual and artistic pretension. Many of them built bungalows and larger houses in the "ostentatious simplicity" of the Arts and Crafts (Craftsman) movement. Almost all of these brown woodsy houses remain, many in almost pristine condition. There are even a few new ones. It is for this reason that we have included so many entries for this section.

1. Laing House, 1935
Harwell H. Harris
1642 Pleasant Way

Simplified Wright, but Harris understood the Japanese modular system much better than the master did.

2. Kempton House, 1961
Lyman Ennis
1685 Poppy Peak Drive

Austere stucco with even more austere slit windows. A late rendering of the Pueblo Revival.

3. Perkins House, 1955
Richard J. Neutra
1540 Poppy Peak Drive

Neutra's ability to make a small space seem large by turning it into the outdoors is seen here at its best.

4. Harris House, 1939
Harwell H. Harris
410 N. Avenue 64

An unpretentious example of this architect's sophistication. Again, Harris evokes Wright but simplifies.

5. John Carr Real Estate Company Building, 1950
John Carr
1400 W. Colorado Boulevard

A Spanish Revival office building with pergola in rear. The design was supposedly based on details taken from the Santa Barbara County Courthouse.

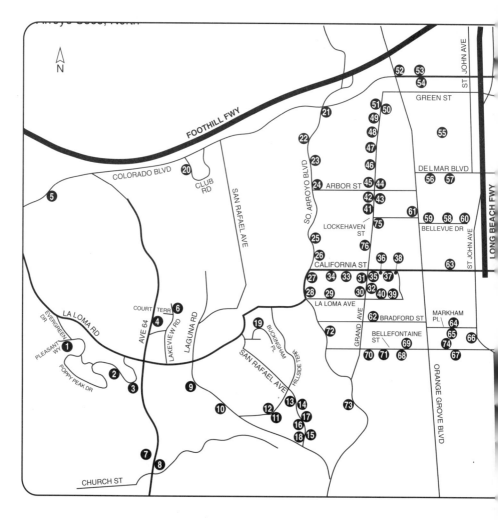

6. Clark House, 1968
Alson Clark
430 Lakeview Road

Spanish Revival with Georgian and other highly innovative touches so that it becomes Postmodern.

7. Greenshaw House, 1907
Joseph Cather Newsom
1102 Lantana Drive

An awkward version of the Mission Revival by an architect who, with his brother Samuel, designed the famed Carson House in Eureka, California. Both of the Newsom brothers kept up with the latest fashion, so it is not surprising to find J. Cather designing Mission Revival buildings in the early 1900s.

8. Church of the Angels, 1889
Arthur Edmund Street;
Ernest A. Coxhead
1100 Avenue 64

This church was erected as a
memorial to Alexander
Campbell-Johnston, a Scot who
bought most of the eastern half of
the Rancho San Rafael and developed it. His wife went to England
to order plans; she chose Street,
the son of the famous Victorian
architect George E. Street, whose
Holmbury Saint Mary's in
Dorking was the model. Street's
drawings were then given to
another Britisher, Ernest A.
Coxhead, who was living in Los
Angeles at the time and who was
semi-official architect for the
Episcopal church in California.
Coxhead took great liberties with
the design, the result being one of
his several masterpieces. The interior is almost precisely the way it

was in the nineteenth century,
and so is the exterior. The 1971
earthquake knocked off the belfry
with its Saxon columns, but this
has now been beautifully restored
(1992; Richard Rose Associates).

9. Gould Garden Pavilion
("Villa Evarno") circa 1925
Raymond Gould
945 Ellington Lane

This building is essentially a garden pavilion that one can live in.
The English gardener, Marion
Cran, in her *Gardens in America*
(1931) describes it: "We break-
fasted over the lake on the terrace
of the 'temple,' which is a spa-
cious room, very Italian in manner. A beautifully furnished room
in the woods; in it his [Gould's]
friends take tea and hear music
looking over his lake and the valley of blossoms."

10. Puelicher House, 1960
Boyd Georgi
901 Laguna Road

An International Style box with
an unusual amount of color in
its bank of louvers.

11. House, 1927
L. C. Brockway
976 Hillside Terrace

A comfortable-looking shingled
English Colonial.

12. Tabor House, 1950
Paul Haynes
969 Hillside Terrace

The horizontality of this
International Style house is carried through with real assurance.

13. Case Study House #10,
1947
Kemper Nomland and
Kemper Nomland Jr.
711 S. San Rafael Avenue

Beautifully sited International
Style.

14. Young House, 1927
George Washington Smith;
A. E. Hanson,
landscape architect
808 S. San Rafael Avenue

A two-story Andalusian house of which you can only gain a few glimpses. Notice the entrance wall, the gate, and the south façade overlooking one of A. E. Hanson's splendid Andalusian gardens, which are no longer intact.

15. Martindale House, 1924
Joseph Kucera
1000 S. San Rafael Avenue

Spanish Revival walled off from the street.

16. Crowell House, 1952
Smith and Williams
(Whitney R. Smith)
949 S. San Rafael Avenue

The architects working in a Japanese mood; one of Pasadena's best 1950s houses.

17. Jevne House, 1913
Eager and Eager
910 S. San Rafael Avenue

A sort of Danish country home in dressed stone.

18. Gallion House, 1956
Arthur B. Gallion
1055 S. San Rafael Avenue

Japanese-style Modern by a city planner and former dean of the USC School of Architecture.

19. Cunningham House, 1980
Pulliam, Matthews, and Associates
969 Buckingham Place

A large cut-into box house with vertical wood sheathing.

Something must be said about the array of houses on San Rafael Avenue north of the intersection with La Loma Road. They are large and private (behind their security systems), and some are fine works of art by Marston and Maybury, Morgan, Walls, and Clements, Paul R. Williams, Reginald D. Johnson, Gordon B. Kaufmann, and other distinguished architects. Almost none can be even vaguely glimpsed from San Rafael Avenue, though there is a tantalizing view of them from Arroyo Boulevard across the Arroyo Seco. All we can say is that we hope you will watch for house tours, particularly those put on by Pasadena Heritage.

Often the San Rafael mansions are the backdrops for movies and television shows and commercials. Naturally the credits never indicate the location.

20. Messler House, circa 1950
Paul Haynes
126 Club Road

A clapboarded house in the Harwell H. Harris tradition.

21. Colorado Street Bridge, 1912–13
Waddell and Harrington (John Alexander Low Waddell, designer and engineer); Mercereau Bridge and Construction Company (John Drake Mercereau, contractor)

Waddell, of the engineering firm of Waddell and Harrington of Kansas City, pioneered reinforced concrete in this monument that he designed to connect Colorado Street in Pasadena to the county road that ran east/west through Eagle Rock. The 1,467.5-foot-long reinforced-concrete bridge has a roadway that is 28 feet wide with 48 lamp clusters lighting the bridge. This long, high concrete bridge spanning the Arroyo was curved so that it would get solid footing. The aesthetic result has been compared to that achieved by the aqueduct at Segovia in Spain. The community became so fond of their monument that, when the bridge needed radical repairs a few years ago, the people of Pasadena demanded that it should be rebuilt and restored as closely as possible to its original appearance. This restoration was completed in late 1993.

22. La Casita del Arroyo, 1934
Myron Hunt
177 S. Arroyo Boulevard

Very uncharacteristic Hunt, this

small meetinghouse was inspired by the Pasadena Garden Club's interest in spurring employment during the depression. The main funds came from the PWA. Hunt donated his services and designed this structure using boulders and sand from the Arroyo, fallen trees from higher up the canyon, and even parts of the bicycle track abandoned after its use in the 1932 Olympics.

23. Barber House, 1925
Roland E. Coate
270 S. Arroyo Boulevard

An attractive Cape Cod Colonial in brick, accompanied by a California version of what a New England garden should be. The landscape architect was Katharine Bashford.

24. House, 1983
Buff and Hensman
Northeast corner of South Arroyo Boulevard and Arbor Street

An elaborate Craftsman bungalow.

25. Cheesewright House #2, 1912
Jeffrey, Van Trees, and Millar
490 S. Arroyo Boulevard

A beautifully sited Craftsman house.

26. Mannheim House, 1913
Attributed to Jean Mannheim
500 S. Arroyo Boulevard

Mannheim, a distinguished regional painter, had earlier been associated with Frank Brangwyn, one of the few painters in the English Arts and Crafts movement. Although Mannheim is usually given credit for the design of his house, the quality of the design and its detailing suggests that he must have had an architect friend.

27

27. Batchelder House, 1909, 1913
Ernest A. Batchelder
626 S. Arroyo Boulevard

A shingled Craftsman house with a brick-terrace entrance and a large second-floor sleeping porch. By the 1920s, Batchelder was one of the country's most successful producers of decorative tile. It all began in the backyard of this house, where his kiln house still stands. He was also a frequent contributor of articles on design and aspects of the Arts and Crafts movement for *The Craftsman* magazine. His wife, a professional pianist, founded the Coleman Chamber Music Association, the oldest such organization in the United States.

28. Clark House, circa 1910
George A. Clark
648 S. Arroyo Boulevard

Another Swiss chalet, well publicized in the periodicals of the time and featured in H. von Holst's *Modern American Homes* (1915). Incidentally, Clark was a haberdasher!

29. Wright House, circa 1909
Timothy Walsh
691 La Loma Avenue

Craftsman with classical touches, illustrated and discussed in *The Craftsman* of January 1910. Walsh was a Boston architect who came out to Los Angeles to do the new Roman Catholic cathedral. The church never got off the drawing boards, but Walsh was quickly converted to the Pasadena style.

30. Austin House, 1909
Grable and Austin, contractors
629 S. Grand Avenue

The architectural historian Clay Lancaster believed that this true (i.e., one-story) bungalow was based on an ancient Lycian house illustrated in the *American Architect and Building News* in 1908. If he is correct, Grable and Austin followed through quickly since this house was published in the *Western Architect* in 1909. An almost identical twin is at 990 Vermont in Oakland.

31. House, circa 1910
Timothy Walsh
619 S. Grand Avenue

A Craftsman chalet; or better, a Bavarian hunting lodge.

32. Volney-Craig House, 1908
Louis B. Easton
620 S. Grand Avenue

A simple Rocky Mountain cabin on the outside, this house exhibits all the Craftsman paraphernalia on the interior—redwood framing and paneling, inglenook, and even a burnt-wood sideboard.

33. Williams House, 1911
Grable and Austin,
contractors/designers
638 W. California Boulevard

This is a fine bungalow in mint condition.

NOTE: In spite of our heavy coverage of this area, we are mentioning only what we consider to be the best examples of the Craftsman architecture here. You should plan to walk Grand Avenue, California Street, Arroyo Boulevard, La Loma Avenue, and Bradford Street.

34. Cheesewright House #1, 1909–10
Jeffrey, Van Trees, and Millar
686 W. California Boulevard

E. J. Cheesewright, an Englishman, was one of the leading interior designers in Southern California. Perhaps he suggested the feeling of a thatched-roof Cotswold cottage for this otherwise Craftsman house. When drawings of the proposed house were first published in 1909, it was described as "the English cottage type."

35. House, 1910
Attributed to Louis B. Easton
550 W. California Boulevard

A fine California bungalow in the Craftsman tradition. In 1990 the house was completely refurbished. Tim Andersen was the restoration architect.

36. Norton House, 1905
Alfred Heineman
540 W. California Boulevard

This house was designed by Alfred three years before he joined his brother Arthur's firm. It has the marks of an early work—simplicity, only a suggestion of Craftsman style. Also, it was at some time remodeled and enlarged. It is significant, however, as a competent work of a young man who got into architecture as a developer and who later would compete with Charles and Henry Greene for commissions. It has been lovingly restored by the present owners—and has a wonderful view of the Arroyo Seco.

37. De Forest House, 1906
Charles and Henry Greene
530 W. California Boulevard

A large Craftsman house; one of the best-preserved specimens of the Greenes' early work.

38. House, 1905
Grable and Austin,
contractors/designers
520 W. California Boulevard

A handsome Craftsman design worthy of comparison with the Greene and Greene next door. Obviously this contracting firm either brought in an architect or had an architect in their office in order to produce a design of this quality.

39. Noble House, circa 1910
475 La Loma Avenue

The Tudor Craftsman mode.

40. Clapp House, 1874
549 La Loma Avenue

A simple but refined Italianate dwelling. One of the oldest buildings in Pasadena, it housed the city's first school. It was moved before the turn of the century from the southwest corner of Orange Grove Boulevard and California Street.

41. Francis House, 1929
Reginald D. Johnson
415 S. Grand Avenue

One of Johnson's best Georgian efforts.

42. Bolt House ("Cobbleoak"), 1893
Seymour Locke and
Jasper Newton Preston
395 S. Grand Avenue

A large cobblestone and shingle house. Another strongly Richardsonian house (1895) by the same firm is at 325 S. Grand Avenue.

34

43. House, 1910
G. Lawrence Stimson
390 S. Grand Avenue

Dressed-up Craftsman, this house is similar in style to Myron Hunt's house at 200 N. Grand Avenue.

44. Post House #2, 1903
Joseph J. Blick
360 S. Grand Avenue

A late Shingle-style structure with Richardsonian touches.

45. Staats House, 1924
Marston and Van Pelt
293 S. Grand Avenue

A French Provincial mansion.

46. Tod Ford House, 1919
Reginald D. Johnson
257 S. Grand Avenue

A grand Mediterranean-style mansion with beautifully landscaped forecourt and impressive gardens terraced into the valley of the Arroyo Seco.

47. Freeman Ford House, 1907
Charles and Henry Greene
215 S. Grand Avenue

This house cannot be seen from the street, but it is one of the Greenes' major works and must be mentioned. The gardens were set out by Robert Gordon Fraser,

48

the landscape architect for the Busch Gardens.

48. Robinson House, 1905
Charles and Henry Greene
195 S. Grand Avenue

The gates have Oriental lanterns, but the house, with its suggestion of half-timbering, seems Tudor. It is being restored with the Ted Wells Studio as advising architect.

49. Shakespeare Club,
circa 1925
**Marston, Van Pelt, and
Maybury (Sylvanus Marston)**
171 S. Grand Avenue

A severe Florentine villa.

50. Vista Grande Townhouses,
1981
Buff and Hensman
72–108 S. Grand Avenue

This linked-together stucco-and-wood style has become very popular in this area, thanks partly to this firm. See also the similar and impressive condominiums by Harrison, Beckhart, and Mill just around the corner at 1 S. Orange Grove Boulevard.

51. Vista del Arroyo Hotel,
1920
**Marston and Van Pelt;
tower,** 1930
George Wiemeyer
125 S. Grand Avenue

This hotel began its life in 1882 as Mrs. Bang's boarding house. Needless to say it prospered, only to suffer a loss of patronage in the 1930s. It was taken over by the federal government during World War II. Today it has been converted for use as an appellate court building. The so-called bungalows in the extensive gardens are mostly by Marston and Myron Hunt.

52. Memorial Flagpole, 1927
**Bertram G. Goodhue
Associates**
*Northeast corner of
Orange Grove and
Colorado Boulevards*

The sculpture at the base is by Lee Lawrie, who worked with Goodhue on many buildings, including the Nebraska State Capitol and the Los Angeles Public Library.

53. Pasadena Museum of Art (now Norton Simon Museum),
1969
Ladd and Kelsey
411 W. Colorado Boulevard

This building, with its curved forms, draws upon the Streamline Moderne of the 1930s, but it has a formal classic quality as to its plan, proportions, and use of materials. The collection it houses is superb. In 1998–99 Frank Gehry (with Greg Walsh) remodeled the galleries in order to exhibit Simon's fabulous collection to greater effect. The almost total re-ordering was a spectacular success. At the same time, landscape architect Nancy Goslee Power redesigned and replanted the grounds with a taste that equals Gehry's. For visiting hours, call (626) 449-6840.

54. Elks Club Building, 1911
**Myron Hunt and
H. C. Chambers**
400 W. Colorado Boulevard

A pleasing variation on Mount Vernon.

55. Ambassador College Campus (formerly)
*The large block bounded by
Green Street, Del Mar and
South Orange Grove
Boulevards, and
St. John Avenue*

In 1950 the World Wide Church of God bought this block on Orange Grove's "Millionaire's Row" in order to provide a campus for its Ambassador College. The new owners saved most of the old houses that were left from the early twentieth century and adapted them for academic use, constructing a few new buildings of varying architectural quality mainly on the north and east sides.

For a variety of reasons the college folded in the nineties, and it stands vacant as of this writing even though the grounds have been kept up beautifully. Redevelopment is almost inevitable, but how much is a bone of contention.

a. Scofield House, 1909
Frederick L. Roehrig
280 S. Orange Grove Boulevard

Roehrig was trained in architecture at Cornell in the late nineteenth century and came to Pasadena during the land boom of the late eighties. He was a rather quirky master of all the styles of his times and went from one to another. In 1905 he had built a fine Arts and Crafts house for Arthur Jerome Eddy, a Chicago lawyer and collector of avant-garde art. It was strongly indebted to the adobe architecture of the Southwest. For the Scofield House he chose a related but much more elaborate version of the Craftsman aesthetic—the Prairie style of Frank Lloyd Wright and other midwestern architects. The interiors are very Wrightian, strongly suggestive of Wright's Dana House in Springfield, Illinois. But the exterior seems more like the work of William Purcell and George Grant Elmslie.

Across the street at the intersection of Del Mar with Orange Grove is another Roehrig house that seems to blend the Queen Anne style with Richardsonian Romanesque detail!

55a

b. Sprague House, 1903
A. A. Sprague
Behind Scofield House

A vast half-timbered Tudor pile.

c. Merritt House, 1905–6
W. F. Thompson

An Italian Renaissance palace set between two large waffle-like grilles near the corner of Green Street and Orange Grove Boulevard. The front porch is a later addition.

d. Information and Administrative Center, 1969
Peter Holstock,
for O. K. Earl Corporation

Influenced by early Yamasaki.

e. Student Center, 1966
Gerd Ernst (for Daniel, Mann, Johnson, and Mendenhall)

A pleasing pavilion.

f. Auditorium, 1974
Daniel, Mann, Johnson, and Mendenhall

This building is already famous for its opulence and good acoustics.

56. Mead House, 1910
Louis B. Easton
380 W. Del Mar Boulevard

A monument of the Craftsman movement by a brother-in-law of Elbert Hubbard. The house was restored in 1979, and a porte cochere was added by the restoration architect, Tim Andersen.

57. Bolton House, 1906
Charles and Henry Greene
370 W. Del Mar Boulevard

The shingle exterior shows only a few signs of the Japanese influence that was to emerge full-blown in the Greenes' work two years later. The staircase bulge was added by Garrett Van Pelt in 1918. The house has gone through many interior changes, but it was restored in 1982 by Tim Andersen.

58. Rhodes House, 1906
W. J. Saunders
365 W. Bellevue Drive

Worthy of Maybeck, this huge Bavarian hunting lodge deserves study.

59. Condominium, 1982
Batey-Mack
371–379 W. Bellevue Drive

Clear stucco abstraction worthy of Irving J. Gill.

60. Jacobs House, 1992
Lee Hershberger
335 W. Bellevue Drive

A really distinguished monument of the current Arts and Crafts revival. This relatively new dwelling and its gardens replace a nondescript house of the 1950s. Particularly noteworthy is the retention of the enormous Moreton Bay fig tree that completes the picture.

61. Wrigley House, 1911
G. Lawrence Stimson
391 S. Orange Grove Boulevard

Mission Revival with delusions of Beaux-Arts grandeur, this mansion, though itself of no great quality, is set in ample gardens that give an idea of the high style once common on Orange Grove Boulevard. It is now the headquarters of the Tournament of Roses Association.

62. Fitzpatrick House, 1980
Lee Hershberger
549 Bradford Street

Craftsman Revival in an area that is worthy of it. Special credit goes to Rodger Whipple, the master carpenter, along with the architect and the imaginative owners.

63. Apartment Building, 1926
Robert H. Ainsworth
339–353 W. California Boulevard

Andalusian Spanish Revival giving variety of design within the uniformity of the U-shaped plan.

64. MacPherson House, 1894
Harry Ridgeway
337 Markham Place

A Georgian Revival dwelling.

65. Blankenhorn-Lamphear House, 1893
Bradbeer and Ferris
346 Markham Place

A beautiful and typical example of the Queen Anne style.

66. McCarthy House, 1937
Donald McMurray
762 Saint John Avenue

If the Long Beach Freeway is completed, this fine Monterey Revival house will be demolished.

67. Hollister House, 1899
Charles and Henry Greene
310 Bellefontaine Street

Early Greene. They tried out the English Colonial Revival and showed their allegiance to the vogues of the eastern seaboard, particularly the work of McKim, Mead, and White.

68. Ware House, 1913
Charles and Henry Greene
460 Bellefontaine Street

Here the Greenes seem to be moving away from their Swiss and Oriental influences. The house looks more like their early work, e.g., the Hollister House.

69. Phillips House, 1906
Charles and Henry Greene
459 Bellefontaine Street

A large, very characteristic brown chalet. The only Greene and Greene style that you do not experience in these Bellefontaine houses is, strangely enough, the Japanese.

70. Thomas House, 1911
Sylvanus Marston
574 Bellefontaine Street

Tudor Craftsman.

71. Marshall-Eagle House (now Mayfield School), 1917
Frederick L. Roehrig
500 Bellefontaine Street

A huge Beaux-Arts mansion whose grounds have been well maintained. The billiard room in the basement is decorated with Batchelder tiles.

72. Swift House, 1927
Donald McMurray
850 S. Arroyo Boulevard

One of the finest Monterey Revival houses in Pasadena.

73. Pergola House, circa 1910
Attributed to Robert Gordon Fraser
1025 S. Arroyo Boulevard

This remains among only a few relics of the Busch Gardens begun in 1903 under Fraser's direction. He had trained at the great Horticultural Gardens in his native Edinburgh. So far as is known, he had no architectural background, but the idea of a platform from which to view Camel's Hump must have been his. Now the circular building has been incorporated in a modest house.

72

74. Buckingham House,
1918–19
Sylvanus Marston
325 Bellefontaine Street

A handsome example of the late–Queen Anne style that Vincent Scully has called the Shingle style. Two more examples are located nearby at 707 and 721 Saint John Avenue. They date from 1890 and 1897, respectively (Frederick L. Roehrig). Both will be demolished if the Long Beach Freeway is completed.

75. Three Houses
Southeast corner of South Grand Avenue and Lockhaven Street

These three houses are move-ons to a property once occupied by the La Solana Inn. The Cosby House is a marvelous Queen Anne extravaganza (1893; Merithew and Ferris) that was originally at 626 W. 30th Street near the USC campus. The owners, with the help of Tim Andersen, restored it, adding some touches.

On the corner at 440 S. Grand is a Shingle-style two-story house designed by W. B. Edwards in 1903. It has an inordinate amount of pizazz as the result of an imaginative paint job. Just south of it is a Colonial Revival that was also moved to this site and restored.

76. Coffey House, 2002
David Serrurier
505 S. Grand Avenue

Somewhat Tudor with a Viking tower as entrance portico, this is an incredibly successful evocation of the 1920s taste, so important in Pasadena's architectural history. See it while you can for the heavy planting will soon screen it from view.

90 • Pasadena—Lower Arroyo Seco, South

When the city of South Pasadena was laid out in 1886, there was a movement to incorporate it with Pasadena. But the good people of this area held out against "the diabolical traffic" in liquor, tolerated by the Presbyterians to the north. South Pasadena was, in the words of historian Hiram Reid, "compelled by sheer necessity for self-protection to incur the expense and trouble of forming a city corporation." The town fought alcohol well into this century. Nevertheless, the town is rich in the domestic architecture of the early twentieth century.

The tradition of otherwise-mindedness also has its rewards. More recently South Pasadena has taken a gallant stand against the Long Beach Freeway that would cut down Meridian Avenue, demolishing old commercial buildings and a fine residential district that includes important Victorian houses, two houses by Greene and Greene, and one by R. M. Schindler.

We do not mean to create ironies, but the simple fact is that freeways, while often destroying major and minor monuments, do not, when properly constructed, divide cities as they seem to do on maps. If elevated, or especially if depressed and bridged, they may actually reduce the traffic flow on surface streets and preserve neighborhoods. The Pasadena Freeway, in spite of its dangerous on-and-off ramps, is almost invisible as it bends out of the Arroyo and through the northern part of South Pasadena. Thus, at the risk of inflaming the passions of people in both Pasadena and South Pasadena, we have included a part of South Pasadena in the following section and then in a later section gone on to move east through the main part of South Pasadena. We do this not to confuse, but to help the knowledgeable admirer of architecture who cares nothing for political boundaries, particularly since they were drawn on the principles of the Anti-Saloon League.

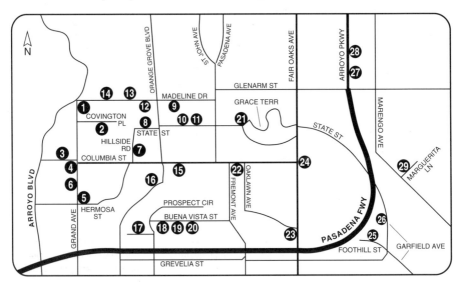

1. House, 1938
Donald McMurray
*Southeast corner of
Grand Avenue and
Madeline Drive
Pasadena*

A Spanish urban house of great
quality. Its model was a seven-
teenth-century house in Antigua,
Guatemala.

2. House, 1950
Leland Evison
*520 Covington Place
Pasadena*

Good conservative Modern with
oiled-redwood exterior.

3. Jeffries House, 1922
Bertram G. Goodhue
*695 Columbia Street
Pasadena*

Unfortunately, when this once-
huge house was divided a few
years ago, the wonderful Churrigueresque entrance was removed.
But we are told that it is stored
somewhere on the grounds. The
house is invisible from the streets
that surround it, but we include it
because of the significance of the
architect and the possibility that it
may sometime be on a special tour.

4. Tanner-Behr House, 1917
Reginald D. Johnson
*Southwest corner of
Columbia Street and
Grand Avenue
South Pasadena*

A rather formidable essay in the
Mediterranean style, now best
viewed from the gate on Grand
Avenue. The two Roman busts at
the tops of the gateposts always
have wreaths around them at
Christmastime. Notice also the
lovely antique pink wall.

5. Koebig House, 1927
H. Roy Kelley
*Northeast corner of Hermosa
Street and Grand Avenue
South Pasadena*

A compact Tudor villa in brick.
This house was frequently published at the time, and in 1928
it won the first prize for a five-
to-eight-room house in a competition sponsored by *House
Beautiful.*

6. House, circa 1925
Donald McMurray
*309 N. Grand Avenue
South Pasadena*

With its scalloped wall and beautiful maintenance, this Spanish
Revival house is almost too good
to be true.

7. Davis House, 1936–37
Roland E. Coate
*1230 Hillside Road
Pasadena*

Federal Revival in painted
brick. Note the arcaded office
on the one-story wing to
the south.

8. Perrin House, 1926
Garvin Hodson
*415 W. State Street
Pasadena*

Monterey Revival with mannered
touches strongly suggesting the
influence of George Washington
Smith.

9. Westridge School, 1906–80
*324 Madeline Drive
Pasadena*

The campus, most of whose
buildings can easily be seen
from the street, is a veritable
museum of the works of Pasadena's architectural worthies.
Remember that the school is
private property. Buildings are
listed in clockwise fashion.

a. Administration Building, 1923
**Marston, Van Pelt, and
Maybury (Sylvanus Marston)**

A modest Tudor Revival structure
by a firm that was more at home
with the congeries of the
Mediterranean.

b. Performing Arts Building, 1909
**Frederick L. Roehrig;
north wing, 1932
Bennett and Haskell;
stage design, 1958
Henry Dreyfuss**

Most of the Roehrig design has
been covered up or remodeled.
The later wing harmonizes with
the Tudor Administration Building. The stage is, of course, the
product of one of the world's
greatest industrial designers
who, incidentally, lived a few
blocks away.

c. Hoffman Gymnasium-Auditorium, 1980
Whitney R. Smith

A shingled box reminiscent of
Smith's Neighborhood Church.

d. Pitcairn House, 1906
**Charles and Henry Greene;
interior remodeled, 1973
Roland E. Coate Jr.,
Tim Andersen, associate;
further restoration, 2000
Pica and Sullivan**

The Greenes in beautiful form.
This building is now a good
example of recycling. The interior
retains many of the old features;
the exterior, with its wonderful
stepped windows reflecting the
interior staircase, remains exactly
as built.

Page 404 (#9d): Pitcairn House.
Photo by Tom Heinz; © 1998 by
Randell L. Makinson Associates

9d

e. Laurie and Susan Frank Art Studio, 1978
Whitney R. Smith;
Seeley G. Mudd Science Building, 1978
Whitney R. Smith

How do you design new buildings next to a major work by the
Greenes? Smith chose shingles
but wisely understated the design,
though the Art Studio may have
been modeled on the Gamble
House garage—a good model.

The landscaping of the south
half of the campus is by Yosh
Kuromiya.

9h

f. Ranney House Classrooms, 1962
**Henry Eggers and
Walter W. Wilkman;**
Gladys Peterson Building, 1962
**Henry Eggers and
Walter W. Wilkman;**
Library (south wing of Administration Building), 1962

**Henry Eggers and
Walter W. Wilkman**

The most "modern"-looking
buildings on the campus.

g. Gertrude Hall Building and Classrooms, 1955
George Vernon Russell

Barely visible from the street
(Madeline Drive), these buildings
are compromises between

Modern architecture and the
Tudor Revival Administration
Building nearby.

h. Braun Science Building
Pica and Sullivan

The school has buildings of every
description. This one is different
from any other. With its extended
eaves and tall windows it seems to
be a Modernist version of the

Italian Villa Style. The view from Orange Grove Boulevard reads dignified yet happy.

10. Mervin House, 1904
Charles and Henry Greene
267 W. State Street

A columned porch decorates this otherwise Craftsman house.

11. Rolland House, 1903
Charles and Henry Greene
225 W. State Street

A Craftsman bungalow (now painted white) with a recessed window in the middle of the roof. Incidentally, Henry Green's own house (demolished) was once across the street.

12. Cravens House, circa 1929
Lewis P. Hobart
430 Madeline Drive

In spite of its present address, this French château by a San Francisco architect is the best remaining example of the Orange Grove lifestyle. It is now Pasadena's Red Cross Headquarters and can be visited from 8:30 A.M. to 5 P.M. on weekdays. The gardens, designed by the Olmsted Brothers, have been subdivided and lost.

13. Old Mill of Banbury Cross, circa 1907; additions later, especially in the 1920s
485 Madeline Drive

The Hansel and Gretel mill was the teahouse in the old Busch Gardens. It cannot be seen from the street but the lych-gate entrance is a fine piece of street furniture.

14. Dunham House, 1956
Carl L. Maston
495 Madeline Drive

The best view of this International Style structure is from Stoneridge Drive.

15. House, circa 1885
919 Columbia Street
South Pasadena

Professor Thaddeus Lowe lived in this expansive Queen Anne villa while his own great house, now demolished, was being built on Orange Grove Boulevard.

16. Porter House, 1875
215 N. Orange Grove Boulevard
South Pasadena

A Queen Anne cottage built by one of the founders of the San Gabriel Orange Grove Association that sold the first eighty-four lots to the so-called "Indiana Colony."

17. Prospect Houses, 1948
Van E. Bailey and
William Gray Purcell
543–545 Prospect Lane
(in the alley just north of
Pasadena Freeway, off
Prospect Circle)
South Pasadena

Rare examples of Purcell's late work. Simple slip-form concrete structures with wide overhanging eaves; somewhat reminiscent of Wright's Usonian houses.

18. House, circa 1895
929 Buena Vista Street
South Pasadena

Huge turn-of-the-century Tudor with lots of shingles. Note also the fine shingled mansion next door at number 917.

19. Garfield House, 1904
Charles and Henry Greene
1001 Buena Vista Street
South Pasadena

The Greenes designed this modest but respectable house for the widow of President James A. Garfield. It is a Craftsman Swiss chalet without the Japanese touches that they were beginning to display in other commissions.

20. Longley House, 1897, 1910
Charles and Henry Greene
1005 Buena Vista Street
South Pasadena

This is a strange but significant work. Here the Greenes were trying their wings in architecture—and they seem to have tried almost everything. It includes Mission-style, Moorish, Richardsonian Romanesque, Asian, and even Georgian Revival elements.

These Buena Vista houses are all in the path of the proposed extension of the Long Beach Freeway and may be demolished in spite of the fact that the Greene and Greene houses are on the National Register.

21. House, circa 1900
135–137 Grace Terrace
South Pasadena

A shingled Mission Revival building constructed as a chauffeur's dwelling for the William Stanton estate. The first floor was once a garage where Pierce Arrows were parked.

Oaklawn Avenue, dating from the early 1900s, has many handsome Craftsman houses. See especially numbers 216, 217, 304, 309, 317, and 325.

22. Oaklawn Gates, 1905
Charles and Henry Greene
Columbia Street, at
Oaklawn Avenue

A Craftsman redwood fence ends in boulder pillars supporting beautiful tile roofs. The ornamental iron gates designed by the Greenes complete the picture.

23. Oaklawn Bridge and
Waiting Station, 1906
Charles and Henry Greene
Oaklawn Avenue at
Fair Oaks Avenue
South Pasadena

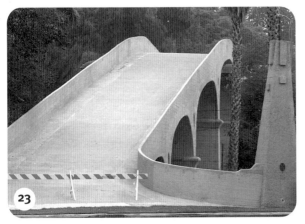

Left: Oaklawn Bridge, 1906
Charles and Henry Greene.
Photo by Jim Brown

Below: Casa de Jose Perez
("Adobe Flores"), 1939, 1849–50.
Photo by Alice Leader

27. Royal Building, 1968
Nyberg and Bissner
*East side of Arroyo Parkway,
north of Glenarm Street*

A stilted pavilion related to
Edward D. Stone's projects
but without his Moorish
screens.

28. Grieger Building, 1972
**Daniel, Mann, Johnson, and
Mendenhall**
900 S. Arroyo Parkway

A strong Streamline Moderne
building of almost monumental
proportions.

The bridge across the tracks of
the Southern Pacific and Santa
Fe Railroads was a sally of the
Greenes into engineering. It has
been restored and turns out to
be a beautiful creation. The waiting station is an amazing concoction of redwood beams with
tile roof.

24. Waiting Station and
Cobblestone Wall, circa 1902
Attributed to T. W. Parkes
*Southeast corner of
Fair Oaks Avenue and
Raymond Hill Road
South Pasadena*

A fine Craftsman shelter where
guests of the Raymond Hotel,
once on the hill above, used to
wait for the "Big Red Cars" on
the Pacific Electric line—a branch
of what was once one of the
greatest rapid transit systems in
the country.

25. Casa de Jose Perez
("Adobe Flores"),
1839, 1849–50
*1804 Foothill Street
South Pasadena*

A single-floor L-shaped adobe
now covered with a tile roof. Used
as Mexican Army headquarters
during the Mexican-American

War, this adobe was restored and
"enhanced" in 1919 by the well-
known exponent of the Spanish
Revival, Carleton M. Winslow Sr.
In the 1920s it was a teahouse
with a high cultural tone. It is
now a private residence.

26. Group of Adobes, 1925–27
Carleton M. Winslow Sr.
*West side of Garfield Avenue,
north of Foothill Street
South Pasadena*

In spite of their late date, these
are much more convincing structures than the previous entry.

29. Spanish Revival Village,
circa 1928
*Marguerita Lane, on the curve
of Marengo Avenue below
Glenarm Street*

A group of very pretty cottages—
actually a bungalow court.

91 • Pasadena—Oak Knoll

Besides Pasadena proper there were other real estate ventures aimed at appeasing the voracious appetites of midwesterners for paradise. The Oak Knoll area, now a part of Pasadena but in the 1880s a separate subdivision, was bought by a Mr. Rosenbaum, a New York speculator, and was laid out by the R. R. Staats Realty Company. Land contours (some determined by earthquake faults!) and native oaks were preserved by curving streets. Oak Knoll was, from the beginning, an area of fine houses on estates originally almost as extensive as those on Orange Grove Boulevard. All of these were broken up in the 1920s so that houses in the Craftsman idiom are cheek to jowl with period revivals.

1. Experimental Dome House ("Bubble House"), 1946
Wallace Neff
1097 S. Los Robles Avenue

A thin-shell concrete dome by this famous exponent of the Spanish Revival. Like many other architects of the World War II years, Neff was looking for a practical low-cost structure that would replace the balloon frame. He started his design experimentation on the "Bubble House" in 1934. His first extensive use of this new form of structure was a colony of twenty units built at Falls Church, Virginia, in 1941.

2. House, circa 1887
Southwest corner of Oakland Avenue and Miles Street

A colorful Queen Anne two-story with picket fence.

3. Flintoft House, circa 1910
G. S. Bliss, contractor
800 S. Oakland Avenue

A two-story Craftsman house. Fine Craftsman houses, some bungalows, pop up elsewhere on this street. See especially numbers 755, 903, 911, and 1315. Bliss constructed many bungalows in Pasadena.

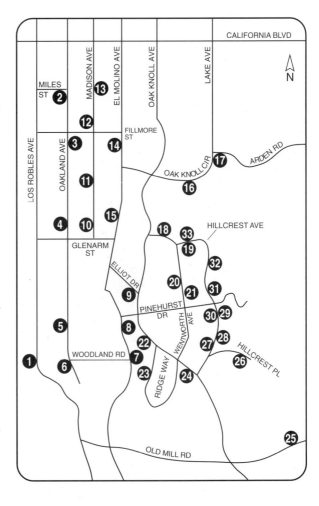

4. Toleston House, 1913
E. P. Zimmerman
965 S. Oakland Avenue

American Georgian with Dutch and Federal elements.

5. House, 1915
Rossiter-Banfield Company
1205 S. Oakland Avenue

A Pueblo Revival house, unusual in this area.

6. Rochester House, circa 1910
T. Beverly Keim
1365 S. Oakland Avenue

The Rochesters chose a Los Angeles architect to design this magnificent Beaux-Arts mansion for them.

7. Grey House, 1911
Elmer Grey
1372 S. El Molino Avenue

Although touches of Italian influence appear in the architect's own house, the broad circular front porch is very Californian. The composition of the rough stucco walls reminds you of Voysey or even Mackintosh. The house is beautifully sited on the hillside.

8. Van Pelt House, 1926
Garrett Van Pelt
1212 S. El Molino Avenue

This important architect chose a variation on a French Provincial theme for his own house.

9. Ross House, 1911
Arthur S. Heineman
(Alfred Heineman, associate)
674 Elliott Drive

The Craftsman aesthetic in its later stage, this house is often mistaken for a work by the Greenes.

10. House, 1910
Sylvanus Marston
1011 S. Madison Avenue

West Coast Prairie style.

11. Ioannes House, 1911
Louis B. Easton
885 S. Madison Avenue

A well-turned effort in Mission-style stucco by an architect who usually used wood.

12. E. J. Blacker House, 1912
Charles and Henry Greene
675 S. Madison Avenue

Obviously this house does not bear comparison with the one that the Greenes had built earlier for another Blacker (see entry #19). It is, nevertheless, a good Craftsman design as is the one (1907) at 805 S. Madison Avenue by Frederick L. Roehrig.

13. Blood House, 1911
654 S. Madison Avenue

An excellent U-plan Craftsman bungalow painted yellow in the latter day.

14. House, circa 1911
Arthur S. Heineman
(Alfred Heineman, associate)
885 S. El Molino Avenue

Although painted, this two-story house still shows its Craftsman origins.

15. Crow-Crocker House, 1909
Charles and Henry Greene
979 S. El Molino Avenue

Actually, this Craftsman masterpiece was designed entirely by Henry Greene.

16. McDonald House, circa 1927
W. F. Staunton
800 Oak Knoll Circle

A good Monterey Revival two-story.

17. "Tara West," 1978
Thornton and Fagan Associates
Southeast corner of Lake Avenue and Arden Road

A folly if there ever was one! It is supposed to be modeled on Scarlett O'Hara's mansion in the late-1930s film *Gone with the Wind.*

18. Garford House, 1919
Marston and Van Pelt
1126 Hillcrest Avenue

A rather dry but dignified version of the Spanish Revival. Just north of it and running along Oak Knoll Avenue is a Japonified gunite wall designed by the Greenes.

19. R. R. Blacker House, 1907
Charles and Henry Greene
1177 Hillcrest Avenue

Like the Gamble House across town, this is one of the very finest of the Greenes' Craftsman-Japanese designs. Its magnificent gardens have been subdivided and built upon. The chauffeur's and gardener's houses, now separate dwellings on Wentworth Avenue, give an idea of the grandeur of the ensemble.

20. Pomeroy House, circa 1913
Arthur S. Heineman
(Alfred Heineman, associate)
1233 Wentworth Avenue

The Craftsman aesthetic, moving directly into a version of Cotswold Hansel and Gretel.

21. Campbell House, 1924
Roland E. Coate
1244 Wentworth Avenue

One of this architect's best Spanish Revival houses.

22. O'Brien House, 1912
Arthur S. Heineman
(Alfred Heineman, associate)
1327 S. Oak Knoll Avenue,
on the corner of
Ridge Way

A beautifully crafted house in the Heineman's special fusion of Asian details with the feeling of a Cotswold cottage.

23. Ledyard House
("Idyllwild") 1909
1361 Ridge Way

An extraordinary Craftsman house framed in logs.

24. Wentworth Hotel
(now Ritz Carleton–
Huntington Hotel), 1906
Charles F. Whittlesey;
expansion, 1913
Myron Hunt;
rebuilding, 1991
McClellan, Cruz, Gaylord
and Associates;
De Bretteville and Polyzoides,
historic architecture
consultants;
The Peridian Group,
landscape architects
1401 S. Oak Knoll Avenue

Whittlesey, well known for his Mission Revival railroad stations and hotels in the Southwest, continued the tradition here in this great hotel, catering to easterners and midwesterners trying to escape wretched winters back home. Henry Huntington, of Southern Pacific Railroad fame,

took over operation and in 1913 commissioned Myron Hunt to expand the central section upward. The result was a rather ungainly façade.

By the 1980s a series of post–World War II remodelings, reflecting changing ownership and management, left the interiors a mess and many of the rooms were substandard. Finally, on the grounds that the building was an earthquake hazard, the great central tower was demolished and rebuilt in the Mission Revival style, but in a bit more coherent version than had hitherto been encountered. The beautiful Whittlesey-designed public rooms—the Venetian and the Georgian—were saved from the wrecking ball and have been restored to their original grandeur, the Venetian being more interesting since it displays

the architect's fondness for the ornamental designs of Louis Sullivan. Also salvaged was a rustic bridge with murals painted in 1933 by Frank M. Moore.

25. El Molino Viejo, 1816
1120 Old Mill Road
San Marino

Built under the direction of Father Zalvidea on the outer limits of the San Gabriel Mission property, it served as a flour mill until a new and presumably more efficient mill put it out of service. It moldered until the 1920s, when it was refurbished and used as a house with painted decoration added to interior walls. Both Myron Hunt and Carleton M. Winslow Sr. were involved in the restoration of the building, and the gardens were restored by Katherine Bashford. Certainly it is one of the most picturesque of the old adobe (also rock and fired-brick) structures remaining in Los Angeles County.

26. Hamish House, 1951
Henry Eggers and
Walter W. Wilkman
940 Hillcrest Place

Actually, all you can see is one wall of the house, but it is a beautiful wall. (Watch the bumps in the road.)

27. Landreth House, circa 1918
Reginald D. Johnson
1385 Hillcrest Avenue

A grand American Classical Revival mansion.

28. Spinks House, 1909
Charles and Henry Greene
1344 Hillcrest Avenue

A blend of barn and Swiss Chalet, with Japanese details. The grounds, restored by Isabelle Greene, the architect's granddaughter, are magnificent.

29. Freeman House, 1913
Arthur S. Heineman
(Alfred Heineman, associate)
1330 Hillcrest Avenue

The once-rolled eaves have now been clipped, but this is still a great Craftsman house. Notice the extensive use of Batchelder tile. There is more inside.

30. Prindle House, 1926, 1928
George Washington Smith
1311 Hillcrest Avenue

Bold Spanish Farmhouse Revival forms mark this house; its tour de force is the garden to the rear.

31. Elliott House, 1925
Wallace Neff
1290 Hillcrest Avenue

Extremely dignified Spanish Revival.

32. Griffith House, 1924
Johnson, Kaufman, and Coate
1275 Hillcrest Avenue

Spanish Revival. See also the house in the same style next door.

33. Cordelia Culbertson
House, 1911
Charles and Henry Greene
1188 Hillcrest Avenue

This gunite-sheathed house with green tile roof seems more Chinese than Japanese. It is roughly U-shaped with a Moorish fountain in the central court. The back of the house, which once looked down on extensive terraced gardens, is almost pure Segovia. Only a suggestion of the extensive gardens remains.

92 • Pasadena, Central Business District

The commercial heart of nineteenth-century Pasadena was at Fair Oaks Avenue and Colorado Boulevard, mostly on Fair Oaks. Indeed, a small and precious fragment remains. But, contrary to early expectations, the main business developed along Colorado Boulevard and the result was a congeries of taste that we have already described. Spanish and Art Deco façades hooked to Victorian structures line the street from Delacey to El Molino Avenues, with an interruption on the south side between Arroyo Parkway and Los Robles.

Colorado Boulevard (Pasadena's main street) was, until the 1950s, pretty much a commercial strip with single-family residential areas spreading behind almost within the same block both north and south. Recently this pattern has changed with the building of hotels, banks, and condominiums to the south of Colorado and the development of the Parsons Engineering firm to the northwest. This new growth has wiped out many neighborhoods and several landmarks, but it has been accompanied by a growing awareness of the importance of old buildings, an awareness that is visible in the restoration of storefronts, the cleaning of the brick backs and alleys, and restrictions on signage. Other indications of responsibility are an extremely active urban conservation program emanating from city hall and a resourceful private support organization, Pasadena Heritage.

1. Ralph M. Parsons Company, Office Tower, 1974
William Pereira Associates
100 W. Walnut Street

Two almost identical office buildings, 1979, 1981
Skidmore, Owings, and Merrill

Sorry to begin this section on a negative note, but the tower in particular is something that should stand as a monument to what should be avoided. Architecturally dull, its bulk is an insult to the fine scale of the older buildings on the skyline. The other two major buildings, designed in Skidmore, Owings, and Merrill's wraparound style, are not much better, though there is a rather striking view of the older one from the picturesque alley to the south of it.

2. Pennsylvania Oil and Tire Warehouse, 1930
Bennett and Haskell
33 Delacey Avenue

The lower portion of the structure has been remodeled, but the tower remains pretty much as it was envisioned by the architects—Art Deco with a Programmatic frieze of automobile wheels. It has been recycled and now houses a Saks Fifth Avenue department store.

3. Friend Paper Company, 1965
Smith and Williams
100 W. Green Street

A surprising place for this sophisticated, typically regionalized (softened), International Style design to have been erected. The deep bays were landscaped by Eckbo, Dean, and Associates.

4. Stahlhuth House, 1907
Charles and Henry Greene
380 S. Pasadena Avenue

Originally you would be unable to distinguish this bungalow from the hundreds of others that once surrounded it. It now has a fine view of the uncompleted Long Beach Freeway.

5. House, 1893
Wood Taylor
101 Bellevue Drive

A charming two-story Queen Anne dwelling with characteristic ornament in the gable. You have to imagine it in its orange grove.

6. Palmetto Court, 1915
A. C. Parlee, builder
100 Palmetto Drive

Fourteen tiny Craftsman bungalows.

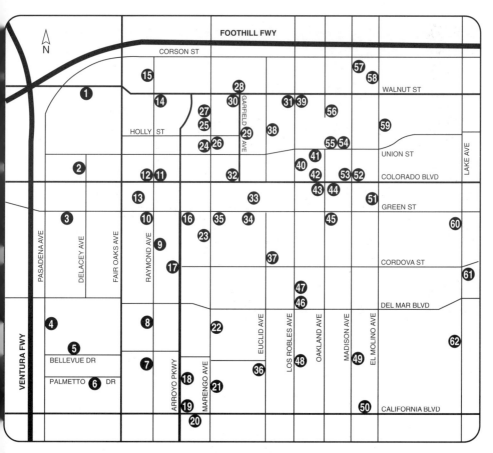

7. Royal Laundry Building, 1927;
addition, circa 1935
Gordon B. Kaufmann
443 S. Raymond Avenue

Restrained Spanish Revival enhanced by a fine tile doorway almost Art Deco in design. The later addition is in Streamline Moderne. All this is on the site of the once-sensational Moorish Revival Lowe's Opera House.

8. Pasadena Humane Society Building, 1932
Robert H. Ainsworth
361 S. Raymond Avenue

A fine Mediterranean-style building. The new addition (1993) is by Kurt Meyer Associates (Clifton P. Allen).

9. Santa Fe (AMTRAK) Railroad Passenger Station, 1935
H. L. Gilman
222 S. Raymond Avenue

The Superchief once stopped here and let out movie stars and other Hollywood types who preferred this station to the one in downtown Los Angeles. Now that the interurban Gold Line has taken over the right-of-way this will become a restaurant. Notice the beautiful Batchelder tile inside.

10

10. Hotel Green (now Castle Green Apartments and Hotel Green Apartments),
1898, 1903
Frederick L. Roehrig
50 E. Green Street,
at the southwest corner of
Raymond Avenue

The Hotel Green, once one of the great resort hotels, has now been converted into apartments and condominiums. Both are very private, but quite often the owners of Castle Green play host to Pasadena Heritage, and it is possible to see the public rooms, almost completely intact with even some of the Moorish furniture in place. These buildings are late additions to an older hotel that was on the other side of Raymond Avenue, but demolished in the 1930s. Thus the "Bridge of Sighs" that once connected the newer buildings to the old is now cut off at the sidewalk. The Staats Company is partly housed in what is left of the old hotel that was

designed by Strange and Carnicle (southeast corner of Raymond and Green). Note the original curved entrance at the corner.

11. United California Bank,
1929
Bennett and Haskell
Northeast corner of
North Raymond Avenue and
East Colorado Boulevard

A crisp brick essay in Art Deco.

11

12. Kinney-Kendall Building,
1897
Charles and Henry Greene;
remodeled, 1925
Bennett and Haskell
65 E. Colorado Boulevard,
at the northwest corner of
North Raymond Avenue

As a result of the 1920s setback and the stripping away of almost all ornament, this rare example of the Greenes' commercial work bears little resemblance to their original ideas. While it was never a great building, the Greene and Greene cult should take it in hand and restore it.

13. Old Pasadena
Fair Oaks and
Raymond Avenues
(two blocks north and south of
Colorado Boulevard)

Here is the commercial heart of old Pasadena. It was pretty badly handled by time, neglect, and remodeling, but the White Block (1887), at one time the city hall, at the southwest corner of Union Street and Fair Oaks Avenue, the Slavin Block next door on Fair Oaks, and the Venetian Revival Building (1887; Harry Ridgeway) farther down the street at number 9–17, have been restored and recycled. A good example of what can be accomplished is the Renaissance Revival Block (1894; Frank Hudson) at 32 S. Raymond Avenue, and there are other good refurbishings all around. Best of all are the brick alleys that have been drawn upon for their highly pictur-esque quality.

14. Entrance to Old Pasadena Public Library, 1887
C. W. Buchanan
Southeast corner of
Walnut Street and
Raymond Avenue

This relic of the Richardsonian Romanesque library remains as a garden ruin at the corner of a small park. Across the street at 145 N. Raymond Avenue is the stunning PWA Moderne California State Armory, now the Armory Gallery. It was designed by Bennett and Haskell, and built in 1932. Notice also the rare

group of clapboard row houses (1901) at the opposite corner.

15. St. Andrew's Roman Catholic Church, 1927
Ross Montgomery
311 N. Raymond Avenue

Early Christian fabric with Romanesque campanile right out of old Ravenna. The rich interior is marvelous, as is the contribu-tion of the church outlines to the cityscape. Best seen from the Foothill Freeway going east at sunset. *The Stations of the Cross* and other murals were painted by Venetian artist Carlo Wostry.

16. BankAmericard Center, 1975
Edward D. Stone
Southeast corner of
Green Street and
Arroyo Parkway

Late Stone, a huge pink marble block without windows (presum-ably because computers do not need light). One wag has sug-gested that it looks like the box that the Conference Center (across Marengo Avenue) came packaged in.

17. Pasadena Winter Garden (now Storage Facility), 1940
Cyril Bennett
Arroyo Parkway at the west end of Cordova Street

Originally a skating rink, this Streamline Moderne mass evokes nostalgia for the FDR era.

18. Bryan's Cleaners, 1938
Eliot Construction Company
544 Arroyo Parkway

A well-turned essay in the Streamline Moderne.

19. Hunt Offices and Display Rooms, 1925
George Hunt
Northeast corner of Arroyo Parkway and California Boulevard

Hunt was the foremost furniture maker to the rich in the 1920s. This Monterey-style structure was good advertising.

20. Architect's Offices, 1929
Wallace Neff and Ernest Torrance
186 E. California Boulevard

Very picturesque, rural Andalusian Spanish, still so, in spite of its sitting behind a gas station. Note the new Spanish Revival apartment house (2001) at the corner of California and Marengo, designed by Polyzoides and Moule.

21. Two Houses, 1905
Louis B. Easton
530, 540 S. Marengo Avenue

Easton, Elbert Hubbard's brother-in-law, built number 540, improvising upon a plan he found in a book. But according to a legend, which should be true even if it isn't, in designing number 530, he cast away precedent and relied on his own best judgment. It is the better of the two, in the Swiss Chalet version of Craftsman

architecture. It has been restored by Pasadena Heritage.

22. Don Carlos Court, 1927
Burrell and Company, builders
374–384 S. Marengo Avenue

A pleasant bungalow court in the Spanish Revival mode. South Marengo still has many bungalow courts. Some are being recycled as this street becomes commercial. Others are in limbo.

23. Stoutenburgh House, circa 1887
J. H. Bradbeer
255 S. Marengo Avenue

A lovely Queen Anne, holding on for dear life against the tides of change. In 1980 it was converted to office use by Tim Andersen, restoration architect.

24. First Baptist Church, 1926
Carleton M. Winslow Sr. and Frederick Kennedy
75 N. Marengo Avenue

Italian Romanesque in exposed concrete with a beautiful tower that adds to the cityscape.

25. Turner and Stevens Mortuary (now Holly Street Grill), 1922
Marston and Van Pelt
95 N. Marengo Avenue

A long, low brick structure in the English Gothic mode.

26. YWCA Building, 1920–22
Julia Morgan
Southeast corner of Marengo Avenue and Holly Street

A disappointing, very bland Mediterranean-style work by a major architect. The addition is, of course, not to be blamed on her. Now abandoned. Across the street is the former YMCA, recycled by Brenda Levin Associates for affordable housing.

27. American Legion Post, 1925
Marston and Van Pelt
131 N. Marengo Avenue

Spanish Renaissance. As the ranks of this once-active American institution dwindle, the future of such fine buildings as this and the even greater one in Hollywood is insecure.

28. Pasadena Public Library, 1927
Myron Hunt and H. C. Chambers
285 E. Walnut Street

Spanish Renaissance. The rich Plateresque entrance beyond the screen on the street is unusual for Hunt, whose works are often on the dry side. A public entrance has been added on the north side of the building, and the interior has been elegantly restored.

29. Pasadena City Hall, 1925–27
John Bakewell Jr. and Arthur Brown Jr.
100 N. Garfield Avenue

One of several exceptions to the rule that Pasadena's best buildings were designed by Pasadena architects, this giant wedding cake is by the San Francisco firm that is responsible for that city's marvelous headquarters. Pasadena was less generous so the interiors are plain in comparison to the earlier San Francisco City Hall, but its central patio with fountain and beautiful garden makes up for the absence of all that marble. The Spanish Baroque dome and western façade are stunning in the late afternoon sun and when lighted at night.

Notice also the handsome Gas Company Building (1929) at the northwest corner of Garfield Avenue and Ramona Street, and

30

across Garfield on the northeast corner, the old Court Buildings (1952; Breo Freeman), the latter distinguished by being well-executed Spanish at so late a date and the former for its rare scraffito-work in the second story.

30. Pasadena Police Department Building, 1989–90
EKONA, planning architect; Robert A. M. Stern, design architect (Stern Ehrenkrantz Ramager); Campbell and Campbell, landscape architects; Robert Irwin, sculptor
Southwest corner of Walnut and Garfield Streets

The architects faced a difficult task in designing this building. The nearby City Hall, Library, and Gas Company Building are so strong in design that they had to choose between being self-effacing or salient. Being rather strong architects themselves, they naturally chose the latter stance, the volutes on the roof being

their big statement. Except for anemic detailing, the building comes off rather well, especially when set off by the small garden and sculpture, not to mention the wall in shades of lavender, now fading.

31. Doubletree Inn, 1989–90
Moore, Ruble and Yudell; Lawrence Halprin, landscape architect; Joyce Kozloff, ceramic designer
Southwest corner of Walnut and Los Robles Streets

Set in the Plaza de las Fuentes (by Halprin) this monster is not the firm's best work. With its round arches, it seems to be playing off the Mission Inn in Riverside. The plaza is much better, setting off the city hall beautifully. The large amount of colorful tilework seems on the gaudy side for Pasadena (but note the old Batchelder tile fountain on the center of the wall).

32. Old Pasadena Post Office, 1913
Oscar Wenderoth; addition, 1938 Marston and Maybury
Northwest corner of Garfield Avenue and Colorado Boulevard

The Italian Renaissance palace is notable not only for its façade with light relief decoration but also for its interior space enclosed in colorful marble walls, paid for by the people of Pasadena, mind you, and not the federal government. The electric blue walls in the rear are recent and lamentable. The building is now a branch of the downright hideous new Central Post Office at Lincoln Avenue and Orange Grove Boulevard.

33. Paseo Colorado
Bounded by Colorado Boulevard to the north, Green Street to the south, Los Robles to the east, and Marengo Avenue to the west

An extraordinary thing has happened here. The Plaza Pasadena, a vast shopping mall built by Kober Associates in 1980, was almost completely demolished in 1998–99 and replaced by this group of buildings, more to the scale of the 1920s structures on the north side of Colorado. Unfortunately the new is just a little bit better than the old. It lacks the attention to detail that is one of the chief requirements of architecture. Except for a partial reopening of the minor axis on Garfield, a part of the original Civic Center plan, the architects (or developers!) have left little open space. Oh yes, they spared one of the chief horrors, the Broadway (now Macy's) department store, as a reminder of the former shopping mall. Its unfenestrated side on Los Robles has been called "the Wailing Wall" with considerable accuracy.

A low-silhouette Italian Renaissance palace that is once again the "City Beautiful" southern anchor of the minor Garfield Avenue axis dominated by City Hall and anchored at the north by the Public Library.

35. Pasadena Convention Center, 1975
John Carl Warnecke
300 E. Green Street

At both sides of the auditorium are what one little old Pasadena lady has called "The Pig Sties," low structures with most of their interior spaces partially underground. The intention of the architect was to avoid competing with the auditorium. Very commendable except that he was in a Brutalist phase and the roofs do intrude.

stepped glass brick. A large ear appears on the roof of this object, so much in contrast with its Craftsman and Spanish neighbors.

37. Masonic Temple, 1926
Bennett and Haskell
200 S. Euclid Avenue

A Beaux-Arts Renaissance structure of great dignity.

38. All Saints Episcopal Church, 1925
Johnson, Kaufman, and Coate (Roland E. Coate);
Parish House and Rectory, 1930
Bennett and Haskell;
interior of Parish House remodeled after fire, 1979
Warren Callister
132 N. Euclid Avenue

English Country Gothic without and within, including Tiffany windows from an earlier church. The Episcopalians seem to have unfailing good taste. The observation applies to the new interiors of the Parish House; joyful is the best word to describe them. The sanctuary has been remodeled (1991) by Kurt Landberg Associates of St. Louis. In order to meet the needs of the modern service, parts of the rood screen were placed in the south transept, and the altar, choir stalls, and pulpit were brought forward. In doing this, only a small area of the original Batchelder tile floor was removed. All in all an extremely sensitive transformation of a church that is in the vanguard of social action.

34. Pasadena Civic Auditorium, 1932
Edwin Bergstrom;
Bennett and Haskell;
J. E. Stanton, decorator
300 E. Green Street

36. Condominiums, 1981
Eric Moss and James Stafford
475 S. Euclid Avenue

Really, in Pasadena? A Postmodern extravaganza in stucco with window panels in

39. First Congregational Church, 1904, 1916
Buchanan and Brockway
Southeast corner of Walnut Street and Los Robles Avenue

A large English Gothic church that dignifies a rather forlorn commercial area.

40. Grace Nicholson Building (now Pacific-Asia Museum), 1924
Marston, Van Pelt, and Maybury
46 N. Los Robles Avenue

A real surprise—a Chinese palace. A dealer in Asian art and books on Asia as well as American Indian artifacts, Ms. Nicholson built it as a shop and home. Later it became the Pasadena Museum of Art until that institution moved to new quarters. Now it is the Pacific-Asia Museum, which has done very well by giving unusually good exhibitions and building a lovely Chinese garden in the central court (1979; Erikson, Peters, Thomas, and Associates).

41. Pasadena Museum of California Art, 2000-2002
Johnson, Favaro
490 E. Union Street (parking under galleries)

This is an unexpected addition

to the museum city of Pasadena. It is the inspiration of Robert and Arlene Oltman, who saw the need for a space devoted solely to the display of California art. The north (entrance) façade is offbeat, but it hardly prepares you for the sensuous undulations of the staircase walls or for the small lobby with its cloud-like chandelier. The galleries have interesting fluctuations in proportions but are simple, as they should be.

42. Warner Building, 1927
Marston and Maybury;
Jess Stanton, designer
481 E. Colorado Boulevard

Most of the marvelous black-and-gold Art Deco seashell and flower ornament has been restored.

43. First United Methodist Church, 1926
Thomas P. Barber
Southwest corner of Oakland Avenue and Colorado Boulevard

On the outside, this English Gothic church is notable for the pleasant entrance court and the lovely tracery of the large east window, best viewed on a Sunday morning. The stained-glass windows throughout the church were fabricated by Roy C. Baillie Studios of Los Angeles. The interior has the usual Methodist central plan with curved pews and curved balcony surrounding the pulpit. But it is the fan vaulting of the ceiling that is remarkable. If you look closely, you will see that the intricate plaster work ingeniously encloses the ventilating system.

44. Singer Building, 1926
Everett Phipps Babcock
520 E. Colorado Boulevard

A good as-yet-unspoiled example of Spanish Revival commercial work.

45. First Church of Christ Scientist, 1909
F. P. Burnham
Southeast corner of Oakland Avenue and Green Street

Like most churches of this denomination, this is a variation on the Neoclassical "Mother Church" in Boston. It is one of the first large exposed-concrete structures in the area. It has recently been restored in the best sense of the word.

46. Throop Memorial Unitarian-Universalist Church, 1923
Frederick Kennedy
Northeast corner of Los Robles Avenue and Del Mar Boulevard

An exposed-concrete (now plastered over) Gothic design that gives sophistication to this area.

47. E. W. Smith House, 1910
Charles and Henry Greene
272 S. Los Robles Avenue, next door to Throop Church

A large two-story Craftsman house that shows very little evidence of the Greenes' Japanese influence. Converted to commercial use without damaging the integrity of the architecture, this building is a model of adaptive reuse.

48. Pages Victorian Court, 1981
Thornton and Fagan Associates
430 S. Los Robles Avenue

Talk about a protest against the Modern movement, this is it—a humorous, not too authentic but still recognizable, Eastlake Revival extravaganza.

49. Pasadena Town Club, 1931
Roland E. Coate
378 S. Madison Avenue

This chaste, one-story Monterey-style building with a good Greek Revival door exudes respectability.

50. Casa Torre Garden Court, 1927
Everett Phipps Babcock
611–627 E. California Boulevard

A two-story, L-shaped Spanish Revival apartment building that looks as if it is about to be gobbled up by Modernism.

51. Pasadena Playhouse, 1924–25
Elmer Grey;
Dwight Gibbs,
with Alson Clark, interiors
37 S. El Molino Avenue

Once the very heart of Pasadena culture, this theater and school came upon hard times in the 1950s and collapsed in the mid-1960s. The wonder is that it is still with us. The theater has been beautifully restored and has resumed its old function and ambience.

52. First Trust Building, 1928
Bennett and Haskell
595 E. Colorado Boulevard, at Madison Avenue

This dignified Renaissance Revival building is most impressive inside. The banking room was decorated by Giovanni Smeraldi and is hung with four large paintings by Alson Clark. Also, this happens to be the first building in Pasadena built to resist earthquakes. In 1971 it met the test.

53. Pasadena Presbyterian Church, 1976
Gougeon-Woodman
Northwest corner of Colorado Boulevard and Madison Avenue

Architectural expressionism at its very height, this church replaces a Collegiate Gothic structure (1906) by F. L. Roehrig that was badly damaged in the 1971 earthquake.

54. Blaisdell Medical Building, 1952
Smith and Williams (Whitney R. Smith)
547 E. Union Street

A small reinforced-concrete building with central patio. Smith was obviously influenced by Wrightian ideas. He did not design the wooden fence.

55. Earl Apartment House, 1912
Charles and Henry Greene
527 E. Union Street

The Greenes working in the Mission style, though they could not resist occasional Asian touches.

56. Blinn House (now Women's City Club), 1905–6
George W. Maher
Oakland Avenue at Ford Place

So far as is known, this is the only house in the West designed by the well-known Chicago architect, a friend of Sullivan and Wright. (Incidentally, Maher's only other western building is, of all things, a combined public library and water tower in Fresno). Stylistically the Blinn House is distantly related to the Mission Revival, though it is hard to place the corner windows on the second floor. The interior, somewhat remodeled, is nevertheless still exciting, particularly the staircase and glazed-tile fireplace.

57. Bungalow Court, 1910
Attributed to Hunt and Grey
270 N. Madison Avenue

A handsome Tudor court.

58. Lukens House, 1886–88
Harry Ridgeway
267 N. El Molino Avenue

This beautifully restored house in its garden is one of the few vestiges of Victorianism left in this part of town. It is Queen Anne with dripping lath-work similar to that on Lucky Baldwin's Guest House in Arcadia.

59. Scottish Rite Cathedral, 1924
Joseph J. Blick
150 N. Madison Avenue

Pre-PWA Classical Moderne with guardian sphinxes.

60. Retail Shops, 1961
Pulliam, Matthews, and Associates
230 S. Lake Avenue

Very civilized International Style, including an outdoor cafe.

61. Bullock's Pasadena (now Macy's), 1947
Wurdeman and Becket; Ruth Shellhorn and Carl McElvy, landscape architects
401 S. Lake Avenue

The design and siting of this posh upper-middle-class store is in many ways unique, even to the California scene. Essentially it appears from Lake Avenue as a building in a park. As was mentioned when it opened in 1947, "Because the new store was planned to serve the people of Pasadena and the San Gabriel Valley, whose lives are spent in garden communities and whose homes express a marked degree of love of the out-of-doors, the architects designed a building in keeping with the garden theme so dear to the dwellers in those prosperous and progressive communities of cultivated estates." (*Southwest Builder and Contractor*, September 26, 1947).

The building extends the Streamline Moderne idiom into the postwar era, but the architects have combined the Streamline with a delicate and sophisticated image of the Regency. The elegance of the interior craftsmanship, now beginning to show wear, evokes the Arts and Crafts tradition. Recently (2003), a new retail center has been built in the old parking lot. It was designed by Johnson, Favaro. In spite of its filling desirable open space, it complements the older building and is, in a word, beautiful.

62. The Burlington Arcade, 1982
Symondz/Deenihan
380 S. Lake Avenue

A galleria of two two-story tiers of shops facing each other, reminiscent of the original London building of the same name. These architects also designed The Commons (1982), a courtyard shopping center up the street near the corner of Green Street. This time they chose the Mansard mode. You will find it impossible to keep from looking up Lake, which is lined with medium high-rise commercial buildings, all of them without exception disappointing. It is incredible that the Design Review Commission for a city that has such a high reputation for good architecture could have allowed this to happen.

93 • East Pasadena

The section of the city east of Lake Avenue and south of the Foothill Freeway is fairly recent Pasadena, with projects of the 1920s and 1930s appearing in the western portion. Then, about Hill Avenue at Pasadena City College, shards of the 1950s begin to pop up, at first on commercial Colorado Boulevard and then south of it in the residential districts. It is easy to brush this stuff off as kitsch culture, but who knows what forthcoming Ph.D. candidate will pronounce it not just significant but profound!

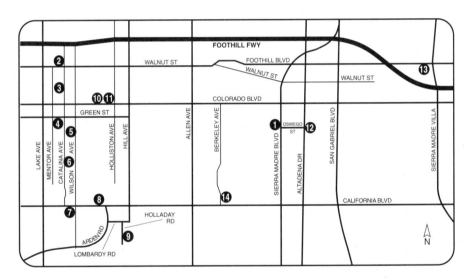

1. House, circa 1915
71–75 Sierra Madre Boulevard

Midwest Prairie-style houses built in the Los Angeles area are rare, and of those built, few remain. Here is an example of the style sheathed in tan-colored brick. It even exhibits Wrightian planters on the top of the columns that support the front pergola. Recently immaculately restored.

2. Trinity Lutheran Church, 1927
Frederick Kennedy Jr.
997 E. Walnut Street, at Catalina Avenue

Vaguely English Gothic in revealed concrete. Kennedy was a strong advocate of concrete construction in the Los Angeles area and his work deserves a careful study.

3. Sanborn House, 1903
Charles and Henry Greene
65 N. Catalina Avenue

This is a large angular Craftsman structure, never very good and made worse by a nasty paint job. But it is by Greene and Greene and significant, for in 1903 they were on the brink of their great creative period.

4. Thatcher Medical Center and other buildings, 1948–49
L. G. Scherer
960 E. Green Street, at Mentor Avenue

A collection of offices, shops, and apartments in the New Orleans Mansard style, rather strange to encounter in Pasadena.

5. Apartment Building, 1963
Pulliam, Matthews, and Associates
241 S. Wilson Avenue

Elegant International Style simplicity on a tree-lined street notable for apartments designed with less sophistication, to put it mildly.

6. House, circa 1915
Arthur S. Heineman (Alfred Heineman, associate)
516 S. Catalina Avenue

The rolled-eave treatment of this house is a trademark of Heineman's work in the teens.

7. Polytechnic School, 1907
Hunt and Grey
1030 E. California Street, at Wilson Avenue

This is probably the first fully realized bungalow school. Not only does it manage to get all the classrooms on one floor, but it also opens these rooms with ranks of doors to the outside, pioneering the idea of the indoor-outdoor school that has won wide popularity in California and elsewhere. The old building has been remodeled, but the idea is still clear.

8. California Institute of Technology (Caltech), 1908–present
California Boulevard, between Wilson and Hill Avenues

The firm of Myron Hunt and

Elmer Grey designed the first campus plan and buildings for Caltech. Their scheme provided a Beaux-Arts axial mall, open at one end and surrounded by two-story Mission Revival structures on the enclosed sides. Their principal building, which terminated the major axis, was Throop Hall (Pasadena Hall) of 1910. After their partnership broke up, Hunt continued work on the campus over a period of eight years, from 1908 through 1915, when he was replaced by Bertram G. Goodhue, who enlarged and elaborated on the original axial plan, making the landscape more Moorish and the buildings more Spanish Churrigueresque. After Goodhue's death in 1924, his firm, Goodhue Associates, continued to design buildings for the campus through the late 1930s. From 1928 through 1938 Beatrix Farrand was the consulting landscape architect for Caltech, and fragments of her various designs remain.

As with most American academic institutions after World War II, the Modern movement entered the scene. The results have added little of merit, and they have done much to destroy the strong character of the original campus plan and its architecture.

The most interesting buildings mentioned here are:

a. Gates Chemistry Laboratory (now Administration Building), 1917
Bertram G. Goodhue and Elmer Grey

Its exterior is dominated by a fine Churrigueresque door. The interior has been recycled (1983) by Bobrow and Thomas; Peter de Bretteville and Stefanos Polyzoides. The Gates Annex

(1927) is by Goodhue Associates and is Spanish mixed with Art Deco.

b. Bridge Physics Laboratory, 1922
Bertram G. Goodhue

Again, rather severe Spanish with relief given by a Churrigueresque entrance.

c. West Court Buildings, 1928–30
Goodhue Associates

The main (Wilson Avenue) entrance to Caltech consists of two long arcaded buildings somewhat reminiscent of the Campo Santo at Pisa. The rows of Italian cypresses in front of them have been cut down, much to the detriment of the original design.

d. Athenaeum (now Faculty Club), 1930
Gordon B. Kaufmann

A marvelous Mediterranean (Italian)-style building without and within.

e. Dormitories, 1931
Gordon B. Kaufmann

Designed around three courtyards, these vaguely Spanish/Italian Romanesque buildings, with capitals in the cloisters featuring the heads of aviators and scientists, are real treasures.

f. Beckman Auditorium, 1963
Edward D. Stone

A fanciful Islamic image evoking late Frank Lloyd Wright.

g. Winnett Student Center, 1998
A. C. Martin Partners

With Gordon Kaufmann's dormitories in mind, the architects remodeled an older building that was incredibly dull. The beautiful result looks more Italian than Spanish.

h. Sherman Fairchild Library, 1997
Moore Ruble Yudell

This building near the Dabney Hall of the Humanities (1928; Goodhue Associates in consultation with Clarence Stein) complements its neighbors' blending of Spanish (even Mayan!) images. A successful example of contextualism. Its reading room is stunning.

i. Avery House, 1996
Moore Ruble Yudell

Tile roofs, arcades, and patio, this dormitory at the southwest corner of Del Mar Boulevard and Holliston Avenue is a return to the Spanish tradition with which the university began its building program.

j. Edyth and Eli Broad Center for the Biological Sciences, 2002
Pei Cobb Freed

In 2000 David Baltimore, the then-new president of Caltech, is supposed to have said that the coming of a new millennium suggested that Caltech deserved a new architecture. The uproar has not yet died down. Indeed, at first it looked as if the fancy East Coast architects were putting up an eyesore, but the Modernist structure—formal yet lively—has turned out very well. The effect has been considerably enhanced by the planting of a grove of mature palm trees at one corner of the building.

9. Hale Solar Laboratory, 1924
Johnson, Kaufmann and Coate (Roland E. Coate)
740 Holladay Road

Here is an oddity and a significant one. This was the private preserve of astronomer George Ellery Hale, who was one of the great cultural leaders in Pasadena, and who, as a Trustee of Caltech, was as responsible as Robert Millikan for bringing Caltech to national eminence. He was also a student of planning and architecture. In the case of this building, the style is Spanish with strong Egyptian overtones befitting the laboratory of an astronomer. No one seems to know who designed the entrance bas-relief of Akhenaton with sun rays. Another bas-relief over the mantel inside is by nationally known sculptor Lee Lawrie. The gardens were laid out by Beatrix Farrand in 1928, but little remains of her design.

California Boulevard, east of Caltech:

This street, extending into San Marino and San Pasqual, has fine houses in the period revivals of the 1920s and 1930s. It is a good place to walk. Even better is Lombardy Road, one block below California; but, since most of Lombardy is in San Marino, we have included it in our San Marino section.

8j

13

10. Austin Automobile Showroom, circa 1927
Austin Company (Cleveland)
1285 E. Colorado Boulevard

Huge gaping jaws full of plate glass are framed by cast-stone Plateresque ornament.

11. Holliston Avenue United Methodist Church, 1899
John C. Austin
Northwest corner of Holliston Avenue and Colorado Boulevard

This large Gothic structure (which looks Richardsonian) was moved stone by stone from its original site at Marengo Avenue and Colorado Boulevard where it had been First Methodist. It lost its tower in the 1971 earthquake, but it otherwise speaks of the late Victorian age. The interior is based on the Akron Plan with its semicircular seating oriented to the northwest corner pulpit area.

12. Pasadena Public Library, Lamanda Park Branch, 1966
Pulliam, Matthews, and Associates
140 S. Altadena Drive, at Oswego Street

Though one-story, the massive concrete post-and-lintel frame makes this building seem monumental. The interior is well-planned for use and beauty.

13. Stuart Pharmaceutical Company, 1957–58
Edward D. Stone; Thomas D. Church, landscape architect
3300 block of East Foothill Boulevard, near Sierra Madre Villa Avenue

This building and the American Embassy in New Delhi are Stone's best designs in the post–World War II era. Like the embassy, the Stuart Building poses as a delicate Islamic box set in a Persian pond. "Despite its sparkling modernity," it was

mentioned in the May 23, 1958, issue of the *Southwest Builder and Contractor:* "The Stuart building has been likened to the Taj Mahal for its beauty and its Asian influence." Church's design for the garden fully acknowledges the mood that Stone was trying to convey. Parking was provided for 300 cars, and Church designed a swimming pool for employees and guests. This impressive ensemble is a significant reminder of the days when industry saw itself as a major patron of the arts. It has fallen on bad times in recent years and is threatened by progress.

14. Ten Spec Houses, circa 1927
Wallace Neff
500 Block of South Berkeley Avenue San Marino

A group of modest-sized Spanish Revival houses by an architect who usually designed much larger ones.

94 • North Pasadena

This area, bounded on the west and south by the Foothill Freeway, on the east by Michillinda Avenue, and on the north by the boundary with Altadena, is listed from west to east, generally alternating streets south/north and north/south.

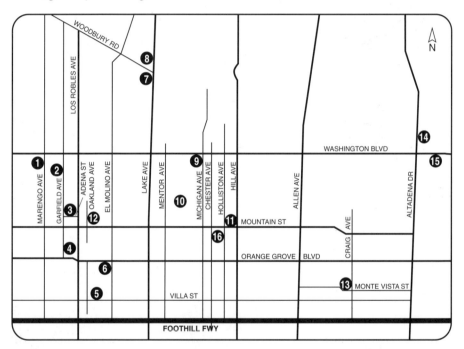

1. Savage House, 1924
Henry Greene

1299–1301 N. Marengo Avenue

A Spanish Revival duplex distinguished only by the name of its architect. It was done after his partnership with his brother, Charles, was dissolved.

2. House, 1891
Frederick L. Roehrig

1247 N. Garfield Avenue

The Anglo-Colonial Revival at its best, this beautifully detailed house awaits restoration.

3. Lewis House ("Mansion Adena"), 1886
Attributed to Eugene Getschell

Northeast corner of Garfield Avenue and Adena Street

This otherwise Queen Anne house sports a Mansard tower.

4. Rust-Smiley House, 1887
E. W. Houghton

730 N. Garfield Avenue

Another good Queen Anne, well set back from the street.

5. Bowen Court, 1913
Arthur S. Heineman
(Alfred Heineman, associate)

539 Villa Street

This is one of the first bungalow courts. It is set in tall trees and extends in an L around to North Oakland Avenue. Note the rustic "playhouse" (now glassed in), which is toward the center of the court. Two other bungalow courts of the same period—one Mission style, the other Craftsman—are at 567 and 572–574 N. Oakland Avenue respectively. The former

is quite simple but retains marvelous Mission-style lanterns in
the center of the court. The
photographer for the image above
was possibly Helen Lukens Gant.

6. House, 1914
*Southwest corner of
Orange Grove Boulevard and
El Molino Avenue*
A huge airplane bungalow on a
boulder base.

7. Westminster Presbyterian Church, 1928
Marston, Van Pelt, and Maybury (Sylvanus Marston)
1757 N. Lake Avenue

Certainly a landmark as Lake
Avenue rises toward the mountains, this church seems vaguely
modeled on St. Maclou at Rouen.

8. St. Elizabeth's Roman Catholic Church, 1924
Wallace Neff
*1849 N. Lake Avenue,
north of Westminster
Presbyterian Church
Altadena*

The monumental but simple façade of this Spanish Revival church is marred only by a bad sculpture of the saint over the door.

9. House, circa 1910
Southwest corner of Michigan Avenue and Washington Boulevard

Mission style with red trim.

10. Bungalow Heaven
Sixteen blocks east of Lake Avenue and bounded by Washington Boulevard, Mentor Avenue, Orange Grove Boulevard, and Chester Avenue.

Almost completely built with bungalows—one- or one-and-a-half-story single-family houses on tree-lined streets of which the best is Michigan. None of the houses is great architecture. They are simply pleasant places to live with their gardens and the unity of scale with few intrusions.

Even more significant, its residents have a conspicuous "pride in place" that makes for a real sense of community. For instance, although near gang-infested areas, the spirit of neighborhood within "heaven" is so strong that there is little trouble with crime or drugs.

The inhabitants, mostly middle-class, are very proud of their houses, which usually date from the teens or twenties and are thus California bungalows, i.e., touched with Japanese and Swiss details. Every year the residents of Bungalow Heaven stage a public tour of several of the houses, with proceeds going toward restoration and neighborhood amenities. It is amusing that so many of these dwellings are now furnished with Craftsman furniture—Stickley and pseudo-Stickley—that the original owners of the houses could not possibly have afforded. But it certainly looks good.

Bungalow Heaven is an official Landmark District of Pasadena and has strict building and renovation codes.

11. Williams House ("Hillmont"), 1887 Harry Ridgeway
Northwest corner of Hill Avenue and Mountain Street

This Queen Anne house of extraordinary quality is set in beautiful grounds. Ridgeway was Pasadena's first professional architect. Hiram Reid in his *History of Pasadena* (circa 1895) wrote that Ridgeway "never wanted any man to be able to point out any structure and say 'that's one of Ridgeway's designs—it shows the earmarks of his style.' He sought and achieved that ideal freedom from style called the artlessness of art."

Just west of the house at 1507 Mountain Street is the utterly nondescript Thum House (1925) by Henry Greene.

12. Gartz Duplex, 1921 Irving J. Gill
950 N. Oakland Avenue

Simple stucco walls and an arch—very characteristic of Gill in a highly puritanical mood.

13. Craig Adobe ("The Hermitage"), circa 1880
2121 Monte Vista Street, just west of Craig Avenue

Except for its walls, this is a Queen Anne cottage with fish-scale shingles in the gable. Most of the "Victorian" details were added in a remodeling (circa 1950) by Earl Hugens.

14. Pasadena Jewish Temple and Center, 1957
1434 N. Altadena Drive, just above Washington Boulevard

Classical Moderne.

15. St. Luke's Hospital, 1934 Gene Verge Sr.
2632 E. Washington Boulevard, near Altadena Drive

Classical Moderne with strong Spanish Revival elements.

16. Hale House, circa 1910
835 N. Holliston Avenue

A sturdy example of the Craftsman aesthetic in a predominantly Swiss Chalet version.

12

95 • Altadena

Altadena is unincorporated, but, as its name implies, it is culturally a higher extension of Pasadena. Here, large estates existed by the late nineteenth century. Although by now almost all of them have been subdivided several times, the relaxed style of living can still be imagined—citrus groves and chicken farms!

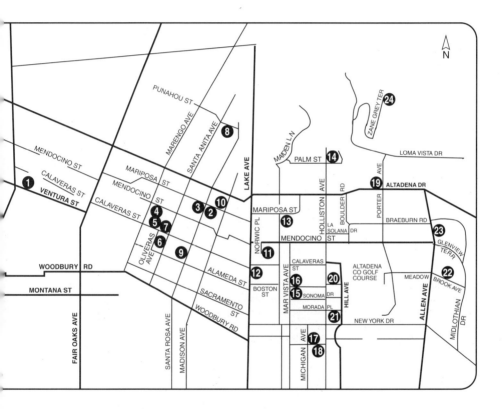

1. House, circa 1906
Louis B. Easton
403 W. Ventura Street, near Lincoln Avenue

By a miracle this Craftsman bunkhouse was not torn down when the C. C. Curtis ranch house was demolished. It is, along with the Volney-Craig House in Pasadena, one of Easton's finest designs, which is to say that it is one of the best examples of the Craftsman aesthetic anywhere.

The house across the street is also probably by Easton. In 1925 additions were made to it by Henry Greene.

2. McNally House, 1888
Frederick L. Roehrig
654 E. Mariposa

A towered, simplified Queen Anne (Shingle-style) building now almost obscured by later building. A. N. McNally (of Rand-McNally) was a commissioner of the World's Columbian Exposition in Chicago in 1893. According to the story, he liked the interior of the Turkish pavilion so much that when it was dismantled he had parts of it crated and sent to Altadena where, presumably with the aid of Roehrig, they were added to the main house as a "smoking room." In fact, remembering Roehrig's Islamic pretensions, we rather imagine that he was the instigator of this delightful enterprise.

3. Altadena Public Library, 1967
Boyd Georgi
600 E. Mariposa Street, at the southwest corner of Santa Rosa Avenue

The International Style box softened by an Asian influence.

4. Hong House, 1917
Myron Hunt
396 E. Mendocino Street, east of Marengo Avenue

A stucco Anglo-Colonial Revival dwelling. Very gracious.

5. Griffith House, 1923
369 E. Calaveras Street

Egyptian Revival. This town has everything! This house was remodeled and enlarged in 1991.

6. Coates House, 1938
Whitney R. Smith
2320 N. Oliveras Avenue

A very simple Modernist structure.

7. Bowen House, 1905
Charles and Henry Greene
443 E. Calaveras Street, at the northwest corner of Santa Anita Avenue

One of the Greenes' best early bungalows, enlarged and almost totally changed at a later date.

8. Lowe House, 1934
Harwell H. Harris
(Carl Anderson, associate)
596 E. Punahou Street, between Santa Anita and Santa Rosa Avenues

An impressive classic of the 1930s. The garage to the street and the L-shaped house enclose the entrance court. Small wood-walled enclosures extend from each bedroom so that it is possible to sleep outdoors in privacy. The feeling is Japanese but also very personally Harris.

9. Case Study House #20, 1958
Buff, Straub, and Hensman
2275 N. Santa Rosa Avenue

An elegant small house set in bosky ("Christmas Tree Lane") surroundings.

10. Woodbury House, 1882
Attributed to Harry Ridgeway; ballroom, 1898
Frederick L. Roehrig
2606 N. Madison Avenue, on the cul-de-sac just north of Mariposa Street

An old ranch house in the Italianate manner.

11. "Little Normandy," 1925
J. Wilmer Hershey
Norwic Place, just east of Lake Avenue, off Mendocino Street

A group of quaint dollhouse dwellings intended to be reminiscent of rural France. Unfortunately, there were some intrusions in the early 1950s.

12. Eliot Junior High School, 1944
Marston and Maybury
2184 N. Lake Avenue

This is essentially a pre–World War II design, realized immediately after the war. It is an example of a stripped Gothic Revival, though the buff-colored brick wall seems to draw it into the warm Modern.

13. Brandt-Serrurier House, 1905
Charles and Henry Greene
1086 Mariposa Street, at the southeast corner of Maiden Lane

A tiny Craftsman bungalow.

14. Gateposts, circa 1910
Northeast corner of Holliston Avenue and Palm Street

An impressive boulder entrance to the old Gillette ranch.

15. Williams House, 1915
Charles and Henry Greene
1145 Sonoma Drive, at the northeast corner of Mar Vista Avenue

The stuccoed house, with its green tile roof, seems almost Spanish until you notice the Asian touches. It is interesting to compare it with the Earl Apartments (1912) and the Cordelia Culbertson House (1911) by the same architects.

16. Mansfield House, 1916
Northeast corner of
Boston Street and
Mar Vista Avenue

A Pueblo Revival bungalow with
matching pergolas jutting from
the central "upper room."

17. Dyment House, 1923
Northeast corner of
Woodbury Road and
Michigan Avenue

A late example of the Mission
style with corner gate.

18. McLean House, 1929
1290 E. Woodbury Road

Mission-style simplicity placed on
an almost monumental rustic
cobblestone base. Very strange.

19. Parsons Bungalow, 1910
Arthur S. Heineman
(Alfred Heineman, associate)
1605 E. Altadena Drive, at
Porter Avenue

This is simply one of the finest,
most characteristic California
bungalows to be found anywhere.
And its siting at a diagonal to the
nearby mountain is spectacular.
In our 1977 *Guide,* it was still at
the corner of Los Robles Avenue
and California Street in Pasadena.
But times change. Incidentally, it
proved impossible to move the
original cobblestone foundations
and pillars, so they were rebuilt
by modern craftsmen. Tim
Andersen was the restoration
architect when the house was
moved in 1980.

There are some fascinating
neighborhoods in this area. You
will not believe Boulder Road,

just west of the above entry, and
nearby La Solana, a street devoted
to the Spanish Revival. Farther
south, Mar Vista Avenue above
and below New York Drive is a
very characteristic pre–World
War I street. The photographer
of the above image was possibly
Helen Lukens Gaut.

20. Keyes Bungalow, 1911
1337 E. Boston Street, west of
Altadena Country Club

A first-rate example of the "airplane bungalow," called that for
its wingspread. It is obvious that
it once was surrounded with
much more open space.

21. Dorland House, 1949
Lloyd Wright
1370 Morada Place, west of
Altadena Country Club

A large glass prow accents the
street façade.

22. Beard House, 1934
Richard J. Neutra
1981 Meadowbrook Road,
between Allen Avenue and
Midlothian Drive

A small but elegant machine-
image house with walls and
roof of H. H. Robertson ribbed-
steel panels.

23. Gunther House, 1923
D. E. Postle Co., designers
1960 Mendocino Lane, facing
Allen Avenue

This is a striking sight—it is
almost as if the street were
designed to show off this rather
unusual and large Mediterranean-
style house here at the east end
of Mendocino. It is extravagantly
lit at Christmas time.

24. Naiditch House, 1994
Dean Nota
3072 Zane Grey Terrace
(best viewed from the end of
Stonehill Drive)

It looks like a battleship cresting
the edge of a wave (cliff).
Certainly strange (and welcome)
in this pleasant neighborhood of
conventional houses.

96 • South Pasadena, Central Section

We have already introduced South Pasadena under the Lower Arroyo Seco, South section. The following listing covers the business district of South Pasadena and its immediate surroundings.

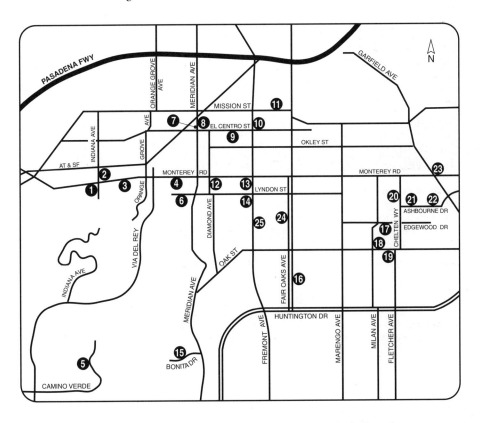

1. House, circa 1910
499 Monterey Road,
at the southwest corner of
Indiana Court

A large Tudor-Craftsman chalet with Mission touches.

2. Bungalow, circa 1900
1102 Indiana Avenue, north of
Monterey Road, near the
Santa Fe Railroad tracks

A marvelous misinterpretation of Vitruvius on a very small scale.

3. Bilike House, 1905–6
Parkinson and Bergstrom
Entrance at 699 Monterey Road

An uphill drive takes you to this Mission Revival house that is now an educational center and church office for the nearby United Methodist Church. Also, the view of Pasadena and the mountains can be magnificent.

4. Two Bungalows, circa 1922
*Northeast corner of
Monterey Road and
Glendon Avenue*

These two Period Revival stucco bungalows of the 1920s express the romantic exoticism of Islam.

5. Chiat House, 1967
Carl Maston
612 Camino Verde

In an area of pleasant but unremarkable houses, this vertically planked Miesian box stands out as one of the best pieces of architecture in South Pasadena.

6. Graham House ("Wynyate") 1887
W. F. Norton
851 Lyndon Street

This triumph of the Queen Anne style was a meeting place for such worthies as John Muir, Mary Austin, and Charles F. Lummis. Imagine it with its porte cochere and tall chimney restored!

7. Meridian Iron Works, circa 1890
913 Meridian Avenue

An example of the Pioneer False Front style, rare in this area.

8. Watering Trough and Wayside Station, 1905
Norman F. Marsh
*On Meridian Avenue,
just across the street from the
Iron Works*

This large boulder cairn was a rest stop for horses and their riders on their way between Los Angeles and Pasadena.

9. South Pasadena Public Library, 1930
Marsh, Smith, and Powell; addition, 1982
Howard H. Morgridge and Associates
1115 El Centro Street

Only the Renaissance Revival façade of the 1930 building has

been retained in the new construction. All traces of the older (1907) Carnegie Library (with dome, of course) have been destroyed. But the new building is harmonious with the old as it now stands.

10. South Pasadena Presbyterian Church (now Grace United Brethren Church), 1906
*Northeast corner of
Fremont Avenue and
El Centro Street*

Mission-style monumentality screening the apse of the much earlier (1886) Pasadena Presbyterian Church that was moved from the site at Colorado and Madison when the 1906 church (demolished) by Frederick L. Roehrig was built.

11. South Pasadena Civic Center, 1985–88
De Bretteville and Polyzoides
*Northwest corner of
Mission Street and
Mound Avenue*

The commission required a complex of a police station, jail, fire station, and council chamber being added to the existing City Hall. The architects chose to organize these various elements around several courtyards and to clothe them in good old Spanish Revival garb with a little Postmodern color thrown in.

12. Cottage, circa 1890
*1103 Monterey Road,
southeast corner of
Diamond Avenue*

A Queen Anne relic.

13. St. James Episcopal Church, 1907
Cram, Goodhue, and Ferguson (Carleton M. Winslow Sr., associate)

*Southwest corner of
Monterey Road and
Fremont Avenue*

Some points of similarity to
the West Point Chapel (by the
same firm) on the outside—
heavy Gothic mixed with
Romanesque—but the interior
is airy and elegant.

14. South Pasadena High School Auditorium, 1937
**Marsh, Smith, and Powell;
Millard Sheets, murals;
Merrell Gage,
sculptured panels**
*Southwest corner of
Fremont Avenue and
Lyndon Street*

PWA Classical Moderne rather
delicately worked. South of the
high school there are some good
streets of bungalows; Ramona
Street has some sophisticated
designs; Diamond Avenue is
another interesting street. East
of Fair Oaks Avenue are more
bungalows and other Craftsman
houses; also, try Milan Avenue.

15. Grokowsky House, 1928
R. M. Schindler
*816 Bonita Drive, off
Meridian Avenue*

An excellent example of
Schindler's early de Stijl phase.

16. 1414 Fair Oaks Building, 1959
**Smith and Williams;
Eckbo, Dean, and Associates,
landscape architects**
1414 Fair Oaks Avenue

A building as a sunscreen, with
gardens and enclosed spaces
underneath. Some unfortunate
alterations have been made by the
recent tenants. This building is
presently in danger of demolition.

17. Spears House, 1925
Ernest Irving Freese
1921 Edgewood Drive

A modest English-style bungalow pays its homage to the
automobile through a dominant
covered driveway and adjoining
entrance porch.

18. Bungalow, circa 1910
*Northeast corner of
Oak Street and
Milan Avenue*

Pictured in Sweet's Bungalows
(circa 1911), the design may be
by the Heinemans.

19. House, circa 1905
*Southwest corner of
Oak Street and
Fletcher Avenue*

Mission style with Oriental
touches.

20. Miltimore House, 1911
Irving J. Gill
1301 Chelten Way

This house is one of Gill's best: puritanical, based on the Mission style. Note the extensive pergolas that provide the transition between house and garden. Also compare this to the houses nearby—very different in imagery but only a little earlier. This section around the intersection of Chelten Way and Ashbourne Drive was once called Ellerslie Park, full of ancient oaks. It was privately developed, with many of the live oaks being saved by curving the streets around them, a perverse twist dear to the hearts of ecologists, old and young.

21. House, 1926
David A. Ogilvie
2000 Ashbourne Drive

The yellow brick walls of this Tudor villa give it a Cotswold feeling.

22. Baer House, 1930
Roland E. Coate
2040 Ashbourne Drive

Spanish Revival somewhat affected by the eastern Anglo-Colonial. It is immersed in foliage.

23. Bixby House, 1925
Roland E. Coate
1148 S. Garfield Avenue,
at the northeast corner of
Monterey Road

This house is one of the first in Southern California to employ the Monterey Revival style. Compared to later uses of this style by Coate, the Bixby House is more Hispanic than Anglo. It was often illustrated and mentioned in regional and national magazines in discussions of that revival in the 1920s and 1930s.

24. Rialto Theater, 1925
L. A. Smith
Northwest corner of
Fair Oaks Avenue and
Okley Street

The exterior, once mildly Plateresque with Baroque touches, is defaced. But the mainly Spanish interior is still intact. Note an Egyptian influence here and there.

25. South Pasadena Women's Improvement Association Clubhouse, 1913
Norman F. Marsh
Northeast corner of
Fremont Avenue and
Rollin Street

A shingled Arts and Crafts building reminding us that the women's club and the Arts and Craft movements flourished at the same time.

20

97 • San Marino

It should be obvious from its architecture that this town, settled on the Henry E. Huntington estate of the same name, is largely inhabited by members of the moneyed class. Its high tone was set by Huntington, who put his house and then his library on a fine prominence with a distant view of the Pacific (still seen occasionally). In the 1920s and 1930s the would-be barons gathered around his regal estate. Even the subdividing of properties in recent years and the consequent building of houses closer and closer together has not really interfered with the picture of opulence. This is the way all people should be able to live, even if they do not wish to do so. Try St. Albans Road north of Huntington Drive to get a feeling for the way of life.

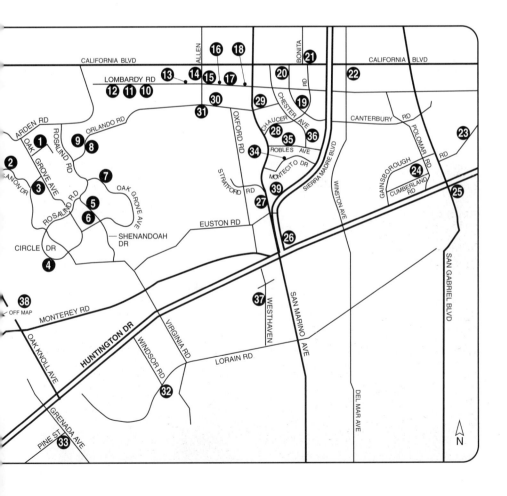

A rule never boldly stated in this book but sometimes implied is that good architecture and a great deal of money are constant companions. In San Marino this rule often breaks down. It is not that there isn't a lot of beautiful building; it is just that the expenditure should have produced more, particularly since nearby Pasadena has always had excellent architects ready to cross the border. As a matter of fact, most of the best work is near Pasadena.

1. House, 1970
B. R. Offenhauser
1045 Oak Grove Place

An unusual and very knowing play on the Mediterranean style.

2. House, 1960
Lynn V. Maudlin
931 Canon Drive

A return to the Japanese-Craftsman tradition. The setting is lovely.

3. Thompson House, 1958
Buff, Straub and Hensman
1030 Canon Drive

A two-story villa in the firm's late-Craftsman style.

4. House, 1932
Roland E. Coate
1435 Circle Drive

A turn at the Georgian Revival.

5. Schuyler Doane House, 1924
Wallace Neff
1180 Shenandoah Road

In part, as a result of the American experience in northern France, the vernacular Norman farmhouse image (or as it was referred to in those years, the "Norman type") came into great popularity. Even at this very early date, Neff mixes our remembrance of fairy tales with the reality of a building. Great expansive roofs come almost to the ground, and a central round tower contains a picturesque exterior staircase.

6. House, 1929
John Atchinson
1215 Shenandoah Road

Tudor finery.

7. Romboz House, 1927
Weston and Weston
1762 Oak Grove Avenue

Spanish Revival (Mudejar) with a gorgeous entrance.

8. House and Outbuildings,
circa 1915
870 Orlando Road

A Mission Revival complex of great interest. It is rare to be able to see all the main buildings from the street. This is a picturesque ensemble with Asian-influenced chimney and green tile roofs.

9. Mays House, 1927
Roland E. Coate
945 Orlando Road

New Orleans, Georgian, and Tudor styles mixed very nicely.

10. Marlow House, 1981
B. R. Offenhauser
1556 Lombardy Road
Pasadena

Recent eastern Anglo-Colonial Revival in the former cutting garden of the Collins House next door.

11. Collins House, 1927
Wallace Neff
1550 Lombardy Road
Pasadena

A solid-looking handsome Mediterranean house set in a well-kept garden.

12. Fong House, 1976
Miller Fong
1500 Lombardy Road
Pasadena

Airy International Style. It fits into the Period Revival neighborhood quite well.

13. Ostoff House, 1924
George Washington Smith
1778 Lombardy Road

A beautiful abstraction of rural Andalusia transferred to opulent suburbia.

14. Baldwin House, 1925
George Washington Smith
665 S. Allen Avenue

Rid yourself of any reservation you may have about the uses of historical imagery. In the hands of an artist, it can produce great things, as this romantic Spanish dwelling and garden attest.

15. Up de Graff House,
circa 1927
Wallace Neff
Northeast corner of
Lombardy Road and
Allen Avenue

Another Spanish Revival masterpiece with a marvelous staircase in front. The hedge on the perimeter of the property has grown considerably since the publication of the last *Guide.*

16. Houses designed by Roland E. Coate:

a. Milligan House, 1928
1850 Lombardy Road

Monterey Revival with a trace of Regency.

b. Le Fens House, 1933
691 Holladay Road

A painted-stone Monterey Revival dwelling with an elegant Greek Revival entrance and sidelights.

c. Pitner House, 1928
1138 Arden Road

A highly refined Monterey Revival.

d. Heath House, 1930
2080 Lombardy Road

A two-story Regency house with an unusual use of fluted piers for the two-story porch.

17. House, 1948
R. H. Ainsworth
1910 Lombardy Road

A Classical Revival giant portico on a delicate Federal (Adamesque) Revival fabric. See 1945 Lombardy Road for an almost identical twin (1941) by the same architect.

18. Bourne House, 1927
Wallace Neff;
Katherine Bashford,
landscape architect
2035 Lombardy Road

One of the finest of Neff's Spanish Revival houses. Here he enlarged the theme of the white, stuccoed, Andalusian farmhouse to a stately villa.

19. Jordan House, 1941
Whitney R. Smith
705 Canterbury Road

A good number of this architect's pre–World War II designs fit into the then-popular California ranch-house mode or that of the Monterey Revival. The Jordan House is a well-carried-out version of the two-story Monterey style.

20. House, circa 1940
Whitney R. Smith
705 Canterbury Road

Monterey style—and good—by an architect best known for his early Modern work.

21. House, circa 1910
580 Bonita Avenue,
at the northeast corner of
California Street

A fine Craftsman house in an otherwise Mediterranean-style area.

22. Fitzgerald House, 1919
Roland E. Coate
708 Winston Avenue

Coate was, of course, always at home with the Monterey style.

23. Packard House, 1924
R. M. Schindler
931 N. Gainsborough Road
Demolished.

24. Day House, 1932
H. Roy Kelley
2871 Cumberland Road

Compact Monterey style.

25. Carver Elementary School, 1947
Marsh, Smith, and Powell
1300 San Gabriel Boulevard, at Huntington Drive

It is interesting to compare this brick International Style school (with its continuation of the indoor-outdoor classroom tradition) with Hunt's and Grey's much earlier (1907) Polytechnic School in Pasadena.

26. Sobieski House, 1946
Harwell H. Harris
1420 Sierra Madre Boulevard, just north of Huntington Drive

The beautifully crafted, two-story shingle-and-wood garage is about all that can be seen from the street.

27. Haigh House, 1948
Wallace Neff
1173 San Marino Avenue

The architect in one of his French Norman moods.

28. House, 1933
Rainer and Adams
2170 Chaucer Road
(visible only from San Marino Avenue gatehouse)

This fine Tudor Revival house with its extensive black-and-white work encourages great expectations for the almost invisible mansion behind it. Records are confusing, but it would appear that the gatehouse came first, and that the mansion was designed (1937) by Girard R. Colcord.

29. Bertololli House, circa 1928
Wallace Neff
2115 Orlando Road

A characteristic Neff Tuscan villa, with an inset second-floor loggia placed above the front entrance.

30. Wallace Neff House, 1929
Wallace Neff
1883 Orlando Road

A larger version of entry number 29, this Tuscan house was even more impressive before the entrance court was changed and the fence added.

31. Henry E. Huntington Art Gallery, Library and Gardens
Entrance is at the end of Allen Avenue at Orlando Road
Gallery (originally the house), 1910
Myron Hunt and Elmer Grey;
Gallery, 1925
Myron Hunt and H. C. Chambers

You will enter through a mildly Beaux-Arts gate and orientation building designed by Whitney Smith (1981). The main Gallery is reserved, academic, Beaux-Arts Neoclassicism. Architecturally, the salient points are the Palladian-like porch and the interior grand staircase. The treasure is the collection, assembled for the railroad magnate by Lord Joseph Duveen. English eighteenth-century painting may not turn you on, but the main gallery—with Lawrence's *Pinkie* on one side and Gainsborough's *Blue Boy* on the other, along with Reynold's *Mrs. Siddons as the Tragic Muse* at the end—is something to behold.

The later, separate library building is also Beaux-Arts with a decidedly French feeling. There is a large exhibition hall where you can gaze at such things as a Gutenberg Bible, Thoreau's manuscript of *Walden,* or an architectural drawing by Thomas Jefferson.

The gardens—French, Shakespearian, Japanese, Cactus, etc.; begun in 1904 by William Hertrich and extended by Wilbur David Cook—are among the most beautiful in the world. The Japanese garden (begun in 1911) is especially fine with a teahouse (1906), much changed, since it was taken from the Japanese Tea Garden that once stood at the northeast corner of California Boulevard and Fair Oaks Avenue in Pasadena. More recently, a Zen garden designed by Robert Watson has been added.

Do not miss the impressive Huntington Mausoleum (1933) designed by America's prominent Beaux-Arts architect, John Russell Pope, designer of the National Gallery in Washington, D.C. Here Pope explores the theme of the circular and domed Classical Temple, a theme he returned to again and again.

Nearby is the Virginia Steele Scott Gallery of American Art (1983–84) designed by Paul Gray (Warner and Gray). It is a sensitive and lively continuation of the Classical tradition of Pope, with its principal space organized around an open dome. Sometimes missed is the annex containing artifacts of the California Arts and Crafts movement, especially the furniture of Charles and Henry Greene. An addition by Frederick Fisher to the Scott gallery is in the works.

32. Sheppard House, 1934
Jock Peters
1390 Lorain Road

A rare executed example in Streamline Moderne of the work of the gifted architect who was the principal interior designer of Bullocks Wilshire in Los Angeles.

33. House, circa 1925
Southwest corner of Pine Street and Granada Avenue Alhambra

The strange Hansel and Gretel feeling of this building suggests that it was designed by the Heineman firm in Pasadena.

34. "The Mosque," 1980
2250 Montecito Drive

This is the name that neighbors have aptly given this house—a little out of place in San Marino.

35. Rupple House, 1938
Roland E. Coate
2225 Robles Avenue

This small, single-floor French-style dwelling is organized around a central motor court. The design is on the stark side but very well carried out.

36. Phillips House, 1934
H. Roy Kelley
940 Chester Avenue

The Streamline Moderne style is neither frequent in this architect's work nor often encountered in San Marino. Kelley's handling of the scale, detailing, and landscape design allows this Modernist house to fit in with the surrounding Period Revival dwellings.

37. Baird House, 1938
H. Roy Kelley
1745 Westhaven Road

One of the popular modes of the Anglo-Colonial Revival in the 1930s was the informal stone-and-wood Pennsylvania Colonial. The Baird house, which was one of several versions of this style by Kelley, was frequently published in the architectural journals and popular shelter magazines of the time.

38. Townley House, 1936
Harold Saxsmith
880 Winthrop Road

In this instance, the Anglo-Colonial image is rendered with the simplicity of the early modern.

39. Stanwyck House, 1940
William D. Holdredge
1300 Sierra Madre Boulevard

The architect managed very well to combine a number of Anglo-Colonial Revival traditions, ranging from Colonial Williamsburg, to the Cape Cod cottage. The house mixes the formal with the informal.

98 • San Gabriel

It all began with the founding of the San Gabriel Mission in 1771, near the present site of Montebello. When the Mission was relocated in 1776, the town also moved. What is left of this later settlement dates from 1791 to 1850, and there is precious little of it. Early photographs show, however, that in the 1890s, West Mission Road was a charming country-town street with adobes and extended pitched roofs over the sidewalks. But in 1913 the residents voted for incorporation and progress. Their decision meant the absolute destruction of the visible past, a process that has continued until fairly recently, leaving few shards other than the Mission which, in spite of its woebegone appearance (and its gift shop, unmatched for its bad taste), is still considerably more convincing than the next in the chain (San Fernando) which has been restored beyond credibility.

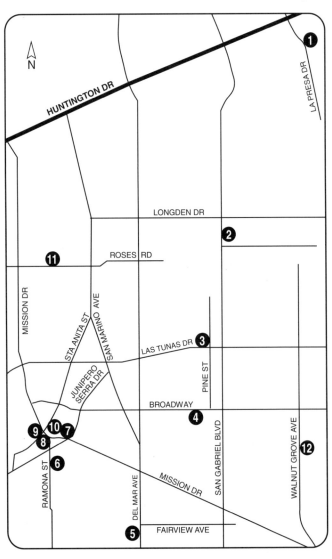

7

1. Rose House, 1862
7020 La Presa Drive, off Huntington Drive

Said to be the oldest frame house in the San Gabriel Valley, it looks the part. It is a simple house without style, but it is neverthe-less picturesque in its beautiful garden.

2. Miller Water Garden,
1925 and later
Bill Miller
6221 N. San Gabriel Boulevard

Driving by, you might think that this was just another nursery, but take time to muse. The garden

furniture takes you back to early California. This is distributed among concrete grottoes, rustic concrete bridges, and rare aquatic plants and fish. There is even a concrete log cabin.

3. San Gabriel Union Church and School, 1936
Northwest corner of Las Tunas Drive and Pine Street

Basically, this building is Classical PWA Moderne with an update of Streamline touches, such as a porch with chrome trim intact.

4. "The Alamo," circa 1929
522 E. Broadway

Yes, this residence has an entrance that vaguely resembles that of the Alamo in San Antonio.

5. San Gabriel Village,
circa 1938
Percy Bitton Limited, developer
Fairview Avenue, west of Del Mar Avenue

This settlement was to have 840 units selling for around $4,000 each. The houses are not much, but efforts at low-cost housing in the 1930s deserve mention.

6. Ortega-Vigare Adobe,
1792–1805
616 S. Ramona Street

Only half of this one-story adobe remains, but it is old in spite of its restored appearance. Originally, the roof was flat and the corridor was completely open.

7. Mission San Gabriel Archangel,
1791–1806 and later
Mission and Junipero Serra Drives

The Mission was established in 1771 and was moved to its present site in 1776. The stone church, begun in 1791, replaced an earlier small adobe church. When first built, the long nave of the church was covered with a barrel vault, but because of earthquake damage, this was replaced by a timber roof in 1804. The building was designed to receive stone vaulting, thus explaining the rows of buttresses that create the fortress-like quality of the church. The square tower that stood to the right of the entrance and much of the fabric of the church were severely damaged in the earthquake of 1812. The church was then partially rebuilt, although the present campanario was not added until 1828.

Over the years the church has gone through several earthquakes, the last major one occurring in 1987. It has been retrofitted and imaginatively restored.

8. San Gabriel City Hall and Municipal Buildings, 1923
Walker and Eisen
Southwest corner of Mission Drive and Ramona Street

Spanish Revival without zest.

9. San Gabriel Civic Auditorium ("Mission Playhouse"), 1923–27
Arthur B. Benton; restored, 1992
De Bretteville and Polyzoides
Northwest corner of Mission Drive and Santa Anita Street

This huge Mission-style building (the prototype was the Mission of San Antonio de Padua near the present town of Jolon) was designed specifically for the production of John Steven McGroarty's *Mission Play*, which presented 3,200 performances between 1912 and 1933. The emblems of Spanish provinces that adorn the interior were given by the king of Spain. The building also houses a fine theater organ.

10. Lopez de Lowther Adobe, 1792–1806
330 S. Santa Anita Street

This single-room-wide gable-roofed adobe was probably one of the Mission outbuildings, and has escaped the wrecker by being on a side street. It is open to the public on Sunday afternoons, 1:00–4:00 P.M.

11. Church of Our Savior (Episcopal), 1872 and later
535 W. Roses Road, near Rosemont Boulevard

Only a portion of this rural English Gothic church is old, but it retains some good Tiffany windows.

12. Sorg House, 1926
R. M. Schindler
5204 N. Walnut Grove Avenue

A tight de Stijl composition, with pergola sunroof and garage. The rows of two-by-six supports suggest the wood-stud wall construction behind the stucco-covered walls.

99 • Sierra Madre

Named by its developer, Nathaniel C. Carter, in 1881, Sierra Madre was intended to be a boomtown, but it never quite made it. It still evokes the image of a midwestern crossroads village at the turn of the century. Its big industry was tuberculosis sanitariums, almost all of which have disappeared. But it attracted more than its share of distinguished architects—Ernest A. Coxhead, Joseph Cather Newsom, Charles and Henry Greene, Timothy Walsh, Irving J. Gill, Wallace Neff, Harwell H. Harris, and John Gougeon.

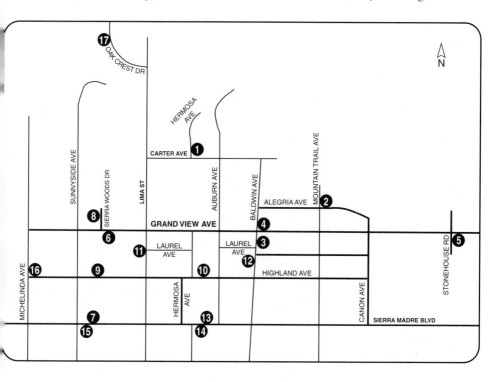

1. Mulvihill House, 1949
Harwell H. Harris
580 N. Hermosa Avenue

Although this house has been remodeled, it still bears comparison with the same Harris's Johnson House in Bel Air of exactly the same year.

2. Sierra Madre Garden
Apartment Houses
(Lewis Courts), 1910
Irving J. Gill
Northeast corner of Mountain Trail and Alegria Avenue

In this project Gill provided an individual terrace and an enclosed porch or loggia for each of the small stucco-walled, two-bedroom bungalows. The open courtyard in the center contained a pergola and a croquet court. The complex is now changed almost beyond recognition and is threatened with demolition, but it is so famous that we felt that we had to include it.

3. Church of the Ascension, 1888
Ernest A. Coxhead
Northeast corner of
Baldwin and Laurel Avenues

One of Coxhead's storybook churches. Some remodeling was done by Carleton M. Winslow Jr., who also designed the parsonage.

4. St. Rita's Church, 1969
John Gougeon
Northeast corner of
Baldwin and
Grand View Avenues

Modern Expressionism with a slight Spanish flavor. Gougeon's later Pasadena Presbyterian Church goes even further.

5. House, circa 1890
Near southeast corner of
Grand View Avenue and
Stonehouse Road
Arcadia

A stone structure, originally built as a maintenance building for the northern section of E. J. "Lucky" Baldwin's extensive ranch.

6. Cabin, circa 1900
468 Grand View Avenue,
east of Sierra Woods Drive

Tiny, vertical board-and-batten building that suggests the back-to-nature atmosphere that Sierra Madre once boasted.

7. Coldwell House, circa 1907
Louis B. Easton
649 Sierra Madre Boulevard

In 1908 a writer in *The Craftsman* magazine wrote that "This house is an admirable illustration of the adaptation of a dwelling to the climate and surroundings, and the preservation of harmony between exterior and interior of the house." It was recently saved from demolition.

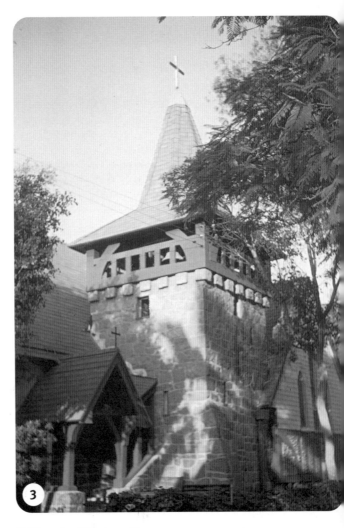

3

8. Edgar Camp House, 1904
Charles and Henry Greene
327 Sierra Woods Drive

One of the Greenes' most picturesque bungalows with later additions. It is partially visible from the street.

9. House, circa 1910
481 Highland Avenue

A long, two-story, shingled Craftsman house with horizontality worthy of the Prairie School.

10. Sierra Madre School, circa 1930
Marsh, Smith, and Powell
North side of Highland Avenue, between Hermosa and Auburn Avenues

Spanish Revival in poured concrete.

11. Pinney House, 1886
Joseph Cather Newsom
225 Lima Street, at the west end of Laurel Avenue

Originally, this building was a large but rather plain hotel on the order of another Newsom hotel still standing in San Dimas. Then in the 1930s, a movie company added the outsized spindle work on the porch and the equally mannerist swan's neck pediment, both from a house being demolished on Wilshire Boulevard in Los Angeles. The result is overwhelming.

12. House, 1911
171 N. Baldwin Avenue
A beautifully maintained, shingled Craftsman house.

13. Church of the Nazarene, 1890
191 W. Sierra Madre Boulevard

A Victorian Gothic structure in wood, somewhat botched around the entrance and, unfortunately, painted white.

14. Congregational Church, 1928
Marsh, Smith, and Powell
170 W. Sierra Madre Boulevard

Some parts of this church are said to date from 1886, but they do not show under the Romanesque exterior.

15. Essick House, circa 1905
550 W. Sierra Madre Boulevard

A large true bungalow (one-story) with flat roof above a thin, horizontal, latticed attic for ventilation.

16. Barlow House (now Alverno School), 1923–24
Wallace Neff
Northeast corner of Michillinda and Highland Avenues

This villa was built by Dr. James Barlow for his wife, who had visited the Villa Collazzi (sometimes attributed to Michelangelo) outside Florence and who wanted a house just like it. Neff gave them what they desired and included a superb southern cortile from which they had magnificent views of the San Gabriel Valley below them through Italian cypresses, palms, and formal gardens.

17. McKinney House ("The Pyramid House"), 1972–74
McKinney
751 Oak Crest Drive

Obviously the virtues of the geometric form of the pyramid were discovered by McKinney a number of years before I. M. Pei employed it at the Louvre. This example is sheathed in metal and glass. Unfortunately you can view the house only from a distance.

100 • Arcadia

This small city is essentially a comfortable upper-middle-class residential community, but it is best known for the Santa Anita Racetrack, where Los Angelenos go to sin, and the Santa Anita Mall, where they go to spend. The acres of asphalt parking lots surrounding the Santa Anita Racetrack are hardly much of a drawing card. But what is a drawing card are the wonderful grandstands designed in 1935 by Gordon B. Kaufmann. Along the front of these is a frieze of horses, riders, and the absolutely necessary palm trees. The motifs of this frieze are entirely two dimensional, being rendered in thin sheets of steel. The original landscape was designed by Tommy Thompson, and some of these plantings remain.

The best thing in town—in fact one of the high points in Los Angeles County—is the County Arboretum, on what was once the old Rancho Santa Anita, the estate of E. J. Baldwin, one of the most eccentric millionaires that California has ever produced. The Arboretum was established in 1947 primarily through the efforts of Dr. Samuel Ayres. Within some 127 acres the plants vary widely from those coming from a temperate zone to the subtropical. One of the interesting features of the park is the *Sunset* magazine gardens, where landscape solutions for the suburban house are presented. In 1989 the small Peacock Cafe, its garden, and its terraces were restored and redesigned by Campbell and Campbell.

The Santa Anita Ranch was granted during the Mexican period to Hugo Reid in 1841. Either just before that date or shortly thereafter, he built an adobe on the ranch. From evidence now available, we know this adobe was a single-floor dwelling with a corridor running along one side, and it was covered by a flat roof. This adobe was later incorporated into a large house. Between 1948 and 1960, the Hugo Reid Adobe was rebuilt; this rebuilding has been updated by the California Conservations Corporation. A new garden of herbs and flowers characteristic of the Mexican period has been planted by the adobe.

In 1875, E. J. "Lucky" Baldwin purchased the rancho, and over the years he extensively planted the area and dredged the picturesque lake. Baldwin was interested in horses, gold mines, real estate, and horticulture. In fact, he was interested in everything, and almost everything he touched turned into gold. Thus, his nickname "Lucky." Having literally struck pay dirt in Northern California, he bought the rancho east of Los Angeles, possibly with the idea of roughing it, for he moved (1875) into the Hugo Reid Adobe and started raising horses—and money! He also planted a wide variety of trees, the nucleus of the arboretum, though now it is much more lush than Lucky would have imagined possible. Incidentally, the grove was the site of the filming of the first Tarzan movies.

Baldwin was also interested in architecture. Like many other Americans, he was excited by the Queen Anne buildings that the British erected for their pavilions at the Philadelphia Centennial Exhibition in 1876. When he returned to California he hired Arthur A. Bennett, one of the architects of the Capitol Building at Sacramento, to design a Queen Anne cottage (1881) as a guest house for the ranch. Although not closely related to the British pavilions and not really Queen Anne, it was and is pretentious both inside and out. The exterior has ornament extracted from Eastlake and is painted to suggest what Vincent Scully has called the "Stick style." There are also Islamic touches. The original features inside are Victorian Baroque with marble fireplaces and art-glass windows that would have been the pride of San Francisco, where they were probably made.

Perhaps more fascinating are the ample stables and dog house in the same style as the exterior of the guest house. Oh yes—a Queen Anne railroad station (1890) that Baldwin built on the Santa Fe right-of-way has now been moved to the grounds.

The California Arboretum Foundation took over its operation of the arboretum in 1948, and the arboretum was opened to the public in 1955. It may be visited every day except Christmas, from 8:30 a.m. to 4:30 p.m., for a small admission charge.

As if grateful for this architectural success, Baldwin married the architect's daughter. The marriage was not so fortunate and the couple soon separated. A previous marriage (there were four) had produced a beloved daughter, Anita, to whom he gave a large section of his ranch to the north. In 1910 she built a large but nondescript house, Anoakia, (designed by Arthur B. Benton), which she proceeded to furnish with large numbers of Tiffany chandeliers and some rather astonishing murals by Maynard Dixon. The chandeliers and murals have been removed and the house and a tiny Greek temple on the grounds have been destroyed in order to make room for a housing tract.

Anita Baldwin's estate has, of course, been subdivided and is now called Santa Anita Oaks. It is a pleasant piece of suburbia that exhibits acre after acre of the California ranch houses of the 1930s and 1940s, as well as some impressive historic-image designs by H. Roy Kelley and others. One of the best of these is the O'Bryan house at 1225 Rodeo Road just north of Foothill Boulevard above Sycamore Avenue. It was designed by Wallace Neff (1939), one of the greatest of the purveyors of the Mediterranean style, who here sheathed his familiar architectural forms in gray shingles. The rest of the area is genially soporific, but lushly so.

Another architectural attraction of Arcadia is an excellent Art Deco retail store building (circa 1932) at 53 Huntington Drive. The relief sculpture on the building is by J. J. Mora.

Clearman's Village at the southwest corner of Huntington Drive and Rosemead Boulevard is worth a look. This is a large-scale, post–World War II drive-in of the early 1950s and later. At first the most striking thing about it is Northwood Inn, a make-believe log cabin with imitation snow on its roof. Deeper observations soon catch other delights, such as a restaurant in the shape of a ship, and many specialty shops in a variety of arrays. See especially, the Spanish Revival gun shop with its tropical-tile roof merging nicely with a snow-covered roof next door.

101 • Monrovia

All of the towns in the shadow of the San Gabriel Mountains owe their existence to the Santa Fe Railroad, which came through the valley in the 1880s. This town is named for a construction engineer, William N. Monroe, who saw the opportunities of this beautiful spot and platted the town in 1886. Though now thoroughly built over, Monrovia still demonstrates its nineteenth-century origins better than most of the San Gabriel Valley communities. Its Victorian houses are sprinkled around town, usually at street corners—evidence of a land speculator's dream that did not materialize until the twentieth century. Old photographs show Queen Anne and Eastlake houses amid orange groves and vineyards. Monrovia must have been lovely.

Like its neighbor, Sierra Madre, Monrovia was a health resort with tuberculosis sanitaria distributed through the upper reaches of the city—a deep irony, for now it gets some of the worst smog in the county, both from friendly Los Angeles and from the industry miserably sprawled to the southwest. The Foothill Freeway that runs through the southern section does nothing to improve the atmosphere. But stop by, if only to see the Aztec Hotel (in the Mayan style!), one of the most exotic things that you will ever encounter.

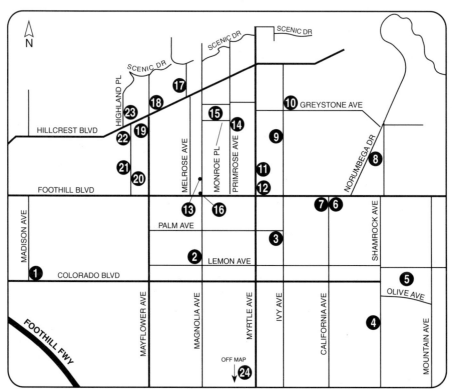

1. Monrovia High School, 1928
John C. Austin and
Frederic M. Ashley
(Austin Whittlesey)
Northeast corner of
Madison Avenue and
Colorado Boulevard

A Palladian façade on an otherwise Spanish Revival building, Whittlesey, the designer, was well known for his books on Spanish architecture.

2. House, circa 1915
423 S. Magnolia Avenue

This remodeled house has all the marks of an Irving J. Gill design.

3. United Methodist Church,
1911;
addition, 1923
Southwest corner of
Ivy and Palm Avenues

An imposing piece of early-twentieth-century Beaux-Arts Neoclassicism.

4. Cottage, circa 1887
823 S. Shamrock Avenue

It is conceivable that this one-and-a-half-story Queen Anne building was designed by one or both of the Newsoms.

5. Park, 1923
Cook and Hill,
landscape architects
Between Shamrock and
Mountain Avenues,
Olive and Lemon Avenues

This is Monrovia's only park of any size—but, of course, there are the mountains!

6. St. Luke's Episcopal
Church, 1926
Carleton M. Winslow Sr.
Southeast corner of
California Avenue and
Foothill Boulevard

A very severe handling of Spanish Romanesque and Gothic in poured concrete. The interior is even more severe.

7. Four Bungalows, circa 1910
Tifal Brothers, builders
Southwest corner of
California Avenue and
Foothill Boulevard

A row of bungalows in mint condition. Actually, there are more, apparently by the same builders, on Wild Rose Avenue on the south side of the same block.

8. Dumond House, circa 1925
270 Norumbega Drive

Pure Hansel and Gretel, the house/studio of an artist.

9. Watt Bungalow, circa 1910
231 N. Ivy Avenue

A flat-roofed single-story house—right out of a bungalow book.

10. Butts House, 1894
Arthur B. Benton
Northeast corner of
Ivy and Greystone Avenues

An angular example of the Shingle style, with a first story of boulders and mannerist touches in the floor above.

11. Burr House, 1893
150 N. Myrtle Avenue

A two-story Queen Anne with a suggestion of the Colonial Revival.

12. United Presbyterian
Church, circa 1926
Harry W. Pierce
Northeast corner of
Myrtle Avenue and
Foothill Boulevard

A Mission Revival tower, but otherwise rather academic Spanish Revival. The interior has hints of the Rococo.

13. Stewart House, circa 1887
117 N. Magnolia Avenue

A two-story Queen Anne dwelling.

14. House, circa 1887
Solon I. Haas
250 N. Primrose Avenue

Another Queen Anne, but this time with a tall, narrow mansard tower, still crowned with iron railing and pinnacles.

15. Monroe House, 1887
225 Monroe Place

This is the Queen Anne house of William N. Monroe, who founded the town and for whom it was named.

16. Aztec Hotel, 1925
Robert Stacy-Judd
Northwest corner of Magnolia Avenue and Foothill Boulevard

Words fail. By the mid-1920s, Stacy-Judd had emerged as one of America's most flamboyant apologists for the pre-Columbian Revival, which he thought, since it was "Native American," should form the basis for a true American style in the future. Here he presents it in cast concrete and stucco. Be sure to take in the lobby.

17. Mills House ("Mills View"), 1887
329 N. Melrose Avenue

It is possible that this house was designed by Joseph Cather Newsom. It has the mark of his outrageous aesthetics in its Queen Anne mass with mansard tower at the southwest corner.

18. Case House, 1887
Northeast corner of Hillcrest Boulevard and Mayflower Avenue

A Queen Anne/Anglo-Colonial (Shingle style) dwelling.

19. Pile House ("Idlewild"), 1887–88
Joseph Cather Newsom
255 N. Mayflower Avenue, near the corner of Hillcrest Boulevard

A two-story Queen Anne with a strange bracket at the corner, the wonderful interiors are well preserved.

20. Mellenthin House, circa 1912
Frank O. Eager
168 Highland Place

A fine, shingled Craftsman house in the Swiss Chalet vein.

21. Everest House, circa 1912
Arthur Kelly
173 Highland Place

Another Craftsman two-story dwelling, almost worthy of Charles and Henry Greene. The Daniels House across the street (number 174) was once by Arthur Kelly.

22. Badger House, circa 1912
Attributed to Arthur Kelly
225 Highland Place

Craftsman shingles again.

23. Wood House, circa 1925
Herbert J. Gerhardt
338 Highland Place

Another evidence of the search for Native America, here realized through the Pueblo Revival.

24. Santa Fe Railroad Passenger Station, circa 1925
William H. Mohr
Just above Duarte Road, on the west side of Myrtle Avenue

A small Hispanic building.

102 • Duarte

This community, founded in 1886 southeast of Monrovia, was once covered with rural estates dating mainly from the teens and twenties. After World War II these succumbed to the growth syndrome and were subdivided. A few good houses remain behind gates and high hedges, but your experience of the "better day" will be only the magnificent trees. Duarte does have a beautiful Mission Revival school (1908) by F. S. Allen at 1247 Buena Vista Street. Its paired towers and pedimented gables are easily visible from the nearby Foothill Freeway, so you won't really even need to slow down.

103 • Bradbury

Very exclusive, mostly behind locked gates. Everything is post–World War II. It does have the honor of having an excellent hilltop house by Frank Lloyd Wright— the Pearce House (1950)—situated, most unfortunately, behind guarded gates at 5 Bradbury Hills Road.

104 • Azusa

Any reader over seventy will remember this town, along with Cucamonga and Anaheim, as one of Jack Benny's stops on his imaginary railroad journeys around Southern California. It was founded in 1887. One of the city's sons, the eminent historian Robert Glass Cleland, wrote that Azusa had "more saloons than Protestants" in the late nineteenth century. And he continued, "So, also, certain priceless gifts—freedom and space, simplicity and leisure, blue skies overhead, and unfailing kindness and friendship in the hearts of our neighbors."

The Civic Center buildings are good examples of the "City Beautiful" movement. The City Hall (1909) looks newer than the wings (1925) that flank it. The little gray stone Iglesia Presbiteriana (circa 1900) nearby at the northwest corner of Alameda Avenue and Foothill Boulevard is picturesque. And the Wells Fargo Bank at the northeast corner of Azusa Avenue and Foothill Boulevard, designed (1918) by Robert H. Orr in a mixture of Romanesque, Classical, and Moderne forms, adds interest to an otherwise uninspiring business district.

105 • Glendora

Whereas Azusa was Presbyterian in its early religious orientation, Glendora, also on the Santa Fe Railroad, was firmly Methodist, a saving grace of nearby Monrovia. Glendora had a strong Dixie element. As late as 1935 the local chapter of the United Daughters of the Confederacy would announce in the Glendora Press an essay contest in which "ten points will be deducted in judging any manuscript that uses the term 'Civil War' when speaking of the War Between the States." Today the sleepy southern crossroads town comes to mind particularly on Glendora Avenue. The northern part of Glendora has simply been taken over by developers for tract housing to the point that the town's original reason for being, its citrus industry, is gone. Surely Citrus College at the west end of town will change its name.

In the foothills behind Glendora there is still some evidence of truck farming. Beautifully tended nurseries cling to the slopes of the hills, as do some Victorian houses, none of great architectural quality. The best work is early-twentieth-century Craftsman. In town the Tudor two-stories (circa 1920) at the northwest corner of Minnesota Avenue and Foothill Boulevard and at the northwest corner of Bennett and Vermont Avenues, and the bungalows (circa 1915) at the northwest corner of Foothill Boulevard and Wabash Avenue and at the southeast corner of Bennett and Vermont Avenues (beautiful beveled-glass door) are cases in point. The modern work at Citrus Junior College by Neptune and Thomas is bland.

106 • San Dimas

Another town inspired by the Santa Fe Railroad and the boom of the 1880s, San Dimas is almost exactly midway between Los Angeles and San Bernardino, to which the railroad had completed its tracks in 1885. As in other boom cities, the first building of consequence was a hotel (1885–87), designed by Joseph Cather Newsom in the Queen Anne style. Again paralleling the history of many such enterprises, the hotel was finished just as the boom collapsed, and it never functioned as a hotel. In 1889 J. W. Walker bought this thirty-room structure and used it as his home. Address: 121 N. San Dimas Avenue.

San Dimas's business street has been remodeled into someone's version of a Wild West town, but the residential streets, with their modest late-nineteenth-century cottages and later bungalows, are pleasant.

San Dimas Hotel, 1885–87; Joseph Cather Newsom

107 • La Verne

Originally named Lordsburg for I. W. Lord, who laid it out in 1888, La Verne was another of the Santa Fe Railroad enterprises based on health and citrus. It is the seat of La Verne University (formerly College), which never made it to Claremont as Pomona did. The best building is the absolutely outlandish (and successful) Student Center and Drama Laboratory (1973), designed by the Shaver Partnership to resemble tents. In fact, the five large episodes *are* tents coated with Teflon. A few new buildings, unassertive but in good taste, give a college atmosphere to the campus. Otherwise the best building in town is the Church of the Brethren (1930) at the southwest corner of 5th and E Streets. It is flamboyant Gothic with suggestions of the Moderne roughed out in reinforced concrete, and was designed by Orr, Strange, and Inslee.

On the west side of La Verne below Foothill Boulevard at the intersection of Moreno Avenue and Gladstone Street is the Water Filtration and Softening Plant (1940), designed by Daniel A. Elliot with monumental Spanish forms in reinforced concrete. It is one of the substations on the 392-mile aqueduct that brings water to Los Angeles from the Colorado River.

La Verne may not have much to offer architecturally, but it has some of the most beautiful trees of any town in the state.

Student Center and Drama Building, 1973, La Verne University; Shaver Partnership

108 • Temple City
El Monte

Mostly depressing, but the Security Savings Bank (1976) by Pulliam, Matthews, and Associates slipped in at Las Tunas Drive and Cloverly Avenue in Temple City. To the south in El Monte, the El Monte High School (1938–39), designed by Marsh, Smith, and Powell through PWA funding at Tyler Avenue and Bodger Street, is a good Moderne work whose best effect is an impressive long, horizontal, cast-concrete bas-relief sculpture by Bartolo Mako on the Administration Building. It depicts *The End of the Santa Fe Trail* beginning with a covered wagon and ending with a coed with tennis racket. There are other panels of relief sculpture, including four on the side of the auditorium that depict industrial activities in El Monte.

While in El Monte you may want to take a look at the Busway Terminal (1973). It was designed by Daniel, Mann, Johnson, and Mendenhall (at the west end of Romano Boulevard near Santa Anita Avenue) to encourage people in the area to give up their cars at the parking lot and ride the buses into Los Angeles. The attempt by architects to achieve absolutely anonymous architecture seems to have reached its complete fulfillment here.

Joseph Weston's Subsistence Homestead Project (1934–35) at Lower Azusa Road, west of Peck Road, in El Monte is one of eight early projects of the New Deal (Subsistence Homesteads, Resettlement Division of the Department of the Interior), which was to relocate people into the country on plots where they could produce their own food. The El Monte Subsistence Homestead project was the one and only example realized in the Los Angeles area. Each of the one hundred houses was situated on three-quarters of an acre. In the August 9, 1935, issue of *Southwest Builder and Contractor,* it was noted that "Seventeen different plans and architectural designs have been used for the houses, distributed to avoid monotony of repetition . . ." It was pointed out in the same issue of this magazine that this project "is not a 'subsistence homestead,' as that term has generally been understood, for the cooperative ideas, involved in other similar projects, is not applied here. Individual owners of homes in this project will provide for themselves independently, producing and utilizing whatever they may grow or raise on their land, as they elect." In style, the houses range from the Anglo-Colonial cottage to the California ranch house. Needless to say, there have been many changes since these houses were built. But a drive through the area reveals a good number of the original houses, most added to, but nonetheless recognizable.

109 • Covina
West Covina
Irwindale

Covina, a product of land speculation in the late 1880s, has real presence in spite of the calculated designs of its political and commercial leaders to destroy it. The area around the intersection of Citrus Avenue with Badillo Street can be brought back in the mind's eye to a better day before modernization took over. How wonderful the broad-eaved Arcade Apartments must have been before their face-lifting! How majestic the Ionic beauty of the First National Bank before its new owners decided to block out its rich architrave with a concrete slab! Thank God for sparing Arthur B. Benton's Holy Trinity Episcopal Church (1910), a shard of a better day. A few Queen Anne cottages remain around the town.

1. Holy Trinity Episcopal Church, 1910
Arthur B. Benton
Northeast corner of
Badillo Street and 3rd Avenue
Covina

Benton has put aside his Mission style (Mission Inn, Riverside) for the Episcopalians' preferred Eastlake-Gothic. The strong tower and fabric of the church was made of stones dragged from the San Gabriel River. The interior is well-wooded and has good stained-glass windows.

2. First National Bank, circa 1918
Train and Williams
Northeast corner of
Citrus Avenue and
College Street
Covina

A well-proportioned Ionic pile, now altered.

3. Masonic Hall, circa 1900
Southwest corner of
2nd Avenue and School Street
Covina

A huge Classical Revival, rather awkward building made of wood. The Masons have as many architectural pretensions as the Episcopalians, and we are glad of that.

4. St. Martha's Episcopal Church, 1956–62
Carleton M. Winslow Jr.
Northeast corner of Lark Ellen Avenue and Service Street
West Covina

Very exotic, the façade is enriched by metal stars suspended a couple of feet in front of the walls and held in place by wires.

5. First Presbyterian Church, circa 1900
5116 Irwindale Avenue
Irwindale

A late Shingle-style church. Boulders form the base of the building, and above this solid earthy base are thin shingle-covered walls for the sanctuary and the corner tower.

6. Our Lady of Guadalupe Church, 1917
16239 Arrow Highway, at Morada Street
Irwindale

A miniature chapel constructed in a Craftsman fashion of river boulders (there are plenty of them in the nearby riverbeds).

7. Ruble House ("The Rock Castle"), 1985
Michael Ruble
844 Live Oaks Avenue
Irwindale

A 1980s folly; a parapeted castle of river boulders and cinder-block walls. What will capture your attention is the seventy-four-foot-high clock and chimes tower.

110 • Industry
La Puente

Industry is what it says it is—an industrial park, although the word park hardly seems appropriate. Much of it is faceless, computerized buildings, eminently forgettable. La Puente seems to be inhabited but has very little else to offer. Here is what we turned up.

1. Puente Hills Mall, 1974
Victor Gruen Associates
Southeast corner of
Pomona Freeway exit and
Azusa Avenue

Nothing really holds this ninety-four-acre shopping center together except the parking lot. A few buildings, especially the Sears store, are noteworthy.

2. Workman Adobe
("Rancho La Puente"),
1842;
altered, 1872
Ezra Kysor;
Temple Hall, circa 1925
Walker and Eisen;
finished by Roy Selden Price
15415 E. Don Julian Road
(take Hacienda Boulevard exit
from Pomona Freeway;
go north to Don Julian Road;
turn west to Rancho entrance)

William Workman ("Don Julian" to his contemporaries) led the first group of Yankees into the Los Angeles area in 1841. Because he had a Mexican wife and thus had a right to claim land, he and his friend John Rowland received the enormous Rancho La Puente, which they shared in common for awhile.

Finally the ranch was divided, Workman taking the western half. As his business ventures prospered in Los Angeles, he decided to remodel his ranch house to resemble what he remembered an English country house looked like. The result was to Gothicize it and remove almost all traces of the simple adobe, at least on the exterior.

Ironically, it was his grandson, Walter P. Temple, who revived the Spanish tradition by building Temple Hall ("La Casa Nueva") next door in the vigorous Spanish Revival (Mediterranean) style—with a Manueline (Portuguese) front door! Temple Hall has been immaculately restored by Raymond Gervigian and is a veritable house museum of the taste of the 1920s.

The grounds also contain the oldest private cemetery in Los Angeles County. In it among the graves of other pioneers are those of Pio Pico and his wife, Maria Ygnacia. The houses and grounds are open (free) to the public Tuesday through Friday, 1:00–4:00 P.M., Saturday and Sunday, 10:00 A.M.– 4:00 P.M. Groups by reservation.

3. The Donut Hole, 1968
John Tindall, Ed McCreany,
and Jesse Hood
Southeast corner of
Elliott Avenue and Amar Road
La Puente
(near Hacienda Boulevard,
north of "Rancho La Puente")

The first of the Donut Hole establishments was built in 1963 in Covina; by the end of the 1960s there were five examples in Southern California. In these Programmatic buildings you drive through the hole in the giant doughnut, pick up your sack of doughnuts, and then exit through a large doughnut at the other end. The whole experience is consummated without your having to get out of your car.

111 • Pomona

Named for the Roman goddess of fruit trees, Pomona was founded in the 1880s, another railroad town—this time the Southern Pacific. It was the commercial center of a very large agricultural region in the east San Gabriel Valley until very recently when changing population and economic patterns turned the area toward housing and industry.

Today, the business district, in spite of some good tries, looks terrible. In 1960 Gruen and Associates, with the best intentions, put in a pedestrian mall along 2nd Street between Gordon and Palomares Streets. It didn't work. Business moved elsewhere. Several banks were built in the late 1960s and a new city hall, public library, and post office were constructed in the same period. While in some cases there is moderately good architecture, they nevertheless demonstrate all the problems of the "City Beautiful" movement that Jane Jacobs so eloquently deplored in her *Death and Life of Great American Cities*. However, there are some fascinating things in Pomona, especially from the turn of the nineteenth into the twentieth century.

1. Xerox Corporation Manufacturing Facility, 1967
Craig Ellwood
800 E. Bonita Avenue, at the southwest corner of Towne Avenue, just above Arrow Highway

Miesian, large, but Spartan, this building just misses the look of having been turned out by a computer.

2. Palomares Adobe, circa 1850–54
491 E. Arrow Highway in Palomares Park

A single-story L-shaped adobe with a shingle hipped roof. A corridor runs around the L, and originally a second corridor faced the patio. The adobe was substantially restored in 1939.

3. Bungalow, circa 1920
178 E. Arrow Highway

An example of the Boulder style much more plentiful in the communities to the north.

4. Los Angeles County Fairgrounds
Northwest corner of McKinley and White Avenues

Most of the buildings date from the mid-1930s and thus have Moderne pretensions. Note particularly the sculpture (1939) near Gate 3—man's tribute to his equine friend—done by Lawrence Tenney Stevens in the heroic style often associated with Nazi art. Remember that this style was not the product of dictatorship (though Mussolini and Hitler went for it) but a more general movement in the history of taste not yet completely analyzed. Everybody will love the Santa Fe Railroad Station (circa 1885) brought from Arcadia. It is a tight mixture of Queen Anne and Stick style, almost dollhouse in scale. Why would Arcadia let this go?

5. La Casa Primera Adobe (Ygnacio Palomares Adobe), circa 1837 and later
Southwest corner of McKinley and North Park Avenues

A single-floor, five-rooms-in-a-line adobe with a corridor along the front and on one side. It is the headquarters of the Pomona Valley Historical Society.

6. House, circa 1887
Southwest corner of Garey and Jefferson Avenues

A big, angular, Queen Anne house with intricate ornament.

7. Pilgrim Congregational Church, 1911
Robert H. Orr
East side of Garey Avenue, between Pasadena and Pearl Streets

A large Gothic complex, including cloister, offices, parish house, etc., all in red brick.

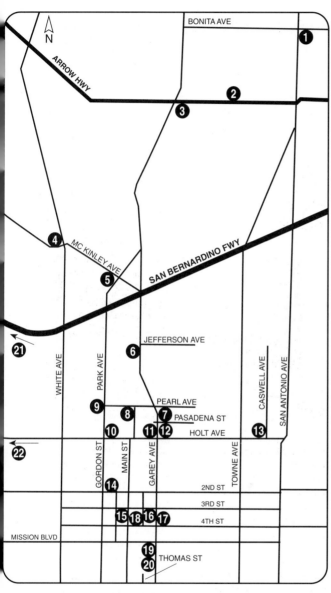

10. House, circa 1887
Northeast corner of
Holt and Park Avenues

Such Queen Anne houses make you realize how marvelous Victorian Pomona must have been. A hideous little building has been dumped in the front yard.

11. First Baptist Church, 1911
Norman F. Marsh
Garey and Holt Avenues

A Beaux-Arts design that would seem to have escaped from one of the turn-of-the-century World's Fairs. A lot of Classical elements have been strung across and around the façade of this structure. The effect is challenging, even unnerving.

12. House, circa 1910
143 Holt Avenue

A two-story Classical Revival house set at a respectable distance from the street.

13. Ebell Club, circa 1910
Ferdinand Davis
Northwest corner of
Holt and Caswell Avenues

This two-story, L-shaped building is a monument to the women's club movement of the turn of the century and to the sober, shingled Craftsman style.

14. Great Western Savings and Loan Association, 1965
Kurt Meyer and Associates
300 Pomona Mall West
(2nd Street)

A big temple with concrete roof slab and concrete columns.

8. House, circa 1900
Southwest corner of
Pearl and Main Streets

Classical Revival with a double-columned two-story portico.

9. Park Place, circa 1920
Park Avenue at Pearl Street

A very unusual compound. Four rows of two-story apartment units, all sheathed in boulders.

15. Seventh-Day Adventist Church, circa 1895
Ferdinand Davis
Southeast corner of
3rd and Gordon Streets

A mad concoction of Queen Anne, Gothic, and Italianate forms mercifully preserved in the midst of progress.

16. Fox Theater, 1931
Balch and Stanberry
Southwest corner of
Garey Avenue and 3rd Street

A late example of Art Deco.

17. Wells Fargo Bank, 1972
Northeast corner of Garey
Avenue and 4th Street

Classical Moderne Revival.

18. Masonic Hall, circa 1900
Ferdinand Davis
Northwest corner of
4th and Thomas Streets

A fancy building with mansard roof. Davis's work needs more study.

19. Pomona City Hall and Council Chambers, 1969
Welton Becket and Associates (B. H. Anderson)
South side of
Mission Boulevard, west of
Garey Avenue

The City Hall is square; the Council Chambers building is round. Both are dull. They are included because they are testaments to the big try.

20. Pomona Central Library, 1965
Welton Becket and Associates (Everett L. Tozier)
Northwest corner of
Garey Avenue and 6th Street

This fussy interpretation of the International Style is not outstanding architecture, but it seems to work.

21

21. California State Polytechnic University, Pomona
Valley Boulevard turn-off from
the San Bernardino Freeway

An agricultural college turned technical in the 1960s, Cal Poly has several interesting modern buildings.

The School of Environmental Design (1971) by Carl Maston is an asymmetrical massing of cubic forms. The Student Health Center (1976) designed by Mosher, Drew, Watson Associates of La Jolla is also well done. Probably the best building on the campus is the Student Union (1976), whose architects were Pulliam, Matthews, and Associates, proponents of the cut-into Box style. The most imposing structure on the campus is the knife-edged CLA Building (1987–92) designed by Antoine Predock (see image above). Assuming that contrast is a good thing, it certainly breaks with the traditional horizontality of the university buildings.

22. Phillips House, 1875
2640 W. Pomona Boulevard, off
Corona Freeway, below
Holt Avenue

An elegant French Second Empire house that seems dreadfully alone in this part of the world.

112 • Diamond Bar

1. South Coast Air Quality Management District Headquarters, 1990–91
Meyer and Allen Associates
21865 E. Copley Drive, off of the Golden Springs Drive Interchange

A Modernist image, for one of Southern California's major "official" environmental bodies. The building has been sensitively sited to take advantage of its smog, the users of the building can (in their spare time) gaze out the windows at the conjunction of the Pomona Freeway, and of course the architect had to design a car park for 1,200 automobiles. As to the design of the building, it is well carried out with remembrances here and there of such great modern buildings of the 1920s as Gropius's Bauhaus at Dessau.

Visually this is one of the biggest hits registered in this *Guide.* How such a revolutionary and brilliant design could pass a school board's scrutiny is a story that we wish we knew. It is as much a theater-piece as Frank Gehry's Walt Disney Concert Hall in central Los Angeles. How it works functionally also needs explaining. There is a lot of concrete. But one of the

orientation to the sun, and skylights have been carefully placed to introduce light internally. It also employs some advanced technology via fuel cells, etc. There are ironic twists in the siting of this building: this eastern section of Los Angeles County gathers more than its share of

2. Diamond Ranch High School, 1999
Morphosis (Thom Mayne)
Exit from Pomona Freeway at Phillips Ranch Road; turn north; in 20 yards you will see the sign to the high school.; go to the top of the hill.

teachers, when asked how she liked it, said that her classroom was the best she had ever worked in.

Surely such a dramatic gesture will encourage young people to think!

113 • Claremont

Claremont was named for its view and for Claremont, New Hampshire, the hometown of one of the directors of the Pacific Land and Improvement Company that settled the property along the Santa Fe Railroad. It was platted in 1887, and by the following year a large hotel was rising to accommodate the visitors who, it was assumed, would soon be thronging the area. Then the "Boom of the Eighties" busted. At first it appeared that the town would also expire.

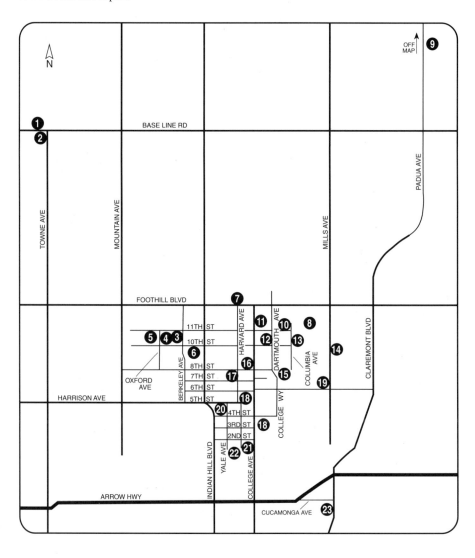

But every economic cloud has a silver lining. A college had been founded by the Congregationalists at Pomona in 1887. Then suddenly, no money! But there was the empty new hotel in nearby Claremont. Pomona College moved into the hotel during Christmas vacation in 1888–89 and named it Sumner Hall in honor of the wife of a Congregational minister. At first it was thought that with good times the college would move back to Pomona, but Claremont proved to be its permanent home. It became the nucleus of a group of "Associated Colleges"—Claremont Graduate School (1925), Scripps College (1926), Claremont Men's (now Claremont-McKenna) College (1946), Harvey Mudd College (1955), and Pitzer College (1963). The Southern California School of Theology, originally connected with the University of Southern California in Los Angeles, is also here, though not formally associated. All of these schools share faculty and libraries.

This is to indicate that even though founded by the Santa Fe Railroad, Claremont has always been a college town—and looks the part except for the area south of the tracks. In fact everything about the town is small and pleasant. The east side is devoted to the colleges and the west side (roughly west of Harvard Avenue) to housing on beautiful tree-lined streets. Claremont is a lively and attractive place on a smog-free day. Like its neighbors, Upland and Ontario, it looks and is civilized.

A note on Base Line Road: this road, which begins in Azusa, gives up in Glendora, picks up again in San Dimas, then stretches in an almost straight east/west line out into the desert. It is a fascinating route to explore. In Los Angeles County it runs through land that was once devoted to citrus and grapes, but now the pitiful orange groves and vineyards are interrupted repeatedly by intervals of tract housing. It is still possible in places to conjure up an older California (1900–1930). Many Craftsman bungalows and Spanish Revival houses remain, as do a few Victorian efforts mainly of the vertical board-and-batten shack variety. The most interesting features of the machine-made landscape are the boulder (cobblestone) pumphouses and reservoirs and barns that remind us that this area was once green. Note especially the stone structures at Benson and Padua Avenues in the Claremont area.

1. Webb School, 1922 and later
1175 W. Baseline Road

This boys' preparatory school was founded in 1922 by Thompson Webb, a native of Tennessee, and his California-born wife, Vivian. The aim was that the boys should live with nature in a gentlemanly manner. Except for Webb's late-Craftsman house, the Spanish Revival was chosen as the style of the early buildings. Apparently Webb and the contractor worked together on these.

The gymnasium is extraordinarily picturesque both inside and out. Recent buildings are mainly by Allen Siple. The Jones Dormitory and the house next to it are by Roland E. Coate Jr. The museum was designed (1965) by Millard Sheets with one of his Neo-WPA murals over the door. The loveliest building on the campus is the Vivian Webb Chapel (1944) that Webb designed as a memorial to his wife. It is a tiny Mission church. Webb, the faculty, the student body, and friends in Claremont literally built it with their own hands. Even the adobe brick was made from the earth of the campus.

Back of the Webb School near the junction of Live Oak Canyon and Summit Roads is a small collection of houses (1960s) designed by Foster Rhodes Jackson, a student of Frank Lloyd Wright. The few that can be seen from the road are impressive.

2

2. Pitzer House, 1910
Robert H. Orr
*Southwest corner of
Towne Avenue and
Base Line Road*

This house is tragically near the
extension of the Foothill Freeway.
Pitzer hired Orr to design a bungalow that would reflect the rustic environment, which can still
be sensed to the north. Orr chose
to sheathe it in boulders. The
plan is essentially a box almost
split by an interior patio whose
walls are encased in boulders and
whose ceiling is the sky. Although
the floor plan seems calculated,
the effect of the arrangement
seems very informal. As usual in a
house of this kind, the most
important rooms, besides the
patio, are the living and dining
rooms, the former having a boulder fireplace framed with art-glass
windows depicting a Dutch boy
and girl. Some additions, lacking
in harmony with the lines and
materials of the old house, have
recently been added.

3. House, circa 1927
*Southwest corner of
Berkeley Avenue and
11th Street*

Probably designed by Helen
Wren, a local architect of talent
who usually worked in the Anglo-
Colonial Revival of which this
Monterey Revival is an intended
offshoot. The street planting is
even better than the house. Praise
water and the absence of Dutch
elm disease!

4. House, circa 1965
Vincent Savoy
*East side of Oxford Avenue,
between 10th and 11th Streets*

A sophisticated International
Style essay in brick and glass.

5. Criley-Patterson House,
circa 1965
Attributed to Vincent Savoy
782 W. 11th Street

Similar to the previous entry.

6. Lincoln House, circa 1927
Helen Wren
472 W. 10th Street

Monterey Revival in miniature.

7. Southern California School
of Theology, 1960–61
Pereira and Luckman
*Entrance is near the intersec-
tion of Harvard Avenue and
Foothill Boulevard*

This is not one of the firm's
greatest works. What a shame
at such a site! The only salient
feature is the Kresge Memorial
Chapel (1961), and it is by
Edward D. Stone!

8. Harvey Mudd College,
1955 and later
**Edward D. Stone;
Heitschmidt and Thompson,
supervising architects**
*Between Columbia and
Mills Avenues*

Stripped Neoclassical in
concrete blocks.

9. Padua Hills

At the northeastern boundary
of Claremont is the entrance to
Padua Avenue. About three miles
north is a tiny community that
grew up around the Padua Hills
Theater and Dining Room, an
institution in Claremont's culture
since the 1920s. Here the stage
version of Helen Hunt Jackson's
Ramona was played. The cluster
of houses on Via Padova includes
the Hansch House (1955) by
Richard J. Neutra at number
4218, and a house (circa 1965)
by Foster Rhodes Jackson at
number 4161.

10. Four College Science
Center, 1970
Caudill, Rowlett, and Scott
*Near the northwest corner of
11th Street and
Columbia Avenue*

Cleaned-up Brutalism, especially
effective set off against the dullness of Harvey Mudd College
nearby.

11. Daggs House, circa 1910
1102 N. College Avenue

A beautifully sited Craftsman house with vertical board-and-batten siding.

12. Garrison Theater, 1963; addition, 1970
Millard Sheets Associates and S. David Underwood
Northeast corner of Dartmouth Avenue and 10th Street

Sheets, once a member of the faculty of the Claremont Colleges, knew modern architecture. He believed that the International Style was too severe. Obvious solution: soften it by giving a Saarinen-inspired classicism some hoopla in the form of mosaics and sculpture. The result is this drama center, strongly related to the Home Savings and Loan Association buildings that he designed or remodeled all over the county in the 1950s and 1960s. There is one of these, in fact, in downtown Claremont.

13. Scripps College, 1926 and later
Gordon B. Kaufmann; Edward Huntsman-Trout, landscape architect

Elizabeth Hubert Malott Commons, 2000; Brenda Levin

Access at Columbia Avenue and 10th Street

Scripps has to be one of the prettiest colleges in the country. It has a small select student body and looks that way largely thanks to Kaufmann, who designed most of the buildings. His Denison Library (1930) is especially well done in the Mediterranean style of most of the campus. The Balch Administration Building (1929) was designed by Sumner Hunt and Silas R. Burns, and fits in beautifully. Note the Shakespearean bas-reliefs by John Gregory that were the casts for those ornamenting the Folger Library in Washington, D.C. Other more recent buildings on the campus were designed by Smith and Williams, Criley and McDowell, and Warnecke and Associates. In the Margaret Fowler Garden of the Scripps Fine Arts Foundation are nine panels painted by Alfredo Ramos Martinez. These are worth a visit. Two new buildings, one a recycling and an extension and the other a brand new dormitory, add more beauty to this lovely campus. In 2000, the old Lang Art Building was made over by Brenda Levin into the Elizabeth

Hubert Malott Commons. It is a beautiful job by an architect who deserves to have a chance to design an all-new building. The Gabrielle Jungels Winkler Dormitory (2001) is in the Spanish or Mediterranean tradition of the rest of the campus and shows that architects can still bring it off when they are creative and knowledgeable.

14. Pitzer College, 1963 and later
Criley and McDowell
Entrance at 9th Street, off Mills Avenue

Not very distinguished in general except for the McConnell Center (1967), which was designed by Killingsworth, Brady, and Associates. Its projecting "rafters" suggest an attempt to break with the International Style. See also the Zetterberg House (1906), a handsome Japanese-influenced Craftsman house that was moved (1977) to the Pitzer campus from 721 Harrison Avenue and restored by faculty and students.

15. Honnold Library, 1952
J. E. Stanton; addition, 1956
Stanton and Stockwell
College Way, at the intersection of Dartmouth and Columbia Avenues

The façade is stripped Moderne so crisp that it has a Regency look. This is the main library of the Associated Colleges.

16. Darling House, 1903
Charles and Henry Greene
Northwest corner of College Avenue and 8th Street

A significant house in the Greenes' oeuvre, for it is one of the first of their houses in the true Craftsman mode—in this case Swiss Chalet with Asian touches.

17. Sugg House, circa 1930
Helen Wren
Northwest corner of
7th Street and Harvard Avenue
This large house is Anglo-Colonial, Wren's favorite style.

east of it is the Harwood Garden (1921) laid out by Ralph Cornell and remaining close to his original ideas. Beyond it is Sumner Hall, the hotel that was Pomona's first building, but it has been so heavily remodeled that it is worth only a glance. Dating from 1908 and looking older is the Carnegie Building designed by Franklin P.

California's most famous murals, *Prometheus* (1930), by Jose Clemente Orozco. In 1960 Honnold and Rex designed a 125-foot-tall Memorial Bell Tower. The Modernist form of this tower, composed of two solid slabs enclosing two surfaces of grillwork, supposedly fitted into the existing Spanish Revival

Smith Campus Center. 1999; Robert A. M. Stern

18. Pomona College,
1887 and later
Ralph Cornell,
landscape architect
Both sides of College Avenue,
between 2nd and 6th Streets

This is the oldest and largest of the colleges with a congeries of styles and architects. The gates (1914) at Sixth Street and College Avenue are by Myron Hunt, as is the Bridges Hall of Music (1915). The latter, based on a Mannerist triumphal arch, is one of Hunt's best buildings. Just

Burnham. The Bridges Auditorium (1931) by San Diego architect William Templeton Johnson is vaguely Romanesque enlivened with a little Art Deco. The interior, with its frescoed ceiling, is a period piece. Also notable is Frary Hall (1929), not for its architecture by Webber and Spaulding but for its murals. Just inside the entrance porch is a striking one by Rico Lebrun (assisted by James Pinto and William Ptaszynski) called *Genesis* (1960). In the dining hall you will find one of

building tradition. It really doesn't accomplish this goal, but the effort was there. The grillwork was designed by Los Angeles sculptor Malcolm Leland. A new building that certainly does fit into the Spanish theme of the campus is the Smith Campus Center (1999) designed by Robert A. M. Stern, who is skilled in contextualism and at the same time is a creative artist.

20

19. Claremont-McKenna (formerly Men's) College, 1948 and later
Allison and Rible
Mills Avenue and 6th Street

Not inspired architecture, but the two residential towers, Fawcett Hall and Claremont Hall (both 1966), designed by Ladd and Kelsey, are worth mentioning because high-rise, even medium high-rise, seems odd in Claremont. Also the scoops taken out of the corners of the buildings seem an obvious planned dig at the International Style.

20. Bungalow, circa 1910
Southeast corner of Yale and Harrison Avenues

Brown in color, of course, with vertical board-and-batten siding. Just behind this house at 428 N. Yale Avenue is another well-maintained Craftsman house.

21. Sumner House, 1887
105 N. College Avenue

A two-story Queen Anne mansion built just before the bust.

22. Santa Fe Railroad Passenger Station, circa 1925
William H. Mohr
1st Street and railroad tracks, just west of the end of Harvard Avenue

This small-scaled Churrigueresque extravaganza has received a new lease on life. Since our last *Guide,* it has been beautifully restored.

23. Russian Village, 1928 and later
South Mills Avenue (approached from the north by Claremont Avenue), just below Arrow Highway

Thirteen picturesque houses built of cast-off materials, such as concrete pavement torn up from

Holt Avenue when it was being repaved. Its creator was Steve Stys, a Pole, who began with 290 S. Mills Avenue. He rather conservatively fashioned it from fieldstone and other materials that he had accumulated, figuring that it cost him thirty-five dollars to build it. Later he went on to use broken concrete, boulders, and, after the Long Beach earthquake of 1933, marble and other parts of the ruins. He did not build all of the thirteen houses, but his imagination obviously dominated the project.

Readings

You can gain some idea of the mountains of literature published on Los Angeles by thumbing through Doyce B. Nunis Jr.'s *Los Angeles and Its Environs in the Twentieth Century* (9,895 entries in 501 pages), and this bibliography covers only the years 1900 through 1973. While every state and every American city had its array of PR sales literature in the nineteenth century, no region or city comes close to equaling the output of literature on Southern California and Los Angeles. And the last quarter century has seen no letdown in the publishing of articles and books about Los Angeles.

The accompanying bibliography lists the writings that we have found most useful in forming our understanding of the built environment of Los Angeles. Periodicals that deal with architecture in Southern California are *Sunset, Westways, Los Angeles Magazine,* and occasional articles that occur in the *Calendar* section of the *Los Angeles Times.* Those specifically devoted to architecture that we have often consulted are *Architectural Digest,* the *L.A. Architect,* and the *Newsletter* of the Los Angeles Forum for Architecture and Urban Design. Older publications are historically of value, such as the *Home Magazine* of the *Los Angeles Times,* and *California Arts and Architecture* (later *Arts and Architecture*).

Magazines no longer published but of great value to us have been *Architect and Engineer, Southwest Builder and Contractor, California Home Owner, Bungalow Magazine, Land of Sunshine* (later *Outwest*), and the all-too-brief *West* magazine of the Sunday *Los Angeles Times.* The real-estate section of the Sunday *Times* has provided clues as to what was occurring in Los Angeles architecture (especially commercial and popular spec architecture). Also, there are those very valuable articles written by the architectural critics at the *Times*

(John Pastier, John Dreyfus, Art Seidenbaum, Sam Hall Kaplan and, more recently, Leon Whiteson, Michael Webb, Aaron Betsky, Suzanne Muchnic, and Nicholai Ouroussoff) and those written by Joseph Giovannini for the *Los Angeles Herald Examiner,* as well as other newspapers and magazines. The Southern California scene in general has been well presented in many of the national magazines such as *Architectural Digest, House and Home, House and Garden,* and *Metropolitan Home.* No longer published but very revealing of Los Angeles and its environs is the environmental planning magazine *Cry California.*

Institutions notable for their collections on Los Angeles architecture (books, runs of magazines, photographs, and other documents) are the Huntington Library; the History Department of the Los Angeles Public Library; the History Division of the Los Angeles County Museum of Natural History; the Los Angeles Cultural Heritage Board; the Pasadena Urban Conservation Program; the UCLA Special Collections, Research Library, Art and Architectural Library; the Art and Architecture Library of the University of Southern California; and the Special Collections Library at the University of California, Santa Barbara.

Original architectural drawings and archives are of great value in the study of architecture in Los Angeles and the Southland. The largest single collection is contained in the Architectural Drawing Collection, University Art Museum, University of California, Santa Barbara. Other collections of drawings are to be found at the Huntington Library (including the Gamble House drawing collection of the University of Southern California) and at the Library, UCLA.

Earlier writings that have continually influenced us are Esther McCoy's *Five California Architects* (first published in 1960; republished in 1975) and Reyner Banham's *Los Angeles: The Architecture of Four Ecologies* (1974). More generally, Robert Venturi and Denise Scott Brown and Charles Moore have informed and inspired us. Their pioneering publications on Los Angeles and vernacular architecture have been continued by John Margolies, Jim Heiman, Rip George, John Chase, and John Beach. Michael Webb in particular has opened up the work of contemporary architects to us.

Abeloe, William N., et al. *Historic Spots in California.* Stanford: 1966.

Allison, David C. "The Work of Myron Hunt." *Architect and Engineer* 53 (April 1918): 38–68.

Amos, Patrick. *At Home with Architecture.* La Jolla: 1983.

Andersen, Timothy J., Eudorah M. Moore, and Robert Winter. *California Design 1910,* 1974. Reprint, Salt Lake City: 1980.

Andre, Herb. "John Byers: Domestic Architecture in Southern California 1919–1960." Master's thesis, University of California, Santa Barbara, 1971.

Anonymous. "California's Contribution to a National Architecture." *The Craftsman* 22 (August 1912): 352–547.

———. *Handbook of Southern California, Los Angeles and San Diego.* New York: 1914.

———. "The Housing Authority of the City of Los Angeles Presents a Solution." *California Arts and Architecture* 60 (May 1943): 47–66.

———. "The Los Angeles 12." *Architectural Record* 160 (August 1976): 81–90.

———. "The Los Angeles Civic Center." *Architect and Engineer* 73 (June 1923): 65–67.

———. "Southern California: The Land of Heart's Desire: Its People, Homes and Pleasure: Art and Architecture." *Los Angeles Morning Herald,* 1912.

———. "Street Art Exploration in Los Angeles." *Sunset* 150 (April 1973): 110–13.

———. "Work of Some Contemporary Los Angeles Architects." *Pencil Points* 22 (May 1941): 306–33.

"Architectural Design Goes West." *Architectural Design* 43, no. 8 (1973).

Atkinson, Janet Erene. *Historical Directory of Los Angeles County.* Jefferson, North Carolina: rev. edition, 1987.

Austin, John C. *Architecture in Southern California.* Los Angeles: 1905.

Austin, Mary. *California: Land of the Sun.* London: 1914.

———. *Land of Little Rain.* Boston: 1903.

Avensleben, Ludolf von. *John Lautner Architect Los Angeles.* Vienna, Austria: 1991.

Baer, Kurt. *Architecture of the California Missions.* Berkeley: 1963.

Bangs, Jean Murray. "Greene and Greene." *Architectural Forum* 89 (October 1948): 80–82.

———. "Los Angeles . . . Know Thyself." *Home Section, Los Angeles Times* (14 October 1961): 4–11.

Banham, Reyner. "L.A.: The Structure Behind the Scene." *Architectural Design* 41 (April 1971): 227–30.

———. "A London–L.A. Love Affair." *West Magazine, Los Angeles Times* (6 June 1974): 9–14.

———. *Los Angeles: The Architecture of Four Ecologies.* London: 1974.

Basten, Fred. *Portrait of a Fabled City.* Los Angeles: 1975.

———. *Santa Monica by the Bay: Its First 100 Years.* Los Angeles: 1974.

Baum, Dwight James. "An Eastern Architect's Impression of Recent Work in Southern California." *Architecture* 38 (July 1918): 177–80.

———. "Ecclesiastical Architecture of California." *American Architect* 34 (July 1928): 71–78.

Baum, George C. "The Spanish Mission Type." *Architectural Styles for Country Houses,* by Henry H. Taylor. New York: 1919.

Baylis, Douglas and Joan Parry. *California Houses of Gordon Drake*. New York: 1956.

Beach, John. "Lloyd Wright's Sowden House." *Fine Home Building* (April/May 1983): 66–73.

Belloli, Jay, ed. *Johnson, Kaufmann, Coate: Partners in the California Style*. Claremont and Santa Barbara: 1992.

———. *Wallace Neff 1895–1982. The Romance of Regional Architecture*. San Marino: 1989.

Benton, Arthur B. "Architecture for the Southwest." *Outwest (The Land of Sunshine)* 4 (February 1896): 126–30.

Beronius, George. "Paradise for Porkers." *Home Magazine, Los Angeles Times* (18 April 1976): 19–21.

———. "Those Astonishing Murals of East Los Angeles." *Home Magazine, Los Angeles Times* (11 April 1976): 12–17, 22–23.

Betsky, Aaron. "Shambles Instead of Shangri-La." *L.A. Architect* (December 1991): 5.

———. "Remaking L.A." *Los Angeles Times Magazine* (15 December 1992): 58–61.

———. *Violated Perfection*. New York: 1990.

Billiteu, Bill. "Simon Rodia's Incredible Towers." *Art News* 78 (April 1979): 92–96.

Bledsoe, Jane. "Added-on Ornament." *Home Sweet Home, American Domestic Vernacular Architecture*, Edited by Charles W. Moore et al. New York: 1983.

Bosley, Edward R. *Greene and Greene*. London: 2000.

Boutelle, Sara Holmes. *Julia Morgan Architect*. New York: 1988.

Bowman, Lynn. *L.A.: Epic of a City*. Los Angeles: 1974.

Boyarsky, Nancy and Bill. "The Highway Game." *West Magazine, Los Angeles Times* (28 February 1971): 7–15.

Bradley, Bill. comp. *Commercial Los Angeles 1925–1947*. Glendale: 1981.

———. *The Last of the Great Stations*. Glendale: 1979.

Brady, Francis. "The Spanish Colonial Revival in California Architecture." Master's thesis, California State University, Long Beach, 1962.

Brantner, Cherri, and Gregory Cloud, eds. "The Essential Pico Blvd." *Scan* 1 (November 1978): 2–7.

Braupton, Ernest. *The Garden Beautiful in California*. Los Angeles: 1946.

Breeze, Carla. *L.A. Deco*. New York: 1991.

Bricker, David. "Cliff May and the California Ranch House after 1945." Master's thesis, University of California, Santa Barbara, 1983.

———. "Ranch Houses Are Not All the Same." *Preserving the Recent Past 2*. Edited by Deborah Staton and William G. Foulck. Washington D.C.: 2000.

Bricker, Lauren Weiss. "The Residential Architecture of Roland E. Coate." Master's thesis, University of California, Santa Barbara, 1982.

Brino, Giovanni. *La Citta Capitalista Los Angeles*. Florence, Italy: 1978.

Brodsly, David. *L.A. Freeway: An Appreciative Essay*. Berkeley: 1981.

Brook, Harry Ellington. *Los Angeles, California: The City and County*. Los Angeles: 1915.

Brown, Robert G. "The California Bungalow in Los Angeles: A Study of Origins and Classification." Master's thesis, University of California, Los Angeles, 1964.

Browne, F. E. *Comfortable Los Angeles Homes and What People Say Who Live in Them*. Los Angeles: 1896.

Bryant, Lynn. "Edward Huntsman-Trout, Landscape Architect." *Review* (Southern California Chapter, Society of Architectural Historians) II, no. 1 (Winter 1983): 1–6.

Buergen, Anne Luise, et al. "Downtown L.A." *L.A. Architect* 5 (February 1979): 3–6.

Burdette, Robert J. *Greater Los Angeles and Southern California*. Chicago: 1906.

———. "The California Mission and Its Influence on Pacific Coast Architecture." *Architect and Engineer* 24 (February 1911): 35–45.

————. "The Work of the Landmark Club of Southern California." *American Institute of Architects Journal* 2 (September 1914): 469–81.

Calistro, Paddy, and Betty Goodwin. *L.A. Inside and Out.* New York: 1992.

California Institute of Technology (Baxter Art Gallery). *Caltech, 1910–1950.* Exhibition catalog with essays by Alice Stone et al. Pasadena: 1983.

Cameron, Robert. *Above Los Angeles.* Los Angeles: 1976.

Campbell, Regula. "Notes on Landscape Design in Southern California." *L.A. Architect* (October 1981): 4–5.

Cardwell, Kenneth H. *Bernard Maybeck Artisan, Architect, Artist.* Salt Lake City: 1977.

Case, Walter. *History of Long Beach and Vicinity.* New York: 1927. Reprint, 1974.

Caughey, John W. and La Ree. *Los Angeles: Biography of a City.* Berkeley: 1976.

Chalk, Warren. "Up the Down-ramp." *Architectural Design* 38 (September 1968): 404–7.

Chapman, John L. *Incredible Los Angeles.* New York: 1967.

Chase, John. "The Garret, the Boardroom, and the Amusement Park." *Journal Los Angeles Institute of Contemporary Art* 4 (1983): 21–27.

————. *Exterior Decoration: Hollywood's Inside-out Houses.* Los Angeles: 1982.

————. "Map Guide to Recent Architecture in L.A." *L.A. Architect* 7 (October 1981): 2, 7.

————. "Typecasting Style: New Condominiums in Santa Monica, California." *Arts & Architecture* 1 (1982): 51–58.

Chase, John, and John Beach. "The Stucco Box." *Home Sweet Home, American Domestic Vernacular Architecture* (1983): 118–29.

Cheney, Charles H. "Palos Verdes: Eight Years of Development." *Architect and Engineer* 100 (January 1930): 35–83.

Clark, Alson. "The Architecture of Los Angeles: An Introduction," *Review* (Southern California Chapter, Society of Architectural Historians) II, no. 1 (Winter 1983): 6–7.

————. "The California Architecture of Gordon Kaufmann." *Review* (Southern California Chapter, Society of Architectural Historians) I, no. 3 (Summer 1982): 1–7.

Clark, David. *L.A. on Foot.* Los Angeles and San Francisco: 1972.

————. *Los Angeles: A City Apart.* Woodland Hills: 1981.

Clark, Robert Judson, and Thomas S. Hines. *Los Angeles Transfer: Architecture in Southern California, 1880–1980.* Los Angeles (William Andrews Clark Memorial Library, UCLA): 1983.

Cleland, Robert Glass. *The Cattle on a Thousand Hills: Southern California, 1850–1880.* San Marino: 1969.

Cohen, Gloria. "Allyn E. Morris, Architect." *L.A. Architect* (May 1982): 2–3.

Coombs, Robert. "The New Victorians." *Westways* 75 (May 1983): 31–33, 69.

Crocker, Donald W. *Within the Vale of Annandale.* Pasadena: 1968.

Crofutt, George A. *Crofutt's New Overland Tourist and Pacific Coast Guide.* Chicago: 1878–79.

Croly, Herbert D. "The California Country House." *Architect and Engineer* 7 (December 1906): 24–39.

Crouch, Dora P., Daniel J. Garr, and Axel I. Mundigo. *Spanish City Planning in North America.* Cambridge, Massachusetts: 1982.

Crump, Spencer. *Ride the Big Red Cars.* Los Angeles: 1962.

Cuff, Dana. *The Provisional City: Los Angeles Stories of Architecture and Urbanism.* Cambridge, Massachusetts: 2000.

Culbertson, Judy, and Tom Randell. *Permanent Californians.* Chelsea, Vermont: 1989.

Current, William R. and Karen. *Greene and Greene, Architects in the Residential Style.* Fort Worth: 1974.

Cutts, Anson B. Jr. "The Hillside Home of Ramon Navarro, A Unique Setting Created by Lloyd Wright." *California Arts and Architecture* 44 (July 1933): 11–13, 31.

Dash, Norman. *Yesterday's Los Angeles.* Miami: 1976.

David, Arthur C. "An Architect of Bungalows in California." *Architectural Record* 20 (October 1906): 306–15.

Davis, Genevieve. *Beverly Hills: An Illustrated History.* Chatsworth: 1988.

Davis, Mike. *City of Quartz.* New York: 1990.

Del Zoppo, Annette, and Jeffrey Stanton. *Venice, California 1904–1930.* Venice: 1978.

Dickinson, R. B. *Los Angeles Today— Architecturally.* Los Angeles: 1896.

Dietz, Lawrence. "Raymond Chandler's L.A." *Western Architect* 32 (August 1969): 87–90.

———. "There Was Once a Woman Who Lived in a Shoe." *West Magazine, Los Angeles Times* (30 November 1969): 12–15.

Direccion General De Arquitectura y Vivienda. *R. M. Schindler Arquitectura.* With articles by Esther McCoy et al. Madrid, Spain: MOPU, 1984.

Diskin, Steve, et al. *Los Angeles at 25 MPH.* New York: 1993.

Duell, Prentice. "The New Era of California Architecture." *Western Architect* 32 (August 1923): 87–90.

Dumke, Glen S. *The Boom of the Eighties in Southern California.* San Marino: 1970.

Dunitz, Robin J. *Street Gallery: Guide to 1000 Los Angeles Murals.* Los Angeles: 1993.

Faulstick, Paul. *A Guide to Claremont Architecture.* Claremont: 1977.

Feldman, Eddy S. *The Art of Street Lighting in Los Angeles.* Los Angeles: 1972.

Fink, Augusta. *Time and the Terraced Land.* Berkeley: 1966.

Flanagan, Barbara. "Terminal Oasis: The Uncanny Survival of Union Station." *L.A. Architect* 6 (February 1980): 2–3.

Flood, Francis B. "A Study of the Architecture of the Period 1868–1900 Existing in Los Angeles in 1940." Master's thesis, University of Southern California, Los Angeles, 1941.

Fogelson, Robert M. *The Fragmented Metropolis Los Angeles, 1850–1930.* Cambridge, Massachusetts: 1967.

Foster, Mark S. "The Model-T, The Hard Sell, and Los Angeles during the 1920s." *Pacific Historical Review* 44 (1975): 459–98.

Frierman, Jay D., and Roberta S. Greenwood. *Historical Archaeology of Nineteenth-Century California.* Los Angeles: 1992.

Gallion, Arthur B. "Architecture of the Los Angeles Region." *Architectural Record* 119 (May 1956): 159–66.

Garr, Daniel. "Hispanic Colonial Settlements in California: Planning and Urban Development on the Frontier, 1769–1850." Ph.D. thesis, Cornell University, Ithaca, 1971.

Gaut, Helen Lukens. A frequent contributor to *The Craftsman* (1901–16) and other journals, she was a Pasadenan who had strong ties to the Arts and Crafts movement. See, as examples:

———. "An Example of Progressive Architecture from the West Coast." *The Craftsman* 18 (June 1910): 380–83.

———. "How the California Bungalow Illustrates the Right Use of Building Materials." *The Craftsman* 19 (November 1910): 200–201.

Gebhard, David. "Architectural Imagery: The Missions and California." *Harvard Architectural Review* 1 (Spring 1980): 136–45.

———. "Architecture in Los Angeles." *Art Forum* 2 (Summer 1964): 10–11.

———. *The Architectural Drawings of R. M. Schindler.* New York: 1993.

———. "California Modernist: Design Stardom at Last." *Metropolitan Home* (October 1989): 93–98.

———. "The Case Study Houses." *Art Forum* 2 (October 1963): 24–25.

———. "Charles Moore and the West Coast." *Architecture and Urbanism* 5 (1978): 45–48.

————. "Civic Presence in California Cities." *Architectural Design* 57 (October 1987): 74–80.

————. *George Washington Smith.* Santa Barbara: 1964.

————. "Getty's Museum." *Architecture Plus* 2 (September–October 1974): 56–61.

————. "L.A., The Stucco Box." *Art in America* 58 (May–June 1970): 130–33.

————. "Los Angeles: An Architectural Tour." *Portfolio* 2 (September–October 1980): 106–9.

————. *Lutah Maria Riggs: A Woman in Architecture, 1921–1980.* Santa Barbara: 1992.

————. "The Monterey Tradition: History Re-ordered." *New Mexico Studies in the Fine Arts* 7 (1982): 14–19.

————. "Preserving the Common Place." *Journal L.A.I.C.A.* 4 (Spring 1983): 50–57.

————. "The Reign of Spain." *Arts & Architecture* 4 (July 1985): 71–76.

————. *Robert Stacy-Judd: Maya Architecture, The Creation of a New Style.* Santa Barbara: 1993.

————, with photographs by Scott Zimmerman. *Romanza: The California Architecture of Frank Lloyd Wright.* San Francisco: 1988.

————. *Schindler.* London and New York, 1972. Reprint, Salt Lake City: 1980.

————. "Some Observations on California's Monterey Tradition." *Journal of the Society of Architectural Historians* 46 (June 1987): 157–170.

————. "The Spanish Colonial Revival in Southern California." *Journal of the Society of Architectural Historians* 26 (May 1967): 131–47.

————. "Tile, Stucco Walls, and Arches; The Spanish Tradition in the Popular American House." *Home Sweet Home, American Domestic Vernacular Architecture.* Edited by Charles W. Moore. New York, 1983.

Gebhard, David, and Harriette Von Breton. *1868–1968: Architecture in California.* Santa Barbara: 1968.

————. *Kem Weber: The Moderne in Southern California, 1920–1941.* Santa Barbara: 1969.

————. *L.A. in the Thirties.* Los Angeles: 1989.

————. *Lloyd Wright, Architect.* Santa Barbara: 1971.

Gebhard, David, and Susan King. *A View of California Architecture, 1960–1976.* San Francisco: 1976.

Gebhard, David, Harriette Von Breton, and Lauren Weiss. *The Architecture of Gregory Ain: The Play Between the Rational and High Art.* Santa Barbara: 1980.

Gebhard, David, Harriette Von Breton, and Robert Winter. *Samuel and Joseph Cather Newsom: Victorian Architectural Imagery in California, 1878–1908.* Santa Barbara: 1979.

Gebhard, David, Lauren Weiss Bricker, and David Bricker. *Fort MacArthur, San Pedro— A Public Report.* Washington, D.C.: 1982.

Gebhard, David, and Robert Winter. *A Guide to Architecture in Los Angeles and Southern California.* Salt Lake City: 1977.

————. *A Guide to Architecture in Southern California.* Los Angeles: 1965.

————. *Architecture in Los Angeles: A Compleat Guide.* Salt Lake City: 1985.

Germany, Lisa. *Harwell Hamilton Harris.* Austin, Texas: 1991.

Gill, Brendan. *The Dream Come True: The Great Houses of Los Angeles.* New York: 1982.

Gill, Irving J. "The Home of the Future: The New Architecture of the West." *The Craftsman* 30 (May 1916): 140–41, 220.

Giovannini, Joseph. As architectural critic for the *Los Angeles Herald Examiner* from 1978 to 1983, Giovannini contributed greatly to our understanding of the local architectural and planning scene:

————. "A Chronicler of California Architecture." *The New York Times* (21 June 1984): 21.

————. "The Environment of Movement." *California History* 60 (Spring 1981): 82–83.

————. *Real Estate As Art: New Architecture in Venice*. Venice: 1984.

Gleen, Constance W. *Egypt in L.A.* Long Beach: 1977.

Gleye, Paul. *The Architecture of Los Angeles*. Los Angeles: 1981.

Goodhue, Bertram G., and Carleton M. Winslow. *The Architecture and the Gardens of the San Diego Exposition*. San Francisco: 1916.

Greene, Charles S. "Bungalows." *The Western Architect* 12 (July 1908): 3.

————. "Impressions of Some Bungalows and Gardens." *The Architect* 10 (December 1915): 251–52, 278.

Grenier, Judson. *A Guide to Historic Places in Los Angeles County*. Dubuque, Iowa: 1978.

Grenier, Judson A., Doyce B. Nunis Jr., and Jean Bruce Poole. *A Guide to Historic Places in Los Angeles County*. Los Angeles: 1978.

Grey, Elmer. "Architecture in Southern California." *Architectural Record* 17 (January 1905): 1–17.

————. "Architecture in Southern California." *Arts and Decoration* 30 (January 1926): 40–41, 78.

————. "Some Country House Architecture in the Far West." *Architectural Record* 51 (January 1922): 308–15.

Griffin, Helen S. "Some Two-Story Adobe Houses of Old California." *Historical Society of Southern California Quarterly* 20 (March 1938): 5–21.

Gudde, Erwin G. *California Place Names: Origin and Etymology of Current Geographic Names*. Berkeley: 1968.

Guinn, J. M. "Los Angeles in the Adobe Age." *Historical Society of Southern California Quarterly* 4 (1897): 49–55.

Haley, A. L. *Modern Apartments*. Los Angeles: ca. 1910.

Halprin, John. *Los Angeles: Improbable City*. New York: 1979.

Hamlin, Talbot F. "California Whys and Wherefores." *Pencil Points* 22 (May 1941): 339–44.

————. "What Makes It American: Architecture in the Southwest and West." *Pencil Points* 20 (December 1939): 762–76.

Hampton, Edgar Lloyd. "Architecture of California." *House and Garden* 51 (February 1927): 104–5, 154, 156.

Hancock, Ralph. *Fabulous Boulevard (Wilshire)*. New York: 1949.

————. *The Forest Lawn Story*. Los Angeles: 1955.

Hannaford, Donald R., and Revel Edwards. *Spanish Colonial or Adobe Architecture in California, 1800–1850*. New York: 1931. Republished, with a preface by David Gebhard, Stamford, Connecticut: 1990.

Hanson, A. E. *An Arcadian Landscape: The California Gardens of A. E. Hanson*. Edited and with an introduction by David Gebhard. Los Angeles: 1984.

————. *Rolling Hills: The Early Years*. Rolling Hills: 1978.

Hanson, Earl, and Paul Beckett. *Los Angeles: Its People and Its Homes*. Los Angeles: 1944.

Harlow, Neal. *Maps and Survey of the Pueblo Lands of Los Angeles*. Los Angeles: 1976.

Harrel, Mary Ann Beach. "The Vernacular Castle." *Home Sweet Home, American Domestic Vernacular Architecture*. Edited by Charles W. Moore. New York: 1983.

Harris, Allen. "Southern California Architects: Walker and Eisen." *Building Review* 22 (October 1922): 43–52.

Harris, Frank and Weston Bonenberger. *A Guide to Contemporary Architecture in Southern California*. Los Angeles: 1951.

Harris, Harwell Hamilton. *Harwell Hamilton Harris—A Collection of His Writings*. Raleigh, North Carolina: 1965.

Hastings, Miles. "The Continuous House." *Sunset* 32 (January 1914): 110–16.

Hatheway, Roger. "El Pueblo: Myth and Realities." *Review* (Southern California Chapter, Society of Architectural Historians) I: 1 (Fall 1981): 1–5.

Hays, William C. "One Story and Open-Air Schoolhouses in California." *Architectural Forum* 27 (September 1917): 57–65.

Heiman, Jim, and Rip George, with an introduction by David Gebhard. *California Crazy.* San Francisco: 1980.

Heisley, George D. "Seeing America: Los Angeles." *Outwest* 30 (March 1909): 193–224.

———. "Seeing America: Some More About Los Angeles." *Outwest* 30 (May 1909): 509–18.

Henstell, Bruce. *Los Angeles: An Illustrated History.* New York: 1980.

———. *Sunshine and Wealth: Los Angeles in the Twenties and Thirties.* San Francisco: 1984.

Hess, Alan. "California Coffee Shops." *Arts & Architecture* 2 (1983): 42–50.

———. *Googie: Fifties Coffee Shop Architecture.* San Francisco: 1985.

———. "Golden Architecture." *Journal Los Angeles Institute of Contemporary Art* (Spring 1983): 28–30.

Hill, Laurence L. *La Reina: Los Angeles in Three Centuries.* Los Angeles: 1929.

Hines, Thomas S. "Housing, Baseball, and Creeping Socialism: The Battle of Chavez Ravine, Los Angeles, 1949–1959." *Journal of Urban History* 8 (February 1982): 123–45.

———. *Irving Gill and the Architecture of Reform.* New York: 2000.

———. *Richard Neutra and the Search for Modern Architecture.* New York: 1982.

Hise, Greg. *Eden by Design: The Olmsted-Bartholomew Plan for the Los Angeles Region.* Berkeley: 2000.

———, ed. *Rethinking Los Angeles.* Thousand Oaks, California: 1996.

Hise, Greg, and William Deverell. *Magnetic Los Angeles: Planning the Twentieth Century Metropolis.* Baltimore: 1997.

History of Los Angeles County. Berkeley: Thompson and West, 1880; reprint, 1959.

Hitchcock, Henry-Russell. "An Eastern Critic Looks at Western Architecture." *California Arts and Architecture* 57 (December 1940): 21–23, 40.

Hoffmann, Donald. *Frank Lloyd Wright's Hollyhock House.* New York: 1992.

Holder, Charles. *Southern California—A Guide Book.* Los Angeles: 1888.

Honnold, Douglas. *Southern California Architecture: 1769–1956.* New York: 1956.

Hopkins, Una Nixon. "The Development of Domestic Architecture on the West Coast." *The Craftsman* 13 (January 1908): 450–57.

Hudson, Karen E. *Paul R. Williams, Architect: Legacy of Style.* New York: 1993.

Hume, H., comp. *Los Angeles, Architecturally.* Los Angeles: 1902.

Humes, Edward. "Downtown is a Bust." *Buzz* 4 (April 1993): 62–67, 101–3.

Hunt, Myron. "Personal Sources of Pacific Coast Architectural Development." *American Architect* 129 (5 January 1926): 51–54.

———. "The Work of Messrs. Allison and Allison." *Architect and Engineer* 42 (1912): 39–75.

Hunter, Paul, and Walter L. Reichardt, eds. *Residential Architecture in Southern California.* Los Angeles: 1939.

Hylen, Arnold. *Bunker Hill: A Los Angeles Landmark.* Los Angeles: 1976.

———. *Los Angeles Before the Freeways.* Los Angeles: 1981.

Inaya, Beata, et al. *The Three Worlds of Los Angeles.* Los Angeles: 1974.

Jackson, Helen Hunt. *Glimpses of California and the Missions.* Boston: 1904.

———. *Ramona.* Boston: 1884.

Jaeger, Roland. "Von Altona nach Los Angeles: Jukob Petlef Peters (1889–1934)." *Architektor in Hamburg: Jahrbuch 1993.* Hamburg, Germany: 1993.

James, George Wharton. *California Romantic and Beautiful.* Boston: 1914.

———. *In and Out of the Old Missions.* Boston: 1927.

Jencks, Charles. *Architecture Today.* London and New York: 1982.

———. *Daydream Houses of Los Angeles.* New York: 1978.

————. "The Los Angeles Silvers." *Urbanism* (October 1976): 13–14.

Jenney, William L. E. "The Old California Missions and Their Influence on Design." *Architect and Engineer* 6 (September 1906): 25–33.

Johnson, Cheryle, et al. *75th Anniversary of the Los Feliz Improvement Association, 1916–1991.* Los Angeles: 1991.

Johnson, Paul, ed. *Los Angeles: Portrait of an Extraordinary City.* Menlo Park: 1968.

Johnson, Reginald D. "Development of Architectural Styles in California." *Architect and Engineer* 87 (October 1926): 108–9.

Jones, A. Quincy, and Frederick E. Emmons. *Builder's Homes for Better Living.* New York: 1957.

Jordy, William H. *Progressive and Academic Ideals at the Turn of the Century.* New York: 1972.

Kamerling, Bruce. *Irving J. Gill, Architect.* San Diego: 1993.

————. *Irving Gill: The Artist as Architect.* San Diego: 1979.

Kammerman, Roy. *L.A. Superlatives.* New York: 1987.

Kaplan, Sam Hall. *Follies: Design and Other Diversions in a Fractured Metropolis.* Santa Monica: 1989.

————. *L.A. Lost and Found.* New York: 1987.

Kapp, Glenn, and Geoff Miller. "Our Backyard Riviera." *Los Angeles* 2 (April 1961): 18–21.

Karasick, Norman M., and Dorothy K. Karasick. *The Oilman's Daughter: A Biography of Aline Barnsdall.* Encino: 1993.

Kennelley, Joe, and Roy Hankey. *Sunset Boulevard: America's Dream Street.* Burbank: 1981.

Kirker, Harold. "California's Architecture and its Relations to Contemporary Trends in Europe and America." *California Historical Society Quarterly* 51 (Winter 1972): 289–305.

————. *California's Architectural Frontier. San Marino: 1960.* Reprint, Salt Lake City: 1973.

Knight, Arthur, and Eliot Elisofon. *The Hollywood Style.* New York: 1969.

Kuehn, Gernot. *Views of Los Angeles.* Los Angeles: 1978.

Lacy, Bill, and Susan deMenli, eds. *Angeles and Franciscans: Innovative Architecture from Los Angeles and San Francisco.* New York: 1992.

Lancaster, Clay. "The American Bungalow." *Art Bulletin* 15 (September 1958): 239–53.

————. *The Japanese Influence in America.* New York: 1963.

Land of Heart's Desire—Southern California: Her People, Homes and Pleasures, Art and Architecture. Los Angeles: Frank F. Peand, 1911.

Laporte, Paul. *Simon Rodia's Towers in Watts.* Los Angeles: 1962.

Lautner, John. "You've Got to Fight for Great Design." *Home Magazine, Los Angeles Times* (14 February 1971): 16–18, 21.

Lazlo, Paul. *Paul Lazlo—Designed in the U.S.A. 1937–1947.* Beverly Hills: 1947.

Le Barthon, J. L. *Our Architecture Morgan and Walls, John Parkinson, Hunt and Eager.* Los Angeles: 1904.

Levick, Melba, and Helaine Kaplan Prentice. *The Gardens of Southern California.* San Francisco: 1991.

Leviseur, Elsa. "California Ecology." *Architectural Review* (April 1991): 52–55.

Lewin, Susan Grant, and Stanley Tigerman. *The California Condition: A Pregnant Architecture.* La Jolla: 1982.

Lewis, Oscar. *Here Lived the Californians.* New York: 1957.

Lindley, Walter, and J. P. Widney. *California of the South.* New York: 1896.

Lingenbrink, William. *Modernistic Architecture.* Los Angeles: undated (ca. 1933).

Littlejohn, David. *Architecture: The Life and Work of Charles W. Moore.* New York: 1984.

Litter, Charles. "A Dream Come True." *California A.I.A.* (June 1939): 28–29.

Long Beach Museum of Art, with an introduction by Jerome Allen Donson. *Arts in California: I: Architecture.* Long Beach: 1957.

Los Angeles Architectural Club. *Yearbook.* Los Angeles: 1910, 1912, 1913.

Los Angeles Chamber of Commerce. *Los Angeles and Vicinity.* Los Angeles: 1904.

Los Angeles Conservancy: The Conservancy has printed a number of tours of Los Angeles. Among them (undated) are the following: *Alvarado Terrace House Tour. Buildings Reborn in Los Angeles. Cruisin' L.A. Old Monrovia House Tour. Would You Believe Hollywood Boulevard? Would You Believe Los Angeles? Los Angeles Conservancy's News* also contains helpful information about architecture and planning in Los Angeles.

Los Angeles Department of Planning. *City Planning in Los Angeles: A History.* Los Angeles: 1964.

Los Angeles Regional Planning Commission. *Annual Reports.* Los Angeles. 1940, 1941, 1942.

———. *A Comprehensive Report on the Master Plan for Highways for Los Angeles County.* Los Angeles: 1941.

———. *Master Plan for Land Use—Inventory and Classification.* Los Angeles: 1941.

Luitjens, Helen. *The Elegant Era.* Palm Desert: 1968.

Luitjens, Helen, and Katherine La Hue. *A Sketch Book of Pacific Palisades, California.* Santa Monica: 1975.

Lummis, Charles F. "The Making of Los Angeles." *Outwest* 30 (April 1909): 227–57. See also his many other articles for this journal and its predecessor, *The Land of Sunshine.*

Mackey, Margaret G. *Los Angeles Proper and Improper.* Los Angeles: 1938.

Makinson, Randell L. *A Guide to the Work of Greene and Greene.* Salt Lake City: 1974.

———. *Greene and Greene: Architecture as a Fine Art.* Salt Lake City: 1977.

———. *Greene and Greene: Furniture and Related Designs.* Salt Lake City: 1979.

———. "Greene and Greene" in *Five California Architects,* by Esther McCoy. New York: 1960.

Margolies, John. *The End of the Road.* New York: 1980.

———. "Roadside Mecca." *Progressive Architecture* 54 (November 1973): 123–28.

———. *Signs of Our Time.* New York: 1993.

Marquez, Ernest. *Port of Los Angeles.* San Marino: 1976.

Marsh, Norman F. "Venice of America." *Architect and Engineer* 3 (January 1906): 19–25.

May, Cliff. *Sunset Western Ranch House.* Menlo Park: 1952.

Mays, Morrow. *Los Angeles.* New York: 1933.

McCawley, William. *The First Angelinos: The Gabrielino Indians of Los Angeles.* Banning, California: 1996.

McClung, William Alexander. *Landscapes of Desire.* Berkeley: 2000.

McClurg, Verner B. *A Catalogue of Small Homes of California.* Hollywood: 1945.

McCoy, Esther. "Charles Greene's Presence." *Review* (Southern California Chapter, Society of Architectural Historians) 1: 2 (Spring 1982): 1–2.

———. *Craig Ellwood, Architect.* New York: 1968.

———. *Five California Architects.* New York; Salt Lake City: 1960, 1975.

———. "The Greenhouse: Energy Efficient Home in Venice, California." *Arts & Architecture* 1: 3 (1982): 45–59.

———. *Irving Gill, 1870–1936.* Los Angeles: 1958.

———. *Modern California Houses: Case Study Houses, 1945–1962.* New York: 1962.

———. *Richard Neutra.* New York: 1960.

———. "R. M. Schindler." *Lotus* 5 (1968): 92–105.

————. *Roots of California Contemporary Architecture*. Los Angeles: 1956.

————. *The Second Generation*. Salt Lake City: 1984.

————. *Vienna to Los Angeles: Two Journeys*. Santa Monica: 1979.

————, with Marvin Rand. "Wilshire Boulevard." *Western Architect and Engineer* 222: 3 (September 1961): 25–51.

McCoy, Esther, and Evelyn Hitchcock. "The Ranch House." *Home Sweet Home, American Domestic Vernacular Architecture*. Edited by Charles W. Moore. New York: 1983.

McGroarty, John Steven. *Los Angeles from the Mountains to the Sea*. Chicago: 1921.

McMillan, Elizabeth. *1929–1979: A Legend Still: Bullocks Wilshire*. Los Angeles: 1979.

————. "Five Basic Classifications of Building Production." *Journal, Los Angeles Institute of Contemporary Art* 4 (Spring 1983): 43–49.

McMillan, Elizabeth, and Leslie Heumann. "Old Venice–New Venice." *Newsletter* (Southern California Chapter, Society of Architectural Historians) 5 (April 1981): 1–6.

McPherson, William. *Homes of Los Angeles City and County*. Los Angeles: 1873.

McWilliams, Carey. *Southern California: An Island on the Land*. Salt Lake City: 1946. Reprinted, with a new introduction, 1973.

Melnick, Robert and Mimi. *Manhole Covers of Los Angeles*. Los Angeles: 1974.

Mikosell, Stephen. *Historic Bridges of California*. Sacramento: 1990.

Millon, Wendy, et al. *The Best of Los Angeles: A Discriminating Guide*. Los Angeles: 1980.

Moore, Charles W. "You Have to Pay for the Public Life." *Perspecta* 9/10 (1966): 57–97.

————. "Plug It in Rameses and See if It Lights Up." *Perspecta* 11 (1967): 33–43.

Moore, Charles W., and Gerald Allen. *Dimensions: Face, Shapes, and Scale in Architecture*. New York: 1976.

Moore, Charles W., Peter Becker, and Regula Campbell. *Los Angeles: The City Observed— A Guide to its Architecture and Landscapes*. New York: 1984.

Moore, Charles W., Kathryn Smith, and Peter Becker, eds. *Home Sweet Home, American Domestic Vernacular Architecture*. New York: 1983.

Moran, Thomas. "L.A. Pop Architecture." *Los Angeles Free Press* 13 (7–8 April 1976): 6–7.

Moran, Thomas, and Tom Sewell. *Fantasy by the Sea: A Visual History of the American Venice*. Venice: 1978.

Morrow, Irving F. "Recent Architecture of Allison and Allison." *Architect and Engineer* 133 (May 1938): 2–34.

————. "The Work of Allison and Allison." *Pacific Coast Architect* 23 (February 1923): 15–21.

Murmann, Eugene O. *California Gardens*. Los Angeles: 1915.

Murphy, Paul Edgar. *American Mercury* 13 (April 1928): 450–53.

Muschamp, Herbert. "The L.A. Museum of Contemporary Art: What's in a Name." *Architectural Record* 187 (May 1987): 83–85, 89.

Nadeau, Remi. *City Makers: The Story of Southern California's First Boom*. Los Angeles: 1965.

————. *Los Angeles, from Mission to Modern City*. New York: 1960.

Nairn, Janet. "Frank Gehry: The Search for 'No Rules' Architecture." *Architectural Record* 159 (June 1976): 95–102.

Neff, Wallace. *Architecture in Southern California*. Chicago: 1964.

Neff, Wallace, Jr., with text by Alson Clark. *Wallace Neff: Architect of California's Golden Age*. Santa Barbara: 1986.

Neuerburg, Norman. *Herculaneum to Malibu*. Malibu, California: 1975.

Neutra, Richard J. "Architecture Conditioned by Engineering and Industry." *Architectural Record* 66 (September 1929): 272–74.

————. *Life and Shape*. New York: 1962.

Newcomb, Rexford. *The Spanish House for America.* Philadelphia: 1927.

———. *Mediterranean Domestic Architecture in the United States.* Cleveland: 1928.

———. *The Old Mission and Historic Houses of California.* Philadelphia: 1925.

———. *Spanish Colonial Architecture in the United States.* New York: 1937.

Newhall, Ruth W. *A California Legend: The Newhall Land and Farming Company.* Valencia: 1992.

Newman, David J., ed. *Postmodernism and Beyond: Architecture as the Critical Art of Contemporary Culture.* Irvine: 1989.

Newsom, Joseph Cather. *Artistic Buildings and Homes of Los Angeles.* San Francisco: 1888. Reprinted, with an introduction by Jenne C. Bennett and a foreword by R. L. Samsell. Los Angeles: 1981

———. *Modern Homes of California.* San Francisco: 1893.

———. *Picturesque and Artistic Homes and Buildings of California.* San Francisco: 1890.

Newsom, Samuel, and Joseph Cather Newsom. *Picturesque California Homes.* 2 volumes. San Francisco: 1884. Reprinted, with an introduction by David Gebhard, Los Angeles: 1978.

Nordhoff, Charles. *California for Pleasure and Residence.* New York: 1878.

Nunis, Doyce B., ed. *Los Angeles and its Environs in the Twentieth Century: A Bibliography of a Metropolis.* Los Angeles: 1973.

Nystrom, Richard Kent. *UCLA, An Interpretation Considering Architecture and Site.* Los Angeles: unpublished, 1968.

Oberhind, Robert. *The Chili Bowls of Los Angeles.* Los Angeles: 1977.

O'Conner, Ben H. "Planning the Supermarket." *Architect and Engineer* 146 (September 1941): 14–19.

O'Flaherty, Joseph. *An End and a Beginning: The South Coast and Los Angeles, 1850–1887.* Hicksville, New York: 1977.

———. *Those Powerful Years: The South Coast and Los Angeles, 1887–1917.* Hicksville, New York: 1978.

O'Sullivan, Judy. *The Pasadena Playhouse.* Pasadena: 1992.

Ostroff, Roberta. "Up Against the Wall." *West Magazine, Los Angeles Times* (31 January 1971): 22–27.

Ouellet, Philip J. *City Planning in Los Angeles: A History.* Los Angeles: 1964.

Ovnick, Merry. *Los Angeles: The End of the Rainbow.* Los Angeles: 1994.

Owen, J. Thomas. "The Church by the Plaza: A History of the Pueblo Church of Los Angeles." *Historical Society of Southern California Quarterly* 42 (June 1960): 186–204.

Padilla, Victoria. *Southern California Gardens.* Berkeley: 1961.

Papademitriou, Peter. "Images from a Silver Screen." *Progressive Architecture* 57 (October 1976): 70–73.

Parker, Robert Miles. "Downtown Los Angeles: Guide Map." *Arts & Architecture* 1 (Fall 1981): 49–53.

———. "Evaluation; Utility and Fantasy in Los Angeles's 'Blue Whale'." *American Institute of Architects Journal* 67 (May 1974): 38–45.

———. *L.A.* San Diego: 1984.

———. "MOCA Builds." *Arts & Architecture* 2 (1983): 31–35.

Pearce, Phyllis M., Claire G. Redford, and Mary Ann Rummel. *Founders and Friends.* Whittier: 1977.

Pelli, Cesar. "Tour Days in May." *Architecture and Urbanism* 45 (September 1974): 19.

Peters, William Fredrick. "Lockwood de Forest, Landscape Architect: Santa Barbara, California, 1896–1949." Master's thesis, University of California, Berkeley, 1980.

Peterson, Kirk. "Eclectic Stucco." *Home Sweet Home, American Domestic Vernacular Architecture.* Edited by Charles M. Moore. New York: 1983.

Phillips California Guide. Los Angeles: Phillips and Co., 1889.

Pildas, Ave. *Art Deco Los Angeles*. New York: 1979.

Pinney, Joyce. *A Pasadena Chronology, 1769–1977: Remembering—When—Where*. Pasadena: 1978.

Pitt, Leonard and Dale. *Los Angeles A to Z: An Encyclopedia of the City and County*. Berkeley: 1997.

Plagens, Peter. "Los Angeles: The Ecology of Evil." *Artforum* 11 (December 1972): 67–76.

———. "The L.A. Connections," *Architectural Design* 43 (August 1973): 571–74.

Polyzoides, Stefanos, Roger Sherwood, and James Tice, with photographs by Julius Shulman. *Courtyard Housing in Los Angeles*. Berkeley: 1982.

Powell, Lawrence Clark. *Land of Fiction*. Los Angeles: 1952.

Price, C. Matlock. "Panama-California Exposition: Bertram G. Goodhue and the Renaissance of Spanish Colonial Architecture." *Architectural Record* 37 (March 1915): 229–51.

Rand, Christopher. *Los Angeles, the Ultimate City*. New York: 1967.

Rand-McNally Guide to Los Angeles and Environs. New York: ca. 1925.

Rawls, James J. "The Californian Mission as Symbol and Myth." *California History* 71 (Fall 1992): 342–61.

Reavill, Gil. *Los Angeles*. Oakland: 1992.

Regan, Michael. *Mansions of Beverly Hills*. Los Angeles: 1966.

———. *Mansions of Los Angeles*. Los Angeles: 1965.

Rey, Felix. "A Tribute to the Mission Style." *Architect and Engineer* 76 (October 1924): 77–78.

Richards, Susan, and Sally R. Simms. "The California Post Offices of Allison and Allison." *Prologue* 20 (Summer 1988): 100–117.

Richey, Elinor. *Remain to Be Seen: Historic Houses Open to the Public*. Berkeley: 1973.

Rickard, J. A. "Los Angeles—The Wonder City of America." *Engineering News Record* 91 (4 October 1923): 554–58.

Rider, Freemont. *Rider's California: A Guide Book for Travelers*. New York: 1925.

Robbins, George W., and Deming L. Tilton, eds. *Los Angeles: Preface to a Master Plan*. Los Angeles: 1941.

Robinson, Charles Mulford. *The City Beautiful—Suggestions for Los Angeles*. Los Angeles: 1909.

———. "Los Angeles Parks." *House and Garden* 10 (September 1906): 114–15.

Robinson, Paul, and Walter Reichardt. *Residential Architecture in Southern California*. Los Angeles: 1939.

Robinson, W. W. *Los Angeles: A Profile*. Norman, Oklahoma: 1968.

———. *Los Angeles from the Days of the Pueblo: A Brief History and Guide to the Plaza Area*. Los Angeles: 1981.

———. *Panorama: A Picture-History of Southern California*. Los Angeles: 1953.

———. *What They Say About Los Angeles*. Pasadena: 1942.

Rochlin, Michael Jacob. *Ancient L.A.* Los Angeles: 1999.

Rolle, Andrew F. *California, A History*. New York: 1963.

Rubin, Barbara. "A Chronology of Architecture in Los Angeles." *Annals of the Association of American Geographers* 67 (1977), 4: 521–37.

Rubin, Barbara, Robert Carlton, and Arnold Rubin. *L.A. In Installments. Forest Lawn*. Santa Monica: 1979.

Ruscha, Edward. *Every Building on the Sunset Strip*. Los Angeles: 1966.

———. *Some Los Angeles Apartments*. Los Angeles: 1965.

———. *Thirty-four Parking Lots*. Los Angeles: 1967.

Salas, Charles G., and Michael S. Roth, eds. *Looking for Los Angeles: Architecture, Film, Photography, and the Urban Landscape.* Los Angeles: 2000.

Sanford, Trent E. *The Architecture of the Southwest.* New York: 1950.

Saylor, Henry H. *Bungalows.* New York: 1917.

Scheid, Ann. *Pasadena: Crown of the Valley.* Northridge: 1986.

Schindler, Pauline, ed. "Special Issue Devoted to Modern Architecture in Southern California." *California Arts and Architecture* 47 (January 1935).

Schmidt-Brummer, Horst. *Venice, California: An Urban Fantasy.* New York: 1973.

Schuyler, Montgomery. "Round About Los Angeles." *Architectural Record* 24 (December 1908): 430–40.

Scott, Mel. *Cities are for People.* Los Angeles: 1942.

———. *Metropolitan Los Angeles: One Community.* Los Angeles: 1949.

Sears, Urmy. "A Community Approaches Its Ideal." *California Arts and Architecture* 38 (June 1930): 19–21, 70, 72.

Seidenbaum, Art. "Los Angeles: The New Neighborhood." *Home Magazine, Los Angeles Times* (31 December 1972): 6–12.

———. *This Is California: Please Keep Out.* New York: 1975.

Seidenbaum, Art, and John Malmin, with a foreword by Will Durant. *Los Angeles 200: A Bicentennial Celebration.* New York: 1980.

Seims, Charles. *Trolley Days in Pasadena.* San Marino: 1982.

Sewell, Elaine K., Ken Tantanaka, and Katherine W. Rinne. "A. Quincy Jones: The Oneness of Architecture." *Process: Architecture* 41 (1983).

Sexton, Randolph W. "A New Yorker's Impression of California Architecture." *California Arts and Architecture* 39 (October 1930): 23–25, 64.

———. *Spanish Influence on American Architecture and Decoration.* New York: 1927.

Sheine, Judith. "Los Angeles Builds on Transportation." *Architecture* 82 (August 1993): 93–99.

Shinn, Charles. *Pacific Coast Rural Handbook.* San Francisco: 1878.

Shulman, Julius. "The Architect's Perspective." *Architectural Digest* (May–June 1962): 72–79.

———. *Cultural-Historic Monuments.* Los Angeles: 1968.

———. "A Photographer's Perspective on Neutra." *American Institute of Architects Journal* 66 (March 1977): 54–61.

Sillo, Terry, and John Manson. *Around Pasadena: An Architectural Study of San Marino, Sierra Madre, and Arcadia.* Pasadena: 1976.

Sitton, Tom, and William Deverell. *Metropolis in the Making: Los Angeles in the 1920s.* Berkeley: 1997.

Smith Elizabeth, ed. *Blueprints for Modern Living: History and Legacy of the Case Study Houses.* Los Angeles: 1989.

Smith, Jack. *The Big Orange.* Los Angeles: 1976.

———. *Jack Smith's L.A.* New York: 1980.

Smith, Kathryn. "Frank Lloyd Wright, Hollyhock House and Olive Hill, 1914–1924." *Journal of the Society of Architectural Historians* 38 (March 1979): 15–33.

———. *Hollyhock House and Olive Hill.* New York: 1992.

Smith, Sarah Bixby. *Adobe Days.* Fresno: 1925, revised 1974.

Soja, Edward W., and Allen J. Scott, eds. *The City: Los Angeles and Urban Theory at the End of the Twentieth Century.* Berkeley: 1998.

Solomon, Barbara Stauffacher. *Good Mourning, California.* New York: 1992.

Spalding, William A., comp. *History and Reminiscences: Los Angeles, City and County, California.* Los Angeles: 1931.

Stacy-Judd, Robert B. "Some Local Examples of Mayan Adaptions." *Architect and Engineer* 116 (February 1934): 21–30.

Starr, Kevin. *Americans and the California Dream.* New York. 1973, Reprint, Salt Lake City: 1980.

———. *Inventing the Dream: California Through the Progressive Era.* New York: 1985.

———. *Material Dreams: Southern California Through the 1920s.* New York: 1990.

Steele, James. *Barnsdale House: Frank Lloyd Wright.* London: 1992.

———. *Los Angeles Architecture: The Contemporary Condition.* London and San Francisco: 1993.

Stein, Achva Benzinberg, and Jacqueline Claire Moxley. "In Defense of Nonnative: The Case of the Eucalyptus." *Landscape Journal* 11 (Spring 1992): 35–50.

Stephens, James C. "The Development of County Planning in California." Master's thesis, University of California, Los Angeles, 1937.

Strand, Janann. *A Greene and Greene Guide.* Pasadena: 1974.

Streatfield, David. *California Gardens: Creating a New Eden.* New York: 1993.

———. "The Evolution of the California Landscape: 1. Settling into Arcadia." *Landscape Architecture* 66 (January 1976): 39–78.

———. "The Evolution of the California Landscape: 2. Arcadia Compromised." *Landscape Architecture* 66 (March 1976): 117–27.

———. "The Evolution of the California Landscape: 3. The Great Promotions." *Landscape Architecture* 66 (May 1977): 229–39.

———. "The Evolution of the California Landscape: 4. Suburbia at the Zenith." *Landscape Architecture* 67 (September 1977): 417–24.

Suisman, Douglas R. *Los Angeles Boulevard: Eight X-Rays of the Body Public.* Los Angeles: 1989.

Sutro, Dirk. *West Coast Waves.* New York: 1993.

Sweeney, Robert L. *Wright in Hollywood.* New York: 1992.

Tomlinson, Russell P. "Mobile Home Parks as a Settlement Type in Los Angeles, Orange, and Riverside Counties." Master's thesis, California State University, Los Angeles, 1968.

Torrance, Bruce. *Hollywood: The First 100 Years.* Hollywood: 1979.

Tracy, Robert Howard. "John Parkinson and the Beaux-Arts City Beautiful Movement in Downtown Los Angeles 1894–1935." Ph.D. thesis, University of California, Los Angeles, 1982.

Trillin, Calvin. "Simon Rodia: Watts Towers." *Naives and Visionaries.* Minneapolis: Walker Art Center, 1974.

Truman, Ben. C. *Semi-Tropical California.* San Francisco: 1874.

———. *Homes and Happiness in the Golden State of California.* San Francisco: 1885.

Van Dyke, Theodore S. *Southern California.* New York: 1886.

Van Petten, O. W. "Westwood: The Case of the Bartered Bride." *West Magazine, Los Angeles Times* (26 October 1969): 23–33.

Vertikoff, Alexander, and Robert Winter. *Hidden L.A.* Salt Lake City: 1998.

Voelkel, Richard. *Architecture: A Window on the Past.* Santa Ana: 1988.

Walker, Derek, ed. *Los Angeles: Architectural Design Profile—AD/USC Look at L.A.* London: 1981.

Warner, Charles Dudley. *Our Italy.* New York: 1891.

Warren, Violet Lockhart. "The Eucalyptus Crusade." *Historical Society of Southern California Quarterly* 51 (March 1961): 31–41.

Weaver, John D. *El Pueblo Grande.* Los Angeles: 1973.

Webb, Michael. *Architecture + Design.* Berkeley: 2000.

Weber, Msgr. Francis J. *Saint Vibiana's Cathedral.* Los Angeles: 1976.

Weitze, Karen. *California's Mission Revival.* Los Angeles: 1983.

Welch, Ileana. *Historic-Cultural Monuments as Designated by the Cultural Heritage Board, Los Angeles.* Los Angeles: 1980.

West, Nathanael. *The Day of the Locust.* New York: 1950.

Whitnall, Gordon. "Tracing the Development of Planning in Los Angeles." *Annual Report of the Los Angeles Planning Commission.* Los Angeles: 1930.

Whittlesey, Charles F. "Concrete Construction." *Architect and Engineer* (December 1905): 43–47.

———. "Reinforced Concrete Construction— Why I Believe in It." *Architect and Engineer* 12 (March 1908): 35–57.

Wiley, Stephen. "Los Angeles: 200 Years, 200 Buildings." *L.A. Architect* 6 (September 1976).

Williams, Paul R. *New Homes of Today.* Hollywood: 1946.

———. *The Small Home of Tomorrow.* Hollywood: 1945.

Wilson, William. "The Colossus of the Roads (The Billboard as Pop Art)." *West Magazine, Los Angeles Times* (31 December 1970): 14–21.

———. "The L.A. Fine Arts Squad: Venice in the Snow and Other Visions." *Art News* 72 (Summer 1973): 28–29.

———. "Where Has All the Neon Gone?" *West Magazine, Los Angeles Times* (19 April 1970): 8–11.

Winter, Robert W. "The Architecture of the City Eclectic." *California History* 60 (Spring 1981): 72–75.

———. "The Arroyo Culture." *California Design 1910.* Pasadena. 1974. Reprint, Salt Lake City, 1980.

———. *The California Bungalow.* Los Angeles: 1980.

———. "The Common American Bungalow." *Home Sweet Home, American Domestic Vernacular Architecture.* Edited by Charles W. Moore. New York: 1983.

———. *Myron Hunt at Occidental College.* Los Angeles: 1986.

———, ed. *Toward A Simpler Way of Life.* Los Angeles: 1997.

Withey, Henry F., and Elsie R. *Biographical Dictionary of American Architects.* Los Angeles: 1956. Reprint, 1970.

Wolfe, Tom. "I Drove Around Los Angeles and It's Crazy: The World is Upside Down." *West Magazine, Los Angeles Times* (1 December 1968): 18–22, 24, 27.

Wood, Ruth K. *The Tourist's California.* Los Angeles: 1915.

Woodbridge, Sally. *Bernard Maybeck, Visionary Architect.* New York: 1992.

———. *California Architecture: Historic American Building Survey.* San Francisco: 1988.

Woollett, William L. "Los Angeles Landmarks." *Historic Preservation* 18 (July–August 1966): 160–63.

Works Progress Administration (WPA). *California: A Guide to the Golden State.* New York: 1939.

———. *A Guide to the City of Los Angeles.* New York: 1941.

Wurman, Richard Saul. *L.A./Access.* Los Angeles: 1982.

Yoch, James J. *Landscaping the American Dream.* New York: 1989.

Young, Betty Lou, and Randy Young. *Pacific Palisades, Where the Mountains Meet the Sea.* Pacific Palisades: 1985.

———. *Rustic Canyon and the Story of the Uplifters.* Santa Monica: 1975.

———. *Street Names of Pacific Palisades.* Pacific Palisades: 1990.

———. *Santa Monica Canyon.* Pacific Palisades: 1997.

Young, Robert B. *Architecture of Robert B. Young.* Los Angeles: 1905.

Zarakov, Barry Neil. "California Planned Communities of the 1920s." Master's thesis, University of California, Santa Barbara, 1977.

Zierer, Clifford M., ed. "San Fernando, A Type of Southern California Town." *Annals of the Association of American Geographers* 24 (1934): 1–28.

Index

f